G Washington

A HISTORY OF
OUR
COUNTRY

A TEXTBOOK FOR HIGH-SCHOOL STUDENTS

· BY

DAVID SAVILLE MUZZEY
Professor of History, Columbia University

GINN AND COMPANY
BOSTON · NEW YORK · CHICAGO · LONDON
ATLANTA · DALLAS · COLUMBUS · SAN FRANCISCO

The Athenaeum Press

GINN AND COMPANY · PROPRIETORS · BOSTON · U. S. A.

INTRODUCTION

The Past in the Present

AT THE OUTSET I invite you to think of American history in a quite new way: not as a series of "lessons" with dates and names and events to be memorized and "recited" upon, but as a story of the past which will help you to understand the world in which you are living. From headlines in the newspapers, titles of magazine articles, radio broadcasts, and discussions at the dinner table you are aware that there are many questions of public interest on which opinions differ. How far the government should interfere with business, by what methods the working class should seek to improve its condition, whether we should join with other nations in the efforts to prevent war, are examples of these questions. You find yourself a member of society, that is, of people associated with one another in many ways to make their common life more secure, prosperous, enlightened, and righteous. You are surrounded by the institutions which society has set up (for the word "institution" means something "set up," or "established") in order to accomplish its aims. There are our governments at Washington and in the forty-eight state capitals and in many hundreds of city halls, our courts of justice, our political parties, our chambers of commerce, our labor unions, our army and navy, our schools and colleges, our churches, newspapers, charity organizations, women's clubs, and numerous other institutions. They are not sudden accidents. They did not spring into being suddenly and in their present shape, as the goddess Athena was fabled to have sprung full-grown and

v

armed from the head of Zeus. Each of them has grown, like plants, from seeds planted in the past. And just as we cannot understand a man's behavior without knowing what influences have contributed to form his character from his earliest days, so we cannot understand our present institutions (which are simply the expression of our social behavior) unless we learn how they have come to be what they are — in other words, unless we know their *history*.

Simply to collect and memorize events of the past is of no more use than to preserve old almanacs. We must try to discover how these events help us to understand the world in which we are living today. The past as a succession of events is gone forever — the past of yesterday as well as the past of Julius Caesar's time. But the past as the story of a nation's growth lives on in the present. So I ask you to think of each of the following units, or topics of study, as a chapter in the *biography* (or life story) of our country. At the beginning of each unit we shall present a brief picture of a condition or an institution existing in our society today, and then reach back into the past to discover how such a condition or institution has come to exist. We shall use the past to explain the present.

Acknowledgment

THE AUTHOR wishes to express his indebtedness to Miss Alice N. Gibbons of the East High School, Rochester, New York, and to Dr. R. J. Langstaff of the Scott High School, Toledo, Ohio, who have read this book in proof, for many valuable suggestions and criticisms.

CONTENTS

Unit Five · *How our Reunited Country Increased in National Wealth and Power*

Unit Six · *How our Country Acquired Distant Possessions and Put Democratic Government to the Test*

Unit Seven · *How our Country was Transformed by the World War*

Unit Eight · *How our Country Sought to Return to "Normalcy"*

COLORED MAPS

★

A LETTER

To High-School Students

My dear young fellow students:

When I was a boy, going to the little wooden church in a New England town, I used to join in singing the old hymn

> "We are living, we are dwelling,
>   In a grand, an awful time;
>   In an age on ages telling
>   To be living is sublime."

The words didn't mean much to me then, but I have thought a good deal about them lately. For certainly the time in which we are living now is more "grand" and "awful" than any that has gone before. It is grand in the power which science has given man to make machines do his once backbreaking labor and to enable him to produce enough, and more than enough, food, fuel, clothing, and shelter to satisfy his needs. It is grand in the opportunities for education furnished by our free schools and colleges, by good books and periodicals, by public libraries and museums, and by the magical radio. But it is also an awful time, because the responsibility of using for the common social good this great power and these opportunities is more keenly felt than it ever has been before.

You are growing up in this age of opportunity and responsibility. In a few years we of the older generation shall have passed on, leaving to you the duty of carrying on the American tradition of a free democracy, of preserving our ideals and remedying our faults. This is Your America. Whatever busi-

ness or profession you may choose to follow, you are all, first and foremost, American citizens. Each of you should think of himself or herself as a person who has inherited a beautiful country estate, and should be proud to keep up that estate and to make such "modern improvements" as will increase its beauty and comforts. You would be ungrateful heirs indeed if you did not care to know who had bequeathed the estate to you, who had planned and built the house, who had labored to keep it in repair for your occupancy, who had extended and beautified its grounds, who had been alert to defend it from marauders and burglars.

If you agree with me, you have already answered the question why you should be eager to study American history. Other subjects of your high-school course are of great value, — science to teach you the operations of nature, languages to introduce you to the great literatures of the ancient and the modern world, mathematics to train your powers of exact thinking, the arts to cultivate your appreciation of beauty and develop your creative talents, — but only the study of history will furnish you with the story of the precious inheritance you have received from the builders of the American nation and provide the background of knowledge necessary for the wise preservation and improvement of your heritage.

Boys and girls have sometimes said to me that they have "had" American history, as if it were measles or chicken pox, which they could have and get over and be henceforth immune from. Now, of course, as children you can learn some dates and names and some picturesque incidents in American history, such as Washington crossing the Delaware or William Penn signing a treaty with the Indians under a spreading oak tree. Do not for a moment think that you are "going over" American history again in the high school, in order to add a few more dates and names to your memory. You are studying a new and fresh subject, not because American history has changed,

but because you *have changed. You have put away childish*
things. You are getting new outlooks on life — new ambitions,
new enthusiasms, new judgments of people and events. Life
broadens and deepens for you. So history, which is the record
of former people's ambitions and enthusiasms, comes to have
a new meaning for you.

This is your book, written to help you to understand your
America better, in order that you may be better equipped to
perform your duties as American citizens. It seeks (1) to fur-
nish you with information so that you may have the necessary
facts on which to base your judgments; (2) to rouse your curi-
osity as to why the builders of America did what they did in
the way they did; (3) to help you to understand our present-
day problems by showing how they have grown out of roots in
the past, how both our ideals and our abuses have grown, the
wheat and the tares; and (4), above all, to increase your
patriotism by inspiring in each of you the desire and deter-
mination to do your part to make your "patria" a fatherland
more and more worthy of the reverence and love of its genera-
tions of sons and daughters to come.

With high hopes of your future, I send each one of you my
hearty greeting.

DAVID S. MUZZEY

COLUMBIA UNIVERSITY

A HISTORY OF
OUR
COUNTRY

★

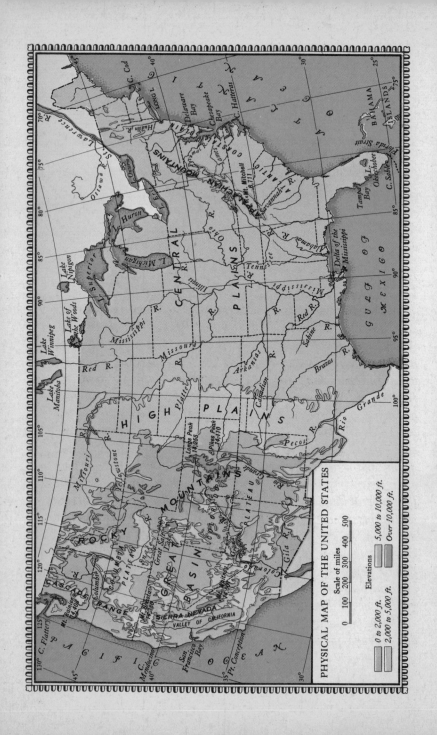

PHYSICAL MAP OF THE UNITED STATES

Scale of miles

0   100   200   300   400   500

Elevations

0 to 2,000 ft.   5,000 to 10,000 ft.

2,000 to 5,000 ft.   Over 10,000 ft.

How our Country was Discovered and Settled

THE LAND AND THE PEOPLE

Breakfast in New York, luncheon in Kansas City, dinner in Los Angeles. The aviator now covers the three thousand miles from the Atlantic to the Pacific coast in less than a summer's day. Passing in the first hour of his flight across the narrow Atlantic plain (the home of the thirteen original states), with its many rivers flowing south and southeast, he soars above the wooded Appalachian range of mountains, extending from the Adirondacks in New York to the state of Alabama, and then has before and beneath him the thousand and more miles of the great Mississippi basin. Over the eastern half of the basin, once covered with dense forests, he looks down upon cities and farms and a network of railroads and highways; but not long after he crosses the Mississippi, the prairies begin to replace the timbered land, the rivers become shallow and sand-choked, the settlements grow sparser, and the Great Plains stretch wider and drier to the foothills of the Rockies. Another flight of nearly a thousand miles carries him above the majestic snow-capped peaks of the Rockies and the Sierras, with the high plateaus between the ranges, and then he descends into the sunlit gardens of the Pacific coast.

What the aviator has done in the smooth flight of a single day took our pioneers more than two centuries to accomplish, as they toiled through the forests with ax and rifle, floated down the "western waters" to the Mississippi, led their wagon trains across the prairies and deserts, fought the stealthy Indians of the forest and the fierce Indians of the plains, and left the bones of their animals and comrades to bleach in the hot sands or to be buried in the drifts of the blizzard. The westward march of the pioneers is the pageant of American democracy. The trader followed the explorer, and the settler followed the trader. The steamboat replaced the raft and flatboat on the rivers. The railroad succeeded the stagecoach and the express rider across the plains and mountains. As each new western frontier opened up new resources (rich bottom lands for farms, vast stands of timber, mines of gold, silver, copper, lead, and iron, apparently exhaustless deposits of coal and oil) each contributed to the story of American life, affecting not only our methods of production, manufacture, trade, and travel but also our laws, our politics, our schools, our churches, our literature, our speech, our diet, and our dress.

About one hundred and twenty-six million people now live in the forty-eight states which form our Union. If they were equally distributed over the three million square miles of the country, there would be a little more than forty inhabitants to the square mile. But our population is very "spotty." The tiny state of Rhode Island has five hundred and sixty-seven people to the square mile, while the state of Nevada, ninety times as large, has less than one inhabitant to the square mile. If the United States were as densely populated as England (seven hundred per square mile), it would contain more than the present total population of the world. The four industrial states of New York, Pennsylvania, Ohio, and Illinois, occupying less than seven per cent of the area of the United States, hold nearly thirty per cent of the population. The four mountain states of Montana, Wyoming, Utah, and Nevada, with fifteen per cent of the area, have only one and one-tenth per cent of the population. Leaving to one side the eleven million eight hundred and fifty thousand Negroes, most of whom are descended from the slaves imported into the country, and the three hundred and thirty-two thousand Indians who have survived the relentless march of the white men across their continent, we find that our population has grown from two main sources: first, from the natural increase and constant westward migration of the settlers who came to our shores (mostly from the British Isles) in the colonial days; and, second, from the heavy European immigration to this land of promise during the nineteenth century. In the seventy years before the World War more than thirty million immigrants arrived in America. Two thirds of them came from Germany, Italy, Ireland, Poland, and Russia. By the census of 1930 there were over thirteen million whites of foreign birth in the United States, and twice that number of foreign or mixed parentage, that is, with either father or mother or both born in alien lands.

America has been called the "melting pot" because of these millions of people of foreign speech and customs who have been thrown in with our native colonial stock, to be fused into a new type of American. Some students of society (sociologists) think that the process has injured our country by introducing a base alloy. Others point to the benefits which the brains and the hands of the immigrants have brought. There is much to be said for each side of the question. But all are agreed that the mixture of peoples in the American melting pot, like the variety of soil and climate in the vast American continent, has had a constant influence upon our history.

Let us now see why and when and how people from the Old World came to discover and settle the land of a New World.

CHAPTER ONE

EUROPE WAKES AND STRETCHES

Europe in the Middle Ages. About five hundred years ago, while our country was still the undisputed hunting ground of Indian tribes, important events were happening in western Europe. The vast Roman Empire had gone to pieces long centuries before, and rude barbarian tribes from beyond the Rhine and the Danube and even from far-off Asia had taken possession of the Roman provinces. The level of civilization then sank rapidly. Trade and commerce ceased, cities crumbled in ruins, roads fell into disrepair, money disappeared, schools were closed, literature degenerated into crude attempts to copy the Greek and Roman writings, and continuous warfare between petty chieftains kept the land in turmoil and made life insecure for the miserable serfs and peasants unless they huddled under the protection of some overlord's stronghold.

Gradually, from about the eleventh century on, the curve of civilization began to rise. The invasions of marauding Huns and Northmen were checked. Towns sprang up on or near the sites of Roman camps or medieval fairs or monasteries. They were walled about for safety, and offered an opportunity for artisans (weavers, shoemakers, bakers, candlemakers, goldsmiths, and the like) to form guilds and ply their trade with the surrounding country. From the Crusades (1096–1270), those unsuccessful expeditions to wrest the grave of Christ at Jerusalem from the infidel Mohammedans, the kings and knights and nobles of Europe brought back the knowledge of a world outside their own narrow limits — always a stimulus to new activities and ideas. Beautiful Gothic cathedrals and guildhalls were built. Students flocked to hear the lectures of the learned men on theology and on the philosophy of the

7

newly discovered "Master" Aristotle. About the year 1300 the Italian poet Dante composed his wonderful epic *The Divine Comedy*, the journey of the soul through hell, purgatory, and paradise. Light was breaking in from many windows upon the darkness of the age of confusion.

The Renaissance. It was not until the fifteenth century, however, that Europe awoke to what we call the modern age. "Renaissance" means "new birth." But a more accurate title for the epoch has been given by the German scholar Voigt, namely, "the Resurrection of Classical Antiquity." During the thousand years of the Middle Ages the views of life held by the ancient Greeks and Romans, as reflected in their myths, dramas, histories, and art, had been buried beneath the teachings of the Christian Church. The Greeks prized beauty, harmony, the human body and mind, and the creative powers of man; but the Middle Ages regarded the "natural man" (that is, he who was not saved by the grace of God through the sacraments of the Holy Catholic Church) as doomed to destruction with all his works. The ancient Greek loved this world, which appealed to his wonder and curiosity; but the medieval Christian despised the world as tainted with Adam's sin, and sought to escape from it into the eternal world beyond the skies. Now, however, the secular (or worldly) interests of man began to emerge. The literature of the ancient poets and philosophers was rediscovered and studied and imitated. Painters, sculptors, engineers, and architects were busy. The joy of human creativeness was felt again, and for its new interest in the works of *man* ("homo") the age was called the age of *Humanism*.

At the same time one of the most important inventions ever made by men came to preserve and spread abroad the achievements of the new age. In 1456 the first printed book (the Bible, which is still the world's "best seller") appeared from the rude press of John Gutenberg at Mainz. Within the next fifty years ten million printed volumes were in circulation in Europe. This "mass production" of books would have been impossible without a cheaper and more convenient material to print them on than the stiff and thickish parchment (sheep or calf skins) on

GUTENBERG'S PRINTING PRESS

which the monks of the Middle Ages wrote their chronicles. The new material was at hand in the paper[1] which the Arabs had taught the Europeans how to make out of a pulp of rags or

[1] Our word "paper" comes from the Latin *papyrus*, the name of a slender reed growing on the banks of the Nile. The stem of the plant was encased in long, thin layers of fiber which were peeled off and pasted together to make a smooth surface to write on. The papyri could be rolled but not folded. Hence the earliest books were in the form of scrolls, like our rolls of wallpaper, and were unwound as they were read. Our word "volume" (from the Latin *volumen*) means a roll. When there came a shortage in the supply of papyrus, a substitute for paper was found in parchment (named from Pergamum, a town in Asia Minor) or vellum

vegetable fibers. One has only to try to imagine a world without newspapers, magazines, or books to realize what Gutenberg's invention of printing with movable type has meant. Almost all our information is derived from what we read or what others read and tell us. Without the printed page we should know little of what is going on in the world today or what has happened in the past. The treasures of literature would be lost except to the few fortunate persons who could afford to buy expensive hand-made copies of manuscripts. The knowledge of science would be confined to scholars who corresponded with one another about their discoveries and theories. Our colleges and universities, without libraries for reading and research, would consist simply of students laboriously copying as much as they could hear and remember of the lectures of their professors. And the great mass of the people, the "reading public" of today, would sink back into the ignorance and barbarism of the "Dark Ages."

Modern States Emerge. In the field of politics also an important development was taking place in western Europe five hundred years ago. The states of England, France, Spain, and Portugal were growing stronger and more united. This was because the king's power steadily grew at the expense of the great feudal lords, — the dukes and counts and bishops and abbots, who, during the Middle Ages, had ruled large portions of the realm, coining their own money, holding their own courts, and leading their own armies. The king, on the other hand, stood as the symbol, or representative, of the whole nation, so

(related to the English word "veal"). It was on this material, prepared from the skins of sheep or calves, that the beautiful illuminated manuscripts of the Middle Ages were written, and parchment is still used for very special documents. Our Declaration of Independence was ordered to be "engrossed on parchment" in July, 1776. Until recently, college graduates received real "sheepskins" for their diplomas, but the classes have grown so large and the colleges so poor that ordinary heavy paper has to do for the diplomas today. The Chinese knew how to make paper from the pulp of rags two thousand years ago, but it was not until the fifteenth century that the art, brought by the Arabs to Spain many years before, became the common property of western Europe. Most of our paper today is made from wood pulp. It is estimated that forty million acres of forest are cut down every year for the purpose; and the pages of a single printing of a New York or Chicago Sunday newspaper, if pinned together, would make a girdle extending all the way around the earth at the equator.

POLIPHILO INCOMINCIA IL SECONDO. LIBRO DI
LA SVA HYPNEROTOMACHIA. NEL QVALE PO‑
LIA ET LVI DISERTABONDI, IN QVALE MODO ET
VARIO CASO NARRANO INTERCALARIAMEN‑
TE IL SVO INAMORAMENTO.

NARRA QVIVI LA DIVA POLIA LA NOBILE ET
ANTIQVA ORIGINE SVA. ET COMO PER LI PREDE
CESSORI SVI TRIVISIO FVE EDIFICATO. ET DI QVEL
LA GENTE LELIA ORIVNDA. ET PER QVALE MO‑
DO DISAVEDVTA ET INSCIA DISCONCIAMENTE
SE INAMOROE DI LEI IL SVO DILECTO POLIPHILO.

E MIE DEBILE VOCE TALE O GRA
tiose & diue Nymphe absone peruenerano &
inconcine alla uostra benigna audiétia, quale
laterrifica raucitate del urinante Esacho al sua‑
ue canto dela piangeuole Philomela. Nondi
meno uolendo io cum tuti gli mei exili cona‑
ti del intellecto, & cum la mia paucula sufficié
tia di satisfare alle uostre piaceuole petitione,
non ristaro al potere. Lequale semota qualuque hesitatione epse piu che
si congruerebbe altronde, dignamente meritano piu uberrimo fluuio di
eloquentia, cum troppo piu rotunda elegantia & cum piu exornata poli
tura di pronútiato, che in me per alcuno pacto non si troua, di coseguire
il suo gratioso affecto. Ma a uui Celibe Nymphe & adme alquáto, quan
túche & confusa & incomptaméte fringultiéte haro in qualche portiun‑
cula gratificato assai. Quando uoluntarosa & diuota a gli desii uostri &
postulato me prestaro piu presto cum lanimo nó mediocre prompto hu‑
mile parendo, che cum enucleata tersa, & uenusta eloquentia placédo. La
prisca dunque & ueterrima geneologia, & prosapia, & il satale mio amore
garrulando ordire. Onde gia essendo nel uostro uenerando conuentuale
conspecto, & uederme sterile & ieiuna di eloquio & ad tanto prestáte & di
uo ceto di uui O Nymphe sedule famularie dil acceso cupidine. Et ítan‑
to bénigno & delecteuole & sacro sito, di sincere aure & florigeri spirami‑
ni afflato. Io acconciamente compulso di assumere uno uenerabile auso,
& tranquillo timore de dire. Dunque auante il tuto uenia date, o bellissi‑
me & beatissime Nymphe a questo mio blacterare & agli semelli & terri‑
geni, & pusilluli Conati, si aduene che in alchuna parte io incautamente

that as the royal *power* gradually caught up with the royal *claims* (that is, as the royal domain, laws, revenues, courts, and armies absorbed those of the feudal lords) a *national conscious-ness* developed. Men became proud of the title of Frenchman or Englishman rather than Burgundian or Kentishman. National patriotism was born. For "king and country," men sought glory in war, riches in the extension of commerce, honor in the cultivation of arts and inventions, and prestige in the planting of the national flag in distant lands.

The Lure of the East. The civilization of western Europe and of America (which was but an extension of western Europe) came by way of Greece and Rome. Most of our ideas of govern-ment, law, art, business, education, and social behavior have their roots in the culture of Greece and Rome. Of the Greeks the poet Shelley wrote,

> On all this world of man inherits
> Their seal is set.[1]

But while western Europe was laboring through the confusion of the Dark Ages, wonderful civilizations existed in the Far East all unknown to our medieval ancestors, or for that matter to the Greeks and Romans themselves. The Chinese had great philosophers and poets; their government was conducted by scholars; their cities were resplendent with palaces, gardens, and temples; their silken fabrics, porcelain ("china") ware, gold, and jewels were of priceless value. As a defense against the Tatars they constructed for fifteen hundred miles along their northern border a Great Wall, in places twenty feet high and fifteen feet broad — an engineering feat which made Hadrian's wall in Britain look like a sand mound built by children on the beach. Their empire under the Mongols extended from the Black Sea to the Pacific Ocean. It was not until the later Middle Ages that western Europe came into contact with the civiliza-

[1] This is not exactly true. Christianity, for example, the chief religion of the Western world, is of Jewish origin, though the doctrines and ceremonies of the Church bear the imprint of Greece and Rome. We also owe to another Semitic people, the Arabs, a great deal in medicine, mathematics, and the natural sciences.

tion of the East through missionaries, traders, and an occasional diplomatic mission.

In 1295 the Venetian merchant Marco Polo returned to his home after seventeen years residence at the court of the Mongol emperor Kublai Khan, and astonished his fellow citizens by the display of gold and jewels and silken garments which he brought with him. Soon afterwards he told the story of his travels in "The Book of Ser Marco Polo," describing the wealth and wonders of the fabulous East. The eyes of all Europe were dazzled by the vision of untold riches. Trade routes with the Orient were opened. Caravans brought the precious goods of India and China across the continent of Asia to ports on the Black Sea and the eastern Mediterranean, whence they were shipped to Venice or Genoa or Marseille and from there distributed along the land routes to the towns of central and northern Europe. It was an expensive way for Paris or London to get their spices, rugs, silks, porcelains, and gems, with the tolls which had to be paid to the Arab and Venetian middlemen (or rehandlers) of the goods. It was a dangerous way, too ; for armed bandits might swoop down upon the caravans in Afghanistan, or pirates seize the treasure ships in the Mediterranean, or robber barons descend from their lairs in Europe to plunder the merchants' pack trains.

Cutting out the Mediterranean. What more natural, then, than that the growing towns which faced on the Atlantic (like Lisbon, Bristol, and Antwerp) should begin to think of finding a *direct* way to the East by sea? Why continue to pay tribute to the Mediterranean merchants if they could send their own ships around Europe to the north or Africa to the south and so bring their precious cargoes home from India and China without exposing them to the expense and danger of the overland journey? This bold idea, which took shape in the fifteenth century, led to one of the most important changes in the world's history. Ever since the days of the Greeks and Romans the inland Mediterranean Sea had been the highway of commerce. Beyond the Pillars of Hercules, as the Straits of Gibraltar were called, lay the ocean, hemming Europe in with its uncharted and terrifying waste of waters. It was the "sea of darkness," fabled to be full

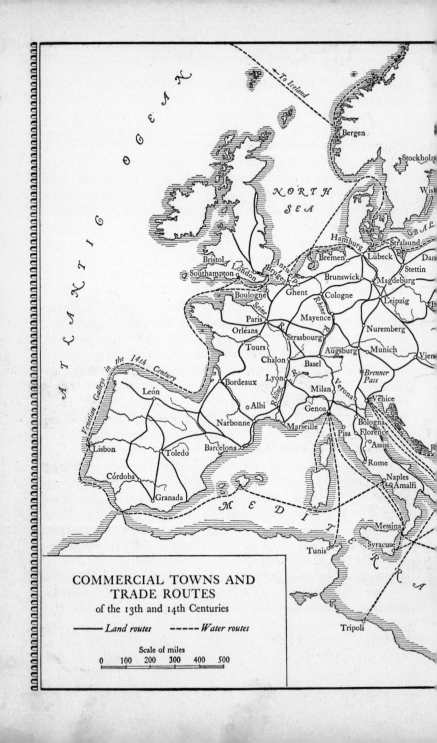

COMMERCIAL TOWNS AND
TRADE ROUTES
of the 13th and 14th Centuries

——— *Land routes*   - - - - *Water routes*

Scale of miles

0   100   200   300   400   500

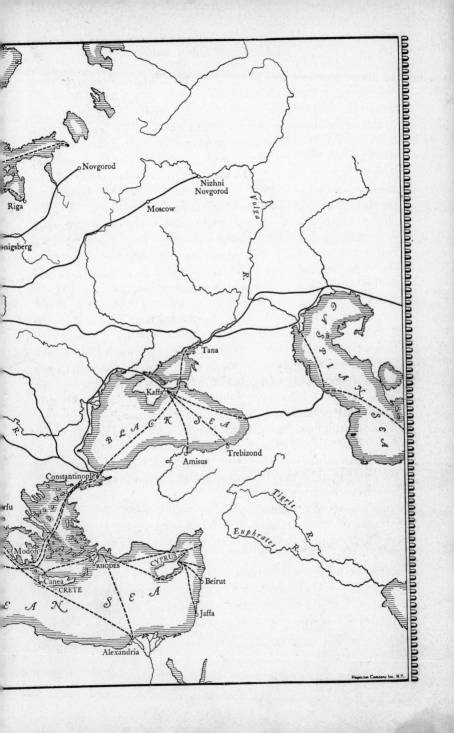

of huge monsters which would devour ships and sailors. The Roman poet Horace wrote that a man must have a heart armored in "triple brass" to dare to venture on the deep.

But in the fifteenth century the sailors began to take the dare. They now had helps to make navigation safer: the compass (perhaps invented by the Chinese) to tell them the direction in which they were going, the astrolabe to measure the height of the sun and so determine their latitude. They had learned to rig their ships to sail against the wind, so that they could easily change their course and return to land if they felt that they were venturing too far into the unknown. But, above all, they had a new *motive* for putting out into the ocean — the lure of the riches of the East. So they began a new stage in world history by making the ocean a highway instead of a barrier. Western Europe, which had faced inward toward the Mediterranean, now began to expand outward from its edges on the Atlantic, and the famous sea which had been for so many centuries the focus of its culture became hardly more than a lake for local traffic.[1] Its once proud cities like Venice and Genoa lost their monopoly of world commerce, and some of them, like Amalfi, shrank into mere fishing villages; while the Atlantic ports were swarming with sailors eager for far adventure.

The Portuguese Navigators. Almost nothing is known or even heard by Americans today of the little state of Portugal, which lies for three hundred miles along the Atlantic coast on the western border of Spain. Yet if it had not been for the Portuguese mariners five centuries ago, America might have long continued to remain unknown to the people of western Europe. For it was the voyages of these mariners which began to reveal the world of continents and oceans which we know today. The Portuguese Prince Henry (1394–1460), called "the Navigator," was the father of maritime exploration. The sea was his hobby. He built a nautical observatory and school on a promontory at the southwestern tip of Portugal. He collected sailing charts and

[1] Until, of course, the Suez Canal, built in 1869, made the Mediterranean a link between the Atlantic and the Indian Ocean, and hence a part of the world's commercial highways.

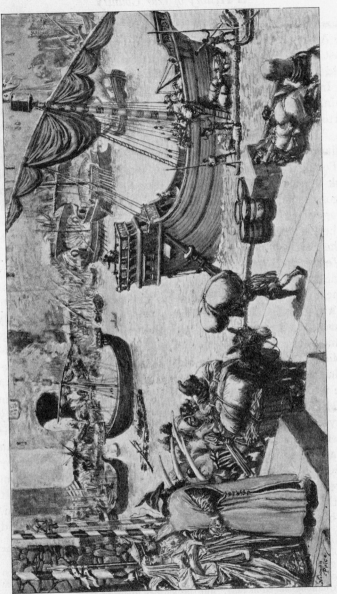

LOADING CARAVAN GOODS IN A MEDITERRANEAN PORT

maps of the known coasts and islands. He sent expeditions to the Azores and Madeira, and his ships crept down the African coast mile by mile. When their route turned eastward along the Gold Coast, they were certain that they were headed straight for India; but after a thousand miles the coast turned south again, apparently interminably. It was not until 1486 that Bartolomeu Dias finally rounded the cape[1] at the bottom of the "Dark Continent." He would have started across the Indian Ocean had not his mutinous crew forced him to return to Portugal. Twelve years later Vasco da Gama finished his work by sailing to Calicut, on the western coast of India. The cargo of spices and gems which he brought back paid for the voyage sixty times over. Da Gama's followers soon pushed on to the East Indies and China. The ocean route to the treasures of the East had been found.

Westward Ho! While the Portuguese were opening the way to the East via the Cape of Good Hope, a new idea was stirring in the minds of the geographers and navigators. Why not try to reach Cathay (China) and Cipango (Japan) by sailing directly *westward*, and thus cut out the twelve-thousand-mile voyage around Africa and across the Indian Ocean? From ancient times scholars had known that the earth is a sphere. A Greek mathematician had calculated its diameter with an error of only a little more than 10 per cent. But his figures had been lost in the Middle Ages, and the geographers of the fifteenth century believed that the eastern shore of Asia was much nearer the western shore of Europe than it really is. A map of the Italian Toscanelli showed Cipango at the place actually occupied by Mexico. Moreover, the scholars of western Europe knew from the reports of Marco Polo and other travelers to the Far East that the cities of China were in the Temperate Zone.[2] Why, then, sail thousands of miles to the south across the equator, around

[1] Dias named the cape "the Cape of Storms," but the king changed it to "the Cape of Good Hope."

[2] A glance at the map of the world will show you that Peiping (Peking) is on the same parallel as Lisbon, and Tokyo on the same parallel as Palos, the port from which Columbus sailed in 1492. But the journey due west from Palos to Tokyo is actually as long as the voyage of the Portuguese via the Cape of Good Hope.

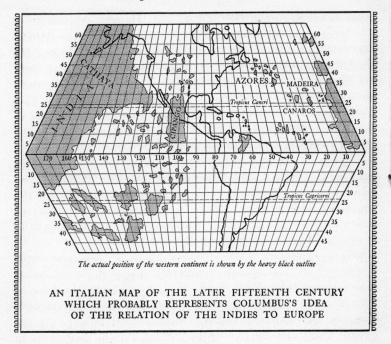

The actual position of the western continent is shown by the heavy black outline

AN ITALIAN MAP OF THE LATER FIFTEENTH CENTURY
WHICH PROBABLY REPRESENTS COLUMBUS'S IDEA
OF THE RELATION OF THE INDIES TO EUROPE

Africa, and thousands of miles more north and east, across the equator again, to reach the land of the Great Khan?

Columbus's Great Voyage. The man who tried out this new idea was Cristoforo Colombo (Christopher Columbus), the son of a prosperous wool-weaver of Genoa.[1] Columbus had followed the sea from his boyhood, making voyages to the eastern Mediterranean, to England, and down the African coast with the Portuguese mariners. He married the daughter of one of these navigators and enlisted in the service of the king of Portugal. He read and reread books on geography and exploration, like Marco Polo's *Travels*, until his mind was full of the scheme of sailing boldly to the west to find the Indies. But when he pro-

---

[1] The attempt has been made recently to prove that Columbus was a native of Spain, but most scholars hold to his Italian origin. He always used the Spanish form of his name, however, Cristóbal Colón.

posed his plan to the Portuguese court in 1482, he was coldly
received. King John was enough impressed by Columbus's
arguments to send a vessel secretly out into the Atlantic; but
the sailors returned in a few days to report that there was nothing to Columbus's crazy project. The navigators were all
absorbed in the African route. So when "God closed the eyes
and ears and senses of the King," Columbus shook the dust of
Portugal from his feet and began an eight-year quest for support
from Ferdinand and Isabella, the sovereigns of united Spain.
They were in the midst of the war to drive the Moors (Arabs)
out of their country, and, while they inclined to favor a project
which promised to beat the Portuguese to the treasure lands of
the East, they were not ready to commit themselves to the
venture nor to grant to the "commoner" Columbus the titles
of honor and the share of wealth and powers of government
which he demanded in the "lands and islands" which he might
discover.[1] The high-spirited Columbus, chafing under the delay,
had actually started for Paris, to seek aid from the king of
France, when a messenger from Queen Isabella overtook him.
The last Moorish stronghold, Granada, had fallen, and the
queen, influenced by one or two courtiers who had faith in
Columbus's idea, had decided to give him her support. "Capit-
ulations," or articles of agreement, were signed on April 17,
1492, granting Columbus all the honors he had demanded, and
the town of Palos was ordered to provide him ships. With the
indispensable aid of the Pinzón brothers, he got his three
"caravels," the *Santa María* (one hundred tons), the *Pinta*
(fifty tons), and the *Niña* (forty tons), and his crews totaling
eighty-eight sailors. They left Palos on August 3, and the
Canary Islands on September 6. With a smooth sea and favoring winds, the voyage across the Atlantic was made in a little

---

[1] Because, in the agreement which Columbus made with the Spanish sovereigns,
nothing was said about India or Cathay, some scholars have believed that
Columbus did not have in mind those regions as his destination. But, since he
carried a letter to the Great Khan and had an interpreter aboard, it seems certain
that he was headed for the Far East. The phrase "lands and islands" may well
have been used as a blind, so as not to arouse the suspicions of the Portuguese.

over five weeks, less than half the time it took the storm-tossed Pilgrim Fathers to reach the coast of Massachusetts in the rickety *Mayflower*, a century and a quarter later. But to the fearful sailors, on the verge of mutiny, the voyage seemed endless. A happy inspiration of Martín Pinzón persuaded Columbus to veer southward on October 7, and five days later the "Admiral," clad in a scarlet cloak and bearing a holy banner, stepped ashore on an island (probably what is now known as Watling Island) in the Bahama group[1] and took possession of the land in the name of the Spanish sovereigns, while the naked savages gazed with awe at their strange visitors.

Columbus Wins Great Renown. As he cruised about, Columbus came upon the island of Cuba, which from its size he believed must be Cipango. He sent his interpreter with presents to find the king, but no signs of golden-roofed palaces or silken-clad grandees appeared — only the same naked natives in their miserable huts. At Christmas time he landed on another large island (Haiti), which he called Hispaniola. Here he built Fort Navidad out of the timbers of his wrecked flagship, the *Santa Maria*, and, leaving about forty men at the fort, sailed for home, on January 16, 1493, in the tiny *Niña*, taking with him ten of the natives and a queer assortment of parrots, lizards, and plants, but no gems, spices, silks, porcelains, or precious metals. If his trophies were meager, however, his claims were great. He insisted, and to his dying day believed, that he had reached the outpost of the rich empire of Cathay. The golden cities which he saw in his imagination he reported as existing in fact. The sovereigns loaded him with honors and made his sons pages at court. The people believed his "tall tales" of teeming cities and near-by mines of gold and silver, because they wanted to believe them; and the stories grew as they were spread abroad to Italy, France, and Germany. Peter Martyr, his chief "pub-

---

[1] Columbus named the island *San Salvador* (Holy Savior). Other names that he bestowed on the islands, like "the Nativity" (*Navidad*), "the Trinity" (*Trinidad*), "Holy Island" (the coast of South America), show how prominent the religious motive was in his expeditions. Indeed, he gave his devout patroness Isabella to believe that the winning of souls for the Holy Church was his chief purpose.

licity agent," wrote to a friend in May, 1493 : "Several days
have passed since Christopher Columbus, a Genoese, returned
from the antipodes . . . loaded with precious merchandise, especially gold which is found in that region." It was a grievous
fault in Columbus to have encouraged such false reports, and
he paid for it grievously.

Disappointment. Three times Columbus returned to the
islands which he called the "Indies," or lands of the East.[1] On
his second voyage (1493-1496) he took more than twelve hundred people on seventeen ships, together with horses, cattle,
sheep, pigs, chickens, seeds, and farm implements, to begin the
real colonization of Hispaniola (Haiti) — the first permanent
settlement of Europeans in the Western Hemisphere. On the
third voyage (1498-1500) he skirted the northern shore of
South America, which he took to be the coast of a large island.
On the fourth voyage (1502-1504) he struck the torrid coast
of Central America, which he explored for weeks, in danger of
death from storms, starvation, and the poisoned arrows of
hostile Indians. For a dozen years he had labored to prove his
faith that he had found the way to the treasure lands of the East.
But he reaped only misfortune and disgrace. His sovereigns lost
confidence in him, and the courtiers jeered him as "the Admiral
of the Mosquitoes, who has discovered lands of vanity and delusion as the graves of Castilian gentlemen." Worst of all, while
he was on his third fruitless voyage, Vasco da Gama had returned from the real Indies with his ships loaded with treasure
for the rival king of Portugal. Columbus came back to Spain
at last in 1504, to find his patroness Isabella dying and his
friends, his fortune, and his reputation gone. He died in poverty
and obscurity two years later, little dreaming that he had
opened the way to a new and mighty world which would be
called by another man's name.

[1] Strangely enough, Columbus's name of "Indies" remained to designate the
islands which surround the Caribbean Sea after it was discovered that the American continents and an ocean much wider than the Atlantic separated them from
the true Indies, which are called the East Indies to distinguish them from our
West Indies. The latter name is a contradiction in terms, for it means "Western
lands of the East."

Why we Celebrate Columbus. Columbus was not the first European to reach the shores of this new world. Before the year 1000 the Norsemen of Scandinavia, in their long open boats with the dragon's head at the prow, had sailed to Iceland, thence to Greenland, and thence to Labrador, completing the arc of stepping-stones which those lands make in the North Atlantic. Leif the Lucky, son of Eric the Red, explored the coast perhaps as far south as Cape Cod, and even spent a winter somewhere on the bleak coast of North America. The Iceland sagas (epic poems) which recount his adventures tell of a region abounding in wild grapes, which he called "Vinland the Good," and of the fright of the "Skraelings" (native Indians) at the sight of the huge, blond-bearded vikings. How often a Norse ship, seeking the settlements of Greenland, may have been driven by the arctic winds to the foggy shores of North America we do not know. Nor was medieval Europe aware of the voyages of these rude and remote people of the north. The stories of Eric and Leif remained hidden in the sagas. America was discovered, but, as Mark Twain humorously remarked, "it did not *stay* discovered." The real discoverer was Columbus, whose voyage of 1492 linked America with the awakened Europe in a continuous and permanent intercourse.

Again, it is often (and truly) said that, if Columbus had not sailed, America would have soon been found by some other navigator. In fact, the Portuguese Cabral, on his way to the East via the Cape of Good Hope in 1500, lost his reckoning and was blown to the eastern shore of Brazil. But the credit for the daring act which first tested the theory that the Indies could be reached by a westward route belongs to Columbus.

> What if the wise men as far back as Ptolemy
> Judged that the earth like an orange was round;
> None of them ever said, "Come along, follow me,
> Sail to the West and the East will be found."

The Pope Draws a Line. The Pope at Rome, as the head of Christian Europe, was recognized as having special authority in the matter of the conversion of heathen peoples. He had already approved the Portuguese claims to the African coast; and, now that Spain had entered into competition with Portugal for the Indies, the Spanish sovereigns asked Pope Alexander VI, who was a Spaniard, to recognize their discoveries too. Accordingly, in 1493, a few weeks after Columbus returned from his first voyage, the Pope issued a "bull" (from *bulla*, a seal) assigning to Portugal all the new lands to be discovered east and to Spain all such lands west of a line drawn from pole to pole one hundred leagues west of the Cape Verde Islands. The two countries accepted the papal division of the world between them in a treaty concluded the next year, only they shifted the line two hundred and seventy leagues farther west. It will be seen from the map (p. 27) that under this agreement all of the American continents except the eastern part of Brazil fell within the Spanish sphere of influence. However, when we say "the American continents" we must remember that in 1494 neither the Pope nor Columbus nor anybody else had the slightest idea that such continents existed.

Why the New World was Named America. That the new world discovered by Columbus did not bear the name of *Columbia* was due chiefly to the fact that Columbus did not believe that he had discovered a new world, but only *a new way to the old world*. A Florentine merchant, Amerigo Vespucci,[1] catching the fever of adventure, gave up his business to join the company of navigators who followed Columbus in the search for the Indies by the western route. On his voyage of 1501, in the service of the king of Portugal, Vespucci sailed down the coast of Brazil for more than two thousand miles. Then, finding himself west of the Pope's demarcation line and in the region assigned to Spain, he steered southeast into the Atlantic until he reached an ice-clad island below the fiftieth degree of latitude. This voyage added two important pieces of knowledge to the new geography. First, it revealed an antarctic region of cold, corresponding to the known arctic north. And, more important still, it showed that not a mere island but a large continent opposite Africa lay in the southern Atlantic ocean. Vespucci was

[1] Pronounced vĕs pōōt′chē.

a good advertiser. He wrote long letters describing the "new world" (*novus mundus*) which he had "discovered," though in reality it was the same South American continent whose northern shore Columbus had touched three years earlier.

Now it happened that the professors of a little college in Lorraine were preparing a new edition of Ptolemy's famous *Geography* in the year 1507, the year after Columbus's death. One of them, Martin Waldseemüller, wrote an Introduction to the work, in which he published some of Vespucci's letters. He also made the suggestion that "since another fourth part of the world (besides Europe, Asia, and Africa) has been discovered by Americus Vespucius, . . . I do not see what fairly hinders us from calling it Amerige or America." Waldseemüller's idea was adopted; and when it was later found that Vespucci's America was not a separate continent lying southeast of Cathay, somewhat in the position of Australia, but was joined by an isthmus to another large continent to the north, the popular name "America" was extended to cover both continents.[1] So it came about that our country was named by a German professor in a French college for an Italian navigator in the service of the king of Portugal. Was it a prophecy of the "melting pot" of the nations which the United States was destined to be?

A New Ocean is Discovered. Wherever Columbus and his followers landed, the Indians told them of lands to the west and south abounding in mines of gold and silver. Expeditions were sent out from the West Indies to the coast of Central and South America to find these treasures. A bold adventurer named Vasco Balboa smuggled himself aboard a ship sailing from Haiti to the

---

[1] The maps on page 29 show how the true location of Vespucci's "new world" was gradually discovered. Then some attempts were made to remedy the injustice done to Columbus. Waldseemüller himself drew a map of the new world in 1513, in which he changed the name from "America" to "Terra Incognita" and added, "This land and the adjacent islands were discovered by Columbus, a Genoese, under the authority of the King of Castile." And in 1571 another geographer proposed that the northern continent be called Columbana and the southern continent America. But the latter name had already become so fixed that it has remained to our own day. It was not until 1609 that the names "North America" and "South America" appeared on the maps; and the Spaniards continued to call the New World the Indies until the middle of the eighteenth century.

Isthmus of Panama by hiding in a cask. On reaching the settlement of Darien on the Isthmus, he seized the government,
and by a course of justice mingled with firmness he saved the
little colony from destruction. In September, 1513, he set out
with a band of Spaniards and Indian guides to find the gold and
silver and the great sea which the natives told him lay beyond
the mountains. For twenty days he toiled through the tropical
jungles of the isthmus, where the white man had never trod,
until he came to a mountain peak from which he gazed down
alone upon the waters of the Pacific Ocean. Four days later he
reached the shore, and, striding out into the sea, took possession
of it and of the coasts it washed in the name of the king of Spain.
Balboa called it the Mar del Sur, or the South Sea. But neither
he nor his men, who

> Looked at each other with a wild surmise
> Silent upon a peak in Darien,

dreamed that they were on the shore of the largest ocean of the
world, which separated them by eight thousand miles from the
golden cities of the Great Khan.

Around the World. That ocean was first crossed by Ferdinand
Magellan, a Portuguese navigator in the service of Spain.
Starting from San Lucar in August, 1519, with five rickety
ships, Magellan aimed to reach the Indies by sailing around
Vespucci's (South) America, as Da Gama had sailed around the
continent of Africa twenty-one years before. Misfortune followed in his wake. The sailors mutinied and two of his ships
deserted before he reached the extremity of South America and
found the narrow, mountain-lined strait which has ever since
borne his name. For five weeks he beat through its winding,
storm-vexed channel, and came out upon a calm sea which, in
grateful relief, he called the "Pacific." But his troubles had
hardly begun. Week after week and month after month he
sailed to the northwest over the apparently boundless waste
of waters. When the last crumbs of their moldy biscuits had
been consumed, the sailors ate the rats which infested the ships,
and when these were gone they soaked and fried the leather of

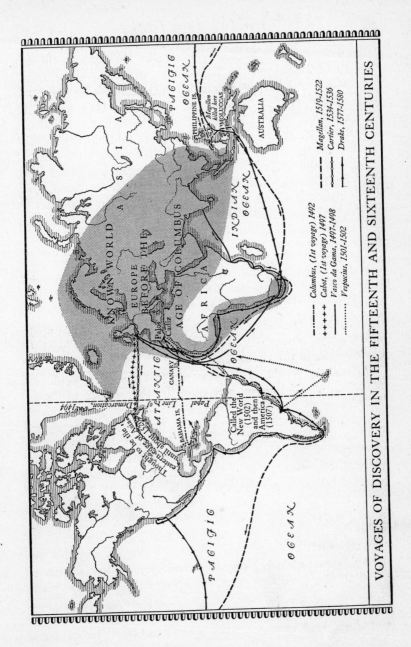

VOYAGES OF DISCOVERY IN THE FIFTEENTH AND SIXTEENTH CENTURIES

the rigging. Twice in the voyage of ten thousand miles land appeared to the eyes of the famished sailors, only to prove a barren rock. Finally, after a hundred days of misery, they came to the inhabited islands off the eastern coast of Asia. Magellan himself was killed in a battle with the natives of the Philippine Islands, and two more of his ships were lost. The *Vittoria* alone, escaping from the pirates of the Moluccas, crossed the Indian Ocean, rounded the Cape of Good Hope, and returned to her starting point of San Lucar in September, 1522. Her crew of eighteen "ghostlike" men made a strange procession as they marched barefoot, with lighted candles in their hands, to pay their vows of thanksgiving at the shrine of Saint Mary of Victory.

The Importance of Magellan's Expedition. The three-year voyage of Magellan's ship was a fitting climax to the series of bold expeditions and wonderful discoveries made by the European navigators in the age of the Renaissance. No other voyage in history can equal it in the contribution it made to man's knowledge of the size, shape, and surface of the earth on which he lives. (1) It proved that the world is a sphere, by actually sailing around it. (2) Magellan fulfilled Columbus's dream of reaching the real Indies by sailing west. (3) The voyage showed how vast a portion of the earth's surface is covered by the waters of the sea. And, most important of all, (4) it revealed that the new world of America was neither an island lying off the coast of Asia nor a large peninsula attached to China (see map, p. 29), but a continent set off by itself, and separated from the old world of Cathay on the west by an ocean more than twice as wide as the one which separated it from the old world of Europe on the east.

Nearly three hundred years were to pass before the true size and shape of the American continents were determined by the explorers of the land.[1] But the location of America in relation to

[1] Because Balboa in 1513 crossed the American continent at the Isthmus of Panama, where the Pacific Ocean is less than fifty miles from the Caribbean Sea, the early geographers naturally believed North America to be much narrower than it really is. It was not until early in the nineteenth century that the first exploring party (of Lewis and Clark) reached the Pacific by the overland route across North America.

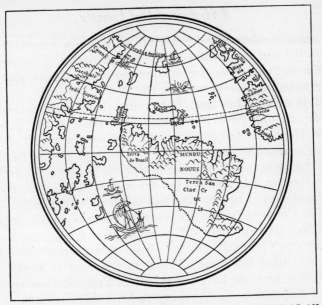

THE LENOX GLOBE (1510) SHOWING THE NEW WORLD AS AN
ISLAND OFF THE COAST OF ASIA

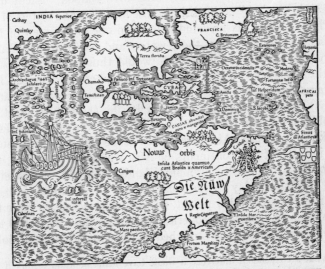

MÜNSTER'S MAP (1540) SHOWING LAND NORTH OF THE
ISTHMUS ATTACHED TO THE NEW WORLD

the other continents and to the oceans was now known. There was a *Western Hemisphere,* destined to be settled by the peoples of Europe, and to develop its own institutions, laws, and customs in its remoteness from the Old World.[1]

All in a Single Lifetime. Only thirty-six years intervened between the day when Bartolomeu Dias rounded the Cape of Good Hope and the day when the eighteen survivors of Magellan's expedition marched barefoot, with candles in hand, to give thanks at the shrine of Saint Mary of Victory. Yet in these few years not only America but the wide world was discovered. A young man of twenty who had sailed with Dias might have been in Columbus's crew six years later on the great voyage of 1492, and six years later still he might have crossed the Indian Ocean with Vasco da Gama to Calicut. At the age of thirty-four he could have sailed with Cabral to the coast of Brazil. At thirty-five he could have taken part in Vespucci's voyage into the far South Atlantic. At thirty-six he could have explored the fever-stricken coast of Central America with Columbus again. At forty-seven he could have stood with Balboa, "silent upon a peak in Darien," and beheld for the first time the waters of the Pacific. At fifty-six he could have been one of the crew of Magellan's *Vittoria* to cross those waters and return to Spain after circumnavigating the globe. He would thus have participated in the discovery of the Western Hemisphere and in the first voyages across the world's three great oceans — the Atlantic (1492), the Indian (1498), and the Pacific (1520). In short, he would have taken part in revealing the outline of the world as we know it today. Much remained to be filled in, to be sure: the interior of the continents of Africa and the Americas, the discovery of Australia and many islands of the sea, the penetration in our own day to the polar regions. But unless we learn to "rocket" to another planet, no man will ever again have the chance to make such discoveries as marked that wonderful age when Europe awoke and stretched its arms to embrace the globe.

[1] What a tremendous difference it would have made in world history if the Chinese and Japanese had been seafaring people who crossed the Pacific eastward to discover and settle the new world of America!

NOTE

The writer realizes that American history is not the only subject that students are taking in the senior year of their high-school course. The English, mathematics, science, and language assignments also have their claims on the student's time. Therefore this book is not burdened with a heavy list of references for outside reading and "projects" of one sort or another, which the student could not possibly find time to accomplish. The text itself is the important thing. If the daily assignments are faithfully prepared and thoroughly mastered, the student will come to the end of the course with an understanding of American history suited to pupils of high-school age.

Just what form the classroom exercises will take must be left to the teacher. They will depend on so many factors (such as the size of the class, the quality of the pupils, the length of the "recitation" period, the equipment of the school in library, maps, movie projectors, etc.) that no directions or suggestions could be given which would fit all cases. The following titles, however, are highly recommended as aids to the text:

1. **For a General Workbook.** HORACE KIDGER, *Directed Studies in American History*; D. C. KNOWLTON, *Making History Graphic*.

2. **For Map Work.** M. C. BISHOP, E. K. ROBINSON, and J. C. WALKER, *Map Work and Study Guide to Accompany Muzzey's "A History of Our Country."*

3. **For Source Material.** A. B. HART, *American History Told by Contemporaries*; D. S. MUZZEY, *Readings in American History*; H. S. COMMAGER, *Documents of American History*. A letter, poem, or extract from a speech or document, selected from this material by the teacher and read aloud by a pupil to the class, would serve not only to make the lesson more vivid but also to train the pupil in a much neglected exercise.

4. **For Linking the Past with the Present.** *The American Observer* (744 Jackson Place, Washington, D.C.), a weekly high-school paper available at one dollar a year to members of clubs of five or more pupils. Besides articles, with illustrations, dealing with subjects of current interest, *The American Observer* has a page on "Historical Backgrounds," which follows the high-school course rather closely, discussing each week some important topic in the student's assignment.

At the end of each chapter will be found a list of the "key words" or terms to be thoroughly understood in the chapter, a few references for supplementary reading, and suggestions for topics for special reports, and some review questions on the text.

A further list of books worth reading, if time permits, will be found in the Bibliography at the end of each unit.

Terms to be Mastered

the Renaissance	the Indies	Magellan
movable type	the Pope's bull	humanism
the national state	the name "America"	the ocean highway
middlemen	the South Sea	

For Supplementary Reading

Edward Channing, *History of the United States*, Vol. I, chaps. i–v; The Pageant of America, Vol. I, chaps. i–vi; Charles Kingsley, *Westward Ho!* John Fiske, *The Discovery of America*, Vol. I, chaps. i–vi; C. L. Becker, *The Beginnings of the American People*, chaps. i, ii.

Topics for Reports

1. **Leif Ericson and the Northmen.** The Pageant of America, Vol. I, chap. i (The Viking Adventurers); M. Hewlett, *Gudrid the Fair*; Justin Winsor, *Narrative and Critical History of America*, Vol. I, pp. 60–69; Olson and Bourne, *The Northmen, Columbus, and Cabot* (Original Narratives of American History); Hart, *Contemporaries*, Vol. I, No. 16.

2. **The Invention of Printing.** George H. Putnam, *Books and their Makers in the Middle Ages*, Vol. I, pp. 348–402; H. G. Aldis, *The Printed Book*, chaps. i–v; R. B. Downs, *The Story of Books* (University of North Carolina Press); *Richards Cyclopedia*, Vol. 23, pp. 6013–6038 (with many very interesting illustrations).

3. **Contemporary Accounts of Columbus's First Voyage.** Olson and Bourne, *The Northmen, Columbus, and Cabot* (Original Narratives of American History), pp. 89–258 (Columbus' Journal); Old South Leaflets, Nos. 29, 33 (descriptions of the voyage by Columbus and his son); Hart, *Contemporaries*, Vol. I, pp. 35–40; Muzzey, *Readings*, pp. 3–10. *America* (a library of original sources, published by the Veterans of Foreign Wars), Vol. I, pp. 134–158.

Questions Suggested by the Chapter

1. Name three things which helped Europe to emerge from the Dark Ages. 2. What influence did the invention of printing have upon the discovery of America? 3. Did the invention of printing have any evil effects? If so, what? 4. What inventions before Columbus's time encouraged ocean voyages? 5. Why did the cities on the Atlantic coast of Europe supplant those on the Mediterranean Sea as centers of trade? 6. Why did Columbus mistake Hispaniola (or Haiti) for Japan? 7. Do you think that our country should have been named "Columbia" instead of "America"? 8. To what part of the Western Hemisphere did the name "America" originally belong? 9. What new geographical knowledge was furnished by the voyage of Vespucius? of Magellan? 10. Show on the map the voyages of Columbus, Vespucius, and Magellan. 11. What important events are marked by the dates 1456, 1486, 1492, 1494, 1501, 1507, 1519–1522?

CHAPTER TWO

A CENTURY OF EXPLORATION

Dreams and Reality. We have seen how the discovery of America was an incident in the expansion of Europe. Let us now leave Europe behind and follow the explorers to the shores of the New World. What did they expect to find here, and what did they actually find? What hardships and dangers did they undergo as they toiled through swamps and jungles, crossed the parched deserts, and climbed the snowcapped mountains in search of the golden realms which the natives always told them lay just a few days' journey farther on? How hopefully did they explore each bay and river, believing that it might lead to the fabled Straits of Anian, which would take them through to the kingdom of Cathay? How persistently did they cling to stories like that of the seven splendid cities founded in a far-western land by seven bishops of Portugal who had fled from the Moorish invaders of the Spanish peninsula in the eighth century?

It would be impossible for us, of course, to trace the journeys or even to mention the names of all the adventurers who came to America in the century following the death of Columbus. Some of them found old empires of enormous wealth in Mexico and Peru, which they conquered and plundered. Many more of them toiled hundreds of miles through the wilderness in the fruitless search for empires which existed only in their imagination. Some were shipwrecked on uncharted coasts, and others were cast ashore to starve or to wander for years at the mercy of the Indians. Some enslaved or massacred the natives ruthlessly, while others braved torture and death to carry the message of Christianity and the sacraments of the Holy Church to the savage tribes. All the qualities of human nature were

33

brought out by these severe tests: courage, endurance, resourcefulness, self-sacrifice, as well as greed, treachery, cruelty, and deceit. It took a century from the death of Columbus for the dreams of glorious conquests and sudden riches to fade before the sober realization that the New World north of the Tropics was a land where primitive nature was disturbed only by the wanderings of sparse Indian tribes. America waited to be settled by permanent colonists from across the sea, and to be subdued to civilization by the pioneers who moved westward from these settlements, with ax and rifle and with wagons filled with household goods.

The American Indians. Before we follow some of the noted explorers of the New World in the sixteenth century, it would be well to see what kind of people they found here. The American Indians [1] are believed by scholars to have come to these continents from northeastern Asia many thousands of years ago, when a solid land bridge, now represented by the chain of the Aleutian Islands, connected Siberia and Alaska. Their high cheekbones, straight black hair, almond-shaped eyes, and beardless faces suggest their relationship to the Mongoloid (Asiatic) race. As they spread southward and eastward in America they grew more "civilized," as we may see if we compare the Eskimos or the "tepee" Indians of British Columbia with the Hopis or Arapahoes of our Southwest, who live in huge "apartment houses," or pueblos, of clay and rock and weave beautiful rugs and make wonderful pottery, glass, and silverware.

It was where the continent narrows into the funnel-shaped region of Mexico and Central America that the Indians developed their highest culture. The temples and palaces, the robes and jewels, the slaves and officials, of the Aztec emperor of Mexico and the Inca king of Peru amazed their Spanish conquerors, as did the ruins of the older and yet more wonderful

[1] The American Indians have been called by the "code name" *Amerinds*, in order to distinguish them from the people who live in India proper. We have seen how Columbus bestowed the name "Indians" upon the natives of the Caribbean, in 1492, because he believed that he had reached the real Indies.

PLAINS INDIANS[1]

civilization of the Mayas, in Yucatan and Guatemala. Still, in that part of America which is now occupied by the United States, the Indians had nowhere advanced beyond the stage of barbarism. They had no written languages. Their only domesticated animal was the dog. Most of them knew how to raise corn, beans, and squashes, and the more intelligent, like the Iroquois tribes of what is now New York State, had a rude sort of government. There were probably not more than from three hundred thousand to three hundred and fifty thousand Indians north of the Gulf of Mexico, and they were constantly on the warpath and shifting their hunting grounds. They had some noble qualities, such as dignity, courage, and endurance, but at bottom they were a treacherous, cruel people who inflicted terrible tortures upon their captured enemies. Except in the

[1] From a painting by Arthur A. Jansson in the American Museum of Natural History.

rarest instances they never adopted the arts, inventions, and ways of civilized living of the white man, for whom their enmity grew more determined and dangerous as they learned to use his firearms and drink his "firewater." Of course, it was impossible that these few hundred thousand natives should stop the spread of the Europeans over the country. That would have been to condemn one of the fairest lands of the earth to the stagnation of barbarism. Nevertheless, the merciless way in which, until fairly recent times, the Indians were enslaved, massacred, driven from their hunting grounds, and cheated by the government (on General Sheridan's principle that "the only good Indian is a dead Indian") has been a chapter of dishonor in the white man's conquest of the continent.[1]

The Spanish Conquistadores. For fifty years and more after Columbus the Spaniards had the field of exploration in the New World to themselves. This monopoly was due to two reasons. In the first place, all of America (except the eastern "nose" of Brazil) lay, as we have seen (p. 24), in that half of the heathen world which was granted to Spain by the papal bull of 1493. Secondly, Spain was the richest and most powerful nation of Europe in the first half of the sixteenth century. Her king was also the ruler of Germany, Austria, the Netherlands, and parts of Italy. In 1519 he was elected as Holy Roman Emperor (Charles V), a proud title which carried the claim of sovereignty over the whole Christian world. His armies defeated the French, the only serious rival power on the continent of Europe. His fleets controlled the Mediterranean. His Council of the Indies at Seville regulated the affairs of the New World, keeping its trade wholly in the hands of Spaniards and watching lest intruders from other nations should attempt to establish settlements on its shores. The court gave charters like that of Columbus to one adventurer after another — and some went without any permission at all — to lead expeditions to the

[1] At the request of scholars who realized how fast the manners and customs of the Indians were disappearing, our government, in 1879, established the Bureau of Ethnology, to study the surviving remains of Indian life. To the reports of this bureau and the researches of scholars and explorers connected with various museums we owe most of our information concerning the Indians.

mainland of America and to set themselves up as viceroys, or governors, of new provinces which they might discover. These explorers all took the proud name of *conquistadores* ("conquerors"). Some of them actually conquered regions of vast wealth; but most of them spent their money and time and often their lives searching among the mud villages of the Indians or the burning sands of the desert for golden cities which existed only in legend.

"Florida," an Elastic Name. The first of the *conquistadores* to set foot within the present boundaries of the United States was Juan Ponce de León, who had come to the Indies with Columbus on his voyage of 1493 and soon afterwards conquered the island of Puerto Rico. Hearing of a magic fountain in the Bahamas which would restore youth to the man who bathed in its waters (there was no limit to the stories which the Spaniards would believe!), Ponce de León left Puerto Rico, with the king's permission, in the spring of 1513, to search for the Fountain of Youth. On Easter morning he came upon a sandy shore which he named Florida, in honor of the day (the *Pascua Florida*, or "Flowering Easter"). He rounded the tip of the peninsula to the Gulf side, and returned to Puerto Rico with only such renewal of his youth as was furnished by the sea voyage and the sight of the natural beauty of the land. Revisiting the coast nine years later, he was mortally wounded by the hostile Indians. Ponce de León's expedition was of no importance except for the new name which it gave to American geography. For, while still calling the Caribbean islands and the mainland to the west and south of them "the Indies," the Spaniards used the name "Florida" to denote all of America extending northward from the Gulf of Mexico, and westward from the Atlantic to the Rocky Mountains. It is the first and most striking example of a process which was repeated again and again in our history, namely, the original use of a term to denote a large area of the United States, and the subsequent narrowing of the term to apply to a single state. Virginia, Louisiana, Missouri, and Oregon are examples of this process which the student will meet later.

The Conquest of Mexico. Six years after Ponce de León's vain search for the Fountain of Youth the Spaniards found a

land of riches which corresponded to their dreams. The boldest
of the *conquistadores*, Hernando Cortes, sailed westward from
Cuba in the spring of 1519, under the authority of Governor
Velásquez, with eleven ships, over five hundred soldiers, sixteen
horses, and ten brass cannon. After various battles with the
natives of the southern shore of the Gulf of Mexico he landed
near the present city of Veracruz. Some two hundred miles up
from the coast, in the high central plateau of Mexico, lay the
capital of the "Emperor" Montezuma, a shining city built on
an island in a lake and connected with the mainland by three
great causeways. The messengers who came down to the coast
with presents of gold and silver to induce Cortes to leave only
increased his excitement and greed by their tales of the power
and wealth of the emperor. And the same messengers took back
to Montezuma terrifying reports of the great ships, the men in
armor, the tubes that spoke like thunder, and the strange
creatures, half beast and half man, that ran swifter than the
wind. For horses had not yet been seen on the mainland of
America, and the natives thought that the horse and rider were
one animal, like the centaurs of old.

There was a Mexican legend that the "fair god" Quetzalcoatl
had sailed away to the east many centuries before and that he
would come back some day to rule the land. Now Montezuma
was divided between piety and fear. Might not the "floating
towers" (the ships) of these strangers be bringing the god back
in the person of the fair-haired Cortes? Or were the strangers
enemies come to conquer and plunder his realm? Cortes did
not leave him long in doubt. In August he began the steep
march into the interior, and early in November he fought his
way into the rich capital. Montezuma was seized and later
murdered. The high altars on which human victims had been
cruelly sacrificed were overthrown. The treasures of gold and
silver, of magnificent robes and jewels and ornaments of ex-
quisite Aztec workmanship, were plundered. Meanwhile Cortes
had defied the authority of Governor Velásquez and set himself
up as lord of Mexico. The treasure which he sent home to the
Spanish court atoned for his rebellion. He had to fight for

several years against the Aztec tribes before his power was safely established and a Spanish colony (the first of many on the mainland of America) was built upon the ruins of the Aztec civilization. In 1539 the conqueror returned to Spain for good, loaded with honor and riches.

The "Cursed Hunger for Gold." Cortes's exploit in Mexico was followed about ten years later (1532–1536) by Francisco Pizarro's conquest of the still richer kingdom of the Incas in Peru. And by the same ruthless course of plunder, murder, and enslavement of the natives another province of "New Spain" was established in America. The silver and gold taken from the mines were conveyed across the Andes by pack trains to the Isthmus of Panama, whence the treasure fleet sailed twice a year for Spain. This "easy wealth" looked like great good fortune for the home country, but it was really a curse. For (1) instead of enriching the country through investment in industry it was squandered by the emperor-king Charles V on his European wars; (2) it made the haughty Spaniards despise work, as beneath the honor of a gentleman; and (3) it led the Spanish explorers in the New World to search with redoubled hope for elusive kingdoms of gold, instead of founding settlements. To find another Mexico or Peru, noblemen spent their fortunes and hundreds of men their lives battling against fever, starvation, shipwreck, hostile Indians, and the pathless wastes of the Western deserts.

A Harrowing Tale. One man's experience of such hardships might have been a warning to the treasure-seekers but for their greed and their readiness to believe the most improbable reports of lying Indians. When Cortes arrived in Spain he found already there a man who had a very different story to tell from his own. This was Cabeza de Vaca, who had been one of a company of three hundred who had started from Cuba to find the fabled cities of wealth — another Mexico perhaps. The explorers had lost their ships on the northern Gulf coast of Florida and built five rickety tubs to replace them. They had coasted along the Gulf shore, past the mouth of the Mississippi, and, separated by storms, one after another of their makeshift craft had gone down. Cabeza de Vaca had been cast ashore on the Texan coast with his shipmates, most of whom perished from starvation or were massacred by the Indians. By some miracle his life had been spared, and he had traveled on foot from tribe to tribe for two thousand miles across what is now the extreme southwest part of the United States. After eight years of wandering, during which he saw "hunchbacked cows" (bison) and rude Indian villages, — but no sign of golden cities, — he had reached a Spanish settlement in Mexico, like one returned from the dead. Back in Spain, he wrote the tale of his sufferings, the first printed account of the Spanish explorations in North America. But Cabeza de Vaca's tale of woe could not take the glamour from Cortes's and Pizarro's achievements. The Spaniards were determined to find treasure.

De Soto and Coronado. The most elaborate of all the Spanish expeditions in the New World was the one conducted by the nobleman Hernando de Soto, who had been a partner with Pizarro in the conquest of Peru. The emperor Charles made him governor of all Florida, and hundreds of nobles and gentlemen were eager to join his expedition. He landed in July, 1539, on the Gulf coast of Florida with a retinue of more than six hundred men, including soldiers, priests, carpenters, and smiths. There were two hundred and thirteen horses, a pack of hunting dogs, and a herd of hogs. Month after month they marched over a great part of what are now the states of Georgia, Alabama, and Mississippi, finding only miserable Indian villages from which they took captives to carry their baggage. In the third year they reached the Mississippi ("alwaies muddie, down which there came continually manie trees and timber"), and, crossing it at a point near the mouth of the Arkansas, went on westward, to wander among the Ozark Mountains. Food supplies gave out. The Indians grew "fiercer than any wild beasts." Threatened by mutiny, De Soto returned to the Mississippi, to die of fever. His body, wrapped in a weighted blanket, was sunk in the river. After a vain attempt to reach Mexico on foot, his followers again returned to the Mississippi and built a fleet of boats on which they floated down seven hundred miles to the

Gulf. Less than half the party which had left Florida with such pomp and confidence four years before finally reached the Spanish settlements.

Meanwhile other expeditions, led by the Franciscan friar Marcos and Francisco Coronado, had gone northward from Mexico in search of the "seven cities of Cibola" and of the Straits of Anian, which they still believed would take them to Asia. They discovered the most wondrous work of nature on our continent, the Grand Canyon of the Colorado, but no more wondrous works of man than the pueblos of the fierce Indian tribes. Coronado penetrated the desert wilderness as far as the present state of Kansas before he gave up his hopes and returned "in sadness" to report his failure to the governor of Mexico.

Spanish America, or "New Spain." For all their expenditure of money and lives, the Spaniards, seventy years after Columbus's great voyage, had not a single settlement in America north of the Gulf of Mexico. They claimed the whole continent, and in a later century their title to all of our country west of the Mississippi was acknowledged. But they did not colonize this region as they did the West Indies, Mexico, and Central and South America. The provinces, or viceroyalties, which they set up in New Spain were governed quite despotically. All the trade was regulated by the "India House" at Seville and forbidden to foreigners. The Roman Catholic religion was the only one allowed. The native Indians and imported Negroes were frightfully treated under the lash of the slave-drivers. The land was in the hands of a few wealthy proprietors. There were no representative assemblies. Yet the Spaniards introduced Western civilization into the New World. They brought horses, cattle, swine, and poultry, built cities and worked farms, opened rich mines of gold and silver, and spread their language, literature, and laws over the southern half of the continent. A flourishing university existed in Mexico City a hundred years before the oldest college (Harvard) in the English colonies was founded. But there is not a single Spanish possession left in the Western Hemisphere today. Spain's colonies on the mainland revolted and established their freedom in the early nine-teenth century, and she lost the last of her West Indian islands when the United States drove her out of Cuba and Puerto Rico in the Spanish-American War, of 1898.

The French Take a Look at the New World. It was not to be expected that the Spaniards could keep the other nations of western Europe out of America indefinitely, especially when the knowledge of the treasure flowing to Spain from the Ameri-can mines roused their envy.[1] In 1524 King Francis I of France (who was at war with Charles V during most of his reign) sent out the Italian navigator Verrazano, who sailed up the Atlan-tic coast from Florida to Nova Scotia, noting the fine harbor of New York on his way. Ten years later Jacques Cartier, a rugged sailor from Brittany, explored the mouth of the St. Lawrence and went up the river as far as the present city of Montreal, where he passed a winter which brought disease and death to many of his men. In 1562 the French Huguenots (Protestants) built a fort and started a colony on the coast of Florida. This was too near the Spaniards for comfort, and they promptly wiped it out, massacring the Frenchmen as both here-tics and trespassers; whereupon a French expedition took revenge by murdering the murderers. It was during this savage little religious war that the Spanish commander Menéndez founded the settlement of St. Augustine (1565), the oldest town in the United States. Nothing came of the French expe-ditions of the sixteenth century, but they showed that there was no respect left for the Pope's bull of 1493. King Francis sar-castically asked to be shown "Father Adam's will" dividing the heathen world between Spain and Portugal.

The Elizabethan "Sea Dogs." The power of Spain declined rapidly in the latter half of the sixteenth century. Her armies were defeated by the French, and the revolt of the Netherlands, secretly aided by England, sapped her strength. For the first thirty years of Queen Elizabeth's reign (1558–1588) England

[1] In 1522 one of the Spanish treasure ships was taken by the French as it was nearing the home port, and its cargo of precious metals was appropriated by the French king.

QUEEN ELIZABETH GOING ON BOARD THE *GOLDEN HIND*

and Spain were nominally at peace, but that did not prevent the English "sea dogs," such as John Hawkins and Francis Drake, from seizing the Spanish ships wherever they met them on the high seas. The queen sent the plunder to the Tower of London, to be "restored" to King Philip II, but, needless to say, it never got back to Spain. Indeed, the wily Elizabeth herself went down to the Deptford docks on the Thames and knighted Francis Drake on the deck of his ship, the *Golden Hind*, after he had made the first English voyage around the world (1577–1580) and had returned laden with the spoils of Spanish galleons. When Philip's patience was exhausted by these "piratical" raids and by the execution of Mary Queen of Scots, Elizabeth's Catholic rival for the English throne, he sent a great fleet to overthrow the exasperating queen and restore her heretical island to the Catholic faith. The defeat of the Spanish Armada in July, 1588, was complete. Such ships as escaped the drubbing which Elizabeth's captains gave them in the English Channel were driven to destruction on the shores of Scotland by terrific storms. England's victory was one of the most important events in modern history, for it gave her the control of the seas and opened the way for the establishment of her colonies on the coast of North America.

Sir Walter Raleigh's Prophecy. During Elizabeth's reign, however, England was too busy building up a strong state at home to make more than a feeble effort to plant colonies beyond the sea. There was more profit in plundering the Spanish treasure fleet. Still, the queen gave a charter to Sir Humphrey Gilbert, in 1578, authorizing him to "inhabit and possess all remote and heathen lands not in the actual possession of any Christian prince." Gilbert was lost at sea after an attempt to found a colony on the bleak coast of Newfoundland. His half-brother, Sir Walter Raleigh, one of Elizabeth's favorite courtiers, inherited his charter, and, in 1585, sent more than a hundred men under Captain Ralph Lane to Roanoke Island, off the coast of North Carolina. Raleigh named the region Virginia, after the virgin Queen Elizabeth, but misfortune dogged his efforts. Lane's adventurers, instead of settling down to work, started hunting for gold and the passage to Asia. They quarreled among themselves and with the Indians, and finally deserted the settlement and sailed home on one of Drake's ships that happened by. A second expedition, including men, women, and children, was sent out the next year by Raleigh, but its fate was even worse. It disappeared entirely, — whether massacred by the Indians or kidnaped by them we do not know.[1] In spite of his failure and his expenditure of many hundred thousand dollars in this venture, Raleigh never lost faith in the colonization of Virginia. "I shall yet live to see it an Inglishe Nation," he declared to Lord Cecil.

Summary. What, then, had been the results of a century of exploration in the New World? By the year 1600 the Spaniards had long been established in the West Indies and on the mainland from Mexico southward. But north of Florida there was not a single colony of Europeans to challenge the dominion of the Indian tribes. French, English, Portuguese, Dutch, and Norwegian fishermen had for years been making their annual voyages to the cod and haddock fishing grounds off the Grand Banks of Newfoundland. The Atlantic shore had been skirted all the way from the Gulf of Mexico to the coast of Labrador. The French had penetrated the St. Lawrence as far as Montreal, and the English had tried to plant a colony on the coast of North Carolina ("Virginia"). The Europeans were as yet only nibbling at the edges of North America. One fact, however, emerged from the century of rival claims and counterclaims: Spain's right to possess the whole Western Hemisphere was no longer respected. Henceforth the portions of America north of Florida would belong to the nations which could successfully colonize them and defend them against European competitors and Indian foes.

[1] One member of this "lost colony" was the infant granddaughter of the governor, John White. She was the first child of English parentage born in America, and was named Virginia (Dare) in honor of her birthplace.

TERMS TO BE MASTERED

Amerinds	Huguenots	New Spain
conquistadores	Spanish Armada	the "lost colony"
Montezuma	the India House	Virginia

FOR SUPPLEMENTARY READING

America, Vol. I, pp. 217–291; H. I. PRIESTLY, *The Coming of the White Man* (SCHLESINGER and FOX, A History of American Life, Vol. I), chaps. i–iii, viii; I. B. RICHMAN, *The Spanish Conquerors*; WILLIAM WOOD, *Elizabethan Sea Dogs*; W. B. MUNRO, *Crusaders of New France* (Vols. II–IV of The Chronicles of America); The Pageant of America, Vol. I, chaps. vi–ix; HART, *Contemporaries*, Vol. I, Nos. 21, 22, 29, 30, 33, 34, 35; MUZZEY, *Readings*, pp. 11–23.

TOPICS FOR REPORTS

1. **The North American Indians.** LIVINGSTON FARRAND, *The Basis of American History*, pp. 195–271; FRANCIS PARKMAN, *The Jesuits in North America*, Introduction, pp. 3–87; JOHN FISKE, *The Discovery of America*, Vol. I, pp. 38–147; HART, *Contemporaries*, Vol. I, Nos. 21, 60, 64, 91.

2. **De Soto's Journey to the Mississippi.** HODGE and LEWIS, *Spanish Explorers in the Southern United States* (Original Narratives of American History), pp. 127–272; E. G. BOURNE, *De Soto* (Trail Makers Series); W. LOWERY, *Spanish Settlements*, pp. 213–252; MUZZEY, *Readings*, pp. 15–18.

3. **Raleigh's Attempt to Found a Colony in Virginia.** MARY JOHNSTON, *Croatan*; H. S. BURRAGE, *Early English and French Voyages* (Original Narratives of American History), pp. 225–323; WILLIAM WOOD, *Elizabethan Sea Dogs*, chap. ix; Old South Leaflets, Nos. 92, 119; HART, *Contemporaries*, Vol. I, No. 32; MUZZEY, *Readings*, pp. 20–23.

QUESTIONS SUGGESTED BY THE CHAPTER

1. What is believed to be the origin of the American Indians? 2. Give some examples of the arts practiced by the more advanced Indians. 3. Distinguish between the present meaning of the terms "Florida" and "Virginia" and their meaning as used in this chapter. 4. Why was the gold and silver brought from the mines of the New World harmful to Spain? 5. How far into the present United States did the Spanish explorers penetrate? 6. What were some of the evils of Spanish government in the New World? 7. When and where was the first permanent European settlement made in the present United States? 8. In what two widely separated regions of America did the French attempt to found settlements in the sixteenth century? 9. Why was the defeat of the Spanish Armada in 1588 an important event for America? 10. Why did England lag behind Spain and France in attempts to colonize the New World? 11. Why do the early maps of North America show the continent much narrower than it really is?

CHAPTER THREE

THE ENGLISH SETTLEMENTS

The history of the United States really began not with the Declaration of Independence of July 4, 1776, but with the founding of the English colonies in America in the seventeenth century. For the groups of homemakers who then settled on our shores from New England to the Carolinas brought with them the seeds of culture which grew into the harvest of our national life. Many other peoples came, to be sure, to add variety and richness to the harvest; but they did not supplant it by the institutions of their homelands. The language, the laws, the forms of government, the ideas of the rights and duties of free citizens as contrasted with unprivileged subjects, even the models of literature, architecture, dress, and manners, — all these were of English origin. They, of course, suffered a "sea change" by being brought across the wide ocean into the wilderness of the New World. But they persisted and took root and spread out over mountains and rivers and plains until our whole land from sea to sea was dominated by a civilization which had been derived from the British Isles. Therefore, though the stories of the Spanish conquerors and the French explorers and missionaries are exciting and picturesque, the more sober chronicles of English settlers deserve our chief interest. We shall study in this chapter the reasons why the English came to America, and the forms of government which they established here.

England Takes to the Sea. At the beginning of the seventeenth century no one would have dreamed that England was destined to build the greatest colonial empire of modern times, with possessions on every continent and in all the seas. For when the last of the Tudor sovereigns, Queen Elizabeth, died in 1603, leaving the throne to James Stuart of Scotland, England did not have a single colony in either hemisphere. The way had been prepared, however, for a great expansion of England. The nation had become "sea-minded." Elizabeth took pride in the navy which her father, Henry VIII, had built, and encouraged the voyages of merchants, traders, and even piratical sea dogs, as a school for sailors to man her fleets, as well as a source of wealth for her kingdom. Commercial companies had been formed in the second half of the sixteenth century to trade with Russia and the Baltic states, Venice, Turkey, and India. A clergyman of Bristol, Richard Hakluyt,[1] wrote enthusiastic accounts of the *Principall Voyages* of English seamen, and in 1584, at the request of Sir Walter Raleigh, published a *Discourse on Western Planting* (colonization) in which he listed more than twenty reasons why Englishmen should "take a hand in the voyages to America." By doing so they would obtain valuable commodities such as naval stores, which they now had to import under heavy duties; they would easily find the passage to China; they would advance the Christian religion by carrying the Gospel to the Indians; and, above all, they would "abate the pride of Spain and pull King Philip down." For, said Hakluyt, "if you touch him in the Indies you touch him in the apple of his eye: take away his treasure which he hath almost out of his West Indies, and his bands of soldiers will soon be dissolved, his purposes defeated and his tyrannie utterly suppressed."[2]

The Attraction of the New World. While overseas commerce was bringing to one class of Englishmen the wealth necessary to support colonial adventures, other classes were finding living in England so difficult that they were ready to try their fortunes in the New World. Many country gentlemen found it hard to keep up their estates, because of the rise of prices which always

---

[1] Pronounced "hăk'lōot."

[2] The student will remember that "the Indies" was the name by which the Spaniards called their American empire. England and Spain were enemies during the whole of Elizabeth's reign, and it was England's victory over the Spanish Armada in 1588 that opened the way for the realization of Hakluyt's advice and of Raleigh's prophecy of "Virginia" (America) as an "Inglishe Nation."

accompanies an increase in the currency (money) of a country. The farmers were in distress, both because of higher rents and taxes and because great tracts of land were being converted into sheep pastures to supply wool for the weavers in Flanders. Since a man with two or three dogs could tend the sheep in a large pasture, the hundreds of men who would have worked on the same land if it had been kept in farms were thrown out of employment. We read in Queen Elizabeth's day of the great increase of idle "rogues and beggars," and of the government's attempt both to relieve them by the "poor laws" and to compel them, by threats of imprisonment and the whipping post, to work for wages which were not enough to keep soul and body together. The English yeomen, proud of their freedom, resented being treated either as objects of charity or as subjects for jail. If Henry VIII's new upstart nobility and the lords of wool had monopolized the land of England, there were broader lands beckoning beyond the Atlantic — lands, moreover, which had enriched the hated Spaniard with shiploads of silver and through which ran somewhere the straits to the fabled wealth of Cathay. There was not yet an English roof over an English head in the New World, where Spain had been established for more than a hundred years. It was time that the English flag should be raised in America. And so patriotism combined with land hunger, the love of adventure, and the hope of riches to furnish the motives for the English colonization of the New World.

James I's Foolish Course. To these worldly motives must be added the Englishman's belief in his right to have and to express his own opinion on political and religious subjects. He acknowledged his allegiance to his sovereign, but he did not believe that to be a good subject he must cease to be a free citizen. He was accustomed to exercise responsibility in local government and to express his mind in Parliament. The great Elizabeth had won the love of her subjects by her intense patriotism, her superb diplomacy, and her wise tolerance. But King James I, the Scotchman, a conceited, narrow-minded, and pigheaded monarch, set out to rule the English people as if they were his humble servants, and not he theirs. He maintained that he owed his throne to God alone and that his words and deeds were no more to be questioned than were God's. James attempted to control his subjects' consciences as well as their political opinions. This was his idea of being a king by "divine right."

James did not dare to disturb the Roman Catholics much, because they were strongly organized and because he wanted to marry his son Charles to the daughter of the Catholic king Philip of Spain. But he persecuted the Puritans, who regarded as idolatrous some of the forms of worship of the Anglican Church of which he was the head, and the more extreme Separatists, who rejected the authority of the bishops and believed that every Christian congregation was an independent church. He declared that he would make them conform or would "harry them out of the land." But Englishmen had tasted too much freedom to submit to such treatment from an autocratic king, especially from a "foreigner" imported from Scotland. And the Protestant doctrine of the individual's responsibility to God alone for his religion had taken too strong a hold in England to be given up at the command of a bishop or a king. Religious persecution did not make the Puritans and Separatists "conform" to the worship of the Anglican Church, but it drove many of them to seek in America a refuge where they could worship God according to the commands of their own conscience.

The Founding of Virginia. In the year 1606 certain "knights, gentlemen, merchants, and other adventurers," one company chiefly from Plymouth and the other from London, received from the king a charter permitting them to plant colonies in America. Three points are to be noted in this charter. First, it gave to the London Company the land between 34° and 41° north latitude, and to the Plymouth Company the land between 38° and 45°, extending a hundred miles inland (map, p. 51). Neither company was to make a settlement within a hundred miles of the other in the common territory between 38° and 41°. Second, it gave to a council of thirteen men, resident in England and appointed by the king, the general management of the companies, while local councils in America were given power to preserve order in the settlements and to regulate trade with the Indians. Third, it provided that the colonists should enjoy "the same liberties, franchises and immunities as if they had been abiding and born within this our realm of England." The Plymouth Company was a failure.[1] But the London Company succeeded in establishing a feeble colony in Virginia, which finally survived to become the first permanent English settlement in the New World — the germ cell of the United States.

In the spring of 1607 three small ships, with one hundred and four colonists aboard, arrived at the capes of Chesapeake Bay, which they named Henry and Charles in honor of the king's sons, and proceeded up the river, which they named the James. About thirty miles from the mouth of the river they landed on a low-lying, heavily

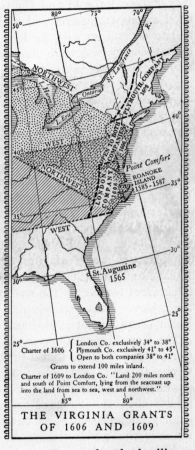

London Co. exclusively 34° to 38°
Charter of 1606 { Plymouth Co. exclusively 41° to 45°
Open to both companies 38° to 41°

Grants to extend 100 miles inland.

Charter of 1609 to London Co. "Land 200 miles north and south of Point Comfort, lying from the seacoast up into the land from sea to sea, west and northwest."

THE VIRGINIA GRANTS
OF 1606 AND 1609

wooded peninsula and began to erect a fort and rude dwellings.

[1] In the summer of 1607 the Plymouth Company sent out one hundred and twenty colonists under George Popham, who started a settlement on the Sagadahoc (Kennebec) River in Maine. A single winter of disease and starvation was enough to reduce the colony by half and send the survivors back to England with "their former hopes frozen to death." No further attempt at colonization was made by the Plymouth Company, whose rights were transferred in 1620 to a new company called the Council for New England.

Their provisions had been nearly exhausted in the five months' voyage, but instead of settling down to cultivate the land they hunted for gold and the passage to China. They quarreled among themselves and with the Indians, on whom they had to depend for such food as they got. If it had not been for the energy and stern discipline of one man, John Smith, who quelled their bickerings and secured supplies of corn from the natives, they would have failed to keep the settlement alive. As it was, more than half the colonists died of fever, starvation, and the arrows of the Indians before the winter was over.

New recruits and supplies came from England in 1608 and 1609, but still the colonists had not learned to provide for their own needs. Of the nine hundred persons who had come to Virginia since the granting of the charter, only one hundred and fifty were alive at the close of 1609; and during the awful "starving time" of the ensuing winter more than half of these died. The miserable remnant of sixty were already aboard their ships in the spring of 1610, abandoning Jamestown to the Indians and the wilderness, when they met Lord De La Warr (Delaware) coming up the river with the supplies which saved the colony. Thus narrowly did Jamestown escape the fate of Raleigh's settlement at Roanoke (p. 45).

The New Virginia Charter. Meanwhile it was evident to the Company in England that if the colony was to continue it must receive better support. In 1609, as a result of glowing advertisements of the wealth and promise of Virginia, the number of stockholders was increased to over six hundred and fifty, including nobles, country gentlemen, tradesmen, and fifty-six of the industrial guilds of London. A new charter from the king granted to the Virginia Company the area bounded on the Atlantic coast by a line running two hundred miles north and two hundred miles south of Point Comfort, and "extending up into the land from sea to sea, west and northwest" (map, p. 51). The quarreling council in Virginia was replaced by a governor, and the affairs of the colony were managed by a "court" in London representing the stockholders. Lord De La

Warr was sent over to Jamestown in 1610 (as we have seen) as its first governor. Under the severe but just rule of his deputy, Sir Thomas Dale, the colony picked up rapidly. A better class of emigrants arrived. A young planter named John Rolfe found a way of curing the harsh-tasting Virginia tobacco so as to make it a very profitable article of export and the basis of the colony's industrial prosperity through the whole colonial period.

About a dozen new settlements, called "cities" or "hundreds," were established in the neighborhood of Jamestown; and in the year 1619 the governor was given instructions to summon two representatives from each of these settlements to Jamestown to make laws for the colony. This little assembly of twenty-two "burgesses" [1] was the parent of our state legislatures and national congress. It met in the log church at Jamestown, and, after a few days' session devoted to the passage of laws for the punishment of idleness, gambling, drunkenness, Sabbath-breaking, and "excess in apparel," adjourned "by reason of extream heat both paste and likely to ensue." In the same year another event fraught with fateful consequences occurred at Jamestown, when a Dutch vessel from the West Indies landed some twenty Negroes in the colony, to be sold as slaves.

Virginia Becomes a Royal Province. By 1624 there were over a thousand inhabitants in Virginia, and the permanence of the colony seemed assured. Yet the returns to the stockholders from the sale of tobacco and the modest manufactures of iron and glass were disappointing. It must be remembered that the colony was started not as an experiment in democracy but as a business investment. Hundreds of thousands of dollars had been put into the enterprise. The dividends were very small. Moreover, King James did not look with favor on the company, since its control was in the hands of the "country party," his opponents in Parliament. The Spanish ambassador at London used his great influence with the king to persuade

---

[1] "Burgess" (or "burgher") was a very old English word to denote a free citizen. The legislature of Virginia was called the House of Burgesses during the whole colonial period.

him that the meetings of the Virginia Company were "hotbeds of sedition" against the royal power. Jealousies and rivalries within the ranks of the company gave its enemies further cause of complaint against it; and when a terrible attack of the Indians in 1622 cost the colony nearly three hundred and fifty lives, the king decided to put an end to the company. His royal judges annulled the charter in 1624, and the king took the government of Virginia into his own hands, appointing a governor and council to rule subject to his orders. However, his son Charles I, who succeeded to the throne in 1625, allowed the House of Burgesses to continue to meet, after a suspension of four years. Thus Virginia furnished the pattern which sooner or later almost all the American colonies reproduced: that of a governor and a small council appointed by the king, and a lawmaking body elected by the people of the colony. The royal rule in Virginia lasted until the American Revolution.

The "Old Dominion." The colony prospered under royal rule. Its population and its exports of tobacco grew rapidly. The ruling class consisted chiefly of the great planters, who acquired hundreds and even thousands of acres of land. There were not many Negro slaves in the seventeenth century. The laborers were for the most part "indentured servants," who had sold their services for a term of years in return for their passage across the Atlantic, together with vagrants picked up by the agents of the "poor laws," and offenders against the barbarous criminal laws of England, who were mercifully sentenced by the judge to transportation to the colonies rather than delivered over to the executioner for stealing a sheep or a silver candlestick. Virginia sided with the "Cavaliers" (Royalists) in the civil war between Charles I and Parliament (1642–1649); and when Charles II was restored to his father's throne (1660), the Burgesses recognized him so promptly and gladly that he called them "the best of his distant children," and quartered the arms of Virginia on the royal shield with the arms of England, Scotland, and Ireland, as a fourth "dominion."

Loyal as they were to their king, however, the colonists guarded their rights as free Englishmen against invasion by the king's appointed officials. They forced one governor to resign and another to dissolve an "old and rotten" House of Burgesses which he had brought under his thumb. And when Governor William Berkeley refused to defend the outlying settlements of the colony against the Susquehanna Indians in 1675 (because of his personal profit from the fur trade), a popular young planter named Nathaniel Bacon raised an army of three hundred volunteers on his own account and not only defeated the Indians but drove Governor Berkeley out of his capital, Jamestown, and set it on fire. Bacon died of fever (or poison) at the moment of his victory, and his "rebellion" collapsed; but, as the first armed resistance to the behavior of English officials in the American colonies, it was prophetic of the great rebellion which took place exactly a century later.

Bacon's Rebellion

The Pilgrim Fathers. While Virginia was founded as a business enterprise by a company of London "adventurers," [1] the second English colony in America had a religious origin. The Separatists (p. 50) were so "harried" by King James's spies and sheriffs that in the year 1608 about a hundred of them from the eastern part of England fled to Holland, which was at that time the only country in Europe where men were not persecuted for their religious beliefs. But these exiles were not entirely happy in their new home, in spite of their freedom to worship as they pleased. Being mostly farmers, they found it hard to adapt themselves to the industrial life of the city of Leiden, where they were settled. Besides, they did not want their children to grow up in a foreign land, where they would forget their native tongue and be tempted to neglect their strict observance of the Sabbath day. They felt like "pilgrims and strangers," longing for a home under the English flag. America beckoned; but the Pilgrims had neither money nor supplies, nor friends at court.

[1] "Adventurers" was the term used for the people in England who subscribed the money to provide ships and supplies for the colonists; while the actual settlers in the colonies were called "planters." Some of the stockholders ("adventurers") might, of course, go to America and become "planters," as in the case of the Massachusetts Bay Colony; but generally the men responsible for financing the company remained in England.

At length they succeeded in getting permission from the Virginia Company to settle within its territory, and found some London "adventurers" who were willing to finance the voyage. On September 16, 1620, the *Mayflower*, a none too stanch ship of one hundred and eighty tons, sailed from Plymouth with thirty-five of the Leiden congregation and nearly twice that number of Londoners who were not Separatists, besides the crew. Dangerously overcrowded, and overladen with furniture, household utensils, and barrels of provisions, the *Mayflower*, after a "longe beating" of sixty-five days, reached the shores of Cape Cod. The colonists were far north of the limits of the Virginia Company's land; but instead of proceeding southward they decided to stay where they were,[1] and, landing on the low, sandy shore of Plymouth harbor (December 21, 1620), they began to build their town.

Before landing, a group of forty-one men had gathered in the cabin of the ship and signed the famous "Mayflower Compact," in which they pledged allegiance to the king and bound themselves to obey "whatever laws, ordinances, acts, constitutions and offices should be thought most meet and convenient for the general good of the Colony." This voluntary agreement was the first instance of "self-determination" in our history. Though they never had a charter from the king, the Plymouth Pilgrims made their own laws and chose their own officials, electing William Bradford (who was also the historian of the "Plimoth Plantation") as their governor year after year.

In the first winter on the bleak New England coast half the colonists died; but when the *Mayflower* sailed back to England the following spring, the survivors all stayed to make America their home. Their profits from fish and furs enabled them in 1627 to take up the debt which they owed to the London mer-

---

[1] Several reasons have been given for this important decision. Bradford says that the *Mayflower* was deterred from sailing south to Virginia because she "fell among dangerous shoulds [shoals] and roring breakers." Other suggestions are that the pilot was ordered to land the settlers within the jurisdiction of the new Council for New England (p. 51, note), and that the Pilgrims had come to fear that their religious liberty would be interfered with if they settled in Virginia, where the Anglican Church was established.

© A. S. Burbank

THE EARLY SETTLEMENT AT PLYMOUTH

chants, thus freeing them from interference by a group which had no sympathy with their desire to found a religious community. The Plymouth Colony, with its few thousand inhabitants scattered in ten small towns (half of which were wiped out by the Narraganset Indians in King Philip's terrible war of 1675), played only a minor part in the political history of New England in the seventeenth century. It was overshadowed by its powerful neighbor of Massachusetts Bay, to which it was finally united by the royal charter of 1691. But the Pilgrim Fathers are revered because of the faith and courage which sent them, for conscience's sake, out into the wilderness beyond the sea, where, in the words of Bradford, there were "no friends to wellcome them nor inns to entertaine or refresh their weather beaten bodys, no houses or much less townes to repaire too, to seek for succoure."

The Massachusetts Bay Colony. After several unsuccessful attempts had been made to establish fishing stations on the north shore of Massachusetts, a group of merchants, ministers, and gentry, mostly Puritans, obtained from the Council for New England, in 1628, a grant of land extending from a point three miles north of the Merrimack River to a point three miles south of the Charles, and westward to the Pacific Ocean (map, p. 59). This New England Company immediately sent over about forty men, who settled at Salem. The next spring the company secured a charter from the king which made it independent of the Council for New England and conferred upon it powers of government like those of the old Virginia Company. "The Governor and Company of Massachusetts Bay in Newe-England," as the new corporation was named in the charter, was to be ruled by a governor, deputy governor, and eighteen "assistants," elected by the "freemen" of the company, who were to meet in a "general court" [1] four times a year, to make laws and ordinances. The Puritan character of the company was reflected by the religious phrases which appeared frequently in the charter, such as that the observance of the Christian faith and the conversion of the Indians to the knowledge of the "onlie true God" were the "principall ende of this Plantacion."

Continued persecution of the Puritans, together with heavy taxes under the despotic "personal rule" of Charles I (1629–1640), now led to an event of great importance in colonial history. A dozen influential members of the Massachusetts Company met at Cambridge, England, in August, 1629, and agreed to go themselves, with their families and belongings, to New England if the company would consent. The company accepted the proposal, John Winthrop was chosen governor, and in 1630 seventeen vessels, carrying more than a thousand colonists, landed at Boston. More than that, *they brought the charter with them*, thus transferring the company and its courts to America, out of the reach of the king's judges who had seized the Virginia charter six years before (p. 54). By this bold act the Puritans made the charter of a trading company in England into the constitution of an almost independent state in Massachusetts. During the troubled decade of the 1630's in England, nearly two hundred ships, carrying twenty thousand colonists, came to Massachusetts Bay. It was the largest, richest, and most self-determined of all the English settlements in America.

[1] The legislature of the state of Massachusetts is still called the General Court.

A line 3 miles north of the source of the Merrimack

MAINE (Granted to Gorges)

Claimed by Massachusetts

Connecticut R.

Merrimack R.

NEW HAMPSHIRE (Granted to Mason)

West to the Pacific

Cape Ann

Salem

Massachusetts

Newtown (Cambridge)

Boston

Bay

Charles R.

West to the Pacific

Springfield

Claimed by Mass.

Cape Cod

Hudson R.

Housatonic R.

Windsor

Hartford

Wethersfield

CONNECTICUT

Thames R.

Providence

RHODE ISLAND

PLYMOUTH

Plymouth

NEW HAVEN

New Haven

Newport

Long Island Sound

LONG ISLAND

········· *Boundaries claimed by Massachusetts*
‒ ‒ ‒ ‒ *Boundaries determined for Massachusetts*
────── *Boundary of the Confederation of New England*

THE NEW ENGLAND SETTLEMENTS

The Rule of the Saints. The main object of the Massachusetts Puritans was to found a colony in which they could enjoy a worship purified of what they called "the idolatrous remnants of popery" in the English Church. They had no intention of allowing *freedom* of worship. Only those who were members of a Puritan church were admitted as "freemen" to a share in the government. It was a sort of religious club. The other four fifths of the inhabitants, the "mutes," might live in the colony,

so long as they did not resist the authorities or speak disrespect-
fully of the ministers; but they had to contribute to the support
of the church and submit to its control of their behavior.

Neither had the Puritan leaders any idea of setting up a
democratic colony in America. They tried to keep the government solely in the hands of the governor and his assistants
(contrary to the provisions of the charter) until the rapid growth
of the colony compelled them in 1634 to admit representatives
from the towns to sit with the assistants in making the laws.
The Reverend John Cotton, the "Patriarch of New England,"
who came from Boston, England, to become the "teacher" of the
church in Boston, Massachusetts, said that democracy was "no
fit government either for church or commonwealth." And John
Winthrop, for many years the governor of the colony, defended
the exclusive rule of the "saints" in the remark that "the best
part is always the least, and of that best part the wiser part
is always the lesser." The ministers and elders of the church
did not hold political office themselves, but they kept strict
watch over the rulers, as they did over the people, of the
colony, to rebuke any departure from the Puritan faith and
worship. They made the laws of Moses the basis of the Body
of Liberties (the law code) of Massachusetts; and they "en-
formed" the government "of the mind of God," not only in
matters of religion but also on such secular questions as the
allotment of land, trials in the courts, and even the conduct of
trade and commerce.

Roger Williams, Apostle of Religious Freedom. The harsh
rule of the Puritan "saints" made living in the colony very
uncomfortable for those who differed from them and who dared
to express their dissent. A brave young pastor of the church
in Salem, Roger Williams, taught that the State had no control over a man's conscience and that, in spite of the royal
charter, the land on which the colonists had settled belonged to
the Indians. For these heresies he was exiled in 1635. Making
his dangerous way southward through the forests in midwinter
from one Indian tribe to another, he arrived at the head of
Narragansett Bay and, purchasing a tract of land from the

Indians, began a settlement which he called Providence, in recognition of God's guidance. Other dissenters from Massachusetts followed, and soon four towns were established. This little colony of "Rhode Island and Providence Plantations" was a true democracy, governed by "the free and voluntary consent of all the free inhabitants." Church and State were completely separated, and all men, of whatever belief, might "walk as their conscience persuaded them, every one in the name of his God."

The scornful orthodox Puritans in Massachusetts called the Rhode Island people "the Lord's debris," and facetiously said that if any man had lost his religion he would be sure to find it in some Rhode Island village. They refused to admit the little colony into the New England Confederation of Massachusetts, Connecticut, Plymouth, and New Haven, which was formed for defense against the Indians and the Dutch. Nevertheless, Rhode Island grew and prospered as an asylum for religious and political liberty. Roger Williams himself secured the recognition of his colony by the English Parliament, and when Charles II was restored to the throne he granted a royal charter to Rhode Island (1663) which it retained as its constitution until 1842 — more than fifty years after it had become a state in the American Union. For his heroic devotion to freedom, far in advance of his age, Roger Williams deserves to be honored as one of the noblest figures in our colonial history.

The Connecticut Settlements. The same year that the Massachusetts rulers drove Roger Williams out of the colony they gave permission to a group of petitioners from several towns to "transport themselves and their estates unto the Ryver of Conecticott, there to reside and inhabit." It was not so much dissatisfaction with the rule of the "saints" as it was the attraction of the rich farming land of the valley of the Connecticut River that caused this exodus from Massachusetts Bay. The emigrants, led by the Cambridge pastor, Thomas Hooker, tramped across the wooded wilderness from the Charles to the Connecticut in the summer of 1636, driving their cattle before them and carrying their household goods on wagons —

the first wave of that mighty westward movement which was to continue through two centuries to the Pacific Ocean. They founded the towns of Hartford, Windsor, and Wethersfield on the "long river," and adopted the "Fundamental Orders," the first constitution framed in America. They did not require a man to be a church member in order to vote, nor did they allow the ministers to control the political life of the colony as they did in Massachusetts.

The Connecticut towns pursued their independent way for a quarter of a century, until (1662), like Rhode Island, they were granted a charter of government by Charles II, which, again like Rhode Island, they retained as their constitution well down into the nineteenth century. By this charter their territory extended westward to the South Sea, or the Pacific Ocean. It was also made to include a number of towns along Long Island Sound, which had been founded, as the colony of New Haven, some years earlier with the double purpose of establishing a strict Puritan colony free from the rule of Massachusetts and a prosperous center of commerce on the Sound.

The Defiant Behavior of Massachusetts. Besides these groups of dissenters who went southward and westward from the neighborhood of Boston to start the settlements of Rhode Island, Connecticut, and New Haven, others went to the north and founded towns in what is now New Hampshire. That region had already been granted to a courtier, however, and Massachusetts had to give up her claim to the towns when Charles II formed them into the royal province of New Hampshire. Still farther north, in Maine, another courtier, Sir Ferdinando Gorges, tried in vain to establish a colony faithful to the king and the Anglican Church, as a rival of Massachusetts. But his heirs were finally compelled to sell their rights to the powerful Bay Company, and Maine remained a province of Massachusetts until 1820. With a wealth and population greater than those of all the other New England colonies combined, Massachusetts dominated the scene. Her will alone prevailed in the New England Confederation (p. 61). Convinced that they were obeying God's commands in the Bible, the Puritan rulers persecuted all those who did not accept their own brand of religion. They drove Episcopalians from the colony, hanged Quakers on Boston Common, and put to death in Salem nineteen persons who were accused by excited children or hysterical women of being witches.[1] In their political conduct too the Massachusetts rulers offended the king by their determination to "obey God rather than man." They coined their own money, omitted the king's name in their legal forms, and ignored the acts of Parliament passed for the regulation of their trade. When Charles II sent commissioners to Boston in 1664 to investigate these matters, they were insulted by a constable in a tavern, and their chairman wrote home, "Our time is lost upon men puffed up with the spirit of independence." A collector of revenue, sent to Boston a few years later, reported that "the King's letters are of no more account in Massachusetts than an old number of the *London Gazette*." Finally Charles's patience was exhausted. He had the Massachusetts charter annulled in his court (1684), and the colony became, like Virginia, a royal province.

Sir Edmund Andros in Boston. The next year James II succeeded his brother Charles II on the English throne. James united New York, New Jersey, and all New England into one great province which should be a solid bulwark against the danger of French and Indian invasion from the north. He sent over Sir Edmund Andros as his governor, to rule this huge province absolutely. Andros was a faithful servant and an upright man, but a harsh, unsympathetic ruler. He tried to seize the charters of Connecticut and Rhode Island, but was baffled by the local patriots in both colonies. He dismissed the assembly of Massachusetts, abolished the colonial courts, introduced the Episcopal worship in Boston, compelled the farmers to pay a fee for the titles to the land which had been allotted to them by the towns, and levied a tax on the land without the consent of the people. He forbade town meetings, those "seed-plots of democracy," to be held except for the election of officers.

---

[1] This momentary outburst of cruelty in Salem in 1692 was only an example of the executions for witchcraft which were common in many parts of Europe in the seventeenth century.

Indignation against Andros had reached a high point when the welcome news arrived in Boston in April, 1689, that James II had been driven from his throne by the "glorious revolution." Andros, left unprotected by the fall of his master, was seized and imprisoned by the outraged leaders of the colony. The town meeting of Boston assumed the government, appointed a committee of safety, and sent envoys to London to learn the will of the new sovereigns, William and Mary of Orange. The "empire" of Andros was broken up. Connecticut and Rhode Island were allowed to resume self-government under their old charters. New York (where a certain Jacob Leisler had seized the power on the news of James II's downfall[1]) and New Jersey received new royal governors. Massachusetts was given a new charter in 1691, which altered the independent Puritan character of the colony in three important respects: (1) the governor was to be appointed by the king instead of elected by the freemen of the colony; (2) liberty of worship was guaranteed to all Protestant sects; (3) the ownership of property and not membership in a Puritan church was made the basis of political rights. Under this charter the Massachusetts colony lived until the American Revolution.

The Proprietary Colony of Maryland. Virginia, Plymouth, and Massachusetts, however varied the motives which brought their settlers to America, had all been financed by trading companies which invited investors to buy their stock. In 1632 appeared the first successful colony of a type which was to supersede the trading company entirely and become the pattern for the colonies founded under the later Stuart kings, Charles II and James II (1660–1689). It is known as a "proprietorship." The king granted to a man or a small group of men (generally courtiers) a tract of land with large powers of government. The proprietors appointed the governors, judges, and councilors of their colonies, organized the courts, authorized lawmaking as-

---

[1] Leisler had no intention of "rebellion," and was willing and ready to hand over authority to the new king's governor when he should arrive at New York. But that cruel governor, Slaughter, provoked by Leisler's assumption of power, had the innocent man hanged as a traitor.

semblies, and drew their revenues from the sale of land to the settlers and the profits of trade. In short, they regarded their colonies as something like large private estates.

In 1632 Charles I granted to George Calvert, Baron of Baltimore, the territory between 40° north latitude and the southern bank of the Potomac (map, p. 67), together with a very liberal charter. No tax was to be levied by the crown on any persons or property within the colony. Laws were to be made "by the proprietor with the advice . . . of the freemen," such laws not to be contrary to the laws of England. The proprietor was only to present to the king two Indian arrows at Easter as a symbol of his allegiance. George Calvert died before the king's seal was affixed to the charter, but in 1634 his son sent a colony of about three hundred gentlemen and laborers to St. Marys, on the shore of Chesapeake Bay. The Stuart kings had a careless habit of granting to courtiers land in America which had already been granted to someone else. Maryland lay wholly within the territory of the Virginia Company as defined by the charter of 1609 (map, p. 51), and Lord Baltimore had to resort to armed force to drive Virginia fur traders from Kent Island in Chesapeake Bay. He had trouble with his own settlers too, because he took the charter to mean that the proprietor was to propose the laws and the freemen accept them, whereas the very first assembly in Maryland insisted on just the opposite view. Baltimore tactfully yielded, and thus the Maryland assembly became a real legislature instead of a body merely to register the decrees of the proprietor's governor.

The Religious Problem in Maryland. Lord Baltimore was a Roman Catholic, and he founded Maryland chiefly for the purpose of providing a refuge in the New World for the members of his faith, who at that time were without any political or civil rights in England. But so few Catholics came to the colony (to which Baltimore admitted Christians of all sects) that they numbered less than one fourth of the population before the province was ten years old. It was in order to protect the Roman Catholic minority from persecution, therefore, that Baltimore got the assembly to pass the Toleration Act (1649), which provided that "no person in this province professing to believe in Jesus Christ shall be in any ways troubled . . . for his or her religion . . . so that they be not unfaithful to the lord proprietary or molest or conspire against the civil government established." This is the first act of religious toleration in the American colonies, though by excluding non-Christians it was less tolerant than Roger Williams's complete religious freedom in Rhode Island. Lord Baltimore even went so far as to appoint a Puritan governor of Maryland in deference to his large majority of Protestant subjects. The strife between Catholics and Protestants in Maryland continued until James II was overthrown in England. Then Maryland was taken away from the Baltimores and put under a royal governor. The Anglican Church was established, and the Catholics, who comprised less than 10 per cent of the population, were deprived of their political rights. However, when the Baltimores turned Protestant the colony was restored to them (1720), and it remained a proprietary province until the American Revolution.

The Carolinas. Owing a debt of both gratitude and money to the Cavaliers who had helped him regain his throne, Charles II, in 1663, granted to a group of eight courtiers the huge tract of land between Virginia and the Spanish settlement of Florida, extending westward to the "South Sea." The object of the proprietors was to build up a prosperous trade in semitropical products, such as silk, wine, ginger, rice, and indigo. They published *A Brief Description* of the province, with a map, setting forth "the Healthfulness of the Air, the Fertility of the Earth and Waters, and the great Pleasure and Profit [that] will accrue to those that shall go thither to enjoy the same." Settlers from Barbados and the British Isles, together with some German and French Huguenots (Protestants), were attracted to the colony by its growing industries and its policy of religious toleration, until by the end of the seventeenth century it had a population of more than fifty thousand.

But the colony did not prosper politically. An elaborate constitution, the "Grand Model," composed by the great English philosopher John Locke, proved utterly unfit for the govern-

CANADA OR NEW FRANCE

GRANTED TO THE DUKE OF YORK, 1664

GRANTED TO GORGES, 1639

GRANTED TO MASON, 1629

NEW ENGLAND

Connecticut R.

IROQUOIS REGION—
NEW YORK'S CLAIMS
RECOGNIZED BY
FRENCH, 1713

Albany

Hartford

GRANTED TO THE DUKE OF YORK, 1664

GRANTED TO PENN, 1681

40°

REGRANTED TO BERKELEY
AND CARTERET, 1664

40°

Disputed by Penn and Baltimore

GRANTED TO
BALTIMORE
1632

Kent I., 1631

Potomac R.

St. Mary's

THE THREE LOWER COUNTIES
ADDED TO PENN'S DOMAIN, 1682

VIRGINIA

Chowan R.

Chesapeake Bay

GRANTED TO A BOARD OF EIGHT NOBLE PROPRIETORS, 1663–1665

GEORGIA GRANTED TO OGLETHORPE, 1732

Savannah R.

Ashley R.

Charles Town

Altamaha R.

*Seven eighths of the Atlantic seaboard
was granted to court favorites between
1632 and 1682*

PROPRIETARY GRANTS
MADE BY THE STUART KINGS

ment of a sparse colony in the American wilderness. The northern settlers on Albemarle Sound and the southern group around Charleston, separated by three hundred miles, went their own ways, until they were recognized in 1711 as the colonies of North Carolina and South Carolina, with a governor for each. Pirates preying on the rich islands of the West Indies used the sheltered coast of North Carolina for their lairs. The Spaniards, who claimed the Carolina territory as their own, incited the Indians to attack the colony on the south. The proprietors, according to the charter, owned the land as feudal lords; and when the assembly of South Carolina tried to take it out of their hands and sell it to settlers, they vetoed the act. The assembly then rebelled against the proprietors and petitioned King George I to be taken under his protection as a royal province (1719). The petition was granted, and ten years later the proprietors sold their rights and interests in both Carolinas to the crown for £50,000.

The Dutch Colony on the Hudson. The best place on the Atlantic coast for the establishment of a colony was the site of New York, with its splendid harbor and bay and its great river leading up to the heart of the fur country. Yet it was not the English but the Dutch who took possession of this choice region. In September, 1609, in search of a passage to Cathay, Henry Hudson, an experienced English navigator in the service of the Dutch East India Company, sailed up the river which bears his name, bartering trinkets, liquor, and firearms for the valuable furs which the Indians brought out in their canoes to his little vessel, the *Half-Moon*. Five years later Fort Orange was built on the present site of Albany. The States-General of Holland created the Dutch West India Company to govern the colony, which was called New Netherland.

The first director-general (governor) arrived at Manhattan in 1623, the date taken to mark the founding of New York City. Shortly afterward the third director-general, Peter Minuit, bought from the Indians the island on which the greatest metropolis of our country now stands, paying for it sixty Dutch guilders (twenty-four dollars), or about one tenth of a cent an acre. The company turned over the settlement of the colony to wealthy proprietors, or "patroons," to whom it gave large estates on both sides of the river, and whom it allowed to exact feudal dues, like rent, tithes, and even days of forced labor, from the settlers whom the patroons brought over. Interested only in profits from the fur trade, the despotic governors neglected to protect the colonists against the Indians and scorned their petitions for a share in the government. The last and ablest of the Dutch governors, crusty old Peter Stuyvesant with the wooden leg, had to give up his claim to the Connecticut valley in 1650, but five years later he swooped down upon a Swedish settlement on the Delaware River and easily reduced it to submission to New Netherland.

New Netherland Becomes New York. Every year the English government realized more clearly the need for getting rid of this Dutch colony, which lay like a wedge between New England and the southern provinces and controlled the profitable fur trade of the Hudson. In 1664, therefore, Charles II, on the verge of a commercial war with Holland, granted to his brother James, duke of York, all the land between the Connecticut and Delaware rivers (map, p. 67). The first knowledge that Director-General Stuyvesant had of this denial of the right of the Dutch to their settlement in America was the appearance of the Duke's fleet in the harbor, with the curt summons to surrender the fort at the foot of Manhattan Island. Stuyvesant stormed and fumed, declaring that he would never surrender; but the leading citizens, knowing that resistance was hopeless, finally persuaded him to yield. New Netherland fell without a blow, and the English flag waved over an unbroken coast from Canada to the Carolinas.[1]

There are still traces in New York of its fifty years of Dutch occupation. The names of the old Knickerbocker families remind us of the patroons' estates, and from the car windows one gets glimpses of high Dutch stoops and quaint market places in the villages along the Hudson.

[1] When its proprietor, the Duke of York, became King James II, in 1685, New York was automatically transformed from a proprietary to a royal province.

Under Dutch rule the colony had had no representative assembly, nor was it until 1683 that the new English proprietor yielded to the pressure (especially from the towns on Long Island founded on the New England model) to grant one. Two years later, on coming to the English throne as James II, he revoked this grant and made New York the pattern of absolute government to which he tried to make all the colonies north of Maryland conform. How his viceroy Andros failed in this plan we have already seen (p. 63). After the confusion following the overthrow of James II and the tragic fate of Leisler (p. 64) was past, New York went on for the rest of the colonial period with governors sent over by the king and with an assembly elected by the people. The Anglican Church was established, but other Protestant sects were allowed to worship freely. Two interesting facts were noted by visitors to New York even in the seventeenth century, namely, the great variety of peoples and languages to be found there, and the absorption of the inhabitants in money-making.

The Jerseys. Even before he had driven the Dutch from his new province, the Duke of York leased the lower part of it, between the Delaware and the Atlantic, to two of his friends, Lord Berkeley and Sir George Carteret. The latter had been governor of the island of Jersey, in the English Channel, and it was in honor of him that the province was called New Jersey. The new proprietors immediately published "Concessions" for their colony — a liberal constitution granting religious liberty and a popular assembly with the control of taxation. The proprietors divided their province into East Jersey (Carteret's) and West Jersey (Berkeley's). Their right to establish a government was constantly disputed by the governors of New York, and their attempts to collect rents from the land were resisted by settlers, many of whom were Puritans from New England. Finally both proprietors grew tired of the strife and sold out their claims to groups of Friends, or Quakers, who, in spite of their peaceful doctrines, could not bring order and harmony into New Jersey politics. In 1702 East and West Jersey were united into a single royal colony, which for thirty-six years thereafter had the same governor as New York though keeping its own legislature and courts. New Jersey was overshadowed by its more powerful neighbors to the north and west, New York and Pennsylvania, by whom it was also hemmed in to narrow geographical limits. Its history during the colonial period was not significant.

The Founding of Pennsylvania. One of the group of Quakers who purchased East Jersey was a young man who was a strange combination of courtier and democrat. His father, the "old" William Penn, had won renown as an admiral in the English navy, and the family stood high in the favor of the Stuart brothers Charles and James. The younger William Penn, while a student at Oxford, became converted to the doctrine of the Quakers, who rejected all ceremonies of religious worship and all authority of priests, bishops, or ministers, obeying only the "inner light" of conscience. Believing in the complete equality of men, they refused to bow or to remove their hats in the presence of magistrates.[1] Neither the angry remonstrances of his father nor persecution and imprisonment by the State could make Penn renounce his new faith. It was in jail that he wrote his famous tract on "The Great Case of Liberty of Conscience." On his release he traveled as a missionary in Holland and Germany, founding Quaker societies.

Penn's father had lent Charles II £16,000, and the king was glad to discharge the debt to the younger Penn by a grant of land in America where he could found a refuge for the persecuted Quakers. So in 1681 William Penn received a royal charter making him proprietor of the territory between New York and Maryland, extending five degrees of longitude west of the Delaware River.[2] Penn called the land "Sylvania"

[1] An amusing incident of Quaker simplicity and directness of speech occurred during the visit of President Washington to New England in the autumn of 1789. The Quaker mayor of Salem greeted him with the words: "Friend Washington, we are glad to see thee and hope thee will enjoy thy visit."

[2] Maryland and Pennsylvania quarreled over the boundary line between them until 1764–1767, when two English surveyors, Mason and Dixon, ran the present line at 39° 43′ 26″ north latitude. This famous Mason and Dixon line formed the boundary between the free and the slave states in the nineteenth century.

(Woodland), but the king insisted on adding "Penn" as a prefix, in honor of the old admiral. Charles II had learned from his troubles with the obstinate colony of Massachusetts not to grant such unlimited powers as had been given to Lord Baltimore. The Penn charter provided that the colony must always keep an agent in London, that the Church of England must be tolerated, that appeals to England from the colonial courts must be allowed, that the king might veto any act of the assembly within five years of its passage, and that taxes might be laid on the colony by the English Parliament. Penn persuaded the Duke of York to cede to him the land which Stuyvesant had seized from the Swedes on the Delaware, and he governed this territory as the "Three Lower Counties," through a deputy, until 1702, when it was given its own assembly as the colony of Delaware. But Delaware remained under the Penns' governors and a part of the proprietary domain of the Penn family until the American Revolution.

Penn's "Holy Experiment." William Penn was the greatest of the founders of the American colonies. He had the liberality of Roger Williams without his impatience, the fervor of the Massachusetts Puritans without their intolerance, and the tact of Lord Baltimore with more industry and ability. He called his undertaking a "holy experiment," believing that a peaceful and prosperous society could exist under a humane government, welcoming people of various nationalities, and tolerating the worship of various creeds. At a time when scores of offenses were punished by death in England, he made murder and treason the only capital crimes in his colony. His prisons, instead of filthy dungeons, were workhouses for the correction and rescue of wrongdoers. His province was the first to raise its voice against slavery, and his fair and kindly treatment of the Indians saved his colony from the horrors of savage raids and massacres. Penn had an eye to business as well. He advertised his province by attractive pamphlets published in England and on the Continent, offering land for sale on easy terms and for rent as low as a penny an acre. In the "Frame of Government" he gave his colony a liberal constitution. He came to America himself

THE OLD PENN HOUSE IN PHILADELPHIA

in 1682 and laid out the town of Philadelphia ("brotherly love"), with its streets at right angles and with ample house plots. A year later there were four thousand "industrious husbandmen, carpenters, masons, weavers and other mechanics in Pennsylvania"; and before the end of the seventeenth century it was the largest and most prosperous colony in America. Its exports of bread, flour, lumber, and beer made those commodities "a drugg in all the markets of the West Indies." Evidently the "holy experiment" was a worldly success.

Nevertheless, after Penn's death there were frequent quarrels between the proprietors, the assembly, and the people of the colony. The Scotch-Irish and Germans who were filling up the western land complained, like the frontiersmen in all the colonies, that they were not getting their fair share of representatives in the legislature at Philadelphia. Moreover, these frontiersmen, who were natural-born fighters, had to bear the attacks of the French and Indians on the border in the wars of the eighteenth century, while the wealthy pacifist Quakers who controlled the government were slow to appropriate money for the defense of the colony. Still another cause of complaint was the exemption of the extensive lands of the Penn family from taxation. Enough of the spirit of the founder prevailed, however, to carry the colony over its difficulties.

The Colony of Georgia. To complete the list of the English colonies which became the thirteen original states of the Union, we must mention Georgia, though it was founded long after the Stuarts had been driven from the English throne. In the year that George Washington was born (1732) James Oglethorpe obtained a charter from King George II granting to a body of trustees for a term of twenty-one years the southern, unsettled part of the old Carolina territory lying between the Savannah and Altamaha rivers. Oglethorpe was a philanthropist who wished to provide a home in the New World for the victims of the harsh English laws which threw a man into prison for a small debt. The Church was eager for the conversion of the Indians on the Carolina borders. Capitalists hoped to make profits out of silk and wine industries introduced into the province. And the English government, drifting into a war with Spain, was glad to have the frontier extended southward to Spanish Florida. So Parliament, the Society for the Propagation of the Gospel, the Bank of England, and many private citizens contributed toward founding the new colony on the banks of the Savannah in 1733. Slavery was forbidden in Georgia in the early days; also the traffic in rum. Still the colony did not prosper as its founder had hoped. Silk and wine culture proved unsuited to the land. When war between England and Spain broke out, Oglethorpe twice descended upon the Spanish post of St. Augustine, in Florida, but was not able to take the fort.

It was not till the close of the French and Indian War, in 1763, that the quarrel over "the debatable land" was ended by the transfer of the province of Florida from Spain to England. Meanwhile, ten years earlier, the trustees of Georgia had been glad to surrender their charter to the king. The valiant Oglethorpe lived till 1785, to see the colony which he had founded a state of the Union, whose independence was recognized by Great Britain and the other powers of Europe.

TABLE OF ENGLISH COLONIES

NAME (the thirteen original states in italic)	FOUNDED BY	DATE	CHARTER	ASSEMBLY	MADE ROYAL	STATUS IN 1775	REMARKS
Virginia	London Company	1607	{ 1606–1609 } 1612	1619	1624	Royal	
Plymouth	Separatists	1620		1639	1691	Royal	Merged with Massachusetts in 1691
Massachusetts	Puritans of the Mass. Bay Co.	1628	1629	1634	1684	Royal	Only royal colony to have its charter restored (1691)
Maryland	Lord Baltimore	1634	1632	1634		Proprietary	A royal province, 1690–1715
Rhode Island	Roger Williams	1636	1663	1647		Self-governing	{ Frustrated Andros's attempt to take away charters, 1686–1687
Connecticut	Emigrants from Massachusetts	1636	1662	1637		Self-governing	
New Haven	Emigrants from Massachusetts	1638		1643			Merged with Connecticut, 1662
Maine	F. Gorges	1641	1639		1691	Royal	Bought by Massachusetts, 1677
North Carolina *South Carolina*	Eight nobles	1663	1663	1669	{ N. 1729 / S. 1729 }	Royal	{ Informally separated, 1691; formally separated with different governors, 1729
New York	(Duke of York)	1664	1664	1683–1685	1685	Royal	Dutch colony of New Netherland, 1622–1664
New Hampshire	John Mason	1664	1639	1680	1679	Royal	Towns absorbed by Massachusetts, 1641–1679
New Jersey	Berkeley and Carteret	1664		1664	1702	Royal	Under the governor of New York till 1738
Pennsylvania	William Penn	1681	1680	1681		Proprietary	A royal province, 1692–1694
Delaware	Swedes	1638		1702		Proprietary	{ Conquered by Dutch, 1655; by English, 1664 / Merged with Pennsylvania, 1682 / Separate governor (1691) and assembly (1702)
Georgia	Jas. Oglethorpe	1732	1732	1733	1752	Royal	

TERMS TO BE MASTERED

Western planting   royal province   proprietorship
divine right of kings General Court   patroons
Burgesses   " the glorious revolution"

FOR SUPPLEMENTARY READING

EDWARD EGGLESTON, *Beginners of a Nation* and *The Transit of Civilization from England to America*; E. B. GREENE, *The Foundations of American Nationality*, chaps. iii–ix; MUZZEY and KROUT, *American History for Colleges*, chap. i; MARY JOHNSTON, *Pioneers of the Old South*; C. M. ANDREWS, *The Fathers of New England*; M. W. GOODWIN, *Dutch and English on the Hudson*; S. G. FISHER, *The Quaker Colonies* (Vols. V–VIII of the Chronicles of America); JOHN FISKE, *Old Virginia and her Neighbors* and *The Beginnings of New England*; T. J. WERTEN-BAKER, *The First Americans* (A History of American Life, Vol. II).

TOPICS FOR REPORTS

1. **Bacon's Rebellion.** H. L. OSGOOD, *The American Colonies in the Seventeenth Century*, Vol. III, pp. 258–278; JOHN FISKE, *Old Virginia and her Neighbors*, Vol. II, pp. 58–107; MARY JOHNSTON, *Prisoners of Hope*; HART, *Contemporaries*, Vol. I, No. 71; MUZZEY, *Readings*, pp. 30–34.

2. **The Pilgrims in Holland and England.** W. E. GRIFFIS, *The Pilgrims in their Three Homes*; H. S. COMMAGER, *Documents of American History*, No. 10; *America*, Vol. II, pp. 101–120; JUSTIN WINSOR, *Narrative and Critical History of America*, Vol. III, pp. 257–265 (with illustrations); MUZZEY, *Readings*, pp. 34–37; HART, *Contemporaries*, Vol. I, No. 97.

3. **Sir Edmund Andros.** *Dictionary of American Biography*, under "Andros"; E. B.ʼ GREENE, *Foundations of American Nationality*, pp. 187–195; C. M. ANDREWS, *The Fathers of New England*, chap. x; JOHN FISKE, *The Beginnings of New England*, chap. vi; HART, *Contemporaries*, Vol. I, No. 136; MUZZEY, *Readings*, pp. 46–50.

4. **The Quakers.** JOHN FISKE, *The Dutch and Quaker Colonies*, Vol. II, pp. 108–114; EDWARD CHANNING, *History of the United States*, Vol. II, pp. 94–126; COMMAGER, *Documents*, No. 26; *America*, Vol. II, pp. 175–180; Old South Leaflets, Nos. 95, 171; HART, *Contemporaries*, Nos. 141, 142; MUZZEY, *Readings*, pp. 63–72.

QUESTIONS SUGGESTED BY THE CHAPTER

1. Why were the dissenters from the Anglican Church called Puritans? 2. What was the difference between the Puritans and the Separatists? 3. Why did people in England leave their home to come to America? 4. Why did the English sovereigns try to make their subjects all worship alike? 5. Why did James I take the charter away from the Virginia Company? 6. What was the difference between the *Mayflower Compact* and the "Fundamental Orders" of Connecticut? 7. Ex-

plain why the Massachusetts Bay Company was more "independent" than the Virginia Company. **8.** What is meant by "the rule of the saints"? **9.** Why was New York superior to Boston as a center of the fur trade? **10.** What changes in the social and political order in Massachusetts were made by the new charter of 1691? **11.** Do you think that Leisler deserved punishment as a rebel? **12.** Compare Rhode Island, Pennsylvania, and Maryland in regard to religious toleration. **13.** Why did the English colonies resent the presence of the Dutch on the Hudson? **14.** What is meant by Penn's "holy experiment"? **15.** When and by whom was the last English colony in America founded?

CHAPTER FOUR

COLONIAL AMERICA

To most Americans of the twentieth century the colonial days seem very remote and strange. Those of us who live in the states along the Atlantic seaboard, which was the only part of our vast country that had a settled colonial life, have many reminders of our seventeenth-century and eighteenth-century forefathers. There are hundreds of colonial houses, with their pillared fronts and dormer windows; slender white church spires overlooking colonial burying grounds in which slanting, moss-covered headstones bear quaintly pious inscriptions; portraits of ancestral worthies in wigs and robes, looking down from the walls of our houses and museums; monuments and markers in almost every town to keep alive the memory of historic events. But, in spite of all these reminders, even the direct heirs of the colonial Americans find it hard to understand the customs and thoughts of people who had no better way of traveling by land than on horseback or in lumbering, springless stagecoaches; who had no light but that furnished by candles or whale-oil lamps; no water except what they drew up from wells or caught in hogsheads from the rain running down the roof; no cities crowded with office buildings and apartment houses; no great mills and factories; no power machines; no railroads, trolleys, automobiles, telephones, telegraphs, kitchen ranges, bathrooms, vacuum cleaners, banks, or stock exchanges.

For all that, the colonial period is as important in our history as the years of childhood and adolescence are in the life of a man. We must remember that it was a long period. More years elapsed between the settlement of Jamestown and the Declaration of Independence than have passed since the inauguration of George Washington as first President of the United

States. During those long, slow colonial years the foundations of the American nation were laid. With their growing population, their cultivation of the abundant land of the New World, their expanding commerce, their increasing political experience, their practice in self-defense against the French, the Spaniards, and the Indians, their establishment of schools and colleges, their creation of new types of architecture, literature, and law, the *English* colonies were gradually transformed into *American* colonies. And from there the step to an independent American nation was a natural one.

We shall study in this chapter the debt which we of the twentieth century owe to colonial America.

Two Colonial Epochs. We may divide the colonial period into two parts at about the year 1690. In the first period, which we have studied in the preceding chapter, all the English colonies (except Georgia) on the mainland of America and in the West Indies were established. Most of the settlers came from England. Although at times there were spurts of emigration which brought several thousands to the colonies, as in the case of Massachusetts from 1628 to 1642, the growth of the population was rather slow. As the seventeenth century drew to a close there were only about three hundred thousand people in the colonies, and the greater part of them stuck pretty closely to the neighborhood of the original settlements: the region about Boston, the Connecticut and Hudson valleys, Philadelphia, the Jamestown peninsula, and Charleston. Intercolonial travel was rare in the absence of roads and the presence of dangerous Indians, each colony being more closely in touch with England and the West Indies than with its nearer neighbors in America. Except for the New England Confederation of 1643 (p. 61), there was no attempt at union or co-operation between the colonies in this first period.

The eighteenth century, however, tells a different story. The population of the colonies grew steadily until it reached some 2,750,000 on the eve of the American Revolution. Religious and political persecution in Europe drove thousands to the New World to swell the natural increase of the large colonial

COLONIAL STAGECOACH

families. Huguenots (Protestants) expelled from France by
Louis XIV's revocation of the Edict of Nantes (1685) came to
New England, New York, and South Carolina. The defeat
of the Scotch supporters of the Stuart cause in 1715 and 1745
sent many Highlanders to America. Germans, fleeing from the
devastation of the Rhinelands by the French armies, flocked
to Penn's colony at the rate of nearly two thousand a year
from 1727 to 1754. Protestants from the north of Ireland (the
Scotch-Irish), oppressed by the harsh English laws against their
industries and commerce, came over to fill in the frontier region
from New Hampshire to the Carolinas, until there were nearly
four hundred thousand of them here at the time of the Revolutionary War. Altogether, the non-English stocks made up more
than a quarter of the population in 1776.

If the colonies were still far from the idea of a political union
for the common good in the first three quarters of the eighteenth
century, they were, nevertheless, coming closer together in
many ways. The spaces between the earlier patches of settlement were filling up. Stage lines and post-office routes were

connecting the chief towns from Portsmouth to Savannah. The
Indian menace disappeared with the ending of the series of wars
that lasted almost uninterrupted from 1690 to 1763. Trade
between the colonies increased rapidly. Commercial firms in
New York and Philadelphia had accounts with firms in Boston
and Charleston. Families of New England and Maryland,
Pennsylvania and the Carolinas, intermarried. Virginians, like
James Madison, were being sent to college in New Jersey
(Princeton). By the middle of the eighteenth century there
were in the colonies many tens of thousands — Germans,
French Huguenots, Scotch-Irish — who had no attachment to
England; and even the descendants of the original settlers were
thinking and speaking of English officials or visitors who came
over as "strangers." The struggling, isolated, sparse English
colonies of the seventeenth century had become the prosperous,
self-reliant American colonies of the eighteenth.

Social Classes. We cannot, of course, study in detail the
history of each of the thirteen colonies which united in 1776 to
form the American nation. Nor is it necessary to do so. For,
in spite of the different circumstances under which they were
founded, the colonies all had certain institutions and certain
experiences in common. The English language, English ideas of
law, and English patterns of government prevailed from New
Hampshire to Georgia. All the colonies had representative
assemblies elected by the people — that is, by such people as
were allowed to vote. The colonies with western frontiers had
a common problem in the rivalry between the "back country"
and the older and more prosperous settlements on the coast,
over such matters as money for defense against the Indians and
a fair proportion of seats in the colonial assemblies. The
merchants in all the colonies had a common interest, and often
a common grievance, in the acts of Parliament and the orders of
the Board of Trade in London governing their commerce with
the mother country, with one another, and with foreigners.

These common problems rather than the events in a particular colony determined the trend of our history in the eighteenth
century. Furthermore, conditions in colonial America made for

WAYSIDE-INN KITCHEN, SUDBURY, MASS.

a less sharp distinction of social classes than prevailed in Europe.
We had no kings or nobles at one end of the social scale, and no
downtrodden serfs or peasants at the other. Land was so
abundant and cheap that even the poor "redemptioner," who
had to sell his services for a term of five or more years in order
to pay his way over to America, could generally acquire a small
farm when he became his own master. There was, to be sure,
a colonial "aristocracy," consisting of the rich merchants of
New England and New York and the great planters of the South,
who went about with powdered hair, ruffles, silk knee breeches,
and silver buckles, receiving the deference of those of humbler
lot. But as it was an aristocracy of wealth and not of birth,
it was constantly broken into by men who made fortunes in
commerce or land speculation or money-changing. As industries like iron and woolen manufactures grew, the number of
wageworkers in mills and factories naturally increased; but
still they were few as compared with the independent "yeomen," or farmers, who comprised over 90 per cent of the
colonial population at the time of the American Revolution.

MONTICELLO

The only classes of white men who lacked the ambition to rise were the lowest of the laborers in the North and the "poor whites" of the Piedmont regions of the South. At the bottom of the social scale were the Negro slaves, who were bought and sold like horses or cattle. Slavery existed in all the colonies, and there were but few voices condemning it as a moral evil. In the North the Negroes were used as house servants and were comparatively few in number. In the South, where their labor was adapted to hot work in the tobacco and rice fields, they increased rapidly during the eighteenth century — many of them brought from Africa by the rum-distillers of Massachusetts and Rhode Island. By 1775 there were more than half a million Negro slaves in the country, all but a few thousands south of Mason and Dixon's line.

Three Types of Colonies. Though the colonies had much in common, we may divide them into three groups in respect to their chief interests and occupations. New England was the land of the Puritans, where religion dominated the scene and the clergy controlled public affairs until the rise of the merchants and lawyers in the eighteenth century. The towns, with church and school as their center, were the units of settlement, and the town meetings the form of local government. The soil was adapted only to small farms, which had to be laboriously cleared of the stones which had been left by the glaciers of the ice age in the distant past. But there was fine timber in the forests for shipbuilding, and the supply of fish in the Northern waters was inexhaustible. So the New Englanders took to the sea. Their stanch, swift ships carried rum to Africa, lumber, shingles, barrel staves, horses, and ironware to the West Indies, and fish to all ports far and near. By the middle of the eighteenth century the little town of Marblehead, Massachusetts, was sending out over a hundred and fifty fishing vessels a year. The sacred cod became the emblem of Boston.

The colonies south of Mason and Dixon's line were in sharp contrast to New England. The Anglican Church was established in all of them, but the harsh rule of the Puritan clergy was missing. Someone described the church in the South as "a gentlemen's club with a faint interest in religion." The county or parish, not the compact town, was the unit of government. Indigo and rice from the swampy coast lands, tobacco from the large plantations extending along the rivers, deerskins from the back country, and pitch and tar from the woods of North Carolina were staple articles of commerce, sent to England and, so far as was permitted by the English laws which we shall notice presently, to the countries of continental Europe. The wealthy planters, with their thousands of acres and many hundred slaves, were far outnumbered by the small farmers with not more than four or five slaves and by the "poor whites"; but they directed public affairs and gave the tone to Southern life. They imported furniture, silver plate, musical instruments, and dress goods from England against their remittances of tobacco, and were generally in debt to the manufacturers of the mother country. They often sent their sons to school at Eton or Oxford.

The middle group of colonies (New York, Pennsylvania, Delaware, and New Jersey) were of a much more varied type

LOADING TOBACCO IN OLD VIRGINIA

than New England and the South. Their population contained more foreign elements, such as Germans, Dutch, Welsh, and Scotch-Irish. They combined both the county and the town government. The large patroons' estates on the Hudson resembled the plantations of the South, except that they employed free white labor instead of Negro slaves. The merchant class rose to wealth and power as in New England. By the middle of the eighteenth century New York and Philadelphia had outdistanced Boston in commerce. The Anglican Church was established in New York and New Jersey, and the Quakers predominated in Pennsylvania. But there were many other religious bodies, such as the Presbyterians, the Dutch Reformed, and the Jews, enjoying freedom of worship. The ablest of the early governors of New York, Thomas Dongan, was an Irish Roman Catholic. Wheat was a chief article of export from these colonies, like fish from New England and tobacco from the South. As the colonial period advanced, however, manufactures developed, and iron, glass, and pottery ware began to compete with such natural products as cereals, furs, lumber, and livestock.

Education in the Colonies. Our present system of free public schools, and even colleges, supported by the state was unknown in colonial days. A smattering of education for the younger children was provided in the private "dame schools" or in schools supported by the churches and missionary societies. The boys, except the few privileged ones who could prepare for college with a tutor, got little schooling beyond the early teens. If they wished to enter a profession, like medicine or law, they learned their trade as apprentices in the office of the lawyer or by making the daily round of calls with the doctor. Girls were not supposed to go to school. The daughters of the wealthy might take private lessons in painting, music, dancing, or French; but the great majority of girls, destined to marry early and rear large families, learned the practical duties of cooking, sewing, preserving, candle-dipping, and the like from their mothers and older sisters in the household.

Massachusetts passed a law in 1647 requiring every town of

HARVARD COLLEGE IN 1726

fifty families to support an elementary school to teach reading, writing, and arithmetic, and every town of a hundred
families to have a "grammar school" in which boys could be
prepared for college. But the records show that many towns
failed to obey the law. More than a century and a quarter
after the founding of Jamestown there were only three colleges
in the colonies: Harvard (1636) in Massachusetts, William
and Mary (1693) in Virginia, and Yale (1701) in Connecticut.
The poverty, hardships, and dangers of life in the early colonial
period made the general spread of education impossible; but
in 1743 Benjamin Franklin could say, "The first drudgery of
settling new colonies is pretty well over, and there are many in
every colony in circumstances which set them at ease to cultivate
the finer arts and improve the common stock of knowledge."
Six new colleges were founded within a few years of Franklin's
prophecy: the College of New Jersey (now Princeton) in 1746,
Franklin's own University of Pennsylvania in 1749, King's
College (now Columbia) in New York in 1754, Rhode Island
(now Brown University) in 1764, Queen's College (now Rutgers)
at New Brunswick, New Jersey, in 1766, and Dartmouth at
Hanover, New Hampshire, in 1769. All but Pennsylvania and

Dartmouth were sectarian — that is, founded under the auspices of a religious denomination.

Arts and Sciences. From the middle years of the eighteenth century on, there were an increasing number of literary and scientific clubs in the colonies. Benjamin Franklin founded the American Philosophical Society in Philadelphia in 1743. Several painters, especially portrait-painters, rose to distinction. Benjamin West, a Pennsylvanian, went to London, where he became the official court painter in 1772, and twenty years later succeeded Sir Joshua Reynolds as president of the Royal Academy. The portraits of Washington by Charles Wilson Peale and Gilbert Stuart are familiar to every American. There were few professional architects in the colonies. Faneuil Hall, the "Cradle of Liberty," in Boston, was designed by a man who kept a paint shop; and Monticello, the most beautiful of all colonial mansions, was planned and built by its versatile owner, Thomas Jefferson (see page 83).

Not until 1765 was the first medical school opened at the college in Philadelphia. Almost nothing was known of the methods of preventing disease. In the absence of sanitation and disinfectants, terrible epidemics of yellow fever claimed thousands of victims. Faces pitted with the marks of smallpox were seen in every community. "The human system," says Professor C. M. Andrews, "was dosed and physicked until it could hold no more. Dismal herbs dispensed by Indian doctors and popular concoctions were taken in large doses by credulous people." George Washington's life was sacrificed to medical ignorance in 1799. He was bled of two quarts of blood by leeches and then "dosed to nausea and blistered to rawness." Even Washington's stout constitution could not stand such heroic treatment.

On the other hand, the colonies produced some geniuses in physical science. Benjamin Franklin (1706–1790), aside from being a great statesman, diplomat, and educator, won worldwide recognition for his researches in electricity and his many practical inventions. Benjamin Thompson, born in Woburn, Massachusetts, became a noted mathematician and military engineer. He was employed in scientific research by the British

BENJAMIN FRANKLIN

war office, and then went to Bavaria, where he held the position of minister of war for eleven years and was raised to the nobility as Count Rumford by the Bavarian ruler.

Books and Newspapers. The tens of thousands of books turned out by our printing presses every year and the stacks of newspapers and magazines piled on our newsstands every day would have bewildered our colonial forefathers. For, except for a comparatively few families whose bookshelves were stocked with the English classics, or for the clergymen and lawyers who gathered a library of theological and legal volumes, the American colonists had neither the time nor the taste for much reading. "Some few towns excepted," wrote John Dickinson on the eve of the Revolution, "we are all tillers of the soil from Nova Scotia to West Florida." Thousands of the country folk could neither read nor write; other thousands could only laboriously con the family Bible or the Farmer's Almanac. Hardly anything that could be called literature was produced in the colonies before the middle of the eighteenth century; and as late as 1827 the Englishman Sydney Smith scornfully asked, "Who reads an American book?" Though there were some private circulating libraries, the free public libraries which are the pride of our cities and towns today were unknown in the colonial period.

The first successful newspaper was the *Boston News-Letter*, appearing in 1704; and within the next half-century all the colonies except New Jersey, Delaware, and Georgia were publishing their *Gazettes* or *Chronicles*. But the colonial newspapers bore little resemblance to the great metropolitan dailies of our own time. They were more like a high-school paper. Generally published once a week in a few hundred copies, their four small pages would contain some stale news brought by the last packet from London, the reprint of an English article, a letter from a citizen who was traveling abroad, an original poem, and sundry advertisements for Indian bitters, a stray horse, or a runaway slave. It was not until the controversy with Great Britain leading to the Revolution grew keen that the American colonies really began to find their voice. Then the articles, pamphlets, and public papers dealing with the crisis won the praise of men on both sides of the Atlantic.

The Zenger Case. Small and dull as the colonial newspaper was, it rendered one great service to the cause of American freedom. In 1734 a German immigrant named John Peter Zenger, the editor of the *New York Weekly Journal*, was haled to court for printing articles criticizing the royal governor, Cosby. Zenger's trial roused an interest that extended far beyond New York. It was a question of whether the press should or should not be free to condemn the acts of public officials. The aged Andrew Hamilton, said to be the ablest lawyer in the colonies, came from Philadelphia to volunteer his services in behalf of Zenger. His powerful plea to the jury, defending "the liberty both of exposing and opposing arbitrary power . . . by speaking and writing the truth," resulted in the acquittal of Zenger amid the cheers of the crowded courtroom. Gouverneur Morris later spoke of the Zenger trial as "the morning star of that liberty which subsequently revolutionized America."

N. E. *Numb.* 17

The Boston News-Letter.

Publiſhed by Authority.

From **Monday** April 17. to **Monday** April 24. 1704.

London Flying-Poſt from Decemb. 2d. to 4th. 1703.

Etters from *Scotland* bring us the Copy of a Sheet lately Printed there, Intituled, *A ſeaſonable Alarm for* Scotland. *In a Letter from a Gentleman in the City, to his Friend in the Country, concerning the preſent Danger of the Kingdom and of the Proteſtant Religion.*

This Letter takes Notice, That Papiſts ſwarm in that Nation, that they traffick more avowedly than formerly, and that of late many Scores of Prieſts & Jeſuites are come thither from France, and gone to the North, to the Highlands & other places of the Country. That the Miniſters of the Highlands and North gave in large Liſts of them to the Committee of the General Aſſembly, to be laid before the Privy-Council.

From all this he infers, That they have hopes of Aſſiſtance from *France*, otherwiſe they would never be ſo impudent, and he gives Reaſons for his Apprehenſions that the *French* King may ſend Troops thither this Winter, 1. Becauſe the *Engliſh* & *Dutch* will not then be at Sea to oppoſe them. 2. He can then beſt ſpare them, the Seaſon of Action beyond Sea being over. 3. The Expectation given him of a conſiderable number to joyn them, may incourage him to the undertaking with fewer Men, if he can but ſend over a ſufficient number of Officers with Arms and Ammunition.

He endeavours in the reſt of his Letters to anſwer the fooliſh Pretences of the Pretender's being a Proteſtant and that he will govern us according to Law. He ſays, that being bred up in the Religion and Politicks of *France*, he is by Education a

THE BOSTON NEWS-LETTER

Amusements and Recreation. There was little time or money to spare for amusements in the early colonial days. In Puritan New England any youthful craving for the joy of life was regarded as a temptation of Satan, and sometimes little children were made to serve as pallbearers at funerals in order that they might be impressed with the brevity of human existence. The Quakers of the middle colonies also frowned upon amusements as frivolous.

The eighteenth century was half over before a theatrical company was allowed to produce a play in Philadelphia. An attempt to give *The Orphan* (a moral play) in a Boston coffee-house in 1750 was forbidden as "tending to discourage industry and frugality and greatly to increase impiety." In the Southern colonies, where the Church of England prevailed, there was little religious prejudice against amusements. We hear of a theater in Williamsburg, Virginia, as early as 1722. Charleston, South Carolina, was the gayest social center in the colonies, with its musical societies, its opera, its balls, fairs, and race tracks. In 1750 Lewis Hallam brought over an excellent dramatic company from London, and for twenty years entertained all the colonies outside of New England with the plays of Shakespeare, Addison, Steele, and other noted English dramatists. On the other hand, there was a coarseness in the recreations of even the "respectable classes" that would be frowned on today. Gentlemen and ladies would spend days in the cruel sport of fox-hunting. Cockfights drew large crowds of gamblers. Hard drinking was regarded neither as an injury to health nor as an offense to morals.

While appreciating the admirable traits of our colonial fore-fathers, — their courage, their thrift, their sturdy spirit of self-determination, — we should also realize that the modern age has brought both a refinement of manners and an improvement in morals. But in one respect these forefathers teach us a wholesome lesson. In their recreations as well as in the more serious concerns of life they did much more for themselves and had much less done for them than we. They worked for themselves; they amused themselves. The age of commercialized entertainment furnished by theater syndicates, managed concerts and lecture tours, prize-ring promoters, and big-league managers was still as far distant as the age of highly specialized industry.

Our Political Debt to the Colonies. After this brief sketch of the social life of the colonies, with its contribution to American education and culture, let us see what we owe the colonial fathers as builders of states, creators of wealth, and defenders of their borders. First of all, we must remember that the colonies were not established as political states. If the trading companies and proprietors were given, in their charters from the king, the power to make laws for the management of their affairs, it was with no idea of freeing them from the king's authority. Their sovereign was in England, and he might take away their charters — as he more than once did. Still, as the charters guaranteed the settlers the rights of Englishmen and as the colonies were three thousand miles distant, it was not strange that they wanted to take more and more responsibility for running their own governments.

The early Stuart kings, James I and Charles I, had so much political and religious trouble with their subjects at home that they had little time to interfere with their subjects in America. But when Charles II was restored to his father's throne in 1660, he entered upon a policy of binding the colonies closer to England both politically and commercially. In the very first year of his reign a Council for Foreign Plantations (colonies) was created to keep the king informed of the conduct of his distant subjects, and the first of a series of Acts of Trade was passed by Parliament to regulate the colonial commerce. We shall turn to these Acts of Trade presently. Here let us notice that the aim of the later Stuarts was to stiffen the control of England over the colonies. The charters granted by Charles II to the Carolinas, New York, the Jerseys, and Pennsylvania[1] contained more definite recognition of the king's authority than did the earlier charters to Virginia, Massachusetts, and Maryland. Royal commissions were sent to the colonies to investigate and report to the Privy Council the behavior of colonial assemblies and courts. Instructions to governors sent out to the colonies were more detailed and strict. We have seen how the attempt was made by James II to unite all of New England, New York, and the Jerseys under the rule of Sir Edmund Andros (p. 63). The number of royal governors increased steadily. In 1682 there were only two royal provinces (Virginia and New Hampshire); but seventy years later all the colonies but five were under royal governors (see map, p. 94), and the governors of the proprietary colonies of Pennsylvania-Delaware and Maryland had to be approved by the king.

The colonists fought most stubbornly to maintain what they considered their rights as Englishmen against the growing power of the king's officials. Their elected assemblies, which had control of the purse strings like the English House of Commons, refused to vote the salary for the governor unless he approved their laws. They began to resist "taxation without representation" nearly a hundred years before the American Revolution.

[1] For the limitations upon the colony of Pennsylvania in Penn's charter of 1681 see page 72.

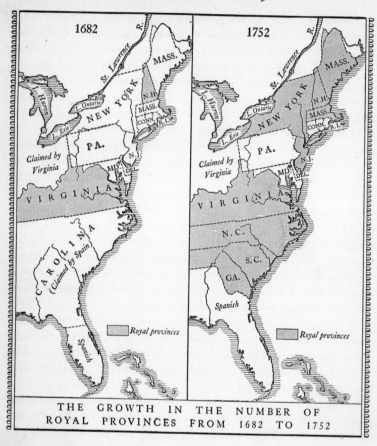

THE GROWTH IN THE NUMBER OF
ROYAL PROVINCES FROM 1682 TO 1752

John Wise and several other leading citizens of Ipswich, Massachusetts, were thrown into prison under Andros for refusing to pay the taxes which he levied upon them without the consent of the town meeting. Several times in the earlier years of the eighteenth century bills were introduced into Parliament to take away all the colonial charters. If this had been done or attempted, it might have provoked open resistance in America long before the Revolution. Two things chiefly prevented such a crisis before George III came to the throne in 1760. First, the Whig ministers in England had enough wholesome respect for the spirit of the colonies not to provoke them by a strict enforcement of the laws regulating their commerce and government; and, second, England needed to stand shoulder to shoulder with the colonies in the defense of their borders in the series of wars with the French and Indians which were waged in the eighteenth century.

The Acts of Trade. Not only did the colonies resist the attempts of the home government to control their politics, but they also opposed the acts of Parliament and the orders of the king's officers to regulate their trade. These acts and orders represented the so-called "mercantile theory" of trade, which the European nations held in the seventeenth and eighteenth centuries. A country's wealth, they thought, was measured by the amount of money in its treasury. Hence more money must be brought into the country than was taken out, to create a "favorable balance of trade." Colonies were useful because they could furnish, free of duties, certain raw materials which the home country did not produce, such as sugar, furs, silk, indigo, and naval supplies; and at the same time the growing population of the colonies would furnish a market for the sale of the goods manufactured by the home country. This is why each country wished to keep the trade of its colonies in its own hands.

In the first year of Charles II's reign (1660) Parliament passed an act specifying that certain "enumerated commodities" produced in the colonies, including tobacco, sugar, cotton wool, indigo, and ginger, could be exported only to England or to English colonies.[1] This act affecting colonial *exports*[2] was fol-

---

[1] The same law re-enacted a Navigation Act, passed in 1651 against the Dutch, requiring that all goods brought from Asia, Africa, and America to ports of the British Empire be carried in vessels built, owned, and manned by British subjects. This act did not harm the colonies, since they were a part of the British Empire.

[2] The original list of "enumerated commodities" did not include the products of the Northern and middle colonies on the American mainland. But later laws extended the list to include ship timber, furs, and copper, as well as more articles from the Southern colonies, such as rice and naval stores. Every addition to the list meant one more commodity that the colonies were not allowed to send directly to the ports of continental Europe.

lowed in 1663 by an act providing that most European goods *imported* into the colonies must first be brought to English ports and there pay a duty before being reshipped to America.[1] Other acts, in 1673 and 1696, imposed heavy penalties for smuggling and introduced into the colonies a number of unwelcome officials to enforce the laws: collectors of revenue; inspectors authorized to search ships, wharves, and warehouses for suspected goods; and judges of special courts to try offenders.

The fact that England had a perfect right to pass such laws and send over such officials did not make them any more acceptable to the colonies. Suppose, for example, that a merchant of Philadelphia sent a cargo of wheat (or any other "nonenumerated commodity") to Italy. He could not bring back olive oil without taking it to England for inspection and the payment of duty. Even though the duty was paid back when the cargo was reshipped to Philadelphia, the merchant had still been obliged to send his ship many miles out of her direct course and to pay the expense of rehandling her cargo in England.

The Molasses Act of 1733. The purpose of the Acts of Trade was to protect British commerce against Spanish, Dutch, and French competition. They were not intended to harm any part of the empire or injure any group of producers.[2] However, if they did work hardship here or there, it was to be borne for the sake of the good of the whole empire. Then came an act which roused indignation because it threatened commercial ruin to one group of the American colonies in order to benefit another group.

The owners of sugar plantations in the British West Indies had a powerful enough lobby in Parliament to get an act passed, in 1733, imposing heavy duties on sugar and molasses imported from the French, Dutch, and Spanish islands of the West Indies into the ports of the American mainland. The merchants of Boston, Newport, New York, Philadelphia, and other com-

[1] On goods which England did not produce or export herself this duty was generally "drawn back," or refunded, when they were reshipped to the colonies.

[2] For example, although tobacco was an "enumerated commodity" which could be exported only to England, the home government gave the tobacco-raising colonies a monopoly of the English market by forbidding the importation of Spanish tobacco into England.

mercial centers had a flourishing trade with the West Indies. The English islands alone could not furnish sufficient molasses for the rum distilleries of Massachusetts and Rhode Island; nor did they provide a large enough market to absorb the fish, lumber, horses, and wheat exported from mainland colonies to the Indies. If trade with the foreign islands were killed, the American merchants could not find the money to pay for the manufactured goods which they imported from England, some of which, such as woolens, hats, and iron products, the colonists were forbidden to make for foreign or intercolonial trade.

The colonies therefore defied the Molasses Act, and for the next thirty years the English ministers were wise enough not to attempt to enforce it. The chief reason for this prudent course was doubtless the rapid increase in the population and wealth of the colonies in the eighteenth century. At the beginning of that century there were not more than three hundred thousand inhabitants scattered from New Hampshire to South Carolina; but by 1760 the number had grown to over a million and a half. In 1700 the total trade of the continental colonies with England was £635,000, or less than one half of the trade between England and the West Indies; but, again, by 1760 the foreign trade of the mainland colonies had increased to £3,000,000, and the imports of these colonies from England were double those of the West Indies. Communities as prosperous as these were not inclined to subordinate their commercial interests to those of the British Empire in general, much less of the West Indies in particular. "If the King of England were encamped on Boston Common with twenty thousand men," said James Otis, "he could not enforce these laws."

The French Menace. Besides defending their local governments and their growing trade against too much interference by acts of Parliament and royal officials, the colonists also rendered valiant aid to the mother country in defending their borders against the French and the Indians. The year after Jamestown was founded, Samuel de Champlain, resuming Jacques Cartier's work of seventy years before (p. 42), established the beginning of the French empire in America by the settlement of Quebec (1608). Then, during the century of the planting and growth of the English colonies along the seaboard of the Atlantic, the French were sending their explorers, fur traders, and fort-builders up through the St. Lawrence valley and the Great Lakes and down the Mississippi,[1] until the lilies of France waved over a vast empire extending in an arc of twenty-five hundred miles from the Gulf of St. Lawrence to the Gulf of Mexico.

For several decades these thinly settled and scattered posts of the French gave the English little concern. They were too remote from the colonies on the Atlantic coast to be competitors; and, besides, the last two Stuart kings (1660–1688) were servile friends of the French monarch, Louis XIV. But when William of Orange came to the English throne, a series of Anglo-French wars began which lasted, with intermissions, for seventy years, and which extended to America.[2] The earlier of these wars took the form of Indian raids on the frontiers of the English colonies or of unsuccessful expeditions of the English and colonials against Quebec. But toward the middle of the eighteenth century the rivalry became more serious.

At that time the English colonists were feeling their way across the barrier of the Alleghenies to the valleys of the rivers which led down to the Ohio and the Mississippi, and at the same time the French were coming down from Lake Erie to secure the Ohio valley and shut the English up between the Alleghenies and the Atlantic. The English governors became increasingly aware of the danger of having the French "running all along by the back" of the colonies; and the rich lands

---

[1] The greatest of the French explorers in America, La Salle, reached the mouth of the Mississippi in 1682, and named the whole basin of the great river Louisiana, in honor of Louis XIV of France.

[2] These wars in America were called King William's War (1689–1697), Queen Anne's War (1702–1714), King George's War (1744–1748), and the French and Indian War (1754–1763). A glorious exploit of the third of these wars was the capture of the great French stronghold Louisburg, on Cape Breton Island, by a force of New England troops commanded by Colonel William Pepperrell of Maine, in 1745. When the English restored this fortress to France in 1748 in exchange for Madras, in India, the colonists resented the transaction as a slur on their sacrifice and courage.

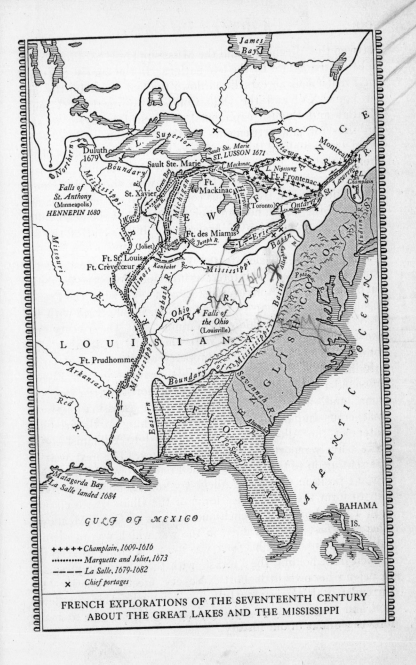

FRENCH EXPLORATIONS OF THE SEVENTEENTH CENTURY
ABOUT THE GREAT LAKES AND THE MISSISSIPPI

between the Alleghenies and the Mississippi now became a prize to be contended for by the two nations. In the same year (1749) the French sent an expedition down the Ohio to claim the land for Louis XV, and the Ohio Company (formed by Virginia planters and English capitalists) dispatched an agent to seek out sites for new settlements on the "western waters." The stolid Indians along the river banks listened to the pleas of the French and the English, and accepted their brandy and rum impartially, little dreaming that they were the dusky chorus at the opening of a tremendous conflict between the two leading nations of the world, not only for the control of the Ohio valley but for the domination of America, of India, and of the sea routes of the world.

Washington's Mission to the French. The contest for the Ohio valley is of special interest as introducing George Washington on the stage of American history. In 1753, when the French began building a chain of forts to connect Lake Erie with the Ohio, Governor Dinwiddie of Virginia sent the twenty-one-year-old major of militia to warn them off the territory "so notoriously known to be the property of the crown of Great Britain." Washington delivered his message to the French commanders at the forts in the wilds of northwestern Pennsylvania, and, after a narrow escape from assassination by a treacherous Indian guide and from drowning in the ice-filled waters of the Allegheny River, returned to Williamsburg to write a lively report of his perilous journey. The next year he was sent again to try to prevent the French from seizing the important position where the Allegheny and Monongahela rivers join to form the Ohio (the "forks of the Ohio"). He clashed with a detachment of French and Indians at Great Meadows, where the first shot was fired in the war which was to disturb three continents. But his force was too weak either to keep the French from holding the "forks" with their Fort Duquesne or to defend his own little Fort Necessity, erected close by. He surrendered his garrison on July 4 — a day which his own devotion and courage, a quarter of a century later, was to make forever glorious in our history.

The Albany Plan of Union. Far-seeing men from William Penn on had been proposing some sort of union for the colonies in the face of the French and Indian menace. Just two weeks before Washington had to surrender Fort Necessity, a congress attended by one hundred and fifty Indians and by delegates from seven of the colonies met at Albany, New York, and listened to a plan proposed by Benjamin Franklin. A Grand Council of forty-eight members, chosen by the colonial legislatures, was to meet annually to regulate Indian affairs, maintain a colonial army, control public lands, pass laws for the general good of the colonies, and levy taxes for the expense of common defense. A president-general, appointed by the king, was to name the high officials and the military commanders. He might also veto the laws passed by the council. Franklin's wise plan was rejected, however, both by the colonies and by the crown; to each it seemed too much of a sacrifice of their rightful authority. Even the danger of war on their borders could not sufficiently overcome the colonies' jealousy of one another and of the royal officials to unite them in a common plan of action.

The French and Indian War. For the first two years the war which opened with Washington's skirmish at Great Meadows went badly for the English. In July, 1755, General Edward Braddock, with an army of British regulars supported by Colonel Washington, marched on Fort Duquesne. Unaccustomed to fighting in the forest behind rocks and trees, Braddock's regulars were almost annihilated, and their brave but rash general was killed. Washington's heroic efforts to rally the troops and stay the wild rout, as he rode about the field with his uniform pierced by bullets, were in vain. Braddock's defeat, together with the loss of Oswego and Fort William Henry the next year, exposed the whole frontier to the attacks of the French and their savage allies. Confusion reigned. Dull, uninformed ministers in London sent incompetent generals to America, who offended the colonial officers by their airs of superiority.

The tide turned in 1757, when William Pitt came into power. Pitt was the greatest English statesman of the eighteenth century. He immediately infused new life into the British armies and fleets spread over half the globe. He removed incompetent commanders and gave the colonial officers their due rank. The Americans responded to his call for hearty co-operation by voting generous supplies of money and troops. In the campaign of 1758 the British and Americans were victorious all along the line. Generals Jeffrey Amherst and James Wolfe recaptured the stronghold of Louisburg, and the French were forced to abandon Fort Duquesne, which was rechristened Fort Pitt (Pittsburgh) in honor of England's great "organizer of victory."

The Fall of Quebec. Then Wolfe and Amherst closed in upon the heart of New France, the former leading a fleet up the St. Lawrence to attack Quebec, and the latter approaching Montreal by the Hudson valley. From June to September, 1759, the British ships lay in the river before the beetling rock of Quebec, while Wolfe vainly sought a landing place for his troops above or below the city. It looked as though the expedition, like earlier similar ones, would end in failure. Then, under cover of the inky darkness of the night of September 12–13, Wolfe embarked five thousand men in small boats with muffled oars, and, escaping the French sentries on the river bank, landed his men at the foot of a narrow, wooded ravine, up which they climbed in single file to the high Plains of Abraham, west of the city. When morning broke, the astonished French commander, the Marquis of Montcalm, saw the redcoats forming their lines of battle before the city and hastened to the attack. A half-hour's desperate fighting gave the British the victory. Both Wolfe and Montcalm were mortally wounded on the field.[1]

---

[1] In the governor's garden in Quebec stands the monument dedicated to these two noble commanders. The inscription which it bears is perhaps the most beautiful expression of commemorative sentiment in the world:

MORTEM VIRTUS COMMUNEM

FAMAM HISTORIA

MONUMENTUM POSTERITAS

DEDIT.

WOLFE   MONTCALM

("Valor gave them a common death, history a common fame, and posterity a common monument.")

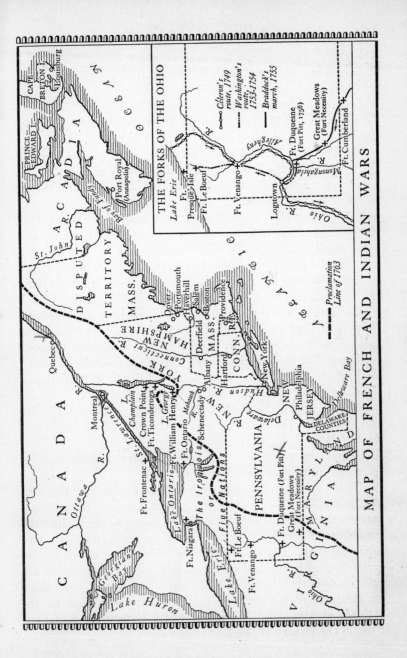

THE FORKS OF THE OHIO

○—○ Céleron's route, 1749
‖‖‖ Washington's route, 1753–1754
† Braddock's march, 1755

Lake Erie
Ft. Presqu'Isle
Ft. Le Boeuf
Ft. Venango
Logstown
Ohio R.
Monongahela R.
Allegheny R.
Ft. Duquesne (Fort Pitt, 1758)
Great Meadows (Fort Necessity)
Ft. Cumberland

CAPE BRETON IT.
Louisburg
PRINCE EDWARD IT.
ACADIA
OCEAN
St. John
Bay of Fundy
Port Royal (Annapolis)
DISPUTED TERRITORY
MASS.
Quebec
CANADA
Ottawa R.
St. Lawrence R.
Montreal
L. Champlain
Crown Point
Ft. Ticonderoga
L. George
Ft. William Henry
Ft. Frontenac
Lake Ontario
Ft. Ontario
Schenectady
Mohawk R.
The Iroquois or Five Nations
Ft. Niagara
Lake Erie
Ft. Le Boeuf
Ft. Venango
Georgian Bay
Lake Huron
NEW YORK
Connecticut R.
Hudson R.
NEW HAMPSHIRE
Dover
Portsmouth
Haverhill
Deerfield
Salem
Boston
Providence
MASS.
CONN.
R.I.
Albany
Hartford
New York
NEW JERSEY
Philadelphia
PENNSYLVANIA
Delaware R.
Delaware Bay
DELAWARE COUNTIES
MARYLAND
VIRGINIA
Ft. Duquesne (Fort Pitt)
Great Meadows (Fort Necessity)
Ft. Venango
Ohio R.

— — — Proclamation Line of 1763

MAP OF FRENCH AND INDIAN WARS

The fall of Quebec was the decisive event of the French and
Indian War. Amherst entered Montreal with little opposition
the next year, and the English fleets completed the downfall
of France and her ally Spain by seizing the rich sugar islands of
Guadeloupe and Martinique in the West Indies, and by capturing Havana in Cuba and Manila in the Philippines.

The Peace of Paris, 1763. The peace, concluded at Paris in
1763, contained the following provisions so far as America was
concerned : France ceded to England all of Canada and the region east of the Mississippi (except the island of New Orleans),
and to her own ally Spain all her claims west of the Mississippi ;
England gave back to France Guadeloupe, Martinique, and
some small islands in the West Indies, and restored Havana
and Manila to Spain, though keeping all of Florida (map,
p. 105). Some of the English statesmen were in favor of taking
the rich sugar island of Guadeloupe and letting the French
retain Canada, arguing that if the French menace were removed
from their borders it would be harder to keep the American
colonies in due submission. And the French minister Choiseul
predicted that the colonies would "shake off their dependence"
on England "as soon as Canada was ceded." But Benjamin
Franklin, citing the hearty support of England by the colonies
during the war, declared that their pride in seeing the English
flag float from the northern seas to the Gulf of Mexico would
double their fidelity to the mother country.

At first this prediction of Franklin's seemed to be correct;
for great enthusiasm over the victory prevailed in the colonies.
Addresses of congratulation were sent to England by the colonial assemblies, the pulpits rang with sermons of joy, and
statues were erected to William Pitt and the king. But the
Frenchman's prophecy turned out to be true, after all. Two
years after the Peace of Paris was signed the colonies were
quarreling with England over taxation ; and at the end of another decade they had begun the war which was to make them
an independent nation. "With the triumph of Wolfe on the
Heights of Abraham," says the English historian J. R. Green,
"began the history of the United States."

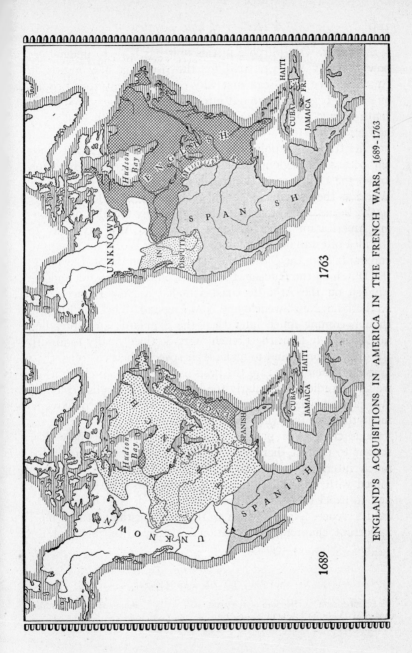

ENGLAND'S ACQUISITIONS IN AMERICA IN THE FRENCH WARS, 1689-1763

Summary. Our purpose in this unit has been to understand how the way was prepared for the rise of a new nation in America. We have seen first why certain adventurous peoples of Europe began to push out into the uncharted seas, about five centuries ago, to find direct water routes to the rich East; then how a new Western world was discovered in this movement and how its true geographical position in respect to the other lands and oceans of the globe was gradually determined. We have followed the explorers of the coasts and the interior of the New World as they sought for fabled realms of gold or for a passage to the Indies. We have noted how gradually the idea of exploring America for riches or for a passage to Asia gave way to the idea of establishing colonies in the New World for groups of emigrants from the Old World. The French on the St. Lawrence, the Dutch on the Hudson, the Swedes on the Delaware, and the English on the Atlantic coast founded a New France, New Netherland, New Sweden, and New England. Since the English, though coming much later than the Spaniards and spreading far less widely than the French, were destined finally to absorb the other colonies and to make their speech, their customs, their laws, and their literature the basis of our American civilization, we have studied particularly the history of the English colonies. We have seen how they were founded, what kinds of government they set up, what were their political fortunes amid the various changes of policies and rulers in England, how they sought to protect their growing trade and prosperity from too much interference by the home government, and how they joined with England to defend their borders from the Indians and to expel the French from the valleys of the Ohio and the St. Lawrence. Now we turn to the study of the first and most important chapter in our national history — the birth of the United States of America.

TERMS TO BE MASTERED

Piedmont region	freedom of the press	enumerated commodities
Board of Trade	Acts of Trade	lobby
redemptioners	taxation without representation	Forks of the Ohio

For Supplementary Reading

C. M. ANDREWS, *Colonial Folkways* (Chronicles of America, Vol. IX); F. J. TURNER, *The Frontier in American History*; G. L. BEER, *The Old Colonial System, 1660–1754*, and *British Colonial Policy, 1754–1763*; O. M. DICKERSON, *American Colonial Government, 1696–1765*; J. H. FINLEY, *The French in the Heart of America*; FRANCIS PARKMAN, *Montcalm and Wolfe*, Vol. II, chaps. xxiv–xxvii; GILBERT PARKER, *The Seats of the Mighty* (a story of the fall of Quebec); HART, *Contemporaries*, Vol. II, Nos. 50–53, 112, 122, 126, 129; MUZZEY, *Readings*, pp. 72–107.

Topics for Reports

1. **A Typical American Colonial Figure.** BENJAMIN FRANKLIN, *Autobiography*.

2. **Colonial Immigration from the Continent of Europe.** S. P. ORTH, *Our Foreigners* (Chronicles of America, Vol. XXXV), pp. 13–18; H. P. FAIRCHILD, *Immigration*, chap. ii; EDWARD CHANNING, *History of the United States*, Vol. II, pp. 402–413; H. I. PRIESTLY, *The Coming of the White Man*, chaps. ix, xi; HART, *Contemporaries*, Vol. I, Nos. 153, 161, 163, 169, and Vol. II, No. 29; MUZZEY, *Readings*, pp. 67–72.

3. **George Washington's Embassy to the French Forts.** FRANCIS PARKMAN, *Montcalm and Wolfe*, Vol. I, pp. 128–161; The Pageant of America, Vol. VI, pp. 66–74; A. B. HULBERT, *Washington's Road* (Historic Highways Series), pp. 85–119; Old South Leaflets, No. 187; MUZZEY, *Readings*, pp. 98–104.

4. **Contrast between the French and the English Ideas of Colonial Government.** FRANCIS PARKMAN, *The Old Régime in Canada*, pp. 257–281; R. G. THWAITES, *France in America* (American Nation Series, Vol. VII), pp. 124–143, and *Jesuit Relations*, Vol. I, pp. 131–147; *America*, Vol. III, pp. 54–61; MUZZEY, *Readings*, pp. 111–117.

5. **Social Life in the Colonies.** C. M. ANDREWS, *Colonial Folkways*; H. SCUDDER, *Men and Manners in America One Hundred Years Ago*; one of ALICE MORSE EARLE's books on colonial customs: *Child Life in Colonial Days*, *Home Life in Colonial Days*, *Stage Coach and Tavern Days*, *Colonial Dames and Goodwives*, *Customs and Fashions in Old New England*.

Questions Suggested by the Chapter

1. Define the terms "favorable balance of trade," "drawback," "salutary neglect." 2. How did the Acts of Trade interfere with colonial commerce? 3. Explain why the New England colonies objected to the Sugar and Molasses Act of 1733. 4. What methods of travel were at the disposal of the colonists? 5. How do you account for the rapid growth of population in the colonies in the eighteenth century? 6. Name three main causes of dispute between the royal governors and their colonial assemblies. 7. Why was the Albany Plan of union a failure? 8. In what respects were the colonies less democratic than our country today? 9. How did the education of girls in colonial times differ from their education today? 10. Name four colleges founded in the eighteenth century. Were there any in the

seventeenth century? **11.** Compare a colonial newspaper with a modern one. **12.** Name three hardships of frontier life in colonial days. **13.** How did a young man get a medical education in the colonies? **14.** Why did the French colonies grow more slowly than the English? **15.** Do you think the French had a better claim to the Ohio valley than the English? If so, why? **16.** Why did some people wish to take Guadeloupe rather than Canada from the French at the close of the French and Indian War? **17.** What were the terms of the peace of 1763? **18.** Explain the quotation from Green at the end of the chapter.

★

Just as the mariner keeps his "bearings" at sea by a constant knowledge of his latitude and longitude, so the student must have a grasp of the setting of events in time and place. Graphs or charts suggested by the teacher or the workbook will help to fix the important dates in memory. The map exercises in BISHOP, ROBINSON, and WALKER's *Map Work and Study Guide* to accompany the present book will provide the necessary geographical setting.

The following list of books, mostly historical novels and biographies, will interest the student who wishes, during week ends or vacation time, to read more about the persons and events studied in this unit:

C. MORRIS, *Heroes of Discovery in America*; D. BYRNE, *Messer Marco Polo*; MARIUS ANDRE, *Columbus*; LEW WALLACE, *The Fair God* (Mexico); RAPHAEL SABATINI, *The Carolinian*; MARY JOHNSTON, *To Have and to Hold* (Virginia); WASHINGTON IRVING, *Knickerbocker's History of New York*; IRVING BACHELLER, *In the Days of Poor Richard*; BERNARD FAŸ, *Franklin, the Apostle of Modern Times*; D. HENDERSON, *Boone of the Wilderness*; J. E. ERNST, *Roger Williams, New England Firebrand*; GILBERT PARKER, *The Power and the Glory* (French explorers); NATHANIEL HAWTHORNE, *The House of the Seven Gables* and *The Scarlet Letter* (New England); W. S. DAVIS, *Gilman of Redford*; H. W. LONGFELLOW, *Evangeline* and *The Courtship of Miles Standish*; B. E. STEVENSON, *Poems of American History*.

[handwritten notes:]
Drums along the Mohawk. Edmonds
Paradise. Forbes
Northwest Passage. — Roberts
Janice Meredith
Hugh Wynne — Free Quaker
Richard Carvel

How our Country Won its Independence and Established a National Government

Every American worthy of the name prizes two bequests which the fathers of the Republic have handed down to us. One is the spirit of liberty, and the other is the Constitution of the United States. Whenever times of trial and strain have come in our history, the best men in all parties and in all parts of our country have been anxious lest we should lose our freedom or see the Constitution "overthrown." We passed through such a time of trial in the early years of the 1930's. There was great distress in business. Banks failed, millions of men were thrown out of employment, and the farmers were driven to desperation by the falling prices of their crops. Still worse distress and confusion in Europe resulted in the setting up of dictatorships in great countries like Russia, Italy, and Germany. Men were willing to sacrifice their liberty for the promise of greater security. Our own government wrestled with the problem of how far it should interfere with the liberty of manufacturers, bankers, brokers, merchants, and farmers to conduct their business as they pleased; how far it should make itself responsible for helping the country out of the Slough of Despond by furnishing work for the unemployed, paying farmers to reduce their production of hogs and cotton, or requiring employers to agree to a certain rate of wages and number of hours for their workers. Some good Americans, like ex-President Hoover, complained that our liberty was being threatened and that the "timbers of the Constitution were cracking" under the strain. Others believed that President Roosevelt's measures would free the energies of the American people by dis-tributing the country's wealth more fairly and that the Constitu-tion was being used as never before to secure one of the objects for which it was framed — "to promote the general welfare." Surely, as good citizens, we ought to know how the Americans gained the freedom which they prize and what kind of Con-stitution they adopted in order "to secure the blessings of liberty to ourselves and our posterity." Those are to be the sub-jects of our study in the present unit.

CHAPTER FIVE

LIBERTY OR LOYALTY?

During the dozen years from the Peace of Paris to the outbreak of the American Revolution the colonies were in a state of intense political excitement. Meetings and conventions were held, resolutions were adopted, pamphlets were written, petitions were sent to England, protests were thundered in speeches and sermons, and sometimes violence was used against the king's officials and their sympathizers. The cause for all this ferment lay in a change of policy on the part of the British government when George III came to the throne, in 1760. George was not a cruel tyrant bent on "oppressing" the colonies, but he was determined to rule as well as to reign. Hence he chose ministers who were ready to do his bidding, and by the lavish bestowal of money and offices he built up in Parliament a party of "King's Friends" who would support the measures which his obedient ministers proposed. The result was the passing of a succession of laws which affected the colonies' trade, currency, courts of justice, legislative assemblies, and, above all, their ideas of the proper form of taxation.

The object of the laws was to bind the parts of the British Empire closer together under the authority of Parliament; but many of the measures seemed to the colonies a deliberate attempt to deprive them of rights which they believed belonged to them as British subjects and which they had been enjoying almost undisturbed during the reigns of the first two Georges. The colonists steadily asserted their loyalty to the king. America was proud to be a part of the great and powerful British Empire. At the same time, the colonists felt the dignity which their growing numbers and wealth inspired. They must not be treated as an inferior part of the empire, to be dictated to by a minister in London who had little understanding of their feelings. It was, then, the attempt to preserve both their loyalty to the British Empire and their own cherished liberties that produced the arguments and resolutions and protests of these dozen years. As the measures of the British government grew stricter the spirit of the colonists grew bolder, until at last the loyalty of the Americans yielded to the strain and they resorted to arms to defend their liberty.

The British Situation in 1763. Great Britain was faced with certain new and serious problems in America at the close of the French war. In the first place, with Canada, the eastern basin of the Mississippi, and Florida in her possession, England had the responsibility of ruling a territory over twice as large as her colonies along the Atlantic seaboard. In the region west of the Alleghenies there were more than two hundred thousand Indians, many of them ready to believe the stories which the French soldiers and traders spread among them, that their new masters the English were planning to rob them of their hunting fields. Indeed, in the very summer of 1763 the great Ottawa chieftain Pontiac, having roused the Indian tribes from Lake Superior to the Gulf of Mexico, captured ten of the fourteen English frontier posts and spread terror through the region west of Pittsburgh.

The English government thought that a standing army of ten thousand men would be necessary to police the trans-Allegheny country and protect the newly organized provinces of Canada and East and West Florida. This task they would not entrust to the thirteen separate colonies, because some of the colonies not only had failed to support the war against the French but had even furnished examples of aiding the enemy by carrying on the forbidden trade with the French and Spanish West Indies.[1] Such laxness in the colonies must be stopped, said the

---

[1] For example, a British admiral told the Board of Trade that he "certainly would have taken Martinique if it had not been for the provisions which the North American vessels, to the knowledge of every Captain in his squadron, supplied to the French islands." William Pitt, who was the firm friend of America, was so indignant at this "treasonable" violation of the Acts of Trade that he gave orders for the British warships to suppress the traffic.

British ministry, and the only way to stop it was to tighten the control of the colonies and manage all the problems of the newly enlarged empire from the center at London.

Moreover, the British debt had been doubled during the war, and the taxes had risen to four shillings in the pound, or 20 per cent. The colonies were rapidly growing in population and wealth. Why should they not help bear the burden of the war which had relieved them of the danger from the French and the Indians? It was not denied that some of the colonies had been generous in their supplies of men and money;[1] still, others had seen fit to make no contribution at all to the war. The matter must not be left to the decision of the individual colonies. There must be some uniform scheme of raising a revenue in America. So the idea of *taxing* the American colonies, often considered but never yet applied by the British government, was now revived and put into operation — with the tragic results which we shall see.

The Royal Proclamation of 1763. Before tackling the questions of colonial taxation, the British government turned its attention to the Western lands. By a proclamation of 1763, King George forbade the colonists to emigrate into the territory west of a line drawn along the crest of the Alleghenies. There was no intention of keeping the Americans out of this region permanently; but "for the present" the British deemed it wise not to give the Indians further cause for discontent by allowing fur traders, land speculators, and settlers to flood in upon their hunting grounds. The disastrous raid of Pontiac must not be repeated. The colonists, however, did not take this view of the matter. The Western land had all been included in their original charters. Some pioneers had already gone into it, and hundreds of families, distressed by the high cost of living brought by the war, and eager to start life anew on the rich lands of the Western

---

[1] Massachusetts, for example, had incurred a debt of £818,000 in the war, and John Hancock, a rich merchant of Boston, declared that he was taxed more heavily than any man in England. Virginia had spent £385,000; Pennsylvania, £313,000; and so on. Still, the fact remained that these contributions had depended on the good will of colonial legislatures, some of which had refused to give any aid at all.

waters, were ready to follow. Companies, such as the Ohio Company of 1749, had been formed to exploit the region. The settlers would be fully able to protect themselves against the Indians. Thus the colonists regarded this attempt of the king to bar their first grand opportunity for westward expansion as a scheme to cheat them of lands which were their rightful inheritance, and to keep them hemmed in between the Alleghenies and the Atlantic coast.

The Grenville Program. George Grenville became prime minister in 1763. He was a conscientious, narrow-minded man, who was determined to make the American colonies realize their obligation to the empire by obeying the Acts of Trade and contributing their due share to the increased imperial expenses. In order to put an end to smuggling, customs officials (many of whom were drawing their salaries and taking their ease in London) were instructed to be at their posts in America and to attend strictly to the collection of the duties. The admiralty courts, in which the cases of illicit trade were tried without a jury, were reorganized, and judges who winked at the unlawful commerce which the Americans were carrying on with Europe and the West Indies were weeded out. Duties were levied on a number of articles, such as silk, wine, and coffee, imported into the colonies from countries outside the British Empire.

The worst blow to the colonial merchants, however, was the enactment of a new Sugar and Molasses Act. We have seen (p. 96) how the old act of 1733, if enforced, would have ruined colonial commerce. The new act, although it reduced the duties on foreign sugar and molasses by half, was still ruinous. The British West Indies could furnish less than two thirds of the molasses necessary for the thirty rum distilleries of Rhode Island, to say nothing of the sixty distilleries of Massachusetts. And unless the colonial merchants had the money which they drew from the French, Spanish, and Dutch islands in payment for the meat, fish, flour, horses, and lumber which they exported thither, they could not settle the large debts which they owed their British creditors for furniture, clothing, ironware, pottery, jewelry, and many other necessities and luxuries which they imported. The ministry was warned that it was killing the goose that laid the golden egg by shutting off the colonial trade with the foreign West Indies. The farmers would be deprived of their best market, the well-to-do would have to cease importing foreign goods, and the people at large, for lack of ready money, would see an end to the prosperity which had been growing for a century. The outlook was made all the worse by a law of the same year (1764) forbidding the colonies to issue paper money to supply the lack of gold and silver.

The Stamp Act. But even if the colonies could have raised the cash to pay the new duties, the amount would not have been half as much as the British ministry expected them to contribute for the military establishment proposed. New sources of revenue must be found. Grenville was eager to find a kind of taxation which would be acceptable to the colonies, and invited their agents to make suggestions. But, as the colonies did not wish *any* kind of taxation, he got no reply. There were men in Parliament also, like Pitt, Burke, and Fox, who believed that taxes should be levied in America only by the colonial assemblies in which the representatives of the people sat. That was their right as British freemen. But these men were outvoted and hooted down by the "King's Friends," who controlled Parliament.

So an act was passed in March, 1765, to go into effect the first of November, requiring stamps costing from a few pence to several shillings to be affixed to all colonial deeds, leases, bills of sale, pamphlets, newspapers, advertisements, mortgages, wills, and contracts. The Stamp Act was one of the major causes of the American Revolution.[1] It stirred the people of the colonies far more deeply than had any previous act, because it was a tax levied by a body thousands of miles away for the sole purpose of raising a revenue. The duties of 1764 might be considered as a part of the regulation of the trade of the empire, which nobody denied Parliament had a right to control; but

[1] The causes of the Revolution were so varied that it would be rash to single out any one as decisive. But all of them arose out of the attempt of England to bind the colonies more closely under the authority of Parliament.

the stamp tax affected the "internal" affairs of the colonies. And, more than that, it affected all classes in the colonies. It was no longer a case of the great merchants in Boston, New York, Philadelphia, or Charleston grumbling about the duty on foreign molasses or the strict measures to prevent smuggling. Now every man in the remotest village of America who wished to mortgage his house or sell a horse or make his will would find added to the lawyer's charge the price of the hated stamp attached to the document. Every publisher of a newspaper or tract would have to affix to it a stamp representing a tax of so many pence per sheet. Before the autumn frosts set in, agents would be arriving from England with bundles of stamps and stamped paper to be distributed through the colonies.

Resistance and Repeal. Grenville and his colleagues had no idea of the hornets' nest that they were stirring in the colonies. The stamp tax had passed Parliament without debate or opposition. Benjamin Franklin, who was in London at the time, though he was opposed to the act, thought that the colonies could no more prevent its going into operation "than they could prevent the sun from setting." He even applied for the position of stamp-distributor for one of his friends in Pennsylvania. But in the colonies resistance was immediate and intense. Practically all the distributors were forced to resign before November, and only in Georgia were the stamps actually used. The merchants of Boston, New York, and Philadelphia agreed not to import English goods, and the trade with Great Britain declined about 25 per cent in a year.

In the colonial assemblies orators denounced the tyranny of "taxation without representation," and an eloquent young lawyer named Patrick Henry, just elected from one of the "backwoods" counties to the Virginia House of Burgesses, defended the right of the colonies to assess their own taxes in a speech with such threatening allusions to King George as to bring the cry of "Treason!" from the more conservative members. Henry secured the passage (by a single vote) of a set of resolutions against the Stamp Act, which were circulated through the colonies. Rioting and violence occurred. The

BOSTONIANS WERE FILLED WITH INDIGNATION AND RESENTMENT
WHEN THEY LEARNED OF THE PASSAGE OF THE STAMP ACT

mansion of Chief Justice Hutchinson [1] of Massachusetts was sacked by a Boston mob, and the gilded coach of Governor Colden of New York (which, as Professor Becker says, "was certainly never designed to carry the stamps") was burned. Most important of the forms of protest was the Stamp Act Congress which met in New York in October, 1765, at the call

[1] Hutchinson, a native of Massachusetts, was an outspoken opponent of the Stamp Act. But he had made himself unpopular because of his defense of writs of assistance. These writs were general warrants given to the royal customs officers to search any storage house or private residences where they suspected that smuggled goods were concealed. James Otis of Boston, in 1761, had made an impassioned speech against these writs which John Adams called the opening act of the Revolution. Among the effects of Hutchinson that were thrown into the street by the mob was the manuscript of his *History of Massachusetts*, which may still be seen in the State House at Boston, with the mud stains on its edges.

of Massachusetts. Nine colonies were represented by twenty-seven delegates. A Declaration of Rights and Grievances was drawn up, and a petition sent to the king and Parliament, protesting against the act as hostile to the "liberties of the colonies."

Influenced by this violent and unexpected resistance from the colonies and by the complaints of the British merchants whose business was being injured, Parliament repealed the Stamp Act in the spring of 1766, after Grenville had gone out of office. The colonies hailed the repeal with great rejoicing and with protestations of loyalty to King George. Nevertheless, they had not won their claim to be exempt from "taxation without representation." For Parliament accompanied the repeal with a Declaratory Act, which stated that it had "full power and authority to . . . bind the colonies and people of America, subjects of the crown of Great Britain, in all cases whatsoever."

The Townshend Duties. The good feeling created by the repeal of the stamp tax was short-lived. The British government had dropped a particular form of taxation, but had no intention of giving up the idea of getting a revenue from the colonies. A change of ministers brought to the fore an aggressive, witty, and persuasive head of the treasury (Chancellor of the Exchequer) in the person of Charles Townshend. Townshend had no sympathy for the Americans, and regarded their objection to being taxed by Parliament as "so much nonsense." He jauntily promised that he could get plenty of revenue from the colonies, and in the summer of 1767 persuaded Parliament to pass acts laying duties on glass, painters' colors, red and white lead, paper, and tea imported into America. At the same time the hated writs of assistance were renewed, and a board of customs commissioners was established at Boston with oversight over the collection of duties at all the American ports. Out of these customs receipts were to be paid the salaries of the royal governors and judges, who were thus to be freed from dependence upon the colonial assemblies for their support. Finally, Parliament interfered directly with local government in America by suspending the New York Assembly for refusing to furnish certain supplies for the king's troops quartered in the province.

This serious set of measures revived all the forms of protest and resistance in the colonies — pamphlets, petitions, smuggling, boycott of British goods, insults to customs officials, and fiery speeches on the British design to reduce the Americans to slavery. Samuel Adams of Boston led the revolt, convinced even thus early that the only remedy for the colonies was complete independence from Great Britain. Adams, who was a tireless organizer and agitator, got the Massachusetts legislature to send out a circular letter to all the towns in the province, inviting them to unite in protest; and when the governor ordered the legislature to recall the letter and make apologies, they refused by a vote of 92 to 17. The new commissioners of customs were so rudely treated in Boston that they asked Commodore Hood at Halifax to send a warship to protect them in their duties. The chief method adopted by the colonies for defeating the Townshend Acts was the refusal to import British goods. By the spring of 1769, nonimportation agreements had been entered into by the merchants of New York, Philadelphia, Charleston, and lesser commercial ports. George Washington [1] presented the Virginia agreement, together with the assertion that the right of taxation belonged exclusively to the House of Burgesses; whereupon the royal governor dissolved the House, only to have the members meet at a private house and adopt the nonimportation agreement. How effective the boycott was may be seen from the figures of the Board of Trade. British imports to the colonies were reduced from £2,157,218 in 1768 to £1,336,122 in 1769.

The "Boston Massacre." Though Benjamin Franklin had told the House of Commons at the time of the Stamp Act that if troops were sent to the colonies to enforce obedience they would not find a revolution there but might very well create one, the warship *Romney* and two regiments of soldiers were sent to Boston, at the governor's request, in the autumn of

---

[1] Washington's advanced position as early as 1769 is shown in a letter which he wrote to his friend George Mason in April of that year: "No man should scruple, or hesitate a moment," he said, "to use arms in defense of so valuable a blessing" as our liberty.

1768. The legislature refused to provide quarters for the troops or furnish them food. Their presence was a constant irritation to the citizens, and the rougher element taunted them with cries of "Lobster!" and "Bloody-backs!" and sometimes pelted them with brickbats.

The inevitable clash came on March 5, 1770, when some British soldiers on guard, taunted by a crowd of jeering men and boys, fired into the group, killing four men and wounding several more. The town and the surrounding country were roused to fury by this deed of bloodshed. Samuel Adams hastened to Acting Governor Hutchinson's house and, with menacing language and gestures, demanded the immediate removal of the soldiers from the town. Hutchinson yielded, and the troops were taken down the harbor to Castle William. The customs commissioners prudently decided to go with them. When the news of these events reached England, the "King's Friends" in Parliament condemned Hutchinson's "cowardly surrender" to the mob spirit and sneeringly dubbed the troops "Sam Adams' regiments." For years the people of Boston celebrated the anniversary of the "massacre" in a meeting in which the orator thundered against British tyranny.

The Flame of Liberty Burns Low. Edmund Burke, a friend of the colonies, spoke of the British ministry as "blundering into a policy one day and backing out of it the next." That is what they had done in the case of the Stamp Act, and now they repeated their behavior. Lord North became prime minister in 1770. He believed that the Townshend duties were not in line with sound colonial policy, because they laid taxes on articles of British manufacture. Furthermore, it was costing far more to collect them than they yielded in revenue to the treasury, and the American boycott was severely injuring British trade. Therefore Lord North secured the repeal of all the Townshend duties except a trifling tax of threepence a pound on tea, which King George insisted should be kept in order to prove that Parliament had the right to tax the colonies. The tea tax actually counted for little, since the colonists smuggled most of their tea in from Holland. It looked now as though friendly

Engrav'd Printed & Sold by PAUL REVERE Boston

"THE BOSTON MASSACRE"

relations with the mother country were restored. The colonial merchants purchased large orders from British firms, sending their imports up from £1,336,122 in 1769 to £4,200,000 in 1771.

Radical leaders, such as Patrick Henry, Thomas Jefferson, and, above all, Samuel Adams, feared that the colonies were losing interest in their rights. The flame of liberty was burning low. Adams sought to revive the flame by keeping up a constant agitation in letters and the newspapers. "It is high time," he wrote, "for the people of this country explicitly to declare whether they will be Freemen or Slaves. . . . Let it be the topic of conversation in every social Club. Let every Town assemble. Let Associations & Combinations be everywhere set up to consult and recover our just Rights." In 1772 he organized Committees of Correspondence in all the towns of the province, and Thomas Jefferson, the next year, extended the idea to all the colonies. Here was the beginning of a possible *united* action of the colonies. Still, the provocative acts of the British government were few in the years from 1770 to 1773,[1] trade was flourishing, and the merchants, who heretofore had been the chief malcontents, were giving up agitation and attending to their business. Even John Hancock grew friendly to Governor Hutchinson.

A Tempest over Tea. It was the genial Lord North and not the fiery Sam Adams who precipitated the next crisis in the colonies. The great East India Company had a monopoly of the importation of tea into England, on which it paid a duty of a shilling a pound. In 1773 the company was in distress. It had seventeen million pounds of tea stored in England on which it could not pay the duty, and which could not be sold there until the duty was paid. Lord North and the king then agreed to the clever scheme of letting the company sell its surplus tea directly to America and be relieved of the shilling duty. Thereby three objects could be accomplished: (1) the company would have a large market in which to dispose of its tea; (2) it could afford to sell the tea in America at a lower price (including the duty of threepence) than was paid for the tea smuggled from Holland; and (3) the duty of threepence a pound collected on the tea in America would bring in a neat sum to the British treasury. So in the autumn of 1773 several ships loaded with East Indian tea sailed for the colonies.

But unfortunately both Lord North and the king had overlooked two very important questions in their clever plan. Would the colonies be bribed by the cheaper price of the British tea into buying it and paying the threepence duty, thus acknowledging the right of Parliament to tax them? Would the merchants who were making a profit by handling the smuggled tea be content to be replaced by the agents of the East India Company,

[1] Most of the trouble in those years was caused by the attempts of the British revenue vessels to prevent smuggling. One such vessel, the *Gaspee*, was boarded and burned by a group of Rhode Islanders in June, 1772, when it ran aground on a sandspit in Narragansett Bay.

who were to have a monopoly of selling the British tea in America? The answer to both these questions was No! When the tea ships reached New York and Philadelphia, their captains were persuaded to return to England without unloading the cargo. At Charleston the tea was landed; but it was stored in the cellar of the exchange building, and three years later sold at auction for the support of the Revolution. In Boston, as usual, came the trouble. Because the tea had been entered at the customs, the officials would not let the ships leave the port without unloading. Governor Hutchinson, whose two sons were among the agents for selling the tea, would not sign a pass for the ships to be released from the customs officers. The people were determined that the tea should not be landed. When persuasion failed, a band of men disguised as Indians boarded the ships on the evening of December 16, ripped open three hundred and forty-two chests of tea, valued at ninety thousand dollars, and threw the contents into the harbor.

The "Intolerable Acts." The "Boston Tea Party" was condemned by many of the leading men of the colonies as an act of lawless violence. But the punishment visited upon the town and the colony was so severe that it made the offense look small. Without inquiring who was to blame for the destruction of the tea, or heeding the offer of more than a hundred merchants of Boston to pay for the tea, Parliament passed acts closing the port of Boston to trade, forbidding town meetings to assemble (except for the regular election of officers) without the consent of the governor, depriving the legislature of the right to choose the governor's council, providing for the quartering of troops again in the colony, and ordering that any officer or soldier of the crown accused of an act of violence in the performance of his duty should be sent to another colony or to England for trial.[1] To these measures of punishment was added the Quebec Act, extending the province of Quebec southward to the Ohio River, thus cutting off the claims of Massachusetts, Connecticut,

[1] This in spite of the fact that at the time of the "Boston Massacre" John Adams and Josiah Quincy had courageously acted as counsel for the British officer in command of the troops and secured his acquittal.

Result ?

Virginia, and New York to their western lands and surrounding these Protestant colonies with a large territory in which the Catholic religion and the French customs of absolute government were established.

By these "Intolerable Acts," as they were called in America, Parliament thought that it was punishing the colony of Massachusetts, but it soon found that it had stirred a whole people to resistance. Wagonloads of food and expressions of sympathy poured into Boston from every colony. The Burgesses of Virginia, meeting in defiance of Governor Dunmore's orders, appointed June 1 (the day on which the Boston Port Bill was to go into effect) as a day of "fasting, humiliation and prayer," and proposed that the colonies should hold an annual congress to consider their common interests. A few days later the Massachusetts legislature invited all the colonies to choose delegates to such a congress. Meanwhile Governor Hutchinson returned to England and was replaced by General Gage, who brought an army of about four thousand men to quarter on the town of Boston. Gage was for severe measures with the colonies. "They will be lyons while we are lambs," he wrote. And George III agreed with him. "The die is cast," the king wrote to Lord North; "the colonies must either triumph or submit."

The Continental Congress. In spite of the efforts of the royal governors to prevent the elections, all the colonies except Georgia chose delegates to the congress of fifty-six men that met at Carpenter's Hall in Philadelphia on September 5, 1774. It was a remarkable assembly. George Washington (chosen as presiding officer), Patrick Henry, and Richard Henry Lee were in the Virginia delegation. John and Samuel Adams attended from Massachusetts; John Dickinson and Joseph Galloway from Pennsylvania; John Jay and Philip Livingston from New York; Roger Sherman from Connecticut; Christopher Gadsden and the Rutledges from South Carolina. Most of them had never met one another before, but they were nevertheless acquainted through their common efforts, in letters, pamphlets, and speeches, to define and defend American rights. One might say that the Continental Congress was the birth of the American *nation*; for it marked the first _united_ appeal of the colonies for the recognition of their ideas of liberty.

Opinions in the Congress ranged all the way from Galloway's scheme of reviving Franklin's Albany Plan of twenty years before (p. 101) to the desire of Samuel Adams and Patrick Henry for independence from Great Britain. The result of the Congress was a compromise between the conservative and the radical views. It published a Declaration of Rights and Grievances asking for a repeal of the acts of Parliament passed since 1763 which were still on the statute books. It sent addresses to the king and people of Great Britain, expressing the loyalty of the colonies; but at the same time it approved resolutions which declared the "Intolerable Acts" void. Most important of all, it adopted the so-called "Association," by which it prohibited trade with Great Britain. Committees chosen in every county and town were to see to it that these boycotting orders were obeyed. The members adjourned in October, after appointing May 10, 1775, as the date for a meeting of a second Continental Congress in case the British government refused to heed the petitions and protests.

Armed Resistance. Before the second Congress met, however, the clash of arms had actually come. The colonial militia had been training for several months. Bands of "minutemen" had been organized, ready to march at a minute's notice to meet any attack of the king's troops. Late in the night of April 18, 1775, Gage sent out a thousand men under Major Pitcairn to seize colonial supplies of powder at Concord, about twenty miles from Boston. But the patriots had learned of the plan, and dispatched Paul Revere and William Dawes on horseback, by different routes, to warn the countryside that the British were coming. When Pitcairn reached Lexington, in the early dawn, he found a company of about seventy minutemen drawn up on the common to dispute his passage. He ordered the "rebels" to disperse. A shot was fired by some unknown soldier. It was the signal for a volley from the British, which killed eight of the minutemen. Pitcairn's troops marched on to Concord, where, at the bridge, they were met

MINUTEMEN GATHERING ON LEXINGTON GREEN[1]

and turned back by the "embattled farmers" who had gathered from the near-by towns. During the long, hot afternoon the British retraced their dusty march, constantly harassed by a deadly fire from behind trees and stone walls, until at last they reached safety in their own lines at Charlestown, with a loss of nearly three hundred men. The news of Lexington and Concord was swiftly carried by Paul Revere to the colonies southward. New England was in a ferment. Farmers, taking down their old flintlocks from the chimney piece, hastened to join the militia surrounding Boston. They came not only from Massachusetts but from New Hampshire, Connecticut, and Rhode Island as well, until in a few days there was a rude and unorganized army of sixteen thousand men holding Gage besieged in the town of Boston.

Bunker Hill. The British had no intention of starting a war when they set out to seize the powder at Concord. Neither

[1] From *The Eve of the Revolution*, one of The Chronicles of America Photoplays. Used by permission of Yale University Press.

had Ethan Allen and his "Green Mountain Boys" when they seized the British fort at Ticonderoga, on Lake Champlain, the very day the Second Continental Congress met (May 10). But the next month the British regulars and the colonial militia faced each other in the bloodiest conflict that had ever been fought on American soil. During the night of June 16 the colonials under Colonel William Prescott fortified Breed's Hill,[1] on the peninsula of Charlestown, only a mile or so across the water from Boston. The next day, after a bombardment from the British warships had failed to dislodge the Americans, General William Howe (who, with Generals Henry Clinton and John Burgoyne, had lately arrived at Boston with reinforcements for Gage) attempted to storm the American position. The redcoats charged up the hill twice, only to meet a galling fire as they neared the breastworks and to be driven back to reform their lines. On the third assault, as the colonials had burned all their powder, the British drove them from the redoubt with bayonets. But the American defeat at Bunker Hill was a moral victory; for it showed that the raw colonial troops could face the regulars without flinching. When Washington heard of the battle he said, "The country is safe." Howe's loss of over a thousand men was double that of the Americans. One eighth of all the British officers killed in the Revolutionary War fell at Bunker Hill. "I wish we could sell them another hill at the same price," was the remark of one of the American officers.

The Congress Declares War. On the receipt of the news of Bunker Hill the Continental Congress at Philadelphia was confronted with a question of the utmost importance. Should it treat the actual warfare in Massachusetts as a local matter, or should it assume responsibility in the name of all the colonies for armed resistance to Great Britain? It took the latter momentous decision. It adopted the colonial troops facing Boston as a Continental Army, and, at the suggestion of John Adams, appointed George Washington of Virginia as commander in

[1] Breed's Hill was a lower height to the east of Bunker Hill. It was on Breed's Hill that the battle was fought, though it has always been called the battle of Bunker Hill.

chief. On July 3 Washington took command of the army at Cambridge, Massachusetts, and three days later Congress issued a spirited declaration of war.

We are reduced to the alternative of choosing an unconditional submission to the tyranny of irritable ministers or resistance by force. The latter is our choice. We have counted the cost of this contest and find nothing so dreadful as voluntary slavery. Our cause is just, our union is perfect. . . . In defence of the freedom which is our birthright we have taken up arms. We shall lay them down when hostility shall cease on the part of our aggressors.

The Crisis. So it had come to open and declared war between Great Britain and the American colonies. In spite of protests of loyalty on the part of the colonists for a decade, in spite of petitions, remonstrances, and legal arguments, the breach had grown wider and wider until it could not be healed. We must appreciate the efforts of the devoted friends of America in Parliament, such as Pitt and Burke, to stem the influence of the "King's Friends," [1] and we must recognize also the arguments of conservatives in America like Galloway, Dickinson, Jay, and Livingston, who clung longer than Washington, Jefferson, Henry, and the Adamses to the belief that the colonies might still secure their rights as British freemen without having to give up their allegiance to the king and the empire.

The question was, Could liberty be reconciled with loyalty? Liberty meant to the colonists the right to control their officials, to extend their commerce without hindrances, and, above all, to vote their taxes in their own elected assemblies. Loyalty meant to King George and his ministers unquestioning obedience to the acts of Parliament, which was the supreme authority of the empire. The two ideas could not be joined in harmony.

[1] For example, Pitt (Lord Chatham after 1766) pleaded with Parliament for the removal of all the British troops in Boston, but his motion secured only eighteen votes in the House of Lords. Burke begged the House of Commons to win the affection of the Americans by giving up the idea of drawing a revenue from the colonies and by admitting them to a full share of the freedom enjoyed by their fellow citizens in Great Britain. "Magnanimity in politics," he said, "is not seldom the truest wisdom; and a great empire and little minds go ill together." But the great statesman's plea for conciliation with America was voted down three to one.

On the British side was the dogged determination to make the colonists submit. "I know what my duty to my country is," wrote King George, "and threats cannot prevent me from doing it to the utmost extent." On the other side was an equally dogged determination not to sacrifice liberty for the sake of preserving the empire. "It is an immense misfortune," said Thomas Jefferson, "to have a king of such a disposition at such a time. There is not in the British empire a man who more cordially loves a union with Great Britain than I do, but, by the God who made me, I will cease to exist before I yield to a connection on such terms as the British parliament propose. And in this I think I speak the sentiments of America."

In August, 1775, Richard Penn arrived in London with a respectful petition from the Continental Congress, asking that the relations between the colonies and Great Britain be restored to the status of 1763. The news of Bunker Hill had already reached England. King George refused to receive either Penn or the petition. Instead, he published a proclamation declaring that his "subjects in the colonies had proceeded to an avowed rebellion by arraying themselves to withstand the execution of the law, and traitorously levying war against him." The colonists were no longer only disobedient children or troublesome agitators. They were rebels in arms, enemies to be conquered — and punished.

Terms to be Mastered

"King's Friends"	Declaratory Act	"Intolerable Acts"
proclamation line	"Sam Adams' regiments"	minutemen
admiralty courts	Committees of Correspondence	rights of British freemen

For Supplementary Reading

Carl Becker, *The Eve of the Revolution* (Chronicles of America, Vol. XI); C. M. Andrews, *The Colonial Background of the American Revolution*; C. H. Van Tyne, *The Causes of the War of Independence*; G. E. Howard, *The Preliminaries of the Revolution* (American Nation Series, Vol. VIII); J. R. Green, *A Short History of the English People*, chap. x; The Pageant of America, Vol. VIII, chap. ii (interesting illustrations); C. A. and M. R. Beard, *The Rise of American Civilization*, Vol. I, chap. v; James T. Adams, *Revolutionary New England*, chaps. xiii–xvii; Hart, *Contemporaries*, Vol. II, Nos. 130–158; Muzzey, *Readings*, pp. 111–132.

Topics for Reports

1. **Pontiac's Rebellion.** Francis Parkman, *The Conspiracy of Pontiac.*

2. **Resistance to the Stamp Act.** *America*, Vol. III, pp. 72–84; H. S. Commager, *Documents of American History*, Nos. 35–40; C. Becker, *The Eve of the Revolution*, chap. vi; Hart, *Contemporaries*, Vol. II, Nos. 141, 142; E. B. Greene, *The Foundations of American Nationality*, pp. 403–412.

3. **"The Boston Tea Party."** John Fiske, *The American Revolution*, Vol. I, pp. 80–93; *America*, Vol. III, pp. 96–105; C. H. Van Tyne, *Causes of the War of Independence*, pp. 369–390; Hart, *Contemporaries*, No. 152.

4. **The Defense of American Rights.** (By James Otis) M. C. Tyler, *The Literary History of the American Revolution*, Vol. I, pp. 30–44; (by Daniel Dulany) ibid. pp. 101–111; (by Jonathan Mayhew) ibid. pp. 121–140; (by Stephen Hopkins) Muzzey, *Readings*, pp. 115–117; (by John Dickinson) ibid. pp. 125–128; (by William Pitt) Hart, *Contemporaries*, Vol. II, No. 142.

Questions Suggested by the Chapter

1. Why did Great Britain want an army in the American colonies? **2.** How did Great Britain subordinate the interests of the mainland colonies to those of the British West Indies? **3.** Why did Great Britain try to keep the colonists out of the land west of the Alleghenies? **4.** What did John Adams mean by saying that molasses was one of the causes of the American Revolution? **5.** What British statesmen were favorable to the American cause? **6.** Why was the Stamp Act more irritating to the Americans than the Acts of Trade? **7.** Why did Parliament repeal the Stamp Act? **8.** What did Samuel Adams do to earn the title of "the great incendiary"? **9.** Explain the difference between the English and the American ideas of representation. **10.** Why were troops sent to Boston in 1768? **11.** How did the "Intolerable Acts" of 1774 differ in purpose from the Grenville and Townshend measures? **12.** Do you think that the men of Boston were justified in destroying the tea? **13.** Why was the Quebec Act offensive to New England? **14.** Who were some of the leading figures, and what were some of the leading measures of the First Continental Congress? **15.** Why did the Americans consider Bunker Hill a virtual victory? **16.** What did the colonists mean by "natural rights"?

CHAPTER SIX

WASHINGTON SEES IT THROUGH

Increasing numbers of men of good will in every civilized country deplore warfare as a means of settling international disputes, and the governments of practically all the countries of the world have signed the Kellogg-Briand Pact of 1928, renouncing war as "an instrument of national policy." War is regarded, even by most of the military men who feel obliged to wage it, as barbarous, wasteful, cruel, and demoralizing. Since the earliest recorded history, however, men have fought in battle, and none can tell how far away is the day when the nations will become sufficiently humanized and civilized to settle their disputes without resort to arms. Wars often fail to bring any lasting benefit to the victors, leaving only the seeds of future wars in the suffering, poverty, hatreds, and desire for revenge which they bring in their train. But if any war is justified by its results, it is the American Revolution. By securing the independence of the United States it gave this new nation the opportunity to establish the first great democracy in history and to put to the proof the doctrine of the fathers that freemen are able to govern themselves, without the authority of kings, nobles, or any other class of "masters."

It is not our purpose in this chapter to describe the campaigns and battles of the American Revolution. Military history is a highly specialized subject which only experts can understand. What interests us here is the part which certain operations of Washington and his generals and certain policies (especially diplomatic) of the Continental Congress had in winning the independence of the American colonies from Great Britain.

Moving toward Independence. The war which opened at Lexington and Concord was not begun for independence. The colonists regarded themselves not as rebels against the king but as defenders of long-established rights which the British ministers and Parliament were denying them. Rhode Island regiments which came up to join Washington's army around Boston even spoke of themselves as "in his Majesty's service." And Congress, in its declaration of war on July 6, 1775, said, "We have not raised armies with the ambitious design of separating from Great Britain and establishing independent states." Moreover, we have the emphatic statements of nearly all the patriot leaders themselves (Washington, Franklin, John Adams, Jefferson, Jay, and dozens more), in the summer of 1775, that they were not aiming at independence. Nevertheless, by the end of the year, events had occurred on both sides of the Atlantic which made it impossible for the colonies to continue to believe that they could obtain their rights *within* the British Empire.

At the moment when Burke made his unsuccessful plea in the Commons for reconciliation with America, Benjamin Franklin was on his way home after ten years' residence in England, convinced that all his efforts to make the British government see the light were useless. Not only did the king reject the petition of Congress and declared his American subjects "rebels," but he hired twenty thousand troops from the petty German princes of Brunswick, Hesse, and Anhalt to help subdue them. When Parliament met in October, it supported the ministry by large majorities, and passed acts strengthening the king's forces in America and forbidding the colonies to trade with any country outside the British Empire. On this side of the water too the ties which bound the colonies to the mother country were snapping. The royal governors from New Hampshire to Georgia were taking refuge on warships off the coast. Their legislatures were refusing to obey them and were converting themselves into popular conventions controlled by the radical leaders. Congress was laboring to increase Washington's army and provide it with food, clothing, and money. Valiant captains of sloops and schooners were attacking British supply ships and seizing barrels of flour and gunpowder. Eighty yoke of oxen were dragging the cannon from Fort Ticonderoga to Cambridge over the December snow, to help keep Howe (who had succeeded Gage) shut up in Boston. Richard Montgomery and Benedict Arnold were invading Canada, one by way of Lake Champlain and the other through the Maine wilderness, to try to win the French "habitants" to the American cause. On the last day of the year, in the midst of a blinding snow storm, Montgomery was killed and Arnold severely wounded in a vain attempt to capture the town of Quebec.

Britain's Authority in the Colonies Comes to an End. Though Congress did not actually vote the separation of the colonies from England until July, 1776, that separation was fully completed months before the vote was taken. In other words, the Declaration of Independence did not *propose* that the colonies should throw off their allegiance to Great Britain, but rather acknowledged before the whole world that they had already done so. They had put an end to the authority of king and Parliament over them. On the first day of the new year (1776) Washington had raised above his camp a flag symbolizing the union of the thirteen colonies.[1] A week later appeared a famous pamphlet from the pen of Thomas Paine, an Englishman who had recently come to America, on Franklin's advice, to help the cause of freedom. Paine's *Common Sense* urged the colonists to put an end to the inconsistency of recognizing King George (whom he called a "royal brute") as their sovereign while they were fighting against his troops. Providence had designed the colonies, he wrote, to be the nucleus of a great American nation, destined to cover a continent and to be an example to the world of a people free from the tyranny of kings and nobles. The future belonged to America. Let her accept her birthright by immediately breaking off all connection with Great Britain. Over one hundred thousand copies of *Common Sense* were quickly sold. Washington spoke of its "sound doctrine and unanswerable reasoning"; and Edmund Randolph declared that, next

---

[1] Washington's flag was not yet the Stars and Stripes. It had the thirteen alternate stripes of red and white, representing the thirteen colonies; but instead of the cluster of white stars on a blue field in the corner, it had the combined crosses of Saint Andrew and Saint George. The Stars and Stripes were first raised over Fort Stanwix the next year.

to King George, Thomas Paine was the man responsible for the declaration of our independence.

Washington brought the long siege of Boston to an end in March, by seizing Dorchester Heights, which commanded the town and the harbor, and forcing Howe to sail away to Halifax, Nova Scotia. With Howe went eleven hundred Tory refugees, representing many of the best families of the province. Boston was delivered, and for the rest of the war Massachusetts and northern New England saw no more of the British redcoats.

To add to Washington's great victory at Boston came three most important acts of Congress, which cut the last threads of dependence upon Great Britain. In March, Silas Deane of Connecticut was sent to France to ask for help in men and money. That is, Congress acted as the agent of an independent nation by entering into diplomatic relations with England's old enemy. In April, Congress opened the ports of America to all the nations of the world, thereby annulling the Acts of Trade by which, for more than a century, Great Britain had sought to keep the colonies' commerce in her own control. Finally, in May, Congress advised all the colonies "to adopt governments that conduce to the happiness and safety of their people," that is, to take no further notice of the royal governors, judges, councilors, customs collectors, or other officials. Surely, after these *acts* of independence nothing was left but to speak the word openly.

The Hesitation of Congress. Yet Congress hesitated to speak that word. On June 7, 1776, Richard Henry Lee of Virginia introduced a resolution consisting of three parts:

> That these united colonies are, and of right ought to be, free and independent states; that they are absolved from all allegiance to the British Crown, and that all political connection between them and the state of Great Britain is, and ought to be, totally dissolved.
>
> That it is expedient forthwith to take the most effectual measures for forming foreign alliances; and
>
> That a plan of confederation be prepared and transmitted to the respective colonies for their consideration and approbation.

John Adams seconded the motion. The debate in Congress was very spirited. Some members, from long attachment to the mother country, were not ready to close the door finally to an agreement. Others were afraid that if their cause should fail they would be executed as traitors. Then, too, it was argued that to declare independence would both divide the colonies and unite the British; for many who were willing to fight for their rights *within* the empire would desert the patriot cause if the empire were broken up; while Englishmen like Pitt and Fox, who sympathized with Americans striving for their liberties as British subjects, would cease to support Americans fighting to establish an independent nation. The argument of John Dickinson of Pennsylvania may be taken as an example of the opposition to independence. Dickinson was in favor of the second and third parts of Lee's resolution, and he was a member of both the committee to seek foreign aid and the committee to prepare a plan of confederation of the colonies. But he thought that until the colonies knew what aid they might expect from abroad (that is, from France), and had bound themselves into a firm union, America was not ready "to advance with majestic steps and assume her station among the sovereigns of the world." To which it was fittingly replied that so long as the colonies remained a part of Great Britain they could expect no help from France, and that a bold declaration of their independence would be just the best way to secure their firm union. If the members of Congress did not all "hang together," said Benjamin Franklin, "they would all hang separately." The views of the bolder spirits prevailed. On July 2, 1776, a day which John Adams declared would be celebrated "as the most memorable epoch in the history of America," [1] Congress adopted Lee's resolutions by a vote of twelve of the thirteen colonies.[2] They were no longer the united colonies of Great Britain but the United States of America.

[1] It is not July 2, however, that we celebrate as the birthday of the American nation, but July 4, the day on which Congress adopted the *Declaration* of Independence, written by Thomas Jefferson, proclaiming to the world the reasons for our separation from Great Britain.

[2] The New York delegates did not vote, because they had no instructions from home. But five days later they received permission to join the other twelve colonies, making the vote on independence unanimous.

The Declaration of Independence. When Lee's resolutions were introduced in June, a committee, including Jefferson, Franklin, John Adams, Roger Sherman, and Robert R. Livingston, had been elected by ballot to prepare a public paper justifying the action of Congress in case it should vote for independence. Thomas Jefferson, who stood highest on the ballot and who was a master of clear and forceful style, was asked to write the declaration. He sat down at his desk in his lodging room at Philadelphia and, "without reference to book or pamphlet," produced the immortal document which, with slight amendments by Adams and Franklin, was accepted by Congress on July 4.[1]

Turn to Appendix I and read the Declaration of Independence carefully, noting its three parts: (1) the assertion of the justice of revolution against a government which denies its people their "unalienable rights"; (2) the long list of oppressive acts of King George III which proved him "unfit to be the ruler of a free people"; and (3) the ringing declaration repeating the words of Lee's motion and pledging the members of Congress to defend the independence of the new nation with their lives, their fortunes, and their sacred honor.

The Declaration of Independence cleared the air. It put an end to the contradiction of fighting against a king while still professing loyalty to him. It called upon the waverers to make their definite choice between allegiance to the United States or to the now foreign and enemy government of Great Britain. It offered France and Spain, jealous rivals of England, the chance to help shatter the proud empire which had defeated them in

---

[1] A famous historical painting represents the members of Congress as pressing forward to sign the Declaration on July 4. As a matter of fact, the only members who signed on that day were the presiding officer, John Hancock (who wrote his name in letters "large enough for King George to read without his spectacles"), and the clerk, Charles Thompson. The Declaration was ordered to be engrossed on parchment on July 19, and most of the members signed it on August 2. Other names were added later. The yellowed parchment, with the original signatures, is now in the Library of Congress, preserved, along with the original document of the Constitution of the United States, in a kind of little shrine and under a glass plate. The desk on which Jefferson wrote the Declaration is preserved in the State Department, at Washington.

INDEPENDENCE HALL

the last war. And, finally, it put spirit into the American army
by giving it a cause supremely worth fighting for. On July 9,
Washington had the Declaration read to his troops in New York,
whither he had moved after compelling Howe to evacuate
Boston. "The General hopes," said the order of the day,
"that this important event will serve as an incentive to every
officer and soldier to act with fidelity and courage, as knowing
that now the peace and safety of this country depend (under
God) solely on the success of our arms."

Washington at Bay. Whatever the general hoped, he knew that a long and hard struggle was ahead. He could have echoed the words of John Adams on July 2: "I am well aware of the toil and blood and treasure that it will cost us to maintain this declaration. . . . Yet through all the gloom I can see the rays of light and glory." On July 12 Admiral Lord Richard Howe landed on Staten Island, in New York Harbor, with reinforcements for his brother, Sir William, who had already come down from Halifax. And when to these were added the troops of General Clinton, just returned from an unsuccessful attempt to capture Fort Moultrie, at Charleston, the British had a well-trained army of thirty-five thousand men to oppose to Washington's force of half that number, composed of raw troops with short-term enlistments.

Washington had no hope of holding New York, but he was determined to make the British fight for every inch of ground he must yield to them. He met them first on Long Island (August 27–28), and after the inevitable defeat he performed a miracle of strategy by ferrying his whole army, with their provisions and military equipment, across the East River to New York under the cover of a fog. Howe followed and forced him out of the city (which the British held till the end of the war) [1] and mile by mile up the Hudson valley. Unable to hold the forts on the river, Washington crossed to the New Jersey side and led his dwindling army southward, vainly imploring General Charles Lee to come to him with reinforcements from the eastern bank of the Hudson. [2]

[1] On September 21 Captain Nathan Hale, of Connecticut, a graduate of Yale College, volunteered to enter the British lines in New York to gather information for Washington. He was captured and treated with the greatest indignity, not even being allowed to write a farewell word to his mother or his fiancée. The next morning he was hanged as a spy, declaring on the scaffold that his only regret was that he had but one life to give for his country.

[2] Lee was a rash, conceited general, who despised Washington in his heart and wanted to succeed him in the command of the army. When he did finally cross the Hudson, after Washington's repeated orders, he allowed himself to be surprised and captured at a farmhouse by a squad of thirty British soldiers, and was taken to New York, where he began to plot with Clinton for the destruction of the American army. His treachery unsuspected, he was exchanged later for a high British officer, and returned to his American command only to make more mischief for Washington, as we shall see.

A Declaration by the Representatives of the UNITED STATES OF AMERICA, *in General Congress assembled*

When in the course of human events it becomes necessary for ~~one~~ people to dissolve the political bands which have connected them with another, and to ~~assume among the powers of the earth that subordination~~ which ~~they have hitherto remained~~, ~~to~~ as -sume among the powers of the earth the ~~equal & independent~~ separate and equal station to which the laws of nature & of nature's god entitle them, a decent respect to the opinions of mankind requires that they should declare the causes which impel them to ~~that~~ the separation

We hold these truths to be ~~sacred & undeniable~~ self-evident, that all men are created equal ~~& independent~~ that ~~from that equal creation they derive~~ they are endowed by their creator with ~~equal~~ rights ~~inherent~~ & inalienable, that ~~these~~ among ~~which~~ are the ~~preservation of~~ life & liberty, & the pursuit of happiness; that to secure these ~~ends~~, rights, go -vernments are instituted among men, deriving their just powers from

FACSIMILE OF THE OPENING LINES OF THE DECLARATION
OF INDEPENDENCE

Washington was pursued all the way across New Jersey by Howe, and just got his last boatloads of men over the Delaware River at Trenton when the British entered the town.

The American army, by this time, was reduced to less than three thousand effective men, shivering on the banks of the Delaware in the December frosts. The American cause looked hopeless. It was the darkest hour of the war. Congress fled from Philadelphia to Baltimore. Thomas Paine sat down in the gloomy American camp to write, in the first number of *The Crisis*, "These are the times that try men's souls." Even the great commander himself nearly lost courage. "If every nerve is not strained to recruit a new army," he wrote to his brother, "I think the game is pretty nearly up."

Trenton and Princeton. But the darkest hour was the hour before the dawn. Ere the river should freeze, and enable the British to cross and annihilate his little army, Washington resolved on a desperate plan. Late on Christmas night, in the midst of a driving storm of sleet, he transported about twenty-three hundred men across the ice-filled river and at daybreak fell upon the Hessians, who were sleeping off their Christmas

WASHINGTON'S
CAMPAIGN OF 1776

revels at Trenton. The town was stormed, the Hessian commander was mortally wounded, and his entire force of nearly a thousand men taken prisoners. Lord Cornwallis — who was about to embark for England, thinking that the war was over — hastened to repair the disaster. Washington, however, outwitted and eluded him, defeating three British regiments at Princeton and sending Cornwallis back in panic to New Brunswick to protect his military stores. Washington then moved up to Morristown, in the Jersey highlands, about thirty miles from New York, to go into winter quarters. In a brilliant campaign of ten days he had recovered the state of New Jersey.

The Howes offered the king's pardon to all Americans who would take an oath of allegiance to Great Britain, and hundreds of New Jersey farmers had accepted the terms, glad to save their skins in what seemed the sure failure of the American cause and to sell their produce to the British for hard gold. But now that the patriots were on top, these renegades hastened to destroy Howe's certificates of pardon, which, if found on them, were likely to cost them a coat of tar and feathers. Lord George Germain, the new British minister of war, sadly confessed that all his hopes "were blasted by the unhappy affair at Trenton," and when Lord Cornwallis made the final surrender of the British army to Washington at Yorktown, in 1781, he complimented the American commander on his "unsurpassed performance" in New Jersey five years before.

The British Blunder of 1777. While Washington was in northern New Jersey, waiting for recruits to come in for the campaign of 1777 and wondering why Howe did not come out from New York and put an end to his army of four thousand men, the British war office was hatching a plan to conquer the state of New York and so cut off New England from the states to the south. General John Burgoyne, with an army of eight thousand British regulars, Hessians, Canadians, and Indians, was to march down from the St. Lawrence, via Lake Champlain and the Hudson, to Albany. Lieutenant Colonel St. Leger was to join him there, coming eastward from Lake Ontario through the Mohawk valley. And at Albany both were to combine with forces sent up the Hudson by Howe.

But no part of the plan succeeded. Howe, either because he failed to get the proper instructions from home [1] or because he thought it more necessary to capture the "rebel capital" of Philadelphia, set sail with the greater part of his army for Chesapeake Bay just as Burgoyne was starting from Canada. St. Leger was turned back at Oriskany by the brave German-American general Herkimer, before he had got halfway to Albany. Burgoyne, confidently marching southward, with his great baggage trains and host of camp followers, found himself more and more entangled in the forests between Lake Champlain and the Hudson. The militia from New York, the newly formed state of Vermont, and the rest of New England swarmed about him like hornets. He tried to beat them off in engagement after engagement, but was finally decisively beaten at Saratoga, and on October 17 surrendered his entire army, reduced to fifty-eight hundred men by defeats and desertions, to General Gates. [2]

[1] The story was that the incompetent, pleasure-loving Germain was so eager to go grouse-shooting in the country that after signing Howe's instructions he put them in a pigeonhole in his desk and forgot them.

[2] Gates was a bombastic, selfish person, who soon was deeply engaged in a plot to get himself made commander in chief instead of Washington. He did not appear on the field of battle at Saratoga. The chief honor for that victory belongs to Benedict Arnold and Daniel Morgan.

Meanwhile Washington had hastened to meet Howe, who landed at the head of Chesapeake Bay to march on Philadelphia. In spite of Washington's efforts in the battles of Brandywine Creek (September 11) and Germantown (October 4), he could not prevent the superior British force from taking the city. But Howe's victory was far more than offset by the loss of Burgoyne's army. His blunder in not co-operating with Burgoyne in the campaign for the Hudson brought results which forced the British to abandon Philadelphia nine months after they had taken it.

The French Alliance. The victory at Saratoga was the turning-point of the war, because it brought as an ally to America the greatest continental power of Europe. The French had welcomed the Declaration of Independence, and had been secretly supplying arms and provisions to America through the agency of an adventurous courtier named Beaumarchais. The wealthy young Marquis of Lafayette had fitted out a ship at his own expense and, in spite of Louis XVI's orders, had sailed in April, 1777, to aid the American cause, carrying a dozen French officers with him. Benjamin Franklin, who was to be as successful in Paris as he had been unsuccessful in London, was urging on the French court the advantages which France would reap from the transfer of America's trade from England to France.

But the Count of Vergennes, the astute foreign minister, was wary of bringing on a war with Great Britain until two objects were attained. First, Spain, which was allied to France by a compact of 1761, must be willing to join. Second, the Americans must furnish proof, by some decided success in arms, that they were likely to be able to maintain the independence which they had declared. He knew that the British ambassador at Paris knew that secret help was going to the Americans; but he put the ambassador off with fair words — and deliberate lies.[1] The news of Saratoga, arriving in December, satisfied

[1] For example, when the British ambassador, Lord Stormont, complained that the American commissioners were being received too frequently and too cordially by Vergennes, the latter blandly replied that a minister's house was like a church, — "anybody might enter, but with no certainty that his prayers would be heard!"

Vergennes on his second point and enabled him to get Spain also to furnish money to the Americans secretly, although Spain waited another year before joining in the war on Great Britain. On February 6, 1778, France threw off the mask and entered into treaties of alliance and commerce with the United States. By the terms of the treaty of alliance, the two nations agreed to open their ports to each other for prizes taken from the enemy, to guarantee each other's possessions in the New World, and not to lay down their arms until the independence of the United States was acknowledged by Great Britain.[1]

The Belated British Offer. The news of Saratoga brought a great change in London as well as in Paris. Even Lord North and the king were ready to make concessions to the Americans. Chatham, in the House of Lords, seeing a war with France loom up, pleaded for immediate peace with America and for bringing all the power of the empire to bear against the old enemy France. But the "die-hards" in Parliament, who railed at Burgoyne for his "cowardly surrender to a mob of poltroons," voted down Chatham's motion by large majorities. He begged the Lords to act at once; but Parliament adjourned for the Christmas holidays, and when it got round to considering North's proposals in February, the French alliance was already concluded. "One of the strangest ironies of history," says Professor N. W. Stephenson, "is this throwing away an empire to save a Christmas recess."

The "olive branch" offered by North on February 17 and adopted by Parliament granted the Americans all that they had asked for before their separation from the empire: no taxes to be laid by Parliament, the repeal of all the obnoxious laws since 1763, amnesty and pardon for those who had been branded as "rebels," and a commission authorized to treat with Congress, the provincial assemblies, or with General Washington himself. However, even if the French alliance had not been concluded, it

---

[1] This treaty with France (which lasted only until 1800) was the only treaty of alliance that the United States ever made. Therefore it is a mistake to speak of "our allies" in the World War. We were "associated" with the "Allied" powers (England, France, Italy, etc.) in the war against Germany and Austria-Hungary, but we had no treaty of alliance with any of them.

is certain that the Americans would not have accepted North's olive branch. Despite Professor Stephenson's epigram, Great Britain had already "thrown away" her empire before the Christmas recess of 1777. North's offer came not a few weeks but two years too late. Before July 2, 1776, the terms might well have been accepted; but since then the Americans would be content with nothing but the acknowledgment of their independence — and that even Chatham was unwilling to grant.

Valley Forge. The spot which Washington chose for his winter encampment on the Schuylkill River, twenty miles above Philadelphia, has become a name to immortalize the sufferings and endurance of the American army. While the British were making the winter gay with balls and pageants in the captured city, Washington's eight thousand men, housed in rude huts which they built from the trees of the surrounding forest, shivering from lack of clothing and blankets, and leaving their bloody footprints on the snow as they toiled dragging the cannon or foraging for firewood, presented a harrowing picture of distress. Valley Forge was a terrible test of their great commander's courage too. Not only did he suffer from the hardships of his soldiers but he had to endure also a personal humiliation. The Congress (which had fled to York before Howe's army) criticized him for retiring from Philadelphia.[1] Odious comparisons were made between his failures at Brandywine and Germantown and Gates's brilliant success at Saratoga. A group of generals and members of Congress joined in a cabal against him, headed by the Irish inspector general Conway, to supplant him by Gates. His repeated supplications for supplies went unheeded.

'Still, there were encouraging signs to offset the gloom at Valley Forge. The sympathy of Europe for the American cause was growing stronger every month. Frederick the Great of Prussia forbade the German troops hired by King George

---

[1] This treatment drew from Washington one of his few sarcastic replies to Congress: "I can assure those gentlemen that it is much easier and less distressing to draw remonstrances in a comfortable room by a good fireside than to occupy a cold, bleak hill, and sleep under frost and snow without clothes or blankets."

WINTER AT VALLEY FORGE

to march through his territory and declared that the chances were a hundred to one that the Americans would win their independence. Baron von Steuben, a veteran of the Prussian wars, arrived at Valley Forge to drill the troops into an efficient army. Franklin, at Paris, was winning over King Louis and Vergennes day by day. At last, on May 6, 1778, came the joyful news of the French alliance, which was celebrated by the firing of thirteen cannon and by such festivities as the meager resources of the camp would allow. Already the Count d'Estaing had sailed for America with twelve ships of the line and a number of regiments. The general feeling prevailed that a new and successful era had opened in the war for American independence.

The Changed Character of the War. A new era had opened indeed. The first effect of the French alliance was the abandonment of Philadelphia by Howe's successor, General Clinton, since the forts on the Delaware were not strong enough to protect the city against D'Estaing's fleet. As Clinton, with seventeen thousand men and a baggage train eight miles long, was marching through New Jersey to New York, the American army met him at Monmouth (June 28) and would have cut his line in twain had not General Charles Lee basely ordered a retreat in the middle of the battle. Washington, hastily summoned by Lafayette, rode up in time to save the day, and ordered Lee to the rear with a blasting rebuke. The treacherous general was court-martialed, suspended from his command for a year, and then dismissed in disgrace from the army. Monmouth was the last general engagement of the war north of Virginia, and the last battle in which Washington took part until he led the combined forces of America and France to the final victory at Yorktown in the autumn of 1781.

With the French alliance, followed by the accession of Spain in 1779 and Holland in 1780 to the league against Great Britain, the war took on a European character. It was no longer merely a civil war between England and her revolted colonies, but a struggle for life for Great Britain against four enemies at once. The British war office in 1778 adopted a new policy. It decided to transfer the seat of war to the Southern states, where it be-

Sir   Paris, Dec. 23. 1776

104.

We beg Leave to acquaint your
Excellency, that we are appointed and
fully impowered by the Congress of the
United States of America, to propose
and negotiate a Treaty of Amity and
Commerce between France and the said
States. × × × × × × × × × × × ×

We request an Audience of your Excell.cy
wherein we may have an Opportunity of
presenting our Credentials; and we flatter
ourselves that the Propositions we are
instructed to make, are such as will not
be found unacceptable.

With the greatest Regard we have
the Honour to be,

Your Excellency's most obedient
and most humble Servants

B Franklin

Silas Deane

Arthur Lee

His Excell.y the Count de Vergennes.

FRANKLIN'S LETTER TO THE COUNT OF VERGENNES

The Earliest Diplomatic Correspondence of the American Congress

lieved that the Loyalists in large numbers were ready to join the British army, and it resolved to prosecute the war with unsparing cruelty in order to punish the Americans for allying themselves with England's old enemy France. They should be treated now as foreign foes to be utterly crushed, and no longer as disobedient subjects to be reclaimed.

The War in the South. Beginning with the capture of Savannah in December, 1778, the British took Augusta and overran the state of Georgia. The old royal governor was restored to office, and the state was declared reunited to the empire. Then, in December, 1779, General Clinton sailed from New York with an army of eighty-five hundred for the conquest of South Carolina. The following May he took Charleston and compelled General Benjamin Lincoln to surrender his whole force of twenty-five hundred men, practically the entire regular American army south of the Potomac. South Carolina, like Georgia, felt the full vengeance of the British officers. Houses and barns of the patriots were burned, livestock slaughtered, crops destroyed, and the unfortunate people driven into prison camps. When Clinton returned to New York, leaving Lord Cornwallis in command in the South, he wrote to Germain, "Few men in South Carolina are not either our prisoners or in arms with us." Against Washington's preference for Greene, Congress sent Gates to supersede Lincoln; but the "hero of Saratoga" suffered the worst defeat of the war at the hands of Cornwallis at Camden, South Carolina, August 16, 1780. His militia "ran like a torrent" before the charges of the British regulars, and Gates ran with them, never stopping until he had reached Charlotte, North Carolina, fifty miles away. The brave Bavarian Baron De Kalb, who had come over with Lafayette in 1777, was mortally wounded in his attempt to save the day for the Americans.[1]

[1] Another distinguished foreign general gave his life for America in the Southern war when Count Casimir Pulaski, a Pole, was mortally wounded in an attempt to recapture Savannah, Georgia, in October, 1779. The great Polish patriot and engineer Thaddeus Kosciusko came to America, on Franklin's recommendation, in 1776 and served Washington through the whole war. It was he who planned the fortifications at Saratoga and West Point.

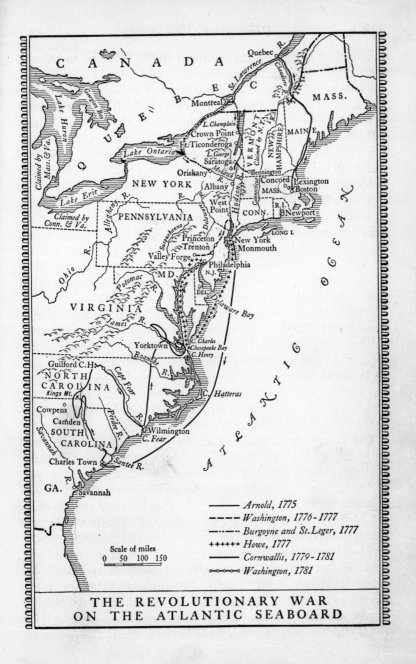

THE REVOLUTIONARY WAR
ON THE ATLANTIC SEABOARD

Arnold, 1775
Washington, 1776–1777
Burgoyne and St. Leger, 1777
++++++ Howe, 1777
Cornwallis, 1779–1781
Washington, 1781

Scale of miles
0   50   100   150

It looked as though the Southern states were lost to the patriot cause. "Three or four hundred good soldiers would finish the business," wrote Colonel Patrick Ferguson, one of the cruelest of Cornwallis's officers, to his chief. But on October 7 several regiments of backwoodsmen from both sides of the Alleghenies, gathered under John Sevier, caught Ferguson's force of twelve hundred Loyalists at King's Mountain, near the northern border of South Carolina, and annihilated it in the bloodiest battle of the war since Bunker Hill.

King's Mountain, said Jefferson, was "the turn of the tide." It struck terror into Cornwallis's army and it aroused the patriots throughout the Carolinas. Irregular bands under Sumter, Pickens, and "the swamp fox" Marion harassed the British at every turn. Nathanael Greene, next to Washington the ablest of the American generals, was sent to replace Gates, and with him went the fiery Daniel Morgan, of Saratoga fame. Morgan redeemed the defeat at Camden by a brilliant victory at Cowpens, South Carolina (January 17, 1781), and he and Greene skillfully maneuvered Cornwallis northward until he was far separated from his base at Charleston. Cornwallis could make no headway against the superior strategy of his opponents, and the summer of 1781 found him just where he had been a year before, namely, in control of the seaboard only. Even the patriot governor and legislature of Georgia had been restored.

The Treachery of Benedict Arnold. While the war was going on in the South, a distressing event took place on the Hudson. Benedict Arnold, who had so distinguished himself for bravery at Quebec and Saratoga, and who was in command at Philadelphia during the winter of 1778–1779, believed that he had not been advanced as rapidly as he deserved to be in the American army. He married a Tory belle of the city, Peggy Shippen, and lived so extravagantly that he began to hanker after British gold. Under the double temptation of ambition and greed, he entered into the pay of General Clinton and in February, 1779, offered to shift his allegiance from the American to the British cause. He easily obtained from Washington the command of the fortress of West Point, on the Hudson, where the American military stores were kept. Major John André, a former beau of Arnold's wife, was chosen by Clinton as the agent to whom Arnold was to hand over the plans of West Point.

The moment selected was when Washington was at Hartford, Connecticut, for the purpose of meeting General Rochambeau, who had arrived at Newport in July, 1780, with six thousand French troops to reinforce the American army. Arnold and André met in the woods on the west bank of the Hudson on September 11, and ten days later André, with the papers in his boots, had nearly reached the British lines when he was stopped by some American pickets at Tarrytown. Arnold was at breakfast when the news of André's capture was brought to him. Without a word or a change of countenance, he rose and fled for refuge to the British warship *Vulture*, anchored in the river. To Washington, who had just arrived at West Point from his interview with Rochambeau, the shock of Arnold's treason was great. "Whom can we trust now?" he sadly remarked to his secretary Hamilton. André was hanged as a spy, in spite of his prayer to be allowed to suffer a less humiliating form of execution. Arnold was made a brigadier general in the British army and given a command in Virginia; but he won no respect among his late foes. He died in London, twenty years later, in poverty and bitter remorse.

The Victory of the *Bon Homme Richard*. To offset Arnold's treason, good tidings came from Europe in the late years of the war. The French were increasingly generous with money, ships, and troops. In September, 1779, John Paul Jones, the hero of the American navy, who had captured more than three hundred British vessels, met the *Serapis* off Flamborough Head, in the North Sea, convoying a British merchant fleet from the Baltic, and in a terrific hand-to-hand battle forced the *Serapis* to strike her colors. Before his own vessel, the *Bon Homme Richard*, went down, he had just time to transfer his crew and his wounded men to the captured British frigate. In February, 1780, Catherine of Russia formed a league of "armed neutrality," to which Sweden, Denmark, and the Netherlands later adhered. It served notice to Great Britain that neutral shipping would defend its rights against unjust seizures and "paper" blockades.[1]

George Rogers Clark's Conquest of the West. But most encouraging of all was the news that came out of the West. George Rogers Clark was a young Virginian who had cast in his lot with the Kentucky settlers. Clark learned through spies that the French and Indians in the Virginian territory north of the Ohio[2] were luke-warm in their allegiance to their new English masters, and he decided to seize this territory for the patriot cause. He went to Williamsburg, where Governor Patrick Henry gave him £1200 in paper currency to raise a force to conquer a region as large as New England, New York, and Pennsylvania combined. Gathering a few hundred men on the upper Ohio, Clark went down the river to within a few miles of its junction with the Mississippi and marched across the southern tip of Illinois territory to surprise the posts at Kaskaskia and Cahokia, which surrendered without a blow. By skillful diplomacy he induced the garrisons and people of the region to accept American sovereignty. When he learned that Colonel Hamilton, the British commander at Detroit, had seized the fort at Vincennes, on the Wabash, he marched in midwinter, with one hundred and thirty picked men, across the icy swamps and bleak hillocks of "the drowned lands" of southern Illinois and compelled the amazed, unprepared Hamilton to surrender his garrison as prisoners of war (February 24, 1779). The capture of Vincennes marked the end of British power north of the Ohio, except for the fur posts on the shores of the Great Lakes.

Cornwallis's Surrender at Yorktown. The year 1781 found the American cause in a desperate situation. The Continental money was worthless; the soldiers were in rags. Washington wrote in his diary that he could hardly begin another campaign

---

[1] A paper blockade means a mere declaration that ports are shut to commerce, without warships' being stationed near the ports to make the blockade actually effective.

[2] The student will remember that Virginia, by her charter of 1609 (p. 52), claimed a region of indefinite extent, reaching "up into the land from sea to sea, west and northwest."

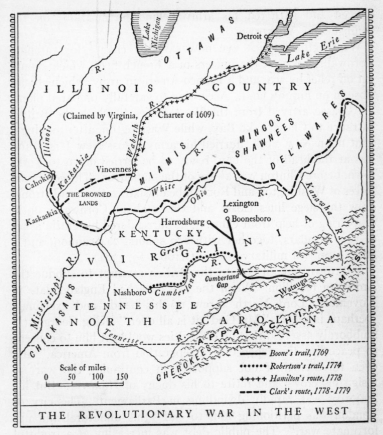

THE REVOLUTIONARY WAR IN THE WEST

without generous help from France. A special envoy was sent
to Paris, and King Louis responded with two million francs in
gold and seven thousand men, brought over by Admiral de
Grasse. Cornwallis, having abandoned the Carolinas, was now
attempting to crush "that boy" Lafayette, who was defending Virginia with a small army of regulars aided by the
militia. Clinton, fearing a combined attack on New York,
by Washington's army and the fleet of De Grasse, ordered
Cornwallis to fortify himself at some point on the Virginian
coast and to send him reinforcements. Cornwallis reluctantly

obeyed and gathered his army behind fortifications on the peninsula of Yorktown.

Washington's quick eye now saw the chance for catching Cornwallis between the pincers of a French fleet, which should cut off relief by sea, and a Franco-American army, which should close in on him by land. According to carefully prepared plans, De Grasse arrived from the West Indies to block the British entrance to Chesapeake Bay, while Washington, after making a feint upon New York, hurried his army across New Jersey and was at the head of the bay, ready to be ferried down to Yorktown, before Clinton was aware of the maneuver. The combined forces of Washington and Rochambeau, sixteen thousand strong, drew the siege lines closer and closer about Cornwallis until, despairing of help from Clinton, he surrendered his entire army of 7250 regulars, together with 850 sailors, 244 cannon, and a large supply of military stores (October 19, 1781).

Yorktown put an end to the British attempt to subdue the American rebellion. When the news reached England, late in November, Lord North threw up his hands and exclaimed (perhaps in relief), "My God! it is all over." King George still stubbornly asserted that no difficulties would get him to consent to peace "at the expense of a separation from America," and even threatened, if not supported in continuing the war, to resign his crown and retire to his duchy of Hanover. But his majority was rapidly dwindling in Parliament. The city of London was petitioning him to end "this unnatural and unfortunate war." The public debt was increasing at a frightful rate, and the French, Spanish, and Dutch ports were closed to British commerce. Finally the headstrong king had to give way. Lord North resigned in March, 1782, and Rockingham came back to power with the sole condition that there should be "no veto to the independence of America." In his cabinet were Fox, Lord Shelburne, and other friends of the American cause. The next month Shelburne's agent, Richard Oswald, was in Paris to consult with Benjamin Franklin on terms of peace.

The Peace Negotiations. In June, 1781, Congress had appointed Franklin, John Adams, John Jay, Henry Laurens, and

Thomas Jefferson [1] as peace commissioners and instructed them to take no step "without the knowledge and concurrence" of the French ministry. Nevertheless, our commissioners, without consulting Vergennes, entered into an agreement with the British on November 30, 1782. Their reasons for thus breaking the letter of their instructions were (1) that England was ready to grant the independence of America, for which the Franco-American treaty of 1778 had been made, whereas (2) France had later bound herself in a treaty with Spain, in which the United States had no part, to continue the war until Spain should have recovered Gibraltar from Great Britain. We considered ourselves in no way pledged to fight on for the benefit of Spain, whose minister at Paris was winning over Vergennes to the scheme of confining the new American republic to the territory between the Alleghenies and the Atlantic.

It took all of Franklin's tact to smooth the ruffled feelings of Vergennes, who accused the American commissioners of bad faith. But he agreed finally to the peace treaty, which was signed at Paris on September 3, 1783. By its terms England acknowledged the independence of the United States, with the Mississippi as our western boundary. The great river was to be open to the shipping of both nations, and the Americans were to share in the Newfoundland fisheries. The British demanded that Congress should restore the confiscated estates of the Loyalists and guarantee the payment of debts owed by Americans to British merchants. But all that our commissioners would promise was that Congress would "recommend" to the states that they restore the property, and would not hinder British creditors from collecting their debts through the courts. Florida was returned to Spain, after having been for twenty years a possession of England (p. 104), and several islands in the West Indies which had been captured by the British were given back to France. It was the United States that came out on top, gaining every point on which our commissioners insisted.

[1] Since Jefferson declined the appointment and Laurens was captured by the British on his way to Europe, the peace negotiations were conducted by Franklin, Adams, and Jay.

The Retirement of Washington. On April 19, 1783, the eighth anniversary of Lexington and Concord, Washington read to his troops the proclamation of Congress announcing the end of hostilities. At no time did his character shine brighter than in the months following his triumph at Yorktown. In scores of letters he urged the establishment of a government strong enough to win the confidence of the states at home and the respect of nations abroad. The treasury was empty, the paper currency was worthless, and the officers and soldiers were unpaid and impatient. One Colonel Nicola wrote Washington in May, 1782, begging him to use the army as Oliver Cromwell had done, to make himself a dictator. But Washington rebuked the writer for daring to suggest a plan so "abhorrent" to his character. The next spring, while the army was in camp at Newburgh on the Hudson, an eloquent address was circulated among the officers, reciting their neglect by Congress and threatening the resort to force to secure their just deserts. Washington immediately summoned the officers to a meeting, put the malcontent Gates in the chair, and, in an address of mingled firmness and pathos,[1] stilled the rising mutiny and won a unanimous vote of confidence in the justice of Congress.

A few months later, in June, Washington spoke to the whole American people by means of a circular letter which he sent to the governor of each state. He entreated his fellow countrymen to lay aside jealousies and to unite in seizing "a fairer opportunity for political happiness than any other nation has ever been blessed with." This was the moment, he warned, to decide "whether the revolution must ultimately be considered a blessing or a curse — not to the present age alone, for with our fate will the destiny of unborn millions be involved."

A few weeks after the treaty of peace was signed, the British evacuated New York, which they had held for seven years, and Washington entered the city amid great rejoicing. On Decem-

---

[1] In the course of his address Washington drew from his pocket a pair of spectacles (which he had never before worn in public), and, as he adjusted them, he quietly remarked: "I have grown gray in your service, and now I am going blind." Generals Schuyler and Knox rode to their quarters together after the meeting unashamed of the tears which they had shed at these words.

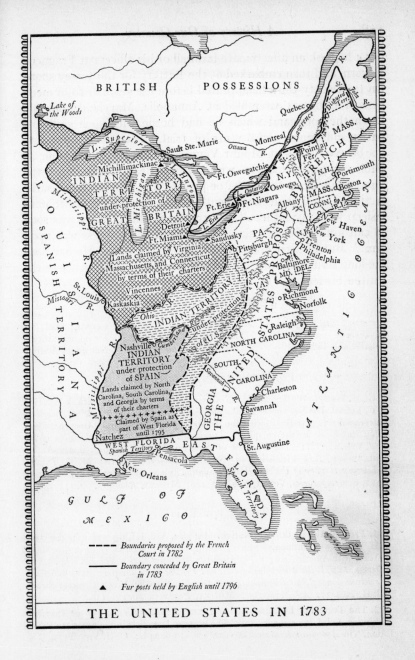

THE UNITED STATES IN 1783

ber 4 he took an affectionate farewell of his officers at Fraunces'
Tavern, and then embarked at the Battery for the Jersey shore.
On the twenty-third he appeared before the score or so of members of Congress assembled at Annapolis, Maryland, and laid
down the command which he had borne with such skill and
patience through eight years of trial. Then he returned to
his beloved acres at Mount Vernon. "I have retired from all
public employment," he wrote to his dear friend Lafayette,
"and shall tread the paths of private life with heartfelt satisfaction. . . . I shall move gently down the stream of life until
I sleep with my fathers." Vain wish! for his country was soon
to call him to other tasks. "The doom of greatness was upon
him." But his first great service was nobly done. He had seen
the long struggle through. He had won the independence of the
United States.

Terms to be Mastered

Common Sense	Hessians	Conway cabal
Loyalists	alliance	armed neutrality
"unalienable rights"	the olive branch	Newburgh Address

For Supplementary Reading

G. M. Wrong, *Washington and his Generals* (Chronicles of America, Vol. XII);
H. C. Lodge, *The Story of the Revolution*; S. G. Fisher, *The Struggle for American
Independence* (sympathetic with the Tories); John Fiske, *The American Revo-
lution* (favorable to the colonies); Theodore Roosevelt, *The Winning of the
West*, Vols. II, III; The Pageant of America, Vol. VI, chaps. vii–x; A. M.
Schlesinger, *New Viewpoints in American History*, chap. vii; M. C. Tyler,
A Literary History of the American Revolution (views of contemporary writers);
Hart, *Contemporaries*, Vol. II, Nos. 130–220; Muzzey, *Readings*, pp. 111–159.

Topics for Reports

1. **French Aid in the Revolution.** *America*, Vol. III, pp. 222–234, 245–253;
C. H. Van Tyne," Influences which Determined the French Government to Make
a Treaty with America in 1778," in *American Historical Review*, Vol. XXI, pp. 528 f.;
J. Jusserand, *With Americans of Past and Present Days*, chap. i; Bernard Faÿ,
The Revolutionary Spirit in France and America, chap. ii; Hart, *Contemporaries*,
Vol. II, Nos. 172, 176, 178, 199; Muzzey, *Readings*, pp. 141–148.

2. **The Tories, or Loyalists.** M. C. Tyler, *A Literary History of the American
Revolution*, Vol. I, pp. 293–383, and " The Party of Loyalists in the American Revolution," in *American Historical Review*, Vol. I, pp. 24 f.; C. H. Van Tyne, *The*

Loyalists in the American Revolution; HART, *Contemporaries*, Vol. II, Nos. 138, 154, 156, 166–169; MUZZEY, *Readings*, pp. 153–159.

3. **The Exploit of George Rogers Clark.** F. J. TURNER, "George Rogers Clark and the Kaskaskia Campaign," in *American Historical Review*, Vol. III, pp. 491 f., 506 f.; F. A. OGG, *The Old Northwest*, chaps. iii, iv; THEODORE ROOSEVELT, *The Winning of the West*, Vol. II, chaps. ii, iii; *America*, Vol. III, pp. 257–266; HART, *Contemporaries*, Vol. II, No. 201; MAURICE THOMPSON, *Alice of Old Vincennes*.

4. **Washington's Trials with the Army and Congress.** JOHN FISKE, *The Critical Period of American History*, pp. 101–119, and *The American Revolution*, Vol. II, pp. 24–46, 62–72; *America*, Vol. III, pp. 130–135, 200–205, 235–244, 282–286; C. H. VAN TYNE, *The American Revolution* (American Nation Series, Vol. IX), pp. 236–247; HART, *Contemporaries*, Vol. II, Nos. 174, 195, 198, 206.

QUESTIONS SUGGESTED BY THE CHAPTER

1. Why did the colonies delay their declaration of independence for more than a year after the Revolutionary War began? **2.** What were the three parts of Lee's resolution of June 7, 1776? **3.** Why did Jefferson lay the blame on George III rather than on Parliament for the revolt of the colonies? **4.** What forms did the opposition to the war take in America? **5.** Why is the Revolution sometimes called a civil war? **6.** What was the British military plan of 1777, and why did it fail? **7.** Why did the war become more serious for the British after Saratoga? **8.** What did John Paul Jones do? **9.** Why was the war west of the Alleghenies important? **10.** How did Admiral de Grasse help Washington and Rochambeau win the final victory at Yorktown? **11.** What were the terms of our alliance with France in 1778? **12.** Do you think that we treated France unfairly in negotiating terms of peace with England in 1782? **13.** Name four important foreign officers who fought for the American cause. **14.** What were the main provisions of the treaty of peace of 1783? **15.** Tell what traits of Washington's character the following names suggest to you: Valley Forge; Trenton; Yorktown; Newburgh.

CHAPTER SEVEN

THE CONFEDERATION AND THE CONSTITUTION

For nearly one hundred and fifty years the American people have been living under a document which furnishes the framework of their national government. This Constitution, as it is called, provides what kind of bodies shall make our national laws; how our President, who is to execute those laws, shall be elected and what powers he shall have; and how disputes, or "cases," arising under the laws shall go to the Federal courts, and in the last instance to the Supreme Court, for their decision. It defines the relations between the United States and the separate states, forbidding the latter to do certain things which a "sovereign" state may do (such as making war or treaties), and it binds all the officials in all the states to obedience to its own provisions. It contains a "Bill of Rights," which defines the liberties of the people which even the national Congress may not infringe. And it provides a method for its own amendment, by three fourths of the states, whenever social, economic, or political conditions in the country seem to make a change in its provisions desirable. It is the oldest written constitution in any country of the world today. Every political party in the history of the United States has vaunted itself as the defender of the Constitution, and the mass of the American people have always regarded it with veneration. But this great document was not dropped down like a scroll from heaven or revealed to any prophet on Mount Sinai. It was the product of a bitter struggle between jealous states and the conflicting views of able statesmen. It was framed in order to remedy evils which threatened to bring our country to the verge of anarchy. In this chapter we shall study the conditions out of which the Constitution grew and shall trace the work of the fathers in composing this charter of "a more perfect Union."

The Continental Congress. Until a few months before the final victory at Yorktown the Revolutionary War was fought under the authority of a body which had no charter or constitution defining its organization or its powers. This Continental Congress had met in May, 1775, at Philadelphia, to discuss what the colonies ought to do if the petition which had been sent to the king the previous autumn were not heeded. But a month before the meeting, war against the king's troops had broken out at Lexington and Concord. Therefore the Congress assumed the powers of government. It raised troops, borrowed money, sent envoys abroad for help, declared the independence of the United States, authorized the states to set up governments of their own, issued millions of dollars of paper currency, and through its many committees managed all the affairs of common interest to the country. It was a sort of general agent for the states, and it was allowed to exercise these powers (which had not been granted to it positively) because, if the war was to be won, the states must all hold together and have a central directing group of men to represent them. Each state (if it pleased) sent members (as many as it pleased) to the Congress; and, as the members were paid by the states, could be recalled at any time by the states, and were expected to act only on instructions from their states, the Congress was naturally a weak and divided body.

So long as the war lasted, the Congress, to be sure, had considerable support and respect from the states; but when the crisis was over, many thought that its work was done. The states could now get along by themselves. They did not want a central government to interfere with their liberty, as the king's officials and the Parliament had done in the colonial days. Members of the Congress quite frequently went back to serve their own state, which they regarded as more important than the Union. The membership dwindled until there were sometimes only a handful present, representing half the states. On the important occasion of Washington's retirement only twenty-three members were gathered at Annapolis to receive him.

why
who
favored

The Need for Union. For more than a hundred years before the Revolution, plans had been suggested for a confederation, or league, of some or all of the colonies. At times these plans had been proposed by the colonies themselves, for united action against the French and Indians; at other times by the British government, for the sake of a better control of the colonies.[1] During the war, Washington, who was "nationally-minded" because he felt the responsibility for the success of the Revolution in all sections of the country, repeatedly urged the need for a closer union. In December, 1778, for example, he wrote to Benjamin Harrison of Virginia: "The states separately are too much engaged in local concerns. Too many of our ablest men are withdrawn from the general councils. . . . Where are Mason, Wythe, Jefferson, Nicholas, Pendleton, Nelson and another [Harrison] I could name?" He compared the government to a clock. What good was it to keep the little wheels (the states) in order, if the great wheel (Congress) that moves the whole was neglected?

Benjamin Franklin too was an ardent advocate of union. At the very beginning of the war, a year before the declaration of independence, he had presented to the first Continental Congress a draft of "Articles of Confederation and Perpetual Union." But the members were still too much interested in securing a peaceful remedy for their grievances from Great Britain to discuss Franklin's plan. When they were ready for independence, however, they turned in earnest to the question of a united government.

You will recall that the third part of Lee's resolution of June 7, 1776, read, "That a plan of confederation be prepared and submitted to the respective colonies for their consideration and approbation." A committee of thirteen (one member from each colony), with John Dickinson of Pennsylvania as chairman,

---

[1] We have already noticed some of these plans; for example, the New England Confederation of 1643 (p. 61), Franklin's Albany Plan of 1754 (p. 101), and the project of James II for uniting the Northern colonies under the rule of Sir Edmund Andros in 1687 (p. 63). Early in the eighteenth century a bill was introduced into Parliament to deprive all the colonies in America of their charters and unite them in a single great colony under one royal governor.

prepared Articles of Confederation, which were approved and adopted by Congress in November, 1777. However, for reasons which we shall notice presently, the Articles were not ratified by the last of the thirteen states, and so put into effect as the law of the land (our first national constitution), until more than three years later.

The Articles of Confederation. The framers of the Articles had a difficult task. Here were thirteen independent states, each one of which was rejoicing in its freedom and was setting up its own government to regulate its taxation, its commerce, its suffrage, its currency, its courts, and a hundred other matters. The states had got rid of royal officials (governors, judges, collectors of customs, and the like), and they had no desire to create another set of officials, beyond their immediate control, to interfere in their affairs. They did not wish a Congress to *govern* them, as the British had done, but only to be their servant and agent in carrying out their will. Even James Madison, who was one of the foremost leaders for a strong central government, declared in 1782 that it was "extravagant" to maintain that "the rights of the British crown" (that is, a sovereign power over America) had been inherited by the Continental Congress. The Articles, therefore, while announcing a "perpetual union" and a "firm league of friendship" between the states, nevertheless declared at the outset that each state retained its "sovereignty, freedom and independence."

Would the states surrender any part of their sovereignty to a central government? If they would not, then, of course, that government could have no power over them, and would not be a real government at all. But the states did agree, in accepting the Articles, to give up certain powers to a "general government." A Congress of one house, to which each state might elect from two to seven members, was to make the laws, and the laws were to be passed not by a majority of the members in Congress but by a majority of the states, each state having one vote. Important laws required the assent of nine of the states, and any alteration of the Articles had to receive the vote of every state. There was no provision for a President or other executive officers, or for United States judges or courts. Congress was to have power to declare war, make treaties, borrow money, settle disputes between the states, regulate the currency, establish a post office and post roads, manage Indian affairs, and, in general, attend to matters which were supposed to concern the interests of all the states taken together. But it had no power to tax the people or collect duties on imports or control commerce. The only way by which it could raise the money necessary to carry on the government was by requesting each state to pay its share, which the states paid or did not pay as they saw fit. To us this "government by supplication," as Gouverneur Morris called it, looks like a very feeble one; but to many men of the time the powers granted to Congress seemed to threaten to "swallow up the states" in the central government. "If the plan now proposed should be adopted," wrote Edward Rutledge of South Carolina, "nothing less than the ruin of some of the colonies [states] will be the consequence."

The States Cede their Western Land Claims. The delay of three years in the ratification of the Articles, however, was due not so much to the fear of giving too much power to Congress as to the question of the ownership of vast tracts of land in the West. The states of Massachusetts, Connecticut, Virginia, North and South Carolina, and Georgia claimed land extending to the Mississippi, by virtue of their "sea to sea" colonial charters. Virginia's claim was strengthened by George Rogers Clark's conquest of the Northwest (p. 152). New York also claimed Western land secured by treaties with the Indians. The other states had no Western land claims, either because, like Rhode Island and New Jersey, they "backed up" on neighboring states or because their western boundary was limited in their charter, like Pennsylvania and Maryland. These "landless" states, led by Maryland, refused to agree to a general government until the others should surrender to Congress their claims to land west of the Alleghenies. It was unfair that Massachusetts or Virginia should keep these large tracts of land for sale to pay off their own debts when the war had been a common undertaking of all the states. New York led the way in 1780;

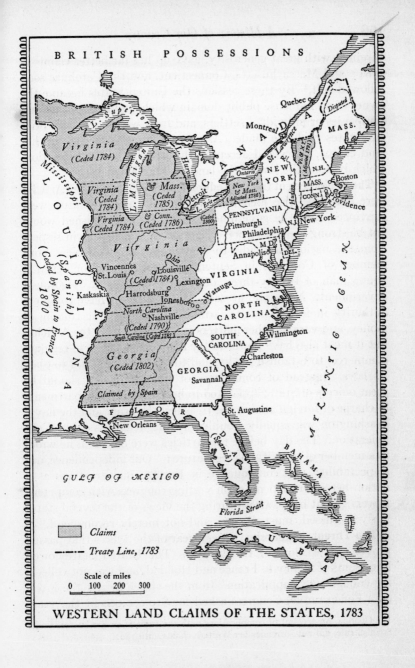

WESTERN LAND CLAIMS OF THE STATES, 1783

Virginia, with great generosity, gave up her far better claims in 1784; and Massachusetts, Connecticut, and the Carolinas soon followed suit.[1] By these cessions the United States became the owner of an immense public domain which could be sold to land companies or individual settlers, and from which new territories and states could be made. As soon as New York gave up her land claims, Maryland accepted the Articles of Confederation, which became the law of the land on March 1, 1781.

The Weakness of the Confederation. Even before the Articles were adopted, wise men like Washington and Hamilton were convinced that the government which they established would not be strong enough to preserve order at home and win respect from the nations abroad. In a famous letter to a New York member of Congress in September, 1780, Hamilton, then a young man of twenty-three, outlined a plan for a "vigorous" government. Not only, he said, must Congress have complete authority in foreign affairs, armies and navies, the coining of money, and various other matters entrusted to it by the Articles, but it must also have power to lay and collect taxes, to regulate commerce, to establish banks, and to compel the states to obey its laws. Instead of committees of Congress there should be great officers of State, appointed to be the heads of departments in charge of foreign affairs, the treasury, the army and the navy. Washington was equally troubled by the weakness of the Confederation. The day before the Articles were adopted, he wrote to a member of the Virginia legislature: "Our independence, our respectability and consequence in Europe, our greatness as a nation hereafter, depend upon vesting congress with competent powers. That body, after hearing the views of the several states fairly discussed, must dictate, and not merely recommend."

The Threat of Anarchy. Every year of the 1780's that passed proved the wisdom of these views. The United States owed large sums of money to France and Holland, and was not collecting enough by "supplication" from the states to pay the interest. For example, Congress asked for $10,000,000 in the years

---

[1] Georgia, on account of complications with the Indians on her borders under Spanish rule, did not surrender her Western claims until 1802.

1781–1783, of which only $1,500,000 was paid by June, 1784. This was not because the people were too poor to support the government but because the government had no authority to tax them. When Congress asked to be allowed to lay a small duty on imports, Rhode Island and New York refused consent. The paper money, or "Continental currency," which Congress issued to the amount of more than $240,000,000, sank in value until it took forty dollars of paper to buy one dollar of silver.[1] Moreover, we had as yet no national coinage, and English, French, Dutch, Spanish, Portuguese, and old colonial pieces of silver and gold circulated in the states with varying values.

Our independence now made us a "foreign" nation in the eyes of Great Britain, with whom five sixths of our commerce was carried on. The British Navigation Acts therefore shut us out of the trade with the West Indies and other parts of the empire; and Congress was powerless to get concessions from Great Britain, because it was not permitted to make commercial agreements in the name of all the states. Not only did the separate states insist on keeping their commerce in their own hands, but they often treated one another like foreign states. New York laid taxes on firewood coming in from Connecticut and on farm produce from New Jersey. The states quarreled over boundaries, debts, river rights, currency values, and a hundred other matters. Pennsylvania actually went to war to drive the Connecticut settlers out of the Wyoming valley. With dismay, men like Washington asked whether we had fought through the long war only to become a collection of thirteen jealous and quarreling little republics. "There must be lodged somewhere a supreme power," he wrote in his letter to the governors in 1783, "without which the union cannot be of long duration, and everything must very rapidly tend to anarchy and confusion." And again, a year later, he wrote, "I predict the worst consequences from a half-starved, limping government, always moving on crutches and tottering at every step."

[1] In 1780 Congress itself acknowledged the worthlessness of the Continental currency by calling it in at the rate of two cents on the dollar. "Not worth a continental" is a slang phrase still used to mean not worth anything at all.

The Attitude of the European Powers. It is little wonder that so weak a government failed to secure the respect of the countries abroad. France, Holland, and England had acknowledged the independence of the United States before the end of 1783, but none of them wanted us to become a strong power, to rival them in wealth and commerce.[1] George III did not send a minister to the United States until 1792, although he graciously received John Adams as our first minister to England in 1785. But when Adams suggested a commercial treaty, the British foreign minister sarcastically asked him whether England was expected to make thirteen treaties or one. Thomas Jefferson, our minister to France from 1785 to 1789, wrote home that he could not get the French government to take Congress seriously. "We are the lowest and most obscure of the whole diplomatic tribe," he moaned. The thrifty Dutch merchants and bankers were fearful that the interest on their loans to the new republic would not be paid. Even the pirates of the Barbary States, on the Mediterranean Sea, plundered our vessels at will because we had no navy to protect the lives and property of our citizens. Furthermore, Great Britain held on to a chain of fur posts, extending from Lake Champlain to Lake Michigan, all situated in territory belonging to the United States by the treaty of peace. The excuse for this act of trespass was that Congress had failed to carry out the treaty by not compelling the states to see to it that the debts owed to British merchants were paid and the property taken from the Loyalists was returned; but the real reason was to keep the fur trade, which amounted to $1,500,000 a year, from being diverted from Montreal to Albany and to maintain control over the Indians of the Northwest.

The Mississippi Valley. In the trans-Allegheny region south of the Ohio the situation was critical. By the end of the Revolu-

[1] We have already seen how our ally France was ready to agree with Spain in shutting the new republic into the narrow strip between the Alleghenies and the Atlantic (p. 155). An English clergyman, Dean Tucker, wrote in 1781 that the idea of America's ever becoming a strong and united empire was "one of the idlest and most visionary notions ever conceived even by writers of romance"; and prophecies were freely made that before long the United States would be begging King George to take them back into the British Empire!

tionary War some twenty-five thousand settlers, following Daniel Boone and other pioneers, had crossed the mountains into the rich lands on the "Western waters," and at the close of the decade of the 1780's they had increased to over one hundred thousand. Farms and homesteads had succeeded the hunters' camps and cabins. The only outlet that these settlements had for their produce was the Mississippi River. According to the treaty of 1783, the Mississippi was to be open to American navigation; but Spain was in possession of both banks of the mouth of the river. Being hostile to the expansion of the United States (p. 155), and wishing to keep the river trade in her own hands, Spain closed the river to Americans — except those with whom she was plotting to detach the West from its allegiance to the United States.[1]

The merchants of the Atlantic coast, jealous of the growth of the West, cared little for the navigation of the Mississippi if they could gain admission to the ports of Spain and her colonies. Our secretary for foreign affairs, John Jay, made a treaty with the Spanish agent Gardoqui, in 1785, by which, in return for entrance into Spanish ports, we were to give up our right to use the Mississippi for twenty-five years. The Jay-Gardoqui Treaty was fortunately defeated in Congress; but the very thought of it so angered the Western settlers that some of them were ready to cast in their lot with Spain, while most of them were in favor of raising troops and driving the Spaniards, together with their Indian allies, out of the land. If they were not supported by their fellow countrymen on the Atlantic seaboard, declared these Western insurgents, they would "throw off their allegiance and look elsewhere for help." There was, indeed, grave danger that we should lose the magnificent domain which had been acknowledged as ours in the peace treaty. "The western states,"

[1] James Wilkinson, later a general in the American army, was one of the rascals in the pay of Spain. The hostility of Spain to the United States was increased when the news leaked out of a secret clause in the treaty of 1783, by which the northern boundary of Florida was to be at 32° 30' north latitude if Great Britain retained the province, but at 31° if Florida should be returned to Spain (as it actually was). Spain asserted her claim to the land between 31° and 32° 30' until 1795 (map, p. 157).

wrote Washington, "stand on a pivot; the touch of a feather will turn them any way."

Social Discontent. Besides the quarrels between the states and the difficulties with foreign nations, there was a great deal of social unrest in the 1780's. The war had brought to the fore a class of newly rich men, who had profiteered by selling supplies to the government. British and French money had found its way into the hands of the wealthy, to encourage extravagance and luxury. On the other hand, the poor were poorer for the war. The farmers who had won the struggle went home, as Washington said, "without a farthing in their pockets." They had believed that liberty would bring them equality and prosperity. But those without property found themselves an inferior class, shut out from the offices and generally deprived of the vote. Moreover, prices had risen so high during the war that the farmers could not afford the necessities of life, while they saw money being drained out of the country to pay for European luxuries. Their houses and farms were mortgaged; and when they had no cash to pay the interest, they saw the lawyers getting rich from fees for foreclosing the mortgages by forced sales of their property.

In some states the radicals got control of the legislature and passed "stay" laws, postponing the collection of debts, and "tender" laws, forcing the creditors to accept paper money in payment.[1] In Massachusetts, where the division between the poor farmers of the western counties and the rich merchants and lawyers of the eastern towns was especially marked, it came to a little civil war. The farmers, under Captain Daniel Shays, a veteran of the Revolution, raised a force of fifteen hundred men, closed the courts at Northampton and Worcester, defied the sheriffs and constables to seize property for debt, and attacked the arsenal at Springfield. Governor Bowdoin finally sent four thousand state militia under General Lincoln, who

---

[1] For example, in Rhode Island, a butcher named John Weeden refused to accept paper money from one of his customers, Trevett. When the case of Trevett *v.* Weeden was brought into the court, the judges roused the fury of the radicals and suffered defeat in the next election by declaring the tender law unconstitutional.

SHAYS AND HIS MEN TAKE POSSESSION OF A COURTHOUSE[1]

[1] From the drawing by Howard Pyle in *A Larger History of the United States*, by Thomas Wentworth Higginson, Harper & Brothers, 1888.

defeated Shays' "army" at Petersham in a pitched battle (on February 25, 1787). Shays' Rebellion was regarded with dismay by men who wanted an efficient national government. "The late turbulent scenes in Massachusetts," wrote James Madison early in 1787, "have done inexpressible injury to the republican character in that part of the United States." Congress had made no effort at all to quell these disorders. Every year showed more clearly that its authority under the Articles of Confederation was sadly inadequate to command the obedience of the states and to ensure the "perpetual" character of the Union.

The Northwest Ordinance. One great service which the Congress of the Confederation performed before it came to an end in 1789 was the organization of the Western territory north of the Ohio which had been ceded to the United States by Massachusetts, Connecticut, New York, and Virginia. By the Land Ordinance of 1785 this region was ordered to be surveyed and laid out in "townships" six miles square, divided, by lines running north and south and other lines running east and west, into thirty-six "sections," each of one square mile, or six hundred and forty acres. The land was to be sold at a dollar an acre, in lots not smaller than a square mile, and one section in each township was to be set aside for the support of education. On July 13, 1787, Congress, following a plan proposed by Jefferson three years earlier,[1] placed the territory under a governor and three judges. When the number of free white inhabitants should reach five thousand, they were to be allowed to elect a legislature and to send to Congress a delegate who should have the right to debate but not to vote; and when the population of a district numbered sixty thousand, it was to be admitted to the Union as a state, on an equal footing with the original thirteen. Not less than three nor more than five states were to be made out of the territory. The Ordinance also provided for religious freedom, full protection of liberty and prop-

---

[1] Jefferson's plan was to be applied to the whole of the region west of the mountains, both north and south of the Ohio. But the Southern lands had not yet been ceded by the states, and the plan was dropped.

erty, encouragement of education, fair treatment of the Indians, and the prohibition of slavery in the territory. The great importance of the Ordinance was that it furnished the pattern for the immense tracts of land later acquired by the United States by war or treaty from France (the Louisiana Purchase), Mexico, and Great Britain (the Oregon territory). All this region (except Texas and California), comprising more than two thirds of the present United States, developed from territorial government into statehood, as the tadpole develops into the frog.[1] Less than a year after the Northwest Ordinance was passed, a company of New Englanders, having purchased one million five hundred thousand acres of land from Congress, went down the Ohio in a fleet of boats appropriately led by the *Mayflower*, and established at Marietta the first settlement in the Northwest Territory.

Steps Leading to the Constitutional Convention. At the very moment when Congress, sitting at New York, was passing the Northwest Ordinance, another body, at Philadelphia, was in the midst of its work preparing a new constitution for the United States. This body, comprising fifty-five very distinguished men ("an assembly of demigods," Thomas Jefferson called them) elected by the legislatures of the states, was the Constitutional Convention. Its meeting on May 25, 1787, was the result of half a dozen years of accumulating proofs that the Articles of Confederation were too weak to hold the Union together, to command obedience from the states at home, or to win respect for the nation abroad.

The immediate steps which led to the convention grew out of the desire of the Potomac Company, in which Washington was interested, to connect the Potomac and the Ohio by a canal, and thus bind the uncertain West closer to the Union. Maryland and Virginia were at odds over the navigation of the Potomac, and commissioners from the two states met in 1785 at Alexandria

[1] The Northwest Ordinance was not followed in all its details in the organization of future territories and their admission as states, but only in its general pattern. For example, Congress did not require a specific number of inhabitants in order that territories might be admitted as states, and slavery was allowed in some of the new territories while forbidden in others.

(adjourning to Mount Vernon at Washington's invitation) to settle the matter. In the course of the discussion it appeared that Pennsylvania and Delaware were also interested,[1] and it was suggested that *all* the states be invited to send delegates to Annapolis, Maryland, the next year, "to consider how far a uniform system of commercial regulation" might "be necessary for their common harmony." Only five states sent delegates to Annapolis in September, 1786. They were too few to take any action. But one of them, Alexander Hamilton of New York, boldy proposed that they should invite the states to send delegates to still another convention, to meet at Philadelphia the following May, "to consider the situation of the United States" in general and to take such measures as would make the government "adequate to the exigencies of the Union."

Now this was an irregular proposal, because Congress alone had the right to suggest any change in the Articles, and even this had to be with the consent of all the states. But, fortunately, Congress accepted the Annapolis proposal and sent out a call to all the states to appoint delegates to a convention in Philadelphia "for the sole and express purpose of revising the Articles of Confederation."

The Great Convention. Rhode Island alone refused to respond to the call. The other states sent a group of men who have not been surpassed in character and ability by any body of equal size in the world's history. From Virginia came Washington (who was unanimously chosen president of the convention), Governor Edmund Randolph, James Madison, and George Mason. Pennsylvania sent Benjamin Franklin, James Wilson, and Robert and Gouverneur Morris. Roger Sherman and Oliver Ellsworth came from Connecticut; Elbridge Gerry and Rufus King from Massachusetts; John Rutledge and the Pinckneys

---

[1] For example, Pennsylvania wanted to construct a canal between Delaware and Chesapeake bays, — an undertaking which would necessitate crossing the northern tip of the state of Delaware. New Jersey also was interested in the project. In fact, there were many plans afoot for joining the Eastern seaboard with the "Western waters." Note that the conference at Alexandria and Mount Vernon took place in the very year that our hold on the West seemed threatened by the Jay-Gardoqui Treaty (p. 169).

from South Carolina; John Dickinson from Delaware; and
Alexander Hamilton from New York. Some of the men who had
been in the front rank in the struggle for independence were
absent. John Adams and Thomas Jefferson were abroad, serving as ministers to England and France. Patrick Henry and
Sam Adams were both opposed to strengthening the central
government. They feared that liberty would be in danger if
the states parted with some of their power, while most of the
men in the convention feared rather such disorders as Shays'
Rebellion and the danger to property from the radical democrats.
The sessions of the convention were held in secret, but the me-
thodical Madison took notes on the debates, writing them out
every evening as a journal. When he died, fifty years later
(the last survivor of the convention), his widow sold the manuscript to Congress for thirty thousand dollars, and it was published at Washington in 1840.

The Work of the Convention. Instead of following the instructions of Congress simply to "revise" the Articles of Confederation, the convention proceeded to make a new constitution. On
May 29 Governor Randolph presented the "Virginia Plan"
(mostly Madison's), which provided for three separate departments of government — the legislative, the executive, and the
judicial. There were to be two houses of Congress; and the
members of the House and the Senate, as well as the President
and the Federal judges, were to be servants of the *United States*,
paid out of the national treasury, and not subject to the authority of any state. There was much debate as to how these officials
were to be chosen, no less than seven different methods being
suggested for the election of the President alone. The smaller
states, fearing that they would be "swallowed up" in the larger
and richer ones, supported a counterplan introduced by William
Paterson of New Jersey, which insisted that the representatives
in Congress (of one house) should still represent the *states* and
not the *nation*, and that each state, regardless of size, should
have an equal number of delegates. There were extremists on
both sides. Some members left the convention because they held
that it had no right to do more than "revise" the Articles, ac-

cording to its instruction by Congress. On the other hand, Alexander Hamilton,[1] in a great speech, urged a more "consolidated" plan than that of Virginia, the President and Senators to hold office for life (like the English king and lords), and the executive to have power to appoint the governors of the states and veto the state laws.

At times it seemed as if the convention would go to pieces in the fierce debates over the division of power between the central government and the states and the conflicting interests of the agricultural South and the industrial, commercial North. But finally all these disputes were settled by a series of "compromises," or bargains. The large states were favored in the House of Representatives, which was to be elected according to population and was to frame the bills for raising revenue (taxation),[2] while in the Senate each state was to have two members, elected by the state legislature. Furthermore, no state was ever to be deprived of its equal representation in the Senate without its own consent. In return for the power granted to Congress to regulate foreign and interstate commerce, the agricultural, slaveholding states of the South were given certain concessions: no duties could be levied on exports (on which the South depended for its wealth), three fifths of the slaves were to be counted as "population" in apportioning a state's representation in the House, and the importation of slaves into the country was not to be interfered with for at least twenty years.

But in spite of the heated debates over these compromises, the points on which the convention agreed far outweighed those on which it differed; else we should not have had a constitution. The large majority of the members were eager to have a national

[1] Governor George Clinton of New York was opposed to a new constitution, and by his influence two men of his own way of thinking, Yates and Lansing, were chosen as Hamilton's colleagues in the convention. They returned to New York when they saw that the constitution was taking shape, leaving Hamilton powerless, because the vote of the state could be cast only by a majority of the delegation.

[2] This provision, however, did not give the House that complete "control of the purse" which the British House of Commons had; for our Senate can amend the revenue bills which come to it from the House, and in doing so it has almost always changed them so much that they are practically new revenue bills originating in the Senate.

government with power to lay taxes, defend the country against foreign foes, preserve order at home, and protect property. Perhaps the most happy device of the whole Constitution was the skillful way in which it secured the obedience of the states to the Federal government. Instead of interfering directly in their affairs or using the army or navy to coerce them, it required the officials in every branch of the state governments to take an oath to support the Constitution as the supreme law of the land (Art. VI). On September 17 the Constitution was finished; and it was signed by thirty-nine of the members of the convention present from the twelve states, only Mason and Randolph of Virginia and Gerry of Massachusetts refusing their signatures.

The Constitution Ratified. The convention recommended to the Congress in New York that the Constitution should be ratified by conventions elected in each state for that express purpose, and provided in Article VII that when nine of the states had ratified the Constitution it should go into effect for those states. Congress submitted the Constitution to the states, the conventions were elected, and the hard battle for ratification began. The men of property, the holders of the government debt, the merchants, and the industrialists were in favor of the new Constitution; not so the farmers, the laborers, and the paper-money men. If left to a vote of the whole people, the Constitution would have been defeated, since the latter classes far outnumbered the former. But, as they had no voice in the election of the state conventions, they could not make their influence felt.

Little Delaware led the way, ratifying by a unanimous vote on December 7, 1787. Pennsylvania, New Jersey, Georgia, and Connecticut soon followed. In some of the states there was a severe struggle. A change of ten votes in the Massachusetts convention, of six votes in the Virginia convention, and of even two votes in the New York convention would have defeated the Constitution in those important states. The narrow victory in New York was won only through the tireless work of Alexander Hamilton, and Washington's great influence was chiefly responsible for winning over the opponents in Virginia. Hamilton made

CELEBRATING THE RATIFICATION OF THE CONSTITUTION

the campaign one of education through the publication (with the aid of Madison and Jay) of a remarkable set of essays, *The Federalist*, explaining the nature of the new Constitution and meeting objections to its provisions. By the end of June, 1788, nine states had ratified, and the Constitution went into effect.[1] The event was hailed with rejoicing. Dinners, processions, illuminations, and jollifications of every sort followed. No one seemed to regret the end of the old government under the Articles of Confederation. It was called the "sloop *Anarchy* which had gone ashore on the rock of Union." "Federal punch" was the favorite brew in the taverns; "Federal hats" were advertised in the shops; and "Federal mixture" was smoked in "Federal pipes."

The Constitution a Wonderful Achievement. By the adoption of the Constitution our country passed, without revolution or military dictatorship, from weakness to strength, from anarchy to order, from death to life. William Pitt, the great prime minister of England, said of it, "It will be the pattern for all future

---

[1] North Carolina did not ratify until November, 1789, when Washington had been President for six months, and Rhode Island remained outside the Union until the spring of 1790. John Adams did not exaggerate the case when he said that "the Constitution was extorted from a reluctant people by a grinding necessity."

constitutions and the admiration of all future ages." And it has, indeed, served as the model for the organization of republican governments on both sides of the Atlantic. Count Alexis de Tocqueville, our distinguished French visitor a century ago (1835), said:

It is new in the history of society to see a great people turn a calm and scrutinizing eye upon itself when apprised that the wheels of its government are stopped; to see it carefully examine the extent of the evil and patiently wait two whole years until a remedy is discovered, to which it voluntarily submits without its costing a tear or a drop of blood from mankind.

And the great English statesman Gladstone called the Constitution "the most wonderful work ever struck off at a given time by the brain and purpose of man."

Analysis of the Constitution. The student should now turn to the text of the Constitution (Appendix II) and study it carefully. Note first that it provides a *framework*, or structure, of government, describing how the members of Congress, the President, and the Federal judges are to be chosen, how long they shall serve, and what qualifications they must have for office. Then note what powers and duties the Constitution prescribes for Congress (Art. I, Sect. 8), for the President (Art. II, Sects. 2 and 3), and for the courts (Art. III). You will see that certain acts are expressly forbidden to the Federal government (Art. I, Sect. 9) and that the states too are denied several powers which they had exercised under the old Confederation (Art. I, Sect. 10). You will note in the first ten amendments to the Constitution, called the Bill of Rights, that the citizens of the United States are guaranteed against interference by the government with some very important rights and privileges. Finally, you will see how the Constitution provides for its own amendment, or alteration (Art. V), and for its supremacy as "the law of the land" (Art. VI).

The Growth of the Constitution. The most thorough knowledge of the text of the Constitution, however, would not tell a person how it actually *works*. For many practices have grown up, through law or custom, which are not mentioned in the

Constitution at all. For example, our great party conventions for the nomination of the President were not invented until 1831, and the power of the Supreme Court to declare acts of Congress or of the state legislatures unconstitutional was not mentioned in the Constitution. There is no legal limit to the number of times a President may be re-elected, but an "unwritten law," or custom, since Washington's day has fixed two terms as the limit. Furthermore, under the so-called "elastic clause," which gives Congress the power to "make all laws which shall be necessary and proper for carrying into execution" its enumerated powers (Art. I, Sect. 8, par. 18), many acts, such as the chartering of a national bank or the issue of paper money, have been performed by Congress without the specific permission of the Constitution.

From the very earliest days of our government there have been two schools of opinion as to the interpretation of the Constitution. The "strict constructionists" have held that the letter of the Constitution must be obeyed, and that Congress and the President must exercise *only* the powers expressly granted to them in Articles I and II. On the other hand, the "loose constructionists," professing themselves equally devoted to the Constitution, contend that it must be interpreted as meaning to give to Congress "implied powers" sufficient to make the Constitution really "the law of the land." With the rise of the great trusts, in the decades after the Civil War, and the growth of industries beyond the limits and control of the states, this question of the authority of the national government became of vast importance. And in our own days of depression we have seen Congress and the President exercising powers that were never dreamed of by the fathers of the Constitution, such as spending large sums of money for relief, providing work for the unemployed, lending money on homes, paying farmers for "plowing under" wheat and cotton, saving banks and railroads from failure, and fixing the value of a gold dollar at sixty cents.

Amendments to the Constitution. Besides being constantly expanded by interpretation, the Constitution has been added to from time to time by amendments. Though twenty-seven hundred amendments have been introduced into Congress, only eleven have been actually adopted since the passage of the Bill of Rights, in 1791 (p. 179). These amendments, with the dates of their adoption, will be found at the end of Appendix II. Three of them (XII, XVII, XX) made changes in the machinery of the government. Three others (XIII, XIV, XV) were occasioned by the extinction of slavery in the Civil War. Two (XVI, XVIII) conferred new powers on the national government. One (XIX) gave the vote to women, and one (XXI) repealed a former amendment (XVIII). Amendments are frequently suggested for political, economic, and social changes, such as having the President elected by a popular vote instead of by an electoral college, government ownership of railroads, telegraphs, and telephones, or a uniform national law of marriage and divorce. But amendments are made rather difficult both by the slow method prescribed by the Constitution and by the reluctance of the states to give up their rights to the national government.

The Inauguration of Washington. With the Constitution adopted, the expiring Congress of the Confederation sent instructions to the states to elect Senators and Representatives to the new Congress of the Constitution, and to appoint electors to choose the new President. Every elector in every state wrote Washington's name first on his ballot. For second place John Adams of Massachusetts received the largest number of votes and thereby became Vice-President. The first Wednesday in March [1] was the date fixed for the inauguration of the new government, but it was well into April before enough of the Congressmen had arrived in New York to form a quorum. On April 30, 1789, George Washington appeared on the balcony of Federal Hall in Wall Street, New York, to take the oath, at the hands of Chancellor R. R. Livingston, to "preserve, protect, and defend the Constitution of the United States," while the throng that filled the streets below shouted "God bless our Washington!" Then, returning to the chamber where the Con-

[1] The first Wednesday in March, 1789, fell on March 4, which was the date for the inauguration of each new administration until it was changed to January 20 by the Twentieth Amendment, adopted in 1933.

THE INAUGURATION OF WASHINGTON[1]

gressmen were assembled, the President read his inaugural
address in a voice "a little tremulous" with the sense of the
responsibilities which rested upon him. "The preservation of
the sacred fire of liberty and the destiny of the republican
model of government," he said, "are justly considered as deeply,
perhaps as finally, staked on the experiment intrusted to the
hands of the American people."

TERMS TO BE MASTERED

Confederation	Western posts	control of the purse
sovereignty	"stay" and "tender" laws	Federalist
Continental currency	Northwest Ordinance	"elastic clause"
Barbary States	Madison's notes	Presidential elector

FOR SUPPLEMENTARY READING

JOHN FISKE, *The Critical Period of American History*; MAX FARRAND, *The
Fathers of the Constitution* (Chronicles of America, Vol. XIII); R. L. SCHUYLER,

[1] From a miniature group by Dwight Franklin in the Museum of the City of
New York.

The Constitution of the United States; A. C. McLaughlin, *The Confederation and the Constitution* (American Nation Series, Vol. X); The Pageant of America, Vol. VIII, pp. 144–160; *America*, Vol. IV, pp. 83–90, 106–145; J. M. Beck, *The Constitution of the United States*, chaps. iii, iv, xv; Charles Warren, *The Making of the Constitution*; H. S. Commager, *Documents of American History*, pp. 120–150; Hart, *Contemporaries*, Vol. IV, Nos. 40, 41, 45, 47, 49, 50, 54, 57–59, 66; Muzzey, *Readings*, pp. 163–182.

TOPICS FOR REPORTS

1. **Foreign Relations under the Confederation.** With England: John Fiske, *The Critical Period of American History*, pp. 131–144; G. S. Callender, *Economic History of the United States*, pp. 210–220; A. C. McLaughlin, *The Western Posts and British Debts* (American Historical Association Report, 1894). With Spain: F. A. Ogg, *The Opening of the Mississippi*, pp. 400–460; A. B. Whittaker, *The Spanish-American Frontier*.

2. **The Public Land of the United States.** R. L. Schuyler, "Working toward a National Domain," in *Political Science Quarterly*, Vol. XXVIII, pp. 496 f.; E. E. Sparks, *The Expansion of the American People*, pp. 118–158; P. J. Treat, *The National Land System*, chaps. i–iii; T. Roosevelt, *The Winning of the West*, Vol. III, pp. 253–269; Hart, *Contemporaries*, Vol. III, Nos. 42, 43, 46.

3. **Opposition to the Constitution.** E. B. Greene, *The Foundations of American Nationality* (ed. of 1935), pp. 603–612; O. G. Libby, *The Geographical Distribution of the Vote on the Federal Constitution*; A. J. Beveridge, *The Life of John Marshall*, chaps. ix–xii; A. C. McLaughlin, *The Confederation and the Constitution*, pp. 277–317; *The Federalist* (ed. P. L. Ford), Introduction, pp. xx–xxix; Hart, *Contemporaries*, Vol. III, Nos. 70, 73, 75.

QUESTIONS SUGGESTED BY THE CHAPTER

1. Compare the Congress of the Confederation and the present Congress of the United States in respect to membership and powers. 2. By what method did the Congress of the Confederation raise money for running the government, and with what success? 3. Why did the paper money of the Confederation sink in value? 4. Why was it important for the central government to regulate foreign commerce? 5. Show that Virginia had better claims than the other states to land west of the Alleghenies. 6. What two important bodies were sitting in the summer of 1787 at Philadelphia and New York? What did each do? 7. What was the name of the first written constitution of the United States? 8. What did Alexander Hamilton contribute to the Constitution? 9. Why was the Mississippi outlet more important for the Western country than for New York? 10. What was the cause of Shays' Rebellion? 11. Explain how our government is "partly national and partly federal." 12. Name three compromises of the Constitution. 13. How does the Constitution ensure the supremacy of the national government without interfering directly with the states? (Be sure you understand this point.) 14. In what states was there a bitter contest over the ratification of the Constitution? 15. Explain "strict construction" and "loose construction" of the Constitution.

CHAPTER EIGHT

LAUNCHING THE GOVERNMENT

When Washington spoke of the "experiment" of the American republic, he used the fitting word. No country of the world had as yet made trial of a form of government by the people themselves, as free citizens choosing their "servants" to fill public office, and not as subjects ruled over by kings, princes, or feudal lords. The success of the American experiment depends chiefly upon an affirmative answer to three questions. First, will the people be wise enough to choose as their public servants men and women who are wholly devoted to the public welfare? Second, will the people be intelligent enough to control their government by the force of an enlightened public opinion? Third, will the people be orderly enough to seek desired changes by the patient remedy of law rather than by the impatient resort to revolution? The men who launched the new government under the Constitution faced a very difficult task. Congress had to create the machinery for raising money, providing for national defense, dealing with the Indian tribes, organizing territories, establishing Federal courts, making trade regulations, carrying on diplomatic relations with foreign nations, and a host of other duties prescribed by the Constitution. The President had to make hundreds of appointments to executive, judicial, and diplomatic offices. The experience of the colonies under British rule and of the states under the Confederation, of course, had furnished many lessons in self-government and provided models for the leaders. But the task of establishing the American republic was, nevertheless, a hard one, and the problems which had to be faced in the first few years under the new Constitution were of tremendous importance, because upon their wise solution depended the success of the "experiment." After a brief

THE CAPITOL AND THE WHITE HOUSE

glance at the condition of the country in 1789, we shall study in this chapter the way in which the chief problems were met.

The United States in 1789. The country over which Washington was unanimously called to preside in 1789 contained a free white population of 3,200,000, with 600,000 Negro slaves, scattered along the Atlantic seaboard from New England to Georgia. Philadelphia, the largest city, had 42,000 inhabitants; New York followed with 32,000; Boston, Charleston, and Baltimore had each passed the 10,000 mark. A steady stream of immigration was pouring into the valleys of the Ohio and the Cumberland across the Alleghenies. In the very summer that the statesmen at Philadelphia were framing the Constitution, a traveler reported that 900 boats had gone down the Ohio from Pittsburgh, carrying 18,000 settlers with their horses, sheep, and cattle, to take up the farm lands which were to be had for a dollar or two an acre. The census of 1790 showed a population of more than 100,000 in what had been the trans-Allegheny districts of Virginia and North Carolina; and these hardy pioneers, imbued with the idea of self-government, were preparing the machinery for statehood and clamoring to be admitted to the Union. North of the Ohio the settlement was somewhat slower, because the 45,000 Indians of that region, encouraged by agents from Canada who wished to keep the fur trade in the hands of the British, were better organized to resist the American advance. All the country west of the Mississippi, as well as the entire shore of the Gulf of Mexico, belonged to Spain. Our country was then but one third the size of the present United States and contained less than one thirtieth of our present population.

Industries and Commerce. What is now a land of great cities joined by a network of railroad and airplane lines, and humming with the whir of thousands of factory wheels and millions of automobile engines, was in Washington's day a land of forests and farms. Over 90 per cent of the inhabitants were tillers of the soil. Shipping and fishing were the only industries of importance. There were, to be sure, a few iron foundries, tanneries, pottery works, and textile mills; but the "Industrial Revolution," which was rapidly making England "the workshop of the world" by the application of steam power to machinery, had not yet reached America. The growth of our foreign trade showed that the depression following the Revolution was over and that the new government was coming into power "on a wave of prosperity." Our imports from Europe nearly doubled (from $9,400,000 to $17,000,000) in the two years 1788–1790. Our exports to Great Britain were already larger than they had been before the war. Trade with China, India, the Baltic, and the African coast was flourishing. Of the forty-six vessels which entered the port of Canton in 1789, eighteen flew the American flag. Men were experimenting with devices for propelling boats by poles and paddles worked by steam and were putting on tracks wagons to be drawn by horses or hauled by windlasses; but it was to be some years still before the steamboat and the railroad ushered in the age of rapid transit. George Washington had no more comfortable or speedy means of travel than did a Roman consul of two thousand years ago — the saddle, the sailboat, or the lumbering, springless stagecoach.

Social Conditions. The United States of 1789 was not what we think of as a *democracy*, that is, a government in which practically every adult citizen has the right to vote and in which the offices are open to rich and poor alike. The various state constitutions excluded probably five sixths of the adult white males from voting, and a much larger proportion from officeholding, by requiring certain religious beliefs or the possession of property in land or money. The Constitution forbade any religious test for holding national office, but allowed only those who could vote for the popular branch of the legislature in their own states to vote for Congressmen or Presidential electors. So a man might be elected President who would not be eligible to be governor of Massachusetts or South Carolina.[1]

Socially the United States was even less democratic. "Al-

---

[1] It was not until 1870 that the United States interfered with the states' right to determine who should vote. The Fifteenth Amendment, of that year, forbade any state to deny the suffrage to the Negro. The Nineteenth Amendment, of 1920, forbade the states to deny the vote to women.

though there are no nobles in America," wrote the secretary of the French legation, "there is a class of men denominated gentlemen who, by reason of their wealth, their talents, their education, their families, or the offices which they hold, aspire to a pre-eminence which the common people refuse to grant them." Powdered wigs, silver buckles, liveried servants, stately courtesy of speech and manners, were the marks of the social elite. Washington instituted a kind of "Republican court" at New York. He drove behind four cream-colored horses in a canary-colored chariot decorated with gilded cupids and emblazoned with the Washington arms, and appeared at levees in black velvet and silk stockings, wearing a sword at his side and his powdered hair in a bag. But for all its brave show it was a harmless aristocracy, without the power or desire to oppress the people with debasing services and crushing taxes. There was no peasant class in America, condemned from generation to generation to remain hewers of wood and drawers of water. Opportunity to rise in the social scale was open to all. Our visitors from Europe were impressed with the general diffusion of a moderate prosperity among the American people.

Washington's Appointments. The new government was put into operation by men who had supported the movement for a new constitution. Eleven of the twenty-two Senators and several of the members of the House in the first Congress had sat in the great convention at Philadelphia. All the new justices of the Supreme Court and most of the judges of the lower Federal courts nominated by the President were friends of the Constitution. For the head of the most important department of the government, the Treasury, Washington chose his friend Alexander Hamilton, an ardent nationalist. Another ex-member of the convention, Governor Edmund Randolph of Virginia, was appointed Attorney-General. The War Department was entrusted to General Henry Knox of Massachusetts, a firm supporter of the new Constitution. Thomas Jefferson was called home from Paris, where he had been minister since 1785, to become our first Secretary of State. Jefferson had followed the debates in Philadelphia with great interest and was on the whole favorable to the Constitution, but he had some misgivings lest the rights of the states should be injured and the interests of the plain people should not be sufficiently consulted. The Secretaries of State, of the Treasury, and of War and the Attorney-General made up the four members of Washington's "cabinet."[1] There was a Post Office Department, dating from colonial times, but the Postmaster-General did not have a seat in the cabinet until 1829. From time to time, as the business of the government required, Congress added new executive departments: the Navy (1798), the Interior (1849), Agriculture (1889), Commerce and Labor (1903). The latter was made into two separate departments in 1913. So at present there are ten secretaries forming the President's "official family," or cabinet.

Funding the National Debt. Alexander Hamilton occupies the center of the stage in Washington's first administration, because as Secretary of the Treasury he had to frame the measures for putting the finances of the country on a sound basis. The debt of the United States in 1789 was fifty-four million dollars. Over ten million dollars of this was owed to our ally France and to the Dutch bankers. The remainder was a domestic debt in the form of paper certificates promising to pay the holder the amount named on the paper. Everyone agreed that the honor of the country required the payment of every dollar of the foreign debt. But Hamilton's proposal to pay the domestic debt also at its full face value was strenuously resisted. The certificates had fallen to a low price on the market, because of a lack of faith that the government would pay them in full.[2]

[1] The "cabinet" was not mentioned in the Constitution as a part of the machinery of the new government. It grew out of the provision (Art. II, Sect. 2) that "he [the President] may requir the opinion, in writing, of the principale officer in each of the executive departments, upon any subject relating to the duties of their respective offices." Washington sometimes consulted the secretaries separately, and sometimes he called them together in a cabinet meeting. They were responsible to him alone, and he could dismiss them at will. They were not, like the members of European cabinets, a group representing the party which has a majority in the legislature. No member of Congress could be a cabinet officer (Art. I, Sect. 6, last sentence).

[2] This lack of confidence was due partly to the sad experience which the country had had with the large issues of paper currency by Congress and the states during the Revolutionary War.

Many honest men had been obliged to sell their certificates for whatever they could get for them in the hard times following the war, and speculators had bought them up at prices as low as fifteen or twenty cents on a dollar. Even though payment of these certificates in full would enrich these speculators, Hamilton insisted that it was necessary in order to preserve the credit of the United States.

He also insisted that the central government should take over the unpaid debts (amounting to about twenty million dollars) which the various states had incurred in prosecuting the war. He argued that, since the war was fought for the benefit of all the states, its whole debt should be paid by the government representing all the states. There was great opposition to this policy of "assumption," because some of the states had already paid their Revolutionary debt, and the measure was defeated in the House by a vote of 31 to 29. But Hamilton was persistent. He buttonholed Jefferson, walking him up and down before the President's house until he persuaded him to get a few of the Southern Congressmen to change their votes, in return for the location of the national capital on the Potomac. Assumption was a shrewd policy, because it taught creditors both at home and abroad to look to the United States rather than to the separate states as the responsible power.

The total debt of about seventy-five million dollars was "funded" by the issue of government bonds bearing interest, some at 6 per cent, some at 3. The bonds were sold to those who had money to invest (bankers, merchants, people of inherited wealth), and so the rich classes were from the beginning attached to the government and interested in its success. Scarcely any of the bonds were held by the people west of the Alleghenies or by the farmers in the upland regions of the original states.

Raising a Revenue. To pay the interest on its bonds, the salaries of its officials and employees, the cost of its army and navy, and other running expenses, the government had to have an income, or revenue. Fortunately, it was no longer obliged to rely upon "requisitions" of money from the states, for Congress now had power to lay and collect taxes. The sale of its public lands also brought money into the Treasury. The first tariff act (July 4, 1789) laid duties ranging from 5 to 15 per cent on over eighty manufactured articles imported into the United States. These duties were collected at the "ports of entry" (at which the foreign articles must be landed) by United States customs officials. The states were not allowed to collect customs duties for themselves, as they had done under the Confederation.

In his great Report on Manufactures (December 5, 1791) Hamilton defended the tariff not only as a source of revenue but also as an encouragement to American manufactures, by "protecting" them against European competition. Furniture, clothing, glassware, and tools could be produced more cheaply in the Old World, where labor was abundant and wages low; and if such articles were allowed to be brought into this country free, our people would never get a start in manufacturing them themselves. We should then remain a nation of farmers, dependent upon foreign countries for many necessities and comforts of life, instead of becoming a land of factories, mills, mines, and cities which would attract immigrants to our shores and provide the growing generations with the opportunity to use their talent and energy in developing our vast natural resources.

A protective tariff (generally many times higher than that advocated by Hamilton) has remained to our own day as an American policy. We shall see in later pages how often it has been a subject of political attack and defense. In addition to the receipts from the land sales and the tariff, the Treasury had a third source of income from internal revenue (or excise) duties. In time of war, when there is need for a rapid increase in revenue, excise duties are levied on a great variety of articles (theater tickets, Pullman berths, steamer fares, soft drinks, etc.); but ordinarily they are confined to a few luxuries like tobacco, wines, and liquors. The tariff and excise duties furnished the Treasury with far the largest part of its receipts until 1913, when Congress began to lay taxes on the incomes of individuals and corporations.

The First National Bank. A businessman does not carry his money around with him or keep it in a box at home, but deposits it in a bank which acts as his "financial agent," cashing his checks, discounting his notes, or making him loans. So Hamilton believed that the government should have an agent for the large amount of financial business which it has to conduct. He therefore got Congress to pass a bill in February, 1791, chartering a United States Bank. The government was to hold one fifth of the Bank's capital of ten million dollars and appoint one fifth of the board of directors. The Bank was to receive on deposit the money which came into the Treasury, and could use this money, like that of the private depositors, for profitable investment. It could also issue notes which were received in payment of all dues to the government, and which circulated in all parts of the country as a uniform national currency. In return for these favors, the Bank had to do the financial business of the Treasury free of charge, to lend the government money when this was needed, and to submit reports on its condition at the request of the Secretary of the Treasury.

Washington hesitated about signing the Bank bill. He asked for written opinions on it from both Hamilton and Jefferson. The former defended it as a "necessary and proper" measure for carrying out the power of Congress to "borrow money on the credit of the United States" and to regulate the currency. Jefferson opposed it because the Constitution nowhere gave Congress the power to establish a bank and because he saw a danger in the government's going into partnership with the wealthy men who would purchase the Bank stock. Secretary Knox agreed with Hamilton, and Attorney-General Randolph with Jefferson. Washington was finally persuaded by the arguments of his Secretary of the Treasury to sign the bill, thus ranging himself with those who believed in the "loose construction" of the Constitution (p. 180). The Bank was chartered for a period of twenty years. On July 4, 1791, its stock was offered to the public at four hundred dollars a share, and in less than two hours after the subscription books were opened every share had been taken.

The Effect of Hamilton's Policies. Many years after Hamilton's death the great Whig statesman Daniel Webster said of him, "He smote the rock of the national resources and abundant streams of revenue gushed forth; he touched the dead corpse of Public Credit and it sprang upon its feet." But however much Hamilton's measures strengthened the finances and credit of the government, they divided the country into two camps, or parties, each shaping its politics according to its social standing or economic interests. On the one side were the farmers, the laborers, the shopkeepers, the artisans, and the Western pioneers, who saw themselves bearing all the burdens of the new order without sharing any of its benefits. They could not buy the government's bonds, but they had to pay the taxes to meet the interest on the bonds; they could not afford Bank stock, which paid 8 per cent dividends, but they had to use currency whose value was determined by the Bank's issues, and pay interest rates which were governed by the Bank's decision. On the other side were the wealthy merchants, manufacturers, and financiers, who were being made still more wealthy by the coupons of the government bonds, the dividends on their Bank stock, and the protective tariff on their manufactures.[1] The anti-Hamiltonians objected also to the power which the central government was assuming at the expense of the states, and feared that, in alliance with the rich, it would use the Constitution to protect property rather than to "provide for the general welfare."

The First Political Parties. The followers of Hamilton came to be called *Federalists*, a name that indicated their belief in a strong Federal (or national) government. Socially, they represented "the rich, the well born and the able," to use John

[1] For example, rich New England received $440,800 out of a total of $1,180,900 in interest on the public debt in 1795. Massachusetts alone received one third more than all the states south of the Potomac, and Connecticut more than Virginia, North Carolina, and Georgia combined. The Bank stock was practically all held by wealthy men in the prosperous centers of the Atlantic seaboard. The tariff was of no benefit to the agricultural regions of the South and West, which contended that the government had no right to encourage one form of industry (manufactures) at the cost of another (farming).

Adams's phrase. The Anti-Federalists, who soon took the name of "Democratic-Republicans" or simply "Republicans," had Thomas Jefferson for their leader. Their chief strength was in the South and the West. They had faith in the mass of the people. They favored agriculture as against manufactures, and the country as against the city. They believed in a "strict" interpretation of the Constitution, and wanted to have the state and local governments kept strong enough to resist any "tyranny" on the part of the national government. Hamilton and Jefferson disagreed violently in the cabinet, and their followers assailed each other bitterly in Congress, in pamphlets, and in the newspapers. The Republicans charged the Hamiltonians with aiming to make the United States a monarchy, like Great Britain; and the Federalists declared that the Jeffersonians would wreck the government by turning it over to the mob.

Had it not been for the respect and affection with which Washington was regarded by the whole people, this party strife might have brought disaster to the government in its infancy. The great President wished to retire to Mount Vernon at the close of his first administration, but both Hamilton and Jefferson implored him to accept a re-election in 1792. He was again the unanimous choice of the electors; but John Adams received only seventy-seven votes for Vice-President, against fifty-five for Republican candidates, and the Republicans elected a majority to sit in the next House of Representatives. The battle of parties had begun.

Our Troublesome Neighbors. It was not domestic discord alone that induced Washington to serve a second term but also, as he put it, "the delicate posture of our foreign affairs." We had embarrassing relations with the three most important nations of western Europe: Great Britain, Spain, and France. The British, our neighbors on the northwest, were, as we have seen (p. 168), still refusing to carry out the treaty of 1783. They still held the fur-trading posts within our territory. Their agents from Canada were furnishing arms and powder to the Indians and encouraging them to resist the advance of the American settlers. Indian raids and massacres were frequent

JOHN JAY

JOHN ADAMS

ALEXANDER HAMILTON

THOMAS JEFFERSON

on the border; and when General Arthur St. Clair, the governor of the Northwest Territory, attempted to punish the Indians, his force of fourteen hundred men was ambushed on the Wabash River, November 4, 1791, and almost annihilated. This terrible defeat, over which Washington wrung his hands in anguish, threatened to expose the whole territory to the vengeance of the savages. The Spaniards, our neighbors across the Mississippi and along the shores of the Gulf of Mexico, still refused to allow our shipping to pass freely through New Orleans and continued to incite the Creeks and Cherokees against our southern border. To have gone to war with either of these powers would have exhausted the strength of the new republic and crippled our reviving commerce. There was need for a strong hand at the helm of government to secure our just rights through peaceful negotiations, — for a man revered at home and respected abroad as only Washington was.

The French Revolution. France was not our neighbor, like England and Spain; but she was our ally, — a fact which proved quite as embarrassing. Only five days after Washington's first inauguration the Estates-General, or national assembly, of France met at Versailles and in the two years 1789–1791 accomplished a wonderful reform by sweeping away many agelong and oppressive privileges exercised by the king, the nobility, and the higher clergy. When the royalists and the aristocrats brought on war through their resistance to the revolution, the government fell into the hands of the extreme radicals, the Jacobins of Paris. Aristocrats and priests were massacred, the monarchy was overthrown for a republic, the imprisoned king was beheaded, and when Washington was inaugurated for his second term (March 4, 1793) the Jacobins were preparing to crush the other factions in the republic and send their leaders to the guillotine in a "reign of terror." Already the radicals, like the Bolshevists of Russia in 1918, had announced a "world revolution" to overturn the governments of Europe and establish their own theories of a democratic society. Great Britain, Spain, and some of the minor powers had joined Austria and Prussia in war against the radical French Republic.

"Citizen" Genêt's Mission. Scarcely a month after his second inauguration Washington was faced with the very serious question of our relations with the new French Republic. On April 8, 1793, its minister to the United States, "Citizen" Edmond Genêt, landed at Charleston and was welcomed in a series of banquets by the Jeffersonians as he proceeded northward to the capital at Philadelphia. The Federalists, disgusted with the violent trend of the French Revolution, were opposed to receiving Genêt as minister.

Yet France was our ally. She had furnished us with the men and money that helped us win our own revolution against Great Britain; and by the treaty of alliance in 1778 we had promised to aid France in defending her West Indian islands if they were attacked by a foreign foe, and to allow her to bring into our ports ships which she should capture in war. Were we bound by our treaty with King Louis XVI's government still to be the ally of the revolutionists who had overthrown and beheaded the king and were at war with Great Britain, — a war into which we should almost certainly be drawn if we allowed the French to use our ports? Washington, with the unanimous agreement of his cabinet, answered this question in the negative when, on April 22, he issued a Proclamation of Neutrality, announcing that it was the policy of the United States to keep aloof from the war in Europe. Genêt, however, ignored the proclamation. He treated the United States as though it were a colony of France. He scolded Washington and the cabinet in petulant letters, appealed to the "true" republicans in America to support their "sister republic" across the Atlantic, and, worst of all, went right on enlisting seamen and fitting out vessels in our ports to prey on British commerce in the West Indies. His conduct finally became so impertinent that even Jefferson, warm as his sympathy was for republican France, agreed with Washington in demanding the recall of "Citizen" Genêt.[1]

[1] Genêt, however, did not return to France. The Jacobins had now got control of the government and were sending to the guillotine the members of the party to which Genêt belonged. So, for his personal safety, the discredited minister was allowed to remain in this country, where he married a daughter of Governor Clinton of New York and lived to a ripe old age.

The Jay Treaty. Genêt's mission and the war between Great Britain and France only served to increase the hostility between the Federalists and the Republicans in our own country. The Federalists, abhorring the violence of the French revolutionists and wishing to preserve our valuable trade with the British Isles, despised the Republicans as "filthy Jacobins." The Republicans retaliated by calling the Federalists aristocratic snobs and "Anglo-men," who deserted the ally that had befriended us and who fawned upon the enemy that had not ceased to injure us. So bitter did the feeling become that Federalists and Republicans would cross the street to avoid meeting each other.

In spite of the Proclamation of Neutrality, we barely escaped war with England when the British began to seize our cargoes going to French ports [1] and to take sailors off our vessels to serve in the British navy. The French faction in the country was clamoring for war with England, and the Republican House of Representatives actually passed a bill cutting off all trade with England, — a bill which was defeated in the Senate only by the casting vote of Vice-President Adams. Washington was determined to have peace. In May, 1794, he sent John Jay, the Chief Justice of the Supreme Court, to London as special envoy to negotiate a treaty. After a year's labor Jay returned with the best terms that he could get. England agreed to give up the fur posts in American territory by June 1, 1796, and to submit to arbitration the questions of disputed boundaries, the damage done to American shipping, and the debts due to British merchants. But she would not open her West Indian ports to American vessels of more than seventy tons or allow them to carry any of the West Indian products to Europe. Neither would she abandon the practice of searching our vessels on the high seas for sailors whom she claimed as British subjects.

A storm of wrath greeted the treaty. Jay, whose patriotism was "as pure as the ermine which clothed his shoulders," was

[1] At the outbreak of its war with England (February, 1793) the French Republic opened its ports in the West Indies to American commerce free of duties. The British refused to allow this free trade, on the basis of the "rule of 1756," which forbade a country in time of war to open to neutrals ports which were closed in time of peace.

accused by the Republicans of selling his country for British gold. Hamilton was stoned in the streets of New York for speaking in favor of the treaty. Even Washington did not escape abuse. He was persuaded, however, that acceptance of the terms, unsatisfactory as they were, was the only way to preserve peace. He sent the treaty to the Senate, where it was barely ratified by the necessary two-thirds vote.

The Pinckney Treaty with Spain. Having come to terms with Great Britain, we had little difficulty in reaching an agreement with our other "troublesome neighbor" in the west, Spain. The all-powerful Spanish minister Godoy feared that the Jay Treaty might lead to an alliance between England and the United States which would drive Spain out of America. When, therefore, our minister at London, Thomas Pinckney, was sent on a special mission to Madrid to take up the question of the navigation of the Mississippi at the point where Jay and Gardoqui had left it a decade before (p. 169), he found Godoy eager to win our friendship. By a treaty concluded in October, 1795, Spain conceded every point that we had been demanding for a dozen years: the free navigation of the Mississippi, the acceptance of 31° north latitude as the southern boundary of the United States, and the "right of deposit," that is, the privilege of transferring cargoes at New Orleans from the river boats to the ocean-going vessels without payment of duty. The treaties of 1795 [1] were of the utmost importance in establishing the security of the new American republic. They enabled Washington to end his administration at peace with the world, in spite of the war which was raging in Europe. We were eventually drawn into the war, to be sure, but not until the United States had had a decade and a half to grow in population and wealth and to have its gristle harden into bone.

The Parting Advice of Washington. As the Presidential election of 1796 approached, Washington, now fully determined to

---

[1] Besides the Jay and Pinckney treaties, we had made in the same year a treaty with the Indians of the Northwest, by which they *surrendered* their claims to most of the present state of Ohio. This treaty of Greenville followed on a complete victory of "Mad Anthony" Wayne over the Indians, which wiped out the disgrace of St. Clair's disaster (p. 196).

Friends, & Fellow Citizens

The period for a new election of a Citizen, to administer the Executive government of the United States, being not far distant and the time actually arrived when your thoughts must be employ ed in designating the person, who is to be cloathed with that important trust ~~for another term~~, it appears to me proper, especially as it may conduce to a more distinct expression of the public voice that I should now apprise you of the resolution I have formed to decline being considered among the number of those, out of whom a choice is to be made. ———

I beg you, at the same time to do me the justice to be assured that this resolution has not been taken, without a strict regard to all the considerations appertaining to the relation, which binds a dutiful Citizen to his country — and that, in withdrawing the tender of service which silence in my situation might imply, I am influenced by no diminution of zeal for your future interest, no deficiency of gratepul respect for your past kindness; but ~~am~~ am supported by a ful conviction

WASHINGTON'S FAREWELL ADDRESS [1]

[1] From Avery's *History of the United States*. Courtesy of Barrows Brothers Company.

end his long service to his country, issued a Farewell Address to his fellow citizens, in which he urged them to remain devoted to the Union and to a republican form of government. In the part of the address most often quoted, he gave the following advice on our relations with the nations across the sea.

Why, by interweaving our destiny with that of any part of Europe, entangle our peace and prosperity in the toils of European ambition, rivalship, interest, humor or caprice? It is our true policy to steer clear of permanent alliances with any portion of the foreign world. . . . The great rule of conduct for us in regard to foreign nations is, in extending our commercial relations, to have with them as little political connection as possible.

These words, in recent years, have been the chief weapon in the hands of the men who have thus far fought successfully against the entrance of the United States into the League of Nations and the World Court.

Washington also warned his fellow countrymen not to allow the bitterness of party strife to divide and weaken the country. But this warning fell on deaf ears. Federalists and Republicans were already at each other's throats, and even Washington himself had gradually gone over completely to the Federalist "faction." Jefferson had resigned from the cabinet at the close of 1793, and was devoting his immense correspondence from Monticello to building up the Republican opposition. As head of the party, he was the Republican candidate in the Presidential election of 1796, while the Federalists supported John Adams. Adams won by a very narrow margin of electoral votes (71 to 68), but, through dissension in the ranks of the Federalists themselves, Jefferson became Vice-President.[1]

---

[1] Why we had a President of one party and a Vice-President of the opposition party in the administration of 1797–1801 is explained thus: Hamilton, who had left the cabinet on January 31, 1795, was not friendly to Adams. The rumor spread that he was trying to get some of the Federalist electors to leave Adams's name off their ballot, so that Thomas Pinckney, who was Adams's running mate, should come in first and Adams second. To prevent this, several of Adams's friends left Pinckney's name off their ballot, with the result that the latter's vote fell below Jefferson's. Thus the ticket elected was Adams and Jefferson, and Hamilton's clever plot to keep Adams out of the Presidency only resulted in putting the Republican Jefferson into the Vice-Presidency. After one more experience (in 1801) of the confusion which might arise from the electors' simply

Our Second President. John Adams was sixty years of age when he succeeded Washington in the difficult task of guiding a young nation which was torn with party strife at home and regarded with none too great respect abroad. He had deserved well of his country in a career of unbroken service since he had entered the first Continental Congress, in 1774. He had been a member of the peace commission of 1783, and our first minister to the courts of Holland and Great Britain. He had proposed the name of Washington as commander of the Continental Army, and that of Jefferson as the draftsman of the Declaration of Independence. His patriotism, rectitude, and courage were beyond question, but he was somewhat irritable, obstinate, and lacking in the tact and patience of his great predecessor. Assured of his own righteous judgment he made little attempt to harmonize conflicting views in his cabinet, in Congress, or in his party. He made the initial mistake of retaining the chief cabinet officers of the close of Washington's administration, who were devoted followers of his personal enemy Hamilton, from whom they almost openly took their orders. On one occasion Secretary of State Timothy Pickering actually apologized to Hamilton for not being able to prevent President Adams from taking certain measures.

The X Y Z Affair. The only European country with which our relations grew worse instead of better during the Adams regime was our ally France. The most corrupt government of the revolutionary years, the so-called Directory, had come into power in France in 1795. Angered by the Jay Treaty (p. 198) and by the recall of our minister James Monroe, who had shown himself too friendly to the radicals, the Directory not only refused to receive C. C. Pinckney, whom Washington sent to replace Monroe, but actually ordered him to leave the country. When the news reached America that her minister had been treated as a common spy, Adams called a special session of Congress

writing two names on their ballot without specifying which one they meant for President and which for Vice-President, the uncertainty was removed by the adoption (in 1804) of the Twelfth Amendment to the Constitution, which provided for naming the President and the Vice-President on the elector's ballot.

and in his opening address declared that we must convince France and the world that we were "not a degraded people, humiliated under a colonial spirit of fear." Still, desirous of peace, Adams, acting on the invitation of the French foreign minister Talleyrand, sent John Marshall and Elbridge Gerry to join Pinckney.

The envoys were courteously received; but presently they were subjected to the most outrageous treatment. Instead of dealing with them openly and honorably, the shameless Talleyrand sent them secret agents who told them that no business would be done until an apology was made for Adams's speech to Congress, a loan was promised from the United States to the French Republic, and a sum of two hundred and fifty thousand dollars was slipped into the hands of the Directors themselves. When they heard these insulting demands, our envoys indignantly refused to pay a penny. Marshall and Pinckney immediately returned to America, to rouse the people to patriotic fervor by the story of their treatment. The Republican Gerry was persuaded by Talleyrand to remain a while longer at Paris, on the pretext that his departure might cause war between the two countries.[1]

A State of War with France. Republicans and Federalists alike rallied to the President's support in his measures to compel respect for our envoys as "representatives of a great, free, powerful, and independent nation." For once in his life John Adams was thoroughly popular. His fellow citizens applauded his vigorous language of defiance, huzzaed for "Adams and Liberty!", shouted the new song "Hail, Columbia!", and adopted as a slogan the toast proposed at a banquet to the returning hero Marshall: "Millions for defense, but not one cent for tribute!" Preparations for war were begun, and Washington was again called to the chief command. The Navy Department was created by Congress.

War was not actually declared, but Congress denounced the

[1] This incident was known as the "X Y Z Affair," because when the Secretary of State submitted the dispatches from Paris he substituted the letters *X*, *Y*, and *Z* for the names of the agents whom Talleyrand had sent to our commissioners.

treaty of 1778 and authorized our ships to prey on French commerce. In the two years 1798–1800 a state of war with France existed, and over eighty French ships were captured. But neither country wanted war. When Talleyrand saw that he could not browbeat the United States, he hastened to assure our minister to Holland that a new American commission would be received with due respect by the French Republic. Adams, to his everlasting credit, resisted the clamor of the Hamiltonian faction for war, and sent envoys to France to reopen negotiations. Four days after they had sailed from Philadelphia, Napoleon Bonaparte overthrew the corrupt Directory. Intent on establishing his despotic power in France and Europe, Napoleon wanted no complications with the United States. He readily agreed, in September, 1800, to a convention by which he gave up the treaty of alliance of 1778 in return for our government's abandonment of all claims for damages to our shipping by French cruisers since 1793. It was a fair bargain, and it enabled us to enter the nineteenth century at peace with all the nations of the world.

The Alien and Sedition Acts. The Federalists rendered great services to the country during the first decade of its history under the Constitution. They set our finances in order and strengthened our credit at home and abroad; they encouraged domestic manufactures and stimulated foreign trade; they maintained the honor of the United States while bringing to a peaceful conclusion serious controversies with England, France, and Spain. By the year 1800 the new government was firmly established. But already the Federalists had signed the death warrant of their party. In the heyday of their power, in the exciting summer of 1798, they had sought to crush the Republican opposition and secure their own party hold on the government by passing a set of laws that caused their downfall.

Since most of the foreigners who came to the country joined the Republicans, the Federalists passed a Naturalization Act, increasing from five to nineteen years the period of residence necessary for a foreigner to become a citizen of the United States. Two Alien Acts followed which gave the President the power for two years to send out of the country any alien whom he thought dangerous to our security, and, in time of war, to deport or arrest at will aliens belonging to an enemy nation. Finally, a Sedition Act, to run to the end of Adams's term, punished with heavy fines or imprisonment any persons found guilty of "combining and conspiring to oppose the execution of the laws, or publishing false, scandalous, or malicious writings against the President, Congress or the government of the United States." It is only fair to say that the wisest of the Federalists, such as Adams, Hamilton, and Marshall, disapproved of these harsh acts, put through Congress by the panicky "hyper-Federalists,"[1] and that the President did not arrest or deport a single alien. However, ten Republican editors were fined or imprisoned under the Sedition Act.

The Virginia and Kentucky Resolutions. The Republicans were quick to take up the challenge. Jefferson and Madison prepared resolutions to be introduced into the legislatures of Kentucky and Virginia, protesting that the Union was a compact made by the several states, and that when the central government exceeded its constitutional power it was the right and duty of the states to "interpose their authority." The Kentucky legislature declared the Alien and Sedition Acts "void and of no effect" and called upon the other states to join in demanding their repeal. When the invitation was rejected, Kentucky passed another resolution, in 1799, to the effect that the rightful remedy for an unconstitutional act of Congress was "nullification by the state sovereignties." The authors of these protests had not the slightest intention of breaking up the Union. Indeed, when a "hyper-Republican" of Virginia proposed that his state should secede, he was roundly rebuked by Jefferson. The resolutions were meant to serve chiefly as campaign material against the Federalists in the election of 1800; and they did serve admirably for that purpose. Their great importance, however,

---

[1] For example, Hamilton wrote to Secretary Wolcott, "Let us not establish tyranny; energy is a very different thing from violence." And Adams remarked sarcastically to another Secretary, McHenry, that there was "as little danger of seeing a French army on our shores as of meeting one in heaven."

lay in the fact that they were the first instance in our history when a state or a group of states claimed the right to nullify an act of the national Congress. As such they dimly foreshadowed secession and the great Civil War of 1861.

The Election of 1800. As the Presidential campaign of 1800 approached, the Federalists found themselves in a sorry condition. Their party was split into the Adams and Hamilton factions. The government expenditures for the possible war with France had increased from six million dollars to over nine million dollars, and the taxes to meet this swollen budget were heavy. Opposition to the Alien and Sedition Acts was strong. On the other hand, Jefferson and his lieutenants had been steadily and skillfully building up the Republican party. After a campaign of mutual slander, in which the Republicans accused the Federalists of running the country in the interests of rich aristocrats who toadied to Great Britain, and the Federalists declared that if Jefferson were elected the country would be turned over to a mob of atheistical and murderous Jacobins, Jefferson and Burr received 73 electoral votes to 65 for Adams and 64 for C. C. Pinckney.

Every Republican elector had meant, when he wrote the two names on his ballot, that Jefferson should be President and Burr Vice-President; but since no elector had thought to omit the name of Burr from his ballot, the two men were tied for first place. The choice between them then had to be made, according to the Constitution (Art. II, Sect. 1, par. 3), by the House of Representatives, each state delegation having one vote. The Federalists controlled enough states in the House to keep Jefferson out of the Presidency, and for thirty-five ballots they blocked his election. Finally, however, through the influence of Hamilton, who thought Burr would be an even worse President than Jefferson, enough Federalists refrained from voting in the House to allow Jefferson to be chosen by ten states to four (February 17, 1801).

Summary. With this first party overturn in our history, which is often called "the Revolution of 1800," and which the victorious Republicans hailed as a return to the principles of the Declaration of Independence, we may pause for a moment to sum up the content of our unit. We began by examining the problem which faced the colonies of how they could preserve their loyalty to the British Empire and at the same time freely develop their commerce and their ideas of self-government, with which many acts of Parliament and many orders of the king interfered. We have seen how they were finally forced to abandon their loyalty in order to preserve their liberty. In the armed conflict which followed, Washington, by his superb courage and endurance, secured the acknowledgment of the independence of the United States. Then came the further problem of welding the thirteen states into an enduring Union. We have seen how the first attempt at a national government under the Articles of Confederation failed because of insufficient power in Congress to compel the obedience and co-operation of the states. The remedy was found in the Constitution of 1787, which created a strong government alongside of and above the state governments, acting on the people as a whole through its national legislative, executive, and judicial departments. Finally, we have studied how this new government, under Presidents Washington and Adams, got fairly started: how its finances were set upon a firm basis by the genius of Alexander Hamilton; how the troubles with our border neighbors England and Spain, and with the Indians under their influence, were met; and how we escaped being drawn into the general European wars of the 1790's as a result of the firm though cautious diplomacy of Washington, Adams, Jay, Morris, Marshall, and the Pinckneys. The years from 1763 to 1801 represent the period of the birth and infancy of the American republic. By the beginning of the nineteenth century we had made good our place in the family of nations. We were prospering in numbers and wealth at home. We were respected abroad. We were a "going concern."

TERMS TO BE MASTERED

Industrial Revolution	excise	nullification
assumption	neutrality	Jacobin
funding	right of deposit	bank stock

FOR SUPPLEMENTARY READING

J. S. BASSETT, *The Federalist System* (American Nation Series, Vol. XI); C. G. BOWERS, *Jefferson and Hamilton*; R. G. ADAMS, *History of the Foreign Policy of the United States*, chaps. v, vi; H. J. FORD, *Washington and his Colleagues* (Chronicles of America, Vol. XIV); F. S. OLIVER, *Alexander Hamilton* and *Essay in Union*; C. A. BEARD, *The Economic Origins of Jeffersonian Democracy*; J. T. ADAMS, *The Adams Family*, pp. 89–115; The Pageant of America, Vol. VIII, pp. 166–203 (interesting illustrations); HART, *Contemporaries*, Vol. III, Nos. 82, 85, 86; MUZZEY, *Readings*, pp. 183–212.

TOPICS FOR REPORTS

1. **Social Conditions in Washington's Day.** R. W. GRISWOLD, *The Republican Court*; EDWARD CHANNING, *History of the United States*, Vol. IV, chap. i; E. S. MACLAY (ed.), *The Journal of William Maclay* (critical of Washington); ALLAN NEVINS, *American Social History as Seen by British Travelers*, pp. 27–63; *America*, Vol. IV, pp. 167–196; MUZZEY, *Readings*, pp. 183–192.

2. **Citizen Genêt's Mission.** C. M. THOMAS, *American Neutrality in 1793*; M. MINNEGERODE, *Jefferson, Friend of France* (favorable to Genêt); J. B. McMASTER, *History of the People of the United States*, Vol. II, pp. 98–113, 136–142; F. J. TURNER, "The Origin of Genêt's Projected Attack on Louisiana and the Floridas," in *American Historical Review*, Vol. III, pp. 650 f.

3. **Alexander Hamilton.** H. J. FORD, *Alexander Hamilton*; C. G. BOWERS, *Jefferson and Hamilton*, chaps. ii–iv; GERTRUDE ATHERTON, *The Conqueror*.

4. **The Virginia and Kentucky Resolutions.** H. S. COMMAGER, *Documents of American History*, pp. 178–184 (text); F. M. ANDERSON, "Contemporary Opinion of the Virginia and Kentucky Resolutions," in *American Historical Review*, Vol. V, pp. 45 f., 225 f.; E. P. POWELL, *Nullification and Secession in the United States*, chap. ii; J. F. McLAUGHLIN, *Matthew Lyon*.

QUESTIONS SUGGESTED BY THE CHAPTER

1. Why did Washington call the new American republic an "experiment"? 2. What were the chief elements of our population in 1790? 3. How does our cabinet differ from the British cabinet? 4. What elements of modern democracy were lacking in Washington's day? 5. Why did Hamilton favor a national debt? 6. What were three main sources of income for the national government under Washington? 7. What favors did the Bank receive from the government, and what services did it render to the government? How did it benefit the

wealthy? **8.** Would you have been a Federalist or a Republican in 1793? Give your reasons. **9.** What benefit to the country did Hamilton see in a protective tariff? **10.** Why was the French treaty of alliance of 1778 embarrassing to us in 1793? **11.** Why was Washington so eager to preserve our neutrality in 1793? **12.** Why did the Jay Treaty meet such bitter opposition? **13.** Explain why Spain yielded to our demands in 1795. **14.** What advice did Washington give on foreign affairs in his Farewell Address? **15.** Explain how we had a President and a Vice-President of different parties in 1797. **16.** When was our Navy Department created? **17.** Why was the election of 1800 thrown into the House of Representatives? **18.** Explain the difference between nullification and secession.

BOOKS WORTH READING ON UNIT II

R. G. THWAITES, *Daniel Boone*; IRVING BACHELLER, *In the Days of Poor Richard*; P. L. FORD, *The True George Washington*; CHARLES COFFIN, *Daughters of the Revolution*; J. F. COOPER, *The Spy* and *The Pilot*; C. C. FRASER, *The Story of John Paul Jones*; WEIR MITCHELL, *Hugh Wynne, Free Quaker*, and *The Red City*; WINSTON CHURCHILL, *Richard Carvel* and *The Crossing*; K. L. ROBERTS, *Arundel*; J. BOYD, *Drums*; H. P. JOHNSTON, *Nathan Hale*; MARY JOHNSTON, *Lewis Rand*.

How the Sections of our Country Began to Contend for their Special Interests

Today the political map of our country comprises forty-eight states of various sizes and shapes like the pieces of a jigsaw puzzle. Each of these states has its constitution, its governor, legislature, and courts, its militia, its system of taxation, its laws controlling a vast number of the interests of its citizens, such as business, the inheritance of property, the definition and punishment of crime, the regulation of marriage and divorce, public education, the care of the poor or insane, and the protection of labor. The Constitution recognized the states as the units combining to form the nation and dealt with them as such. For example, it guaranteed to each of the states a republican form of government, and protection against invasion or domestic violence; it forbade them to exercise certain powers; it gave each of them two seats in the national Senate; it allowed each to choose its Presidential electors by any method that the state legislature might prescribe; and it declared that no state should be divided without its own consent. It was natural that the states should have this prominence in the earliest days of our republic, because of their separate origins as colonies. Each had its own interests, its own long history of colonial traditions, and hence its intense local patriotism. Thomas Jefferson at the close of the Revolution spoke of Virginia as "my country."

The political map still remains, but over it has been gradually drawn another map which has made the boundaries of the states grow fainter and fainter. This is the economic map of the

United States. It shows areas or sections of the country, in which nature (climate, rainfall, soil, mineral deposits, forests, mountain chains, and the like) has favored a kind of occupation and hence a set of interests different from those of other areas or sections. These sections may comprise a number of states, like the "cotton kingdom" of the South, the manufacturing area north of the Potomac and east of the Mississippi, the great wheat fields of the Northwest, the fruit gardens of the Pacific slope, the mining camps of the Rockies. At the opening of the nineteenth century there were but sixteen states in the Union, and Kentucky and Tennessee were the only ones that touched the Mississippi on the west. There were no broad highways or railroads or air lines to bind these states together. The peculiar interests of the different sections had hardly begun to take form. Cotton had not yet become the staple product of the South, for the cotton gin had been invented only seven years before. Manufactures, as Hamilton's report of 1791 shows, were still in their infancy. In the West, where the sectional feeling was strongest on account of the "troublesome neighbors" England and Spain, the pioneer communities were still clearing the dense forests and living in rude cabins. But with the growth of population and the necessity of making a living by carrying on the industries best suited to the regions in which the various groups of population lived, there began to emerge a sense of the conflicting interests of the different sections of the country. How strong that sense is today we can see in the struggle of the Western farmers against the Eastern bankers, or of the Southern cotton-growers against the Northern iron-manufacturers.

In the present unit, covering the period from Thomas Jefferson's administration to Andrew Jackson's, we shall see how this sectional rivalry grew more and more conscious and determined, how it crept into all the great questions of the day — territorial expansion, a second war with England, the tariff, the Bank, and the beginnings of the ominous struggle over the extension of slavery.

CHAPTER NINE

JEFFERSON MAKES A GREAT BARGAIN

The New Capital and the New President. In the summer of 1800 the capital had been removed from Philadelphia to the banks of the Potomac, where the foundations of the noble city of Washington were being laid in the District of Columbia, a tract of land ten miles square which had been presented to the government by the states of Virginia and Maryland.[1] The Presidential mansion (the "White House") was still unfinished. More than a mile to the eastward the masons were at work on the wings of the Capitol building. Instead of the stately Pennsylvania Avenue which now connects the Capitol with the White House, there was a muddy road, "scarcely more than a footpath cut through the bushes and briars," by which ran the sluggish Tiber Creek. A few cheerless boardinghouses harbored the members of Congress, who longed for the gay society of Philadelphia which they had left behind. "We need nothing here," wrote Gouverneur Morris, "but houses, men, women, and other little trifles of the kind to make our city perfect."

The new President, with his democratic manners and his ill-fitting, snuff-stained apparel, presented a striking contrast to the "pomp and ceremony" of Washington and Adams. He abandoned the coach and six horses, and rode horseback or walked in the streets of the capital. Instead of addressing Congress in person, like the king speaking to Parliament from the throne, he sent a message to be read by the clerk.[2] The stiff

[1] The capital lay in the part of the District ceded by Maryland. The smaller piece of the District south of the Potomac was returned to Virginia in 1846.

[2] President Wilson in 1913 revived Washington's and Adams's custom of reading their messages to Congress in person. Coolidge and Hoover went back to Jefferson's practice; but President Roosevelt began again to address Congress in person in January, 1934.

weekly levees were succeeded by informal receptions, to which the public thronged to shake the President's hand. The British minister Merry was shocked when Jefferson received him in negligee, with slippers worn down at the heels, and Merry's secretary compared the President to "a tall, large-boned farmer," — a description which Jefferson would probably have considered flattering, since he believed that the independent, self-respecting farmers were the saving element in our population.

Jefferson's Moderation. It soon appeared that the scare-mongers who had prophesied a revolution in case Jefferson were elected had grossly misjudged their man. In his inaugural address the new President praised our "just and solid republican government" as a "successful experiment," and declared that Federalists and Republicans were all brethren in their common devotion to the Union. He promised "equal and exact justice to men of every shade of political and religious opinion"; friendship with all nations, but no alliances; respect for the rights of the states, while still preserving "the general [national] government in all its constitutional vigor"; freedom of speech, press, and elections; and economy and honesty in the management of the country's finances. If Jefferson's opponents feared or his followers hoped that he would attack the financial system which Hamilton had set up (Bank, tariff, public funds), they were equally mistaken. The Naturalization Act (p. 204) and a tax on whisky which had started a riot, known as the Whisky Rebellion of 1794, among the farmers of western Pennsylvania, were repealed. The offenders imprisoned or fined under the Sedition Act were pardoned. The army and navy were reduced, and Jefferson's Secretary of the Treasury, Albert Gallatin, a native of Switzerland, applied the savings to the payment of the public debt, which he estimated would be entirely paid off by the year 1817. These reforms could hardly be called a "revolution."

Hectoring the Judges. There was one point, however, at which Jefferson made a direct attack on the policy of his predecessor. At the very close of Adams's administration the Federalists, defeated in the elections for the Presidency and Congress, tried to keep control of the third branch of the government. They created sixteen new Federal judgeships and a number of minor judicial offices, which were of course to be filled with Federalist appointees. The new judges were called "the midnight judges," [1] because President Adams was still busy signing their commissions late in the evening of his last day in office.

Jefferson considered this attempt of the defeated Federalists to retain "a dead clutch on the patronage" as indecent, and sent word to the officials whose commissions had not yet been delivered to consider their appointments as never having been made. His first Congress repealed the Judiciary Act in 1802. But the Republicans were not content with this. They instituted impeachment proceedings against several Federal judges. The famous case was that of the Maryland justice Samuel Chase of the Supreme Court, who had made himself offensive to the Republicans by his bitter denunciation of the "Jacobins" in his charges to the juries in the sedition cases. The trial of Chase before the Senate was an exciting and colorful event, attracting the attention of the whole country. His acquittal, though it sorely disappointed the Republicans, was a fortunate thing, because, however unbecoming Justice Chase's conduct had been, it certainly did not fall under the definition of "treason, bribery, or other crimes and misdemeanors" for which civil officers of the United States might be impeached under the Constitution (Art. II, Sect. 4).[2]

Marbury *v.* Madison. A still more important practice in our government resulted from the quarrel of the Republicans with the judiciary. One of Adams's "midnight" appointees as a justice of the peace in the District of Columbia was a certain

---

[1] This phrase gave rise to the myth that Jefferson's newly appointed Attorney-General, Levi Lincoln, stood over President Adams's desk on the night of March 3, 1801, with a watch in his hand, and when the hour of midnight arrived ordered Adams to lay down his pen.

[2] "Civil officers" means those in the executive and judicial departments of the United States. Military officers are tried by court martial. Members of Congress are not subject to impeachment, but they may be expelled from either House or Senate by a two-thirds vote of their colleagues. Since the Chase trial no Federal official (if we except the disgraceful partisan attack on President Andrew Johnson in 1868) has been impeached for his political opinions.

William Marbury. Marbury brought suit against Jefferson's Secretary of State, Madison, to compel him to deliver the commission which Adams had not had time to sign. When the case of Marbury *v.* Madison came before the Supreme Court, in February, 1803, it brought a momentous decision from the great Federalist John Marshall, who had been appointed Chief Justice by Adams early in 1801. The court refused to order the delivery of Marbury's commission. In his decision Marshall declared that the section of the Judiciary Act of 1789 to which Marbury appealed was contrary to the Constitution and hence null and void.

This was the first instance in which the Supreme Court pronounced a law of Congress unconstitutional. If the framers of the Constitution intended to give the court this power, they at least did not say so in the document itself. It was a power that the court *assumed* as guardian of the Constitution, and that the court has exercised ever since. It has elevated the court to the position of supremacy in our government. For the court decides not only how a law of Congress or of a state is to be *interpreted* but also whether such a law is to be allowed to remain on the statute books or not. Moreover, since the court decides by a simple majority vote, the opinion of a single justice can determine what is law for one hundred and twenty-five million people when the court (as it has frequently done in important cases) hands down a five-to-four decision.[1] In no other self-governing country in the world is such power given to so small a group of men.

Warnings from the West. While the Republican Congress was thus seeking to bring economy into the government and to limit the Federal power to the advantage of the states, the Republican President took a step which cost the government more money at a single stroke than the Federalists had spent in any two years, and which stretched the Federal power far beyond any of the measures of Alexander Hamilton. To understand this extraordinary departure from Republican principles on the

---

[1] A recent example occurred in February, 1935, when the Supreme Court (five to four) upheld the law of Congress which allowed the President to reduce the value of gold in a dollar from one hundred to sixty cents. This means that the government and private corporations can pay their bonds in sixty-cent dollars.

part of Jefferson we must look to the West. Rumors were current early in 1802 that Napoleon Bonaparte, now undisputed master of France, had forced Spain to cede to him the vast region of Louisiana, or the whole western valley of the Mississippi and the island of New Orleans.

Now to have the western bank and the mouth of the great river in the hands of the mighty Napoleon was a danger of which Jefferson was immediately aware. It would re-establish on our border a neighbor more troublesome than England and Spain had been. "The moment France takes possession of New Orleans," wrote Jefferson to our minister in Paris, "we must marry ourselves to the British fleet and nation." This from a Republican President! His fears were realized when the news came, late in 1802, that the Spanish official at New Orleans had closed the port to American shipping (doubtless at Napoleon's behest), thus breaking the Pinckney Treaty of 1795 (p. 199).

The seriousness of the situation lay in the fact that our country beyond the Alleghenies was filling up rapidly. Over two hundred thousand settlers had gone into Kentucky. Ohio was ready for statehood. The free navigation of the Mississippi meant everything to these Westerners, who had no railroads to carry their products eastward over the mountains. The exports from the port of New Orleans in 1802 — sugar, cotton, tobacco, flour, cider, apples, bacon, pork, and lead — amounted to millions of dollars. That was the only outlet for the export of the surplus produce of three eighths of the area of our country. The Westerners belonged almost to a man to that sturdy, self-respecting class of farmers whom Jefferson regarded as the backbone of the country. They supported the Republican party. They must not be left with the choice between economic ruin and dependence on the favor of Napoleon. Something must be done for them to keep them faithful to the Union.

The Louisiana Purchase. Jefferson hoped to solve the problem by purchasing New Orleans from Napoleon. For this purpose he secured an appropriation of two million dollars from Congress, and sent James Monroe to Paris to aid our minister Livingston in the negotiations, "upon which," he wrote, "the future destinies of our country hang." Before Monroe arrived at the French capital, however, the situation in Europe and the mind of Napoleon had changed. Renewal of the war between France and England was imminent. An army which Napoleon had sent out to conquer Santo Domingo, in the West Indies, as the basis for his new colonial empire in America, was destroyed by yellow fever and the stubborn resistance of the natives under the brave Negro leader Toussaint l'Ouverture.

Napoleon knew that when the war with England broke out anew, he could not defend Louisiana. For these reasons he suddenly decided to sell the whole province to the United States. Our envoys, who were prepared to offer $2,000,000 for New Orleans, were dumfounded by the invitation to buy all of Louisiana, a region, extending from the Gulf of Mexico to Canada and from the Mississippi to the Rocky Mountains, which would double the size of the United States. The price set by Napoleon's agent Marbois was 100,000,000 francs, or somewhat less than $20,000,000. After some haggling the figure was reduced to 80,000,000 francs,[1] and Livingston and Monroe accepted the terms. As they put their names, with Marbois's, to the Louisiana Purchase treaty on May 2, 1803, Livingston remarked: "We have lived long, but this is the noblest work of our whole lives. From this day the United States take their place among the powers of the first rank."

Jefferson's Dilemma. When the treaty reached Washington in midsummer, it was Jefferson's turn to be dumfounded. He knew that his envoys had made an excellent bargain in this "greatest real estate transaction in history," but he could find no clause in the Constitution that authorized the President to buy foreign territory. He admitted that, "strict constructionist" as he was, he had "done an act beyond the Constitution." At first, he prepared an amendment to the Constitution, by

[1] Of this sum of approximately $14,500,000 Napoleon was to be paid $11,250,000 in United States bonds, and the remainder was to be held in the Treasury of the United States to satisfy the claims of our own citizens for damage to their trade by the French cruisers. For many decades after the Louisiana Purchase, American citizens were applying to the government at Washington for the payment of their "French claims."

Monroe   *Livingston*   *Marbois*

SIGNING THE LOUISIANA PURCHASE TREATY

which the people might sanction what he had done. But his friends in Congress persuaded him that this was unwise, because during the long delay necessary for the ratification of such an amendment, with the opposition which the Federalists would surely raise, Napoleon might again change his mind and deprive us of our fine bargain. So Jefferson simply appealed to the "good sense" of the people to approve an act which he had performed for their benefit; and the people as a whole were with him. To be sure, the Federalist minority objected to the treaty from every point of view: it violated the Constitution; the payment of so large a sum of money to one belligerent power was virtually a breach of neutrality; Napoleon's title to Louisiana was not clear; and all that we had bought at this huge price was "the authority to make war on Spain." But the Federalist opposition was unavailing. The Senate immediately ratified the treaty by a vote of 24 to 7; and the House, by 89 to 23, voted the $11,250,000 of 6 per cent bonds. There was no doubt of the popularity of the Louisiana Purchase.

The Significance of the Purchase. The purchase of Louisiana was the most important event in our history during the first half of the nineteenth century. It added nearly a million square miles to our territory, at a cost of less than three cents an acre. Except for the extreme southern tip of the region, which is now the state of Louisiana, it contained hardly any white inhabitants; but today it has a population of twenty-three million, living in the fifteen states of the Union that have been carved out of it in whole or in part (map, p. 222), and its wealth in farm values alone is more than a thousand times the purchase price. These grand results of Jefferson's bargain could not, of course, be foreseen in 1803. The significance of the purchase then was that it relieved the tension in the West by bringing the whole Mississippi Valley into American possession. The great river became the undisturbed highway for the rapidly increasing products of the trans-Allegheny country. New Orleans rose to be "the Queen City" of the South, and retained her crown and scepter until the Erie Canal and then the railroads began to carry the Western freight across or through the mountain

An Editorial on the
Lousiana Purchase
A cartoon on the Louisiana
Purchase

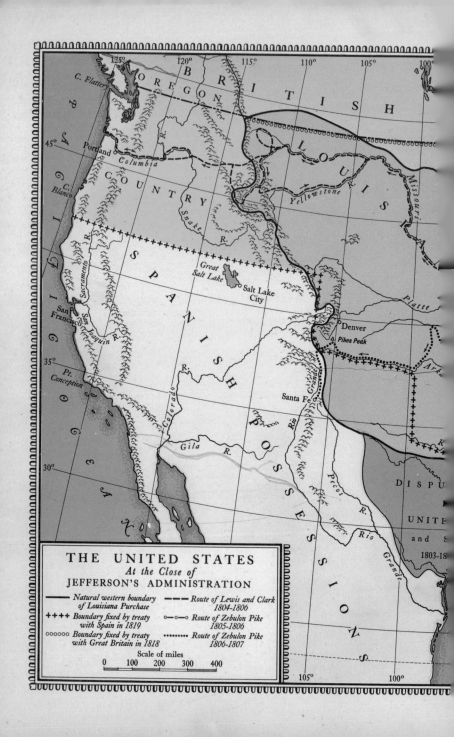

THE UNITED STATES
At the Close of
JEFFERSON'S ADMINISTRATION

——— Natural western boundary of Louisiana Purchase

– – – Route of Lewis and Clark 1804–1806

++++ Boundary fixed by treaty with Spain in 1819

∘–∘–∘ Route of Zebulon Pike 1805–1806

∘∘∘∘∘ Boundary fixed by treaty with Great Britain in 1818

•••••• Route of Zebulon Pike 1806–1807

Scale of miles
0   100   200   300   400

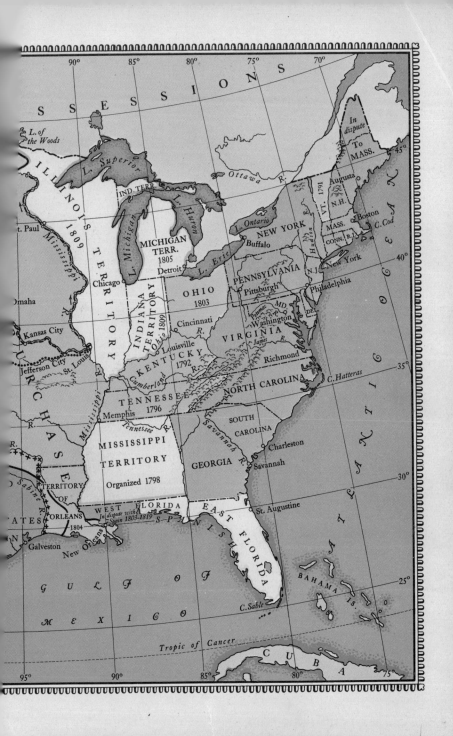

barrier to the Atlantic ports. Another decade and more was to pass, and there was to be fighting on both borders, before we were rid of the troubles caused by our British neighbors in the Northwest and the Spanish on the Gulf shore. But the danger which had been threatening ever since the treaty of 1783, that the pioneer communities of the West might secede from a government which did not protect their interests against Spanish or French neighbors, was past when the great Mississippi became an American stream.

The Federalist Protest. If the Louisiana Purchase relieved the economic tension in one section of the country, however, it increased the political tension in another section. The Federalists, whose strength lay chiefly in New England and New York, were bitterly opposed to the Louisiana treaty. They were jealous of the growth of Jefferson's popularity in the West, and they favored friendly relations with England rather than with France. They saw in this acquisition of a huge Western territory, whose inhabitants, according to the treaty, were to be brought into the Union with all the rights of American citizens, a threat to the political supremacy of the old states on the Atlantic seaboard. New Republican states would multiply in the West until their Representatives and Senators came to dominate Congress, where they would pass laws favorable to the farmers and debtors and injurious to the commercial and banking interests of the East.

In the spring of 1804 some New England Federalists, under the lead of Senator Timothy Pickering of Massachusetts, went so far as to plan a separate Northern confederacy. They even approached Vice-President Burr, promising him the presidency of the proposed confederacy if he would bring New York into it. We need not take this movement of the "hyper-Federalists" of New England too seriously. It was easily nipped in the bud by the stern disapproval of Hamilton [1] and other true nationalists.

---

[1] Hamilton's hostility to Aaron Burr in this plot, following his success in keeping Burr out of the Presidency in 1801, led Burr to challenge him to a duel. The two men met with pistols on Weehawken Heights, on the Hudson (July 11, 1804), and Hamilton fell mortally wounded by Burr's first shot.

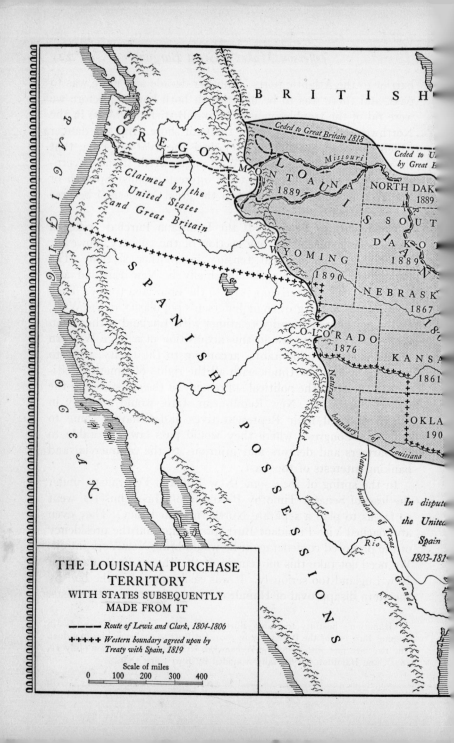

THE LOUISIANA PURCHASE
TERRITORY
WITH STATES SUBSEQUENTLY
MADE FROM IT

– – – – – *Route of Lewis and Clark, 1804–1806*

+ + + + + *Western boundary agreed upon by
Treaty with Spain, 1819*

Scale of miles

0   100   200   300   400

POSSESSIONS

L. Superior

St. Lawrence R.

In dispute

...SOTA
1858

I O W A
1846

L. Michigan

L. Huron

L. Ontario

L. Erie

MISSOURI
1821

UNITED STATES

Ohio R.

1783

...RCHASE

...MA

ARKANSAS
1836

...tween
...tes and

Sabine R.

LOUISIANA
1812

Mississippi R.

In dispute
with Spain

SPANISH TERRITORY

ATLANTIC OCEAN

G U L F   O F

M E X I C O

But it is interesting to note that the first definite proposal of secession from the Union came not from the South but from New England.

The West Florida Tangle. The Louisiana Purchase gave rise to a boundary dispute which was not settled for fifteen years. Just what territory we had bought from Napoleon in 1803 was far from clear in the language of the treaty, where it was described as having "the same extent that it now has in the hands of Spain [1] and that it had when France possessed it." The "Louisiana" which France possessed before she lost her territory on the mainland of America in 1763 (p. 104) included a strip of land along the Gulf of Mexico east of the Mississippi (colored blue on the map, p. 220). This strip went to England in the treaty of 1763 and was made into the British province of West Florida. Twenty years later it was ceded, together with East Florida, by England to Spain; so in 1803 it was "in the hands of Spain," but as a part of *Florida* and not of *Louisiana*. Indeed, for forty years it had not been considered a part of Louisiana. Neither Napoleon who sold, nor Monroe and Livingston who bought, Louisiana believed that it included West Florida.

But Jefferson was determined to have the province. He easily persuaded himself by historical researches at Monticello in the summer of 1803 that we had bought West Florida, and the next year, in spite of the angry protests of the Spanish minister at Washington, he got Congress to make the waters and shore of Mobile Bay (in West Florida) into a United States customs district. This first assertion of United States authority in a region claimed by a foreign power was followed in 1810 by the "occupation" of West Florida under Jefferson's successor Madison and by the incorporation of part of that territory in the new state of Louisiana in 1812. It was the beginning of a not always peaceful penetration of the United States into the Latin-American countries which has continued to our own days.

[1] Napoleon had not had Louisiana formally transferred from Spain to France. The Spanish flag was still floating above the government building in New Orleans when Napoleon sold Louisiana to the United States. It gave place to the French flag on November 30, 1804, and a few days later the French tricolor was hauled down and the Stars and Stripes raised in its stead.

The Lewis and Clark Expedition. The acquisition of Louisiana roused the interest of our people in the great Western wilderness which stretched two thousand miles from the Mississippi to the Pacific coast. A few weeks after the purchase, Jefferson, who was an ardent advocate of expansion, got Congress to appropriate twenty-five hundred dollars "to send intelligent officers with ten or twelve men, to explore even to the western ocean," and to study the Indian tribes, the botany, the geology, and the animals of the region. It seemed not to trouble the President much that the expedition, after passing the Rockies, would be trespassing on territory that did not belong to the United States. He selected his private secretary Meriwether Lewis to lead the expedition, with William Clark, the younger brother of George Rogers Clark, for his lieutenant.

Lewis and Clark, with a company of about forty men, started westward from the mouth of the Missouri River in the spring of 1804. They ascended the river to its source, crossed the "Great Divide" of the Rockies, and, descending the Columbia River, in the summer of 1805 reached the Pacific, which Clark called "the roreing otean." A New England sea captain named Gray had discovered the mouth of the Columbia as early as 1791, but this expedition of Lewis and Clark constituted our best claim to the great region of the Northwest known as Oregon.

About the same time (1805–1807) another explorer, Captain Zebulon M. Pike, traveled to the upper Mississippi, then through the lands of Indians and buffaloes as far west as the Rockies (Pikes Peak), and into the Spanish territory of Mexico on the south. Maps and descriptions of these regions began to make our people acquainted with the vast territory west of the Missouri which one day would be made into states of the Union.

The Barbary Pirates. We were at peace with the nations of Europe in these opening years of the nineteenth century, and our commerce and wealth were increasing so rapidly that Secretary Gallatin had no difficulty in meeting the payments for the Louisiana Purchase out of the ordinary receipts of the Treasury. But there was one foreign problem that grew more serious as our commerce expanded. For many years the rulers of the Barbary States, on the north coast of Africa (Morocco, Algiers, Tunis, and Tripoli), had been in the habit of seizing the ships which entered the Mediterranean Sea and holding their crews for ransom. The European nations paid tribute to these pirates and kidnapers, as a cheap substitute for war; and we had done the same, distributing to them, in the decade 1790–1800, "presents" amounting to two million dollars.

Jefferson was determined to put an end to the graft and insults of these "racketeers." [1] In spite of his devotion to peace and economy, he sent squadrons to punish the pirates. [2] It was a costly business, for which Congress imposed a special $2\frac{1}{2}$ per cent duty on imports as a "Mediterranean fund." But the results justified the sacrifice. For when our government finally made peace with Tripoli, in January, 1805, it put an end to the piratical raids not only upon our own shipping in the Mediterranean but also upon that of the maritime nations of Europe. It was a true international service that our navy thus performed during Jefferson's first administration.

The Election of 1804. Meanwhile Jefferson had been triumphantly re-elected over his Federalist opponent, General C. C. Pinckney. The Federalists, in their vain opposition to the Louisiana Purchase and westward expansion, had dwindled into a faction with hardly any strength outside New England, and even there the Republicans had been gaining steadily every month. In 1800 Jefferson had received only a single electoral vote (from Vermont) in New England; but in 1804 he carried all the New England states except Connecticut. Aaron Burr, defeated in his candidacy for the governorship of New York

[1] This modern term exactly applies to the conduct of the Barbary rulers. For example, on one occasion the dey of Algiers compelled the very American vessel (her name was the *George Washington*!) that was bringing him tribute money to raise the Algerian flag at her masthead and sail to Constantinople for him on an errand to the Sultan of Turkey.

[2] No deed of John Paul Jones in the Revolution was more daring than the exploit of young Lieutenant Stephen Decatur, who, with a few men in a light boat, ran into the harbor of Tripoli in the night of February 16, 1804, boarded the frigate *Philadelphia*, which had fallen into the hands of the pirates, overpowered her crew, set fire to her hull, and rowed back to his ship in the midst of a terrific bombardment from the Tripolitan batteries.

and under indictment in two states for his murder of Hamilton, was dropped from the Vice-Presidency in favor of Governor George Clinton of New York. Of the 176 electoral votes cast, Jefferson received all but 14. It was a Republican "landslide."

The Situation in the West. While Federalist judges were being impeached and our diplomats were negotiating at Paris and our sailors fighting in the Mediterranean, the country between the Alleghenies and the Mississippi was filling up. Nearly ten thousand emigrants had gone to the new Mississippi Territory, established in 1798. Ohio, with a population of fifty-five thousand, was admitted to the Union as the seventeenth state in February, 1803. The year before, Georgia, the last of the original seaboard states, had ceded to the United States her land claims west of the Alleghenies. In January, 1805, a territorial assembly met in Indiana, under the governorship of William Henry Harrison, and the new territory of Michigan was set up under Governor William Hull. By an act of Congress, land offices had been established on the Ohio frontier for the sale of public land in lots of three hundred and twenty acres, at two dollars an acre, for which the emigrant might pay in four yearly installments. Though the Indian danger west of Ohio was not yet past, the demand for land on credit was a sure sign that the small farmer was beginning to replace the hunter, the ranger, and the speculator on the western frontier.

The Flood Tide of Prosperity. Few administrations in our history have been as successful as Jefferson's first term. Our foreign trade had increased 100 per cent, and the customs receipts so far outran Gallatin's estimates that our debt was reduced by twenty-five million dollars, in spite of the purchase of Louisiana. Except for what Jefferson called "bickerings with Spain" over West Florida, our relations with the European nations were friendly. The commissioners under the Jay Treaty (p. 198) had satisfied the British merchants by awarding them $2,664,000 in payment of long-standing debts from American citizens. We had compelled respect for the American flag beyond the Strait of Gibraltar. We had opened the vista of a continental domain for settlement west of the great Mississippi.

The factious opposition of a few Federalists was drowned in the general chorus of approval for the policies of the President, whose election four years before had provoked the prophecy of the ruin of our commerce, the end of efficient government, and the destruction of the social order. When Thomas Jefferson took the oath of office a second time, on March 4, 1805, he could congratulate his fellow countrymen that "not a cloud appeared on the horizon."

TERMS TO BE MASTERED

"midnight judges"	French claims	the great divide
impeachment	hyper-Federalists	"Mediterranean fund"
Louisiana	West Florida	land office

FOR SUPPLEMENTARY READING

EDWARD CHANNING, *History of the United States*, Vol. IV, chaps. x–xx, and *The Jeffersonian System* (American Nation Series, Vol. XII); ALLEN JOHNSON, *Jefferson and his Colleagues* (Chronicles of America, Vol. XV); J. K. HOSMER, *The History of the Louisiana Purchase*; F. L. PAXSON, *The History of the American Frontier*, chaps. xv, xvi; F. A. OGG, *The Opening of the Mississippi*, chaps. x–xv; EMERSON HOUGH, *The Magnificent Adventure* (the Lewis and Clark expedition); E. E. SPARKS, *The Expansion of the American People*, chap. xv; The Pageant of America, pp. 204–213; *America*, Vol. IV, pp. 266–303; HART, *Contemporaries*, Vol. III, Nos. 106–115; MUZZEY, *Readings*, pp. 212–222.

TOPICS FOR REPORTS

1. **Jeffersonian Republicanism.** EDWARD STANWOOD, *History of the Presidency*, chap. vi; M. C. CRAWFORD, *Romantic Days in the Early Republic*, chap. iii; W. WILSON, *History of the American People*, Vol. III, pp. 163–180; A. JOHNSON, *Jefferson and his Colleagues*, chap. i; HART, *Contemporaries*, Vol. III, Nos. 106–108, 110.

2. **The Louisiana Purchase.** T. ROOSEVELT, *The Winning of the West*, Vol. IV, pp. 258–307; R. PAGE, *Dramatic Moments in American Diplomacy*, chap. vi; HENRY ADAMS, *History of the United States in the Administrations of Jefferson and Madison*, Vol. II, pp. 116–134; H. S. COMMAGER, *Documents of American History*, p. 190; HART, *Contemporaries*, Vol. III, Nos. 111–113.

3. **The Lewis and Clark Expedition.** R. G. THWAITES (ed.), *The Journals of the Lewis and Clark Expedition* and *Rocky Mountain Explorations*, pp. 92–187; N. BROOKS, *First Across the Continent*; AGNES C. LAUT, *Pathfinders*, pp. 307–333; *America*, Vol. V, pp. 38–65; T. ROOSEVELT, *The Winning of the West*, Vol. IV, pp. 308–328.

QUESTIONS SUGGESTED BY THE CHAPTER

1. Why are political parties necessary? **2.** What part of the Federalist system was changed when Jefferson came into office? **3.** For what can an official of the United States be impeached? **4.** Did Franklin D. Roosevelt follow Jefferson's or Wilson's practice in communicating with Congress? **5.** What was the importance of the decision in the case of Marbury v. Madison? **6.** Why did Napoleon decide to sell Louisiana? **7.** Why did the Federalists object to the purchase of Louisiana? **8.** What was the plot of the "Essex Junto" in 1804? **9.** Show that West Florida was not a part of Louisiana in 1803. **10.** What international service did Jefferson render in his first administration? **11.** Why did New York surpass New Orleans as a port for foreign trade? **12.** On what terms was public land sold by the government under the law of 1800? **13.** Why did Aaron Burr kill Alexander Hamilton? **14.** Give examples illustrating the growth of the West in Jefferson's day. **15.** What accounts for the triumphant re-election of Jefferson in 1804?

CHAPTER TEN

OUR SECOND WAR FOR INDEPENDENCE

John Randolph and the "Quids." The clouds gathered thick and fast, however, in Jefferson's second administration, until they finally broke in war under his successor Madison. First of all, opposition to Jefferson developed among the Congressmen of his own party, as it generally does in the case of a vigorous President. The leader of the opposition was John Randolph of Roanoke (Virginia), a distant connection of Jefferson's, who in 1801 became chairman of the Ways and Means Committee in the House. Randolph was a nervous skeleton of a man, with a shrill voice and a biting tongue which heaped abuse and ridicule upon his foes. He was an extreme partisan, a "simon-pure" Republican, who believed that his party should run the government for the interests of the agricultural South as the Federalists had run it for the interests of the commercial North. He had no sympathy with Jefferson's conciliatory policy. Why should a Republican President let the Federalist tariff, Bank, and national debt stand undisturbed? Why should he go to the New England states to select most of his cabinet officers? Why be so ready to save the investments of Northern speculators in Yazoo land? [1]

[1] The legislature of Georgia in 1795 had sold thirty-five million acres of land on the Mississippi and Yazoo rivers to land companies at a cent and a half an acre. It was a corrupt transaction, in which many of the members of the legislature were themselves interested. The next year a reform legislature annulled the sale. When Georgia surrendered her Western land to the United States in 1802, speculators in the North who had bought Yazoo land asked the government at Washington to recognize their titles. Jefferson appointed three members of his cabinet to investigate the claims, and they recommended that five million acres in Mississippi Territory be set aside to satisfy the claimants. Randolph fought the "Yazoo men" bitterly and successfully until he lost his seat in Congress (to Jefferson's son-in-law!) in 1812.

When Jefferson sent his regular message to Congress, on December 2, 1805, recommending military preparation to resist Spanish "aggression" in West Florida, and followed it up a few days later with a secret message asking for two million dollars with which to purchase Florida, Randolph's fury burst forth. Why should we appropriate money to buy West Florida if we had already purchased it from Napoleon? Let us fight for it openly and honestly if we were entitled to it, but not drift into a war with Spain by constant bickering over the province. Jefferson got his two million dollars, but at the cost of a split in his party. Though there were 112 Republicans to 27 Federalists in the House, the bill secured a majority of only 22 votes; and the two million dollars was still unused when Jefferson went out of office. Randolph and his "Quids"[1] were a constant thorn in Jefferson's side, as Hamilton and his clique had been in Adams's.

The Burr Conspiracy. Still more troublesome to the President's peace of mind was the conduct of the ex-Vice-President Aaron Burr. Just what Burr intended to do is uncertain to this day — whether to establish an independent state in the Mississippi Valley, or to seize the city of New Orleans and carve out an empire for the Burr "dynasty" in Spanish territory, or to attempt the conquest of Mexico, or simply to plant a colony on the Red River. At any rate, after trying to draw the British and Spanish ministers at Washington into his scheme, he collected men, money, and arms on an island in the Ohio, and cajoled several prominent persons in the West to give him their support in what they supposed would be a chastisement of the hated Spaniards.

Just as Burr was ready to move his men down the Ohio, Jefferson sent out a proclamation for the arrest of "sundry persons" who were "conspiring to set on foot a military enterprise against the dominions of Spain." Burr kept on down the Mississippi, however, until he learned that he had been betrayed

---

[1] The name "Quids" was given to the faction by Randolph himself, who said that he and his followers represented a *tertium quid*, which is the Latin phrase for something different from two recognized things — in this case the two regular political parties.

by one of his fellow conspirators, General Wilkinson. He was seized while trying to escape into Spanish Florida and was sent to Richmond for trial on the charge of levying war against the United States. The eyes of the whole country were fixed on Richmond when the trial began in August, 1807. Jefferson was eager to have Burr convicted and did everything in his power to aid the prosecution. But Jefferson's foes were in charge of the proceedings, with Chief Justice Marshall as the judge and John Randolph as foreman of the jury. Burr was acquitted of treason, but the verdict convinced few of his fellow citizens of his innocence. He lived on for nearly thirty years, finally dying in poverty and obscurity in New York at the age of eighty (1836).

The *Chesapeake* Affair. Shortly before the Burr trial opened in Richmond, an event occurred off the Virginia coast which threw the country into a state of excitement such as had not been experienced since the first shots of the Revolution were fired on Lexington Green. Our frigate *Chesapeake*, Captain Barron commanding, weighed anchor from Norfolk, Virginia, on June 22, 1807, bound for the Mediterranean service. Her guns were still unmounted and her decks were littered with tackle. The British warship *Leopard* overhauled her outside the capes and ordered her to stop and be searched for British deserters in her crew. When Barron replied that he had no deserters, the *Leopard* poured a broadside of shot into the *Chesapeake*, killing three men and wounding eighteen more. Barron, unprepared to resist, struck his colors after firing a single gun, lighted by a coal brought from the ship's galley. Then the British officers took four alleged deserters from the American frigate and left her to crawl back to Norfolk with her rigging torn and her hull riddled by solid shot. To understand this outrage upon an American warship perpetrated by a nation at peace with us, it is necessary to review the course of our foreign affairs in the years immediately preceding; for it was foreign entanglements and not domestic discord that brought the woes which afflicted our country during the second administration of Jefferson and the two terms of his successor, Madison.

British Orders and French Decrees. In the spring of 1803 war between England and France was renewed. It was to last a dozen years, until the final overthrow of the mighty Corsican adventurer at Waterloo. In October, 1805, Lord Nelson destroyed the combined French and Spanish fleets off Cape Trafalgar; and a few weeks later Napoleon annihilated the Russian and Austrian armies at Austerlitz. England was now mistress of the seas, and Napoleon was master of the continent of Europe. Each of the powers now tried to starve the other out by shutting off his commerce. The British issued Orders in Council, forbidding neutral ships to trade with ports under Napoleon's control on the Continent, and Napoleon replied with imperial Decrees authorizing the seizure of ships which traded with the British Isles or allowed themselves to be searched by a British cruiser.

The commerce of the United States was threatened with ruin by these Orders and Decrees. As a neutral nation we had profited from the general war in Europe by building up a flourishing foreign trade. In the years from 1789 to 1805 our imports had increased from $20,000,000 to $77,000,000, and our exports had grown from $23,000,000 to $80,000,000.[1] Nine tenths of the shipping was carried under the American flag. In the year 1805, 70,000 tons were added to our merchant marine, requiring the addition of 4200 seamen. Sailors' wages rose from $8 to $24 a month. Hundreds of foreigners, mostly British, became naturalized in order to enjoy the better pay, better food, and more humane treatment which they found on American vessels.

---

[1] A large part of these exports were goods carried on so-called "broken voyages." For example, a cargo of sugar might be brought from the French West Indies in an American ship, landed at an American port (paying the duties), and then reshipped to a port in France. The British admiralty court in 1801 had decided that such trade was legal, considering that landing and paying duty in an American port made the cargo an American cargo. But in 1805, in the famous *Essex* case, a higher British court reversed this decision and held to the doctrine of the "continuous voyage." This meant that, regardless of stopping on the way in America, the cargo of sugar was a French cargo, since it came from a French port and was destined finally to be landed at a French port. Therefore the American ship, as illegally carrying a French cargo, was liable to seizure by the British cruisers. It meant the ruin of our large West Indian carrying trade.

The Impressment of American Seamen. Napoleon had no more respect for American rights on the seas than England did. He seized our ships in his Continental ports and sold their cargoes for the benefit of his imperial treasury. But he was not able to do us as much damage as the British were, because he did not have the cruisers to capture our merchantmen on the high seas or to hover off our coasts, to search our ships for deserting sailors. In her desperate struggle with Napoleon, Great Britain needed every man she could get to serve her navy. It mattered little to her that the sailor had an American naturalization paper, because her law did not allow a British citizen to transfer his allegiance to another country. Furthermore, many of the naturalization papers were forged. Just how many *bona fide* American citizens were taken off our ships by the British impressment officers it is impossible to say. But shortly before we went to war with Great Britain in 1812, President Madison sent Congress a report on the subject in which he listed more than six thousand cases of American seamen who had been "impressed and held in bondage" by the British during the preceding three years. It was not so easy to distinguish between an American and an Englishman as between an American and a Frenchman, and we may be sure that in case of doubt the British officer claimed the sailor.

Jefferson's Embarrassment. We see now why the firing on the *Chesapeake* and the forcible removal of four of her crew roused such a storm of fury in our country. Jefferson immediately issued a proclamation excluding British warships from our waters, and sent orders to our minister Monroe in London to demand an apology for the attack on the *Chesapeake*. There was little to be hoped for from England, however. A Tory Parliament had been elected in April. It was determined to let nothing stand in the way of crushing Napoleon. Britannia ruled the waves, and there should be no neutral rights. The Tory press spoke of America as "an insignificant and puny power," which could not be allowed to "mutilate Britain's proud sovereignty of the ocean." The reply of the British foreign secretary, George Canning, to Jefferson's demand for an apology reached Washington in December.

IMPRESSING AN AMERICAN SAILOR

Canning was willing to discuss making amends for the outrage committed upon the *Chesapeake*; indeed, the admiral whose orders were responsible for that outrage had already been dismissed from his command on the American coast. But on the general question of the right of search and impressment the British ministry would not yield an inch. A new Order in Council had made every neutral vessel that did not touch at a British port and pay duties there subject to seizure. As Henry Adams, the foremost authority on this period, says: "From the moment Mr. Canning and his party assumed power, the fate of Jefferson's administration was sealed. America had no alternative but submission or war."

The Embargo. Submission and war, however, were equally distasteful to Jefferson. Even if he had wished war, the reduced size of our navy made the defense of our coasts against a British fleet impossible. When Secretary of State Madison wrote a complaint against Great Britain's outrages upon our ships and sailors, John Randolph sneered at it as "a shilling pamphlet launched against 800 vessels of war." Jefferson determined to try a method of "peaceful coercion," to bring both Canning and Napoleon to terms. Our commerce was flourishing. Even in the year 1807, when the seizures of our cargoes were most numerous, our exports totaled $108,000,000 and our imports $138,000,000 — the largest volume of foreign trade in our history until 1835. The warehouses of Antwerp, Cádiz, Lisbon, and Hamburg were filled with goods brought in American ships. Jefferson believed that our trade was so indispensable to both England and France that the threat of its interruption would make them repeal their Orders and Decrees and respect American neutrality. Every member of his cabinet agreed with him.

Therefore, on December 17, 1807, he recommended to Congress an act prohibiting any American vessel from sailing for a foreign port. Congress immediately passed the Embargo Act, by large majorities. But instead of cowing England and France into a change of policy, the act only roused a storm of opposition in America, for it threatened to destroy the commerce which it was designed to protect. Rather than have their ships tied up at the wharves and their merchandise spoiling in warehouses, many merchants of New England and New York preferred to disobey the embargo and run the risk of the capture of their cargoes at sea. Even so, our foreign trade during the "embargo year" of 1808 shrank to less than one third of its value in 1807. Thousands of workers in the shipping ports were thrown out of employment, and the farmers saw the demand for their products for export to Europe fall off sharply. These farmers and laborers formed the chief support of Jefferson's party in the Northern states, but they began to fall away from him when unemployment and distress overtook them. Congress had given Jefferson power to enforce the embargo; but when he called on Governor Tompkins of New York to use the militia to prevent the smuggling of produce across the border, to be exported from the Canadian ports, he was accused of resorting to the same military "tyranny" that the Hamiltonians had used in quelling the Whisky Rebellion (p. 214).

Resistance to the Embargo. Whether or not the embargo, if strictly enforced, would have caused the European powers to respect our rights in order to regain our trade we cannot say. But it was evident with every month that passed that the embargo was growing more intolerable at home. What was the sense, cried the merchants, of ruining our own trade for the sake of punishing Europe? The shipowners disobeyed the embargo. Town meetings in New England passed resolutions against it, and Jefferson confessed later that he "felt the foundations of the government shaken under his feet" by their action. There was even talk of the secession of New England from the Union, as there had been five years before when Louisiana was purchased (p. 221). A confidential agent of Canning's, named George Rose, was hobnobbing with Senator Pickering and the Federalists, who told him that the embargo would send the Republicans down to defeat and that the friends of England would soon be in the saddle again. Moreover, the stanch Jeffersonian frontiersmen of the West, who were convinced that the British in Canada were arming the Indians against them, had little use for such milk-and-water measures as an embargo. They were already talking of driving the British out of Canada.[1]

[1] The governors of Indiana and Michigan territories reported conferences between the British and the Indians on the Canadian border in the autumn of 1807, and John Randolph (probably to embarrass Jefferson) made a speech in favor of the invasion of Canada. The Kentucky legislature, in the summer of 1808, passed a resolution pledging "our honor, our blood and our treasure" to protect the peace and dignity of the Union against "foreign invasion," and "to chastise and bring to reason our haughty and imperious foes." The frontiersmen in the South were equally inflamed against the Spanish in Florida, who shut off the direct access of Mississippi Territory and Georgia to the Gulf of Mexico.

The Embargo Repealed. Politics also played its part in the fate of the embargo. The year 1808 was a Presidential year. Jefferson was determined that his Secretary of State, James Madison, should succeed him. He was able to secure Madison's nomination by the Republican caucus of Congress, in spite of bitter opposition from Virginia, Pennsylvania, New York, and New England; but the election looked so doubtful in June, 1808, that Secretary Gallatin wrote, "The Federalists will turn us out by the 4th of March next." His fears proved unfounded. The South and West stood by Madison, who defeated his Federalist opponent, General C. C. Pinckney of South Carolina, by 122 electoral votes to 47. But Madison lost every New England state except Vermont. The Republican Congress became convinced that the embargo was driving a wedge into their party which would split it. On March 1, 1809, three days before Jefferson left office,[1] they repealed the embargo, substituting for it a Nonintercourse Act to apply only to Great Britain and France, and authorizing the President, in case either of those countries should cease to violate our neutral rights, to reopen trade with that country.

Madison's Weak Diplomacy. The new President was a mild, scholarly man, unfitted by temperament to control the factions which vexed his cabinet and his party in Congress. Besides, he was so anxious to preserve peace with England and France that he allowed himself to be imposed upon by both nations. His administration was but a few weeks old when he committed a blunder which made our relations with England worse than ever.

The new British minister to Washington, David Erskine, was instructed by Canning to offer to withdraw the Orders in Council on condition that we should still permit British cruisers to seize American ships which traded with countries which obeyed Napoleon's Decrees. Erskine, a liberal Whig with an American wife, eager to restore harmony between the two

---

[1] Jefferson was disgusted with the failure of the embargo, which he continued to believe would have forced Great Britain and France to respect our rights. Over a year later he wrote to Henry Dearborn that the "fatal measure" of repeal was "the immediate parent of all our present evils," and that it had "reduced us to a low standing in the eyes of the world."

AMERICAN SHIPS SAILING AFTER THE REPEAL OF THE EMBARGO

English-speaking countries, failed to communicate the whole of his instructions to our government; and Madison, without asking to see Erskine's full instructions, issued a proclamation on April 19 reopening trade with Great Britain on the tenth of the following June. The merchants were jubilant. They dispatched scores of ships to British ports, laden with cotton, lumber, grain, and tobacco. They praised Madison as a statesman who had succeeded where Jefferson failed. Then came the reckoning. The moment Canning heard what Erskine had done, he disavowed the arrangement and recalled his minister. Nothing was left for Madison to do but to issue a second proclamation restoring the Nonintercourse Act against Great Britain.

That act expired in 1810. Thereupon Congress tried a new experiment. On May 1 it passed Macon's Bill No. 2, throwing open our commerce again to all the world, but authorizing the

President, in case either Great Britain or France should withdraw its edicts against our commerce before March 3, 1811, to revive nonintercourse with the other power. This time it was the wily and faithless Napoleon who hoodwinked Madison. On August 5, 1810, his foreign minister, in a letter filled with protestations of love for the American people, announced that the Berlin and Milan Decrees had been revoked, and called upon Madison to revive nonintercourse with Great Britain. A careful diplomatic check on Napoleon's behavior would have shown that he was still seizing American ships and proclaiming the Decrees to be "permanent laws of the Empire." Lord Wellesley, who had succeeded Canning, warned us truly that Napoleon had no intention of keeping his promise. Yet Madison again jumped at the chance of coercing Great Britain by proclamation. He announced that unless she repealed her Orders in Council before February 2, 1811, we would forbid all trade with her and her colonies. The day came and went without any word from London. The proclamation was issued by Madison, and a month later Congress ratified it by a large majority. There is perhaps no more pitiable exhibition of American diplomacy than that furnished in the years 1809–1811.

Drifting into War. The mid-term elections of 1810 sent to Congress a group of men who represented the spirit of the frontier. They were young, aggressive, and intensely nationalistic. They demanded that the weak and shifting diplomacy which was humiliating the United States in the eyes of Europe should come to an end. Their leader was Henry Clay, who had migrated from Virginia in his twentieth year (1796) to the new state of Kentucky, where he rose rapidly to be the leading lawyer and most influential citizen. Clay and his companion spirits were indignant at the seizure of American ships and the impressment of American sailors. But, as representatives of the frontier, they were especially incensed over the encouragement which the hostile Indians were receiving from British and Spanish agents. The West would never be free to develop its magnificent resources until the Indian danger was removed by the expulsion of the British from Upper Canada and of the

Spanish from Florida. John Randolph ridiculed these belligerent enthusiasts as the "boys" and the "War Hawks," but neither his sarcasm nor the timid caution of the President could check their appeal to national honor.

Before Congress met in November, 1811, and elected Henry Clay Speaker of the House, three events had occurred which made war with England more probable. First, our minister William Pinkney, tired of fruitless negotiations with Lord Wellesley, quitted London and left us without official representation at the Court of St. James's at the moment we needed it most. Then, on May 16, our frigate *President*, which was patrolling the coast to protect our sailors from impressment, met the British sloop of war *Little Belt*, and, after a brisk battle of a quarter of an hour, forced her to surrender. The victory was hailed as a complete revenge for the *Chesapeake* outrage. The third event was the appearance of the first steamboat on the Ohio River,[1] which promised a rapid two-way traffic between Pittsburgh and New Orleans, and so made it more than ever necessary to free the whole Mississippi Valley from the Indian menace.

The Battle of Tippecanoe. Three days after Congress met, a fourth event occurred to feed the fires of anti-British sentiment. Two able brothers of the Shawnee tribe, Tecumseh and the Prophet, determined to form a great Indian confederacy to resist the further encroachment of the whites upon the lands which the Great Spirit had given them for their hunting grounds. They established their headquarters on the Wabash River, near Tippecanoe Creek, to bid defiance to William Henry Harrison, the governor of the territory of Indiana. Harrison moved with a force of nine hundred men to the neighborhood of the Indian town. On November 7, 1811, while Tecumseh was in the South, stirring up the Creeks and Cherokees to join the confederacy, the Prophet made an attack on Harrison's force.

---

[1] The steamboat, after various experiments with wheels, paddles, and pushing poles worked by steam power, had been finally recognized as a success when, on August 11–12, 1807, Robert Fulton's *Clermont*, a side-wheeler, made the 146-mile trip from New York to Albany in 32 hours.

The Indians were repulsed, and the next day they abandoned their village, which Harrison entered and burned. Tecumseh fled to the British in Canada. Harrison strengthened the belief of the West that British officials had been inciting the Indians on our frontier ever since St. Clair's defeat of twenty years before (p. 196), by reporting the capture of new guns and "ample supplies of the best British glazed powder" at Tippecanoe, evidently obtained from the king's stores at Malden.

The Declaration of War. During the winter of 1811–1812 the war spirit grew steadily in the West and South, while the commercial class in the East resisted it both as an interruption to their trade and as a threat of the political supremacy of the farmer and pioneer communities in case we should win the victory. Henry Clay descended from the Speaker's chair to urge the war in fiery speeches. Canada was ours for the taking. It would be a mere matter of marching to drive the British out. A thousand riflemen from Kentucky alone could do the trick. The other "War Hawks" whipped up the confidence, pride, and patriotism of the people. President Madison was swept along in the current. Congress voted to increase the army by fifteen thousand men, accept fifty thousand volunteers, refit our frigates *Adams, Constellation*, and *Chesapeake*, and raise a loan of eleven million dollars in 6 per cent bonds. Moreover, 1812 was a Presidential year, and it was rumored (though denied by Clay) that the "War Hawks" were threatening Madison with a defeat for renomination if he refused to pursue a spirited policy.

The President was renominated by the Republican caucus on May 18, and the next day news arrived from England that the British ministry would make no change in the Orders in Council until it should be convinced that Napoleon had repealed his Decrees in good faith. This dispatch, wrote Madison many years later, was "the more immediate impulse to the war." Forced, as he said, to choose between war and degradation, the President sent a message to Congress on June 1, 1812, in which he reviewed "the injuries and indignities which had been heaped upon our country" by Great Britain, and recommended Congress to make a decision which should be "worthy of the enlightened and patriotic councils of a virtuous, a free, and a powerful nation." The hand was Madison's, but the voice was Henry Clay's. Congress, by a vote of 79 to 49 in the House and 19 to 13 in the Senate, declared for war,[1] and on June 18 Madison signed the fateful bill. "I flung forward the flag of my country," said the aged Madison a quarter of a century later, "sure that the people would press onward and defend it."

A Needless War. There is no doubt that Great Britain had for several years given us cause for war, as had Napoleon too. Yet our declaration of war in 1812 was an act of folly. A wise and statesmanlike administration at Washington must have seen that events both in England and on the continent of Europe gave promise that our grievances would cease very soon. In fact, they were less acute in 1812 than at any other time since the attack on the *Chesapeake* five years before. We had been patient in the years of great trial; we lost our patience when relief was at hand.

England did not want war with us. The burden of her debt had risen to nearly four billion dollars in resisting Napoleon. Her exports declined by 33 per cent in the year 1811, and she needed our trade, which was worth sixty million dollars a year to her. If the special envoy whose appointment the "War Hawks" blocked early in 1812 had been allowed to go to London, he would have found Parliament already debating the question of repealing the Orders in Council; and if the dispatches of our able minister at St. Petersburg, John Quincy Adams, had been studied with care, they would have shown that Russia's refusal to close her Baltic ports at Napoleon's order foreshadowed the end of the "Continental System" and the beginning of the downfall of the French emperor. We should have heeded the repeated messages of Jonathan Russell from Paris to the President that it was "the great object of Napoleon's policy to entangle us in a

---

[1] This vote showed a far larger opposition than the votes committing us to any other of our foreign wars. On the Mexican War, of 1846, the vote was 174 to 14 in the House and 40 to 2 in the Senate; on the Spanish War, in 1898, the votes were 324 to 19 and 67 to 21 respectively; and we entered the World War by a vote of 373 to 50 in the House and 86 to 6 in the Senate.

war with England," so that his own hands might be freer to accomplish the enslavement of Europe; and Madison, even at the cost of a renomination, should have resisted the pressure of the frontiersmen to drive us into war with the British for the alluring prospect of the conquest of Canada.

In fact, the friends of American conciliation won in Parliament, and Lord Castlereagh announced on June 16, two days before Congress declared war, that the Orders in Council would be repealed. There was no Atlantic cable, however, to flash the news to Washington. So the needless war between the sister nations of the English tongue began just as Napoleon was leading his army of half a million men across the Russian border, hoping to crush the last great European power that dared to resist his despotic will.

A Divided Country. The United States was wholly unprepared for the war which had been precipitated by the frontier expansionists. Though we had more than a million male white citizens of military age in 1812, the War Department could never put an army of more than ten to fifteen thousand soldiers in the field. Less than 10 per cent of the fifty thousand volunteers whom the President was authorized to enlist responded to his call. The generals were men averaging sixty years of age, some of whom had seen no service since the Revolution and some of whom had never commanded a regiment. Winfield Scott spoke of the old officers as "sunk in sloth, ignorance or habits of intemperate drinking . . . decayed gentlemen utterly unfit for any military purpose whatever." Our navy consisted of less than a score of frigates and sloops, built in the days of Washington and Adams, with one hundred and seventy small gunboats (Jefferson's hobby) which were intended for coast defense but were useless outside of smooth water; while the British had eleven ships of the line and ninety other warcraft at their American stations.

There was enough wealth in the country to finance the war easily; but it was concentrated chiefly in the commercial regions of the East, which were bitterly opposed to the war. Half the money in the country was held by the bankers of New England, but they refused to support "Mr. Madison's war" — which they might better have called "Mr. Clay's war." They subscribed less than $1,000,000 of the $11,000,000 loan of 1812, and during the entire war contributed only $3,000,000 of the $41,000,000 paid into the Treasury. Moreover, New York and the New England states refused to let their militia serve outside their own boundaries, their legislatures and town meetings denounced the war openly, and their farmers sold beef, pork, and flour to the British armies in Canada.

The election of November, 1812, shows how sharply the country was divided. The most powerful politician of New York, De Witt Clinton, went over to the Federalists and ran against Madison as a peace candidate. He received all the New England votes except Vermont's 8, together with 46 votes from the middle Atlantic states north of Virginia, making a total of 89. Madison's 128 votes came from the South and West, together with Pennsylvania. Indeed, it was only the 25 votes from the latter state that saved him from defeat.

The War on the Canadian Frontier. Having studied the causes which brought our country into the War of 1812, we need devote only a few paragraphs to the military and naval events of the war. It started with the confident movement for the "conquest" of Canada. The attack was to be delivered at four points (map, p. 246): from Lake Champlain down to the St. Lawrence and Montreal; at Kingston, where Lake Ontario narrows to the river; and at both the eastern and western ends of Lake Erie. Every one of these plans failed through lack of teamwork among the American armies, continual quarrels between the generals, and the refusal of the militia to leave their own states.

The series of disasters opened on the western front, when the aged Governor William Hull of Michigan Territory, in a panic, surrendered the post of Detroit to 700 British troops, without striking a blow (August 16, 1812).[1] The fall of Detroit meant

---

[1] General Hull was tried by court-martial for cowardice and condemned to be shot; but President Madison pardoned him for his services in the Revolution — and his gray hairs.

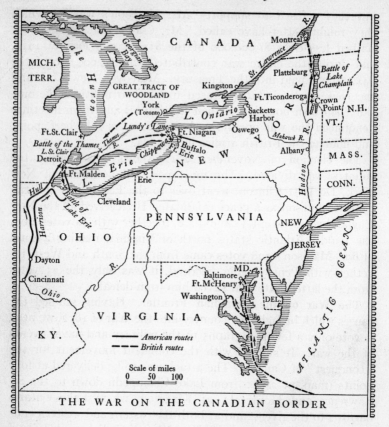

THE WAR ON THE CANADIAN BORDER

the British occupation of our entire western frontier extending from Lake Erie to the Mississippi River.

It was more than a year before the damage of Hull's surrender was repaired by the brilliant victory of Captain Oliver H. Perry's fleet over a British squadron on Lake Erie (September 10, 1813). Perry's exploit forced the British to abandon Detroit and retire eastward along the north shore of the lake. General William Henry Harrison pursued them with ten thousand Kentuckian volunteers and, overtaking them on the Thames River, completely routed them (October 5, 1813). The British commander Proctor barely escaped capture, and the great Tecumseh was among the slain. The Indian menace on our western border was removed. As for the operations of our quarreling generals of regulars and militia farther East (Lakes Ontario and Champlain), they were a complete failure during the first two years of the war.

The Naval War. It was expected when the war started that our troops would have little difficulty in conquering Canada, but that our tiny navy would be powerless against the great British fleet. It turned out the other way. The miserable failure on the Canadian border was offset by the exploits of our frigates *President*, *United States*, and *Constitution* ("Old Ironsides"). Three days after his uncle's disgraceful surrender of Detroit, Captain Isaac Hull, in the *Constitution*, met the British brig *Guerrière* off the north-Atlantic coast, and in a spirited battle of half an hour reduced her to a floating wreck. Even the New England Federalists could not repress the rejoicing over this challenge to England's sea power at the beginning of the war. Our other naval commanders, such as Decatur and Bainbridge, hastened to emulate the exploit of Hull. In six months they forced three British frigates and two sloops of war to strike their colors, while they themselves lost only the eighteen-gun *Wasp*.

But in the end the enormous superiority of the British fleet in numbers prevailed. All but two of our frigates were either captured or penned up in our ports. British cruisers drew a stringent blockade about our coast from New London southward. By the close of 1813 we had no vessels left to defend our shores, and the British could land pretty much where they would. Exports from New York fell from over $12,000,000 in 1811 to $200,000 in 1814, and those from Virginia from $4,800,000 to $17,500. From Long Island Sound to the Savannah River foreign trade was paralyzed. On the other hand, our swift-sailing privateers harassed the British merchant marine on all its far-flung lines of world commerce, and captured some thirteen hundred ships and cargoes valued at about $40,000,000. The British had boasted at the beginning of the war that they would not let an

American craft cross from New York to Staten Island; but before the war was over they themselves were paying 15 per cent insurance on vessels crossing the English Channel.

Great Britain Takes the Offensive. During 1812 and 1813 the British had been more concerned over Napoleon's fortunes in Europe than over the war in America, which was, after all, but a footnote to the great Napoleonic drama. But with Napoleon's abdication and exile to Elba, in April, 1814, England was free to adopt an aggressive policy toward the United States. The plan consisted of three parts: an invasion of New York along Burgoyne's old route via Lake Champlain; attacks on Washington and other cities of the Atlantic coast; and an expedition to seize New Orleans and detach the Mississippi Valley from the Union. The plan failed eventually in all its parts, just as the American plan for the conquest of Canada had failed.[1] The British were unable to get a permanent foothold inside the borders of the United States.

The "Star-Spangled Banner." With their control of the sea the British not only blocked our commerce but landed parties at will to burn towns and pillage farms along the coast. They even "annexed" the whole of Maine down to the Penobscot River as a British province. As a climax to their marauding expeditions, Major General Ross, with four thousand men, landed on the banks of the Potomac and marched on the undefended city of Washington. A force of hastily gathered militia was easily swept aside by Ross's regulars at Bladensburg, seven miles from the capital (August 24, 1814), and President Madison, gathering such valuables as he could, fled for refuge to the Virginia side while the British set fire to the Capitol, the White House, and several other public buildings. After

---

[1] The final attempt at the conquest of Canada was made in the midsummer of 1814, when two new and energetic American generals, Jacob Brown and Winfield Scott, crossed the Niagara River with fifty-five hundred men and, at Chippawa (July 5), drove the British forces from the field. Three weeks later Brown fought a furious battle at Lundy's Lane, a few miles down the river, in which the Americans again had the advantage until darkness finally forced Brown to retire, leaving the British in possession of the field. In November the Americans withdrew to their own side of the Niagara for good.

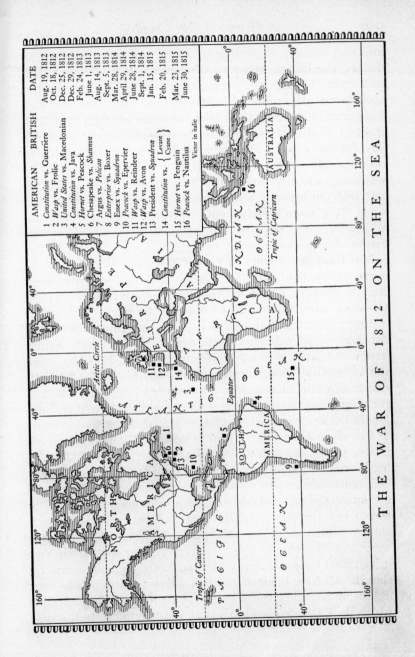

THE WAR OF 1812 ON THE SEA

	AMERICAN	BRITISH	DATE
1	*Constitution* vs. Guerrière		Aug. 19, 1812
2	*Wasp* vs. Frolic		Oct. 18, 1812
3	*United States* vs. Macedonian		Dec. 25, 1812
4	*Constitution* vs. Java		Dec. 29, 1812
5	*Hornet* vs. Peacock		Feb. 24, 1813
6	Chesapeake vs. *Shannon*		June 1, 1813
7	Argus vs. *Pelican*		Aug. 14, 1813
8	*Enterprise* vs. Boxer		Sept. 5, 1813
9	*Essex* vs. Squadron		Mar. 28, 1814
10	*Peacock* vs. Epervier		April 29, 1814
11	*Wasp* vs. Reindeer		June 28, 1814
12	*Wasp* vs. Avon		Sept. 1, 1814
13	President vs. *Squadron*		Jan. 15, 1815
14	*Constitution* vs. { Levant / Cyane }		Feb. 20, 1815
15	*Hornet* vs. Penguin		Mar. 23, 1815
16	*Peacock* vs. Nautilus		June 30, 1815

Victor in italic

inflicting damage amounting to about one and a half million dollars, the British sailed up Chesapeake Bay to repeat their raid upon the important commercial city of Baltimore. But their troops were repulsed before the city in a battle in which Ross was killed, and their fleet, after an all-night bombardment of Fort McHenry (September 13–14), headed down the bay for the capes. The young Francis Scott Key was being detained aboard one of the British ships that night. He watched anxiously "through the perilous night" while the fort held out against the continuous firing from the fleet. And when "the morn's early light" revealed that "our flag was still there" he composed our national anthem, "The Star-Spangled Banner."

Macdonough's Victory on Lake Champlain. While Ross was approaching Baltimore, Sir George Prevost, with the finest British army ever sent to America, was advancing from the Canadian border to Lake Champlain, to repeat with better success the march of Burgoyne in 1777. Arriving at the strong American fortifications at Plattsburg, he waited for the British fleet on the lake to enter Plattsburg Bay and help him storm the works. But young Lieutenant Thomas Macdonough, a veteran of the Tripolitan war (p. 226), stationed his inferior fleet at the entrance of the bay and so skillfully outmaneuvered and outfought the British squadron that he gained as decisive a victory as Perry's on Lake Erie. The next day (September 12) Prevost, unable to proceed with the Americans in command of the lake, led his ten thousand troops back to Canada.

Macdonough's victory was not only the most brilliant naval exploit of the war but also the most encouraging in point of time. For the American fortunes had reached their lowest ebb by September, 1814. The public buildings of Washington were in ashes. The Treasury was empty. Our war vessels were driven from the ocean, our coasts blockaded, and our commerce ruined. All New England and half a dozen states besides were discussing how they could secure for themselves the protection which the distracted government at Washington seemed unable

THE *CONSTITUTION*

to provide.[1] It looked as if our envoys who were then negotiating a treaty of peace at Ghent, in Belgium, would have to submit to the humiliating terms which the British commissioners proposed. But MacDonough's victory changed all that. It not only saved New England and New York from falling into the hands of the British but encouraged our commissioners at Ghent to stand firmly against the British demands.

The Battle of New Orleans. The third part of the British plan of operation for 1814 was, as we have seen (p. 248), the conquest of the valley of the Mississippi, which they mistakenly believed to be lukewarm in its attachment to the Union. A British army of nearly ten thousand men, of whom half were veteran troops just released from service against Napoleon's armies in the Spanish peninsula, descended upon New Orleans in December, 1814. They were commanded by the Duke of Wellington's brother-in-law, Sir Edward Pakenham. Jackson, hastening from his quarters at Mobile,[1] reached New Orleans a few days before Pakenham's advance troops landed on the shore of Lake Borgne, only fifteen miles from the city. When Pakenham's veterans, despising alike Jackson's hasty fortifications of cotton bales and the men behind them, delivered a frontal attack on January 8, 1815, the unerring fire of the Western riflemen mowed them down like grass. In the battle of less than twenty minutes the British lost their com-

[1] The only heartening event of the summer occurred in the Southwest. The Creek Indians in Mississippi Territory, stirred up by Spanish agents from Florida and by Tecumseh's visit (p. 241), had taken up the hatchet in 1813 and massacred two hundred and fifty Americans at Fort Mims, on the lower Alabama River. General Andrew Jackson, a Tennessee frontiersman who liked nothing better than an Indian hunt, completely broke the power of the Creeks in the battle of Horseshoe Bend and compelled them to sign the Treaty of Fort Jackson, by which they surrendered to the United States two thirds of their lands in Alabama. The Mississippi Territory was thus cleared of the Indian danger, as the Northwest Territory had been cleared by Harrison's victory at Tippecanoe. Jackson pressed on to occupy Mobile and, marching into Spanish East Florida, raised the American flag over Pensacola. Jackson's exploits, for which he was elevated to the rank of major general in the regular army and given command of the military district of the Southwest, were only incidental to the war between the United States and Great Britain; but as a blow to England's ally Spain they contributed to American influence at the peace table at Ghent.

mander and over two thousand men (as against seventy-one for Jackson), and their shattered army re-embarked on Lake Borgne and sailed away to the eastward while Jackson entered the city in triumph. Henceforth he was "the hero of New Orleans." He was rewarded with the governorship of Florida, a seat in the United States Senate, and finally the Presidency of the United States (1829).

The Treaty of Ghent. Had the Atlantic cable existed in 1814, the battle of New Orleans would not have been fought, and the most masterful of our Presidents from Washington to Lincoln might never have sat in the White House. For on the very evening before Pakenham arrived off New Orleans, the British and American commissioners at Ghent had signed a treaty of peace (December 24, 1814). The treaty provided simply for a return to the conditions which had existed before the war. Boundaries, fisheries, and the navigation of the Mississippi were left open for further negotiations. Impressment was passed over in silence. The treaty reached Washington on February 14, 1815, and three days later it was unanimously ratified by the Senate, amid universal rejoicing. The real reason why the Americans were so well satisfied with the peace was that the grievances which had drawn them into the war had ceased to exist. The danger of the Indians on our western frontier had been removed. The overthrow of Napoleon had made the British seizures of our ships and impressment of our sailors no longer necessary. The War of 1812, though precipitated by Henry Clay and the "War Hawks," had been caused by Napoleon Bonaparte. When he fell, the obstacles to peace fell, too.

The Hartford Convention. The Federalists of New England were especially bitter in their opposition to the policies of Jefferson and Madison. They condemned the acquisition of Louisiana, defied the Embargo and Nonintercourse Acts, and thundered against "Mr. Madison's war." "Organize a peace party," read an address of the legislature to the people of Massachusetts a week after the war was declared; "express your sentiments without fear and let the sound of your disapprobation of this war be loud and deep. . . . Let there be no volunteering except for defensive war." The long discontent culminated in a call sent out by Massachusetts to the other New England states for a convention to meet at Hartford, Connecticut, on December 15, 1814, "to unite in such measures for our safety as the times demand and the principles of justice and the law of self-preservation will justify."

Twenty-three delegates, from Massachusetts, Connecticut, and Rhode Island, met at the time and place appointed. Their sessions were secret. They adopted resolutions, like those of Virginia and Kentucky in 1798, to the effect that when the Constitution was violated it was the duty of the states to "interpose their authority for the preservation of their liberties." They proposed seven amendments to the Constitution: (1) to abolish the clause which gave the South the privilege of counting three fifths of the slaves in the population upon which representation in Congress was based; (2) to require a two-thirds vote of Congress to admit new states to the Union;[1] (3) embargoes to be laid for only sixty days; (4) nonintercourse to be proclaimed only by a two-thirds vote of Congress; (5) the same two-thirds vote to be necessary for the declaration of war; (6) no naturalized citizen to be eligible to national office; and (7) no President to have a second term or to be succeeded by a President from the same state (this to put an end to the "Virginia dynasty").

There was nothing "treasonable" in these propositions, and there was no purpose of secession in the convention, as its enemies charged. But the members hoped and believed that the war would fail under Madison's weak leadership,[2] and they made the mistake of obstructing the war as a party measure when it had become in reality a struggle of the nation for its life.

[1] This amendment, if adopted, would have permitted thirteen Senators (one more than a third of the number at the time) to prevent adding to the Union as a state a single new community of the growing West.

[2] For example, Daniel Webster, later the great Whig Senator from Massachusetts, wrote in December, 1814: "The Government cannot last under this war in the hands of these men [Madison and his cabinet and Congress] another twelve months. Not that opposition will break it down, but it will break itself down. It will go out. This is my sober opinion."

Soon after the convention adjourned three of its members set out for Washington as "ambassadors" to the government. But when they reached Baltimore, news of Jackson's victory at New Orleans came, and the morning after their arrival in Washington (February 14) came the still more joyful news of the treaty of peace. There was nothing left for the "ambassadors" to do but to go home. Though the proceedings of the Hartford Convention were published a few years later, and Otis spent the rest of his long life defending the lawfulness of those proceedings, the country at large continued to regard them as unpatriotic and seditious. Nothing else contributed so much to the death of the Federalist party as the Hartford Convention.

The Completion of our Independence. The close of the War of 1812 marks an epoch in American history. The war itself, as a military event, was of minor account. The armies were small, and our losses were less than five thousand in a population of eight million. The enemy never penetrated more than a few miles into our territory and, with the exception of Washington, never held one of our cities for even a day.

Yet the effects of the war upon the government and people of America were far-reaching. Ever since the second inauguration of Washington we had been hardly more than a makeweight in the politics and wars of Europe. Our parties were English and French, "Anglomen" and "Jacobins." Our independence was acknowledged on paper but not respected in practice. The energies of the administration at Washington were absorbed by the endeavors to preserve the peace and honor of the country in the face of constant insults and injuries from abroad. One expedient after another was tried to force or coax Great Britain and France to respect our neutral rights. Special envoys and commissions followed one another across the Atlantic. We made seven treaties with foreign nations and fought two wars in the period 1794–1814. Many of our most prominent statesmen were drafted to serve their country in foreign capitals. The eyes of the people were turned seaward to greet the swift packets bringing good news or bad from London, Paris, and Madrid.

But with the "universal peace" of 1815 there came a sharp change. America struck out on a new path — the path of full national consciousness. We turned our back on Europe and began in earnest to grapple with the problems of our own growing country and the development of our vast national domain. The War of 1812 marked the completion of our independence.

TERMS TO BE MASTERED

"Yazoo men"	impressment	right of search
Orders in Council	embargo	peaceful coercion
continuous voyage	militia	the "Virginia dynasty"

FOR SUPPLEMENTARY READING

R. D. PAINE, *The Fight for a Free Sea* (Chronicles of America, Vol. XXVII); C. A. and M. R. BEARD, *The Rise of American Civilization*, Vol. I, chap. ix; JULIUS PRATT, *The Expansionists of 1812*; WANDELL and MINNIGERODE, *Aaron Burr*, Vol. II, pp. 173–232; L. M. SEARS, *Jefferson and the Embargo*; THEODORE ROOSEVELT, *The Naval War of 1812*; F. L. PAXSON, *History of the American Frontier*, chaps. xi–xiv; K. C. BABCOCK, *The Rise of American Nationality* (American Nation Series, Vol. XIII), chaps. iv–x; H. S. COMMAGER, *Documents of American History*, pp. 195–205; *America*, Vol. V, pp. 116–269; HART, *Contemporaries*, Vol. III, Nos. 116–129; MUZZEY, *Readings*, pp. 222–231.

TOPICS FOR REPORTS

1. **The Conspiracy of Aaron Burr.** J. B. McMASTER, *History of the People of the United States*, Vol. III, chap. xv; J. S. BASSETT, *The Life of Andrew Jackson*, Vol. I, chap. iv; WANDELL and MINNIGERODE, *Aaron Burr*, Vol. II, pp. 31–81; W. F. McCALEB, *The Aaron Burr Conspiracy*; *America*, Vol. V, pp. 71–77; JAMES PARTON, *The Life and Times of Aaron Burr*, chaps. xviii–xxvi.

2. **The Effect of the Napoleonic War on American Trade.** CLIVE DAY, *A History of Commerce*, chap. xlvii; H. U. FAULKNER, *American Economic History*, pp. 246–254; HENRY ADAMS, *The History of the United States in the Administrations of Jefferson and Madison*, Vol. III, chaps. xv–xviii; EDWARD CHANNING, *History of the United States*, Vol. IV, pp. 352–378; HART, *Contemporaries*, Vol. III, Nos. 118, 120–122, 129.

3. **The Hartford Convention.** H. C. LODGE, *George Cabot*, chaps. x–xiii; S. E. MORISON, *The Life and Letters of Harrison Gray Otis*, Vol. II, pp. 78–199; E. P. POWELL, *Nullification and Secession in the United States*, chap. v; *American Historical Review*, Vol. IX, pp. 96–104; HENRY ADAMS, *Documents Relating to New England Federalism*; H. S. COMMAGER, *Documents of American History*, pp. 209–211; J. T. ADAMS, *New England in the Republic*, pp. 281–301.

Questions Suggested by the Chapter

1. Why did John Randolph criticize President Jefferson? **2.** Why was Jefferson so eager to have Burr convicted? **3.** What different theories of Burr's intentions are there? **4.** On what ground was Burr acquitted? **5.** What does naturalization mean? **6.** What did Jefferson think would be the effect of the embargo? **7.** Explain why New England resisted the embargo. **8.** What two methods for securing our commercial rights were tried after the repeal of the embargo? **9.** How did Canada and Florida figure in the causes of the War of 1812? **10.** Why did we go to war with England and not with France in 1812? **11.** What was the origin of "The Star-Spangled Banner"? **12.** Who opposed the admission of the state of Louisiana to the Union, and why? **13.** Why was MacDonough's victory on Lake Champlain so important? **14.** What was the condition of the American navy at the close of the war? **15.** Contrast Washington's and Jefferson's methods of averting war. **16.** What was decided by the Treaty of Ghent? **17.** Outline the demands of the Hartford Convention. **18.** Why is the War of 1812 called our "second war for independence"?

CHAPTER ELEVEN

SECTIONAL RIVALRY

Two Currents. The War of 1812 revealed weaknesses in our government — in political authority, in defense, in finances, and in respect at home and abroad — almost as alarming as those of the days of the old Confederation of the 1780's. The fate of our country hung in the balance in the last months of the war. "The shock of a severe defeat at New Orleans or a complete rupture at Ghent might have loosed even the slender ties holding the administration together, and sent the fragments of a discredited government flying from the capital, just as the march of the British had dispersed the President and his cabinet in the preceding summer."

The first effect of the war, therefore, was to start a strong current of national sentiment to which every part of the country contributed. The time had come for North, South, and West to rally to the support of an adequate central government. The antinationalist protests of states or groups of states which had constantly found expression, from the Virginia and Kentucky Resolutions of 1798 to the Hartford Convention of 1814, were now condemned as manifesting a narrow and selfishly unpatriotic spirit.

Yet this current of enthusiastic nationalism was hardly under way when it was met, slowed up, and finally stopped by a countercurrent of sectional rivalry. By the middle of the decade of the 1820's the East, the South, and the West were arrayed against one another, each section conscious of its own economic interests and striving to secure them at the expense of the others. We shall first study the measures of the "new nationalism" of the three or four years immediately following the war, and then turn to the conflicting currents of sectional strife.

The Second National Bank. The Jeffersonian era may be said to have come to a close with President Madison's annual message of December, 1815, which called for a liberal provision for national defense, new frigates for the navy, a standing army, national aid for the construction of roads and canals, encouragement to manufacturers by a protective tariff, and even the re-establishment of the National Bank. The response of Congress to the President's message was hearty. A committee reported a bill for the charter of a bank with a capital of thirty-five million dollars, with all the features of Hamilton's bank of 1791. Southern statesmen who had argued against the constitutionality of the old bank now declared that any such discussion was "a useless consumption of time." Henry Clay, who had fought the recharter of the Bank in 1811, now descended from the Speaker's chair to support the Bank by the very arguments which Hamilton had used. The bill passed both houses of Congress and was signed by Madison on April 10, 1816.

During the preceding five years the currency of the country had been in a deplorable condition. State banks had multiplied threefold. They had been hailed as "the pillars of the nation" in 1811, but now they were denounced as the "caterpillars" of the nation. They had issued more than one hundred million dollars of bank notes, with only fifteen million dollars of real money in their vaults; and in the dark days of 1814 all but the well-managed banks of the Northeastern states had been forced to "suspend specie payment," that is, to refuse to redeem their notes in gold or silver. The creation of the new bank quickly remedied these evils. In less than three years over 40 per cent of the state bank notes disappeared from circulation, replaced by the national bank notes of uniform and guaranteed value; and the state banks which survived were obliged to resume specie payment.

The Tariff of 1816. Seventeen days after the Bank bill became law, Madison signed another bill which gave even stronger proof of the nationalistic spirit. While our foreign trade was suffering from embargo, nonintercourse, and war, large amounts of capital which had hitherto been invested in shipping were diverted to manufacturing. By the close of 1815 there were already one hundred and forty cotton mills within a radius of thirty miles of Providence, Rhode Island ; and pioneer industries of iron and of wool and cotton were scattered through the Ohio valley from Pittsburgh to Cincinnati. The British manufacturers, who had supplied the American market ever since colonial days, did not wish to lose it now. As Lord Brougham said in Parliament, they must "stifle in the cradle those rising manufactures in the United States which the war has forced into existence." Even before the Senate had ratified the peace treaty of Ghent, British ships were waiting off Sandy Hook laden with goods made by the cheap labor of England, to "dump" on the American market at lower prices than those at which the same goods could be produced in the new American factories and mills. In the single year the British sent over ninety million dollars' worth of merchandise to "stifle" our "rising manufactures."

In order to protect these "infant industries" against British competition, Congress passed a tariff act (April, 1816) which made permanent the double duties that had been imposed as a war measure in 1812. All the sections of the country contributed to the large majority by which the bill was passed in the House, North Carolina and Louisiana being the only states that did not cast a vote in its favor.

Measures of Defense. To avoid a repetition of the humiliating experience with the militia of the states during the war, Congress voted to maintain a regular army of ten thousand men, and the President appointed Jacob Brown and Andrew Jackson as major generals for the Northern and Southern sections respectively. Jefferson's useless gunboats were sold, and appropriations were made for new warships to guard our coasts and our shipping. Altogether, about four and a half million dollars was voted for the army and navy. Our coast defenses were strengthened, our interior forts were remanned, taxes were levied on foreign vessels using our ports, and only ships of American registry were allowed to engage in trade between one port of the United States and another.

The Election of 1816. The popular approval of the nationalistic program of 1816 was shown in the Presidential election in November. The declining Federalists, the party of the Hartford Convention, made but a feeble attempt to recover the control of the government by the aristocratic faction of "the rich, the wellborn and the able." Their candidate, Rufus King, of New York, spoke of his canvass as "a fruitless struggle." "The Federalists of our age," he confessed mournfully, "must be content with the past." All that remained to them, he said to his son, was "to support the least wicked section of the Republicans in case of a division among them." Massachusetts, Connecticut, and Delaware were the only states that cast their electoral votes (34) for King. The 183 votes from the other nineteen states of the Union went to the Republican candidate, James Monroe of Virginia. It was the last time that the Federalists put up a candidate for the Presidency. Their party was dead.

The Need for Improved Roads. One of the lessons of the war was the need for better means of transporting goods and troops. The soldiers of Hull, Harrison, Scott, and Jackson had to toil through forests and carry their supplies over rough trails through the wilderness. The farm products of the growing West could find an outlet only by slow and expensive haulage across the Alleghenies or by the long voyage down the Mississippi and through the Gulf of Mexico. It cost one hundred and fifty dollars a ton and took a month to carry goods from Baltimore to Cincinnati. The roads in the Ohio valley were so poor that it did not pay to raise grain or hogs fifty miles from a navigable river. Peter B. Porter, of New York, warned the country, in a speech in Congress in 1811, that the Union might separate into an eastern and a western half unless measures were speedily taken to bind together the farmers on one side of the mountains and the manufacturers and merchants on the other; and President Madison, in his last annual message (December, 1816), urged Congress to turn its attention to "a comprehensive system of roads and canals such as will have the effect of drawing more closely together every part of our country."

Calhoun's Bonus Bill. A few days later John C. Calhoun introduced a bill to devote the $1,500,000 bonus which the Bank was to pay for its charter, together with the interest which the government was to receive on its $7,000,000 of Bank stock, to such "internal improvements" as the building of roads and canals. "We are great and rapidly, I was about to say fearfully, growing," said Calhoun. "The extent of our country exposes us to the greatest of all calamities next to the loss of liberty — *disunion.* . . . Let us bind the Republic together with roads and canals." The Bonus Bill passed Congress in February, 1817. It reached Madison the day before his retirement from office and was vetoed by him, not because he disapproved of its object but because he thought that an amendment to the Constitution would be necessary to give Congress the right to spend the public money for purposes not set down among its powers. Madison's successor Monroe felt the same way; and since there was no hope of getting a two-thirds vote in Congress to override the Presidential veto, the projects for internal improvements at national expense fell through. Such projects were taken up by the states, however, the most notable of them being the Erie Canal connecting the Great Lakes with the Hudson River.[1]

Adjustments with Great Britain and Spain. Not only the acts of Congress but the negotiations of the State Department and the decisions of the Supreme Court strengthened the national government in the years immediately following the war. Monroe's Secretary of State, John Quincy Adams, was one of the ablest officials in our country's history. In 1817 we entered

[1] The Erie Canal is a monument to the energetic governor of New York, De Witt Clinton. It was begun on July 4, 1817, and completed in 1825, when Clinton staged the pageant of "the marriage of the Lakes and the Atlantic" by pouring a cask of water brought from Lake Erie into New York Harbor. The canal, constructed at a cost to the state of seven million dollars, immediately reduced freight rates from Buffalo to New York from one hundred dollars to fifteen dollars a ton and doubled the value of farm products in western New York and the Ohio valley. It stimulated the growth of the cities on the Lakes (Buffalo, Cleveland, Detroit, Chicago) in rivalry with the river cities of Pittsburgh, Cincinnati, and St. Louis, and made New York the great commercial metropolis of the country.

MISSOURI TERR.

MISSISSIPPI TERRITORY

Huntsville
Oct. 12, 1813

✗ Horseshoe Bend

SOUTH CAROLINA

GEORGIA

✝ Ft. Jackson
Apr. 18, 1814

June 1, 1818

Ft. Scott, March 9, 1818

LOUISIANA

Mississippi R.

Pearl R.

Mobile
Aug. 15, 1814

Alabama R.

Chattahoochee R.

Savannah R.

E A S T

St. Marks

Suwanee
F. Apr. 17, 1818

New Orleans
Dec. 2, 1814

Pensacola
May 24, 1818

Ft. Gadsden
March 16, 1818
May 2, 1818

F L O R I D A

GULF OF MEXICO

- - - *Jackson's routes*

J A C K S O N   I N   F L O R I D A

into an agreement with England (maintained to this day) by which each country pledged itself not to keep vessels of war on the Great Lakes; and the next year we made a treaty running the boundary line between the United States and Canada along the forty-ninth parallel from the Lake of the Woods to the Rocky Mountains (map, p. 222) and providing for the joint occupation of the Oregon territory from the Rockies to the Pacific for a period of ten years.

The most satisfactory stroke of diplomacy in Monroe's administration, however, was the settlement of the long-standing quarrel with Spain. That power had promised, in the Pinckney Treaty of 1795 (p. 199), to prevent the Indians of Florida from marauding our borders, but had miserably failed to keep its word. Acting on instructions from Washington to pursue the Indians into Spanish territory if necessary, General Jackson swept across East Florida, capturing the Spanish strongholds of Pensacola, Gadsden, and St. Marks, executing two British agents who were inciting the Indians to murder and pillage, and returned to Tennessee in May, 1818, leaving Florida a conquered province. Secretary Adams, though not approving all of Jackson's acts, upheld him against the criticism of Secretary of War Calhoun and other members of the cabinet, and persuaded the President to send an ultimatum to Spain. "The duty of this government to protect the persons and property of our fellow citizens on the borders of the United States is imperative — it *must* be discharged," wrote Adams to our minister at Madrid.

Confronted with this ultimatum and embarrassed by the revolt of her colonies in Central and South America, Spain decided to abandon Florida to the United States. The treaty of cession was signed at Washington in 1819. We agreed to assume the claims of our citizens against Spain for damage done to our commerce during the Napoleonic Wars, to the amount of about five million dollars. By the same treaty the boundary line between the Louisiana Purchase territory and the Spanish domain to the west of it, which had not been determined at the time of the purchase in 1803, was fixed by a line running in a stairlike course from the mouth of the Sabine River to the point where the forty-second parallel of latitude meets the Pacific coast (map, p. 222). A few years later (1824) Adams negotiated a treaty with Russia in which that power agreed to accept the parallel of 54° 40′ as the southern limit of its province of Alaska.

John Marshall's Decisions. As a final contribution to the trend of nationalism in these years we must notice a series of decisions by the Supreme Court under its great Federalist Chief Justice, John Marshall. Alexander Hamilton had thought that the Federal judiciary would be the weakest department of our government, because it had control of "neither the purse nor the sword." But it turned out to be the strongest department, since, as guardian and interpreter of the Constitution, the Supreme Court has the final say as to what is or is not the law of the land. There is no appeal from its decision.

We have already seen that in the case of Marbury *v.* Madison (1803) the Court ruled that a part of an act of Congress was unconstitutional (p. 215). In Fletcher *v.* Peck (1810) Marshall

JOHN MARSHALL

R.S. Supreme Court overruled State Courts

and his colleagues had also annulled a law of the state legislature
of Georgia. But until the end of the War of 1812 only three
or four important cases had come before the Court. Now, however, with the attention of the country turned to its own internal development, the cases came thick and fast.

In Martin *v*. Hunter's Lessee (1816) Marshall overruled the
highest court of Virginia in its contention that the case could
not be appealed to the Supreme Court. Three years later, in the
Dartmouth College case, he annulled a law of the legislature of
New Hampshire altering the charter of the college, on the ground
that the charter was a "contract" and that states were forbidden by the Constitution (Art. I, Sect. 10) to "pass any law
impairing the obligation of contracts." In the same year (1819)
came Marshall's most famous decision, in the case of McCulloch
v. Maryland, in which the Court forbade the state of Maryland

to lay a tax on the business of the branch of the United States Bank in Baltimore. "The power to tax is the power to destroy," said Marshall, and no state had the right to control or hinder the operations of a national institution established within its borders. Finally, in the famous "Steamboat Case" of Gibbons *v.* Odgen (1824) the Court destroyed the monopoly granted to Robert Livingston and Robert Fulton by the legislature of New York to control the navigation of the Hudson and of New York harbor and bay. All these decisions of the Court strengthened the power of the national government at the expense of the states.

The "Era of Good Feeling." A few weeks after his inauguration President Monroe set out for a tour of the North and West. His reception in New England was so enthusiastic that a witty writer compared it to "the adoration of the Wise Men of the East." In Boston, the very citadel of Federalism, honors were heaped upon this friend of Jefferson's, who had done so much to encourage "Mr. Madison's war." The Boston *Centinel*, which had appeared with mourning borders when Jefferson was elected, now spoke of Monroe as the herald of "an era of good feeling." The phrase pleased the President, who repeated it frequently on his tour until it caught the fancy of the American people. It has been used ever since to denote the period of Monroe's Presidency. A happy augury of the national spirit was the raising of our new flag over the Capitol on April 13, 1818.[1] When the election of 1820 approached, there was no rival candidate to oppose Monroe in the field. The Federalists had been merged in the nationalized Republican party. Monroe was re-elected with only one dissenting electoral vote.

Sectional Interests. We turn now to the other side of the picture. In spite of the wave of national enthusiasm which fol-

---

[1] On June 14 (Flag Day), 1777, Congress had adopted the first American flag — thirteen alternate stripes of white and red, and a circle of thirteen white stars on a blue square in the upper left-hand corner. By an act of April 4, 1818, it was provided that a new star should be added for each new state admitted to the Union. At first the stars were arranged in the form of a large star, but later they were set in horizontal lines on the field of blue. There are now six lines of eight stars each, representing the forty-eight states.

lowed the War of 1812, our country was far from being the unified nation that it is today. There were no railroads, automobiles, air routes, telegraphs, telephones, or radios to bind the remotest parts of the land together in commerce, ideas, and mutual acquaintance.

We must think of the country in the years of Monroe's administration as a great geographical framework containing rather isolated communities, in which different types of inhabitants and occupations and inherited traditions prevailed. These differences gave rise to conflicting ideas on a great number of questions. Were the agricultural or the commercial and industrial interests the more important? What kind of currency or what types of banks were preferable? Should the government at Washington help to develop the more "backward" parts of the country or leave them to fend for themselves? Did "democracy" mean that all adult male citizens, regardless of their birth, wealth, or religious opinions, should have the privilege of voting and of holding office? Had the national government the right to forbid slavery in the territory of the United States west of the Mississippi?

The growth of our population and prosperity after 1815 served only to intensify the devotion of each of the sections of the country to what it felt to be its own peculiar needs; and, quite naturally, each section did its best to shape the policy of the government to favor its own needs. This is why practically all the nationalistic measures which we have noted in the first half of this chapter (tariff, Bank, government aid in road-building and canal-building,[1] the expanding power of the Federal judiciary) became subjects of bitter controversy as the decade of the 1820's proceeded. The "era of good feeling" yielded rapidly to an era of bad feeling.

The Industrial East. We have already seen what a change the war made in the economic life of the region north of the

---

[1] By 1820 Congress had passed ten acts appropriating altogether over one and a half million dollars for such "internal improvements." Several of the states also (New York, Pennsylvania, South Carolina) spent large sums for roads, canals, and river improvements.

A SOUTHERN MANSION

Potomac by diverting capital from shipping into manufacturing. New England, New York, New Jersey, and eastern Pennsylvania became the center of an industrial section of the country which gradually extended out into the Ohio valley. For a time the shipping interests of the seaport centers, such as Salem, Boston, Newport, New York, Philadelphia, and Baltimore, tried to encourage foreign commerce as against the development of manufactures. They wanted freedom of trade. Daniel Webster, of Massachusetts, for example, voted against the tariff bills until 1828. But the industrial interests gained steadily, and by the middle 1820's they became the dominant interests of the section. The manufacturers wanted, first of all, a high tariff to protect their industries against British competition. In order to have an abundant supply of laborers for their mills and factories, they favored immigration and opposed the rapid settlement of the West, which drew men off into the wilderness. They wished to see a large population growing up within easy reach

ELI WHITNEY AND THE COTTON GIN

of the manufacturing centers, so that they might have a market for the consumption of the goods which they produced. Finally, they wanted a sound currency and banking system to protect business credit.

The Planters of the South. The interests of the South were quite different from those of the North. They had been determined by the invention of a Connecticut schoolteacher named Eli Whitney, who had been obliged to go South for his health. As he watched the Negro slaves on a Georgia plantation laboriously picking the seeds from the cotton fiber, his Yankee ingenuity led him to devise a machine which enabled a man to clean three hundred pounds of cotton from the seeds in the same time that it had taken to clean a single pound by hand. Whitney's cotton "gin" (engine) was one of the most fateful inventions in history; for it made the production of cotton so profitable that the plantation system, and therewith slave labor, was fixed upon the South. The cotton crop increased from 2,000,000 pounds in 1791 to 40,000,000 pounds in 1801, to 80,000,000 pounds in 1811, and to 177,000,000 pounds in 1821. Because cotton culture exhausts the soil rapidly, the planters were always looking for fresh lands. They quickly spread into the fertile regions of the Mississippi Territory (which Andrew Jackson had freed from the Indian danger), and by 1821 more than a third of the cotton crop was being raised in the states west of the Alleghenies.

Since manufacturing was excluded from the South by the plantation system, there was no need for a protective tariff. The planter bought his clothing, tools, furniture, and other manufactured goods from the North or from Europe. The tariff was a burden upon him, because it raised the price of every such article that he bought, thus enriching the Northern manufacturer at his expense. That the tariff made higher wages possible and so increased the buying power of the laborers was no argument in its favor; for his laborers were slaves to whom he paid no wages, but for whom he had to supply tools, clothing, and food. He was not particularly interested in the prosperity of the New England cotton mills, because they used only about one fourth of the Southern cotton crop. The planter's chief markets were in Europe, and he wanted to exchange his cotton freely for the manufactured goods of Europe and the North at prices which were not increased 10, 20, or 30 per cent by the tariff.

The New West. In contrast to the industrial system of the East and the plantation system of the South, the West presented a pioneer society, with its own peculiar needs and interests. The ever westward-moving frontier has been one of the most important influences in American history. The frontier bred a type of settlers who, in their struggle to subdue the wild forests and the wilder savages, became self-reliant, resourceful, and courageous. As it had little attraction for people of wealth or social distinction, it developed a stark democracy. One man was as good as another politically and socially. The real test was whether he could swing an ax, tame a horse, bring down a squirrel with his long-barreled rifle, meet the wily attack of the Indian, and keep steady under a load of corn whisky. When the

MOVING INTO THE WEST

hindrances to the settlement of the West were removed (pp. 241, 252 note), a great flood of emigrants poured through the passes of the Allegheny Mountains and down the "western waters" to the rich bottom lands of the Mississippi Valley. "The old America seems to be breaking up and moving westward," wrote an English visitor in 1817.

Five new Western states were added to the Union in six years: Indiana (1816), Mississippi (1817), Illinois (1818), Alabama (1819), and Missouri (1821). In the decade 1810–1820 these communities were growing by leaps and bounds, while the population of the older states remained almost stationary.[1] By the census of 1820 more than a quarter of our population (2,600,000 out of 9,600,000) dwelt in the trans-Allegheny states, which

[1] The census reports for 1810 and 1820 give the following figures:

	MASSACHUSETTS	NEW YORK	VIRGINIA	INDIANA	MISSOURI	MISSISSIPPI
1810	472,040	995,049	974,600	24,520	19,783	40,352
1820	523,287	1,373,812	1,065,386	147,178	66,586	75,448

sent 16 of the 46 Senators and 47 of the 213 Representatives to Congress. The greatest need of these Western communities was better means of transportation to get their surplus products to the Eastern markets. Being too poor themselves to build the necessary roads and canals, they looked to the government for help. But, just as the Southern planters resented being taxed by a tariff to encourage Northern manufacturers, so the Eastern capitalists did not relish being taxed by "internal improvement" schemes to develop the Western country, which was attracting emigrants by the thousands and so making labor scarce and costly.

Clay's "American System." Nationally-minded statesmen, like Henry Clay and John Quincy Adams, hoped that the conflicting interests of the various sections might be reconciled. Clay especially urged that we should no longer have regard to Europe but should build up "a genuine American policy." He would encourage the manufactures of the North by a high tariff and so create a large industrial population to consume the agricultural products of the West and to spin and weave the raw cotton of the South. From the money brought into the Treasury by the tariff duties he would spend generous sums for the improvement of roads, canals, and rivers, to bring the food products of the West to the industrial centers of the North and the cotton and tobacco plantations of the South. He favored the National Bank as the guardian of a sound and uniform currency.

But the attempt to satisfy all the sections at one time was as hopeless as squaring the circle. Each section saw the advantages to the others and the disadvantages to itself. The North approved the tariff and the Bank, but not internal improvements. The South was glad to get its bacon and flour cheaper, but that did not offset the higher cost of the tariff-protected manufactured goods. The West was grateful for the promise of better roads, but, as a debtor community, wanted the abundant and cheap money and credit furnished by the state banks.

The Slavery Question. Before these countercurrents of sectional interests grew strong enough to stem the current of

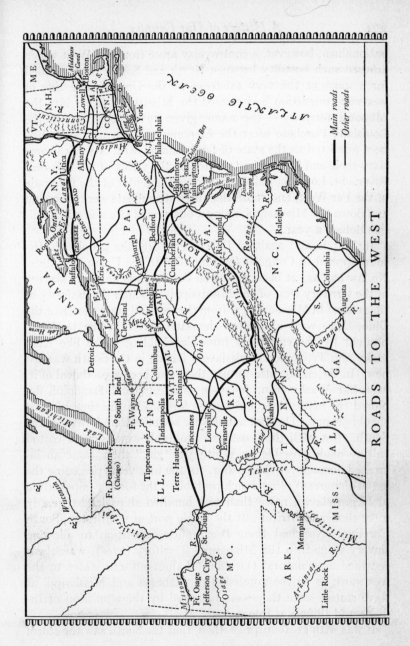

ROADS TO THE WEST

nationalism, however, a controversy arose from the West which aroused such hostility between North and South as threatened for a moment the very existence of the Union. The tide of westward migration had crossed the Mississippi River into the Missouri territory — the name given to all the rest of the Louisiana Purchase after the extreme southern part of it had been admitted as the state of Louisiana in 1812. By 1818 some sixty thousand settlers had pushed up the valley of the Missouri River. St. Louis had already become the center of the fur trade of the Far West, and more than fifty steamboats were plying up and down the Mississippi, doing a business of two and a half million dollars a year.

In March, and again in December, 1818, the people of Missouri applied to Congress for admission to the Union as a state. No law had as yet been passed on the question of Negro slavery in the territory west of the Mississippi. Though the majority of the settlers in Missouri were from the free-soil states north of the Ohio, there were about ten thousand slaves in the territory, brought by the emigrants from slaveholding states like Kentucky and Tennessee. Antislavery feeling in the South was not new. In the eighteenth century there had been a good deal of it. Men like Washington, Jefferson, Madison, and Randolph deplored the institution, and looked forward to the time when it should die out. The first antislavery societies were formed in the South. But with the great and profitable expansion of cotton culture made possible by Whitney's "gin," there came an increased demand for slave labor. In the four years preceding the act of Congress (1807) which prohibited the further importation of Negro slaves, more than two hundred ships landed nearly forty thousand Africans at the single port of Charleston, South Carolina. Nor had there been much opposition to allowing slavery to go into the Mississippi Territory (1798), which was regarded as a natural extension of the Southern states to the westward, or to the admission of Alabama and Mississippi as slave states, since they were balanced by the admission of Indiana and Illinois as free states.

It was with great surprise, then, that the South saw the storm of protest against the extension of slavery which was roused by the bill for the admission of Missouri. Representative James Tallmadge of New York immediately proposed an amendment to the bill "that the further introduction of slavery . . . be prohibited . . . and that all children born within the said state after admission thereof into the Union shall be free at the age of twenty-five years." The amendment passed the House but was promptly rejected by the Senate; and Congress expired on March 4, 1819, with Missouri's application for statehood still pending.

The Missouri Debates. During the summer and autumn of 1819 the question of permitting slavery to enter Missouri absorbed the attention of the country. State legislatures and heated mass meetings passed resolutions on the subject, and when Congress met in December it was overwhelmed with petitions for and against the Tallmadge amendment. Passion ran high, and the words "disunion" and "civil war" were boldly uttered. The aged Jefferson wrote that the sudden strife woke him like the alarm of a fire-bell in the night. John Quincy Adams set down in his *Diary* that the battle between North and South might as well come now on this issue of slavery; and Howell Cobb, of Georgia, warned Tallmadge on the floor of Congress that he had kindled "a fire which only seas of blood could extinguish."

For several reasons the question of the admission of Missouri with or without slavery was of special importance. In the first place, there was an equal number (eleven each) of free and slave states in the Union at the close of 1819, making an even balance in the Senate between the sections north and south of Mason and Dixon's line. Secondly, the admission of Missouri with slavery would set a precedent for future states to be carved out of the Louisiana Purchase. Thirdly, the purchase treaty of 1803 had guaranteed to the inhabitants of the territory "protection of their liberties, property and religion." Could Congress now in fairness deprive the planters in Missouri of their "property" in slaves by providing for the emancipation of all the Negroes born in the new state? Did the clause of the Constitution which reads, "New States may be admitted by Congress into this Union" (Art. IV, Sect. 3) give Congress the power to prescribe what kind of property the inhabitants of those states should hold or not hold? And did the clause giving Congress the power "to dispose of and make all needful rules and regulations respecting the territory or other property belonging to the United States" mean to include as "needful" the "regulation" of the occupations and the domestic relations of the inhabitants? The Northern orators in the Senate answered these questions in the affirmative. They pointed to the Northwest Ordinance of 1787 (p. 172), which had excluded slavery from the territory north of the Ohio. The Southern orators were as determined on the other side. Congress might admit or refuse to admit Missouri, they conceded, but, if admitted, the state must be as free as Massachusetts or South Carolina to choose its own form of social and economic life. Otherwise, it would not be the equal of its sister states. The territory of the United States was the common possession of all the states, and the slaveholding ones had just as much right to extend their "peculiar institution" into that common territory as the free-soil ones had to send their settlers into it. It was not for Congress to decide whether a state should be slave or free, nor for fanatics of the North to cast aspersions upon the social system of the South!

The Missouri Compromise. A way out of the dangerous situation was found in the spring of 1820. Maine, which had been a part of Massachusetts ever since the Bay Colony had purchased it from the heirs of Sir Ferdinando Gorges in 1677, had got the consent of Massachusetts to a separation. Accordingly, in December, 1819, Maine, with an antislavery constitution already framed, applied to Congress for admission as a state of the Union. The Senate now combined the Maine and Missouri bills and substituted for the Tallmadge amendment one by Senator Thomas of Illinois excluding slavery "forever" from the Louisiana Purchase north of the parallel 36° 30′ (the southern boundary of Missouri), except for the state of Missouri itself. The House, by the close vote of 90 to 87, accepted this compromise both because it still preserved the equal balance of the free and the

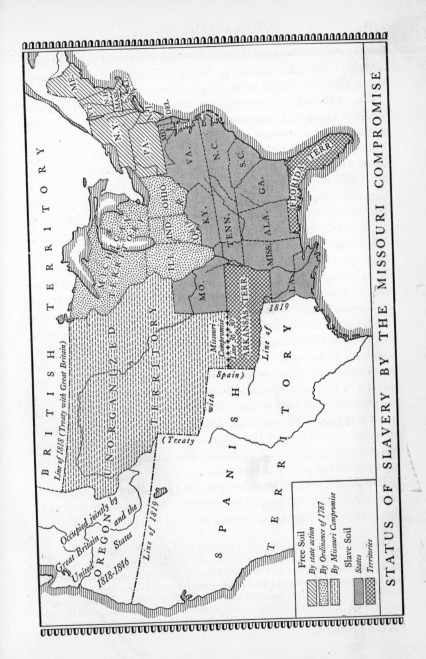

STATUS OF SLAVERY BY THE MISSOURI COMPROMISE

BRITISH TERRITORY

Line of 1818 (Treaty with Great Britain)

ME.

N.H.
MASS.
CONN.
N.Y.
R.I.
N.J.
PA.
DEL.

VA.
N.C.
S.C.
GA.
FLORIDA TERR.
KY.
TENN.
ALA.
MISS.
LA.

OHIO
IND.
ILL.

MICHIGAN TERRITORY

MO.
ARKANSAS TERR.

Missouri Compromise
Line 36° 30'

Line of 1819

SPANISH TERRITORY

UNORGANIZED TERRITORY

(Treaty with Spain)

Occupied jointly by
Great Britain and the
United States
1818-1846

OREGON

Line of 1819

Free Soil
  By state action
  By Ordinance of 1787
  By Missouri Compromise
Slave Soil
  States
  Territories

slave states and because it made free soil of five sixths of the vast Louisiana Purchase territory. Early in March, 1820, President Monroe signed the bill admitting the two states.[1]

Why were all the seventy-five votes in the House from the South in favor of a compromise which still recognized the right of Congress to exclude slavery from territory of the United States, and by far the largest part of such territory at that? There are several possible answers. First, the South may have regarded "a bird in the hand as worth two in the bush." With Missouri safely in the Union as a slave state, they would take their chances on getting Congress to admit slavery into new states to the north and west of Missouri when the time came for their formation. That time seemed very remote in 1820. An army officer traveling in upper Louisiana in that year reported that the country was a desert "almost wholly unfit for cultivation." Indeed, as late as 1850 there were only about a thousand white inhabitants in the territory dedicated to freedom by the Missouri Compromise. Again, the South may have yielded, as Professor Channing suggests, because of its sincere love of the Union. The national enthusiasm was perhaps at its peak in this year of the undisputed re-election of President Monroe. Neither section of the country could look with anything but horror on the possibility of civil strife. Nevertheless, the compromise was but a stopgap. The South still held to its belief in the righteousness and desirability of the extension of slavery, and the North was equally convinced that slavery was a curse which should be kept out of the national territories.

The Monroe Doctrine. In spite of their diverging interests, however, all the sections of the country were proud of the prestige which the increasing population and wealth of the United

[1] Missouri was not actually admitted until August, 1821. The reason for the delay was that she put a clause in her constitution excluding free Negroes from the state. Since Negroes had the privileges of citizens in some states of the North, this clause violated the first paragraph of Article IV, Section 2, of the national constitution. It was not until Henry Clay had negotiated a second Missouri Compromise, by which the state promised never to interpret the clause in such a way as to deprive a citizen of his "privileges and immunities," that Missouri was finally admitted.

States enabled them to take among the nations. This confidence was shown nowhere more clearly than in the proclamation of the Monroe Doctrine.

The "Holy Alliance" had been formed in 1815 by the sovereigns of Russia, Austria, and Prussia, for the purpose of restoring the absolute, divine-right authority of the thrones which had been so shaken by the French Revolution and the Napoleonic Wars. During those wars the Spanish colonies in America, from the Isthmus of Panama to Cape Horn, had thrown off the yoke of the mother country and declared themselves independent republics. When the Alliance (made the Quadruple Alliance by the accession of France) began to listen to the plea of the king of Spain for help in recovering his rebellious colonies, our government, at the suggestion of the British foreign minister Canning, stepped in to prevent such a move.

In his annual message to Congress, on December 2, 1823, President Monroe declared that this western hemisphere was no longer open to colonization by European powers and that any attempt of those powers to extend their system (the Holy Alliance) to any portion of the American continents would be "viewed as the manifestation of an unfriendly disposition toward the United States." We would not meddle with European politics, and in return Europe must not disturb the political status of the republics on this side of the ocean. Thus, from recognizing the independence of our sister American republics in 1822, we proceeded to guarantee that independence against European interference.

The Monroe Doctrine of "America for the Americans" has ever since been regarded a cornerstone of our foreign policy. It has been emphasized by every President since Monroe, and American public opinion compelled the insertion of an article respecting the Monroe Doctrine into the Covenant of the League of Nations in 1919. But while forbidding Europe to interfere with the Latin-American republics, the Doctrine said nothing about interference with their politics or finances or wars and revolutions by the United States. Such interference, as we shall see in later pages, has been very frequent since the end of the nineteenth century, and it has been generally disliked by Latin America. Our sister republics to the south want our good will, and even our protection against European aggression if such protection should be necessary; but they do not want to be dictated to and overshadowed by "the great colossus of the North." They would convert the Monroe Doctrine into a Pan-American doctrine, in which all the American republics, including the United States, stand on an equal footing.

The Favorite Sons. The campaign for the election of a successor to Monroe in 1824 showed how strong the rivalry of the sections had become. It was not a contest of parties, for since the fall of the Federalists in 1816 the Republican party had stood without a rival in the field. It was, rather, a struggle between North, South, and West to get possession of the government. Each section had its favorite sons to put forward. The New England states nominated the experienced and conscientious Secretary of State, John Quincy Adams of Massachusetts. Tennessee put up her great military hero Andrew Jackson, who was acclaimed by mass meetings in various parts of the country. Kentucky put forward her brilliant orator and statesman Henry Clay, who was promptly accepted by the legislatures of Missouri, Illinois, Ohio, and Louisiana. South Carolina supported her most distinguished son, John C. Calhoun. President Monroe's own preference was for his Secretary of the Treasury, William H. Crawford of Georgia.

Long before the voting took place in November, 1824, it was almost certain that no one of these five candidates would receive a majority in the Electoral College.[1] As it turned out, Jackson had 99 votes (32 less than a majority), Adams 84, Crawford 41, and Clay 37. According to the Constitution

---

[1] It was not until seven years later (1831) that the present method was adopted — that of selecting the Presidential candidate in a national nominating convention several months before the election. It is interesting to note, however, that in the winter of 1824 this method was proposed by a paper in Pennsylvania: "We believe that the best method would be a convention of delegates from all the states of the Union." Only, said the writer, this would be "entirely impracticable from the immense extent of our country and the great expense." There were no railroads as yet, and it took two weeks to make the journey from St. Louis or New Orleans to Washington.

ALASKA

CANADA

OREGON

UNITED
STATES

MEXICO

ATLANTIC

OCEAN

WEST INDIES

BELIZE

CENTRAL
AMERICA

COLOMBIA

BR. GUIANA
DUT. GUIANA
FR. GUIANA

PACIFIC

PERU

BRAZIL

OCEAN

CHILE

LA PLATA

PARAGUAY

English territory

Latin-American Republics

Russian territory

Territory claimed by England
and the United States

THE AMERICAN CONTINENTS IN 1823

(Amendment XII), the House of Representatives then had to choose a President from the three highest names on the list, each state having a single vote and a majority of the states (twelve) being necessary for a choice. Clay, being out of the race, threw his support to Adams rather than to Jackson, both because the former was more in sympathy with his own views on the tariff, the Bank, internal improvements, and other points of the "American System," and because he did not wish to see his Western rival, the "military chieftain," in the White House. Adams won on the first ballot in the House, receiving the votes of thirteen states, as opposed to 7 for Jackson and 4 for Crawford. It was a perfectly fair and constitutional election, and Andrew Jackson was one of the first to congratulate Adams on his inauguration day.

The "Corrupt Bargain" Charge However, when Adams appointed Clay as his Secretary of State, the wrath of the Jackson men flared up. They accused Clay of having sold his support to Adams in return for the promise of the first place in the cabinet. It was a lie. Clay had declared two months before the electoral votes were counted that he should support Adams. But Jackson believed the charge to the day of his death, twenty years later. He resigned his seat in the Senate and began a four-year campaign to oust Adams and Clay and the whole "dynasty of secretaries" from power, and to restore the government to servants of the people's choice. His able lieutenants in all parts of the country kept harping on the theme that Jackson had been unjustly deprived of the Presidency in 1825. He had received the largest number of electoral and popular votes. What had become of democracy if the will of the people could be thwarted by the maneuvers of the House and a corrupt bargain between two ambitious politicians? As a matter of fact, the claim that Jackson was "the people's choice" in 1824 had hardly any more foundation than the charge of a "corrupt bargain." Jackson did have, to be sure, some 153,000 popular votes to 114,000 for Adams. But in six states, containing a fourth of the population of the country, there was no popular vote at all. The Presidential electors were chosen by the legislatures in these six states, and the only one of them to give its vote to Jackson was South Carolina.

The "Tariff of Abominations." Not only was Adams's administration vexed by the continuous campaign of slander waged by the Jackson managers, but it met with opposition in Congress to every one of its policies. The Republican party, which had seemed so united in the "era of good feeling," was now split into two wings, or factions. The Adams-Clay wing, or the National Republicans, continued to support the nationalistic policies of the decade following the War of 1812; while the Calhoun-Crawford wing returned to the old states-rights doctrines of Jefferson, opposing the tariff as detrimental to the interests of the South and realizing the danger to slavery in the extension of the national power over the territories.

The unpopular Adams was the victim of this clash of factions. Like his father, John Adams, he refused to play politics when all the men around him were absorbed in the game. He would not dismiss officials who opposed him, even a member of his cabinet. The Senate, presided over by Calhoun (on whom the sections had united for the Vice-Presidency), held up his appointments, Congress frowned on his plans for internal improvements, and the governor of Georgia defied him when he tried to defend the claims of the Cherokee Indians to their treaty lands within the state.

But the most troublesome subject during his whole term was the tariff. The Northern manufacturers had kept up the rates in the bills of 1820 and 1824; and in their convention at Harrisburg, Pennsylvania, in 1827, they demanded still higher protection. The South protested vigorously. They were not strong enough to keep a new tariff bill out of Congress in 1828, but they resorted to a shrewd trick to defeat it. Instead of seeking to lower the rates, they joined with the farmers of the West in adding duties on the raw materials (such as wool, hemp, flax, and iron ore) which the manufacturers needed, hoping thereby to get the Northern industrialists disgusted enough with the bill to vote against it. But the trick did not work. The North swallowed the bill with all its inconvenient additions. It passed both houses of Congress by narrow margins and was signed by President Adams on May 19, 1828. When this "Tariff of Abominations," which carried the highest duties in our history until the Civil War, was passed, flags were flown at half-mast in Charleston. Southern orators advised boycotting all trade with the protected states and even recommended the resignation of the Southern members from Congress. McDuffie of South Carolina called the Stamp Act of 1765 and the tariff of 1828 "kindred acts of despotism." And an excited journalist wrote that it was high time "to prepare for a secession from the Union." Vice-President Calhoun presented to the legislature of South Carolina his famous "Exposition and Protest" (December, 1828), in which he argued that the tariff act was unconstitutional and grossly sectional. He revived the doctrine of the Virginia and Kentucky Resolutions of 1798, declaring that the states should be the judges of whether or not Congress was overstepping its powers. Any state might challenge an act of Congress and appeal to its sister states for a verdict. Then Congress must secure the votes of three fourths of the states in ratification of an amendment giving it the power in dispute.

The Triumph of Andrew Jackson. The year of the "Tariff of Abominations" was also the year of the Presidential election, and the Jackson men joined heartily in the game of boosting the Western rates, in the hope of discrediting Adams with the Eastern manufacturers. The sarcastic John Randolph remarked that the tariff bill "had nothing to do with manufactures except the manufacture of a President." In the election, which took place a few weeks before Calhoun laid his "Exposition and Protest" before the legislature of his state, Jackson won a complete victory. Every state west of the Alleghenies and south of the Potomac gave him its entire vote, and he had all the electors of Pennsylvania, 20 out of 36 in New York, and 5 out of 11 in Maryland besides — a total of 178 to 83 for Adams. Calhoun, who had been re-elected Vice-President, advised the South to wait, before taking any radical action on the tariff, to see what the new President would do.

So the industrial North and the agricultural South stood facing each other in a hostile truce while the West celebrated its boisterous triumph. It had put an end to the "dynasty" of aristocrats and scholars from Virginia and New England. For the first time in our history, a President from west of the Alleghenies, a plain man of the people, frontiersman, Indian-fighter, with no training in political science and with the passions and prejudices of "the untamed West," would sit in the seat of Washington, Jefferson, and Adams. On inauguration day the "common people" flocked from hundreds of miles to invade the White House, standing with muddy boots on the damask-covered chairs, spilling orange punch on the costly carpets, and almost suffocating the old hero of New Orleans as they pressed round him to shake his hand. Dignified statesmen like Daniel Webster and Justice Story might deplore the opening of the reign of "King Mob," the disgusted Adams might slip out of the White House on the evening of March 3 and refuse to attend the inauguration of the "barbarian"[1] who was supplanting him; but the masses of the common people, the laborers and farmers and shopkeepers, into whose hands the ballot was being thrust,[2] rejoiced that with Andrew Jackson was inaugurated the rule of American democracy pure and undefiled.

[1] When Harvard College conferred the degree of Doctor of Laws upon President Jackson at its commencement exercises of June, 1833, Adams, then a member of the House of Representatives, declined to appear. "Myself an affectionate child of our Alma Mater," he wrote, "I would not be present to witness her disgrace in conferring her highest literary honors upon a barbarian who could not write a sentence of grammar and hardly could spell his own name"(!). It is interesting to note that exactly a century later (1933) criticisms of the same sort were heard when Harvard gave the same degree to another self-made man of the "people," ex-Governor Alfred E. Smith.

[2] Every one of the new states that came into the Union after the adoption of the Constitution (except Tennessee) had manhood suffrage from the day of its entrance; and by 1828 all but five of the original thirteen states had abolished property qualifications for voting or holding office. The number of voters in proportion to the population was increasing rapidly when Jackson came into the Presidency.

Terms to be Mastered

specie payments	protective tariff	Holy Alliance
internal improvements	the "American System"	"Exposition and Protest"
obligations of contracts	Tallmadge amendment	nationalism

For Supplementary Reading

J. W. Burgess, *The Middle Period*, chaps. i–viii; F. J. Turner, *The Rise of the New West* (American Nation Series, Vol. XIV); R. E. Riegel, *America Moves West*, chaps. xv–xvii; E. S. Corwin, *John Marshall and the Constitution* (Chronicles of America, Vol. XVI); Carl Schurz, *Henry Clay*, Vol. I, pp. 126–310; Jesse Macy, *The Antislavery Crusade* (Chronicles of America, Vol. XXVIII), chaps. i–v; J. A. Woodburn, *The Historical Significance of the Missouri Compromise* (American Historical Association Report, 1893, pp. 249–298); A. B. Hart, *The Monroe Doctrine, an Interpretation*; Edward Stanwood, *American Tariff Controversies in the Nineteenth Century*, chap. viii; H. S. Commager, *Documents of American History*, pp. 213–232; *America*, Vol. V, pp. 285–318; Hart, *Contemporaries*, Vol. III, Nos. 130–150; Muzzey, *Readings*, pp. 235–264.

Topics for Reports

1. Early Travel to the West. F. J. Turner, *The Frontier in American History*, chaps. iii–v; Constance Skinner, *Pioneers of the Old Southwest* (Chronicles of America, Vol. XVIII), chaps. v, x, xi; F. A. Ogg, *The Old Northwest* (Chronicles, Vol. XIX), chaps. vi, vii; Timothy Flint, *Recollections of the Last Ten Years* (1826); Morris Birbeck, *Notes on a Journey in America* (1827); James Hall, *Letters from the West* (1828); Muzzey, *Readings*, pp. 247–254.

2. American Antislavery Sentiment in the Eighteenth Century. J. F. Rhodes, *History of the United States from the Compromise of 1850*, Vol. I, pp. 12–27; Thomas Jefferson, *Notes on Virginia*; J. Macy, *The Antislavery Crusade*, chaps. i–iii; William Birney, *James G. Birney, His Life and Times*, Appendix C; Hart, *Contemporaries*, Vol. II, Nos. 102, 103, 106.

3. Modern Interpretations of the Monroe Doctrine. Reuben Clark, *The Monroe Doctrine* (Government Printing Office, Washington); D. Y. Thomas, *One Hundred Years of the Monroe Doctrine*; A. C. Coolidge, *The United States as a World Power*, pp. 95–110; J. B. Moore, *American Diplomacy*, pp. 152–167; *Harper's Magazine*, Vol. CIX, pp. 857 f.; W. R. Shepherd, *The Hispanic Nations of the New World* (Chronicles of America, Vol. L), chaps. xi, xii, and "The Monroe Doctrine Reconsidered," in *Political Science Quarterly*, Vol. XXXIX, pp. 35–66.

4. John Marshall's Famous Decision in McCulloch v. Maryland. A. J. Beveridge, *The Life of John Marshall*, Vol. IV, pp. 282–339; *America*, Vol. V, pp. 297–304; A. B. Magruder, *John Marshall* (American Statesmen Series), chap. x; G. Hunt, *Writings of James Madison*, Vol. VIII, pp. 447–453; Hart, *Contemporaries*, Vol. III, No. 133. Text of the decision in Commager, *Documents of American History*, pp. 213–220.

QUESTIONS SUGGESTED BY THE CHAPTER

1. What weaknesses in America did the War of 1812 reveal? 2. What effect did the war have on industries? 3. What was the object of the tariff of 1816? 4. What factors aided westward migration after the war? 5. What new states were admitted to the Union between 1815 and 1821? 6. Why was the admission of Missouri delayed for a year? 7. What was the object of the Bonus Bill? 8. Why did the Federalist party die out? 9. Why did Jackson invade East Florida? 10. Trace the boundary lines laid down by the treaty of 1818 with England; by that of 1819 with Spain. 11. What was Clay's "American System"? 12. Show how the South depended on the North, on the West, and on England. 13. Why was the Supreme Court's decision in Gibbons *v.* Ogden of great importance? 14. What change was made in our flag in 1818? 15. Why did not the Missouri Compromise settle the slavery question? 16. Distinguish between the Tallmadge and the Thomas amendment. 17. How did the protective tariff harm the South? 18. Why did the question of slavery in Missouri seem so much more important than the question of slavery in Alabama? 19. Was the Monroe Doctrine a law? a treaty? Did we violate it when we entered the World War? when Wilson signed the Treaty of Versailles? 20. Indicate to which of the following cases the Monroe Doctrine would apply: (*a*) a revolution in Chile setting up a king; (*b*) the immigration of Germans into Brazil; (*c*) a war between Peru and Colombia; (*d*) the overthrow of the Argentine government by a French expedition; (*e*) the establishment of a naval station on the coast of Venezuela by Japan. 21. Do you think Jackson was the "people's choice" in 1824? 22. Compare Calhoun's "Exposition and Protest" with Jefferson's Kentucky Resolutions. 23. Why was John Quincy Adams's administration beset with difficulties?

CHAPTER TWELVE

THE JACKSONIAN ERA

The New Democracy. The masses who hailed the advent of Andrew Jackson were not mistaken in their belief that a new type of democracy had come into power. The "revolution" of 1828 was more thorough than the "revolution" of 1800, because, while Jefferson held that the common man should be given the opportunity through education and training to fit himself to take part in the government, Jackson declared that such education and training were of trifling account. "The duties of all public officers are . . . so plain and simple," he said, "that men of intelligence may readily qualify themselves for their performance." Jefferson, the aristocratic Virginian scholar and statesman, believed that the competent should rule, subject always to the vigilant and free criticism of the people at large. Jackson, the assertive, self-made frontiersman, believed that government should be *by* the people as well as *for* the people, and hence that the offices should be "passed around," in order to give as many as possible a share. It was chiefly the growing influence of the new West that gave strength to the Jacksonian democracy. By 1828 nine of the twenty-four states of the Union lay west of the Allegheny Mountains, and they contained more than one third of the 12,600,000 inhabitants of the country. In these pioneer communities differences of social rank disappeared. The voice and opinion of the Western pioneer were worth as much as those of any aristocratic merchant or planter in Boston or Charleston. These Westerners were, in Professor Turner's phrase, "men with bark on." Though not one in a hundred had probably ever heard of Emerson, they would have readily agreed with his saying "Europe extends to the Alleghenies; America lies beyond."

The Labor Class. The West was not the only factor in the development of the new democracy, however. The growth of manufactures in the Eastern states since the second war with England had given rise to a laboring class (swelled by immigration from Europe) which was becoming conscious of its strength and was demanding legislation for its social and economic improvement. The factory system took away the independence of the worker and made him a cog in a great machine. He was no longer the master of his own tools but the servant of the expensive tools owned by the capitalists. He had to enter the factory gates when the whistle blew, and had to work from twelve to fifteen hours a day in such quarters and for such wages as the management provided. Women and children generally toiled beside the men to eke out a living. Women comprised half the operatives in the cotton mills of New England, and children of six or eight years of age worked from daylight to dark for a dollar a week, "growing up," as one pathetic petition put it, "as ignorant as Arabs of the desert."

Trade unions had existed for many years, and strikes had not been infrequent; but they were feeble and local affairs before the extension of the suffrage gave some political influence to the working class. In the very year of Jackson's election the trade unions of Philadelphia organized a Workingmen's party and put up candidates for local offices. What was more natural than that the class which was demanding higher wages, shorter hours of work, free public education, and more sanitary conditions in mills and factories should flock to the support of Andrew Jackson, the plain man of the people? It was their votes in the industrial section of the country that ensured his election. Without his votes from New York and Pennsylvania he would have been defeated.

Reform Movements. The age was marked also by a number of efforts for the improvement of the physical, moral, and mental condition of the people. Excessive drinking was a curse of American society in the early nineteenth century. Vast quantities of raw corn whisky were consumed by the Western frontiersmen, while rum, brandy, fiery punches, and strong wines were as common as butter or salt on the tables of the merchants and planters. Even the ordination of a minister of the Gospel often provided a sideboard stocked with a variety of strong liquors. It was in 1826 that the first organized movement for total abstinence was started in Boston. From that time on, temperance and total-abstinence societies spread rapidly through the country.

In 1827 a gifted Scotchwoman, Frances Wright, created a great sensation by appearing on the lecture platform, in a day when it was expected that women should be modestly busy in the kitchen or modestly idle in the parlor. "Fanny" Wright boldly discussed temperance, slavery, prison reform, the care of the insane, and the rights of women. In spite of ridicule and insult, other apostles of the liberation of women from social and legal bondage, like the Grimké sisters of South Carolina and the eloquent Quakeress Lucretia Mott, pleaded their cause from the lecture platform.

In 1828 William Ladd, of New Hampshire, founded the American Peace Society. This society anticipated by nearly a century the program of Woodrow Wilson for an international guarantee against war. He advocated a Congress of the Nations, meeting at fixed periods, and the establishment of a World Court to decide disputes arising between the countries. These are but a few of the movements of the time which, with the campaigns for popular education, for the abolition of slavery, for the release of debtors from prison, for the safeguarding of health in the factories, and for the humane treatment of patients in hospitals and asylums, testify to the new interest in the welfare of the "common man."

The New Politics. Thomas Jefferson[1] believed that the life of American democracy depended upon the class of free, self-reliant owners of the soil who would keep a watchful eye on their public servants, to guard against any invasion of their "unalienable rights" of "life, liberty, and the pursuit of happi-

---

[1] By a curious coincidence, Jefferson and John Adams both died on July 4, 1826, the fiftieth anniversary of the Declaration of Independence. Jefferson was eighty-three years old and Adams ninety-one.

ness." Once let men become herded in cities (the plague spots of civilization), they would degenerate into an idle, vicious, turbulent "proletariat" easily led by demagogues. Just the thing that Jefferson feared was beginning to take place in the Jacksonian era. The factory system was gathering hundreds of thousands of "hands" into the industrial centers of the North. Immigrants from Europe, attracted now not so much by the land as by the chance for a job in a mill, began to pour in by the tens of thousands to take the place of the Americans who preferred to go West rather than work for a boss.

These immigrants furnished a cheap labor supply, and, being rapidly naturalized and enfranchised, offered the politicians a rich harvest of votes. Politics, the science of government, came to be more and more the game of capturing the offices. The art of flattering the people rather than of instructing them was cultivated. All the tricks of political advertising — catchwords, cartoons, badges, banners, stump speeches, clubs, and rallies — were used to catch votes. And public office, when once attained, was looked on not so much as an honorable position of civic responsibility as a source of patronage with which to reward the faithful "party workers." William L. Marcy, of New York, in a debate in the United States Senate in 1832, made the remark "To the victors belong the spoils." This famous proverb, borrowed from the Romans, gave the name to the vicious "spoils system," which cursed our government for half a century after Jackson's accession. It meant that with every change of administration the civil servants of the defeated party, however long or faithful their service had been, were turned out of office to make way for adherents of the victorious party.

The New President. The man who was elected to the Presidency at this important time of ferment, which marked "the rise of the common man" in politics and industry and social planning, was a sharp contrast to his predecessors, not only in speech and manners but in his ideas of the nature of the first office in the land. Our former Presidents had considered themselves as "executives," to carry out the laws made by Congress. They respected the "checks and balances" of the Constitution,

CARTOON OF THE CAMPAIGN OF 1832

by which Congress and the President had a mutual control over each other's actions, with the Federal judiciary, the Supreme Court, as the final authority. But Jackson had little regard for Congress, since the "aristocratic" House had kept him out of the Presidency in 1825; and he had no awe of the Supreme Court. He believed that the President had as much right as Congress or the Court to decide what laws were desirable or constitutional. So he vetoed more acts of Congress than all his predecessors put together, and on one occasion defied the Supreme Court with the remark "John Marshall has made his decision; now let him enforce it." Indeed, Jackson considered that his own will was the will of the American people. They had chosen him to be their spokesman. He liked to think of himself as a Roman tribune, the officer elected by the masses of plebeians to sit by the door of the aristocratic Senate and shout his veto of laws injurious to the interests of the commoners.

Jackson's character and patriotism were above reproach, but his intense devotion to what he believed to be good for the country often led him to the hasty and untrue judgment that those who were opposed to his policies were enemies of the country.

He was seldom without a quarrel, personal or public; but, on the other hand, no President has ever had a more devoted band of followers. His sharply etched personality, the glamour of his military achievements, and the vigor of his championship of "the forgotten man" gathered the elements of the new democracy to him in enthusiastic devotion, as the magnet gathers the iron filings in its field. And because everyone had to be either decidedly for or against Andrew Jackson, his partisans were no more ardent than his enemies. For the latter Jackson was a conceited demagogue, pandering to the people in his lust for one-man power, and threatening the balance of the government by his contempt for Congress and the Supreme Court. A cartoon represented him as "King Andrew the First," clothed in ermine and trampling the Constitution under his feet.

Jackson's Quarrel with Calhoun. Before many months of his administration had passed, Jackson had a quarrel with Vice-President Calhoun which led to the most serious consequences. It started with the President's disapproval of Mrs. Calhoun's attitude in a social feud which was raging in Washington.[1] Calhoun's enemies seized on this favorable moment to discredit him with the President and kill his ambitious plan to succeed Jackson in the next election. They unearthed and brought to Jackson's attention the fact that Calhoun (not Adams, as Jackson had thought) was the member of Monroe's cabinet who had proposed to censure Jackson for his invasion of Florida in 1818 (p. 263). The President demanded an explanation from Calhoun, and when the latter tried to evade the question with lame excuses, Jackson struck him off the list of even his speaking acquaintances, and reorganized his cabinet by excluding Calhoun's friends.

The rift between the South Carolina leader and the President was still further widened by the latter's failure to lead a crusade against the protective tariff.

[1] Secretary of War Eaton had married a sprightly tavern-keeper's daughter, Peggy O'Neal, whom the wives of some of the cabinet members, led by Mrs. Calhoun, refused to recognize socially. Jackson, whose own departed wife had been maligned, sprang to the defense of Mrs. Eaton.

WEBSTER, AS HE STOOD TO REPLY TO HAYNE'S ATTACK ON THE
NORTH, BEFORE A CROWDED SENATE, JANUARY 26, 1830

The Webster-Hayne Debate. Meanwhile a scene had been
enacted in the Senate of the United States which greatly inflamed the hostile feeling between North and South. An act
of Congress in 1820 had reduced the price of the public lands
and authorized their sale in parcels as small as eighty acres.
The low price was tempting speculators to buy up large tracts
of land and hold them for a rise. When Senator Foot of Connecticut proposed a resolution in December, 1829, that no more
public land should be put on the market for a time, a lively
debate followed. Southern and Western members of Congress
attributed the resolution to the selfishness of the Eastern manufacturers, who, they said wanted to stop migration to the West in
order to keep a mass of cheap laborers for their factories at home.

During the debate Senator Robert Hayne of South Carolina
left the subject of the public land to indulge in a bitter denunciation of the North in general and of Massachusetts in particular for its selfish policy of sectionalism. In the course of a long

speech, on January 21, 1830, he set forth for the first time in the halls of Congress Calhoun's doctrine of the "compact." The states, he maintained, had entered into a compact, or agreement, creating the Federal government, and had voluntarily conferred upon it certain powers. As the originators of the compact, the states were the proper judges of whether the Federal government had exceeded the powers granted to it or not. Calhoun, in his "Exposition and Protest" (p. 284), had shown the way in which the states should interpose their authority to annul "unconstitutional" laws of Congress.

Daniel Webster's reply to Hayne on January 26–27 was perhaps the most powerful speech ever delivered in Congress. After defending his state of Massachusetts against the charge of selfish sectionalism, Webster proceeded to the defense of the national government. It was no mere league of states, as the Southern orators claimed. Not the states but the *people* had made the Union. "It is, sir, the people's Constitution, the people's government, made for the people, made by the people, answerable to the people." [1] If Congress exceeded its powers, there was an arbiter appointed by the Constitution itself, namely, the Supreme Court, to declare a law void. This authority could not be given to a state or a group of states. Pennsylvania would annul one law, Alabama another, Virginia a third, and so on. Congress would become a mockery, the Constitution a mere "rope of sand." The Union would fall apart, and the states would return to the frightful anarchy which followed the Revolutionary War, while our flag, now the "gorgeous ensign of the republic," would droop, with its stripes erased and its stars obscured, over the "broken and dishonored fragments of a once glorious Union."

[1] A big, rawboned farmer's son in Indiana, just approaching his twenty-first birthday, read and pondered Webster's speech as it appeared in a Louisville paper. Abraham Lincoln little thought, as he trudged a few days later beside the oxcart which was carrying his thriftless father's family goods across the border into Illinois, that upon him would be placed the burden, a generation after, of preserving the Union for which Webster so magnificently pleaded. Even the words of the Massachusetts orator remained in Lincoln's memory; for the "government of the people, by the people, for the people" in Lincoln's Gettysburg Address of 1863 is but a paraphrase of Webster's language quoted in the text.

Jackson's Toast. The President, of course, could have no part in the great debate in the Senate, but a few weeks later an opportunity came for him to show where he stood on the question of the nation versus the states. The Southerners in Washington arranged a banquet for Jefferson's birthday (April 13), planning to use the occasion to claim the author of the Kentucky Resolutions as the sponsor of the doctrine put forward by Calhoun and Hayne. Jackson attended the dinner; and when, as chief magistrate, he was called on for the first toast, he lifted his glass and, looking Calhoun straight in the eyes, proposed, "Our Federal Union — it *must* and *shall* be preserved!" The Vice-President rose and drank the toast with the rest, his glass trembling in his hand. The excitement was intense. All the company knew that the President's sharp words were a direct challenge to the South Carolinian. "An order to arrest Calhoun where he sat," wrote one of the diners, "could not have come with more staggering, blinding force." The Vice-President accepted the challenge as he rose to give the second toast: "The Union — next to our liberty most dear!" Then, after a moment's delay, he added, "May we all remember that it can only be preserved by respecting the rights of the states and by distributing equally the benefits and burdens of the Union." The issue was clear. For Calhoun and Hayne the Union, though they sincerely professed their love for it, threatened, if not curbed by the paramount authority of the states, to endanger liberty. For Jackson and Webster the Union, superior to the states, was the only guarantee of liberty.

Nullification. In the summer of 1832 a new tariff bill was passed by Congress and signed by the President. Its rates were lower than those of the "Tariff of Abominations," but still it was highly protective. The Southern members of Congress wrote home that no relief was to be expected from Washington. A convention met at Columbia, South Carolina, in November, 1832, and by the decisive vote of 136 to 26 declared the tariff acts of 1828 and 1832 "null, void, and no law." The people of the state were ordered to pay no duties under these laws after February 1, 1833. At the same time the convention de-

ANDREW JACKSON

JOHN C. CALHOUN

HENRY CLAY

JOHN QUINCY ADAMS

clared that any attempt of Congress to enforce the tariff laws in South Carolina would be "a just cause for the secession of the state from the Union." The legislature approved the work of the convention, and the governor called for ten thousand volunteers to defend the state. When the nullifiers were warned by the Union men that their course might lead to war, they contemptuously asked these "submission men" whether "the descendants of the heroes of 1776 should be afraid to fight!" Jackson answered the nullifiers on December 10 in a spirited proclamation: "I consider the power to annul a law of the United States, assumed by one state, incompatible with the existence of the Union . . . inconsistent with every principle on which the Constitution was founded, and destructive of the great object for which it was formed." To the collector of the port of Charleston he wrote: "I will meet treason at the threshold. . . . In forty days I will have fifty thousand men in the state of South Carolina to enforce the law."

Civil Strife Averted. The situation at the opening of 1833 was extremely critical. Jackson had been triumphantly re-elected over Henry Clay. He was at the height of his power, and no one doubted that he would make good his threat to put down nullification by force of arms if the necessity came. Calhoun had resigned the Vice-Presidency to carry his fight for states' rights to the floor of the United States Senate, taking the seat vacated by Hayne, who had been elected governor of South Carolina. Calhoun's hope that the other states of the South would support nullification was disappointed. Georgia [1] and North Carolina stood firmly by Jackson. Virginia sent a delegation to South Carolina to persuade the nullifiers to repeal the ordinance. Mississippi denounced the doctrine of nullification as "subversive of the Constitution." Other states made no reply to South Carolina's appeal for co-operation.

Calhoun saw that he had gone too far. He was receiving

[1] Georgia was grateful to the President for his defense of her right to survey for sale the lands of the Cherokee Indians lying within the state. Jackson could be counted on to take the part of the white man against the Indian on any occasion. It was in this controversy that he defied Chief Justice Marshall to enforce the decision of the Supreme Court in favor of the Cherokees (p. 292).

disquieting warnings of the punishment which awaited "traitors" to the Union. He was ready for compromise, and in his anxiety he turned to the very man who had been most responsible for the tariffs that had driven South Carolina to defiance of the government, namely, Henry Clay. It was a common enmity to Jackson that united Calhoun and Clay. The latter, smarting from his defeat in the Presidential campaign and having no desire to see the "military chieftain" in the White House directing an army against South Carolina, worked out a compromise tariff, by which the rates were to be reduced gradually over a period of nine years until they reached the levels of 1816. The bill was signed by Jackson on March 2, 1833, and pronounced acceptable by Calhoun. By his advice, when the Columbia convention reconvened, a few days later, it rescinded the nullification ordinance by an overwhelming vote. At the same time it rejected a "Force Bill" which had been passed by Congress along with the compromise tariff, and which authorized the President "to employ the army and navy of the United States to collect duties in South Carolina."

With nullification repealed, the Force Bill was an empty threat. Both sides claimed the victory — South Carolina for having compelled Congress to lower the tariff, and the Union men for having forced South Carolina to repeal the ordinance of nullification. But a compromise is not a settlement when principles are in conflict. Jackson's strong hand and Clay's parliamentary skill had averted civil strife; but, as in the case of the Missouri Compromise a dozen years earlier, the clash between the warring interests of the sections had only been postponed. The language of nullification was not forgotten in South Carolina. Twenty years later it was revived and intensified in a struggle far more serious than that over tariff rates — the great slavery controversy which precipitated the Civil War.

Jackson's War on the Bank. As the professed foe of monopoly and privilege, Jackson waged a bitter war against the second Bank of the United States (p. 259). This institution was very prosperous under its able president, Nicholas Biddle of Philadelphia. In addition to $8,000,000 of the government's money, it held some $6,000,000 in deposits of private persons. It paid handsome dividends to its stockholders, and its shares of $100 par value often sold as high as $140 each. Besides the parent bank in Philadelphia, "with its marble palace and hundreds of clerks," there were twenty-five branches in the towns and cities of the Union. Many of its shares were owned by foreigners, and its notes were as good as gold not only in every part of the United States but in all the great financial centers of the world. The flourishing condition of the Bank, however, was just the thing which made it the more dangerous enemy of the people, in Jackson's eyes. If it had been poor and weak, he might have left it alone; but he could not endure a rich and powerful institution which he believed was corrupt and undemocratic, — corrupt because it used its great wealth to aid with loans and credit only those businessmen and statesmen whose political opinions it approved; and undemocratic because it employed the public funds, raised by taxes upon the people, to make more money for the rich who could afford to buy its shares. Naturally, these wealthy men did not come from the pioneer states west of the Alleghenies.

The Bank's charter would not expire until 1836, and Biddle was in favor of "lying low" like Brer Rabbit, hoping that a truce could be arranged with the President. But Henry Clay thought he saw a chance to defeat Jackson on the Bank issue in the campaign of 1832. Clay had been unanimously nominated for the Presidency by the National Republican convention at Baltimore on December 12, 1831. A few months later he succeeded in getting a bill through Congress for the recharter of the Bank, believing that if Jackson should dare to veto the bill he would lose enough votes in the East to cost him the election.

The recharter bill went to the President on July 4, 1832, and six days later was returned to Congress with a veto which, in Biddle's words, "had all the fury of a chained panther biting the bars of his cage." Webster, Clay, and Biddle were jubilant. They thought that Jackson had signed his own political death warrant. But never were men more mistaken. In the autumn elections state after state gave its vote for the "old hero" who had defied the power of the money kings. Clay carried only six states, with a total of 49 votes. The rest of the states (save Vermont and Virginia [1]) cast their 219 votes for Jackson.

The Removal of the Deposits. Had it not been for Clay's folly in precipitating the question of the recharter four years before it was due, the Bank might have weathered the opposition of Jackson and been a steadying influence in the financial confusion which came after its destruction. But, having been provoked to the battle and having won a decisive victory, the President was determined to put an end to "Emperor Biddle's Monster," as he called the Bank. A clause in its charter allowed the Secretary of the Treasury to discontinue placing the government's balances in the Bank if he gave satisfactory reasons to Congress for so doing. Jackson had to promote one Secretary of the Treasury to the State Department and dismiss another before he found in Roger B. Taney, of Maryland, one who would obey his orders to boycott the Bank.

On October 1, 1833, Taney announced that after that date the government would make no more deposits in the Bank and would gradually withdraw the money which it had there for the payment of its current expenses. When Congress met the next month, the Senate declared that Taney's reasons for removing the deposits were "unsatisfactory," refused to ratify his appointment as Secretary, and spread on its minutes a censure of President Jackson.[2] But all this manifestation of spite did not help the Bank. Deprived of the government's patronage, it had to call in its loans and curtail its business. It struggled along until its charter expired in 1836, when Biddle got it rechartered

[1] The Virginia electors cast their votes for John B. Floyd in 1832, and Vermont was carried by William Wirt, the candidate of the first of our "third parties," the Antimasons. This party, which, like most third parties, lasted but a few months, was started by the excitement caused by the murder of a certain William Morgan, who had written a book exposing the secrets of the Freemasons.

[2] The Senate had no right to pass a resolution of censure upon the President. Its condemnation of his actions is limited to trying him on impeachment charges regularly brought before it by the House. Jackson's champion in the Senate, Thomas H. Benton, of Missouri, finally succeeded in having the offensive resolution expunged from the journal, after an exciting debate mingled with hisses from the gallery, on January 16, 1837.

as a state bank by the legislature of Pennsylvania. But, like many of the state banks, it failed to survive the panic which overtook the country under Jackson's successor.

A Masterful President. Theodore Roosevelt used to say that our Presidents were of two types: the Jackson-Lincoln kind (with whom he classed himself), and the Buchanan-Taft kind. The former asserted their leadership in the name of the American people; the latter deferred more to Congress and to the letter of the Constitution. Perhaps no other President has been so completely a master of the situation, in both domestic and foreign policies, as was Jackson in his second term. After his negotiations with Great Britain had secured the abolition of tonnage duties on our trade with the West Indies, he won a great diplomatic victory over France by forcing the government of Louis Philippe to pay us 23,500,000 francs in claims of our citizens for American property seized by Napoleon.

At home Jackson swept out of his path every opponent and rival. The elegant Biddle had scornfully written: "This worthy President thinks that because he has scalped Indians, . . . he is to have his way with the Bank. He is mistaken." But it was Biddle who was mistaken, and who died in chagrin the year after his Bank of Pennsylvania went down. Henry Clay sought revenge for his defeat in 1832 by securing the Senate's rejection of Taney as Secretary of the Treasury. But two years later, on Marshall's death (1835), Clay saw Taney raised to the Chief-Justiceship of the Supreme Court. Calhoun, smarting from Jackson's exclusion of his friends from the cabinet, had used his casting vote in the Senate to defeat Van Buren's nomination as minister to England. But in 1833 he saw Van Buren occupying his own former seat as Vice-President and presiding over the Senate that had rejected his appointment to London. Jackson emerged victorious from every attack on his policies. In the eyes of the common people he was a demigod. "General Jackson may be President for life, if he wishes," wrote William Wirt. But Jackson did not wish another term. In the spring of 1835 a convention of his party (now called Democrats) met at Baltimore and on his instructions nominated Van Buren for his successor.

The Election of Van Buren. Meanwhile Jackson's enemies had formed a coalition against him and in 1834 had taken the name of "Whigs." The Whigs were held together by no stronger tie than a common hostility to the President. They comprised National Republicans, like Clay and Webster, who condemned Jackson's vetoes of the Bank charter and bills for "internal improvements"; states-rights men, like Calhoun and Tyler, who resented his threat to South Carolina in the nullification controversy; "Native Americans," who saw a danger in the numbers of easily naturalized immigrants flocking to our shores to join the Democratic party and become the political tools of the "bosses";[1] and the conservative classes generally, who abhorred Jackson's highhanded conduct in snubbing Congress and the Supreme Court, in making wholesale removals from office, and in surrounding himself with a little group of politicians and newspapermen (the "Kitchen Cabinet") who could be counted upon "to sneeze every time that he took a pinch of snuff."

The Whigs, in 1836, held no national convention, published no platform, put up no candidate against Van Buren. Instead, they adopted the "favorite sons" method of 1824 (p. 280), letting the various state legislatures name their candidates and hoping that by so dividing the electoral vote among the sections they could prevent Van Buren from getting a majority and throw the choice into the House of Representatives. But Jackson's influence behind his favorite was too strong for the Whigs. Van Buren carried fifteen states, with a clear majority of 46 electoral votes.[2] In his inaugural address he declared that he would

---

[1] Until the Jacksonian era the immigrants to America did not number more than about ten thousand a year, but from that time on they came in ever-increasing hordes. In the early 1830's our rising manufactures could count on the addition of some fifty thousand new "hands" a year to supply the place of the independent Americans who preferred seeking their fortunes in the West to working at low wages for a boss. Of course, the new immigrants were at the mercy of the political as well as of the industrial boss.

[2] Van Buren's running mate, Colonel R. M. Johnson, of Kentucky, failed to receive a majority of the electoral votes, however, and the choice of a Vice-President was, for the only time in our history, thrown into the Senate, which chose Johnson on the first ballot.

"tread in the footsteps of his illustrious predecessor." It looked as though Andrew Jackson had entered by proxy on a third term.

The Panic of 1837. Before Martin Van Buren got fairly started on the path of his "illustrious predecessor," however, he ran into a storm which washed the footprints out completely. The period of Jackson's second term had been one of reckless overconfidence in our country's rapid growth. We were completely out of debt in 1834, and the customs duties were producing large surpluses in the Treasury. Our foreign trade in 1835 surpassed for the first time the figures of the great boom year (1807) preceding Jefferson's embargo (p. 236). The sales of public lands, which were less than $2,000,000 in 1830, jumped to $14,000,000 in 1835, and to $24,000,000 in 1836. The purchasers, or speculators, paid for this land in notes of the Western state banks, which had multiplied rapidly since Jackson's attack on the United States Bank. Soon the national treasury was overflowing with this unsound currency.

On July 11, 1836, Jackson issued his famous "Specie Circular," forbidding the Treasury to receive anything but gold and silver (specie) or bank notes based thereon, in payment for public lands. The Specie Circular was the needle that pricked the bubble of speculation. The state banks did not have the specie to redeem their notes, and the boom of the West collapsed. Land sales dropped to less than a million dollars. Building operations ceased. Long lines of rails were left to rust in the Western wilderness. Thousands of laborers were thrown out of employment. By the close of May, 1837, all the banks in the country had suspended specie payment, and by September almost all the factories in the Eastern states were closed. Over six hundred banks failed, including many of the eighty-nine "pet banks" in which the government had deposited its money after Taney's order of 1833 (p. 301). A blight on the wheat crop sent the price of flour up to twelve dollars a barrel and started riots among the starving laborers, who broke into the warehouses of New York and Philadelphia. For four or five years the country suffered in the throes of the worst panic in its history, with the possible exception of the one from which we are now struggling to emerge.

The Ferment of Unrest. Financial and industrial depression was not the only trial that Van Buren had to meet. Ever since William Lloyd Garrison had published the first number of *The Liberator* in Boston (January 1, 1831), in his crusade against Negro slavery, the abolitionists had been driving the Southerners to defend the institution as an economic good, a social necessity, and even a divine order, rooted in human nature and sanctioned by the Word of God. When the apologists for slavery pointed to its recognition in the Constitution, Garrison publicly burned a copy of the Constitution on Boston Common, calling it "a covenant with death and an agreement with hell." When a "gag rule" passed Congress in May, 1836, forbidding the reception of any petitions against slavery, John Quincy Adams, no friend of abolition before,[1] protested that it was "a direct violation of the Constitution of the United States (Amendment I), of the rules of this House and of the rights of my constituents." When the citizens of Charleston, South Carolina, seized and burned a mail sack full of abolitionist documents in 1835, Congress upheld Postmaster-General Kendall in his refusal to compel the postmasters of the South to deliver such mail.

Another cause of unrest lay in the attempt of the expansionists North and South to bring Texas (which had revolted from Mexico and secured its independence in 1836) into the Union. Van Buren's opposition to the annexation of Texas, as likely to bring on war with Mexico, earned for him the reputation of cowardice in the eyes of the expansionists.

Finally, the President was accused of the unpardonable sin in an American official, namely, of truckling to Great Britain. During a Canadian rebellion in 1837 the English had seized and burned an American vessel, the *Caroline*, which was illegally transporting men and supplies from Vermont and upper New York to aid the rebels. Our people on the border, claiming that

---

[1] For example, he had voted in the Senate in 1807 against the bill to prohibit the slave trade, and as peace commissioner at Ghent in 1814 he had insisted that the British pay for the slaves which they had taken from the Southern plantations.

an American had been killed on the *Caroline*, clamored for war; but by skillful diplomacy Van Buren averted trouble, at the expense of his unpopularity with the jingoes.

"Tippecanoe and Tyler Too." During the whole of Van Buren's administration the Whigs were laying their plans to turn him out of the White House. In their national convention at Harrisburg, Pennsylvania, in December, 1839, they passed over Henry Clay, the towering genius and virtual founder of the party, much to his chagrin, and nominated General Harrison, the hero of Tippecanoe (p. 241). John Tyler, of Virginia, was named for Vice-President, simply to get votes in the South; for Tyler was a states-rights man, an anti-Bank man, and a low-tariff man, whose only bond of sympathy with the Whigs was hatred for Andrew Jackson. The convention published no platform, because the party had no program except to dish Van Buren.

A Democratic newspaper man made the sneering comment on Harrison: "Give him a barrel of hard cider, settle a pension of two thousand dollars a year on him, and my word for it, he will sit for the remainder of his days in his log cabin by the side of a sea-coal fire, studying moral philosophy." The Whigs cleverly converted the sneer into a campaign slogan, proclaiming the simple tastes and virtuous poverty of their candidate (who actually lived in comfort on a two-thousand-acre farm in Ohio), in contrast to the aristocratic Van Buren, who was reveling in dainty fare and costly wines in the White House, callous to the sufferings which his misrule had brought upon the people. Log cabins were erected for Whig headquarters, and barrels of hard cider were on tap at Whig rallies all over the country. Men and boys rolled huge balls from town to town, to symbolize the majorities that would be rolled up for Harrison, and roared out their campaign songs of "Tippecanoe and Tyler Too," "Van, Van, is a used-up Man," and

> Farewell, dear Van,
> You're not our man.
> To guide the ship
> We'll try old Tip.

CAMPAIGN PROCESSION OF 1840

At no other time in our history has there been such a campaign of "ballyhoo." In the place of sober discussion of the tariff, the Bank, states' rights, and other planks in the Democratic platform, the Whigs offered only boisterous appeals to emotion and prejudice. "We were sung down, lied down, drunk down," scornfully remarked a Democratic paper. Harrison and Tyler carried all but seven states, with 234 electoral votes to 60 for Van Buren. In the excitement of the campaign the appearance of a new party which polled but 7000 votes passed almost unnoticed. But the Liberty party, pledged to the extinction of slavery, was destined to grow through a score of years into the mighty force which shattered the Whigs into fragments and sent the Democrats down to a long defeat.

The End of an Era. The Whig victory of 1840 marks the end of the Jacksonian era. That era had been ushered in by the election of a soldier hero, a representative of the new West, standing as the champion of the plain people against an "aristocratic" government at Washington. It was ended by exactly another such victory. To the old hero of seventy-three, in his retirement at the "Hermitage" in Tennessee, the log cabins and cider barrels, the rolling balls, and the uproarious songs of 1840 must have been a pathetic reminder of the hickory poles and stamped waistcoats and huzzas for New Orleans and Pensacola of a dozen years before.

The Jacksonian era was perhaps the period of all our history most fruitful in democratic changes, with its enlargement of the suffrage, its extension of elective offices, its revised state constitutions, its national nominating conventions, its organization of labor, and its discussion — on the lecture platform, in the pulpits, and especially in the multiplying issue of cheap newspapers — of the burning questions of the day. It was an era of humanitarian reform in debtors' laws, in prisons and asylums, in the curricula of schools, in the encouragement of temperance, in the agitation for the abolition of slavery. It was an era of inventions in industry and commerce that have done more to change the course of history than many a war or treaty. The patenting of the McCormick reaper in 1834 was the prophecy that our great wheat fields of the West would one day produce enough to feed half the world. The utilization of the anthracite-coal deposits of Pennsylvania in the process of iron-smelting in 1836 foreshadowed the mighty age of steel which has succeeded our fathers' age of wood. The application of the screw propeller to ocean steamers in 1839 opened the way for the *Normandie* and the *Queen Mary*. Chief of all, the appearance of the steam locomotive on the thirteen-mile track of the Baltimore and Ohio Railroad in 1830 gave promise of the network of over two hundred and fifty thousand miles of railway track which covers our country today.

ABOVE, LOCOMOTIVE OF 1830; BELOW, LOCOMOTIVE AND TRAIN
OF 1830 COMPARED WITH A MODERN LOCOMOTIVE

Summary. In this unit, covering the forty years from the beginning of the Jeffersonian era to the end of the Jacksonian era, the central theme has been the emergence of sectional interests. The way in which the people of any region make their living is the chief factor in determining their views as to how the government should be run. Not only are their politics influenced by this "economic factor," but their whole culture — their literature, their art, their schools, their songs, their dress, their speech, and even their religion — is colored by it.

We have seen how three such main economic and cultural regions developed in the United States during the first half of the nineteenth century. In the North manufactures gradually gained the supremacy over farming and shipping, this resulting in the demand for high tariffs for the protection of industry, cheap labor to feed the mills and factories, stable banks to furnish credit, and a strong government at Washington to keep power in the hands of the "wealthy and well born." The South, on the other hand, gave up its early hopes of becoming an industrial community and devoted itself to the profitable cultivation of cotton ("the Cotton Kingdom"). The planters became an aristocracy. But, unlike the Northern barons of the factories and the banks, they resisted the tariff, which increased the cost of the tools, clothing, and food that they had to provide for their slaves; sought fresh lands in the West, to replace the soil so rapidly exhausted by the cotton crops; and fought for the rights of the states against the central government at Washington. The faster-growing population of the North and West had given these sections a majority in Congress which seemed more and more determined to restrict the spread of slavery. Finally, there was the marvelously growing section beyond the Alleghenies, the new West of the adventurous, self-confident pioneers, adding state after state to the Union, and sending its waves of democratic influence back to the old communities of the seaboard. The West was poor in money, but rich in hope and courage. It asked for a cheap currency, for easy credit, for protection against Indians and their foreign instigators on its borders, and especially for the improvement at public expense of the means of commerce (roads, rivers, canals) in order to get its abundant farm products to the markets of the East and overseas.

We have seen how the rivalry of these sections to further their own interests in the conduct of our government entered into every debate of Congress and every act of the executive; how the North antagonized the South, and the South complained of the narrow selfishness of the North; and how the West, courted by both, twice (1828, 1840) swept the country to put an "unspoiled son of the people" into the White House. The lesson of these years is that, though one flag floats over our land, America became, and has remained, a country of such diverse occupations and interests in its various regions that it is a very difficult thing to make national laws which do not seem partial or unfair to one section or another.

TERMS TO BE MASTERED

trade union	states' rights	"Kitchen Cabinet"
proletariat	Force Bill	"Specie Circular"
spoils system	removal of deposits	"gag rule"
compact	Whigs	Jacksonian democracy

FOR SUPPLEMENTARY READING

F. A. OGG, *The Reign of Andrew Jackson* (Chronicles of America, Vol. XX); WILLIAM MACDONALD, *Jacksonian Democracy* (the American Nation Series, Vol. XV); The Pageant of America, Vol. VIII, pp. 237–264 (interesting illustrations); C. G. BOWERS, *The Party Battles of the Jackson Period*; M. B. SMITH, *The First Forty Years of Washington Society*, pp. 281–298; S. P. ORTH, *The Boss and the Machine* (Chronicles of America, Vol. XLIII), chap. ii; C. R. FISH, *The Rise of the Common Man* (A History of American Life, Vol. VI), chaps. i–v; D. F. HOUSTON, *A Critical Study of Nullification in South Carolina* (Harvard Historical Studies, Vol. III); R. C. H. CATTERALL, *The Second Bank of the United States*; America, Vol. VI, pp. 43–65, 71–103, 111–117, 156–173, 180–194; R. C. MCGRANE, *The Panic of 1837*; HART, *Contemporaries*, Vol. III, Nos. 158–163, 174–178, 180; MUZZEY, *Readings*, pp. 265–288.

TOPICS FOR REPORTS

1. **Women's Rights.** H. A. BRUCE, *Women in the Making of America*; Mary R. BEARD, *America Through Women's Eyes*, chap. iv; EDITH ABBOTT, *Women in Industry: a Study in American Economic History*, pp. 36–85; J. W. TAYLOR, *Before Vassar Opened*; K. PORTER, *History of Suffrage in the United States*, pp. 135–145.

2. **Labor Conditions in the Jacksonian Era.** S. P. ORTH, *The Armies of Labor*, chap. ii; MARY R. BEARD, *A Short History of the American Labor Movement*, chaps. iii–vi; R. T. ELY, *The Labor Movement in America*, pp. 7–60; EDWARD CHANNING, *History of the United States*, Vol. V, pp. 94–118; J. R. COMMONS, "Labor Organizations and Labor Politics," in *Quarterly Journal of Economics*, Vol. XXI, pp. 323 f.

3. **The Origin of the Whig Party.** EDWARD STANWOOD, *History of the Presidency*, Vol. I, chaps. xv, xvi; H. J. FORD, *Rise and Growth of American Politics*, chaps. xiii–xv; E. M. CARROLL, *The Origins of the Whig Party*; A. C. COLE, *The Whig Party in the South*, chaps. i, ii; A. D. MORSE, "The Political Influence of Andrew Jackson," in *Political Science Quarterly*, Vol. I, pp. 153 f.

4. **The Earliest Railroads.** E. R. JOHNSON, *American Railway Transportation*, chap. ii; C. F. ADAMS, *Railroads, their Origin and Problems*, chaps. i, ii; J. B. MCMASTER, *History of the People of the United States*, Vol. VI, pp. 77–95; H. U. FAULKNER, *American Economic History*, pp. 325–333; HART, *Contemporaries*, Vol. III, Nos. 165, 166.

QUESTIONS SUGGESTED BY THE CHAPTER

1. How did Jackson's idea of democracy differ from Jefferson's? 2. When and by whom was the first American peace society founded? 3. How did the factory system affect the lives of the workers? 4. What social reforms did "Fanny" Wright advocate? 5. What was Jackson's conception of the Presidency? 6. What was Calhoun's theory of the relation of the national government to the states? 7. Show how it differed from Webster's. 8. What subject started the Webster-Hayne debates? 9. Why did South Carolina claim that she had won in the nullification controversy? 10. How did the new democratic West influence the older states? 11. Why was Jackson opposed to the Bank? 12. What caused the panic of 1837? 13. Why did the sale of public lands drop sharply in 1837? 14. What successes in foreign policy marked Jackson's term? 15. Why did the antislavery movement die out in the South? 16. Why were the abolitionists persecuted in the North? 17. Why was it easier for England to get rid of slavery in the West Indies than for the United States to get rid of it in the South? 18. What new party appeared in the election of 1840? 19. Name some of the reforms of the Jacksonian era; some of the inventions. 20. Why was Jackson less popular in New England in 1835 than in 1832?

BOOKS WORTH READING ON UNIT III

E. SNOW and H. A. GOSNELL, *On the Decks of "Old Ironsides"*; GILBERT CHINARD, *Thomas Jefferson, The Apostle of Americanism*; F. J. TURNER, *The Frontier in American History*; IRVING BACHELLER, *D'ri and I* and *The Light in the Clearing*; K. L. ROBERTS, *The Lively Lady*; G. BROOKS, *Dames and Daughters of the Young Republic*; C. T. BRADY, *For the Freedom of the Sea*; D. T. LYNCH, *An Epoch and a Man* (Van Buren); G. HUNT, *Life in America One Hundred Years Ago*; W. E. DODD, *Statesmen of the Old South*; M. DILLON, *The Patience of John Morland*; S. G. FISHER, *The True Daniel Webster*; E. B. STEVENSON, *Poems of American History*.

How our Union was Enlarged, Endangered, and Preserved

The threefold motto of the American republic is "Liberty, Democracy, and Union!" These three objects were not all gained at once. Our forefathers who fought the Revolution and set up the government (*Unit II*) were intent upon securing Liberty — freedom from British interference with their trade, the disposition of their lands, the assessment of their taxes, and the laws of their colonial assemblies generally. They were not concerned with extending political rights or social recognition to the masses of the people, who, they believed, should be content with the station in which Providence had placed them, and should regard their educated leaders with obedient awe. It was not until the Jacksonian era of a century ago that the second term, Democracy, was really added to our motto. Then, as we have seen (*Unit III*), the influence of the Western frontier spirit, the increase of the laboring class in the industrial centers, and the influx of immigrants to swell the masses of voters organized by the political bosses brought about "the rise of the common man." The offices, even to the Presidency, were thrown open to all. One man was as good as another. Birth, wealth, and education were frowned upon as "aristocratic" pretensions. The good thing about this new democracy was that it opened the way to a career for the latent genius of men of humble origin, like Abraham Lincoln. The bad thing was the opportunity it gave to the demagogue to rise to power by flattering the ignorance of the masses or purchasing their votes. The third ideal of our motto, Union, was won only after the ordeal of a terrible civil war (1861–1865), in which eleven states of the South fought to establish a Confederacy independent of the government at Washington. The main theme of the present unit will be the gathering and bursting of the storm which threatened to engulf the Union. We shall see how our expansion to the Rio Grande and the Pacific coast reopened the controversy over the status of slavery in the territories of the West, which was thought to have been "forever" settled by the Missouri Compromise of 1820 (p. 276); how further compromise and attempts at compromise failed to satisfy the determined leaders on each side of Mason and Dixon's line; how the South, at last despairing of getting what it believed to be its rights under the Constitution, seceded from the Union and resorted to arms to gain its independence; and how, after four years of desperate struggle, the superior resources of the North in money, food, transportation, military supplies, and man power won the victory. In the first "critical period" of our history, just following the Revolution, it had been a question of whether the "United States" should be thirteen nations or one. This second crisis determined that the one nation then formed under the Constitution should remain united and indivisible. Various parts of our country have had, and still have, their grievances against the government at Washington. But since Lee laid down his sword at Appomattox in 1865, no state or group of states has sought to remedy its grievances by withdrawing from the Union.

Identifications
1 Names   4 dates
2 terms
3 places

attitude of Van Buren + Taylor
toward the annexation of Texas.
Reports - Defense of the Alamo.
Hoists Discovery of Gold in Calif.
With The Matanuska Valley

CHAPTER THIRTEEN

THE ADVANCE TO THE PACIFIC

The Far West. Let us go back now a score of years from the triumph of the Whigs in 1840, to see what was going on in the vast region to the west of the Mississippi while the Congress was discussing tariffs and banks, nullification, the sale of public lands, improvements in transportation, and petitions for the abolition of slavery. The trans-Mississippi region, which now comprises more than two thirds of the area of the United States, consisted then of three parts. West and south of the boundary line of the treaty of 1819 (p. 264) was Spanish territory, including the present states of California, Nevada, Utah, Arizona, New Mexico, Texas, most of Colorado, and small parts of Wyoming, Kansas, and Oklahoma. Between the Mississippi and the Rockies, east and north of the line of 1819, extended the great territory purchased from Napoleon in 1803, from which a dozen agricultural and mining states were eventually to be carved. West of the Rockies, above the forty-second parallel of latitude, lay the Oregon country, including what are now British Columbia and our states of Washington, Oregon, and Idaho, and parts of Montana and Wyoming, — a country which we had agreed, by the treaty of 1818, to share on equal terms with Great Britain (p. 263).

There were only a few thousand whites and half-breeds in the Spanish domains of the Southwest, scattered among the trading posts or the Indian missions of California. In Oregon the Hudson's Bay Company and the American Fur Company, with their posts on the Columbia River, competed for the peltries which they sent to China in exchange for silk, tea, and precious stones to be sold in the cities of our Eastern states. Hunters and trappers penetrated the wilderness of the upper

Missouri, pushing their canoes into the creeks to reach the
beaver lodges, and bringing down to St. Louis thousands of
dollars' worth of furs for the markets in Europe. There was
little attempt made to settle the region between the Missouri
and the Rockies, which contained hardly a thousand white inhabitants by the middle of the nineteenth century. Except for
the trails of the hunters and an occasional military exploring
expedition, it was given over to the dense herds of bison and
the fierce tribes of the Plains Indians. From the time of Monroe's administration our government had been moving the
Indian tribes from the eastern side of the Mississippi to reservations across the river, where they were guaranteed the possession of their inferior lands "forever." [1] They were thought to
be beyond the frontier of American settlement.

Major Stephen H. Long, returning to St. Louis from an
expedition to the headwaters of the Platte and Arkansas rivers
in 1820, reported the country as "almost wholly unfit for cultivation and, of course, uninhabitable by a people depending
upon agriculture for their subsistence. . . . The scarcity of wood
and water, almost universally prevalent, will prove an insuper-
able obstacle in the way of settling the country. . . . This region,
however, viewed as a frontier, may prove of infinite importance
to the United States, inasmuch as it is calculated to serve as a
barrier to prevent too great an extension of our population westward"! Such pessimistic descriptions of a region now smiling
with fields of wheat and corn served to retard for years the development of the Western plains and to cause them to be
labeled on the maps of a century ago as "the Great American
Desert."

The Santa Fe Trail. The year after Major Long made his
discouraging report, exciting news came from the Southwest.
Mexico joined the long list of Spanish-American colonies in the
New World in throwing off the yoke of the mother country and

---

[1] The removal of the tribes was not always an easy matter. The Sacs and Foxes,
under their remarkable chief Black Hawk, defended their lands in Illinois in a
war in which Abraham Lincoln served as a captain (1832). The Seminoles in
Florida resisted removal beyond the Mississippi for more than a decade.

establishing an independent republic. This meant that the strict Spanish law forbidding foreigners to trade with her colonies was at an end for Mexico, and that the Spanish guards on the United States border line of 1819 would be removed. An enterprising Missourian, Captain William Becknell, was quick to see the opportunities of trade with Santa Fe, which for years had had no outlet but the port of Veracruz, more than a thousand miles to the south. Becknell, in the autumn of 1821, opened the famous trade route from Independence, Missouri, across the broad plains of Kansas and a corner of Texas, to Santa Fe in New Mexico. Year by year the caravans of covered wagons and pack horses fought their way through the hostile Indians that infested the trail, and brought their cotton goods, their silks, their hats and shoes, their iron tools, their clocks and cutlery and glassware, to sell for furs and gold. In the year 1828 a hundred wagons, carrying a hundred thousand dollars' worth of merchandise, passed over the trail, to be welcomed as they drove into the town with the cries of "Los Americanos!" "Los Carros!" In 1829 President Jackson ordered four infantry companies to escort the caravan to the Mexican border, and the danger of Indian attacks ceased. The profitable trade over the Santa Fe Trail continued until the eve of our war with Mexico (1846). The trail is followed in part today by the route of the Atchison, Topeka, and Santa Fe Railroad.

The Road to Oregon. Meantime hardy explorers were defying the blizzards and grizzlies of the Rocky Mountains, the attacks of the fierce Indian tribes, and the arid wastes of sands covered with sagebrush and cactus as they threaded their way through the passes of the Great Divide and followed the courses of the boiling rivers. The most significant movement of Far-Western travel was the migration to Oregon.

About the year 1830 that distant region began to exert upon the imagination of the Easterners a powerful spell, in which the appeal of the magnificent climate and natural resources of the country, the lure of trade with the Orient, and missionary zeal for the conversion of the natives were equally mixed. In 1831 Nathaniel J. Wyeth, of Massachusetts, organized a trading

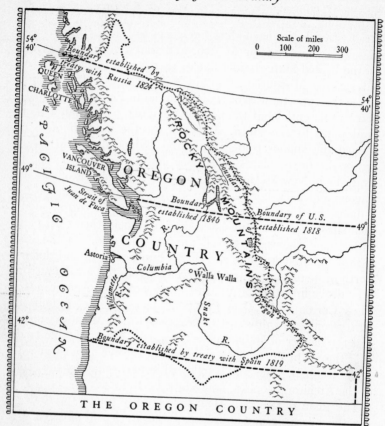

THE OREGON COUNTRY

company for the Columbia valley, and the next year he led a small group overland to Oregon. His route, which became famous as the Oregon Trail, led from Independence on the Missouri River, up the Platte River and through the South Pass in the Rockies of Wyoming, to Fort Hall (Idaho), and thence down the Snake River to the Columbia.[1] Over the Oregon Trail went various missionaries: Jason and Daniel Lee, sent out

[1] A little west of the South Pass the trail forked, the lower branch leading southwest through the salt plains of the Central Basin and over the Sierras to California.

by the Methodists in 1834; Dr. Marcus Whitman[1] and H. H. Spalding, with their wives, the first white women to cross the Rockies, sent by the American Board of Missions in 1836; and Father Pierre de Smet, the affable and learned Jesuit, bent on establishing a mission in the Bitter Root valley in 1840.

By 1843 there were about a thousand settlers in Oregon, but as yet Congress had made no move to take them under the protection of the United States. So, following the example of our pioneer communities for half a century past, they held a convention in an old barn belonging to one of the missions, and drew up a constitution "for the purposes of mutual protection and to secure peace and prosperity among ourselves . . . until such time as the United States of America extend their jurisdiction over us." The next year brought fifteen hundred new emigrants, and the following year more than three thousand were added. It was evident that the government at Washington could neglect the distant "republic" of Oregon no longer.

Americans in Texas. Long before the migration to Oregon got under way, the constant urge of westward expansion was sending thousands of land-hungry pioneers from the Mississippi Valley across the Sabine and Red rivers into Texas. This movement was favored by three circumstances. First, there were many American statesmen, such as Adams, Clay, and Benton, who believed that Texas was included in the Louisiana Purchase of 1803 and who resented its "surrender" to Spain in the treaty of 1819. Second, Congress passed an act in 1820, just at the moment when the hard times caused by the panic of 1819 were driving people to seek relief by moving to new lands in the West, requiring payment *in cash*, at $1.25 an acre, for public land, which had theretofore been sold on credit. Third, the new state of Mexico, of which Texas was a part, encouraged the settlement of Americans on Texan land during the 1820's

[1] Dr. Whitman was a tireless worker for the development of Oregon. When there was some danger that the Board would discontinue its mission there, he made the long trip back to the East on horseback alone, to plead for the continuance of the settlement. It was this trip that led to the long-accepted "legend" of how Whitman "saved Oregon" from the British by persuading the authorities at Washington to push the American claims to the Columbia valley.

by granting them large tracts on the sole condition of their recognizing the authority of the Mexican law.

The result was that, while there were not more than three thousand white colonists in Texas at the end of Spanish rule over the province, the single decade 1821–1830 brought over twelve thousand Americans. "It may be easily foreseen," wrote our distinguished French visitor Alexis de Tocqueville in 1835, "that if Mexico takes no step to check this change, the province of Texas will soon cease to belong to her." But the Mexican government had already reversed its policy of generous welcome to American immigrants. By an edict of 1829 it forbade slavery in Mexican territory, though many of the American settlers were slaveholders from Tennessee, Mississippi, and Alabama; and in the following year it prohibited all further immigration into Texas from the United States.

Texas Wins its Independence. Incensed by this treatment and encouraged by their American neighbors across the Sabine, the Texans, three quarters of whom were Americans, declared their independence of Mexico on March 2, 1836. Santa Anna, the new Mexican president, a man of perfidious and cruel character, led an army in person to punish the rebellious province. At the Alamo, a mission building in San Antonio, he exterminated the garrison of one hundred and sixty-six Texans, not even sparing the sick in the hospital ward. A little further on, at Goliad, the defenders were massacred in cold blood after their surrender. Santa Anna was met at the San Jacinto River on April 21 by a force of about seven hundred and fifty Texan volunteers under General Sam Houston ("the Raven"), a veteran of the War of 1812 and an ex-governor of Tennessee. The Mexican army was routed and Santa Anna taken prisoner. The independence of Texas was won. A republic was set up, with Houston as president, and a constitution was adopted modeled on those of the American states. Slavery was legitimized in the new republic, but slaves could be imported only from the United States. President Houston, the legislature, and the people of Texas were in favor of immediate annexation to the United States.

THE OREGON TRAIL[1]

[1] From "The Covered Wagon," by Paramount Pictures, Inc.

The Question of Annexation. There was a widespread sentiment in the United States too in favor of the annexation of
Texas. Besides those who thought it our patriotic duty to take
under our legal protection a province so largely populated by
our own fellow citizens, there were the expansionists who believed that it was the "manifest destiny" of the American flag
to fly over the territory to the Rio Grande and the Pacific.
Furthermore, the purchasers of Texan land scrip thought that
their investments would be safer under American law, and the
Southern planters coveted the fertile soil of Texas for the extension of their cotton culture.

President Adams had offered Mexico a million dollars for
Texas in 1825, and President Jackson had raised Adams's offer
to five million dollars. Indeed, it was rumored that Jackson
himself encouraged the Texan revolution of 1836 because of
Mexico's rejection of his offer. Though this charge was false, it
is nevertheless probable that if the Texans had won the victory
of San Jacinto and their independence at any other time than
the spring of 1836, their overtures for annexation to the United
States would have been accepted. But in 1836 the abolitionist
controversy was raging (p. 305). It was a Presidential year, and
Jackson was determined not to endanger the chances of his
candidate Van Buren by adding a large slaveholding state to
the Union, and perhaps precipitating a war with Mexico besides. For Mexico was as firm in refusing to acknowledge the
independence of Texas as she had been in refusing to sell it. So,
although we recognized the republic of Texas in 1837 and maintained diplomatic relations with it, the question of annexation
slumbered during the administration of Van Buren, who was
opposed to the extension of slave territory, and played no part
in the turbulent election of 1840 which overthrew the Jacksonian
regime (p. 306).

Tyler and the Whigs. The Whig victory of 1840 soon turned
to ashes. President Harrison died a few weeks after his inauguration. Vice-President Tyler, who then entered the White
House, was a states-rights Virginia Democrat, who would never
have been put on the Harrison ticket by the Whig leaders if

they had dreamed that he would have any more to do with the administration than to preside over the Senate in dignified obscurity. Henry Clay expected to manage the "ship of state," with President Harrison as a sort of ornamental figurehead. Clay declined Harrison's offer of the Secretaryship of State, preferring to remain as Whig leader in the Senate. He had already drawn up an elaborate plan of legislation (his "general orders to Congress") for the restoration of the National Bank, the increase of the tariff, and the distribution of the money from land sales in the states for the furtherance of internal improvements — in short, the revival of the "American System" (p. 272). When President Tyler wrecked this program by twice vetoing a Bank bill and refusing to support the distribution scheme or a tariff high enough to create a surplus in the Treasury, he was read out of the Whig party, to which he had never really belonged, as a "traitor" and "apostate" and a miserable "President by accident." Clay resigned from the Senate in disgust in 1842, and all the Whig members of the cabinet, except Secretary of State Daniel Webster, followed him into retirement.

The Webster-Ashburton Treaty. Webster remained at his post partly because he did not wish to seem to take orders from Clay and partly because he was engaged in an important diplomatic negotiation with Great Britain, which he wished to bring to a happy conclusion.

Our relations with England were, in fact, more strained in 1841 than they had been at any other time since the War of 1812. Many British investors had lost money in the depression following the panic of 1837 and the repudiation of their bonds by several states of the Union. The *Caroline* affair (p. 305) was still rankling in the breasts of the jingoes. The Southern planters were incensed because the authorities of the British island of Nassau had set at liberty a shipload of slaves who had mutinied on board the brig *Creole*, killed the captain, overpowered the crew, and brought the brig into the British port. The swelling stream of American immigration into Oregon was threatening to sweep away the equal rights of the British there, as guaranteed by the terms of the joint occupation. Finally, war had actually broken out between the lumbermen of Maine and New Brunswick over the location of the northeastern boundary between the United States and Canada as determined by the treaty of 1783. A fortunate change in British politics in 1841 brought Lord Aberdeen, a friend of the United States, into the Foreign Office.

In the summer of 1842 Aberdeen sent Lord Ashburton (also a friend of America and a personal friend of Webster) to Washington, where, in pleasantly informal discussions, most of the points of controversy were settled. The Webster-Ashburton Treaty fixed our northeastern boundary in its present location, dividing the twelve thousand square miles of territory in dispute almost equally between New Brunswick and Maine. In the spring of 1843 Webster, being unable to work longer in harmony with the administration, also resigned his cabinet position. But two years later he re-entered the Senate.

The Texas Question Reopened. With both the great Whig leaders out of the way, Tyler, who was an ardent annexationist, turned his attention to Texas and looked for support to the men of the South. Upshur of Virginia, who succeeded Webster, began negotiations with Texas; and when he was killed by the explosion of a cannon on the warship *Princeton*, his work was taken up by an even more ardent annexationist, John C. Calhoun. Meantime the English government was giving unmistakable proof of its determination to keep Texas out of the Union. Mexico owed about fifteen million dollars to British capitalists, for which lands to the north and west of the Rio Grande had been mortgaged. Besides, an independent state of Texas under British protection would furnish England with plentiful supplies of cotton and a market for her manufactures, unhampered by the tariff of the United States. Finally, Lord Aberdeen wrote a letter to the British minister in Washington, in which he expressed the hope that slavery would be kept out of Texas, as it had been abolished in the British West Indies. England even went so far, in 1843, as to promise a large loan to Texas and to secure the recognition of her independence from

Mexico if she would consent to remain a free-soil republic independent of the United States.

But, in spite of these offers, the Texans still favored annexation. In April, 1844, Calhoun completed a treaty with the Texan minister providing for the reception of Texas not as a *state* but as a *territory* of the United States. She was to surrender her public lands, but in return she was to have her debt, to an amount not exceeding ten million dollars, assumed by the national government. As Texas lay almost wholly below the Missouri Compromise line of 36° 30′, it would presumably be a slaveholding territory. So, at least, it was understood by John Quincy Adams, who wrote in his diary for April 22, "The treaty for the annexation of Texas to this Union was this day sent into the Senate; and with it went the freedom of the human race."

But Adams's gloomy prophecy was premature, for the Senate, on June 8, rejected Calhoun's treaty by the decisive vote of 16 to 35. That only 16 votes could be found for the treaty in a Senate which contained 26 members from the states of the South shows that the plan to annex Texas cannot be regarded simply as a "gigantic conspiracy" to add slave territory to the Union. Disapproval of Calhoun's highhanded methods, hostility to the land speculators, the doubt whether the Constitution allowed the executive to annex an independent foreign state to the Union, and fear of inviting a war with Mexico were the main reasons for the defeat of the treaty.

The Election of 1844. While Calhoun's treaty was being discussed in the Senate, the national conventions met to select their candidates for the Presidential campaign. Henry Clay was unanimously nominated by the Whigs at Baltimore, May 1, on a platform which, by his own request, was silent on the subject of Texan annexation. The Democrats also met at Baltimore, on May 27. It was expected that Van Buren would be their nominee, for about three fourths of the Democratic state conventions had instructed their delegates to Baltimore to support him. But on April 27 he had courageously published a letter opposing the annexation of Texas, which turned many of the

Southern delegates against him. At that, he had the majority of the votes on the first ballot, but could not command the two-thirds vote necessary for nomination in a Democratic convention. On the ninth ballot the convention unanimously nominated James K. Polk, of Tennessee, a man not hitherto considered as "Presidential timber," though he had been Speaker of the House and governor of his state.[1] The platform announced that our title to the whole of the Oregon territory was "clear and unquestionable," and that "the reoccupation of Oregon and the reannexation of Texas at the earliest practicable period" were "great American measures."[2] This clever combination of Oregon and Texas was intended to win both free-soilers and slaveholders for the ticket.

Clay had also published a letter on April 27 (when he thought that Van Buren would be the Democratic candidate), opposing annexation; but when he found himself running against the avowed annexationist Polk he changed his tune and wrote that he "would be glad to see Texas admitted on fair terms" and that "slavery ought not to affect the question one way or another." This shifty behavior caused enough antislavery Whigs in New York and Michigan to vote for James G. Birney, the candidate of the Liberty party, to enable Polk to carry those two states and therewith the election. It was a bitter pill for the brilliant and confident Clay to meet defeat in his third campaign for the Presidency at the hands of so obscure and mediocre a candidate as Polk. The election, however, was very close, in spite of the electoral figures of 170 to 105; for Polk's popular plurality was less than 40,000 in a vote of nearly 3,000,000. He carried seven Northern states to Clay's six, and eight Southern states to Clay's five. It was the "abolitionist" vote for Birney that defeated Clay. With the 41 votes from New York and

[1] Polk was the first example of the "dark horse" in a national convention. The term was borrowed from the race track. An unexpected candidate who finally secured the nomination was likened to a horse which came up from behind and won the race.

[2] The "re" in the Democratic slogan of 1844 meant that we already owned Oregon and that we had purchased Texas from Napoleon in 1803. Neither of these claims was justified by the facts of the case.

Michigan he would have won the election over Polk by a margin of 17 electoral votes.

The Annexation of Texas. Despite the narrowness of Polk's victory, President Tyler, in his December message to Congress, declared that "by the election a controlling majority of the people and a large majority of the states [!] had declared in favor of immediate annexation." He was not even willing to wait for Polk to come into office to carry out this alleged "mandate" from the American people. In February, 1845, he secured the passage of a resolution in both houses of Congress for the annexation of Texas to the Union. He signed the resolution on March 1, three days before he left office, and immediately dispatched a messenger to Texas with the offer. Texas was to be admitted as a state on condition that she should frame and submit to Congress an acceptable constitution before January 1, 1846. She was to surrender all her public buildings, defenses, ports, and harbors to the United States, retaining her public lands and her debts. Four additional states might be carved out of her immense area, with her consent. Slavery was to be prohibited in the small part of her territory north of the line of 36° 30'.

The redoubled efforts of Great Britain and Mexico to prevent the annexation of Texas were of no avail. The people of Texas ratified their new constitution with less than fifty dissenting votes; Congress received the new state by large majorities in both the Senate and the House of Representatives; and President Polk signed the act of admission on December 29, 1845. A few weeks later the blue flag of Texas, with its lone white star, — the emblem under which the republic had lived its uncertain life for ten years, — was hauled down, and in its place were raised the Stars and Stripes.

The Oregon Treaty. With Texas safely in the Union, Polk turned to the other campaign pledge, that of the "reoccupation" of Oregon. We had already proposed a division of the territory along the line of 49° north latitude, which would give us most of the valley of the Columbia River; but the British government refused the proposition. Now with Polk asserting our claim to the whole of Oregon up to the Alaska (Russian) boundary of 54° 40′, and with the apostles of "manifest destiny" shouting, "All of Oregon or none!" and "Fifty-four forty or fight!" it looked as if we should come to blows with Great Britain. Besides, the Northern expansionists were accusing the Southern Congressmen of growing cold to the "reoccupation" of free-soil Oregon now that they had secured the "reannexation" of slaveholding Texas. "Texas and Oregon," cried Hannegan of Indiana, "were born in the same instant, nursed in the same cradle — the Baltimore convention — and they were at the same instant adopted by the Democracy throughout the land. There was not a moment's hesitation until Texas was admitted; but at the moment she was admitted the peculiar friends of Texas turned and were doing all they could to strangle Oregon."

In April, 1846, Congress authorized the President to end the treaty of 1827 for the joint occupation of Oregon, and a month later Polk gave formal notice of the termination to the British government. But there was a good deal of bluff in all this. Neither Congress nor the President had any intention of going to war with England over a difference of five degrees of latitude in our northwestern boundary, especially at the very moment when war with Mexico over our incorporation of Texas was certain.[1] So when, at a hint from our minister in London, Great Britain sent over the draft of a treaty dividing Oregon on the parallel of 49° from the Rockies to the waters of the Pacific, Polk accepted it and the Senate ratified it by a vote of 41 to 14. The arch-expansionists, like Hannegan, might storm at what they regarded as the cowardice of a government which marched its troops to the borders of a weak Mexico but which retreated from Oregon in the face of a strong England. They overlooked, however, the simple fact that we had no more claim to the Oregon of 54° 40′ than we had to China.

[1] It was on the day after Congress voted to terminate the agreement with Great Britain for the joint occupation of Oregon that the first armed clash between Mexican and American troops on the Rio Grande took place (p. 330). It was not until more than two weeks later, however, that Congress declared war on Mexico.

Polk's Negotiations with Mexico. For many years preceding Polk's Presidency our relations with Mexico had been strained. We had tried to collect claims for injuries to the persons and property of our citizens resulting from the revolutionary disturbances which so frequently vexed the Mexican Republic. In 1837 Jackson had actually broken off relations with Mexico and threatened to send a warship to Veracruz to enforce our claims. The aid furnished by Americans in securing and defending the independence of Texas was another cause of friction. But the chief grievance of Mexico was the annexation of Texas to the United States. As early as November, 1843, the Mexican minister at Washington had notified our Secretary of State that if we should "commit the unheard-of aggression" of seizing "an integral part of Mexican territory," he would consider his mission at Washington at an end, since his government was "resolved to declare war so soon as it received information of such an act." Though his government did not declare war when the resolution for the annexation of Texas was signed by Tyler, diplomatic relations between Mexico and the United States were immediately broken off.

Polk tried to renew them in the autumn of 1845, sending John Slidell of New Orleans to Mexico to adjust the claims and the Texan boundary and to offer Mexico as much as thirty million dollars for her vast territory of New Mexico and California, over which she had but feeble control. But Mexico was just then entering upon another revolution, and neither of the rivals for the presidency was willing to risk his popularity by making any concessions to the United States. Slidell was refused an audience, and, after lingering hopefully in Mexico for many weeks, he returned to New Orleans.

General Zachary Taylor, with two thousand regular troops, was in Texas in the summer of 1845 to protect that state against a Mexican invasion. When the news of Slidell's rejection reached Washington in January, 1846, Taylor was ordered to advance to the Rio Grande, which we insisted was the southern boundary of Texas. Taylor built a fort opposite Matamoros as a warning to the Mexicans not to cross the river. When he refused to withdraw to the Nueces River [1] at the order of the Mexican commander, a Mexican detachment crossed the Rio Grande and ambushed a scouting party of Americans under Captain Thornton, killing or wounding sixteen of them (April 24, 1846).

The Declaration of War. On receiving the news of the attack on Captain Thornton, Polk sent a special message to Congress, declaring that war already existed "by the act of Mexico herself," in spite of all our efforts to prevent it. "After reiterated menaces," he said, "Mexico has passed the boundary of the United States . . . and shed American blood on American soil." He asked for soldiers and money to prosecute the war. There was some opposition from Whig Congressmen who took the view that the United States was the aggressive party by moving its troops into the disputed area between the Nueces and the Rio Grande. But the opposition was feeble. On the day of the President's message the House passed a bill for the enlistment of fifty thousand troops and the appropriation of ten million dollars, by a vote of 174 to 14. The vote next day in the Senate was 40 to 2. On May 13 Polk signed the bill, and the gates of war were opened. Except for New England, where the abolitionist spirit was strong, the country responded with enthusiasm to the call for troops. Soon twenty-three thousand volunteers from the Western and Southern states were in arms. The cry was, "Ho for the halls of Montezuma!"

The Americans Seize New Mexico and California. As soon as the war broke out, Colonel Stephen S. Kearney, at Fort Leavenworth, Kansas, was ordered to invade New Mexico. Setting out with eighteen hundred men near the end of June, and toiling over hundreds of miles of arid country, Kearny entered Santa Fe in August. The mixed Mexican and Indian force of four thou-

---

[1] To be consistent, Mexico should have demanded that Taylor withdraw his army not beyond the Nueces but beyond the Sabine River. For according to her claim the whole of Texas was still Mexican territory. On the other hand, when Santa Anna had been captured at the battle of San Jacinto, in 1836 (p. 320), he had made a treaty with the victorious Texans recognizing the Rio Grande as the boundary of their state — a treaty which the Mexican congress rejected because it had been concluded under force.

sand retreated before him without a show of resistance. Raising the American flag, he declared the territory of New Mexico "incorporated into the United States," and absolved its inhabitants from their allegiance to Mexico. A few days later he published a code of laws for the territory. Then he started for California, where he joined with Captain John C. Frémont in completing the conquest of that beautiful Mexican province.[1]

Taylor's Victory at Buena Vista. While California and New Mexico were thus being brought under the American flag, General Taylor was penetrating the northern provinces of Mexico. He had already occupied the capitals of several of these provinces when the government at Washington adopted a new plan to end the war. An expedition under General Winfield Scott was to land at Veracruz, on the Gulf of Mexico, and march directly upon the Mexican capital. Half of Taylor's army of ten thousand was assigned to Scott. Learning from an intercepted letter of the plans for the Veracruz expedition, the Mexican dictator, Santa Anna, swept northward with his great "Army of Liberation," twenty thousand strong, to drive Taylor's reduced forces back across the Rio Grande. The two armies met on February 22, 1847, near the ranch of Buena Vista. After two days of furious battle the shattered Mexican army left the field under the shadow of night. Buena Vista was a glorious victory in the face of tremendous odds, against the largest army that American troops had ever met. It made Zachary Taylor the next President of the United States.

Scott Takes the Mexican Capital. Meanwhile Scott's troops were being conveyed down the Gulf of Mexico to Veracruz, where they landed in March and began their romantic march of three hundred miles up through the mountains to the Mexican capital. Santa Anna had hastened back from Buena Vista to oppose Scott's advance with an army of thirteen thousand men.

[1] Frémont, a young captain of engineers, was on one of those exploring expeditions in the Far West which won him the name of "the Pathfinder." In the summer of 1846, without orders from Washington, he and his band of "shaggy-bearded" men had set up an American Republic of California under the famous "Bear Flag." When news of the outbreak of the war reached Frémont, he hauled down the Bear Flag and raised the Stars and Stripes in its place.

After he had been driven from the heights of Cerro Gordo, however, by a brilliant flanking movement planned by Robert E. Lee, he ceased to be a menace, and the American troops were only occasionally troubled by guerrilla bands. As to the civilian population, they welcomed rather than resented the presence of the Americans. Scott posed as their liberator from the faction-ridden government, and his orders to treat persons and property with respect and to pay liberally for all supplies furnished by the peasants were strictly obeyed.

Polk had sent Nicholas Trist, the chief clerk of the State Department, to join Scott's headquarters and to offer peace and a money payment to Mexico any moment that she was ready to give up her claims to Texas, New Mexico, and California. When Scott reached the outskirts of Mexico City, in August, he granted an armistice for the discussion of Trist's offer. But the Mexican government not only refused to part with its northern provinces (though they were in secure possession of the Americans) but even demanded that the United States pay damages for the invasion of her territory. Trist was ordered home, the war was resumed, and Scott, after storming the strong defenses of the city, looked down, as Cortes had done three centuries before, upon the splendid capital now at his mercy. The Mexican troops withdrew from the city, and the council sent its capitulation to the American headquarters. At dawn of September 14, 1847, our troops, "decorated with mud and the red stains of battle," entered the gates and raised the American flag above the palace, while General Scott mounted the stairway of the "halls of the Montezumas" to write his dispatch of victory.

The Treaty of Guadalupe-Hidalgo. The fall of Mexico City eliminated Santa Anna and brought to power a government desirous of peace. Trist had remained in Mexico, in spite of his recall, and on February 2, 1848, he concluded with the new Mexican commissioners the Treaty of Guadalupe-Hidalgo. Mexico acknowledged our title to Texas, New Mexico, and California, and in return we paid her $15,000,000 and assumed claims of our citizens against Mexico for $3,250,000 more. Some

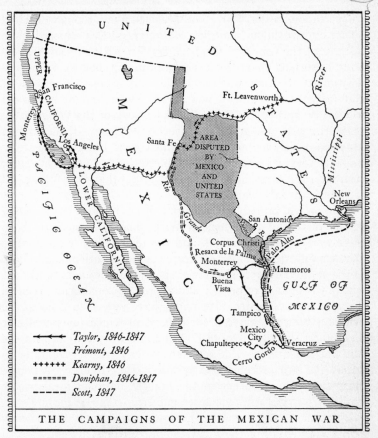

Taylor, 1846-1847
Frémont, 1846
Kearny, 1846
Doniphan, 1846-1847
Scott, 1847

THE CAMPAIGNS OF THE MEXICAN WAR

members of the cabinet, including Secretary of State Buchanan, wanted to take all or part of Mexico proper, but Polk held firmly to the line of the Rio Grande. In the Senate the treaty was opposed by expansionists who wanted more territory, antislavery men who wanted no territory, and Whigs who were chagrined that Polk should have finished up his program so successfully at the opening of the Presidential year. Nevertheless, the treaty was ratified by a vote of 38 to 14, only three more than the necessary two thirds.

Opposition to the War. The Mexican War, though declared by an overwhelming majority of Congress, was opposed more bitterly at the time and has been condemned more severely by later historians than any other war in our history. The opposition at the time was partly the honest moral objection of abolitionists [1] to acquiring new territory which might be opened to slavery, and partly the political jealousy of the Whigs, who, in their newspapers and their speeches in Congress, encouraged Mexican resistance to a war which was being successfully waged under a Democratic administration. [2] Later historians, with few exceptions, have taken the ground that Polk "goaded" the Mexicans into war.

Opinion will probably always remain divided on the question of the justice of the Mexican War. The grievances on both sides were of long standing, and the disputes over boundaries were complicated. A man of greater tact and patience than Polk in the White House might have kept the expansionist sentiment within the bounds of peace; and a more reasonable and reliable government at Mexico City might have agreed in time to the generous offer we made it for distant provinces over which it had only a shadow of control. But those who contend that the war was not dishonorable can hardly deny that it was unfortunate. The only recompense of war is that it unites a people more firmly in devotion to the highest national ideals. The result of our victories which we gained in 1846–1847, however, was not the peaceful and harmonious development of the newly acquired territory of the Far West but bitter strife and discord

---

[1] See, for example James Russell Lowell's "The Present Crisis" and *The Biglow Papers*.

[2] Corwin of Ohio, for example, hoped that the Mexicans would "welcome the American soldiers to hospitable graves." Clay, Webster, and the other "Mexican Whigs" were accused of giving more aid and comfort to the enemy than if they "had arrayed ten thousand Mexicans against Scott." Abraham Lincoln, serving his single term in Congress (1847–1849), presented his famous "spot resolutions," challenging Polk to name the spot of American soil on which the Mexicans had shed American blood. That most of the Whig opposition to "Mr. Polk's war" had the purely partisan character of the New Englanders' opposition to "Mr. Madison's war" in 1812 is shown by the fact that the Whig party took both the victorious Whig generals as candidates for the Presidency — Taylor in 1848 and Scott in 1852.

Ewing Galloway

MISSION AT SANTA BARBARA, CALIFORNIA

over its status in the Union. The fruits of the Mexican War, like the apples of Sodom, turned to ashes in our mouth.

The Program of Expansion Completed. With the annexation of Texas (1845), the acquisition of Oregon to the forty-ninth parallel (1846), and the cession of New Mexico and California (1848), the continental boundaries of the United States reached practically their present limits.[1] The work of westward extension was done. Expansion, the watchword of the decade 1840–1850, was dropped from our vocabulary for fifty years, and the attention of the nation was directed toward finding a plan on which the new territory could be organized with satisfaction to the conflicting interests of the free and slave sections of our country.

[1] A small strip of land south of the Gila River — southern Arizona — was bought from Mexico in 1853 because it offered the best route for a railroad across the southern Rockies to the Pacific coast. The large sum of ten million dollars paid for this "Gadsden Purchase" was regarded by some critics of the Mexican War as "conscience money" paid to Mexico for the provinces which we had taken from her five years before.

TERMS TO BE MASTERED

Great American Desert	"manifest destiny"	"Fifty-four forty"
Great Divide	"dark horse"	Bear Flag
the Alamo	"reannexation" of Texas	armistice
"spot resolutions"	joint resolution	Gadsden Purchase

FOR SUPPLEMENTARY READING

E. E. SPARKS, *The Expansion of the American People*, chap. xxv; The Pageant of America, Vol. VIII, pp. 271–281; G. P. GARRISON, *Westward Extension* (American Nation Series, Vol. XVII); N. W. STEPHENSON, *Texas and the Mexican War* (Chronicles of America, Vol. XXIV); W. E. DODD, *Expansion and Conflict*, chaps. vii–ix; EDWARD CHANNING, *History of the United States*, Vol. V, chaps. xv–xviii; ALLAN NEVINS (ed.), *Polk, the Diary of a President*; W. J. GHENT, *The Road to Oregon*; America, Vol. VI, pp. 200–226, 231–238, 281–290, 313–318; Vol. VII, pp. 13–105; HART, *Contemporaries*, Vol. III, Nos. 185–189; Vol. IV, Nos. 7–22; MUZZEY, *Readings*, pp. 312–334.

TOPICS FOR REPORTS

1. **American Pioneers in Texas.** G. P. GARRISON, "The First Stage of the Movement for the Americanization of Texas," in *American Historical Review*, Vol. X, pp. 72–96; HENRY BRUCE, *The Life of General Houston*, pp. 64–156; W. B. DEWER, *Letters from an Early Settler of Texas*; E. C. BARKER, *Life of Stephen F. Austin*; G. P. GARRISON, *Texas, a Contest of Civilizations*, pp. 137–169.

2. **The Legend of Marcus Whitman.** E. G. BOURNE, "The Legend of Marcus Whitman," in *American Historical Review*, Vol. VI, pp. 276–300; JAMES SCHOULER, *History of the United States*, Vol. IV, pp. 504–514; WILLIAM BARROWS, *Oregon*, pp. 160–254; H. H. BANCROFT, *Works*, Vol. XXIX, pp. 391–424, 446–469, 508–554.

3. **The Webster-Ashburton Treaty.** H. C. LODGE, *Daniel Webster*, pp. 241–263; JARED SPARKS, "The Webster-Ashburton Treaty," in *North American Review*, Vol. LIV, pp. 452 f.; E. D. ADAMS, "Lord Ashburton and the Treaty of Washington," in *American Historical Review*, Vol. XVII, pp. 746–782; H. S. COMMAGER, *Documents of American History*, pp. 298–300; H. S. BURRAGE, *Maine in the Northeastern Boundary Controversy*.

4. **John C. Frémont, "the Pathfinder."** R. G. THWAITES, *Rocky Mountain Exploration*, pp. 228–243; J. C. FRÉMONT, *Memoirs of my Life*; JESSIE B. FRÉMONT, *Souvenirs of my Time*, pp. 189–209; ALLAN NEVINS, *Frémont, the West's Greatest Adventurer*, Vol. I, chaps. iii, vii, viii, x–xiv, xvi, xix, xx; JOHN BIDWELL, "Frémont and the Conquest of California," in *Century Magazine*, Vol. XIX, pp. 518–525, 759–780, with interesting illustrations.

Questions Suggested by the Chapter

1. What did the term "Oregon" mean in 1840? 2. How did our government treat the Indian tribes a hundred years ago? 3. What was the route of the Santa Fe trail? of the Oregon trail? 4. Who discovered the Great Salt Lake, and when? 5. On what did Benton base our claim to Texas? 6. Why did the annexation of Texas hang fire during Van Buren's administration? 7. Why was England interested in keeping Texas out of the United States? 8. Explain Clay's "straddle" on the annexation of Texas. Why have American historians usually condemned the Mexican War? 9. Was Tyler a "traitor" to the Whigs? 10. Why did Webster remain in Tyler's cabinet after Clay's followers had resigned? 11. What does the phrase "Mexican Whigs" mean? 12. Why was the conquest of New Mexico and California so easy? 13. How was the controversy with England over Oregon settled? 14. Why was Calhoun's treaty for the annexation of Texas rejected by the Senate? 15. On what terms did Texas enter the Union in 1845? 16. How was opposition to the Mexican War expressed at the time? 17. What were the terms of the treaty ending the war?

CHAPTER FOURTEEN

THE BUSINESSMAN'S PEACE

The New Far West. An area larger than the United States of 1783 or the Louisiana region purchased from Napoleon in 1803 was added to our territory between 1846 and 1848.[1] The land varied in value. Between the rich cotton areas of Texas and the smiling valleys of California lay the arid plateaus and majestic canyons of the Rockies. In Oregon fine timber and farm lands were awaiting the settler. The sudden acquisition of the Pacific coast from Puget Sound to San Diego opened upon our view the great western ocean and made us neighbors of China and Japan. The new region, though sparsely populated by white men, was still not entirely unknown; for ever since the days of Lewis and Clark's expedition adventurous explorers and emigrant trains had been beating into roads the Indian trails to Santa Fe, Oregon, and California. Groups of immigrants, obeying the American instinct for self-government, had set up little "republics" on the Columbia, the Sacramento, or the Rio Grande, waiting for the United States to take them under its protection. Now that the whole Far West was ours by formal treaties, it was incumbent upon the government at Washington to provide for its proper political organization. President Polk had already urged Congress in his message of December, 1846, to erect Oregon into a territory, and as soon as we acquired New Mexico and California he recommended a territorial government for these provinces also.

---

[1] AREA OF UNITED STATES BEFORE 1845

ADDITIONS, 1845–1848

	Sq. Miles			Sq. Miles
Original area, 1783	(about) 830,000	Texas, 1845	(about)	390,000
Louisiana Purchase, 1803 . .	" 875,000	Oregon, 1846	"	290,000
Florida Purchase, 1819	" 65,000	Mexican Cession, 1848. . . .	"	520,000
	1,770,000			1,200,000

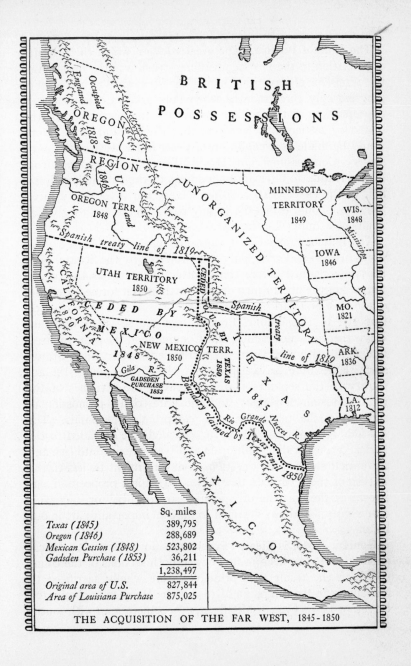

THE ACQUISITION OF THE FAR WEST, 1845-1850

	Sq. miles
Texas (1845)	389,795
Oregon (1846)	288,689
Mexican Cession (1848)	523,802
Gadsden Purchase (1853)	36,211
	1,238,497
Original area of U.S.	827,844
Area of Louisiana Purchase	875,025

The Wilmot Proviso. The great rock on which the peaceful organization of the new acquisitions struck was the question of the admission of slavery to them. The Mexican War had been in progress only three months when Polk asked Congress for an appropriation of two million dollars for the negotiation of the boundary settlement. Knowing that the demand for territory would be made as a condition of peace with Mexico, the anti-slavery Congressmen got David Wilmot, a Democrat from Pennsylvania, to offer an amendment to the two-million-dollar bill, to the effect that "neither slavery nor involuntary servitude . . . should ever exist in any part" of the territory which might be acquired by the war.

The Wilmot Proviso, as it was called, passed the House several times in 1846 and 1847, only to be rejected by the Senate. The Proviso remained before the country, however, as the official demand of the liberty men of the North, and it formed the basis of the Free-Soil party of 1848 and the Republican party of 1854. Opposed to the Wilmot Proviso was the so-called Calhoun-Davis theory, which denied that Congress had the right to interfere at all with slavery in the territories of the United States, since slaves were private property which came under the authority of the separate states. Between the extremes of the total exclusion of slavery and the unrestricted permission of slavery in the territories were compromise proposals. The Missouri Compromise line of 36° 30' might be extended to the Pacific coast, dividing California and New Mexico into free and slave sections. Or the question of slavery might be left to the settlers of the territories themselves. This last proposition was known as the doctrine of "popular sovereignty" or "squatter sovereignty," and was destined to play an important part in our history.

General Taylor is Elected President. Both the great political parties wanted to keep in favor with both sections of the country, with the result that principles were wholly sacrificed to maneuvers in the campaign of 1848. The Democrats nominated Governor Lewis Cass of Michigan, a "northern man with southern principles," popularly known as a "doughface." [1] The platform defended the Mexican War as "just and necessary" and denied the power of Congress to interfere with the domestic institutions (slavery) of the states. Every attempt to discuss the Wilmot Proviso was shouted down in the convention. The Whigs, in spite of their denunciation of the war, nominated the hero of Buena Vista. General Taylor was a Louisiana sugar planter and the owner of three hundred slaves. But he repudiated the extreme proslavery doctrine of Calhoun and of his son-in-law Jefferson Davis. He had had no experience in political affairs, and had not even voted for some years. When asked for his opinions on the Bank and the tariff, he replied with blunt honesty that he had "had no time to investigate" those questions. The Whigs simply counted on his brilliant record in the war to sweep him into office. "Old Rough and Ready" was the campaign cry that recalled the "Tippecanoe and Tyler Too" of eight years before.

The issues of the Bank, the tariff, and internal improvements, on which Whigs and Democrats were formerly divided, had faded into the background,[2] but the lines of the new struggle over slavery, cutting across both parties, were not yet sharply drawn. Each party was angling for votes wherever they could be found — the Whigs with the bait of a Louisiana slaveholder whose military glory commended him to the free North, and the Democrats with a Northern frontiersman whose views on slavery were not offensive to the South.

In striking contrast to this attempt of both the great parties to dodge the main question, the new Free-Soil party declared against the erection of another slave territory or the admission

[1] This was a name fastened upon Northerners who supported Southern measures for the sake of preserving peace. It was coined by the sarcastic John Randolph, and it implied that the men so designated had so little conviction of their own that their faces could be molded into any shape.

[2] The Bank question was settled by the final establishment of the Subtreasury system in 1846, by which the government moneys were kept in its own vaults in various cities. The government remained wholly divorced from the banks until the Civil War. The Walker tariff of 1846 agreed upon moderate rates which were not disturbed for eleven years.

of another slave state (the Wilmot Proviso doctrine). The Free-Soilers nominated Martin Van Buren of New York, who took away enough votes from Cass in that state to give its 36 electoral votes and therewith the election itself to Taylor. Taylor carried seven free states and eight slave states; Cass carried eight free states and seven slave states.[1] The Free-Soilers won no state, but elected to the House of Representatives 13 members who would hold the balance of power between the 112 Democrats and the 105 Whigs in the Thirty-first Congress (1849–1851).

El Dorado. President Polk's term ended on March 4, 1849, without any step's having been taken by Congress for the organization of California and New Mexico. While Congress was thus deadlocked over the question of slavery in the Mexican cession, events occurred on the Pacific coast which gave a new aspect to the question.

A few days before the treaty with Mexico was signed, gold was discovered in the Sacramento valley of California. As the news of the richness of the deposits spread, a wild rush to the gold fields began. Men from every walk of life — merchants, farmers, lawyers, shopkeepers, sailors, ministers, servants — abandoned their pursuits to stake out claims in the "diggings," from which they often took a fortune in a few weeks. Thousands came by wagon across the plains, braving starvation, the fever of the alkali wastes, and the attacks of the Indians, and leaving a tell-tale track of broken wagons, dead animals, and human bones. Other thousands came by sea, enduring the buffetings of the six months' voyage around Cape Horn, or crossing the pestilence-laden Isthmus of Panama to battle like crazy men for a place on the dirty, rickety steamers plying up the California coast. The immigration in the single year 1849 raised the population of California from six thousand to over eighty-five thousand souls. The "forty-niners," as these gold-seekers were called, were largely from the free states of the North. Consequently, when

[1] The slave and free states were still evenly matched, at fifteen each, in November, 1848. Since the admission of Maine and Missouri in 1820–1821, the three slave states of Arkansas (1836), Florida (1845), and Texas (1846) had been balanced by the three free states of Michigan (1837), Iowa (1846), and Wisconsin (1848).

WASHING GOLD ON A RIVER NEAR SACRAMENTO, CALIFORNIA

delegates elected by the Californian immigrants met in a convention in September, 1849, they drew up a state constitution excluding slavery by a unanimous vote. When Congress met in December, therefore, California was no longer waiting to be organized as a territory but was asking for admission to the Union as a state with a free constitution.

Henry Clay Proposes a Settlement of the Slavery Question. There was little chance that Congress would heed President Taylor's plea to "abstain from exciting topics of a sectional character." The members from North and South had come to Washington determined to uphold their respective demands on the slavery issue. In the Senate, where for the last time the great triumvirate of Calhoun, Clay, and Webster met, heated resolutions on the "exciting topic" were introduced by several prominent leaders. It looked as if chaos would rule the session when, on January 29, 1850, Clay rose to propose a set of compromise measures to secure "the peace, concord, and harmony of the Union."

After an absence of seven years, Clay had returned to Washington, at the age of seventy-four, racked with the cough of

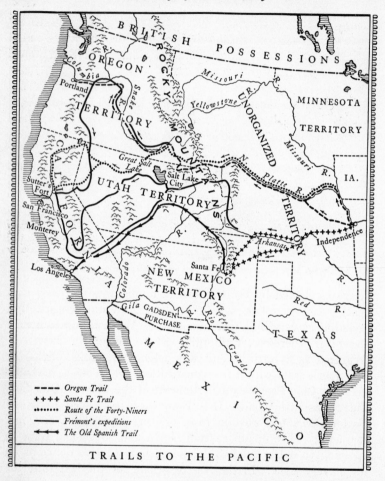

TRAILS TO THE PACIFIC

advanced consumption, to devote his last service to pouring oil
on the troubled waters of sectional strife. The "Omnibus Bill"
which he defended in the opening speech of the greatest debate
ever heard in the halls of Congress consisted of five main proposals: (1) California should be admitted as a free state;
(2) territorial governments should be established in the rest of
the Mexican cession (Utah on the north and New Mexico on the

south) without restrictions as to slavery; (3) the area of the slaveholding state of Texas should be cut down from 379,000 to 264,000 square miles, but in return she should receive ten million dollars to pay her war debt contracted before 1845; (4) the slave trade should be prohibited in the District of Columbia, but slavery itself should not be abolished in the District without the consent of Maryland;[1] and (5) a new fugitive-slave law should be passed making the recovery of runaway slaves much easier than under the old law of 1793.

We can realize what a difficult task Clay had undertaken when we compare the demands of the radical leaders of the North and the South on these questions.

On the question of	The South demanded	The North demanded
(1) California	organization as a territory, admitting slavery	immediate admission as a free state
(2) New Mexico	legalization of slavery by Congress (at least below 36°30′)	the application of the Wilmot Proviso
(3) Texas	the same boundaries as the Texan republic claimed in 1836	a reduction in the size of Texas without any money compensation
(4) District of Columbia	no interference with slavery by Congress	abolition of slavery
(5) Fugitive slaves	a strict law enforced by national authority, with no jury trial for Negroes	jury trial for every Negro claimed as a fugitive slave

Clay held out the olive branch to both sections "of this distracted and unhappy country." No sacrifice was too great to preserve the Union of the fathers. Secession could mean only war — war "ferocious and bloody, implacable and exterminating."

The Debate in the Senate. Calhoun was to speak on the fourth of March. Too enfeebled by the ravages of consumption to take the floor himself, he sat swathed in flannels in his seat while his carefully prepared speech was read by his colleague Senator Mason. Calhoun too loved the Union and dreaded the

---

[1] The student will recall that the District of Columbia was formed from land donated to the government by Maryland and Virginia, and that the Virginia part had been ceded back to that state in 1846 (p. 213, note 1).

word "secession." But the Union as it now existed, he said, was no longer a guarantee of the liberties of the South. The equilibrium between the sections had already been destroyed by the aggressions of the North. She alone was to blame. No institution of hers was attacked, no threat against her property was made, no stigma was cast on the moral character of her citizens. The South asked only her plain rights under the Constitution. She had nothing to compromise or concede. It lay with the North to cease all agitation against slavery if our republic were not to be dissolved into warring factions. It was Calhoun's last word. Before the month had closed he had passed beyond all earthly strife.

Daniel Webster spoke to crowded galleries on the seventh of March. He had put himself on record as opposed to the extension of slavery "irrespective of lines and latitudes"; but now, realizing the great danger to the Union, he supported Clay's compromise at every point. There was no possibility, he said, that slavery would ever actually invade the deserts and plateaus of New Mexico. Of what use, then, to "reaffirm an ordinance of nature or re-enact the will of God" by insisting on the Wilmot Proviso, which the South looked on as a "taunt and a reproach." As to the abolitionist societies, they "had produced nothing good or valuable in their operations for twenty years." Webster was severely denounced by the antislavery zealots for his "treachery" to the cause; but the conservative businessmen of the North approved his stand and circulated two hundred thousand copies of his speech of March 7.

Two other notable speeches followed. William H. Seward, a new Whig Senator from New York, appealed to "a higher law than the Constitution," namely, the law of human freedom. Salmon P. Chase, a Democrat of Ohio, denounced the compromise as a cowardly surrender to the threats of the South, denying Calhoun's charge that the North was the aggressor.

What was Gained by the Compromise of 1850. The great debate seemed no nearer its end in July than it had been in February. President Taylor, who was much under Seward's influence, would do nothing to hasten the passage of the Omnibus Bill. But Taylor's death, on July 9, 1850, brought into the

White House Millard Fillmore of New York, who favored the compromise. Clay's measures were passed by both houses and signed by the President in August and September.

It is difficult to say which side profited most by the Compromise of 1850. By the admission of California as a free state the North finally got control of the Senate, in which the balance between free and slave states had been maintained for thirty years; on the other hand, the new Fugitive-Slave Act put the whole power of the Federal government behind the South for the return of its runaway Negroes. The South gained admission for slaveholders into the territories of New Mexico and Utah, but it was a region into which slavery was never likely to go. The abolition of the slave trade in the District of Columbia relieved the free-soil Congressmen from the spectacle of chain gangs of Negroes being driven to the Southern cotton fields under the very shadow of the Capitol.

But apart from the question of the gains to either side, it is probable that the Compromise postponed secession for a decade. A convention of nine Southern states had met at Nashville, Tennessee, in June, at Calhoun's suggestion. A majority of the delegates had declared that Congress had no power to exclude slavery from the territories, and some had denounced compromise of any sort and advised secession. With the passage of the Clay measures, however, the South in general agreed that the "sectional controversy" was finally settled. The status of slavery had now been determined in every square mile of our domain from the Atlantic to the Pacific. When Congress met in December, 1850, Clay secured the signatures of forty members to a pledge that they would support no man for public office who refused to abide by his Compromise. If only North and South would carry out the pact faithfully, there need be no occasion for further trouble.

The "Underground Railroad." It was the new law for the return of fugitive slaves that kept the country in a ferment, in spite of the pleas of conservatives like Daniel Webster and Stephen A. Douglas for the law's observance. For several years there had been in operation in New York, in Pennsylvania, and all along the northern bank of the Ohio a system called the "underground railroad," whose object was to give help to Negroes escaping across Mason and Dixon's line into the free states. Prominent citizens were engaged in this work, offering their barns and sheds as "stations" on the "underground," and passing the fugitive along from station to station until he reached the Canadian border.

The people of the free states felt fairly secure in breaking the old fugitive-slave law of 1793, because that law depended on the state authorities for its execution. The new law of 1850, however, if strictly enforced, would have closed every station on the "underground." At the order of the United States marshal all good citizens of a state must help in capturing the fugitive, who was neither allowed to testify in his own behalf nor given a jury trial. The magistrate before whom the Negro was brought was given twice as large a fee for handing him over to the master who claimed him as he was for declaring the Negro free.

The antislavery men of the North were incensed at the new law. Ralph Waldo Emerson wrote in his diary, "I will not obey it!" State after state passed Personal Liberty Acts guaranteeing fugitives protection and a fair trial. In 1852 Harriet Beecher Stowe, sister of the famous preacher Henry Ward Beecher, wrote a pathetic but highly exaggerated novel, *Uncle Tom's Cabin*, portraying the cruelties practiced by the slave-driver, and imploring "the Christian and humane people of the North" not to accept the Fugitive-Slave Act. Her novel, selling by hundreds of thousands, so influenced public opinion that President Lincoln, meeting her later in the White House, greeted her as "the little woman who brought on the Civil War."

Both Parties Agree to the Compromise. The only chance of preventing the two great national parties from being split into Northern and Southern factions was the acceptance of the Compromise of 1850 as a *finality*. The Democrats, in their convention of June 1, 1852, pledged themselves heartily to "abide by and adhere to a faithful execution of" the Compromise measures, and nominated General Franklin Pierce of New Hampshire, a man of winning personality and a creditable record as a legislator

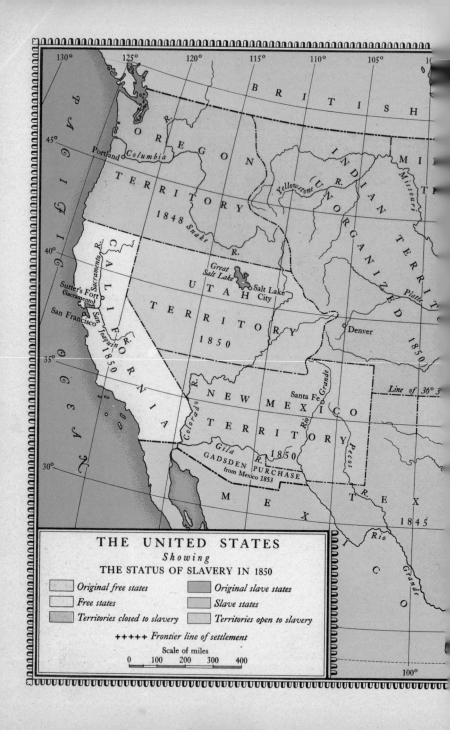

THE UNITED STATES

Showing

THE STATUS OF SLAVERY IN 1850

Original free states

Free states

Territories closed to slavery

Original slave states

Slave states

Territories open to slavery

+++++ Frontier line of settlement

Scale of miles

0   100   200   300   400

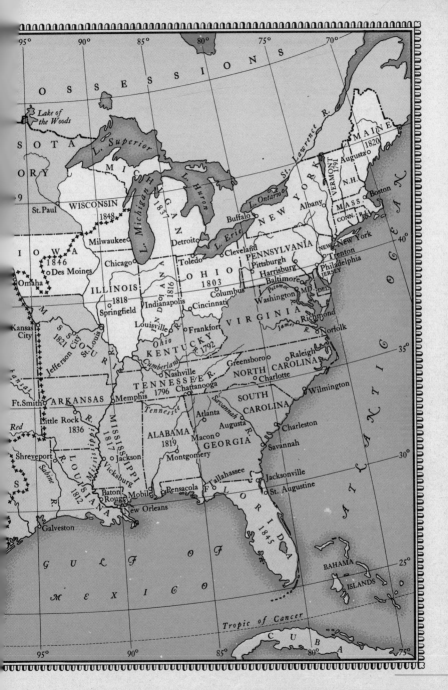

and soldier. The Whigs were in a worse condition than the Democrats. Their great founder and leader for a score of years, Henry Clay, was on his deathbed when the convention assembled. Webster, next in reputation, had ruined his chances with the free-soil element in the party by his support of the Compromise of 1850. It was not until the fifty-third ballot that General Winfield Scott won the nomination. The Whig platform too accepted the finality of the Compromise measures and "deprecated all further agitation" of the slavery question.

But the Whigs failed to repeat the triumphs of 1840 and 1848 with their third military hero. Scott was suspected of a leaning toward free-soil principles and was "knifed" by the Whig leaders of the South. He carried only the four states of Vermont, Massachusetts, Kentucky, and Tennessee, with 42 electoral votes to 254 for Pierce. Harmony was the key word of the new President's inaugural address as he took the oath of office before the throng about the eastern portico of the Capitol on March 4, 1853. The Compromise measures of 1850, he said, were "strictly constitutional and to be unhesitatingly carried into effect," and he fervently hoped that no sectional ambition or fanatical excitement might again "threaten the durability of our institutions or obscure the light of our prosperity."

The Truce of 1850–1854. When President Pierce mentioned "the light of our prosperity," he struck a responsive chord in the industrial and commercial life of the country. The businessmen were tired of the agitation over slavery which Benton, thirty years before, had compared to the plague of frogs in Egypt.

An era of great economic prosperity was opening. Gold was coming from the rich diggings in California at the rate of over $50,000,000 a year, and two thirds of it was going abroad to pay for the excess of our imports over our exports. Our wheat fields were being extended westward into Wisconsin, Iowa, and Minnesota; and the surplus, mounting up rapidly from 100,000,000 bushels, was finding a market in England and on the continent of Europe. Cotton was the wealth of the South. By 1850 the value of the crop was over $100,000,000, and it comprised nearly 50 per cent of the exports of the country. Such figures led the Southerners to believe that the plantation system was the basis of the prosperity of the country. "Cotton is king!" they said. "In the 3,000,000 bags of cotton that slave labor annually throws upon the world, we are doing more to advance civilization than all the canting philanthropists of New and Old England will do in centuries."

From 1830 to 1848 only 6000 miles of railroad had been built in the United States, but the next decade saw more than 16,500 miles added. The New York Central and the Erie reached the Great Lakes in 1850 and 1851. The next year the Pennsylvania entered Pittsburgh, and in 1853 the Baltimore and Ohio was extended to Wheeling, West Virginia. By the close of Pierce's term the railroads from the East touched the Mississippi at ten points, furnishing transportation for the farm products of the West to the Atlantic ports in place of the long voyage down the river and through the Gulf of Mexico.[1]

Our foreign trade, over 70 per cent of which was carried in American ships, was flourishing. In 1850 Great Britain repealed the last of her Navigation Acts, and an exciting rivalry began between the fast Yankee clippers and the British vessels for the trade in the teas and spices of the Orient. In 1853 Congress granted an annual subsidy of $858,000 to the Collins Line to compete with the British Cunard Line, and in that year the tonnage of our merchant marine surpassed that of Great Britain by 15 per cent.

The census of 1850 showed that we had grown from a seaboard population of less than 4,000,000 in Washington's day to a continental people of over 23,000,000, nearly half of whom lived in the great valley of the Mississippi or on the Pacific coast. The statistics of our banks, mills, farms, railroads, and shipping all showed rapidly rising curves. No wonder that the manufacturers, merchants, bankers, railroad-promoters, and cotton-

[1] This substitution of the east-and-west railroad traffic for the north-and-south river traffic had the very important effect also of binding the upper Mississippi valley more closely to the East than to the South in its political sympathies — a fact which proved to be of the greatest significance when the Civil War came.

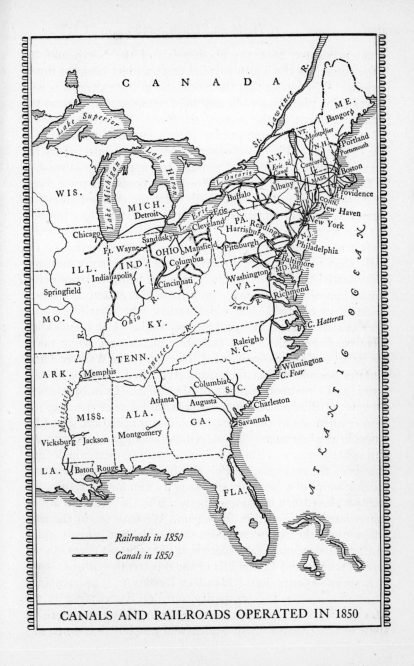

CANALS AND RAILROADS OPERATED IN 1850

planters wanted both the abolitionists of the North and the "fire-eaters" of the South to quiet down and let business thrive in peace! No wonder that the moderates in state after state won elections on platforms endorsing the Compromise of 1850 as the final settlement of the slavery question! The truce of 1850–1854 was a businessman's peace. For a moment it looked as if the optimism of Pierce's inaugural address were justified by the facts. Another "era of good feeling" had apparently dawned.

Discord Increases between North and South. A truce, however, brings no peace unless both sides are satisfied; and, as James A. Garfield remarked, "Unsettled questions have no pity for the repose of a nation." The "good feeling" of the early 1850's was as hollow and deceptive as the good feeling of the early 1820's. The apparent success of the Compromise measures only incited the extremists in North and South to more determined opposition. Language grew more violent and counsels of resistance more bold. The older leaders, with their respect for the Constitution and the spirit of compromise which it embodies, were passing off the scene, and their places were being taken by impatient and assertive men, like Benjamin Wade of Ohio, Charles Sumner of Massachusetts, William L. Yancey of Alabama, and Governor Quitman of Mississippi. Even Stephen A. Douglas of Illinois, the foremost political figure of the 1850's, a sincere advocate of the Constitution and conciliation, urged his cause in the language of abuse, vituperation, and sarcasm. All through the years of the truce, incidents occurred which foreshadowed the renewal of strife. Hardly a month passed without a disturbance in a Northern city over a claim for the return of a fugitive slave, or a meeting of hotheads in the South to advise immediate secession from the Union. We shall see in the next chapter how the flimsy truce was shattered. But before turning to that story we must take some note of important events in our foreign relations at the middle of the nineteenth century.

America Asserts her "Manifest Destiny." The combined effect of our economic prosperity, our decisive victories in the Mexican War, and our expansion to the Pacific was to nourish a spirit of boastfulness in our leaders and people. Statesmen like

CLIPPER SHIPS AT SOUTH STREET IN THE 1850'S, NEW YORK[1]

[1] By courtesy of the Museum of the City of New York.

Cass, Douglas, Clay, and Webster talked of the destiny of the American flag to float over the whole continent from Hudson Bay to the Isthmus of Panama, and of the superiority of our free democratic government over the "effete monarchies" of the Old World. The failure of the potato crops in Ireland in 1845 and 1846, and the revolutions of 1848 which convulsed the leading states of continental Europe, sent to our shores hundreds of thousands of immigrants who were welcomed to the "land of liberty."

Our government was quick to express its sympathy for peoples struggling for their freedom from European despotism. In December, 1850, our Secretary of State, Daniel Webster, sent a defiant reply to the Austrian representative at Washington, who had complained of the sympathy we showed to Hungary in her struggle for freedom: "The power of this Republic at the present moment is spread over a region one of the richest and most fertile on the globe, and of an extent in comparison with which the possessions of the House of Hapsburg are but a patch on the earth's surface." When the Hungarian patriot, General Louis Kossuth, came to America the next year, he was received by Congress and the people with a welcome only less enthusiastic than that given to Lafayette a quarter of a century before.

In the summer of 1853 Douglas made a trip abroad and probably expressed the sentiment of a large proportion of his fellow countrymen when he wrote: "Europe is tottering to the verge of dissolution. When you visit her, the objects which enlist your attention are the relics of past greatness, the broken columns erected to departed power." And Henry Clay, on his deathbed, wrote to Kossuth that "for the cause of liberty, we should keep our lamp burning brightly on this western shore, as a light to all nations." The Americans of the mid-century were no more modest than was Woodrow Wilson at the time of the World War in their idea of the role of the United States as an example of justice to an erring world.

We Become Interested in an Isthmian Canal. The most imposing work of man in the Western Hemisphere is the Panama Canal, through whose locks and Gatun Lake and Culebra Cut thousands of ships pass every year between the Atlantic and the Pacific. How the United States acquired the Canal Zone and built the canal early in the present century will be told in a later chapter. That was the completion of a project which had been dreamed of for three centuries, ever since the explorers had discovered how the continent of North America tapers down rapidly at its southern end to a mere ribbon of land, fifty miles wide, connecting it with its sister continent of South America.

Our expansion to the Pacific coast and the rush of the gold-seekers to California roused great interest in a canal route across the Isthmus toward the middle of the nineteenth century. For example, we made a treaty with the republic of New Granada (now Colombia), in 1846, giving us permission to build a road, railroad, or canal across the Isthmus of Panama, in return for which we guaranteed the sovereignty of New Granada over the Isthmus, as well as freedom of transit for all nations on equal terms. Three years later we made similar treaties with Nicaragua and Honduras. In these negotiations we came into collision with the British, who had a colony on the coast of Nicaragua and seemed to be planning to extend their "protectorate" over the Isthmus. Both nations being willing, however, to come to an agreement on the building of a canal, the British sent over Sir Henry Bulwer as a special envoy for that purpose.

The Clayton-Bulwer Treaty. After several months of nego-tiation, Sir Henry and our Secretary of State, John M. Clayton, signed a treaty on April 19, 1850, "for facilitating and protecting the construction of a ship canal between the Atlantic and Pacific oceans." Both parties pledged themselves never to obtain ex-clusive control over such a canal, nor to erect fortifications on it, nor to acquire any colonies in Central America. They were to protect any company that should build the canal and to guar-antee the neutrality of the canal when built. The canal was to be maintained "for the benefit of mankind on equal terms to all." In spite of these liberal provisions, trouble between the United States and Great Britain in Central America did not come to an end. The British held on to the colony in Nicaragua and even annexed some islands off the coast of Honduras (1852), and the next year an American war vessel bombarded a British port in Nicaragua. Had it not been for more important questions for both governments in 1854,[1] the Central American issue might not have sunk so suddenly into insignificance.

Our Interest in Cuba. The most critical incident in our mid-century diplomacy concerned Cuba. Ever since the days of Thomas Jefferson expansionists had prophesied that the island must eventually belong to the United States. As our interest in the Caribbean region grew with the annexation of Florida and Texas, and as the South saw the opportunity for the westward extension of slavery shut off by the geography of New Mexico and the dedication of Oregon and California to free soil, Cuba offered a tempting bait. Not only must that rich island guarding the entrance to the Gulf of Mexico not be allowed to fall into the hands of any strong European power, but from the Southern point of view its acquisition would be very desirable. It might be carved into five fertile slave states, which would add ten members to the United States Senate. President Polk offered Spain one hundred million for the island, only to be met with the proud reply from Madrid that the Spanish government would " rather see Cuba sunk in the ocean than transferred to any power."

We Have Trouble with Spain. Still, the Spanish rule was oppressive, and Cuba was in a chronic state of revolt. In 1850 and 1851, a Venezuelan adventurer named López organized "filibustering"[2] expeditions at New Orleans to seize Cuba by force; and in this lawless course he was encouraged not only by some of the influential Southerners but even by meetings of sympathizers in Philadelphia, Pittsburgh, and New York. When the news came of the capture and execution of López and about fifty of his band, including some young men of prominent Southern families, a mob attacked the Spanish consulate at New Orleans, tore down the ensign of Castile, and defaced the por-

---

[1] Namely, the re-opening of the struggle over the extension of slavery into the territories, by the Kansas-Nebraska Act (to be studied in the next chapter), and England's participation in the Crimean War.

[2] This word denotes a forcible attempt to seize some advantage without the support of law.

trait of Queen Isabella. Fillmore's Secretary of State, Daniel Webster, sent an apology to Madrid for this insult to Spain, "committed in the heat of blood"; but Fillmore's successor, Pierce, seemed to invite further trouble deliberately by appointing as minister to Madrid the fiery Pierre Soulé of Louisiana, who had advocated the annexation of Cuba in the Senate and had lauded the "heroic" López. Soon after his arrival in Spain, Soulé sent a blustering ultimatum to the court, threatening to demand his passports unless reparation should be made within forty-eight hours for the seizure of a cargo of cotton on the American vessel *Black Warrior* in the port of Havana. The cautious Secretary Marcy, however, did not support Soulé in his extravagant demand, but ordered him to confer with Buchanan and Mason, our ministers to England and France, on the best policy for our government to pursue in regard to Spain and Cuba.

The Ostend Manifesto. The three ministers met at Ostend, in Belgium, in the summer of 1854. Both Buchanan and Mason were annexationists, though more moderate than Soulé. Both had been members of Polk's cabinet, and Buchanan, as Secretary of State, had made Spain the offer of one hundred million dollars for Cuba. But at Ostend they were persuaded by Soulé to put their names to the most disgraceful public paper in all our history. This Ostend Manifesto, after asserting that the possession of Cuba was necessary for the peace of the United States, concluded with the statement that "if Spain, dead to the voice of her own interests and moved by pride and a false sense of honor, refused to sell Cuba," then we should be "justified by every law human and divine" in taking the island from her by force. There was, of course, no law, human or divine, that could justify the language of the Ostend Manifesto or the deed of pure robbery which it proposed. Secretary Marcy very properly disowned the Ostend Manifesto and compelled Soulé to resign. A few months later Spain apologized for the seizure of the *Black Warrior* and restored her cargo to her owners. It was to be a far more serious event in Havana harbor forty-four years later — the destruction of the American battleship *Maine* — that was to precipitate the war which cost Spain "the Pearl of the Antilles."

The Compromise of 1850 Breaks Down. In spite of political platforms and pledges, in spite of the desperate efforts of the conservatives on both sides of Mason and Dixon's line to preserve an atmosphere of peace in which the business of the country could flourish, the question of slavery would not down. The "plague of frogs" still rested on the land, and infested every measure of public policy proposed. When the South sought expansion in the only direction possible, the North resisted it as simply a move to gain territory for the creation of more slave states. When Northerners proposed plans for the development of the West by building railroads and granting free land to settlers, the South saw in such plans only the determination to create a great free-soil empire in the West, which would ensure the permanent inferiority of the slaveholding South. The old political parties were separating into Northern and Southern wings, and new parties were already formed to gather recruits from the old parties on the issues of slavery, temperance, immigration, and Roman Catholicism. We shall see in the next chapter how the first of these issues absorbed all the others and resulted in the sharp division between the sections of our country north and south of Mason and Dixon's line.

TERMS TO BE MASTERED

Wilmot Proviso	"Omnibus Bill"	protectorate
"squatter sovereignty"	"underground railway"	filibuster
Subtreasury	Yankee clipper	Ostend Manifesto

FOR SUPPLEMENTARY READING

EDWARD CHANNING, *History of the United States*, Vol. VI, chaps. iv–ix; T. C. SMITH, *Parties and Slavery* (American Nation Series, Vol. XVIII); S. E. WHITE, *The Forty-Niners* (Chronicles of America, Vol. XXV); W. E. DODD, *The Cotton Kingdom* (Chronicles, Vol. XXVII); CARL SCHURZ, *Henry Clay*, Vol. II, chap. xxiv; A. H. CLARK, *The Clipper Ship Era, 1843–1869*; C. R. FISH, *The Rise of the Common Man* (A History of American Life, Vol. VI), chaps. xxiv, xxv; R. F. NICHOLS, *Franklin Pierce*; The Pageant of America, Vol. VIII, pp. 282–298; H. S. COMMAGER, *Documents of American History*, pp. 319–327; *America*, Vol. VII, pp. 114–170; HART, *Contemporaries*, Vol. IV, Nos. 15–24; MUZZEY, *Readings*, pp. 335–356.

TOPICS FOR REPORTS

1. **Gold and Politics in California.** J. S. HITTELL, "The Discovery of Gold in California," in *Century Magazine*, Vol. XIX, pp. 525–536; EMERSON HOUGH, *The Passing of the Frontier* (Chronicles of America, Vol. XXVI), chap. v; WALTER COLTON, *Three Years in California*, pp. 242–290; BRET HARTE, *The Luck of Roaring Camp*; HART, *Contemporaries*, Vol. IV, No. 18; MUZZEY, *Readings*, pp. 335–340.

2. **Industrial Prosperity in the Fifties.** J. F. RHODES, *History of the United States from the Compromise of 1850*, Vol. III, pp. 1–56; D. R. DEWEY, *The Financial History of the United States*, pp. 248–274; G. S. CALLENDER, *Readings in the Economic History of the United States*, pp. 738–793; A. C. COLE, *The Irrepressible Conflict* (A History of American Life, Vol. VII), chaps. i, v, viii.

3. **Mid-century Plans for an Isthmian Canal.** W. J. JOHNSON, *Four Centuries of the Panama Canal*, pp. 51–77; I. D. TRAVIS, *The History of the Clayton-Bulwer Treaty* (Michigan Political Science Publications, Vol. II, No. 8); J. B. MCMASTER, *History of the People of the United States*, Vol. VII, pp. 552–557; J. H. LATANÉ, *The Diplomatic Relations of the United States and Spanish America*, pp. 176–195; H. S. COMMAGER, *Documents*, pp. 326–327.

4. **Daniel Webster's Seventh-of-March Speech.** ALEXANDER JOHNSTON, *American Orations*, Vol. II, pp. 161–201; H. C. LODGE, *Daniel Webster*, pp. 301–332; J. F. RHODES, *History of the United States*, Vol. I, pp. 137–161; W. C. WILKINSON, "Daniel Webster and the Compromise of 1850," in *Scribner's Magazine*, Vol. XII, pp. 411–425; HART, *Contemporaries*, Vol. IV, Nos. 20, 21.

QUESTIONS SUGGESTED BY THE CHAPTER

1. Distinguish between the Liberty party and the Free-Soil party. 2. Name three plans proposed for the status of slavery in the territory secured by the Mexican War. 3. Why did Webster support and Calhoun oppose the Compromise of 1850? 4. What part of the compromise gave most offense to the North? most satisfaction to the South? 5. Do you think the North gained most, or the South, by the compromise? Give your reasons. 6. How did California settle the slavery question? 7. What did Seward mean by a "higher law" than the Constitution? 8. What was the effect of Taylor's death on the Compromise of 1850? 9. What effect did the railroad-building of the 1850's have on the commerce of the Mississippi Valley? 10. What clause of the Constitution gave Congress authority over the territories? 11. What did the case of Prigg *v.* Pennsylvania in 1842 decide? 12. How do you account for Scott's bad defeat in 1852? 13. Explain what the Southern planters meant by the phrase "Cotton is king"? 14. What was the condition of our overseas trade in the 1850's? 15. How did Daniel Webster emphasize the prestige of the United States when he was Secretary of State? 16. What trouble with England did we have in the decade of the 1850's? 17. Why did the South want Cuba? 18. Why was the Ostend Manifesto a "disgraceful" paper? 19. What was the story of López? 20. On what questions besides slavery did the North and the South differ in regard to the West?

seize of L. P. territory
why it occupy attention
now

THE HOUSE DIVIDED

A Fateful Conference. In his first message to Congress on December 5, 1853, President Pierce spoke of the sense of repose and security that had come to the public mind with the passage of the Compromise of 1850, and added, "That this repose is to suffer no shock during my official term, if I have the power to prevent it, those who placed me here may be assured." Yet less than fifty days after giving this pledge, Pierce was closeted with his Secretary of War, Jefferson Davis, and the chairman of the Senate Committee on Territories, Stephen A. Douglas, lending the approval of the administration to a measure which was destined not only to disturb the country's repose but to head it straight toward civil war.

The subject of this fateful conference at the White House was a bill reported by Douglas to the Senate eighteen days before for the territorial organization of the region between the Missouri River and the Rockies, north of the parallel of 36° 30′. This vast area of nearly five hundred thousand square miles was larger than all the free states of the Union east of the Rockies combined. Little attention had been paid to it since we had acquired it in the Louisiana Purchase of 1803. It had been given over to various Indian tribes and contained only a scant thousand of white inhabitants residing at scattered military posts. It had not been considered important enough to have any figures of its population or resources included in the census of 1850. But now, with our power established on the Pacific coast and the need for the better protection of the increasing westward migration on the Oregon, California, and Santa Fe trails, this middle region began to occupy the attention of the government.

The Kansas-Nebraska Bill. The bill reported to the Senate by Douglas for the erection of the territory of Nebraska did not mention the Missouri Compromise of 1820, by which that region had been forever dedicated to free soil; but it provided that "all questions pertaining to slavery in the Territories and the new States to be formed therefrom are to be left to the decision of the people residing therein." That is, it applied to a part of the old Louisiana territory from which slavery had been excluded thirty-four years earlier the "popular sovereignty" doctrine which had been adopted in 1850 for the new territory acquired from Mexico. Senator Dixon of Kentucky insisted that the bill be amended so as to include a direct repeal of the Missouri Compromise. Douglas knew that such a stand would cost him the support of many free-soil Democrats of the North, but he yielded to Dixon's proposal, relying on the support of a pro-Southern administration.[1] So, the day after the assuring conference with Pierce and Davis at the White House, Douglas submitted in the place of the Nebraska Bill a Kansas-Nebraska Bill, providing for the creation of two territories divided by the fortieth parallel of north latitude, with the idea that slavery might go into the southern one (Kansas), while the larger northern one (Nebraska) would probably be free soil. The new bill also repealed the slavery restriction of the Missouri Compromise, declaring it "inoperative" and "superseded by the principles of the legislation of 1850."

The Triumph of Douglas. A storm of opposition in the North greeted this proposal to annul the Missouri Compromise. The day after the Kansas-Nebraska Bill was reported, the anti-slavery men in Congress, led by Senator Chase of Ohio, issued a protest entitled "The Appeal of the Independent Democrats,"

---

[1] Though Pierce was from the free state of New Hampshire, his sympathies were with the South. Jefferson Davis of Mississippi, the Secretary of War, and Caleb Cushing of Massachusetts, the Attorney General, the most influential members of the cabinet, were both strong states-rights and proslavery men. The Secretaries of the Treasury and the Navy were conservative Southerners. Marcy of New York (Secretary of State) held aloof from the slavery question. Incidentally, Pierce's cabinet was the only one in our whole history that remained unchanged during the entire Presidential term.

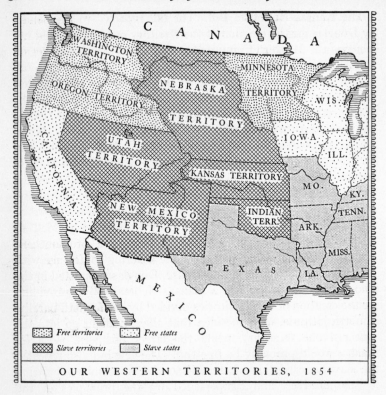

OUR WESTERN TERRITORIES, 1854

in which they denounced the bill as "a gross violation of a sacred pledge" and "part and parcel of an atrocious plot" to turn a large and undeveloped area of our country into "a dreary region of despotism inhabited by masters and slaves." The legislatures of half a dozen Northern states sent petitions to Congress protesting against the passage of the bill. Douglas was reviled as a traitor,[1] a Judas, a Benedict Arnold, who had sold himself to the South in the hope of the Presidential nomination. He was burned in effigy so frequently that he said he could travel from Boston to Chicago in the light of the fires.

[1] Douglas himself, a short time before the passage of the Compromise of 1850, had spoken of the Missouri Compromise as "canonized in the hearts of the American people."

But Douglas was not a man to be daunted by opposition. Aggressive, ingenious, and confident, he rose to his greatest heights as a debater the harder the fight grew. Almost unaided, he met the arguments of the anti-Nebraska men on the floor of the Senate, day after day, with a vigor and tact which won even from his adversaries expressions of admiration. On March 4, 1854, after a continuous session of seventeen hours, Douglas carried his bill through the Senate by a vote of 37 to 14. In the House the heavier strength of the North prolonged the battle for two and a half months; but finally, under the skillful management of Alexander H. Stephens of Georgia, the bill passed by the narrow margin of 113 to 100 votes. On May 30 it was signed by President Pierce.

What Were the Motives of Douglas? James Ford Rhodes says that the Kansas-Nebraska Act was "the most momentous measure that passed Congress from the day that the Senators and Representatives first met to the outbreak of the Civil War," and another distinguished historian of the period, Professor John W. Burgess, calls it "probably the greatest error which the Congress of the United States ever committed." It is worth while, therefore, to ask what were the motives of the man who was responsible for the passage of this "momentous measure."

Rhodes's theory has been accepted widely, namely, that "the action of the Senator from Illinois was a bid for Southern support in the next Democratic convention." It is true that Douglas was ambitious for the Presidency and that the men who were likely to be his chief competitors for the nomination were all courting the South.[1] But Douglas was too good a politician not to know that his doctrine of "popular sovereignty" would lose him as much support in the North as it gained for him in the South; also that the Southern leaders, like Jefferson Davis, would not

[1] President Pierce was hand in glove with Jefferson Davis. Buchanan was lending support to the acquisition of Cuba. Marcy was cautious, but favorable to Southern expansion. Cass was an avowed "doughface" (p. 341, note 1). Moreover, Douglas had a handicap to overcome in the South because he was a farmer's son born in the abolitionist state of Vermont.

be content with a scheme which allowed the settlers of a territory to exclude slavery from it by their votes.

Nor was Douglas interested in the question of the extinction or the preservation of slavery. He said that he did not care whether slavery was "voted up or voted down" in the new territories. But he believed that it was in accord with the spirit of American democracy to let the people themselves decide whether they would have slavery or freedom in the locality where they lived. It was a mistake, he said, to separate the country into two hostile sections by the line of 36° 30′ or any other geographical division. North and South had got along together for many generations, one region free, the other slave. Why could they not continue to live in peace with their different institutions? This was the blind spot in Douglas's vision. He had no appreciation of the moral objection to slavery which was agitating the North and provoking an answering defense of the moral value of slavery in the South. He was particularly interested in a railroad to the West, with its eastern terminus at Chicago; and it was to secure the support of the South for his railroad that he was willing to open to slavery the territory through which it would run.

The New Republican Party. While the Kansas-Nebraska Bill was being debated in the Senate, a group of Northern Whigs, anti-Nebraska Democrats, and Free-soilers met at Ripon, Wisconsin, and resolved that if the bill passed they would organize a new party to resist the extension of slavery. They suggested the name "Republican,"[1] which was taken up and popularized by Horace Greeley's *New York Tribune*. On July 6, 1854, the party was launched at a meeting in a grove of oaks on the outskirts of Jackson, Michigan. Its platform declared that

---

[1] The two-party system has always prevailed in the United States. In spite of the extent of our country and the diverse interests of its various sections, the vast majority of our citizens have supported one or the other of the two strong, well-organized parties. These parties, since the 1850's, have been the Republicans and the Democrats. Many other ("third") parties have been formed, such as Greenbackers, Socialists, Laborites, Populists, Progressives, Farmer-Laborers, etc.; but no one of them (except possibly the Progressives under Theodore Roosevelt in 1912) has ever had the slightest chance of electing a President.

slavery was "a great moral, social, and political evil," demanded the repeal of the Kansas-Nebraska Act and the Fugitive-Slave Law of 1850, and resolved to sink all political differences and unite in the battle against slavery until the fight was won. It nominated a full state ticket of Republican candidates who were elected in November, together with four Michigan Congressmen.

During the summer and autumn of 1854, conventions in other states (Maine, Vermont, Massachusetts, Ohio, New York) met to organize Republican or Anti-Nebraska parties; and the elections in November showed that a revolution had taken place in politics. The great Whig party was shattered, its Northern members going by thousands into the Republican ranks, and its Southern members, unable to stand alone, drifting toward the Democrats. It never put up another candidate for the Presidency. The Democratic party stood the shock better, but it was hard hit. Of the 42 Northern Democrats who voted for the Kansas-Nebraska Bill, only 7 were re-elected to Congress in 1854, and the Democratic majority of 84 in the House was changed into a minority of 75. Moreover, when Douglas intro-

and in only three instances (1892, 1912, 1924) have they carried a single state. Since the names "Republican" and "Democrat" were used in the earlier years of our history with somewhat different meanings from those they have had since 1854, the following table will be of use to the student.

DATE			PAGE
1791–1792	FEDERALISTS v. (for strong national government)	DEMOCRATIC REPUBLICANS (for strictly limited national government)	
1793		dropped the name "Democratic" and became simply the Republicans	193
c. 1816	died out, leaving only the		
c. 1820		REPUBLICANS ("era of good feeling")	266
	who split on the question of "internal improvements," such as national aid for the construction of canals and roads, and the charter of the National Bank, into two wings:		267
1825–1830	NATIONAL REPUBLICANS v. the nucleus of a new party which, in opposition to Jackson, took the name of	DEMOCRATIC REPUBLICANS who dropped the name "Republican" and became simply	282
1834	WHIGS v.	(Jacksonian) DEMOCRATS	303
	On the great question of slavery the Whig party went to pieces soon after 1850, and the present Republican party was organized.		364

duced his bill the Democrats seemed to be in secure control of the Northwestern states. Every one of the Senators and all but five of the Representatives from Indiana, Illinois, Michigan, Wisconsin, and Iowa belonged to the party of the administration. The immense influence of Douglas kept Illinois in the Democratic column in the election of 1856; but Michigan, Wisconsin, and Iowa went over to the Republicans forthwith, and only Indiana remained permanently in the "doubtful column." It was Stephen A. Douglas who called the Republican party into being.

"Bleeding Kansas." When the Kansas-Nebraska Bill became law, Douglas boasted that "the struggle over slavery was forever banished from the halls of Congress to the Western plains." He was wrong about the halls of Congress but right about the Western plains. Since the settlers were to decide the question of slavery or free soil, a rivalry for the control of the territory began at once. "Come on, then, gentlemen of the Slave States!" cried Seward. "We will engage in a competition for the virgin soil of Kansas, and God give the victory to the side that is stronger in numbers as it is in the right!"

Free-soil emigrants from New England and proslavery men from Missouri founded rival towns in Kansas; and when Pierce's governor, Andrew H. Reeder, arrived in the territory in October, 1854, he found the stage set for civil war. It was impossible to hold free and fair elections for the legislature or for a delegate to Congress. President Pierce confessed that he was "haunted day and night" by the situation.

It was inevitable that deeds of violence should occur. When a free-state man attempted to assassinate a proslavery sheriff as he rode into the free-soil town of Lawrence to arrest a murderer, the storm broke. An armed band of Missourians descended upon Lawrence and sacked the town. In revenge, the fanatical abolitionist John Brown led a small group of men, including his four sons, to a proslavery settlement on Pottawatomie Creek, where they dragged five men from their beds at dead of night and massacred them in cold blood. Bands of armed rioters marched up and down the land like the factional "armies" of a Central American republic. Farmers went in groups, armed to the teeth, to till their fields. No herd was safe from plunder, and no house or barn from the torch. Over two hundred lives were lost and two million dollars' worth of property destroyed.

Charles Sumner is Assaulted in the Senate. So much for the "Western plains." Was it calmer in the "halls of Congress"? The ashes of Lawrence were still hot when an outrageous deed of violence was perpetrated in the United States Senate. Charles Sumner of Massachusetts, a man of powerful intellect and unbounded self-esteem, had delivered a speech in the Senate called "The Crime against Kansas." It was a fierce attack on the pro-slavery men in the territory and their abettors in the South, abounding in personal abuse. Sumner especially singled out for his venomous onslaught Senator A. P. Butler of South Carolina, who was ill at the time and absent from his seat. Two days later Representative Preston Brooks, a relative of Butler's, entered the Senate chamber late in the afternoon, when Sumner was bent over his desk at work, and beat him savagely with a heavy gutta-percha cane. Sumner struggled to rise to his feet, wrenching his desk from the floor, but he was too dazed to offer much resistance to his assailant, who continued to rain blows upon him until he fell to the floor unconscious. A motion to expel Brooks from the House failed to get the necessary two-thirds vote; but he resigned and appealed to his constituents in South Carolina, who re-elected him with only six dissenting votes. He was toasted at banquets in the South and presented with numerous souvenir canes. Sumner was gradually restored to health by the skill of European doctors; but it was not until December, 1859, that he was able again to take his seat in the Senate, which had been kept vacant for him by the Massachusetts legislature.

The Nominating Conventions of 1856. In the week following the sack of Lawrence, the murders on the Pottawatomie, and the assault on Sumner, the Democratic national convention met at Cincinnati. The delegates took care not to nominate any candidate who could be held responsible for the strife in Kansas, which was then at its height. Passing over both Pierce and Douglas, they chose James Buchanan, a dignified and conservative Pennsylvanian, who had been Secretary of State under Polk and who had been absent from the country as minister to England when the Kansas struggle was precipitated. His "availability" consisted chiefly in the negative facts that he had no connection with Kansas and no abolitionist leanings which would make him offensive to the South.

The first national convention of the Republican party was held at Philadelphia on June 17. Its platform declared that it was "both the right and duty of Congress" to legislate for the territories of the United States, abolishing in them "the twin relics of barbarism," slavery and polygamy.[1] It demanded the immediate admission of Kansas as a free state. Instead of choosing a man of political experience, like Seward or Chase, the convention nominated John C. Frémont of California, whose romantic career as the "Pathfinder" of the Far West and the "Conqueror of California" had won him a reputation far in excess of his abilities.

There was also a third party in the field, the Native American, or "Know-Nothing," party. This had grown out of the Order of the Star-Spangled Banner, a secret association formed in 1853 to combat the influence of immigrants, especially those of the Roman Catholic faith, in our politics. It got its nickname from the reply "I don't know" which its members made to any inquiry about its activities. In the troubled days of the middle 1850's the Native Americans attracted a good many wavering Whigs and some Democrats to their ranks, and carried a number of state elections. But in the Presidential election of 1856 their candidate Fillmore won only the state of Maryland.

Buchanan is Elected President. There were frequent warnings that the triumph of the "Black Republican" ticket of

---

[1] The Mormons were a sect founded in 1827 by Joseph Smith, who claimed to have discovered on a hillside near Palmyra, New York, a divine revelation written on plates of gold. They made converts rapidly. After attempting to found settlements in Ohio, Missouri, and Illinois, they migrated in 1847, under their new leader Brigham Young, to the valley of the Great Salt Lake, Utah, which was then Mexican territory. The next year, by the Mexican cession, they came again under the jurisdiction of the United States. Though the Mormons established a peaceful and prosperous community at Salt Lake City, their practice of plural marriages, or polygamy, made them offensive to our government.

Frémont and Dayton would mean the dissolution of the Union. "To the fifteen states of the South," said Rufus Choate of Massachusetts, "Frémont's government would appear an alien government, and, worse than that, a hostile government." On the other hand, every week of the continuance of the disturbances in Kansas was making converts for the Republicans. Three things saved the election for the Democrats: the tireless campaigning of Douglas, the fear of the business interests that the Republicans would disturb prosperity by rash legislation,[1] and the restoration of something like order in Kansas by Pierce's use of Federal troops — a confession of the failure of "popular sovereignty." Buchanan carried the South, together with California, Illinois, Indiana, New Jersey, and Pennsylvania. His electoral vote was 174 to 114 for Frémont. Still, the Republicans in their first national campaign had made a remarkable fight, winning eleven states and polling 1,341,264 votes to 1,838,169 for Buchanan. They closed their ranks and rallied for the next battle, cheered by John G. Whittier's marching song:

> Then sound again the bugles,
> Call the muster-roll anew;
> If months have well-nigh won the field,
> What may not four years do?

The Dred Scott Case Stirs the Country. Two days after President Buchanan, in his inaugural address, had expressed his hope that the long agitation over slavery was now "approaching its end," the Supreme Court handed down one of the most famous decisions in its history (March 6, 1857). In 1834 Dr. Emerson, an army surgeon stationed at St. Louis, had taken his slave Dred Scott into the free state of Illinois and then across the Mississippi into the free part of the Louisiana territory.

---

[1] If this fear seems strange to a generation for which the Republican party is the party of the "big business" interests, it must be remembered that at its origin the party was composed of "come-outers" who were as radical in their attitude toward the chief social question of their day (slavery) as are Socialists or Communists in facing the absorbing question of our own day (capitalism). In fact, the early Republicans were regarded by the conservatives of 1856 much as the Socialists are regarded by the conservatives of today.

Some years after their return to St. Louis, Dred Scott sued Dr. Emerson's widow for his freedom, on the ground that his residence on free soil had emancipated him. The highest court of Missouri denied his suit. Then Scott came into the possession of a New Yorker named Sandford, and his case went to the Federal circuit court of Missouri,[1] which reaffirmed the decision of the state court, namely, that Scott still remained a slave and, as a noncitizen, had no right to bring suit.

The case finally came up to the United States Supreme Court, which had only to determine whether there had been any error in the procedure of the Federal court in Missouri. It decided that there had not, and there the case should have ended. But Chief Justice Roger B. Taney of Maryland, with the support of all but two of his colleagues on the bench, went on to deliver an elaborate opinion, *obiter dictum*,[2] on the status of the Negro, hoping thereby to put an end to the slavery agitation. The Negro, said Taney, was not a citizen. The Constitution was made for white men only. The Missouri Compromise was unconstitutional, because a slave was the property of his owner and the Constitution nowhere gave Congress the right to deprive a citizen of the United States of that kind of property. The South rejoiced that at last the highest tribunal of the land had endorsed the proslavery doctrine of Calhoun and Davis. But the Northern press spoke of the "soiled ermine of the judicial robes." "The people of the United States," said Seward, "never can and never will accept principles so unconstitutional and abhorrent."

The Panic of 1857. To add to the unrest caused by the Dred Scott decision, a severe panic overtook the country in the first summer of Buchanan's administration. Extravagant spending, overbuilding of railroads, and overextension of bank credits

---

. [1] If a citizen of one state sues a citizen of another state, the case is tried in a Federal court (Constitution, Art. III, Sect. 2). Of course the Negro slave, Dred Scott, did not start this case himself. It was managed and financed by abolitionists who wanted to test the position of the courts on slavery.

[2] *Obiter dictum* (literally "spoken by the way") means an added opinion of the judge, that is, one not called for in deciding what the law is in the special case before the court.

brought the crash. Banks failed, specie payments were suspended, mills and factories closed, and thousands of unemployed paraded the streets with banners demanding "work or bread."

Buchanan Supports Fraud in Kansas. Worse even than the panic, from which the country began to recover the next year, was the renewal of trouble in Kansas. In spite of four governors sent to the territory within three years, in spite of the Federal troops employed by Pierce, the proslavery and free-soil factions were as hostile to each other as ever.

When a convention met at Lecompton in September, 1857, to draw up a constitution under which Kansas might come into the Union as a state, the proslavery men got control. Realizing that the constitution which they had framed would be rejected if honestly submitted to the people of Kansas for a vote, they resorted to a piece of trickery. They allowed a popular vote only on the question whether the constitution should be adopted "with slavery" or "without slavery." The former phrase meant that slaves might be brought into Kansas without limit; the latter, that no *more* slaves should be brought in. In either case the slaves already there would remain slaves. The free-soilers refused to go to the polls to vote on this tricky proposition, and the result was that the Lecompton Constitution was adopted. It was clear, however, that the great majority of the people of Kansas did not want slavery. For when the Lecompton Constitution *as a whole* was submitted to them two weeks later, they rejected it by 10,000 votes.

Douglas Breaks with the Administration. President Buchanan had pledged himself in his inaugural address "to secure to every resident inhabitant of Kansas the free and independent expression of his opinion" on the subject of slavery. But now he sent the fraudulent Lecompton Constitution to Congress, with a special message urging its adoption as a test of fidelity to the administration. Douglas, who had done more [than any other man to make Buchanan President, immediately protested against the Lecompton fraud as a "travesty and mockery" of the doctrine of "popular sovereignty," which had been written into the Democratic platform of 1856. A new constitution must be

DOUGLAS

BUCHANAN

framed in Kansas and submitted to an honest vote of the people there. The government had no right to force either slavery or freedom upon them. That was a question for them to decide. Douglas withstood Buchanan to his face; and when the latter threatened him: "Mr. Douglas, I wish you to remember that no Democrat ever yet differed from an administration of his own choice without being crushed," Douglas retorted, "Mr. President, I wish *you* to remember that General Jackson is dead." The President tried to "crush" Douglas by withdrawing all official patronage from him, but the Illinois Senator was undaunted. He joined forces with the free-soil Republicans in Congress to defeat the admission of Kansas under the fraudulent Lecompton Constitution.[1]

Lincoln and Douglas. Douglas's second term as Senator was about to expire, and he returned to Illinois in the summer of 1858 to seek re-election. His Republican rival for the Senator-

[1] Kansas remained a territory (theoretically open to slavery by the Dred Scott decision) until the withdrawal of the Southern members of Congress on the eve of the Civil War. On January 21, 1861, the turbulent seven years' history of Kansas Territory came to a close with its quiet admission to the Union as a free state.

ship was Abraham Lincoln, a former Whig who had joined the Republicans on the Kansas-Nebraska issue and risen to be their leading politician in the state. Douglas and Lincoln had known each other for twenty years. They were both poor farmers' sons who had come to Illinois as young men and engaged in the practice of the law. They were alike, too, in their ambition to make a name for themselves in politics and in their intense devotion to the Union. But here the resemblance ceased. While Douglas had been in the United States Senate for more than a decade and had twice been a serious competitor for the Presidential nomination, Lincoln's national honors had been limited to a single term (1847–1849) as a Whig member of Congress.

In appearance, temper, and character the two men were exact opposites: Lincoln very tall, lanky, awkward, reflective, slow in speech and motion; Douglas scarcely five feet in height, thickset, agile, volcanic in utterance, impetuous in gesture. Neither was an extremist in his views on slavery, Douglas being as far removed from the "fire-eaters" of the South as Lincoln was from the abolitionists of the North. But while Douglas believed that the free and slave states could continue to live together in peace, and cared not whether slavery was "voted up or voted down," Lincoln was certain that slavery was a moral wrong and that the Union could not last unless slavery were eventually abolished. In his speech before the Illinois convention which nominated him for the Senatorship[1] in June, 1858, he said: "A house divided against itself cannot stand. I believe this government cannot endure permanently half slave and half free. I do not expect the Union to be dissolved. I do not expect the house to fall, but I do expect it will cease to be divided." Douglas misrepresented this prophecy of Lincoln's as a plea for "a war of the sections until one or the other shall be subdued," and

[1] Many eastern Republicans, including the influential Horace Greeley of the *New York Tribune*, thought Douglas's re-election should be unopposed in Illinois because of his brave stand against Buchanan. But the Illinois Republicans could not go back on their principles by supporting the author of the Kansas-Nebraska Act. They were as firmly opposed to Douglas's plan of letting the people of a territory determine whether they would have slavery or not as to Buchanan's attempt to force slavery upon them.

criticized Lincoln's declared opposition to the Dred Scott decision as an appeal from the judgment of the Supreme Court of the land to "the decision of a tumultuous town meeting."

The Lincoln-Douglas Debates. After several haphazard attacks and answers to each other in separate localities, Douglas and Lincoln agreed, at the latter's invitation, to meet on the same platform to argue the question of slavery in a series of joint debates. Seven such debates were held between August and October, 1858, one in each of the electoral districts of the state. Their immediate object was to influence the people in the election of the legislature which was to choose the United States Senator. The rivals spoke from a platform in the open air before thousands, who drove miles in buggies and carryalls from the towns and farms of the districts. But the real audience extended far beyond the borders of Illinois. Long extracts from the speeches were published in the papers of Boston, New York, St. Louis, and Cincinnati. Douglas kept harping on Lincoln's "house divided" speech as an incitement to civil strife, and upon the fairness, the democracy, and the "Americanism" of his own doctrine of "popular sovereignty," if honestly applied. Lincoln insisted that the territories must be kept as future homes for free white settlers, but at the same time made it clear that he was opposed to interfering with slavery in the states where it was established.

The high point of the debates was reached at Freeport (August 27), when Lincoln asked Douglas whether the people of a territory of the United States could lawfully exclude slavery from its limits prior to the formation of a state constitution. If Douglas answered Yes, he would seem to defy the Dred Scott decision; if he answered No, he would repudiate his own doctrine of "popular sovereignty." Douglas held to his doctrine, claiming that it did not annul the Dred Scott decision; for, he said, even though the Supreme Court decided that slavery was lawful in a territory, the institution "could not exist anywhere for a day or an hour" without the support of "local police regulations." That is, by failing to pass laws for the protection of slavery the legislature of the territory could in fact exclude it.

THE LINCOLN-DOUGLAS DEBATE

This was Douglas's famous "Freeport Doctrine," which Lincoln later summed up in the witticism: "Then a thing may be legally driven away from a place where it has a legal right to be." Douglas won the Senatorship by the narrow margin of eight votes, but he had ruined his chances of Southern support for the Presidency — as Lincoln meant that he should.

The "Irrepressible Conflict." Every public question had now come to be regarded solely from the standpoint of its bearing on the great sectional issue. When the Northerners tried to get a Pacific-railroad bill passed, Iverson of Georgia declared that the Union would soon be dissolved, and refused to vote for a road "which would lie outside a Southern confederacy." When a Homestead Bill was passed by the House, with only three affirmative votes from the slaveholding states, it was defeated in the Senate because the South saw in this measure, giving "land to the landless," only national encouragement to the free-soil emigration which had robbed them of Kansas. When the Southerners again attempted to purchase Cuba, and a commercial congress at Vicksburg resolved that "all laws, state or national, forbidding the African slave trade, ought to be repealed," Wade of Ohio sneered at the South's demand for "niggers for the niggerless."[1]

As the strife grew more bitter the debates grew more menacing. Concession was looked on as "treason" to one's section. Douglas warned Davis that he could not get the vote of a single Northern state on his doctrine that the national government must use force, if necessary, to protect slavery in the territories; and Davis replied that Douglas could not get a single vote in Mississippi for popular sovereignty. In a speech of fierce denunciation against slavery at Rochester, New York, Seward spoke of the "irrepressible conflict between opposing and enduring forces."

[1] It cost the planter fifteen hundred dollars or more to buy a first-class slave from Virginia or Kentucky, while he could have plenty from the Guinea coast for a third of that figure. American slave ships were bringing their cargoes into Southern ports in open defiance of the laws making the slave trade piracy; and no juries could be found in the South to indict their captains or owners. Douglas declared that no less than fifteen thousand African slaves were landed in the Southern ports in the year 1859.

John Brown's Raid. John Brown, whose murderous deed in Kansas we have already described (p. 366), believed that he was commissioned by God to free the slaves. Collecting some four thousand dollars from abolitionist sympathizers, and a band of about twenty armed followers, Brown conceived the wild plan of persuading slaves to leave their masters and flee to "camps of freedom" in the Appalachian Mountains. In October, 1859, he seized the United States arsenal at Harpers Ferry, Virginia, at the junction of the Potomac and Shenandoah rivers, and, raiding the premises of a few neighboring planters, forcibly "freed" about thirty of their slaves. The Negroes were huddled together with his men in the arsenal, bewildered, and more like captives than newly baptized freemen, when a detachment of United States marines under the command of Colonel Robert E. Lee arrived on the scene, battered down the doors of the arsenal, and easily made captives of such of Brown's band as had not been killed in the "siege." Brown himself, severely wounded, was promptly tried for treason in a Virginia court, and, entering no defense but his divine commission, was condemned and hanged. His courage, dignity, and composure in the face of death could not alter the fact that his raid at Harpers Ferry was the rash deed of a fanatic. In the eyes of the Southerners it was a widespread plot to incite a slave rebellion, supported by the Republican leaders; while abolitionists like Emerson and Theodore Parker glorified Brown as a martyr, and Thoreau even compared him to Christ on the Cross. Northern regiments in the Civil War marched to the song

> John Brown's body lies a-moldering in the grave,
> His soul goes marching on.

Lincoln Speaks at Cooper Union. Congress met on December 5, 1859, three days after John Brown was hanged. In the House, which contained 109 Republicans and 101 Democrats, a battle of two months was waged over the choice of a Speaker.[1] In-

---

[1] This was because John Sherman of Ohio, the candidate of the Republicans, had endorsed a book entitled *The Present Crisis in the South and How to Meet It*, written by Hilton R. Helper, a "poor white" of North Carolina. Helper aimed to prove (by figures which were not always accurate) that industry was being

sults were hurled across the aisle, challenges to duels were exchanged, and many of the members went to the sessions armed with revolvers. On February 2, 1860, Jefferson Davis introduced into the Senate a set of resolutions which were intended as a final statement of the terms on which the South would remain in the Union. The Northern states must repeal their Personal Liberty Acts; the Fugitive-Slave Law must be enforced; Congress must protect slavery in every territory of the United States; and Douglas's Freeport Doctrine must be repudiated.

On the twenty-seventh of the same month Lincoln made a notable address in Cooper Union, New York City. The debates with Douglas had brought Lincoln a national reputation, but the Eastern Republicans had not yet given him a place beside Seward and Sumner. His clothes were ill-fitting, his voice was high and thin, and his gestures were awkward as he stood before the cultured audience of New York. But all these things were forgotten as he proceeded, with accurate knowledge, clear exposition, and great charity, to expound the Republican doctrine. He showed that Congress had repeatedly made laws to control slavery in the territories, and that the South had accepted such laws; that no particle of proof could be brought to show that the Republican party had anything to do with John Brown's raid; that the threat of the "fire-eaters" to break up the Union if a Republican President were elected had no justification. He concluded with a ringing appeal to the men of the North to stand by their principles in the faith that "right makes might." The Cooper Union speech was an answer to Davis's resolutions, and it made Lincoln a serious candidate for the Republican nomination.

The Democratic Party is Split. The great conventions of 1860, which were to nominate candidates for the most important Presidential election in our history, began with the meeting of the Democrats at Charleston, South Carolina, on April 23. The committee on the platform approved the Davis resolutions, but

ruined in the South by the slave owners, who formed less than 10 per cent of the white population; and he appealed to the great mass of non-slaveholders to join with the Republicans in getting rid of the evil.

the majority of the delegates supported Douglas, who was the unanimous choice of the Northern Democrats. Thereupon the Alabama delegation, led by the ardent secessionist William L. Yancey, marched out of the hall, followed by the majority of the delegates from South Carolina, Georgia, Florida, Mississippi, Louisiana, Arkansas, and Texas. Since in the diminished convention Douglas failed to get the two-thirds vote necessary for nomination, the members adjourned, to meet again at Baltimore on June 18. There again the convention split, the "regulars" nominating Douglas, and the "bolters" naming John C. Breckinridge of Kentucky. With two Democratic tickets in the field to divide the Northern and Southern vote of the party, the victory of the Republicans was made almost certain. Alexander H. Stephens of Georgia, one of the ablest statesmen of the South and a foe of secession, declared that "within a twelvemonth of the disruption of the Democratic convention at Charleston the nation would be engaged in a bloody civil war." And so it was.

The Election of Abraham Lincoln. Meanwhile the Republican convention had met (May 16) at Chicago in the huge structure called the Wigwam, which was packed with ten thousand wildly excited delegates and spectators. Senator William H. Seward of New York was the favored candidate, and he confidently expected the nomination, leading Lincoln by $173\frac{1}{2}$ votes to 102 on the first ballot. But Seward was handicapped in the East by his pronounced sympathy with the abolitionists and his savage attacks on the "Know-Nothings," while the West was solidly behind their homespun hero, "Honest Abe." Lincoln was nominated on the third ballot, and the convention went wild with joy.

The platform not only reasserted the free-soil doctrine, condemning the Lecompton fraud and the Dred Scott decision, but cleverly appealed to the business interests also, by advocating the construction of a Pacific railroad, national aid for river and harbor improvements, and a protective tariff to encourage home manufactures. Thus the Chicago "bargain," as Professor Beard calls the platform, was a sort of combination of William Lloyd Garrison and Henry Clay.

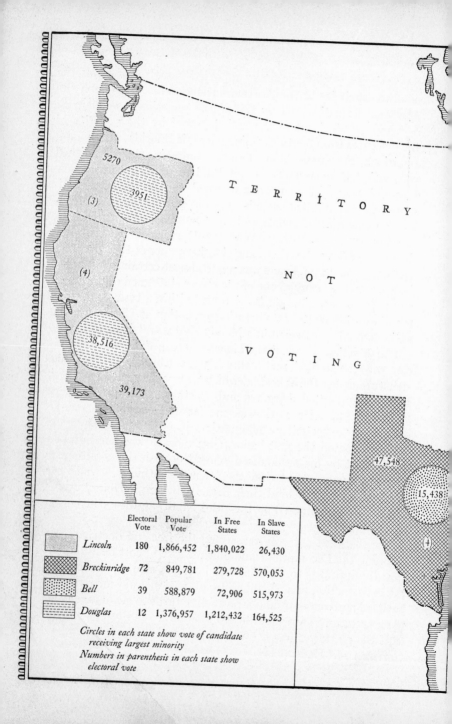

5270

(3)

3951

(4)

38,516

39,173

T E R R I T O R Y

N O T

V O T I N G

47,548

15,438

(4)

		Electoral Vote	Popular Vote	In Free States	In Slave States
	Lincoln	180	1,866,452	1,840,022	26,430
	Breckinridge	72	849,781	279,728	570,053
	Bell	39	588,879	72,906	515,973
	Douglas	12	1,376,957	1,212,432	164,525

Circles in each state show vote of candidate
    receiving largest minority
Numbers in parenthesis in each state show
    electoral vote

THE PRESIDENTIAL
ELECTION OF 1860

There was a fourth party, made up of the remnants of the Southern Whigs and of the Know-Nothings chiefly, which sought to avoid the slavery issue, and ran on the noncommittal platform of "the maintenance of the Union and the Constitution and the enforcement of the laws." The Constitutional-Unionists, as they were called, nominated John Bell of Tennessee and Edward Everett of Massachusetts.

A study of the map on pages 380–381 will show how Lincoln carried the election on November 6. Note the following points : (1) Lincoln, in spite of his overwhelming majority in the electoral college, received only about 40 per cent of the popular vote ; (2) Douglas, though he was repudiated by the administration and carried only one state and part of another, rolled up a very large popular vote in the Northern states ; (3) the three stanch Unionist candidates together polled four and a half times as many votes as Breckinridge ; and (4) even in the slave states Breckinridge received only 45 per cent of the votes, or 115,000 less than Douglas and Bell combined, which shows that the South as a whole was not in favor of secession in November, 1860.

The Southern Confederacy. These figures could hardly be taken as a mandate to the Southern extremists to dissolve the Union. Yet South Carolina proceeded immediately to the work. Its legislature,[1] as soon as it heard of Lincoln's election, called a convention which met at Charleston on December 20 and, by the unanimous vote of its 169 members, passed the famous Ordinance of Secession, repealing the act of May 23, 1778, by which it had ratified the Constitution, and declaring that "the Union now subsisting between South Carolina and the other states, under the name of the United States of America, is hereby dissolved."

Within six weeks Mississippi, Florida, Alabama, Louisiana, Georgia, and Texas had severed their connection with the Union, and delegates from all these "sovereign states" except Texas

[1] South Carolina was the only state in 1860 that chose its Presidential electors by the legislature. In all the other states they were chosen by popular vote. The South Carolina legislature, having chosen its electors on November 6, remained in session until it heard the result of the vote in the other states, and then sent out the call for the secessionist convention.

THE INAUGURATION OF JEFFERSON DAVIS AT RICHMOND,
FEBRUARY 22, 1862

(where the secession ordinance had to be submitted to a popular vote) met at Montgomery, Alabama, on February 4, 1861, and organized the new Confederacy. Jefferson Davis of Mississippi was chosen president, and Alexander H. Stephens of Georgia vice-president. The Confederate Constitution was patterned rather closely upon that of the United States,[1] except that the president was to serve a single term of six years, the cabinet members were to have the right to speak on the floor of congress, slavery was expressly sanctioned, and no protective duties were to be levied. A Confederate flag, the "Stars and Bars," was adopted. A tax of one eighth of a cent a pound on exported cotton was levied. President Davis was authorized to raise an army of one hundred thousand men and secure a loan of fifteen million dollars. A committee was sent abroad to seek the friendship and alliance of European courts. Both Davis and Stephens believed that the South would have to fight "a long and bloody war" to establish its independence.

THE STARS AND BARS

Attempts to Avert Civil War. Meanwhile the greatest confusion prevailed at Washington. President Buchanan was "floundering about in a sea of perplexity," only hoping that his term might come to an end before the storm broke. In his last message to Congress (December 4, 1860) he denied the right of secession: "The framers of this government never intended to plant in its bosom the seeds of its own destruction. . . . Secession is neither more nor less than revolution." But at the same time he declared that the government had no right to compel a state to remain in the Union. Three members of his cabinet avowed their belief in the right of secession, more than a month before South Carolina acted, but Buchanan did

---

[1] The Confederate and the United States constitution are printed in parallel columns in Woodrow Wilson's *History of the American People*, Vol. IV, Appendix. The Civil War, of course, prevented the Confederate constitution from going into full effect.

not dismiss them. Abolitionists, such as Garrison and Phillips, were glad to see the "sinful" slaveholding South separate itself from the Union. Pacifists, like Greeley, would let the cotton states "go in peace" rather than engage in a hideous war to "pin" them to the rest of the states "by bayonets."

In Congress desperate attempts were made to engineer another compromise between the sections. Senator John J. Crittenden of Kentucky, Clay's successor, proposed a set of "unamendable amendments" to the Constitution, extending the Missouri Compromise line of 36° 30′ to the Pacific as the dividing line between slavery and free soil, legalizing the domestic slave trade, and pledging the government to pay for escaped fugitive slaves. To these amendments were added resolutions upholding the Fugitive-Slave Law of 1850 but modifying it to make it more acceptable to the North, recommending the repeal of the Personal Liberty Acts, and suppressing the African slave trade. A committee of thirteen — including Senators of all shades of opinion, from Wade and Seward to Davis and Toombs — discussed the Crittenden Compromise earnestly, but could not agree. The Republicans, backed by President-elect Lincoln, held firmly to their refusal to allow slavery to go into territories below 36° 30′, and with them voted Davis and Toombs, who just as firmly refused to exclude slavery above 36° 30′. The only outcome of the long discussion was the recommendation of a constitutional amendment making slavery inviolable in the states where it was established by law. This proposed Thirteenth Amendment to the Constitution was passed by a two-thirds majority in both houses (February 28, 1861) and submitted to the states; but by that time the Southern Confederacy was already established, and only two states took the trouble to ratify the amendment.

Lincoln Faces a Crisis. It was a serious situation that confronted Abraham Lincoln when he was sworn into the Presidency on March 4, 1861. A rival government in the South had been in operation for a full month. All the military property in the seven Confederate states, except one or two forts, had been seized by the secessionists. From Congress and the executive departments at Washington, from Federal offices all through the North, from army and navy posts, Southerners were departing daily to cast in their fortunes with the cause of their states. Many voices in the North were bidding them Godspeed. Most serious of all, Major Robert Anderson, with a little garrison of eighty-three men in Fort Sumter, in Charleston harbor, was writing to the War Department that his stores of food were almost exhausted.[1]

Lincoln's inaugural address was a reassertion of his kindly feeling toward the South and a plea for calmness and brotherly love. He declared that he must hold the forts and property of the United States in the South and collect the duties under the law; but he disclaimed any intention to disturb the institutions or invade the rights of the South. "In your hands, my dissatisfied fellow-countrymen, and not in mine," he said, turning to his Southern hearers, "is the momentous issue of civil war. The Government will not assail you. You can have no conflict without being yourselves the aggressors. You have no oath registered in heaven to destroy the government, while I shall have the most solemn one to 'preserve, protect and defend it.'" In a moving closing word he appealed to the common memories of the North and the South, which, like "mystic chords . . . stretching from every battle-field and patriot grave to every living heart and hearthstone all over this broad land, will yet swell the chorus of the Union, when again touched, as surely they will be, by the better angels of our nature."

The Fall of Fort Sumter. A few days after his inauguration, Lincoln laid before his cabinet the critical situation in Charleston harbor. He was determined that Major Anderson should

[1] Major Anderson had moved his garrison from Fort Moultrie to the stronger Fort Sumter a few days after the secession of South Carolina. The authorities of the state took this to be a warlike act and demanded that the garrison be sent back to Fort Moultrie. Buchanan refused to yield to commissioners from the "sovereign state" of South Carolina who came to Washington to treat with the government for the surrender of the Federal property in their state. He even sent a merchant vessel, the *Star of the West*, with provisions for Anderson's garrison in Fort Sumter. The ship was turned back by fire from the guns on Morris Island (January 8, 1861), and for the remaining two months of his term the President took no further step to disturb the "truce" in Charleston harbor.

THE BOMBARDMENT OF FORT SUMTER

not be starved out. Therefore, with the approval of all but two of his cabinet members, he notified Governor Pickens of South Carolina on April 8 that he would send provisions to the fort. The Confederate government at Montgomery then ordered General Beauregard, who was in command of seven thousand troops at Charleston, to demand the immediate surrender of Fort Sumter. Anderson refused to abandon his post, and, just before dawn of April 12, 1861, the batteries on Sullivan's, James, and Morris islands opened fire upon the fort. The bombardment lasted all day and at intervals through the night of rain and wind that followed, while cheering throngs lined the esplanade which ran along the Charleston sea front. After maintaining the unequal contest for thirty-two hours, with the fort in flames and his men tortured by heat and smoke, Anderson surrendered on the afternoon of Saturday, April 13. The next day he saluted the tattered Union flag and marched his half-suffocated garrison out of the fort to embark for New York on the few Federal vessels which during the entire bombardment had been rolling in the heavy sea beyond the bar, unable to come to his relief.

The firing on Fort Sumter opened the Civil War. On April 15 Lincoln called on the states for seventy-five thousand militia to suppress resistance to the laws of the United States by groups of men too numerous and powerful to be dealt with by the civil authorities. None of the governors of the slave states heeded the President's call, but the response of the North was instantaneous. "The first gun at Fort Sumter," wrote James Russell Lowell, "brought all the free states to their feet as one man." Party lines were obliterated. Douglas, the leader of a million and a half Democrats, hastened to the White House to grasp Lincoln's hand and pledge him his utmost support. Ex-Presidents Pierce and Buchanan, hitherto ruled by Southern sympathies, became strong Unionists. Editors like Horace Greeley, preachers like Henry Ward Beecher, statesmen like Edward Everett, who had lately found the idea of coercing the Southern states abhorrent, now joined in the call to arms. The South was no less ardent. Volunteers flocked to answer President Davis's proclamation for an army of one hundred thousand, and the Con-

ABRAHAM LINCOLN

federate Congress met in extra session to pass measures for the military, financial, and industrial security of the Confederacy. So the men of the North and the men of Dixie confronted one another in arms. The "irrepressible conflict" had come. Two systems of social and economic life, mutually contemptuous and destructive, were grimly determined to fight out on the field of battle the question which forty years of compromise had failed to solve.

TERMS TO BE MASTERED

slavery restriction
"doubtful column"
territorial delegate
availability

Native American party
"Black Republicans"
obiter dictum
popular sovereignty

Freeport Doctrine
"bolters"
Personal Liberty Acts
"the irrepressible conflict"

FOR SUPPLEMENTARY READING

T. C. SMITH, *Parties and Slavery* (American Nation Series, Vol. XVIII); J. W. BURGESS, *The Middle Period*, chaps. xviii–xxii, and *The Civil War and the Constitution*, Vol. I, chaps. i–vi; W. E. DODD, *Expansion and Conflict*, chaps. x–xii, and *The Cotton Kingdom* (Chronicles of America, Vol. XXVII); N. W. STEPHENSON, *Abraham Lincoln and the Union* (Chronicles, Vol. XXIX), chaps. i–v; ALLEN JOHNSON, *The Life of Stephen A. Douglas*; G. F. MILTON, *The Eve of Conflict*, chaps. vii–xxxiii; P. O. RAY, *The Repeal of the Missouri Compromise*; CHARLES WARREN, *The Supreme Court in United States History*, Vol. III, chap. xxvi; E. D. FITE, *The Presidential Campaign of 1860*; G. H. PUTNAM (ed.), *The Political Debates between Abraham Lincoln and Stephen A. Douglas*; H. S. COMMAGER, *Documents of American History*, pp. 329–361; *America*, Vol. VII, pp. 205–291; *The Pageant of America*, Vol. VIII, pp. 282–327 (for illustrations); HART, *Contemporaries*, Vol. IV, Nos. 29–52; MUZZEY, *Readings*, pp. 359–407.

TOPICS FOR REPORTS

1. **Bleeding Kansas.** CHARLES ROBINSON, *The Kansas Conflict*, chaps. v–xiii; L. W. SPRING, *Kansas, the Prelude to the War for the Union*, chaps. iii–xii; O. G. VILLARD, *John Brown, a Biography Fifty Years After*, pp. 79–226; W. L. FLEMING, "The Buford Expedition to Kansas," in *American Historical Review*, Vol. VI, pp. 38–48; JOHN G. WHITTIER, *Brown of Ossawattomie*; HART, *Contemporaries*, Vol. IV, Nos. 36–40; *America*, Vol. VII, pp. 221–228.

2. **The Birth of the Republican Party.** FRANCIS CURTIS, *The Republican Party*, Vol. I, pp. 172–234; A. D. MORSE, "The Republican Party," in *Political Science Quarterly*, Vol. VII, pp. 522–535; W. E. DODD, "The Fight for the Northwest," in *American Historical Review*, Vol. XVI, pp. 744–788; EDWARD STANWOOD, *History of the Presidency*, chaps. xix, xx; NICOLAY and HAY, *The Works of Abraham Lincoln*, Vol. I, pp. 178–226; ALLEN JOHNSON, *Stephen A. Douglas*, pp. 260–280.

3. **The Southern Argument for Secession.** R. R. Russell, *The Economic Aspects of Southern Sectionalism*, chaps. i–ix; A. P. Upshur, *The Nature of the Federal Government* (The South in the Building of the Nation, Vol. IV, pp. 466–486); E. A. Pollard, *The Lost Cause*, chap. i; Edward Channing, *History of the United States*, Vol. VI, pp. 256–270; Hart, *Contemporaries*, Vol. IV, Nos. 54, 55; Commager, *Documents*, pp. 362, 371, 372; Muzzey, *Readings*, pp. 394–399.

4. **The Nomination of Abraham Lincoln.** E. D. Fite, *The Presidential Campaign of 1860*, pp. 117–131; J. F. Rhodes, *The History of the United States from the Compromise of 1850*, Vol. II, pp. 456–473; Nicolay and Hay, *Abraham Lincoln, a History*, Vol. II, pp. 255–278; G. W. Julian, "The First Republican National Convention," in *American Historical Review*, Vol. IV, pp. 313–322; Murat Halstead, *Caucuses of 1860*, pp. 141–154; *America*, Vol. VII, pp. 279–286.

QUESTIONS SUGGESTED BY THE CHAPTER

1. What "sacred pledge" did the Kansas-Nebraska Act violate? **2.** What motives have been attributed to Douglas for his eagerness to get the act passed? **3.** What were Douglas's views on the subject of slavery? **4.** In what state was the new Republican party organized? What was its platform? **5.** Why did the Southerners condemn the Emigrant Aid Society? **6.** What were the tenets of the "Know-Nothings"? **7.** What factors helped the election of Buchanan in 1856? **8.** Show how the Dred Scott decision was embarrassing to Douglas. **9.** What was the connection between the Dred Scott decision and the Missouri Compromise? **10.** Analyze Lincoln's Cooper Union speech. **11.** What was the "fraud" in the Lecompton Constitution? **12.** Why was Lincoln nominated, rather than Seward, in 1860? **13.** Why were the Lincoln-Douglas debates held? **14.** What was the subject of the debates? **15.** Why did the South wish to reopen the slave trade? **16.** What was John Brown's object at Harpers Ferry? **17.** What does the map of the election of 1860 show in regard to slavery? **18.** Compare the views of Garrison, Buchanan, and Greeley on the subject of secession. **19.** What were some of the differences between the Confederate constitution and the constitution of the United States? **20.** What instances of threatened secession before 1860 can you recall? **21.** What amendment to the Constitution was proposed to avert the breach between the North and the South? **22.** What appeal to the South did Lincoln make in his inaugural address?

CHAPTER SIXTEEN

THE CIVIL WAR [1]

How we shall Study the War. We have dealt more fully with the reasons why the North and the South drifted farther and farther apart until the break came than we shall deal with the military events of the war itself. For, in the first place, it is most important for the student to understand the *causes* of great upheavals in our history, and, in the second place, the actual handling of armies on the march or in battle is a special science with which only the military experts are competent to deal. *The Official Records of the Union and Confederate Armies and Navies in the War of the Rebellion*, published by the government at Washington, fill more than one hundred and thirty bulky volumes and chronicle over a thousand engagements, of which about one hundred and fifty are important enough to be called "battles." Most of these we must pass over in silence, to sketch in outline only the few great campaigns on which the fortunes of the Republic hung.

Two things the student must constantly bear in mind: the great superiority of the North in resources, and the advantage to the South of fighting an almost exclusively defensive war on her own soil. The population of the free states and the border slave states which did not secede was twenty-two million, as against five and a half million whites in the Confederacy. In money, bank credit, manufactures, and the all-important factor of railroads, which could move men and supplies to any point at will, the North had even more than a four-to-one preponderance.

[1] "The War of the Secession," "the War Between the States," and "the War for Southern Independence" are other titles used. The official title used by the United States government was "the War of the Rebellion," and in the North it was the custom to call the Southerners "rebels" until the passions roused by the war began to cool.

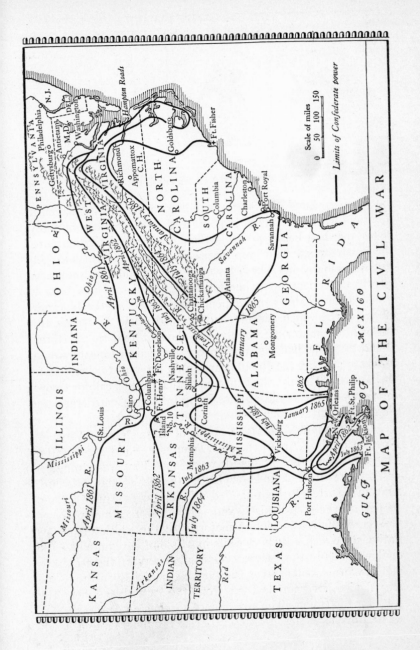

MAP OF THE CIVIL WAR

Scale of miles
0 50 100 150
—— Limits of Confederate power

A GROUP OF WAR ENVELOPES

On the other hand, the South, standing on the defensive against invasion, was more united in spirit and, in the opinion of many historians, had better generals than the North. Furthermore, the South expected aid from three sources — all of which proved disappointing. First, she believed that England and France, so largely dependent upon her for their supplies of raw cotton, would acknowledge her independence and break the blockade of her ports, which Lincoln had decreed a few days after the fall of Fort Sumter. Secondly, she thought that the Northern Democrats, who had cast 1,370,000 votes against Lincoln, would refuse to support the Republicans in an attempt to "subjugate the South." Thirdly, she expected that Lincoln's call for troops for that purpose would at once bring into the Confederacy the eight slave states which had not seceded.

The Confederacy Enlarged. Four of these states — Virginia, North Carolina, Arkansas, and Tennessee — did secede after Lincoln began preparations for war; and there was strong secessionist sentiment in Maryland, Kentucky, and Missouri. Lincoln resorted to high-handed military arrests in Maryland to thwart the secessionists, and used great tact and patience to secure finally a Unionist majority in the legislature of his native state of Kentucky; while in Missouri it required a little civil war before the "Home Guards" (many of them citizens of German descent) under Captain Nathaniel Lyon drove the secessionist governor Jackson from the capital and held the state for the Union. The secession of Virginia on April 17, 1861, was an event of the first importance. It brought the Confed-

Secession States
S.C. Miss, Ala, La. Georgia, Tex. Va
N.C. Ark + Tenn.

M. K. Mo Fla

SLAVE CABINS

eracy up to the banks of the Potomac, where the "Stars and Bars" could be seen from the windows of the White House. The Confederate capital was moved from Montgomery to Richmond, and Virginia became the chief battleground of the war from the first engagement at Manassas to the surrender of Lee at Appomattox. In Robert E. Lee, also, Virginia gave the South her greatest general. Lee was the son of the distinguished Revolutionary general "Light-Horse Harry" Lee, and was himself a gifted commander and a gentleman of spotless character — generous, sincere, and brave. He had already been tendered the command of the Union army by Lincoln, but he felt that he could not draw his sword against his native state, which he believed had "never parted with her sovereign right to demand the ultimate allegiance of her citizens." He loved the Union and hated slavery. Yet after an agonizing mental struggle, he resigned his commission in the United States army to accept the command of the state troops of Virginia. A year later he was made general of the Confederate army in Virginia, and toward the close of the war he was appointed by President Davis general in chief of all the Confederate forces in the field.

DAKOTA
TERRITORY

MINN.

WIS.

NEBRASKA TERR.

IOWA

COLO.
TERR.

KANSAS

ILL. IND. OHIO

N. Y.

PA.

ME.

VT. N.H.
MASS.
CONN. R.I.

N.J.
MD. DEL.

VA.
April 17, 1861

NEW
MEXICO
TERR.

INDIAN
TERR.

ARK.
May 6,
1861

TENN.
June 8, 1861

KY.

Richmond

N.C.
May 20, 1861

S.C.
Dec. 20,
1860

TEXAS
Feb. 1, 1861

MISS. ALA. GA.
Jan. 9, Jan. 11, Jan. 19,
1861 1861 1861

L'A.
Jan. 26,
1861

M O

Montgomery

FLA.
Jan. 10,
1861

☐ *States seceding before the fall
  of Fort Sumter*
⫶ *States seceding after the fall
  of Fort Sumter*
▨ *Slave states remaining loyal*
☐ *Free states (with California
  and Oregon)*

HOW THE SOUTHERN CONFEDERACY WAS
ENLARGED AFTER THE FALL OF FORT SUMTER

The First Battle of Bull Run (Manassas). The Confederate Congress was called to meet at Richmond on July 20, and the overconfident North, cheered by the success of General George B. McClellan in clearing the "rebels" out of West Virginia,[1] demanded that the war should be ended before the Confederate Congress met. Though the thirty thousand troops which Gen-

[1] Forty-eight counties in the western, mountainous part of Virginia voted against secession in May, 1861; and when Governor Letcher sent troops to coerce them, they "seceded from secession" and set up a new state which they called Kanawha. Lincoln sent General George B. McClellan, of the Department of the Ohio, to drive the Confederates out of the region, which he did with complete success. In 1863 Congress admitted these counties into the Union as the state of West Virginia, though this action was a violation of the Constitution (Art. IV, Sect. 3, par. 1).

eral Irvin McDowell had at Washington were not yet properly organized or drilled, their three months' term of enlistment was about to expire, and President Lincoln and General Scott yielded to the popular clamor "On to Richmond!" McDowell's "grand army" set out in high spirits, accompanied by several Congressmen and government officials who went to see "the rebellion crushed by a single blow." McDowell met General Joseph E. Johnston's force of twenty-two thousand at Manassas Junction, a little town on Bull Run (stream) about thirty-five miles southwest of Washington (July 21). Until early afternoon the battle favored the Union side, and reports were sent back to Washington of a glorious victory. But when both armies were exhausted by nearly ten hours of fighting, fresh Confederate troops arrived on the field and decided the day. By sundown McDowell's army, thoroughly defeated and demoralized, was mingling with the panic-stricken civilians in a wild fight for safety to the fortifications of the capital. It was for his firm stand at a critical point in this battle that General Thomas J. Jackson, Lee's ablest lieutenant, earned the nickname of "Stonewall Jackson" which has clung to him ever since.

Complications with England. The defeat at Bull Run had a sobering effect on the North. McClellan, the hero of West Virginia, was put in command of the troops which poured into the camp of his Army of the Potomac by tens of thousands at the President's call. The Southerners, elated by their victory, strengthened the fortifications around Richmond and prepared to hold their front, which extended westward to forts on the lower Cumberland and Tennessee rivers and the middle Mississippi. There were no more major battles in 1861. Each side was girding itself for a long and bitter struggle.

Especially keen was the competition for the sympathy of foreign nations, especially of Great Britain. There the North appealed to a nation which had abolished slavery in its colonies, and the South to a nation which needed cotton. Lincoln sent as minister to England Charles Francis Adams, the son and grandson of former Presidents of the United States. On the day of Adams's arrival in England (May 13) Queen Victoria's government recognized the belligerency[1] of the Confederacy. This action it had a perfect right to take; but, coming as it did before Adams had a chance to explain Lincoln's theory of secession (see note), the British recognition of the South's belligerency was resented by the North as a hasty and unfriendly act.

The *Trent* Affair. A far more serious incident occurred in the autumn of the same year. The government at Richmond had appointed Messrs. Mason and Slidell as commissioners to England and France, respectively, to attempt to win official support for the Confederacy. The commissioners eluded the blockade and boarded the British steamer *Trent* at Havana. On November 8 Captain Wilkes of the United States sloop of war *San Jacinto* stopped the *Trent* on the high seas, forcibly removed the commissioners from her deck, and brought them to New York, whence they were removed as prisoners to Fort Warren in Boston harbor. Wilkes's deed was hailed with rejoicing at the North, and the South was in high hopes that this insult to the British flag would involve Lincoln's government in a war with England. British troops were, in fact, dispatched to Canada. But the sober sense of Lincoln and Seward realized that Wilkes's rash deed was a violation of the rights of vessels of neutral nations, in defense of which we had ourselves gone to war with England in 1812. Therefore, when Seward apologized for the seizure and assured the British minister that the prisoners in Fort Warren would be "cheerfully liberated" and allowed to resume their voyage, the British government was satisfied, and the blockade of the Southern ports continued.

The *Virginia* and the *Monitor*. In the spring of 1862 the Confederates attempted to break the blockade of their coasts, which extended from Virginia to Texas. They raised the frigate

[1] This did not mean recognizing the *independence* of the Confederacy but only its right to be treated according to the rules of warfare between two acknowledged powers, such as the exchange of prisoners and the willingness of the military and civil authorities on each side to deal with the enemy on terms of official respect. At the beginning of the war Lincoln held the idea that the Southerners were insurgents and that those captured in arms should be punished as traitors. But he soon realized that he must recognize so numerous and united a people as the Confederacy as a belligerent power, exchanging prisoners of war with them and dealing with them, as occasions arose, through official channels.

THE BATTLE OF THE *MONITOR* AND THE *VIRGINIA*

Merrimac, which had been sunk at the Norfolk (Virginia) navy yard, and converted her into an ironclad by covering her sides with a sloping roof of four-inch iron plates and attaching a powerful iron ram to her bow. On March 8, this strange craft, rechristened the *Virginia*, entered Hampton Roads and proceeded to destroy the wooden ships of the Federal fleet, whose shots glanced off her sides like pebbles from a sling. After sinking the *Cumberland* and setting the *Congress* aflame with red-hot balls, the *Virginia* was forced by the tide to return to her moorings, intending to finish the destruction of Union vessels the next day and perhaps proceed up the Potomac to shell the city of Washington. Panic reigned in the capital. But before dawn an even stranger craft steamed into Hampton Roads. This was the *Monitor*, a small ironclad designed by the Swedish engineer John Ericsson for the Federal navy. From the deck of the *Monitor*, which was almost flush with the water, rose a revolving turret armed with two eleven-inch guns. She was said to look like "a cheesebox on a raft." The *Monitor* put herself between the *Virginia* and the wooden ships, and after a spectacular duel, in which neither ironclad did much harm to the other, the *Virginia* withdrew again to Norfolk. The Union blockade was saved; but this first fight in history between ironclad vessels made wooden ships as obsolete for naval warfare as Noah's Ark.[1]

The Peninsular Campaign. General McClellan, the new commander of the Army of the Potomac, was a graduate of West Point, not yet thirty-five years old, a magnificent organizer, a tireless worker, and the idol of his troops. When Lee was asked after the war who was the ablest Union general that he had encountered, he replied, "McClellan, by all odds." Yet in the spring of 1862 McClellan seems to have been almost paralyzed by the responsibility of commanding an army which had grown to nearly one hundred and eighty thousand men. He became a prey to the obsession that the greatly inferior forces of Lee and Johnston outnumbered his own, and berated the "imbecile" administration at Washington for not sending him reinforcements.

It was not until the beginning of April, 1862, that McClellan, after repeated orders from the War Department and President Lincoln to advance on Richmond, began to move. But instead of marching on Richmond directly, he ferried his huge army down the Potomac and Chesapeake Bay to the end of the peninsula between the York and James rivers and started a slow and cautious movement up the peninsula toward the Confederate capital. At the end of May he was in sight of the church spires of Richmond, less than five miles away. For weeks President Davis, the cabinet, and a majority of the citizens of Richmond were expecting to hear the Federal batteries thundering at the defenses of the city. But McClellan, still laboring under the delusion that he "would have to fight an army of a hundred thousand men" to take Richmond, and still clamoring for reinforcements for his own army of more than a hundred thousand,[2] resorted again to the defensive.

[1] Neither of these queer vessels was destined to last long. When the Confederates evacuated Norfolk in May, they blew up the *Virginia*; and the *Monitor*, unable to stand the rough seas, sank in a storm off Cape Hatteras in December.

[2] The reason why McClellan received no reinforcements, and even had McDowell's corps of forty thousand men held on the Potomac to defend Washington, was Stonewall Jackson. This third great Virginian general, with Lee and

Hard pressed by Johnston and Lee and by the dashing Confederate cavalry commander J. E. B. ("Jeb") Stuart, he skillfully drew his forces together on the south side of the peninsula, beat off a furious Confederate attack at Malvern Hill (July 1), and led his army back to the bank of the James River, within the protection of the Federal gunboats. The famous Peninsular Campaign was over. The war was fifteen months old, and the Stars and Bars still floated over the Confederate capital. McClellan had missed the opportunity that comes but once in a man's career. But, in spite of the disappointment at Washington and the many demands for a more aggressive general in McClellan's place, Lincoln allowed him to remain in command of the Army of the Potomac.

SEAT OF WAR IN EASTERN
VIRGINIA, 1861-1865

Federal Victories in the West. Meantime, McClellan's failure in Virginia was offset by a series of Union successes on the Cumberland, Tennessee, and Mississippi rivers. These operations brought into prominence the greatest general of the North, Ulysses S. Grant. Grant was a West-Pointer who had served with credit in the Mexican War but had resigned from the army a few years later and sunk into obscurity and poverty, deepened by habits of intemperance. The outbreak of the Civil War

Johnston, conducted a miraculous campaign in the Shenandoah valley in May and June, with seventeen thousand men, defeating three times that number of Federals under Frémont, Banks, and Shields, and so threatening the capital that the eyes of the administration were drawn off the Army of the Potomac. "The fate of Richmond," says an able critic of the war, "was decided not on the banks of the Chickahominy, but by the waters of the Shenandoah."

found him, at the age of thirty-nine, earning eight hundred dollars a year as a clerk in his father's hardware and leather store in Galena, Illinois, and made him the military hero of the North and President of the United States.

THE WAR IN THE MISSISSIPPI VALLEY

Grant's first exploit revealed the qualities which brought his success: a genius for discovering the vulnerable positions of the enemy; a silent, grim, cool courage which mounted as dangers and difficulties thickened; and a habit of pressing on to his objective after either victory or defeat. Forts Henry and Donelson, on the northern border of Tennessee, were Confederate strongholds guarding the lower Tennessee and Cumberland rivers, where they approach within a dozen miles of each other before emptying into the Ohio. On February 6, 1862, with the aid of a fleet of gunboats under Flag Officer A. H. Foote, Grant captured Fort Henry, and ten days later he compelled the surrender of the more formidable Fort Donelson, with fourteen thousand prisoners.

General D. C. Buell then occupied Nashville without a blow, while the Union gunboats went down the Mississippi to the high bluffs of Vicksburg, and Grant conveyed his army of forty thousand up the Tennessee to Pittsburg Landing (Shiloh). Here he was suddenly attacked by Albert S. Johnston, the Confederate commander in the West, and driven back to the river bank in a furious battle (April 6), in which Johnston lost his life. The next day, with reinforcements from Buell's army, Grant drove the Confederates from the field.

In the blackness of the night of April 23 Captain David G. Farragut ran by forts Jackson and St. Philip at the mouth of the Mississippi and captured the city of New Orleans. These victories made Kentucky safe for the Union, cleared the Confederates out of western Tennessee, and left the South in control of only the one hundred and twenty-five miles of the Mississippi between Vicksburg and Port Hudson.

LEE'S INVASIONS OF THE NORTH

— Antietam Campaign, Sept. 1862
--- Gettysburg Campaign, June-July 1863

The First Confederate Offensive — Antietam. During the first year of the war the South acted on the defensive, and on the eastern front General Lee, with his great corps of lieutenants, — "Stonewall" Jackson, Longstreet, Ewell, the Hills, and Stuart, — outwitted and repulsed the Union commanders at every point. After McClellan's failure to take Richmond, the rest of the Union forces in the east were combined into the new Army of Virginia, under General John Pope, who assumed command with a boastful confidence born of his recent successes on the Mississippi. But before Pope could march on Richmond and "end the war" he was caught at Bull Run by Lee and Jackson (August 29–30) and was as completely routed as McDowell's green troops had been on the same field thirteen months before (p. 396). The light of Pope's burning wagon trains was visible from the Capitol at Washington, and the city was again in panic. Repeated reverses in battle were causing a strong reaction against the Lincoln administration. The war was costing two million dollars a day and apparently accomplishing nothing.

Enlistments were falling off and desertions increasing. The half-billion-dollar issue of 6 per cent government bonds was not selling well. The Congressional elections were approaching.

On the other side of Mason and Dixon's line, hope was high in the late summer of 1862. It was the "one brief space in Confederate history that was pure sunshine." A great triple offensive was planned. Lee's victorious army was to invade Maryland, winning that state for the Confederacy and threatening the Federal capital, while Bragg and Van Dorn were to expel the Union troops from Kentucky, Tennessee, and Mississippi and regain control of the great river. Before the autumn frosts the triple offensive had failed at every point. Lee crossed the Potomac on September 4, with fifty-five thousand picked troops singing "Maryland, my Maryland," and was met at Sharpsburg, near Antietam Creek, by McClellan with eighty-five thousand men. All day long on September 17 the battle swayed back and forth, and at nightfall Lee still held his position. But he had suffered too severely to continue his invasion. On the nineteenth he led his army back across the Potomac — except for the eleven thousand men left on the field of battle. McClellan's losses had been even larger. He had checked Lee in the "bloodiest battle of the war," but Lincoln's disappointment that he had allowed the Confederate army to get back to Virginia soil was keen.

The Emancipation Proclamation. At the beginning of the war Congress had resolved that the war was to be waged not to subjugate the South nor to free the slaves there, but solely to preserve the Union. Lincoln, though always believing that slavery was a curse, also maintained that the preservation of the Union was his "paramount object," and that any action he took in regard to slavery was governed by what he judged its effect would be upon the task of reclaiming the seceded states. Still, there was great pressure brought to bear upon him to make the war a crusade against slavery. Two of his generals were rebuked for issuing proclamations freeing the slaves in their departments. His minister to Spain, Carl Schurz, wrote home that the sympathy of Europe could be won only by a

And by virtue of the power and for the purpose aforesaid, I do order and declare that all persons held as slaves within said designated States, and parts of States, are, and henceforward shall be free;

And upon this act, sincerely believed to be an act of justice, warranted by the Constitution upon military necessity, I invoke the considerate judgment of mankind, and the gracious favor of Almighty God.

L. S.   Independence of the United States of America the eighty-seventh.

Abraham Lincoln

THE CLOSING LINES OF THE EMANCIPATION PROCLAMATION

frank declaration that the object of the war was the abolition of slavery. Horace Greeley urged the same course in his *Tribune* editorial entitled "The Prayer of Twenty Millions."

Lincoln was sensitive to public opinion, but he believed that an avowed abolitionist war would drive the loyal slave states of Missouri, Kentucky, and Maryland into the Confederacy. He tried his best to get these states to accept payment for their slaves in United States bonds, hoping that their example would induce the seceded states to do likewise.[1] But when this plan

[1] Congress was ready to appropriate for the purchase of the four hundred and thirty thousand slaves in the border states at three hundred dollars apiece, which would have cost the government less than the expense of two months of war;

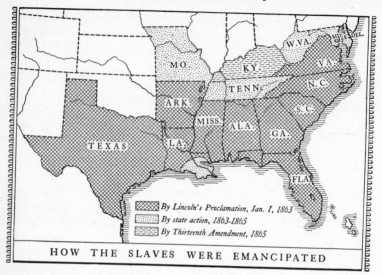

By Lincoln's Proclamation, Jan. 1, 1863
By state action, 1863-1865
By Thirteenth Amendment, 1865

HOW THE SLAVES WERE EMANCIPATED

of "compensated emancipation" was rejected, in the summer of 1862, Lincoln decided, as commander in chief of the army and navy, to strike a blow at the military power of the "rebels" by depriving them of (or "confiscating") their slave property. At Seward's advice, he postponed such action until the North should win a victory in the field. Then, six days after McClellan had checked Lee at Antietam (September 23), Lincoln published the Emancipation Proclamation, declaring that on January 1, 1863, "all persons held as slaves within any State or designated part of a State, the people whereof shall then be in rebellion against the United States, shall be then, henceforth and forever free." Note that Lincoln did not "strike the shackles" from all the slaves but only from those whose masters were "in rebellion against the United States." The Emancipation Proclamation did not free a slave in Delaware, Kentucky, Missouri, or Maryland.[1]

but even if the border states had consented, it would probably have had no effect on the Confederacy. In April, 1862, Congress abolished slavery in the District of Columbia, and in June prohibited slavery in the territories, thus nullifying the Dred Scott decision.

[1] The slaves in Missouri and Maryland were freed by state action; in Delaware and Kentucky, by the Thirteenth Amendment to the Constitution.

Discouragement and "Defeatism." The year 1863, which was really to decide the fate of the great contest, opened darkly for both sides. The South had failed to win Maryland or to regain the ground lost in the West. Her hopes of recognition by England and France were fast fading, and the blockade of her ports was depriving her of the food, clothing, munitions, and railroad equipment necessary for the vigorous prosecution of the war. Unable to raise by taxation or loans more than a fraction of the cash needed to meet the current expenses of the war, she had already resorted to the printing of hundreds of millions of dollars of paper money (inflation), which declined in value until it took a thousand dollars to buy a barrel of flour, and four hundred dollars to buy a pair of shoes. Finally, though the Southern generals worked together splendidly under their great leader Robert E. Lee, there was serious political opposition to President Davis — especially in the original seaboard states of the South, which clung to their doctrine of states' rights and failed to realize that a successful war can be waged only by a unified power. At one time the governors of North Carolina and Georgia even threatened (like the New England states in the War of 1812) to refuse to allow their soldiers to serve outside the state; and all through the South there were protests against the Conscription Act of the spring of 1862.

The North, for all its great resources, was also a prey to discouragement. The first half of 1863 marked the lowest ebb in its military fortunes. Lincoln had finally replaced the slow-moving McClellan by General Ambrose E. Burnside, who met a terrible defeat in a rash attempt to storm Lee's impregnable position on Marye's Heights, above Fredericksburg, on the Rappahannock River (December 13, 1862). Burnside's successor, Joseph ("Fighting Joe") Hooker, was badly beaten at Chancellorsville[1] (May 3-5, 1863), yielding the command of the Army of the Potomac in turn to General George G. Meade. Lincoln, after

---

[1] It was at Chancellorsville that "Stonewall" Jackson, riding in the twilight with some of his staff officers, was mistaken by Confederate sharpshooters for a Union officer and fatally wounded. His loss was one of the severest blows to the Southern cause.

two years of the war, was still looking for a general to match against Lee. The Northern President was also hectored by political opponents and military critics. Mounting taxes, repeated defeats at the front, the lengthening casualty lists of Shiloh, Antietam, Fredericksburg, and Chancellorsville, had cooled the first fine ardor of the North in support of the war. The Democrats carried the important states of New York, Ohio, Pennsylvania, Indiana, Illinois, and Wisconsin in the elections of 1862 and gained thirty-two seats in the House. "Defeatism" was rife. Carloads of civilian clothing were being smuggled into the Union lines to aid deserters to escape. Voluntary enlistments fell so low that in March, 1863, the draft was resorted to, causing riots in many cities, notably in New York, where, in July, over fifteen hundred men were killed before the riots were suppressed by Federal troops sent from Meade's army in Pennsylvania. Clement L. Vallandigham, the famous "Copperhead" (war opponent) Congressman from Ohio, declared in a public speech: "You have not conquered the South; you never will. The war for the Union ... is a bloody and costly failure. Money you have expended without limit, and blood poured out like water. Defeat, debt, taxation and sepulchres — these are your only trophies."[1]

Gettysburg. This distress in the North, and a final hope of obtaining recognition from abroad,[2] now led Davis and Lee to launch their boldest stroke of the war. Lee crossed the Potomac on June 15, 1863, with a splendid army of seventy thousand, to seek the great victory which would terrorize Washington, close the vaults of the Northern bankers, and wreck the sorely

[1] Vallandigham was arrested by General Burnside and sent by Lincoln into the Confederate lines. He later ran for governor of Ohio on a pacifist ticket, but was defeated by one hundred thousand votes.

[2] The French emperor Napoleon III was working hard to get Lord Palmerston to join him in recognizing the independence of the Confederacy. Napoleon had conceived the scheme of setting up a French empire in Mexico and had sent over an army of thirty-five thousand troops, which took Mexico City in June, 1863. Lee's victory at Chancellorsville the month before had revived the faith of British sympathizers with the South, and a motion for the recognition of the Confederacy was pending in Parliament when Lee started on his second invasion of the North.

GENERAL ROBERT E. LEE

tried government of Lincoln. He met Meade's army of eighty thousand at the little town of Gettysburg, in southern Pennsylvania, in the greatest battle of the war (July 1-3, 1863). Lee had the advantage in the first day's battle, before Meade's positions were firmly established; and had "Stonewall" Jackson been at his right hand to follow up the gains by a prompt attack on the Union center early on July 2, there might have been a different story to tell. Time was the very essence of the situation; yet Longstreet failed to obey Lee's orders to hurry his corps to the front. It was not till the afternoon of the third day, when the hope of driving the reinforced Federals from either Culp's Hill on the north or the Round Top on the south of Cemetery Ridge was gone, that Lee made the last desperate bid for victory by sending General Pickett's gallant division of fifteen thousand infantry across the plain to storm the Union center. Steadily they pressed on and up the slope of the ridge, in the face of a sheet of flame from Hancock's batteries, leaving the ground "carpeted with the dead." A hundred men, led by the intrepid Armistead, scaled the fortifications and planted the Stars and Bars within the Union lines — the high-water mark of the Confederacy. But mortal courage could not endure the hail of canister and shrapnel from the Union guns. The line of gray wavered, halted, bent slowly backward, then broke in flight. The day, the battle, and the Southern cause were lost!

The Fall of Vicksburg. On the evening of the "glorious fourth" of July, while the North was celebrating its victory, Lee began his dismal retreat to the Potomac in a pouring rain. His grief and chagrin would have been doubled if he had known that on that same fourth of July General Pemberton had surrendered to Grant the great stronghold of Vicksburg, with one hundred and seventy cannon, fifty thousand small arms, and thirty thousand prisoners of war. The reduction of this last Confederate hold upon the Mississippi was the achievement of a marvelous campaign of eight months by Grant and his chief lieutenant, William T. Sherman. Baffled in his attempt to take Vicksburg from the river approach, Grant had moved his army to the west side of the Mississippi and made his slow way through the treacherous, fever-laden bayous of Louisiana to a point thirty-five miles below the city, while Admiral Porter daringly ran his supply barges by night beneath the batteries on the Vicksburg bluffs. Crossing again to the Mississippi side of the river, Grant marched northward, cutting the railroad that supplied Vicksburg from the east, intercepting General Joseph E. Johnston, who was bringing an army of fifteen thousand to Pemberton's relief, and then turning westward to throw his troops in a besieging line of twenty-five miles around the city. For six weeks the doomed city held out, until the inhabitants were reduced to eating rats and mules, many families taking refuge in caves hewn out of the hard clay of the bluffs to escape the shells from Grant's batteries on the shore and Porter's gunboats on the river. Then, with all hope of relief from Johnston gone, and with his soldiers staggering in the trenches from starvation, Pemberton surrendered. Five days later Port Hudson, the last Confederate post on the river, capitulated, and, in the words of Lincoln, "the Father of Waters" went again "unvexed to the sea." The Confederacy was cut in twain; the bridge over which supplies had come from Texas and Mexico was closed. Adopting the old New England custom, Lincoln appointed the last Thursday in November as a day of national Thanksgiving — a day still observed annually by proclamation of the President.

The "Anaconda Policy." Gettysburg and Vicksburg marked the turning-point of the war, and should have marked its end. For the South was beaten then. To be sure, she did not acknowledge defeat, but struggled on valiantly for nearly two years more in a defensive war "to the last ditch." The Confederate bonds which had been bought in large quantities in England and France sank from 95 to 37 on the news of the Northern victories. The motion pending in the British Parliament for the recognition of the Confederacy (p. 408, note 2) was withdrawn, and the emperor Napoleon abandoned his schemes for intervention. On the other hand, the North adopted a unified plan of conducting the war after Gettysburg and Vicksburg. This was the "anaconda policy," by which the Union armies were to wrap themselves around the Confederacy as the anaconda wraps its coils around its victim, squeezing out its life. Grant and Sherman were to move eastward from the Mississippi, while the Army of the Potomac was to press down upon Richmond.

Chickamauga and Chattanooga. The program west of the Alleghenies was completed before the close of 1863. The Confederate general Bragg, who, after the failure of his drive into Kentucky (p. 404), had been forced back to Chattanooga, drew his opponent Rosecrans across the Tennessee River into the mountains of the northwest corner of Georgia, where he turned on him suddenly at Chickamauga Creek (September 20, 1863) and completely routed him. The defeat might have wrecked the anaconda policy had it not been for the intrepid conduct of the Union general George H. Thomas, a Virginian, who held the left wing firmly against repeated assaults of superior Confederate numbers all through the afternoon and earned the title of "the Rock of Chickamauga." Rosecrans was replaced by Thomas, who was soon joined by reinforcements from the victorious armies on the Mississippi.

Grant, who, as a reward for Vicksburg, had been made a major general and put in command of all the armies of the West, arrived at Chattanooga on October 23 and began the brilliant operations which were to culminate in the three days' battle of Chattanooga (November 23–25), which dislodged Bragg's veterans from their strong position on the heights across the Tennessee River (Lookout Mountain and Missionary Ridge) and sent them in full retreat down the eastern slopes. The victory of Chattanooga made the state of Tennessee safe for the Union, broke the power of the Confederacy west of the Alleghenies, and left the North only the task of subduing the old seaboard states of the South. The Confederates had their backs to the wall. Never after Chattanooga did their armies advance as they had at Shiloh and Manassas, at Antietam and Gettysburg, confident of achieving the victory which should establish the independence of the Confederacy. The public men of the South, from President Davis down, continued to speak in brave language; but the optimism of the political rostrum, the pulpit, and the press did not ring true. It was kept up under a forced draft. "We all knew from the beginning of 1864," wrote George Cary Eggleston in *A Rebel's Recollections*, "that the war was hopeless."

Grant Moves on Richmond. On March 9, 1864, Grant was made lieutenant general and given the command, under the President, of all the armies of the United States. He made his headquarters with the Army of the Potomac, and appointed Sherman as his successor in command of the armies of the West. On the night of May 3 Grant crossed the Rapidan and began to fight his way through the Wilderness, where Hooker had been defeated at Chancellorsville just a year before (p. 407). Though his losses were heavy, Grant steadily hammered his way toward Richmond. "I propose to fight it out on this line, if it takes all summer," he telegraphed to Halleck at Washington. At Cold Harbor (June 3) he lost seven thousand men in an hour in an

"PHIL" SHERIDAN

"JEB" STUART

WILLIAM T. SHERMAN

JOSEPH E. JOHNSTON

GEORGE B. McCLELLAN

BRAXTON BRAGG

assault on Lee's strongly fortified position almost as rash as Burnside's at Fredericksburg (p. 407). Then, avoiding the strong defenses of Richmond, he took his army to the south side of the James River and laid siege to the important railroad junction of Petersburg. In the Wilderness campaign of forty days Grant had sacrificed fifty-five thousand men (almost as many as Lee had in his entire army), but he had at least shown his great opponent the novel sight of a Union commander who did not retreat when he was repulsed or rest when he was victorious.

The Re-election of Lincoln. Five days after the slaughter at Cold Harbor, Lincoln was renominated at Baltimore, the name "Union party" being substituted for "Republican" in order to win the votes of the war Democrats. During the next two months the skies looked dark for the Union cause. Grant was making no headway against Petersburg. Sherman, advancing slowly into Georgia, was repulsed at Kenesaw Mountain by Johnston (June 27). The Confederate cavalry general Jubal A. Early, operating against inferior Union commanders in the Shenandoah valley, crossed the Potomac and threatened the defenses of Washington (July 11). Lincoln himself in mid-August thought it "extremely probable" that his administration would go down to defeat under the repeated military failures. The Democrats, meeting at Chicago on August 22, nominated General McClellan on a platform containing the plank (written by the Copperhead Vallandigham)

After four years of failure to restore the Union by the experiment of war . . . justice, humanity, liberty and the public welfare demand that immediate efforts be made for the cessation of hostilities . . . and peace be restored on the basis of the federal union of the states.[1]

In the autumn, however, the skies cleared for the administration. On August 23 Admiral Farragut's daring capture of the forts of Mobile Bay deprived the Confederacy of its last stronghold on the Gulf of Mexico. On September 3 Sherman entered Atlanta. And on October 19 General Philip Sheridan,

[1] It is only fair to McClellan to say that he repudiated the plank calling the war a failure, declaring that he "could not look his old soldiers in the face" if he ran on such a platform.

ULYSSES S. GRANT

GENERAL ULYSSES S. GRANT

by his dashing ride "from Winchester twenty miles away," turned the Union defeat at Cedar Creek into victory and drove Early's cavalry from the Shenandoah valley. These victories, in Seward's words, "knocked the bottom out of the Chicago [Democratic] platform." Lincoln was re-elected in November by an electoral vote of 212 to 21, carrying every state but New Jersey, Delaware, and Kentucky. But his popular vote was only 400,000 more than McClellan's in a total of 4,000,000.

Sherman's March to the Sea. When Atlanta fell, General J. B. Hood (who had replaced Johnston), thinking to draw Sherman back from further invasion of Georgia and to regain Tennessee, made a dash northward against General Thomas, who had been left to protect Nashville and Chattanooga. But Sherman trusted the reliable Thomas to take care of Tennessee and started with sixty thousand men on his famous march "from Atlanta to the sea," three hundred miles across the state of Georgia.

It was more like a continuous picnic of three months than a campaign. The soldiers lived on the fat of the land — the newly

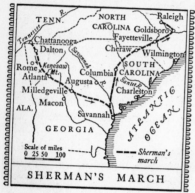

SHERMAN'S MARCH

gathered harvests of corn and grain, an abundance of chickens, turkeys, ducks, pigs, and sweet potatoes. Sherman entered on the march with the grim determination to make the state of Georgia "an example to rebels," and he carried out his threat. Railroads were torn up, public buildings, depots, and machine shops burned, stores of cotton destroyed, ten thousand horses and mules taken, and the military resources of the state damaged beyond repair.[1] Reaching the coast in December, Sherman broke through the feeble defenses of Savannah, and on Christmas evening Lincoln received a telegram from him announcing "as a Christmas gift the city of Savannah, with 150 heavy guns, plenty of ammunition and about 25,000 bales of cotton." Thomas had already annihilated Hood's army at Nashville.

The Fall of Richmond. The plight of the Confederacy could no longer be concealed. Desertions were frequent, food was scarce, Union money was circulating in spite of the prohibition of the government, and Negroes began to be recruited in the army. Public men in increasing numbers were convinced that further resistance was useless. A delegation headed by the vice-president, Alexander H. Stephens, met Lincoln and Seward at Hampton Roads, Virginia, on February 3, 1865, to discuss terms. Lincoln insisted on two points: the restoration of the Union and the abolition of slavery. But the Southerners rejected these terms as "unconditional submission to the mercy

---

[1] Had Sherman's army confined itself to the destruction of property useful in war, there could have been no objection to its behavior. But discipline was lax, and the wanton destruction of private property by camp followers, Negroes, and "bummers" made Sherman's name a byword throughout the South.

of conquerors," and the conference broke up. "I can have no common country with the Yankees," declared Davis; and Lee also advised the continuance of the war.

Sherman and Grant resumed operations. The former marched north through South Carolina, leaving the state capital, Columbia, in ashes behind him.[1] Late in March, Grant renewed his attack on Petersburg. The stronghold fell on Sunday, April 2. Jefferson Davis was at worship in St. Paul's Church in Richmond when a whispered message was brought to him that the city must be evacuated. Hastily collecting his papers, he left Richmond for Danville with his cabinet and several of his staff officers. The next day the Union troops entered the city, followed by President Lincoln, who spoke words of conciliation and kindness in "the enemy's capital." Lee tried to get his dwindling army to the hilly country in the western part of Virginia, where he believed he could still maintain a defensive warfare; but Sheridan's cavalry, spreading out along the Appomattox valley, headed him off, defeating his hungry and exhausted soldiers at Five Forks. On April 7 the Union commander wrote to him, "General, the result of the last week must convince you of the hopelessness of further resistance." Brought to a standstill, Lee consented to listen to Grant's terms of surrender.

The Collapse of the Confederacy. The two great generals met in a farmhouse at Appomattox on April 9. After a few minutes of friendly conversation recalling the days of their comradeship in the Mexican War, Grant wrote out the terms of surrender in a few sentences. The Army of Northern Virginia was to lay down its arms, but the officers were to retain their side-arms and horses. The cavalry and artillery horses also were left, to be used "for the spring plowing" as Grant put it. Lee immediately signed the terms, with a gracious acknowledgment of their generosity. With the surrender of his 26,765 veterans, the submission of the other forces of the Confederacy was only a matter

---

[1] Whether the city was set on fire by Sherman's soldiers the morning they entered it (February 19) or caught from bales of cotton kindled by the inhabitants themselves, to prevent their falling into the hands of the Union army, is a question which is still disputed.

GRANT PRESENTS TO LEE THE TERMS OF THE SURRENDER[1]

of days. Johnston surrendered his army of 37,000 to Sherman at Durham, North Carolina, on April 26, and Generals "Dick" Taylor in Alabama and Kirby Smith in Arkansas turned over their armies to the Union commanders in the Southwest. In all, 174,000 Confederate soldiers laid down their arms.[2] They had fought a valiant fight. The courage of the men and the self-sacrificing devotion of the women remain a cherished tradition in Dixie Land. But there are few, if any, of the children of those who fought for the "lost cause" who would wish today that the outcome of the war had been different — none who would not now echo the final benediction of Jefferson Davis on our common Union: "Esto perpetua!" May it endure for ever!

[1] From "Dixie," one of the Chronicles of America Photoplays. Used by permission of Yale University Press.

[2] Jefferson Davis was captured on May 10 at Irwinsville, Georgia, and imprisoned for two years at Fortress Monroe. After his release he lived quietly in the South until December 6, 1889, never asking for pardon from the government of the United States.

7 ~ Apl '65

Genl

I have recd your note
of this date, Though not enter
taining the opinion you express
of the hopelessness of further resis
-tance on the part of the Army
of N. Va — I reciprocate your
desire to avoid useless effusion
of blood, I therefore before Consider
ing your proposition ask
the terms you will offer on
Condition of its Surrender

Very respy your Obt Servt

R E Lee
Genl

Lt Genl U. S. Grant
Commd Armies of the U. States

LEE'S LETTER TO GRANT RESPECTING THE SURRENDER OF
THE CONFEDERATE ARMY OF NORTHERN VIRGINIA

Good Friday, April 14, was a memorable day in our history. It was the fourth anniversary of the surrender of Fort Sumter. A celebration was held at Charleston, and General Robert Anderson raised above the fort the same tattered flag which he had hauled down after Beauregard's bombardment in 1861. William Lloyd Garrison was present, and the liberated slaves strewed flowers in his path. He spoke at a banquet held that evening. Did the echoes of his voice reach a grave over which stood a marble stone engraved with the single word "Calhoun"?

The Assassination of Lincoln. That same evening President Lincoln was sitting in a box at Ford's Theater in Washington when a demented actor named John Wilkes Booth stepped into the box and shot him in the back of the head.[1] Lincoln was carried to a private house across the street, where he lingered without regaining consciousness until a few minutes past seven o'clock the next morning. He had brought the storm-tossed ship of state safely into port. The exultant shores were ringing with the people's praise and thanksgiving. But in the hour of victory the great captain lay upon the deck, "fallen cold and dead." Lincoln's name is linked with the immortal Washington's in the hearts of his countrymen; for he was the savior of our country, as Washington was its founder and father.

> Our children shall behold his fame,
> The kindly-earnest, brave, foreseeing man,
> Sagacious, patient, dreading praise, not blame,
> New birth of our new soil, the first American.

Summary. The central theme of this unit has been the constantly increasing strife over slavery during the twenty years

---

[1] The assassination of Lincoln was part of a deep-laid plot to kill several high officials of the Union. Secretary Seward, who was in bed suffering from a runaway accident, was stabbed severely the same night, but recovered. Grant too was marked for death, but the assassin lost his nerve after jumping on the general's carriage step and seeing his face through the window. As Booth leaped down onto the stage after firing his fatal shot, his spur caught in the folds of the American flag which decorated the Presidential box, and he fell, breaking his leg. He made his escape from the theater on a horse that was waiting at the stage door, but was soon afterward trapped in a barn in Virginia and shot. The other conspirators in the plot, including a woman, Mrs. Surratt, were apprehended and executed.

preceding the Civil War, and the great struggle in arms which resulted in the abolition of slavery and the preservation of the Union. We have seen that the conflict arose not as a direct issue between North and South (which had lived for eighty years in peace with their different systems of labor) but as a contest between the two sections over the question of extending slavery into the new territory of the West. This question was raised in connection with every advance of our frontier to the Rio Grande and the Pacific under the expansionist program of Tyler and Polk — the annexation of Texas, the acquisition of California and New Mexico from Mexico, and the partition of Oregon with Great Britain. We have seen how the Compromise of 1850, though supported by both the great political parties in the hope of quieting the persistent question of slavery, broke down a few years later, and how Douglas's Kansas-Nebraska Bill of 1854 and the Supreme Court's decision in the Dred Scott case of 1857 put an end to compromise and opened the whole territory of the West to slavery. We have seen how the struggle between the free-soilers and the slavery men for Kansas, supplemented by deeds of violence such as the assault on Sumner and John Brown's raid at Harpers Ferry, aroused the passions on both sides of Mason and Dixon's line to a point where a peaceful settlement was impossible. In spite of the moderate counsels of men like Lincoln and Douglas, the North and the South drew farther apart in their mutual misunderstanding and hatred until the latter section sought its independence by seceding from the Union. We have seen, finally, how President Lincoln refused to let the states of the new southern Confederacy "depart in peace" and how a bitter civil war was waged for four years to compel them to abandon their demand for independence and acknowledge the authority and flag of our common Union.

TERMS TO BE MASTERED

border states	compensated emancipation	"anaconda policy"
belligerency	confiscation	conscription
blockade	Copperhead	Union party

For Supplementary Reading

J. F. RHODES, *The Civil War*; EDWARD CHANNING, *History of the United States*, Vol. VI, chaps. x–xx; WILLIAM WOOD, *Captains of the Civil War* (Chronicles of America, Vol. XXXI); N. W. STEPHENSON, *The Day of the Confederacy* (Chronicles, Vol. XXX); JOHN FISKE, *The Mississippi Valley in the Civil War*; E. C. SMITH, *The Borderland in the Civil War*; J. K. HOSMER, *The Appeal to Arms* and *The Outcome of the Civil War* (American Nation Series, Vols. XX, XXI); LORD CHARNWOOD, *Abraham Lincoln*, chaps. vii–xi; D. S. FREEMAN, *R. E. Lee*, Vols. II, III; E. D. FITE, *Social and Industrial Conditions in the North during the Civil War*; The Pageant of America, Vol. IX, pp. 9–42 (for illustrations); *America*, Vol. VIII; H. S. COMMAGER, *Documents of American History*, pp. 376–429; HART, *Contemporaries*, Vol. IV, Nos. 75–140; MUZZEY, *Readings*, pp. 408–450.

Topics for Reports

1. Efforts at Compromise, 1860–1861. NICOLAY and HAY, *Abraham Lincoln, A History*, Vol. III, pp. 214–238; W. G. BROWN, *The Lower South in American History*, pp. 83–112; MRS. C. COLEMAN, *The Life of John J. Crittenden*, Vol. II, pp. 224–260; F. E. CHADWICK, *The Causes of the Civil War* (American Nation Series, Vol. XIX), chaps. xi–xvi; HART, *Contemporaries*, Vol. IV, Nos. 63–69.

2. The *Trent* Affair. *America*, Vol. VIII, pp. 79–88; C. F. ADAMS, *Charles Francis Adams*, pp. 210–239; FREDERICK BANCROFT, *The Life of William H. Seward*, Vol. II, pp. 223–253; W. C. FORD (ed.), *A Cycle of Adams Letters, 1861–1865*, Vol. I, pp. 75–114; LORD NEWTON, *Lord Lyons. A Record of British Diplomacy*, Vol. I, pp. 55–62; C. F. ADAMS, *The Trent Affair* (Massachusetts Historical Society, Proceedings, Vol. XLV), pp. 148–157; MUZZEY, *Readings*, pp. 414–421.

3. The Draft Riots in New York. J. F. RHODES, *History of the United States from the Compromise of 1850*, Vol. IV, pp. 320–332; J. R. GILMORE, *Personal Recollections of Abraham Lincoln*, chap. xiv; J. B. FRYE, *New York and the Conscription of 1863*; J. T. HEADLEY, *Great Riots of New York*, pp. 136–288; HART, *Contemporaries*, Vol. IV, No. 121.

4. Life in the South during the War. J. C. REED, *Economic Conditions in the South during the Civil War* (The South in the Building of the Nation, Vol. V); J. B. JONES, *A Rebel War Clerk's Diary*; N. W. STEPHENSON, *The Day of the Confederacy*, pp. 99–111; MRS. ROGER A. PRYOR, *Reminiscences of Peace and War*, chaps. ix–xxvi; MARY B. CHESNUT, *A Diary from Dixie*; J. K. HOSMER, *The Outcome of the Civil War*, pp. 269–289; DAVID DODGE, "The Cave Dwellers of the Confederacy," in *Atlantic Monthly*, Vol. LVIII, pp. 514–521; HART, *Contemporaries*, Vol. IV, Nos. 141–144.

Questions Suggested by the Chapter

1. What advantages did the North have over the South in 1860? **2.** What three sources of help did the South count on in vain? **3.** Why did Robert E. Lee join the Confederacy? **4.** How did "Stonewall" Jackson get his nickname?

5. Why was Captain Wilkes's seizure of the envoys on the *Trent* illegal? **6.** Why did McClellan quarrel with the government at Washington? **7.** Trace three main steps in the Union control of the Mississippi. **8.** Why was the blockade so serious for the South? **9.** Why did the upper classes in England favor the South? **10.** What slaves did the Emancipation Proclamation free? **11.** How was the Confederate offensive of 1862 checked? **12.** What effort did Lincoln make to free the slaves before he issued the Emancipation Proclamation? **13.** What opposition did President Davis meet with in the Southern states? **14.** What were the causes of discouragement in the North in the spring of 1863? **15.** What events at the beginning of July, 1863, marked the turning-point of the war? **16.** What was the origin of our national Thanksgiving Day? **17.** Why was Lincoln doubtful of re-election in 1864? **17.** What military events assured his re-election? **18.** Describe the Hampton Roads conference. **19.** What were the terms of Lee's surrender at Appomattox? **20.** Contrast the generalship of McClellan and Grant. **21.** Show that the assassination of Lincoln was a part of a larger plot.

Books Worth Reading on Unit IV

EMERSON HOUGH, *North of 36*, and *The Covered Wagon*; WILLA CATHER, *O Pioneers!*, *My Antonia*, and *Death Comes for the Archbishop*; W. P. WEBB, *The Great Plains*; FRANCIS PARKMAN, *The Oregon Trail*; JAMES R. LOWELL, *The Biglow Papers*; M. MINNEGERODE, *The Fabulous Forties*; T. N. PAGE, *In Ole Virginia*; WINSTON CHURCHILL, *The Crisis*; I. BACHELLER, *A Man for the Ages*; JAMES BOYD, *Marching On*; H. B. STOWE, *Uncle Tom's Cabin*, and *Dred*; S. V. BENÊT, *John Brown's Body*; MARY JOHNSTON, *The Long Roll*; STARK YOUNG, *So Red the Rose*; J. FOX, *The Little Shepherd of Kingdom Come*; W. E. WOODWARD, *Meet General Grant*.

How our Reunited Country Increased in National Wealth and Power

The nations of the Old World commonly regard America as the "land of the almighty dollar." They believe that we are so absorbed in the mad race to get rich quickly that we miss the finer things in life, which can be cultivated only in an atmosphere of leisure, reflection, the creative arts of good taste. They point to the crudeness of our literature, the ugliness of our cities, the commercialized theater and movies, the "education" of our young men for selling something to somebody for a profit, the absorption of the businessman in money-making to the neglect of his duties as a good citizen and companionable husband, and to many more shortcomings of like nature. If there is enough truth in these charges to make a cultivated American wince, he knows that the cultivated European is mistaking a passing phase of our civilization for a permanent character. It is not so much the love of money as the satisfaction of developing the rich resources of our country that has animated our great "captains of industry." In the decades immediately following the Civil War we realized the boundless extent of these resources in forests, mines, oil deposits, Western farm lands, cattle ranges, and coal fields. Ambitious men were ready to invest the money which they had made during the war in exploiting these resources, and capital flowed into the country from Europe to help build the railroads, equip the farms and ranches, and dig the mines. Hundreds of thousands of Americans went West to take up the homesteads which the government gave them, and immigrants from the Old World flocked to our shores. States and territories west of the Missouri River increased in population from fivefold to fourteenfold during the quarter of a century following the war. Men who invested money in grain, cattle, lumber, oil, copper, and silver could hardly help growing rich. At the same time the bankers, the manufacturers, and the merchants of the East were building up great fortunes, and business was making its influence felt more and more powerfully in Congress and the state governments. We shall study in this unit the restoration of the Union and the growth of our modern industrial prosperity.

CHAPTER SEVENTEEN

RECONSTRUCTION

Striking the Balance. The Civil War settled some problems which had been vexing the nation for years, but it opened others no less vexing. It determined (1) that we were to continue to be one country under the Stars and Stripes, (2) that the authority of the government at Washington was to be supreme over the "rights" of the states, and (3) that slavery was at an end in our land. On the other hand, it raised the questions of (1) how the seceded states were to be restored to the Union, (2) what should be done with the freed Negroes, (3) how the war should be paid for, and (4) what settlement should be made with Great Britain for the damages which cruisers built in her shipyards had done to the commerce of the United States. These problems of political and economic reconstruction occupied the attention of our government during the decade following Lee's surrender at Appomattox, while the South was struggling with the poverty and destitution left in the wake of the war and while the capitalists of the North were laying the bases of their fabulous fortunes, undisturbed by the party wrangles at Washington.

The Problem of Political Reconstruction. The immediate question was what was the political status of the states of the secession. Were they still states of the Union, in spite of their four years' struggle to break away from it? Or had they lost their rights as states and become territories, for the government at Washington to readmit as states on conditions which it saw fit? Or, again, was the South merely a "conquered province" like New Mexico in 1848, for example, to be disposed of according to the will of the conquerors? Furthermore, whose business was it to deal with the South? If the war had been only a "rebellion" of numerous individuals who needed to be pardoned, the President, who had the power of pardon, was obviously the person to act. If, however, the Southern states had really been out of the Union, their readmission seemed to be the business of Congress, which under the Constitution had the sole right to admit states to the Union.

Lincoln, from the beginning of the war, held to the "Presidential" theory. In a proclamation of December, 1863, he had declared that when 10 per cent of the voters of 1860 in any of the seceded states should form a loyal government and accept the legislation of Congress on the subject of slavery, he would recognize that government as legal. Such governments had actually been set up in Tennessee, Arkansas, and Louisiana during the war. But Congress did not accept Lincoln's plan. In 1864 it substituted its own conditions for the readmission of the states, providing that 50 per cent of the voters must take the oath of loyalty and excluding the Confederate leaders from voting or officeholding. Lincoln refused to sign this bill, and the war ended without any decision on the political status of the South. It is certain that if Lincoln had lived until the meeting of the new Congress in December, 1865, he would have had on his hands the struggle with Congress which he passed on to his successor.

The Johnson Governments. That successor was Andrew Johnson of Tennessee, a man of humble origin and scant education like Lincoln, but lacking Lincoln's tact, sympathy, conciliatory spirit, and capacity for steady intellectual and moral growth. Johnson hated the slave-owners and, though a states-rights Democrat, was intensely devoted to the Union. He had been the only member of Congress from the seceded states who remained in his seat at Washington in 1861. Lincoln had appointed him military governor of Tennessee, and had asked to have him put on the Union ticket as Vice-President in 1864, partly to reward him for his loyalty and partly to save the Republican party from the reproach of being called "sectional" in again choosing both its candidates from the Northern states, as it had done in 1856 and 1860.

Johnson proceeded during the summer and autumn of 1865 (when Congress was not in session) to carry out the plan of Lincoln. On May 29 he issued a proclamation of amnesty to all persons engaged in rebellion against the United States, with the exception of prominent classes, who were invited, however, to apply to the President for pardon, which would be "liberally extended." He appointed military governors, after Lincoln's pattern, in North and South Carolina, Georgia, Florida, Alabama, Mississippi, and Texas. He ordered conventions to be held in those states, which repealed the ordinances of secession and framed new constitutions. State officers were elected. Legislatures were chosen, which (with the exception of South Carolina) repudiated their debts incurred in the war and (with the exception of Mississippi) ratified the Thirteenth Amendment abolishing slavery. When Congress met in December, Senators and Representatives from all the states of the secession except Texas were at Washington, ready to take their seats. It was a critical moment in our history. If Congress had admitted them, our country would have been spared a disgraceful chapter in its history.

Johnson's Work Rejected. Thaddeus Stevens of Pennsylvania, a harsh, vindictive man of seventy-three, who believed that the South should be severely punished for its "rebellion," ruled the House of Representatives with a rod of iron. He instructed the clerk to omit the names of the Southerners in the roll call, and the Senate, under the lead of Charles Sumner of Massachusetts, an ardent believer in Negro equality, took the same course. The reasons for this action were various. First, these so-called "radical" Republicans hated Johnson for his Southern birth and his defiance of Congress in going ahead with his reconstruction policy during the recess of Congress. Secondly, they feared that if the Southern members were admitted they would join with the Northern Democrats and oust the Republicans from power; and, thirdly, that this same combination would revive the states-rights and free-trade doctrines of the Democrats and repeal the protective-tariff acts that had been passed for the benefit of the Northern industrialists during the war.

Moreover, they resented the behavior of the South in the summer of 1865. The Johnson governments had passed certain laws called the "black codes" for the control of the ex-slaves, especially the vagrancy and apprentice laws which assigned idle and homeless Negroes to "guardians" — often their former masters — for whom they must work without wages. Northerners interpreted these laws as an attempt to put the Negroes back into slavery. The Southerners, however, regarded them as necessary measures of social protection; for few of the liberated slaves had any sense of responsibility, and none had the capital to begin a life of industrial freedom. They believed that the Day of Jubilee had arrived and that the plantations of their former masters were to be divided among them as a Christmas gift, every Negro receiving "forty acres and a mule." They were encouraged in these ideas by some rascally politicians who came down from the North,[1] posing as their guides and protectors but really poisoning their minds against the only people who could help them to get a start in their new life of freedom. A final offense of the South in the eyes of the radicals was the sending of some of the foremost men of the Confederacy (including its vice-president, Alexander H. Stephens) up to Washington to take their seats in Congress and help run the government which they had been trying for four years to destroy.

The Breach between Johnson and Congress. Thoroughly enraged at the radicals for wrecking his governments in the South, Johnson entered into a bitter quarrel with Congress, which lasted to the end of his administration. Making a speech from the balcony of the White House on Washington's birthday, 1866, he attacked Stevens and Sumner by name, accusing them

---

[1] These men were called "carpetbaggers," because they were said to have brought all their belongings to the South in the cheap kind of valise of that day made out of carpet material. The Southerners who acted with them for their own profit and political advancement were called "scalawags." They are not to be confused with the many good men and women who went South to work honestly for the education and protection of the Negroes. Before the close of the war (March 3, 1865) Congress had created a Freedmen's Bureau in the War Department, to help provide the emancipated blacks with food, clothing, shelter, and opportunities for work. Unfortunately, some of the representatives of the Bureau were hardly better than the carpetbaggers, tempting the Negroes away from work into politics.

of seeking to destroy the South and to rob the President of his legal powers and even to encourage his assassination. The radicals replied in kind, calling the President a tyrant, a traitor, an ignoramus, and a drunken brute.

Johnson had the support of important Republicans in 1866, like General Grant, Secretary Seward, Welles, and McCulloch, — whom he had retained from Lincoln's cabinet, — and several influential members of both houses of Congress [1]; and he might have built up a party to offset the radicals if he had known how to exercise patience and good temper. But he was so violent and abusive in his language that he alienated those who were disposed to be his friends instead of winning over his enemies. For example, in the congressional campaign of the autumn of 1866 he made a visit to the West, a "swing around the circle," during which he disgusted Grant, Seward, and the other members of the party by indulging in coarse and angry personal arguments with his hecklers in public audiences. The result of the election was an overwhelming anti-Johnson majority returned to Congress, which overrode his vetoes by a three-to-one vote. Henceforth he was a man without a party.

The Fourteenth Amendment. When Thaddeus Stevens had excluded the Southern Representatives from Congress, he moved the appointment of a committee of fifteen, ostensibly to inquire into the right of the states of the "so-called late Confederacy" to representation, but really to draw up a Congressional plan of reconstruction. In April, 1866, the committee reported, and on June 13 Congress passed, the Fourteenth Amendment to the Constitution. It declared that "all persons born or naturalized in the United States" were "citizens of the United States and of the State wherein they reside," and forbade any state to deprive them of their privileges as citizens. It reduced the representation in Congress of any state which denied the Negro the right to vote, and it disqualified the leaders of the Con-

---

[1] For example, when Congress passed an act continuing the operation and enlarging the powers of the Freedmen's Bureau in February, 1866, Johnson had enough votes in Congress to uphold his veto of the measure. But it was his last victory over the radicals.

THADDEUS STEVENS

federacy from holding Federal or state office. Finally, it forbade the payment of the Confederate debt and guaranteed the payment of the United States debt. The disqualifying clause was harsh; but the rest of the amendment furnished a fair basis for the reconstruction of the South, and even the penalties imposed on the Confederate leaders could be removed by a two-thirds vote of Congress. Tennessee promptly accepted the amendment and was restored to full statehood. All the other states of the secession, however, following the advice of President Johnson, rejected the amendment by the almost unanimous votes of their legislatures. Thus the Fourteenth Amendment failed to secure the three fourths of the states necessary for its ratification.[1]

[1] Of course, it was inconsistent for Congress to ask these states to ratify the amendment as if they were in the Union and at the same time to keep them out of the Union by refusing to seat their Representatives and Senators. But the radicals did not allow logic to stand in their way.

The Reconstruction Act. The radical Congress now determined on severe punishment for the "sinful ten" states which had rejected the amendment. On March 2, 1867, it passed (over Johnson's veto), the terrible Reconstruction Act, which grouped the ten states into five military districts, each ruled by a major general of the army supported by United States troops. The Johnson governments were swept away. The major generals were to summon conventions in the states under their control, to frame new constitutions. Negroes were to participate on an equality with the eligible whites in making the new constitutions and in sitting in the new legislatures. When a constitution providing for Negro suffrage had been framed and accepted by Congress, and when the legislature elected under it had ratified the Fourteenth Amendment and that amendment had become part of the Constitution, then, and only then, would the state be received into the Union.

With the aid of Federal soldiers and the Negro vote, governments were set up in seven of the states by the midsummer of 1868, in time to secure their votes for the Republican ticket in the Presidential election of November. But these governments were sorry affairs, ruled by carpetbaggers, scalawags, and their Negro allies, supported by Northern bayonets. In the legislature of South Carolina, for example, there were ninety-eight Negroes to fifty-seven whites, and only twenty-two of the members could read and write. Two thirds of the members paid no taxes at all, and the rest only trifling amounts; yet they spent the people's money lavishly, voting themselves large salaries, installing expensive furnishings in the capitol, and wasting millions on projects for railroads, canals, and public works, from which they reaped large sums in graft. The debt of the state increased from five million dollars in 1868 to nearly twenty million dollars in 1872. The same story was repeated, with variations, in the other reconstructed states.

The Ku-Klux Klan. Deprived of any legal means of defense against such iniquitous government, the South naturally resorted to intimidation. Secret organizations, chief of which was the Ku-Klux Klan, took advantage of the Negroes' superstition and fear to force them back into a position of social and political obscurity. Bands of young men on horseback, robed in ghostly white sheets, spread terror through the Negro quarters at night and posted on trees and fences horrible warnings to carpetbaggers and scalawags to leave the country if they wished to live. Negroes were beaten and scalawags were shot. Exaggerated reports of these deeds of violence were spread through the North and used by the radical politicians to justify the tightening of military rule in the South.

The Impeachment of Johnson. Not content with reducing President Johnson to political impotence, the radicals were determined to drive him out of the White House. On the same day (March 2, 1867) that it destroyed the President's governments in the South by the Reconstruction Act, Congress passed the Tenure of Office Act, which took from him the privilege, exercised by every President since Washington's day, of dismissing the members of his own cabinet at his pleasure. It was an outrageous measure, designed merely as a trap to catch Johnson in a "violation" of the law and hence furnish a reason for bringing an accusation against him. When, therefore, the President dismissed his Secretary of War Stanton, who was a virtual spy in the cabinet in close alliance with the radicals in Congress, the House of Representatives impeached Johnson of "high crimes and misdemeanors." The Senate tried the case from March 30 to May 26, 1868; but, in spite of the frantic efforts of the radicals to secure a conviction, seven Republican Senators were honorable enough to place justice before partisan hatred and to vote with the twelve Democrats for the President's acquittal, making the vote (35 to 19) fall one short of the two thirds necessary for conviction. By this narrow margin the country was saved from the disgrace of using a clause of the Constitution as a weapon of personal and political vengeance against the highest officer of the land.

President Grant Supports the Radicals. During the impeachment trial the Republican convention had met at Chicago (May 20) and unanimously nominated General Grant for the Presidency, endorsing the radical program of reconstruction.

Grant won a decisive victory over his Democratic rival, Governor Horatio Seymour of New York, in the electoral college (214 to 80), carrying every state in the North except New York, New Jersey, and Oregon, and every state of the reconstructed South except Georgia and Louisiana. However, his popular majority was only 300,000 in a vote of 5,700,000, and but for the 650,000 Negro votes cast for him in the South he would have fallen behind Seymour at the polls. Warned by these figures how necessary it was to retain the colored vote, the radical Republicans added a Fifteenth Amendment to the Constitution (ratified March 30, 1870), forbidding the United States or any state to deny the right of voting to any citizen on account of "race, color, or previous condition of servitude." They also prevailed upon Grant, who was without training in statesmanship and allowed himself to be flattered, deceived, and imposed upon by designing politicians, to support the military coercion of the South.[1] He approved enforcement acts (1870, 1871) punishing infractions of the Fourteenth and Fifteenth Amendments, recommended the Ku-Klux Act for the forcible suppression of the Klan, and in the autumn of 1871 put nine counties of South Carolina under martial law. The net result of the policy of the President who had accepted his nomination with the noble words "Let us have peace!" was to encourage further strife and bloodshed in the South. The very trenches which his troops had occupied at Vicksburg in 1863 were the scene ten years later of an armed conflict between the whites and the Negroes.

The Restoration of Home Rule in the South. The unnatural reconstruction governments could not last, unless the North was prepared to support them indefinitely by Federal troops; and every year saw more people in the North growing disgusted with the terrible misgovernment of the carpetbaggers, until

[1] Grant had been generous to the South at Appomattox and after, reporting to President Johnson in the summer of 1865 that the great mass of the Southerners accepted the outcome of the war "in good faith." Yet as President he fell into the crafty hands of the radicals and, in the words of Professor Dunning, "dwindled from the leader of the people to the figurehead of a party." No one doubts his honesty and patriotism, but few historians today regard him as anything but a failure in the Presidency.

even Grant himself turned a deaf ear to their request for more soldiers. Every year also saw a new crop of young white voters to whom the disqualifying clause of the Fourteenth Amendment did not apply, and a falling off of the Negro vote in spite of the Fifteenth Amendment. The Democrats, in their platform of 1868, had already declared that the issues of slavery and secession were "settled for all time," and had demanded the restoration of all the states to their former rights in the Union. By 1871 Virginia, North Carolina, and Georgia were already under white rule. The next year public opinion in the North compelled the Republicans to pass the Amnesty Act, removing the political disqualifications from all but about five hundred of the Southerners. In 1874 the whites carried Alabama, Arkansas, and Texas, and in 1875 Mississippi. Only Louisiana, South Carolina, and Florida remained under carpetbagger control; and when President Hayes succeeded Grant, in the spring of 1877, he withdrew the last of the Federal troops from these states, which immediately reverted to "home rule." The distressing drama of political reconstruction was over. Thaddeus Stevens and Charles Sumner were in their graves. The South would never have cherished resentment against the North for the defeat of 1861–1865 on the battlefield; but many years were to elapse before they could either forgive or forget the bitter punishment meted out to them by the reconstruction acts.

The Plight of the South. The sting and smart of these acts was more keenly felt in the South because of her economic ruin by the war. Her credit was gone. The bonds which she had sold at home and abroad, pledging the cotton crop in payment, were worthless. The Fourteenth Amendment forbade the United States or any state government to pay the Confederate debt. Some money came down from the North, to be sure, to buy the plantations which their bankrupt owners were obliged to sell at a great sacrifice; and the high price of cotton in Europe at the close of the war helped to prevent an absolute currency famine. But the formerly rich planters, who had spent their money for taxes or bonds in support of the Confederacy, lacked the capital to pay for tools, fertilizers, and animals, or to pay wages to the freed slaves, or to keep up their estates. Many of the large plantations were broken up into small holdings and rented to "shareholders" or "croppers," who paid a part of the crop for their equipment, and were generally deep in debt to the storekeepers and moneylenders for their seeds, tools, food, and clothing. Since cotton was a crop which could not be stolen or eaten by the raisers, their creditors insisted on its cultivation to the exclusion of fruit or grain, thus prolonging the one-crop system in the South.

Furthermore, the time and energy which the Southerners should have had to devote to their economic recovery was absorbed in the struggle to wrest political control from the carpetbaggers and keep the Negroes in their social place. It was not until white rule was restored and the Federal troops were withdrawn that capital began to flow freely into the South to build cotton mills, uncover iron deposits, plant fruit orchards, and exploit the magnificent forests of pine, oak, and cypress. As President Hayes's decoration of the graves of the Confederate soldiers at Chattanooga on Memorial Day, 1877, may be taken as the symbol of the close of the epoch of slavery, secession, and civil strife, so the Atlanta Industrial Exposition of 1881 may stand as the symbol of the new South of cotton spindles, iron foundries, and metropolitan cities.

Banks, Bonds, and Currency. While the war brought exhaustion and destitution to the South, it acted as a stimulus to industry in the North. With a far larger amount of money in her bank vaults and a far smaller proportion of her able-bodied men called into the ranks, the North could easily pay the taxes and man the industries required by the war. The large government orders for food, clothing, blankets, horses, munitions, and arms kept the factories busy and created a new aristocracy of wealth — too often a "shoddy" aristocracy, so named because they furnished paper-soled shoes and cheap substitutes for wool (shoddy) to the army.

The government used three methods for paying for the war. First, it levied taxes in the form of increased duties on imports, internal-revenue taxes on the sale of a great variety of articles, and a tax on incomes above a certain figure. But war is too expensive to run by the pay-as-you-go method of taxation, and much of the largest source of income was the sale of interest-bearing government bonds, the principal of which was to be paid by the United States Treasury at the end of say twenty or thirty years. In order to sell the bonds more easily, Secretary of the Treasury Chase in 1863 created the national-bank system. Any group of five men who furnished a specified capital could be granted a charter by the national government to organize a banking business if they purchased United States bonds and deposited them at Washington. Then they were allowed to issue notes (bank bills) up to the value of 90 per cent of the bonds. Thus, in addition to the interest which they received on the bonds from the government, they also made a profit by lending their notes (or credit) for interest. And, the notes, being secured by the bonds deposited at Washington, formed a safe currency for the public, whether the bank issuing them failed or not.

These two methods, of taxation and bond issues, were good financing; but in its need for ready money early in the war, before the taxes came in or the bonds were sold, Congress resorted to a third device which has always been a plague to the governments that have yielded to the temptation of using it. That was the printing of paper money, not based on gold or silver in the Treasury, and making it "legal tender," or lawful money for the payment of public and private obligations. Early in 1862 the government issued $250,000,000 of these United States notes, or "greenbacks," which were legal tender except for the payment of customs duties and of interest on the government bonds. Further issues raised the amount of greenbacks to $450,000,000. Naturally, this "currency," as it was commonly called, rose and fell in value, as compared with gold, as the fortunes of the war and the confidence of the people in its successful outcome fluctuated.[1]

[1] Altogether, taxes contributed about $667,000,000 to the expense of the war, while over $2,000,000,000 came from the sale of bonds. In the World War, which cost the government at Washington over ten times as much as the Civil War, it was President Wilson's purpose to raise one third of the money by taxation and

The Greenback Controversy. The greenbacks had been issued as an emergency currency; and when the war was over, the government proposed returning to specie payments, that is, calling in the greenbacks and substituting gold for them. The Secretary of the Treasury had already begun this process when a cry went up from the farmers and the debtor class generally. The prices of their products had risen in terms of the cheaper currency, and they had incurred their debts (mortgages on their property or capital to equip their new homesteads) in that currency. Now to be asked to pay back a gold dollar worth a hundred cents for a borrowed paper dollar worth thirty-five cents in gold seemed to them like robbery on the part of their creditors, the bankers and moneylenders of the East. Moreover, these same bankers had bought the government bonds with greenbacks while receiving the interest on them in gold; and for the Treasury to pay the principal of the bonds (that is, to "redeem" them) in gold seemed like a pure gift from the government to the bankers. So began the demand not only that the Treasury cease calling in the greenbacks but that it actually issue more of them.

A battle royal was waged between debtor and creditor, inflationist and contractionist, paper and gold. The Democratic platform of 1868 advocated the payment of the bonds in paper. The Republicans, who had become the party of the wealthy since the war, insisted on the payment in gold. One of the evil effects of the situation was the constant speculation in the price of gold. The noted Wall Street gamblers Jay Gould and "Jim" Fisk even drew President Grant's brother-in-law Corbin into a plot to corner the gold supply, and caused the failure of hundreds of brokers' firms on "Black Friday," September 23, 1869. When the Democrats, in the election of 1874, captured the House for the first time since the Civil War, the Republicans made haste in their last session to pass the Resumption Act (January, 1875),

---

the other two thirds by bond sales. We did not resort to the issue of paper money in that war. About $10,000,000,000 was raised by taxation and $22,000,000,000 by the Liberty and Victory loans. Our debt at the close of the World War was $26,000,000,000 as against a debt of $2,846,000,000 left by the Civil War.

providing for the redemption of the greenbacks in gold on January 1, 1879. The Greenbackers still tried to defeat resumption, putting a party into the field in the Presidential election of 1876. But they received only a little over eighty thousand votes. Thus the election of Hayes, which marked the end of the reconstruction policy in the South, also spelled the defeat of the paper-money inflationists.[1]

Diplomatic Problems. Finally, in addition to settling the political status of the South and the Negro and the financial status of the nation's currency, the government at Washington had to deal with certain problems in our relations to foreign countries at the close of the war. Most of the European nations were friendly to the North during the war, especially Russia, whose Czar, Alexander II, having emancipated the serfs in his own country, was in sympathy with the liberation of the slaves. Russian fleets visited New York and San Francisco during the war as a mark of friendly recognition. In 1867 we requited Russia by purchasing from her, at her request, the colony of Alaska, our first "foreign" possession. Secretary Seward was widely blamed for spending $7,200,000 for the "Arctic waste" ("Seward's ice-box") at a time when the government was burdened with a war debt of nearly $3,000,000,000. But it turned out to be an excellent bargain. The gold alone taken from the Yukon valley since 1897 has paid for Alaska many times over. In contrast to this friendly dealing with Russia, however, were our strained relations with France and England at the close of the war.

Napoleon III's Mexican " Empire." The French emperor Napoleon III was eager to aid in the disruption of the United States. He was jealous of the rising power of the American republic and cherished schemes of completing his uncle's project of establishing a new French empire in North America (p. 217). He attempted again and again to get the British government to join him in intervening in favor of the Confederacy. He re-

---

[1] This does not mean that the inflationists gave up the battle. On the contrary, they have been waging it ever since; and many Congressmen have from time to time urged the issue of billions of dollars of paper money for the relief of the debtor class or the payment of a bonus to the veterans of the World War.

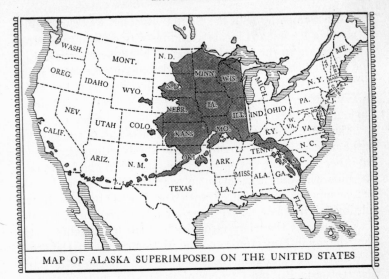

MAP OF ALASKA SUPERIMPOSED ON THE UNITED STATES

ceived President Davis's special envoy John Slidell (p. 398) with conspicuous favor, permitting him to contract for the building of cruisers in the French ports. He was the chief factor in floating the only large Confederate loan in Europe. Finally, he defied the Monroe Doctrine by sending an army into Mexico to overthrow the government and place his puppet " emperor," the Austrian archduke Maximilian, on the throne. Secretary Seward warned Napoleon to keep his hands off Mexico; but Lincoln's administration, in spite of taunts from the South for its "arrant cowardice" in not defending the Monroe Doctrine, refused to be diverted from its main task of prosecuting the war. The moment peace came, however, fifty thousand Federal troops under General Sheridan were sent to the Mexican border to compel the withdrawal of the French army. Napoleon had overshot the mark. The liberals in France were condemning his Mexican venture. War between Austria and Prussia was impending, in which France might be involved. So Napoleon called home his troops in the summer of 1866, abandoning his protégé and tool Maximilian to the Mexican patriots, who seized and executed him (June 19, 1867).

British Sympathy with the South. England was the country with which President Lincoln's administration had trouble from the beginning to the end of the war. The upper classes in England favored the South, and Mr. Gladstone congratulated Jefferson Davis in a public speech in 1862 on having created an army, a navy, and a new nation. The letters of Lincoln's minister to England, Charles Francis Adams, and of his brilliant son and secretary Henry Adams, are filled with instances of the hostility of the officials and the aristocracy to the Northern cause. On the other hand, the common people, and even the laborers in the mills who were thrown out of work by the stoppage of the cotton supply, sympathized with the North, because it was fighting for free labor. We have already noted the complaint of the North at the hasty recognition of the belligerency of the Confederacy in May, 1861, and the friction caused by the arrest of Mason and Slidell on the *Trent* in November of the same year (p. 398). But most serious of all was the controversy over cruisers built in British shipyards to prey on the commerce of the United States.

The Confederate Commerce-Destroyers. Though an act of Parliament of 1819 forbade any subject of the realm to "equip, furnish, fit out or arm any ship to be employed in the service of a foreign state, to commit hostilities against any state at peace with Great Britain," James Bullock of Georgia (an uncle of Theodore Roosevelt), who was the Confederate agent in England, persuaded the crown lawyers that the act would not be violated if the ship were only "built" in England, and "equipped" and "armed" outside the realm. On the strength of this quibble the shipbuilders of the Clyde and the Mersey set to work. In the spring of 1862 several newly built cruisers sailed from England to various ports outside the realm, there to receive their armaments, enlist their crews, and be turned over to the command of Confederate captains. Adams made repeated protests against this breach of neutrality, pointing out that the destination and purpose of the cruisers were perfectly well known to the British government. Finally, to prevent the delivery of two powerful ironclad rams which were being built for the Confederacy in the summer of 1863, Adams wrote to Lord Russell on September 5, "It would be superfluous in me to point out to your Lordship that this is war." But the ministry, coming at last to its senses, had already ordered the detention of the rams two days before. However, it was like locking the stable door after the horse had escaped. Already about a score of commerce-raiders were on the high seas, and they destroyed more than two hundred and fifty vessels during the war, reducing the American merchant marine by some five hundred thousand tons. In fact, they practically swept our merchant fleet from the ocean. In 1860 about 70 per cent of our foreign trade was carried in American ships; by 1865 the figure had sunk to 26 per cent. The *Alabama* alone destroyed more than sixty merchant ships before she was sunk by the United States ship *Kearsarge* in a spectacular battle off the coast of France (June 16, 1864). The *Shenandoah* was still roaming the Pacific in search of her prey when the news reached her, several weeks after the surrender of Lee, that the Civil War was over.

The *Alabama* Claims. For seven years after the war our claims against Great Britain for the damages done by these commerce-destroyers hung fire. President Johnson's new minister to England negotiated an agreement providing for a general arbitration of the disputes between the two countries, without mentioning the *Alabama*; but the Senate rejected the proposal by a vote of 54 to 1. At the same time Charles Sumner of Massachusetts, the chairman of the Foreign Relations Committee of the Senate, delivered a long speech in which he presented an outrageous bill of damages against Great Britain. The items were: $15,000,000 for vessels destroyed, $100,000,000 for driving our commerce from the ocean, and $2,000,000,000 (or half the cost of the war) for "indirect damages," that is, for doubling the duration of the war by her aid to the Confederacy. Sumner was anxious to force Great Britain out of North America, and suggested that she might pay this staggering bill of $2,125,000,000 by ceding Canada to the United States. Of course, the British statesmen treated this demand with amused contempt. Even President Grant, who had a quarrel with Sumner because the latter was defeating his pet scheme for the annexation of the island of Santo Domingo to the United States, spoke of the "indirect damage humbug."

Still Sumner's exorbitant demand was widely approved in our country, and it made difficult the task of our Secretary of State in coming to a reasonable agreement with Great Britain. It was not till the outbreak of the great Franco-Prussian War in Europe, in which England might be involved, that the British ministry declared itself "disposed to enter upon negotiations." Besides, President Grant had threatened that our government would take over the claims against England and press them. Accordingly, on May 8, 1871, American and British commissioners signed a treaty at Washington, providing for the settlement of some fishery and boundary disputes and agreeing to submit the *Alabama* claims to an arbitration tribunal to meet at Geneva, Switzerland.

The Geneva Tribunal. Besides the British representative (Lord Cockburn) and the American (Charles Francis Adams), the tribunal contained a distinguished statesman from each of the countries of Switzerland, Italy, and Brazil. At first the United States counsel, in order to play up to the anti-British feeling in America, presented the full bill of damages. But the tribunal promptly rejected Sumner's claim, admitting only the question of actual losses caused by the operations of the destroyers. It decided, by a unanimous vote in the case of the *Alabama* and by a four-to-one vote and a three-to-two vote in the cases of the *Florida* and the *Shenandoah* respectively, that Great Britain had been guilty of a breach of the neutrality laws, and it awarded damages of $15,500,000 to the United States (September 14, 1872). Lord Cockburn alone dissented from the verdict, with considerable show of bad feeling. The other matters of dispute were settled shortly afterward. Great Britain was awarded about $2,000,000 for injuries to the property and persons of her subjects during the Civil War, and $5,500,000 for our infringement of her fishing rights on the North Atlantic coast. The northwest boundary of the United States through

Puget Sound was referred for settlement to the new emperor of Germany, William I. The peaceful adjustment of these claims and counterclaims of the two great nations of English speech was one of the grandest accomplishments of the nineteenth century. It was the first important case of arbitration in our history, and it remains as a landmark on the road of progress toward the substitution of frank discussion and "sweet reasonableness" for the appeal to arms in the disputes which arise between nations.

The Liberal Republican Movement. The American victory at Geneva came just in time to help re-elect Grant in November, 1872, and offset a threatening revolt in the Republican party. Disgusted with the prolongation of the policy of vengeance toward the South, the travesty of the reconstruction governments, the enforcement acts supported by bayonets, the insolence of the "shoddy" aristocracy, the disgrace of "Black Friday," corruption in high places of government, the mania for speculation, and the general low tone of public morality which followed the war, a group of Republicans, headed by Carl Schurz, started a reform movement in Missouri in 1870. Their aims were amnesty for the South, reduction of the tariff, and the purification of the government from those sinister elements which they saw controlling the President and Congress. Their slogan was, "Anything to beat Grant!" They held a convention at Cincinnati in the spring of 1872, but dissensions in their own ranks (too often the curse of reform movements) prevented their nominating a strong candidate, such as Charles Francis Adams. Instead, they chose Horace Greeley, whom Rhodes called "a preposterous candidate." For Greeley was a high protectionist, an enemy of civil-service reform, a bitter foe of the Democrats whom the Liberals hoped to get to join them in the fight on Grant. In fact, the only point on which Greeley agreed with the Liberals was amnesty for the South. "Let us clasp hands across the bloody chasm!"

The Democrats in their convention at Baltimore accepted Greeley, in their desire to "beat Grant"; but the Liberal Republicans gave him only lukewarm support. In a campaign of unusual bitterness and slander, in which Greeley remarked that he was uncertain whether he was running for the Presidency or the penitentiary, the regular Republicans won a crushing victory. Grant carried every state of the North and West, together with eight of the former slave states, receiving 272 electoral votes to 66 for Greeley. The Republicans, who had seen their majority in the House reduced from 97 to 35 in the mid-term elections of 1870, now raised their majority to 105 and secured 49 seats in the Senate to 24 for the combined Liberals and Democrats.

The " Nadir of National Disgrace." The second administration of President Grant is a period which no lover of his country can study without a sense of shame and sorrow. It revealed to the public a series of scandals that fully justified the charges brought against the politicians in power by the Liberals of 1872. One after another, ugly facts were brought out by investigating committees of Congress, which showed what demoralization in public life had been caused by the greed, the recklessness, the vulgarity, that had followed in the wake of the war. In 1873 the Crédit Mobilier scandal broke out. A company by that name, formed for the construction of our first transcontinental railroad (the Union Pacific, completed in 1869) was found to have bribed the Vice-President and several members of Congress by the free distribution of stock. The same year occurred the "salary grab" or "back-pay steal," by which the greedy Congressmen voted themselves a 50 per cent increase of salary, to apply even to the session just coming to a close. There followed the next year the revelation of the whisky frauds, in which a corrupt ring of distillers and internal-revenue officers had cheated the government out of hundreds of thousands of dollars. In 1876 the Secretary of War, W. W. Belknap, was impeached and tried by the Senate on the charge of reaping large profits from the sale of licenses to corrupt agents who stole the supplies voted for the Indian posts in the West. Belknap both confessed his guilt and escaped condemnation by the Senate by hastily resigning his office. These are but a few examples of the scandals in the national, state, and municipal governments (such as

"Boss" Tweed's looting of the city of New York) which led a distinguished historian of the period to call it "the nadir [lowest point] of national disgrace." To crown it all, a severe panic broke out in 1873, as a result of reckless overspeculation, dishonest banking, railroad wrecking, graft, and general get-rich-quick methods of business. The panic lasted for five years, shutting down mills and factories and bringing unemployment and starvation to thousands of workers.

The Disputed Election. It was not surprising that in the midst of such conditions the administration suffered a severe defeat in the elections of 1874, which returned a large majority of Democrats to the House, giving them control of that body for the first time since the Civil War. It was a warning to the Republicans that the time was past when they could appeal to the voters on the old issue of "the crime of the rebellion" and, on the plea of having saved the country, could rule it as they pleased. In their convention at Cincinnati in 1876 they passed over the brilliant James G. Blaine, who belonged to the group that was suspected of aiding and supporting the evil practices of grafters, and nominated Governor Rutherford B. Hayes of Ohio, a man of unquestioned honesty and of conciliatory views on the Southern question. The Democrats named Governor Samuel J. Tilden of New York, who had won a national reputation for his exposure of the rascality of the Tweed ring in New York city.

The election was the most exciting in our history. Late in the evening of election day it was almost certain that Tilden had been chosen. He had 184 votes — only one less than the majority necessary. Twenty votes were in dispute, because the three Southern states which were still under military control (South Carolina, Louisiana, and Florida) had sent a double set of returns up to Washington, one certifying that Hayes electors had been chosen, the other that the majority of the state votes had been cast for Tilden.[1] There was no provision in the Con-

[1] Another disputed vote came from the state of Oregon, where it was discovered that the Republicans had put a postmaster on the list of electors, overlooking the provision of the Constitution that no person holding a Federal office might serve as an elector. The state had clearly voted for Hayes, however, and the commission did the fair thing in awarding it to him.

stitution or any law of Congress for deciding which set of returns was legal. The Constitution simply says (Amendment XII), "The president of the Senate shall, in the presence of the Senate and the House of Representatives, open all the certificates, and the votes shall then be counted." Ferry, the president of the Senate, was a Republican. If he had the right to choose which set of votes he would *count*, as well as "open," he would naturally take the Hayes certificates and declare Hayes elected by a vote of 185 to 184. If, on the other hand, the disputed votes were thrown out, or a single one of them counted for Tilden, the latter would be elected President; for the House, which has the right of choosing the President in case there is no majority in the electoral college, was Democratic.

The Electoral Commission. It was not until late in January, 1877, only a few weeks before the inauguration of the new President was due, that Congress found a way out of the muddle by creating a commission of fifteen to determine which of the disputed sets of returns should be accepted. The commission consisted of five Senators (three Republicans, two Democrats), five Representatives (three Democrats, two Republicans), and five members of the Supreme Court (two Republicans, two Democrats, and a fifth to be chosen by the other four). It was fully expected that Justice David Davis of Illinois, an Independent, would be chosen as the fifth member from the Court. But he escaped the responsibility of casting the deciding vote on the commission by hastily accepting an election by the Illinois legislature to the United States Senate. As there were only Republican members left on the Supreme Bench to choose from, the commission was perforce made up of eight Republicans and seven Democrats. It voted in every case, by eight to seven, to count the Hayes certificates, and was supported in every case by the Republican Senate. Hence, since the law creating the commission had provided that its decision should be final unless rejected by *both* houses of Congress, Hayes was declared elected by a single vote, two days before the inauguration (March 2, 1877).

Whether the votes of the three Southern states rightfully

belonged to Hayes or to Tilden is a question over which historians have differed ever since the disputed election. Committees of both parties who were sent down into these states to investigate the election found evidences of fraud and intimidation on both sides. Carpetbagger returning boards had undoubtedly thrown out Democratic ballots, and Democrats had forcibly prevented the Negroes (Republicans) from casting their votes at the polls. Which of these frauds outweighed the other it is impossible to say. Nor was it of great importance whether Hayes or Tilden was inaugurated in March, 1877. What was of importance, however, was the fact that the year which opened the second century of American independence found a nation so securely established in the habits of orderly government that a man whom more than half the country believed to have been fairly defeated on election day could be inaugurated four months later without a sign of civil commotion.

The End of an Era. The advent of Hayes marked the end of the reconstruction era. It was not merely that the new President withdrew the last of the Federal troops from the South in April, 1877, and the next month decorated the graves of the Confederate dead at Chattanooga. It was rather that the government came now into the hands of men who saw the necessity of laying aside the old issues of "rebellion" and grappling with the problems of politics and economics raised by the marvelous expansion of our country's industries since the war. William M. Evarts, who had defended Johnson in the impeachment trial, was made Secretary of State. Carl Schurz, the leader of the Liberal Republican movement of 1872, was appointed Secretary of the Interior. The administration applied itself to cleaning up graft and incompetence in the customhouse of New York and to weeding out rascality in the disposal of the public lands and the treatment of the Indians. Hayes was sneered at by the "Stalwarts," the Republican old guard, as a "goody-goody," an "old granny," and a President by fraud; but he went calmly on his way of rectitude and gave the country one of its best administrations. He was faithful to his motto "He serves his party best who serves his country

best." The symbol of the new era was the great Centennial
Exposition at Philadelphia, held during the summer of 1876 in
celebration of the hundredth anniversary of the Declaration of
Independence. The whirling wheels of machinery, the exhibits
of the products of our farms and forests and mines, and many
new and interesting inventions all invited the hundreds of
thousands of visitors to share in the thrill of citizenship in a
country which promised boundless opportunities for wealth and
achievement.

Terms to be Mastered

Johnson governments	impeachment	arbitration
amnesty	"croppers"	"indirect damages"
"black codes"	greenbacks	carpetbaggers
Freedmen's Bureau	resumption	Electoral Commission

For Supplementary Reading

W. A. Dunning, *Reconstruction, Political and Economic* (American Nation
Series, Vol. XXII) and *Essays on the Civil War and Reconstruction*; W. L. Fleming, *The Sequel of Appomattox* (Chronicles of America, Vol. XXXII); H. K.
Beal, *The Critical Year, a Study of Andrew Johnson and Reconstruction*;
C. G. Bowers, *The Tragic Era;* The Pageant of America, Vol. IX, pp. 44-109
(for interesting illustrations); *America*, Vol. IX, pp. 13-125, 143-166, 221-225;
Holland Thompson, *The New South* (Chronicles of America, Vol. XLII), chaps.
i-iii; S. J. Buck, *The Agrarian Crusade* (Chronicles of America, Vol. XLV), chaps.
i-iii; P. L. Haworth, *The Hayes-Tilden Disputed Election*; Hamlin Garland,
Ulysses Grant; his Life and Character, chaps. xxxix-l; G. F. Milton, *The Age of Hate*,
chaps. ix, xvi-xxv; H. J. Eckenrode, *Rutherford B. Hayes, Statesman of Reunion*,
chaps. vi-ix; Hilary Herbert, *Why the Solid South?* chaps. ii-vi, xii-xiv;
H. S. Commager, *Documents of American History*, Vol. II, pp. 1-84; Hart,
Contemporaries, Vol. IV, Nos. 141-157, 168, 169, 174, 175; Muzzey, *Readings*,
pp. 453-494.

Topics for Reports

1. **The Freedmen's Bureau.** Commager, *Documents*, Vol. II, pp. 1, 12 (text
of bill and veto); Fleming, *The Sequel of Appomattox*, pp. 89-117; P. S. Pierce,
The Freedmen's Bureau (University of Iowa Studies, 1904); G. W. Williams,
History of the Negro Race in America from 1619 to 1880, Vol. II, chaps. xxiv-xxvii.

2. **The Geneva Tribunal.** J. F. Rhodes, *History of the United States from
the Compromise of 1850*, Vol. VI, pp. 335-376; John Morley, *Life of Gladstone*,
Vol. II, chap. ix; C. F. Adams, *Lee at Appomattox and Other Papers*, pp. 31-198;
Hart, *Contemporaries*, Vol. IV, No. 175; *America*, Vol. IX, pp. 115-125; Muzzey,
Readings, pp. 471-478.

3. The Disputed Election of 1876. EDWARD STANWOOD, *History of the Presidency*, Vol. I, pp. 356–393; H. J. ECKENRODE, *Rutherford B. Hayes*, pp. 139–234; ALLAN NEVINS, *Abram S. Hewitt*, chaps. xvii–xx; JOHN BIGELOW, *Life of Samuel J. Tilden*, Vol. II, chaps. i, vi; M. H. NORTHRUP, "A Grave Crisis in American History," in *Century Magazine*, October, 1901; HART, *Contemporaries*, Vol. IV, No. 159.

4. Southern Industry after the War. F. L. PAXSON, *The New Nation*, pp. 192–207; HOLLAND THOMPSON, *The New South* (Chronicles of America, Vol. XLII); The Pageant of America, Vol. V, pp. 152–159; ALLAN NEVINS, *The Emergence of Modern America* (A History of American Life, Vol. VIII), chaps. i, xiii; T. M. YOUNG, *The American Cotton Industry*, pp. 54–99; HART, *Contemporaries*, Vol. IV, Nos. 141–143.

QUESTIONS SUGGESTED BY THE CHAPTER

1. Name three questions that were settled by the Civil War, and three questions that were opened by it. **2.** What was the "Presidential" theory of reconstruction? **3.** Do you think that Lincoln would have been more successful than Johnson in restoring the Southern states to the Union? Give your reasons. **4.** What services to the Union had Johnson performed during the war? **5.** Point out the exact difference between the Fourteenth and the Fifteenth Amendment on the subject of Negro suffrage. **6.** Why did the Southern states reject the Fourteenth Amendment? **7.** What act of Congress was responsible for the presence of Negroes in the legislatures of the Southern states? **8.** What means did the South take to protect itself against the carpetbaggers and scalawags? **9.** How do you account for the rapid recovery of white rule in the South? **10.** What happened to the great plantations in the South after the war? **11.** Why did the "radicals" want to make the Negro a voter? **12.** On what charge was Johnson impeached? **13.** What was the real reason for the impeachment? **14.** In what three ways did the North find the money for the conduct of the war? Did the South use the same means? Did our government use all these means in the World War? **15.** Why did the farmers and the debtors want a cheap currency (greenbacks)? **16.** Compare the government's treatment of the greenbacks in 1875 with its treatment of the Continental paper currency after the American Revolution. **17.** What reforms did the Liberal Republican movement of 1872 seek to accomplish? **18.** Why did the Democrats accept Greeley for their candidate in 1872? **19.** What was the Crédit Mobilier scandal? **20.** Why did the electoral college fail to choose a President in 1877? in 1825? in 1801? **21.** Do you think that Tilden was "cheated out of the Presidency" in 1877? Give the reason for your answer. **22.** What trouble did Napoleon III make for the United States during the Civil War? **23.** How large a bill did Charles Sumner wish to present to Great Britain for the damages which she caused the United States during the war? How large a bill did she pay? **24.** How did Hayes put an end to reconstruction immediately after his inauguration?

CHAPTER EIGHTEEN

THE NEW INDUSTRIAL AGE

Our "Economic Revolution." If history recorded only the
political activities of the government, we could pass over the
later decades of the nineteenth century in a few pages. Five
presidents occupied the White House between the inauguration of Hayes in 1877 and the inauguration of McKinley
twenty years later: Hayes, Garfield, Arthur, Cleveland, Harrison, and Cleveland again. Hundreds of Congressmen and Senators came to Washington, served their terms, and departed.
The struggle between the two great political parties for office
(occasionally seriously disturbed by the threat of a third party
to oust them both) went on as usual, each party trying to convince the public by campaign oratory and a flood of propaganda
"literature" that the election of the candidates of the opposing
party would mean the ruin of the Republic. Meantime, beneath
this surface froth of politics, there was going on one of the most
remarkable transformations of a country's economic and social
life that history has ever known. We were changed from a people
of small farmers and manufacturers, producing food and goods
for local consumption, into a land of highly organized industries,
densely populated cities, hordes of immigrant laborers, bonanza
farms and cattle ranges, magically rising El Dorados of gold
and silver and oil and steel, and a thickening network of railroads. The bases for this transformation were laid in the years
when the government was busy winning the war and adjusting
those problems arising from the war, which we have studied in
the last chapter. Little attention was paid then to the steadily
growing power of the bankers, the manufacturers, the railroad-
builders, the mining kings, the oil barons, the iron and steel
masters, the Morgans, the Astors, the Vanderbilts, the Goulds,

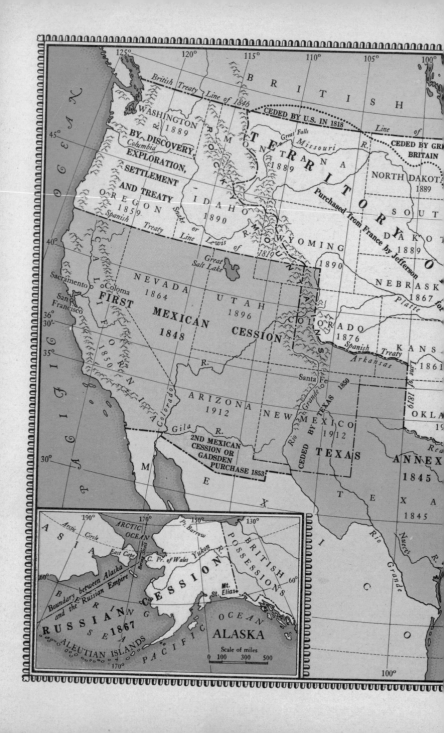

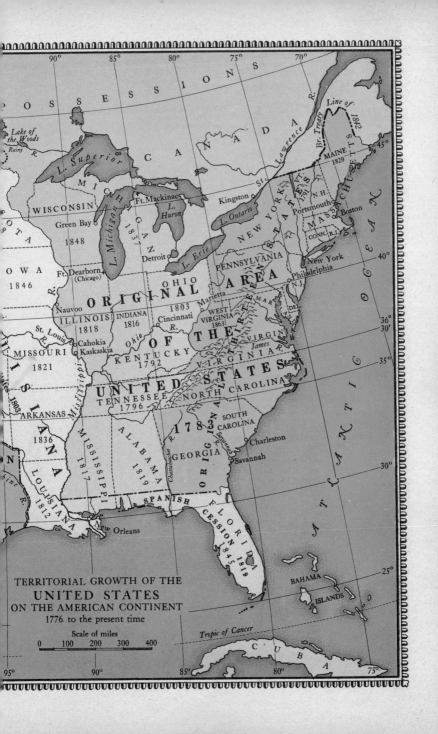

TERRITORIAL GROWTH OF THE
UNITED STATES
ON THE AMERICAN CONTINENT
1776 to the present time

Scale of miles
0   100   200   300   400

the Hills, the Joneses, the Rockefellers, the Carnegies, and the other "captains of industry" who were marshaling our "economic revolution."

The Great West. It was in the undeveloped and almost unexplored West that the opportunities for building the great postwar fortunes were found. While the people of the North were hanging on the news from the battlefields, a steady stream of emigrants were making their way to the farm lands, the cattle ranges, and the mining camps that lay beyond the "frontier"; that is, beyond the irregular line, extending from western Minnesota to the Gulf of Mexico, which marked an average population of two persons to the square mile. The trans-Missouri traffic multiplied sevenfold during the four years of the war, and in the same period the boundary lines of the future states of Colorado, Nevada, Arizona, Idaho, Montana, and the Dakotas were marked out. On May 20, 1862, Lincoln signed the Homestead Act, granting a farm of one hunderd and sixty acres, free of charge, to any citizen of the United States over twenty-one years of age who would settle upon it and cultivate it for five years. Millions of acres were homesteaded in the next few years, but more than a billion acres, or half the area of the country, still remained in the public domain.

President Johnson thought that it would take six hundred years for this domain to be occupied; but before the century had closed, the United States census (1890) announced that the frontier had disappeared. The herds of buffaloes which had blackened the country had been exterminated. The tribes of Indians who had roamed the plains had been subdued and driven sullenly into government reservations. Nine new Western states had been added to the Union. History has no parallel to the rapidity with which this imperial domain of a million and a half square miles was changed from the wilderness home of the wild beast and the painted savage into a land of wheat fields, ranches, mining and loggers' camps, and towns ambitious to become great cities.

The Union Pacific. Six weeks after the passage of the Homestead Act, Lincoln signed the first of the bills for government

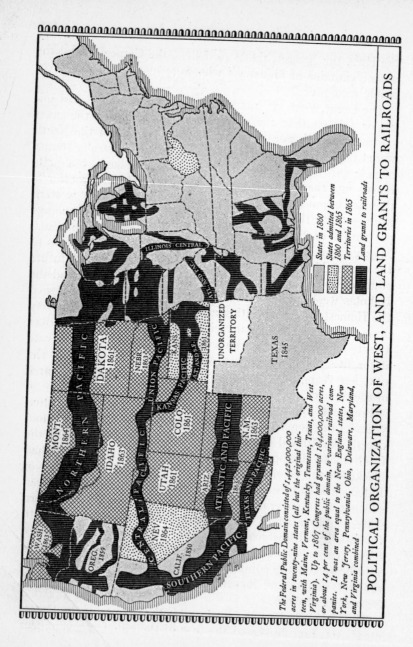

The Federal Public Domain consisted of 1,442,000,000 acres in twenty-nine states (all but the original thirteen, with Maine, Vermont, Kentucky, Tennessee, Texas, and West Virginia). Up to 1867 Congress had granted 184,000,000 acres, or about 14 per cent of the public domain, to various railroad companies. It was an area equal to the New England states, New York, New Jersey, Pennsylvania, Ohio, Delaware, Maryland, and Virginia combined.

POLITICAL ORGANIZATION OF WEST, AND LAND GRANTS TO RAILROADS

BUFFALO HERD STOPPING TRAIN ON PRAIRIES

aid in building a transcontinental railroad. The Union Pacific
Company was to build westward from Omaha, Nebraska, and
the Central Pacific eastward from Sacramento, California, until
their tracks met. Half the public land in a strip ten miles
wide on both sides of the track was given to the companies, and
a government bonus in 6 per cent bonds was added for each mile
of track completed: $16,000 a mile over the prairies, $32,000
a mile across the arid plateaus between the Rockies and the
Sierras, and $48,000 a mile through the towering mountains.
One hundred million dollars' worth of stock was offered to the
public at $1000 a share. Though the land grant was doubled
and further favors were given to the companies by an act of
1864, capital was wary of investing in the project. The war
had ended before the first rail was actually laid on July 10, 1865.
Even then there were plenty of sensible people who maintained
that it was an impossible task to lay iron bands across eighteen
hundred miles, from the Missouri to the Pacific, through vast
deserts and over yawning chasms and precipitous ledges. Gen-

eral Sherman declared in 1865 that he "would not buy a ticket on the Pacific Railroad for his youngest grandchild"; yet the general himself lived long enough to have his choice of buying a ticket to the Pacific coast over any one of five great railroad systems. From 1866 on, the work progressed rapidly, giving employment on the eastern end to thousands of soldiers returning from the war, while gangs of coolies imported from China labored on the Central Pacific. The tracks met at Promontory Point near Ogden, Utah, on May 10, 1869, where the last rail was fastened to a tie of California laurel by a golden spike, and the locomotives drew together "until their noses touched."[1]

The first through train from California to New York arrived at the Hudson River station on July 29, after a run of six and a half days. Ben Holladay's famous "Overland" stagecoaches, lumbering across prairies, deserts, and mountains and fighting off the attacks of highwaymen and Indians in their month's journey from Kansas to the coast, and the dashing riders of the "Pony Express," carrying the mail from the Missouri to San Francisco in ten days,— these now became a story of the past, to be preserved only in the Wild West shows and the modern movies. The effects of this wonderful achievement, which brought the two shores of the country within a week of each other, were immediately felt. Our trade with China and Japan increased 100 per cent in the next three years. The freight carried by the Central Pacific jumped from 1,700,000 pounds in the first ten months of 1870 to over 13,000,000 pounds in 1871. A "Pacific fever" invaded Congress, and other transcontinental railroad companies which had been granted lands or subsidies by the government — the Kansas Pacific, the Southern Pacific, the Atlantic and Pacific, the St. Paul and Pacific, the Northern

---

[1] The ceremonies were impressive. President Leland Stanford of the Central Pacific and Vice-President Durant of the Union Pacific drove in the golden spike with alternate strokes of a silver-headed hammer which was connected with wires that carried the sound to every telegraph office in the country. The spike of gold, inscribed with the names of the dignitaries of the occasion, is still preserved in the museum of the Wells Fargo Express Company at San Francisco. It was exhibited at the California Pacific Exposition of 1935 at San Diego.

Pacific — were stimulated to complete their tracks. But wild-cat financing and the panic of 1873 brought disaster to most of them.

The Atlantic Cable. While the railway was joining the oceans that bounded the New World, the electric cable was laid beneath the Atlantic to join the New World to the Old. The credit for this feat is due to the scientific work of Commander Matthew F. Maury of Virginia, our greatest authority on ocean geography, and to the perseverance of Cyrus W. Field, who was ridiculed as a dreamer and abused as a fraud. Field succeeded in getting a cable laid in 1858, but it broke in less than a month. Nothing daunted, he worked on in the face of opposition and of the competition of a rival promoter, Perry M. Collins, who was building a telegraph line up to Alaska to connect with a four-hundred-mile cable across Bering Sea to Siberia. It was not till 1866 that Field was able to raise the capital to renew his attempt to lay an Atlantic cable. In July of that year he succeeded in joining Trinity Bay, Newfoundland, with the Irish coast and in opening telegraphic communication with Europe, which has been uninterrupted ever since. The "visionary" Field was now hailed as a "modern Columbus." Congress, which had favored the Collins scheme, presented Field with a gold medal. Queen Victoria even considered conferring knighthood upon him.

Agricultural Development. Most important of all the bases of the economic revolution following the war was the growth of large-scale farming. The impetus was given by the war itself, with its demand for food for two million soldiers and sailors, and by the need of Great Britain and France for Northern wheat as well as for Southern cotton. The Homestead Act; the rapid succession of inventions in agricultural machinery for sowing, cultivating, fertilizing, reaping, and binding; and the lengthening lines of railroad for transporting the crops — all hastened the process. The McCormick reaper played its part in the winning of the war no less than did the armies of Grant and Sherman. In the decade of the sixties over 600,000 new farms were started. Our exports of wheat and corn in the decade preceding the war were 52,000,000 and 55,000,000 bushels respec-

McCORMICK'S FIRST REAPER

tively. By 1880 these figures had risen to 552,000,000 bushels of wheat and 436,000,000 bushels of corn. The value of farm property and implements in that year was $12,587,000,000, or more than a quarter of our national wealth; and in the single decade 1870–1880 the number of American farms grew from 2,659,985 to 4,008,907, bringing under cultivation a new acreage equal to the combined area of Great Britain and France. The population of Kansas had increased eightfold and that of Nebraska fourteenfold since the beginning of the war. We were already supplying half the needs of the wheat-importing countries of the world.

The Mining Frontier. Next to farming, the mining of the precious metals was the most important industry of the West. Ever since the mad rush of the "forty-niners" to California (p. 342) every new discovery of gold, silver, copper, or lead in the foothills of the great mountain system which extended from Montana to Arizona drew its crowds of prospectors, diggers, gamblers, and desperadoes to the scene. In the decade of the sixties the Rockies from the Mexican to the Canadian border were dotted with mining camps and "boom cities." Before the close of the war Colorado had sent over $10,000,000 of gold to the United States mint, and Nevada's Comstock lode was yielding $20,000,000 of silver annually. In 1874 gold was discovered in the Black Hills of Dakota Territory, a part of the Sioux Indian reservation; and the Indians had to retire before the rush of speculators, who raised the population of the territory 853 per cent in a decade.[1] Alder Gulch (Virginia City) in Montana, Stray Horse Gulch (Leadville) in Colorado, and a hundred other camps scattered along the mining frontier repeated the same story. It was, said an Eastern writer, "one vast field of bewildering wealth." Mark Twain, who arrived in Carson City, Nevada, late in 1861, described the country as "fabulously rich in gold, silver, copper, lead, coal, iron, quicksilver, . . . thieves, murderers, desperadoes, ladies, children, lawyers, Christians, Chinamen, Spaniards, gamblers, sharpers, coyotes, poets, preachers, and jackass rabbits." The states of California, Colorado, and Nevada produced 90 per cent of the country's gold and 73.5 per cent of its silver in 1880. The gold was readily absorbed as a basis of our expanding business; but the silver, of which over a thousand tons were mined in 1880, depreciated steadily in value. Thereby the stage was set for a great battle for the recognition of silver as an equal partner with gold in our currency — a battle which we shall study later.

The Cow Country. Between the agricultural frontier and the new mining frontier of the Rockies there was a region several

[1] A sad incident in the removal of the Sioux was the massacre of General George A. Custer, with his force of 264 men, by the Indians under Chief Sitting Bull at the Little Big Horn River in Montana (June 25, 1876). Angered by the invasion of their hunting grounds by the whites and the wholesale slaughter of the buffaloes on which they depended for their meat, clothing, tent skins, and bowstrings, the Indians again and again went on the war path. It took twenty years of fighting by some of the best generals of the Civil War and cost the government over twenty million dollars before the red men were finally pacified. It was not till 1887 that the government, by the Dawes Act, repudiated the opinion of General Sheridan that "the only good Indian is a dead Indian," conferring citizenship and a homestead upon the head of any Indian family who would substitute allegiance to the United States for allegiance to his tribe.

hundred miles in width in which the great grass-covered plains offered admirable grazing fields. The stock-raisers of Texas, as soon as the war was over, began to send droves of long-horned cattle "north of 36" to fatten on the plains before they were sold to the packers and shippers for the Eastern markets. In 1871 more than six hundred thousand cattle crossed the Red River on the "long drive" northward. Huge cattle ranches paralleled the mining camps all the way from western Kansas to Montana, and the cowboy in his leather "chaps" and broad sombrero, rounding up the branded cattle of his own drove at the close of the grazing season, became one of the most picturesque figures in American life. So long as the cow country remained open land, roamed over by the buffalo and the Indian, the cattlemen and ranchers reaped large profits. But when the farmers and sheep-raisers began to encroach upon the "open range," staking out their claims under the Homestead Act and enclosing their farms with wire fences to protect their stock against wolves and thieves, the cowboy had to give way to the settled and prosaic farmer.

Big Business. While the West was yielding its treasures from farm, forest, and mine, and the "prostrate South" was struggling to repair the damages done by the war, the bankers, manufacturers, railroad promoters, and merchants of the North were building up large fortunes. The trend of business was toward combination into larger and larger units. In place of the modest factories of ante-bellum times, run by a few workers under the personal supervision of the owners, came huge industrial plants covering acres of ground and costing millions of dollars, equipped with expensive machines tended by thousands of laborers under a hired "boss." The rise of big business was due to several factors. In the first place, it was profitable to combine in a single organization the various steps in the manufacture of a finished article, such as the digging, transportation, smelting, refining, and rolling of the iron ore to convert it into a steel rail, in order to escape the taxes which the government laid on the separate processes. Then, too, a vast amount of capital had been created by the government during the war by its issue of over two billion dollars' worth of bonds, most of which were in the hands of the bankers, who were permitted by law, as we have seen (p. 438), to use them as a basis for loans to the manufacturers, the railroad-builders, the oil-refiners, and the other "captains of industry."

3 Again, unrestricted immigration brought swarms of aliens to our shores after the war to supply "hands" for the new industries. A law of Congress passed in 1864 allowed the unlimited importation of laborers. In 1863 only 80,000 immigrants had come to America. The number rose to 320,000 in 1866, to 380,000 in 1870, and to 420,000 in 1873, before the great panic came to send the figures down below the 200,000 mark. In Philadelphia alone over 180 new manufacturing plants were established in the last two years of the war. The value of our manufactured products increased 200 per cent in the period from 1860 to 1880, and certain sections of the country became great centers of special industries, such as the steel region about Pittsburgh and the textile sections of southern New England.

The Standard Oil Company. It would take volumes to describe the formation and operation of these various combinations, or "trusts," in transportation, banking, and lumbering, and in the steel, coal, petroleum, leather, whisky, sugar, textile, and other industries. We may select the Standard Oil Company as one of the oldest and most typical of them. Toward the close of the Civil War, John D. Rockefeller, a successful young business man in Cleveland, Ohio, became interested in the possibilities of petroleum, which had begun to "gush" from wells drilled in western Pennsylvania in 1859. Rockefeller set out to control the petroleum business. In 1865 his Standard Oil Company of Cleveland was operating on the modest capital of one hundred thousand dollars. Five years later he organized the Standard Oil Company of Ohio, with a capital of one million dollars, and had control of most of the refining business of the state. Another five years and he had absorbed the important refineries in New York, Philadelphia, and Baltimore, and was controlling nearly 90 per cent of the refinery business of the country. In 1882 the great Standard Oil trust was incorporated

OIL CREEK IN 1865

under the laws of New Jersey, consolidating all the subsid-er iary Standard companies and putting their shares into the hands of nine trustees, with Mr. Rockefeller as the dominant director.

Meantime, to the business of refining had been added the drilling of oil fields, the making of barrels, the transportation of oil by hundreds of miles of pipe lines — in short, all the operations of the production of oil "from the wells to the lamps." The methods of the company were mercilessly efficient. Competitors who refused to sell out at Rockefeller's figures were frozen out by price cuts in their region. The company held the whip hand over the oil-carrying railroads, such as the Erie, the Pennsylvania, and the New York Central, dictating what rates they should charge and compelling them to raise the rates to other shippers, on pain of losing the enormous Standard business if they refused. An investigating committee of the New York legislature in 1879 declared that the railroads had paid ten million dollars in rebates to the Standard Oil Company.

Big Business and the Government. These great business corporations got their start in the days when the government at Washington was busy fighting the war and solving the postwar problems of reconstruction. Lincoln, Grant, Stevens, Sumner, Wade, Wilson, Seward, Blaine, and the like were winding up the affairs of a generation in which sectionalism, slavery, secession, and war were the burning questions, and they had little time or inclination to attend to the new order which was growing up under their very eyes. If they got involved in railroad schemes or the manipulations of Wall Street, it was as private individuals seeking profitable investments. Moreover, the Constitution gave little power to the executive or to Congress to deal with industrial questions. It was framed for a nation of three million people whose main occupations were farming and shipping. It contained no mention of corporations, trusts, monopolies, steel mills, pipe lines, telegraphs, or railroads. Such things were in the far-distant future. Besides, unlimited opportunity for American genius and inventiveness to make the most it could of itself and for itself, unhampered by the interference of the state, was a part of the American creed of liberty. Therefore, while the *political* supremacy of the government at Washington had grown steadily until its triumph in the Civil War, there had been no similar development of the *economic* supremacy of the government with which we are so familiar today.

Big business, then, "just growed," like Topsy, and its swelling wealth was regarded as the natural reward of "rugged individualism." But if the government did not interfere with business, business soon began to interfere with the government. The wealth of the corporations enabled them to maintain paid agents (lobbyists) at Washington to prevent any action by Congress detrimental to their interests. The legislatures of many of the state governments were practically under their control. They sometimes bought state judges. They appealed to the Supreme Court to declare unconstitutional, under the Fourteenth Amendment, state laws which they claimed deprived them of their property "without due process of law." It was not until exactly a century after the framing of the Constitution that Congress, in 1887, passed the first national law aiming at the control of the large corporations, namely, the Interstate Commerce Act, which regulated the conduct of the great railroad systems.

The Organization of Labor. Along with the consolidation of business went a parallel movement in the organization of labor. Unions of workers in the same crafts, such as carpenters, tailors, or shoemakers, had existed from the earliest days of the Republic, like the guilds of the Middle Ages or the laborers' associations of ancient Greece and Rome. Indeed, we have records of strikes of workmen in Egyptian days. The object of the unions was to keep up the standards of workmanship in the craft and to secure fair wages and hours of labor from the employers. As early as 1799 the "cordwainers" (shoemakers) of Philadelphia conducted a strike, and in 1834 an attempt was made in New York to unite the workers in various crafts into a general organization of "the productive classes of the country." But the time was not yet ripe for such a movement. It was only in the great industrial age ushered in by the Civil War that labor began in earnest to work under devoted leaders for the improvement of its condition through united effort. During the war the unions multiplied fourfold, and claimed a membership of two hundred thousand at its close.

In 1869 the garment-cutters of Philadelphia organized the Knights of Labor, which aimed to bring together all the workers, skilled and unskilled, into one big union for their mutual protection against "the aggression of employers." With such mottoes as "The injury of one is the concern of all" and "Labor is the only creator of values and capital," the Knights began to work for an eight-hour day, the abolition of child labor, the settlement of industrial disputes by arbitration, and the encouragement of co-operative stores and factories. They soon grew to a membership of six hundred thousand; but they were hampered by the great number of ignorant and unskilled wage-earners in their ranks and could not hold together the immigrants of different languages and nationalities, the communists and anarchists, and the gangs of contract laborers whom they enrolled. Radical agitators led them into violence in railroad and industrial strikes.

The Knights, therefore, gradually lost leadership, to be succeeded by the American Federation of Labor, which owed its organization in 1881 chiefly to a remarkable Jew of English birth, a member of the cigar-makers' union of New York, named Samuel Gompers. The A. F. of L., of which Gompers was elected president every year but one from 1885 to his death in 1924, was an aristocratic organization as compared with the Knights. It comprised the workers in the skilled crafts of the United States and Canada, and it left to each craft union a large direction of its own affairs. Moreover, it refrained from politics and from any socialistic schemes of overturning the government, and devoted itself wholly to securing better economic conditions for the workers: higher wages, shorter hours, security of positions, sanitary conditions in the factories, protection of women and children against overwork, the right of collective bargaining with employers, the recognition of the unions by legislatures and courts. Though the Federation never contained more than a small fraction of the workers of the country in its dues-paying membership,[1] such important organizations as the railroad brotherhoods and the miners' federations being outside its ranks, it nevertheless exerted an influence in the industrial world far beyond what its numbers would seem to justify.

Labor and Politics. Although the American Federation of Labor kept out of politics, another organization for the improvement of the lot of the masses adopted the European plan of capturing the government at the polls. Karl Marx, in his *Communist Manifesto*, had called upon the working men of all lands to unite: "You have nothing to lose but your chains!" In his great work on *Capital* he had predicted that the workers would take political power away from the "bourgeoisie" (the middle class) and convert the capitalistic countries into socialist states in which classes should disappear and the wealth should

[1] Until the end of the nineteenth century the membership did not pass the 250,000 mark, but it had mounted to 1,500,000 by 1905 and to 2,000,000 by 1915. During the World War its growth was astonishing, reaching a membership of more than 4,000,000 in 1920.

Marx;
Socialist

belong to the laborers who created it. Marx found followers in America, chiefly among the immigrants who, fleeing from the revolutions of the Old World, dreamed of starting a revolution in the New World. In 1872 a "National Labor Reform" party was organized, which entered the Presidential campaign with a platform declaring that "our government is wholly perverted from its true design. . . . In this beneficent country of unlimited resources, with the land annually groaning beneath the products of human effort, the mass of the people have no supply beyond their daily wants and are compelled . . . to become paupers and vagrants." The candidate of the party, however, polled less than thirty thousand votes. A few years later (1877) a "Socialist Labor" party was formed, also based on the Marxian doctrines and made up largely of radical immigrant workingmen. It appeared in several Presidential elections up to the close of the century; but it never could command more than a handful of votes.

Debs
+
socialism

Not even the more American "Socialist" party, organized in 1901 and led in five campaigns by the genial and persuasive Eugene V. Debs, could make much impression on a country in which the ideas of individualism and the opportunity of men to rise by their own efforts from the ranks of the workers to independence and wealth were so strong as in America. The Socialists, to be sure, polled nearly a million votes in 1912, and had visions of capturing the government in the near future; but they were split by the World War, and even under so able a leader as Norman Thomas they could not equal their 1912 vote twenty years later. They never carried a state in a Presidential election, and sent only an occasional member to the House of Representatives.

The Grangers. While the workers in the various trades were thus striving to improve their condition through federations and political action, a somewhat similar movement was taking place in the agricultural industry. Almost at the same moment that the Knights of Labor were organized, Oliver H. Kelley, a clerk in the government service at Washington, started a kind of farmers' league called the Patrons of Husbandry (1867). The object of the association was to spread agricultural educa-

GRANGE MEETING IN THE WEST ABOUT 1875

tion and create social fellowship among the farmers. The "grange," as the local unit was called, was a kind of club where the farmers met with their families to enjoy games and a picnic supper and listen to a lecture on improved methods of fertilization or discuss a plan for "chipping in" to buy a new reaper.

At first the Grangers took no part in politics. They welcomed the new railroads which increased the value of their land and furnished transportation for their products. By 1875 there were thirty thousand granges in the country, and in the upper Mississippi Valley (Illinois, Wisconsin, Minnesota, Iowa), where more than one third of the wheat was grown, they boasted a membership of over half a million. In California they organized cooperative banks. In Iowa they built grain elevators and started the manufacture of farm machinery. But these ventures failed because they lacked the money to compete with the industrial capitalists. The farmer was naturally a self-dependent, hardworking man, whose wife and children joined in the labor of the field and the home. He would have liked to see Jefferson's dream of the "free and independent yeoman" realized in the land; but he soon discovered that the time for that was past. Expensive farm machinery, the monopoly of land by absentee owners, the rising price of fertile acres after the frontier began to be filled up, the mounting interest charges on his farm mortgages, all threatened to reduce him to the condition of a tenant working the land for a master, like the croppers and shareholders of the South. The granges then became political organizations, seeking to get control of state legislatures to enact laws for the farmers' relief and protection.

The Granger Laws. In about a dozen Western states parties were formed under such names as "Independent," "National," "Reform," and "Anti-Monopoly," to fight for the control of railroad and grain-elevator rates, for lower interest on loans from the Eastern bankers, and for a cheap currency. Beginning with Illinois in 1870, the farmers won the legislatures of several of these states and passed a number of measures known as granger laws. Of course they could not tamper with the currency, because the Constitution gave to Congress alone the

power to "coin money and regulate the value thereof" and forbade the states to "emit bills of credit" (that is, to print paper
money) or to "make anything but gold and silver coin a tender
in the payment of debts." Their representatives in Congress
fought hard to have the greenbacks continued as national currency and increased in volume; but, as we have seen, it was a
losing battle (p. 439). Nor could the farmers prevent the decline
in the price of their corn and grain which occurred in the decade
of the 1870's. That was partly due to the return of peace in
Europe after the cycle of Bismarck's wars, the renewed cultivation of the fields of France, Austria, and Germany by the
released soldiers, the competition of large harvests in Russia
and the Argentine, and partly to the panic of 1873, which
reduced the buying power of the industrial masses. The farmer
saw his wheat, which had sold for $2.85 a bushel in 1867, sink
to less than $1.00 a bushel ten years later, and he was burning
his corn as fuel because he could get only fifteen cents a bushel
for it in the market.

Not understanding the complicated causes of his misfortunes,
the farmer attributed them wholly to the wickedness of the
Eastern bankers who were stopping the supply of cheap money
(the greenbacks) and to the railroads and grain elevators which
were charging such rates for transportation and storage as they
pleased. The state legislatures could not get at the Eastern
bankers, but they passed a series of laws regulating the freight
and elevator rates. These granger laws, however, proved in-
effective. The railroads quite generally refused to obey them.
State courts, more under the influence of the "interests" than
were the legislatures, declared the laws unconstitutional; and
when the granger cases finally reached the Supreme Court, the
decision was against the farmers' cause.[1]

[1] At first the Supreme Court was favorable to the grangers, deciding in the cases
of Munn v. Illinois (1876) and of Peik v. the Chicago and Northwestern Railroad
(1877) that a state had a right to fix the rates of the grain elevators and to regulate
railroad rates within the state, even though such regulation might affect persons
outside the state. However, nine years later, in the famous case of the Wabash
Railroad v. the State of Illinois (1886), the Court reversed the latter decision and declared that the power to regulate interstate commerce belonged to Congress alone.

The Agitation for Reform. In spite of the meager political results of the agitation of the Greenbackers, the Laborites, and the Grangers in the two decades following the Civil War, their influence looms larger as we look back through the perspective of more than half a century. Though many of the remedies they proposed may have been unsound, at least they saw the evils which accompanied the greedy profit-making and the unrestricted business methods of the new industrial age. They were advance heralds in the struggle for a more just and humane social order, as their fathers had been the pioneers in opening up the wealth of the West. They assailed monopoly and privilege as a denial of the democratic ideal set up by the fathers of the Republic. The government was too much absorbed in the political questions of a passing generation; they scolded and pestered it into realizing that there were important economic and social matters which should receive its attention. They were ridiculed as cranks and condemned as disturbing radicals — as some of them doubtless were.[1] Nevertheless, the leaven of their protest continued to work in other forms of organizations which we shall study in later pages, until many of their demands ceased to be regarded as the vagaries of madmen and were enacted into sober law.

Women in Industry. Our sketch of the new industrial age would be incomplete without a mention of the part which women came to play in it. The story of women's struggle for the right to be treated as the equals of men in the eyes of the law runs all through our history. They had to fight for the control of their own property, the right to their own earnings, admission into colleges and universities, entrance into the professions, service on juries, and participation in political life. Little by little they won their way. In 1869 Susan B. Anthony urged the

[1] For example, a conservative Democratic paper in Iowa sarcastically proposed a platform of two planks for the Greenback-Labor party, which was running General James B. Weaver for President in 1880: "The Treasury of the United States shall pay fifty dollars a month for life to all persons resident in the United States who have worked for forty-eight years and are tired," and "so much of the third chapter of Genesis as is contained in the words, 'In the sweat of thy face shalt thou eat bread until thou return unto the ground,' be and hereby is repealed."

inclusion in the Fifteenth Amendment of the word "sex," in addition to "race, color, or previous condition of servitude," as a ground on which the privilege of voting might not be denied by any state. In the same year the territory of Wyoming gave the ballot to women. The concentration of industry in large establishments offered women a variety of employment outside the home, and the increasing number of women coming from the institutions of higher learning furnished capable workers in many fields. No longer were domestic service, schoolteaching, keeping boarders, bookbinding, and spinning in the cotton mills the only occupations open to women, as they were when Harriet Martineau visited our country in 1840. A number of women were beginning to find their way into the professions as doctors, lawyers, and preachers. Thousands were going into the business world to earn their living under practically the same conditions as men.

Fifteen per cent of the women of the country were engaged in gainful occupations as early as 1870, and the number increased steadily until it reached 20 per cent at the close of the century. It is true that women were frequently looked upon by the men rather as intruders than as partners. Their wages were lower. They were not admitted to the unions. They were regarded as eking out the earnings of their husbands if married, and, if single, as seeking a temporary job until they got married. Their place was still supposed to be "in the home" instead of in the turmoil of politics and the tussle of industry; their interests, "children, cooking, and church." But these ideas were coming to be regarded as old-fashioned and "Victorian" as the century drew to its close. Most of the social hindrances to a woman's taking a job were done away with, and she came to share increasingly in the labors of man.

TERMS TO BE MASTERED

frontier	trusts	Grangers
homestead	lobby	Socialism
"the long drive"	rebate	tenant farmer
the open range	trade union	women's rights

For Supplementary Reading

C. D. Wright, *The Industrial Evolution of the United States*, chaps. xiii, xiv, xxii; E. E. Sparks, *National Development* (American Nation Series, Vol. XXIII), chaps. ii–v, xiv, xv; John Moody, *The Railroad Builders* (Chronicles of America, Vol. XXXVIII), chaps. i, vi, and *The Masters of Capital* (Chronicles of America, Vol. XLI), chaps. iii, iv; The Pageant of America, Vol. V, chaps. v, vi, xiv; Mary R. Beard, *Short History of the Labor Movement*, chaps. vii, viii, and *America through Women's Eyes*, chaps. iv, x–xii; Allan Nevins, *The Emergence of Modern America*, chaps. ii, iv, v, vi, xii, xiv; B. J. Hendricks, *The Age of Big Business* (Chronicles of America, Vol. XXXIX), chaps. i–iii; S. P. Orth, *The Armies of Labor* (Chronicles of America, Vol. XL), chap. iv; Mark Sullivan, *Our Times*, Vol. II, pp. 255–306; J. F. Johnson, *We and our Work*, chap. xvii; Samuel Gompers, *Seventy Years of Life and Labor, an Autobiography*; S. J. Buck, *The Agrarian Crusade* (Chronicles of America, Vol. XL), chaps. i–viii; Hart, *Contemporaries*, Vol. IV, Nos. 162, 163, 169; Muzzey, *Readings*, pp. 481–494.

Topics for Reports

1. **The Union Pacific Railroad.** E. P. Oberholtzer, *History of the United States since the Civil War*, Vol. I, pp. 319–330, Vol. II, pp. 474–484, 598–609; G. M. Dodge, *How we Built the Union Pacific Railroad*; H. U. Faulkner, *American Economic History*, pp. 452–465; John Moody, *The Railroad Builders*, chaps. vi, ix; J. P. Davis, *The Union Pacific Railway*; F. L. Paxson, *Pacific Railroads and the Disappearance of the Frontier* (American Historical Association Report, 1907, Vol. I), pp. 105 f.

2. **The Mining Frontier.** H. H. Bancroft, *The Pacific States of North America*, Vol. XXV, chaps. v, vi; R. W. Raymond, *The Mining Industry of the Rocky Mountains*; C. H. Shinn, *The Story of a Mine*; R. L. Stevenson, *The Amateur Emigrant* and *The Silverado Squatters*; Mary M. Matthews, *Ten Years in Nevada*; A. D. Tallent, *The Black Hills*; T. J. Dinsdale, *Vigilantes of Montana*.

3. **The Granger Legislation.** C. F. Adams, Jr., "The Granger Movement," in *North American Review*, Vol. CXX, pp. 394 f.; K. L. Butterfield, *Farmer's Social Organizations* (Cyclopaedia of American Agriculture, Vol. IV, pp. 289 f.); T. A. McNeal, *When Kansas was Young*; A. D. Adams, "Reasonable Rates," in *Journal of Political Economy*, Vol. XII, pp. 79 f.; C. W. Riesen, "Outcome of the Granger Movement," in *Popular Science Monthly*, Vol. XXXII, pp. 201 f.; D. C. Cloud, *Monopolies and the People*.

4. **The Rise of the Trusts.** H. D. Lloyd, *Wealth Against Commonwealth*, pp. 373–388; M. Josephson, *The Robber Barons*, chaps. i–v; H. U. Faulkner, *American Economic History*, pp. 516–536; H. R. Seager, *Introduction to Economics*, pp. 476–509; R. T. Ely, *The Labor Movement in America*, pp. 1–38; Hacker and Kendrick, *The United States since 1865*, chaps. vii–xii, xiv–xvi; B. J. Hendrick, *The Age of Big Business*, chap. i.

QUESTIONS SUGGESTED BY THE CHAPTER

1. Why was the government so slow to take notice of the rise of big business in the United States? **2.** What favors did the government grant to the Union Pacific Railroad? **3.** What was the "Pacific fever"? **4.** What part did the McCormick reaper play in the fortunes of the Civil War? **5.** Had the government ever given away land to individuals before the Homestead Act? If so, to whom? **6.** Contrast the mining frontier with the agricultural frontier. **7.** What quarrel had the cattlemen with the farmers? **8.** When and by whom was the Atlantic cable laid? **9.** What factors favored the consolidation of business during the Civil War? **10.** What change in its Indian policy did the government make in the Dawes Act of 1887? **11.** Contrast the Knights of Labor with the American Federation of Labor. **12.** Name two important labor organizations that are not in the American Federation of Labor. **13.** What have been the chief demands of organized labor? **14.** Why do you think Socialism has not won more adherents in the United States? **15.** What remedies were the Grangers seeking? **16.** How did the Supreme Court disappoint the Grangers in 1886? **17.** What kinds of "co-operation" did the farmers try to establish? **18.** What political right did Susan B. Anthony seek for women? **19.** What changes in the economic condition of women took place after the Civil War? **20.** When and by what act did the government begin to regulate the railroads? **21.** What was wrong in the practice of rebates? **22.** Why did many farmers sink to the position of tenants?

CHAPTER NINETEEN

FUTILE PARTY BATTLES

From Hayes to Harrison. Let us now turn to a study of the political events of this period when the industries of the country were advancing with such gigantic strides. From the Civil War on to the end of the century, except for the two terms of Grover Cleveland, Republican Presidents sat in the White House. The predominance of the Republican party is not hard to understand. It was the party of Lincoln and Grant, the party that had saved the Union and abolished slavery. Its leaders constantly appealed to the people to "vote as they had shot." Of course, there were many Democrats too who had supported the Union cause. But, after all, the Democratic party was the party of Jefferson Davis; and the Republicans maintained that even if not all the Democrats were disloyal, at least all the disloyalists were Democrats. Besides their appeal to patriotism, the Republicans had certain other advantages for prolonging their power. It was they who had given away homesteads to the farmers of the West and made large grants of public land to the railroads. It was they who had thousands of offices to bestow and who were paying millions of dollars a year in pensions to the veterans of the Grand Army of the Republic. It was they who had bought the $2,500,000,000 of government bonds which established the close connection between the great bankers and the Treasury of the United States. Every candidate that they elected to the Presidency from the inauguration of Hayes in 1877 to that of McKinley in 1897 had been an officer in the Civil War. Indeed, when one considers all these props of their power, the wonder is not that they held it so long but that the Democrats were ever able to shake it.

When the Republicans abused their power, however, by their

cruel reconstruction policy and by the scandals of the Grant regime, they began to lose the confidence of the people. The Democrats captured the House of Representatives in 1874 and held it for sixteen of the twenty-two years following, while the Republicans kept control of the Senate except for the brief period 1893–1895. With Congress thus divided, it was impossible to carry out any consistent program of legislation. The period from Hayes to Harrison (1877–1893), which we shall review in this chapter, was perhaps the most barren dozen years in our history as regards important laws. There was plenty of bitter party strife, but it seemed to be connected with keeping in power when one was in and getting into power when one was out. James Bryce, the English scholar and statesman who visited our country in the 1880's and wrote in his *American Commonwealth* the most illuminating account of our government, said: "Neither party has any clear-cut principles. . . . Both certainly have war-cries, organization, interests enlisted in their support. But those interests are in the main the interests of getting and keeping the patronage of the government."

The Railroad Strike of 1877. President Hayes was beset with difficulties during his whole term. He had been nominated at Cincinnati in 1876 only because it was impossible to break the deadlock between the supporters of General Grant and James G. Blaine, neither of whom wanted a reform administration. He offended the "Stalwart" Republicans by withdrawing the Federal troops from the South (p. 449). His opposition to the greenbacks alienated the Western farmers and debtors. The Democratic papers charged him with having stolen the election from Tilden, and the Democratic House threatened to investigate his title to the Presidency. He had been in office but a few months when a railroad strike, the most violent in all our history, broke out. The long depression following the panic of 1873 hit the railroads hard. They engaged in cut-throat competition for such traffic as there was, often carrying freight at less than it cost them. When the Baltimore and Ohio, in July, 1877, announced a 10 per cent cut in wages (the fourth cut since 1870) for all men receiving more than a dollar a day, the storm broke.

On the day the cut was to take effect, a strike began at Martinsburg, West Virginia, and spread rapidly through fourteen states from New York to Kansas and Texas. The militia was called out in West Virginia, Maryland, and Pennsylvania to quell the rioting; and when it proved unable to handle the situation, the President sent United States troops, under the command of General Hancock, to Baltimore to restore order. Chicago, Columbus, Buffalo, Reading (Pennsylvania), St. Louis, and other cities were the scene of rioting and bloodshed. But the worst of all occurred at Pittsburgh, where ten million dollars' worth of property in cars, buildings, and freight was destroyed and the strikers and troops fought pitched battles in the streets, resulting in the death or wounding of more than fifty men. It was not till the end of August that the last Federal troops left the city.

At the same time a strike of eight thousand anthracite miners in eastern Pennsylvania terrorized the region about Scranton, where the "Molly Maguires," a secret society of Irish, had for some years been assassinating unpopular bosses and superintendents. These scenes of violence, in which for the first time troops were called upon to suppress labor disorders, shocked the country. Men began to ask if America was to witness the horrors of the Paris Commune of 1870, with barricades and battles in the streets.

The Silver Question Emerges. When the law of 1875 made the greenbacks all redeemable in gold on January 1, 1879 (p. 439), the Westerners fell back upon silver as the cheap form of currency. Silver and gold had both been recognized as money since the beginning of the government, at the ratio of one ounce of gold to about sixteen ounces of silver. But in 1873 silver was "demonetized," which means that the government stopped coining silver dollars. The reason for this was that for some years silver had been worth more than one sixteenth as much as gold, and therefore the silver-miners, instead of bringing their silver to the mint to be coined, had sold it to the silversmiths. Now, however, with the enormously increased output of silver from the mining frontier (p. 458), its price in the world market fell rapidly, and the mine-owners clamored to have the government take it at the old ratio of sixteen to one. They spoke of the demonetization of silver as "the crime of 1873," and they were joined by the farmers and debtors for the reasons we have already noted (p. 439). Richard P. Bland ("Silver Dick") of Missouri introduced a bill into the House, at the beginning of Hayes's first Congress, providing for the unlimited, or "free," coinage of silver at the rate of sixteen to one. The bill was modified by Senator Allison of Iowa, so that the government should be obliged to take only two million dollars' worth of silver a month to coin into dollars. In February, 1878, the Bland-Allison Bill passed both houses of Congress by large majorities. President Hayes vetoed it, because, he said, it would be dishonest for the government to make and use "dollars" of less value than the ones in which the people understood that the public debt would be paid. Congress, however, passed the bill over the veto, and thus pledged our government to buy at least twenty-four million dollars' worth of silver every year to coin into "dollars" which were worth in 1878 less than ninety cents in gold.

The "Spoils System." The great army of officials and clerks in the executive department of the government, such as postmasters and customs-collectors, make up what is called the civil service. It had been the custom, especially since President Jackson's day, to bestow these offices on persons who had worked hard for the success of the party, without too much regard for their fitness for the office. "To the victors belong the spoils" was the motto adopted by both parties, and every change of administration saw a wild scramble at Washington for postmasterships, collectorships, judgeships, surveyorships, and the like. Moreover, the men who were rewarded with the offices were expected to pay a percentage of their salary as an assessment, or "voluntary contribution," for the party's campaign expenses. Ever since the Civil War, reformers like Carl Schurz and George W. Curtis had tried to stir Congress to abolish this corrupt "spoils system." In 1871 they succeeded in getting a law passed authorizing the President to appoint a commission to make rules for the reform of the civil service. Grant appointed the commission ; but it could do little in the face of the opposition of the "Stalwarts," who sneered at the "snivel service" and called the reformers hypocrites. President Grant himself was not interested in reform of the civil service; and when Congress failed to make any further appropriation for the work of the commission in 1875, he let the whole matter drop.

Hayes and Civil-Service Reform. Grant's successor, however, was determined to purify the civil service. He revived the commission of 1871. He wrote to his Secretary of the Treasury, John Sherman, that no assessments should be allowed in his department and that no officeholders should be permitted to take part in the management of political campaigns. He supported Secretary Schurz in thoroughgoing reforms in the Department of the Interior. He removed Chester A. Arthur and Alonzo B. Cornell from positions in the New York customhouse because they were using their office to build up the Republican machine in the state of New York, which was dominated by the United States Senator, Roscoe Conkling. Though Hayes was not able to get any favorable legislation from Congress on the subject, his efforts for civil-service reform aroused interest and sympathy all over the country. Civil-service-reform leagues were formed in over thirty of the states during his administration, and a national organization was launched at Newport, Rhode Island, in 1881.

The Election of 1880. No President ever deserved re-election more than Hayes. He had given the country a clean and honest administration. But, aside from his own declaration that he would not accept a second term, his independence of the machine and party politics had made his renomination in 1880 impossible. General Grant had returned in 1879 from a trip around the world, in which he had been received with royal honors by the sovereigns of Europe and Asia. A trio of "Stalwart" Senators (Conkling of New York, Cameron of Pennsylvania, and Logan of Illinois) were determined to put him in the White House again, in spite of the popular prejudice against a President's serving a third term. Grant's chief rivals in the

A COMMON SIGHT IN THE POLITICAL ANTEROOMS BEFORE THE PASSAGE OF THE CIVIL-SERVICE ACT[1]

[1] Drawn by W. T. Smedley for *Harper's Weekly.*

Republican convention at Chicago were Senator James G. Blaine of Maine and Secretary of the Treasury John Sherman of Ohio. Both were extremely able men, with long records of public service; but Blaine was the most brilliant and "magnetic" politician of the age. He had barely missed the Presidential nomination in 1876, because of suspicions that he had used his high position as Speaker of the House to favor some railroad deals in which he was personally interested. But his devoted followers clung to him through thick and thin, cherishing until the last year of his life (1892) the hope of seating him in the White House.

Grant and Blaine ran neck and neck in the convention of 1880 for thirty-five ballots, when the deadlock was broken by the selection of James A. Garfield of Ohio, who had been sent to the convention to work for Sherman. Chester A. Arthur of New York was nominated for Vice-President, to satisfy the "Stalwart" Conkling-Grant faction. The Democrats named General Winfield S. Hancock, like Garfield a gallant soldier, but wholly without Garfield's experience as a statesman.[1] Garfield was elected by 214 votes to 155, but his popular majority was less than 8000. It was the first election since 1860 in which all the states of the South were able to express their choice freely. Embittered against the Republican party for its reconstruction policy, these states cast a solid vote for the Democratic candidate (though he was the victor of Gettysburg!), and for a quarter of a century thereafter the

[1] Garfield is one of the best examples of America's self-made men. He had worked his way up from the tow path of an Ohio canal and from odd jobs as a carpenter and farm hand until he had saved enough to go to Williams College. At the age of twenty-six he was made president of a small college in Ohio, and two years later he was elected to the Ohio state senate (1859). He joined the Union army as the colonel of a regiment largely made up of his own students, and was promoted to a major-generalship for his gallant conduct in General Thomas's famous stand at Chickamauga (p. 411). At Lincoln's request he entered Congress in December, 1863, where he became the undisputed leader of the House after Blaine's transfer to the Senate (1876). In the midsummer of 1880 Garfield had the unique honor of being at the same time a member of the House, a Senator-elect, and the Republican nominee for the Presidency.

"solid South" was found in the Democratic column in every Presidential election.[1]

The Assassination of Garfield. The choice of Garfield, instead of reconciling the Republican factions, resulted in bitter strife. "Stalwarts" like Conkling had supported him and done much to secure his election; but he refused to fulfill the promises they claimed he had made to them during the campaign. He appointed Conkling's chief enemy, Blaine, as Secretary of State, and removed the collector of the port of New York to make place for one of the leaders of the Blaine forces in the convention of 1880, William H. Robertson. Stung by this "ingratitude," Conkling and Platt resigned their seats in the Senate and vainly appealed, with Vice-President Arthur's help, to the legislature of New York for re-election. Factional spirit ran high and culminated in a dastardly crime. On the morning of July 2, 1881, as President Garfield, accompanied by Blaine, entered the railroad station at Washington to take the train for a college reunion at Williamstown, he was shot in the back by a cowardly wretch named Guiteau, who had been seeking an office and who boasted that he was a "Stalwart" and wanted to see Arthur in the Presidential chair. After lingering in great pain through the summer, Garfield died at Elberon, New Jersey, on September 19, the anniversary of Chickamauga.

The Pendleton Civil-Service Act. The accidental elevation of "Chet" Arthur to the Presidency seemed like a calamity to the friends of good government. John Sherman had written just after the convention: "The nomination of Arthur as vice president is a ridiculous burlesque. It attaches to the ticket all the odium of machine politics." Yet this former companion of the bosses and spoilsmen rose to a stature of dignity under the responsibilities of his great office, and gave the country an honest,

[1] McKinley, Roosevelt, and Taft sometimes carried former border slave states (Kentucky, Maryland, Delaware, Missouri) in elections from 1896 on; but it was not until 1920 that the Republican candidate Harding won a state of the former Confederacy (Tennessee), and not until 1928 that the Republican Hoover carried states which had been put under the military regime of the Reconstruction Acts of 1867 (Virginia, North Carolina, Florida, and Texas). These states went back to the Democrats in 1932.

JAMES A. GARFIELD

RUTHERFORD B. HAYES

CHESTER A. ARTHUR

CARL SCHURZ

vigorous, and efficient administration. He insisted on fair terms to China in the act of 1882 for the restriction of Chinese immigration to the United States.[1] He tried to prevent the raid on the Treasury by his veto of "pork barrel" bills, which appropriated huge sums for small harbors and unnavigable rivers. He advocated a fair revision of the tariff. He laid the foundation for our modern navy of ironclads. Most significant of all, though he had been dismissed from the New York customhouse by Hayes for his abuse of the patronage, three years later he signed the act which has been called "the Magna Carta of Civil Service Reform."

Guiteau's pistol shot had roused the country to a realization of the disgraceful state of the civil service. Following the recommendation of Arthur in his Presidential message of December, 1882, George H. Pendleton, a Democratic Senator from Ohio, introduced a bill providing for a commission to classify the grades of the civil service and devise a system of competitive examinations for the selection of the candidates. The bill also forbade political assessments, as well as removals from office for failure to make "voluntary" contributions to political campaigns. The bill was passed by large majorities in both houses and signed by Arthur (January 16, 1883). The President showed his sincerity in the cause by appointing an ardent reformer as chairman of the Civil Service Commission, promulgating a set of rules for the faithful execution of the act, and himself putting about fifteen thousand government employees into the classified service before he left office.

[1] Thousands of Chinese coolies had been imported to work on the construction of the Central Pacific Railroad. By 1870 there were over seventy thousand Chinese in the country, nearly five sixths of them in California. Their low standard of living aroused the hostility of American labor, and there began a crusade against them, led by Dennis Kearney, the "sand lots" orator of San Francisco. "Four dollars a day and roast beef" and "The Chinese must go" were the slogans. President Hayes secured the consent of China to our "regulation, limitation, or suspension" of Chinese immigration, and on the basis of this agreement Congress forbade the entrance of Chinese laborers into the country for twenty years. Arthur vetoed the bill on the ground that the "suspension" of immigration for twenty years was equivalent to a prohibition of it. He forced Congress to reduce the period to ten years. But he might as well have signed the original bill, for at the close of the ten-year period Congress renewed the exclusion of the Chinese by the Geary Act.

The Nomination of Blaine. Arthur, like Hayes, deserved a renomination; and, unlike Hayes, he was eager for it. But he too had offended many Republican leaders, especially the powerful Blaine, by his independent course. During his brief period as Secretary of State (March to December, 1881), Blaine had increased his popularity by a vigorous assertion of the prestige of the United States. He had tried to get Great Britain to give up the Clayton-Bulwer Treaty of 1850 (p. 355) and leave to the United States the sole ownership and control of any Isthmian canal. He had intervened in Peru and Chile in support of American claims to nitrate and guano beds, in which he was accused of being personally interested. His most cherished plan was for a league of the countries of Latin America, under the leadership of the United States, to work out common policies on trade, tariffs, currency, copyrights, weights and measures, public health, and a number of other economic and social questions. He had, with Arthur's approval, sent invitations in November, 1881, to the states of Central and South America to attend a Pan-American congress at Washington the next year. But when Blaine left office in December, his successor Frelinghuysen was instructed to cancel the invitations. Whereupon Blaine wrote an indignant open letter to the President, charging him with "humiliating this government before the European powers," and retired to private life to write his *Twenty Years of Congress*.

In 1884 the way seemed clear for Blaine to realize his ambition for the Presidency. His bitter enemy Conkling, who had kept him from the nomination in 1880, was now "out of politics," practicing law in New York. Grant's political ambitions were over, and he was struggling to avoid bankruptcy in a rascally brokerage firm with which he had foolishly allowed himself to become connected. Platt had forgotten or forgiven his grievance of 1881 against Garfield's Secretary of State, and announced his intention to support Blaine. Arthur's following outside of New York, and apart from the Southern delegates who were bound to the administration by patronage, was negligible. Blaine was nominated on the fourth ballot. Some reform delegates to the convention (among whom was the young Theodore Roosevelt) opposed Blaine's nomination because of his railroad deals and his hostility to civil-service reform; but they had no candidate to vie with him in popularity. Immediately after his nomination many of them began to work to defeat his election. These reformers, led by a number of prominent citizens of New York and New England, were called "Mugwumps" — an Indian word meaning "big chief" — because they were accused of pretending to be superior to the "regular" members of the party. The "Mugwumps" had the support of several influential Republican newspapers and of many of the leading clergymen and educators of the country. They met in conferences in Boston and New York to denounce Blaine, inviting the Democrats to nominate a candidate for whom public-spirited citizens could conscientiously vote.

Grover Cleveland. The Democrats responded by nominating Grover Cleveland, governor of New York. Cleveland was the son of a poor Presbyterian minister. He had grown up in western New York, supporting himself as best he could by tending a country store, teaching in an asylum for the blind, and acting as a clerk in a lawyer's office in Buffalo. Here he studied law, was admitted to the bar, entered politics, and slowly worked his way up to be elected mayor of Buffalo in his forty-fifth year (1881). His administration of the office was so honest, able, and courageous that it brought him the Democratic nomination for governor the next year. He carried the state by the unprecedented plurality of 192,000 votes, and as governor showed the fearless opposition to the corrupt machine politicians that had won him the title of the "veto mayor" of Buffalo. The motto to which he lived up during his entire political career of thirty years was "a public office is a public trust." He had none of the arts of the politician, and did not care how the acts which he believed right might affect his own political fortunes. On the day of his election as governor he wrote to his brother: "The obligation on my side is to perform the duties assigned me with an eye single to the interests of my employers (the people of the state). I shall have no ideas of reëlection or higher political preferment in my head, but be very thankful and happy if I can well serve one term as the people's Governor." By nature and training Cleveland was the very opposite of his rival for the election. Blaine was brilliant, genial, and daring; Cleveland was deliberate, patient, plodding, but firm as a rock when he had made his decision.

The Campaign of 1884. The "Mugwump" campaign of 1884 was perhaps the most bitter and disgraceful one in our whole history, conducted, as the New York *Nation* said, "in a spirit worthy of the back stairways of a tenement house." Every nook and corner of the public and private life of the candidates was ransacked for scandals to be retailed to the people in newspaper articles, pamphlets, cartoons, speeches, and sermons. Blaine was depicted as a crook who had enriched himself by accepting bribes from railroad promoters and selling their worthless bonds to his friends. Cleveland was called a drunkard and libertine, a vulgar politician who had been transferred from the back parlor of a Buffalo saloon to the executive mansion at Albany. The election on November 4 was very close, turning on the pivotal state of New York, which the Cleveland electors won by 1149 votes out of a total of 1,127,169. Blaine's followers claimed that fraudulent counting of the returns in Brooklyn and Long Island had cheated him out of the election; but he accepted the result with good grace, declaring that the country had had trial enough in passing through one disputed election (1876).

Blaine's defeat has usually been attributed to an incident which occurred at a reception given to him by a group of clergymen at the Fifth Avenue Hotel in New York a few days before the election, when a Presbyterian minister named Burchard called the Democrats the party of "rum, Romanism, and rebellion." If Blaine heard the remark, he did not rebuke Burchard; and this insult to Roman Catholics, by classing them with drunkards and rebels, was taken up by their clergy and laymen all through the state. The remark was even attributed to Blaine himself by some papers, though Blaine's own mother was a Catholic and he had never spoken with anything but respect of the Church. The incident undoubtedly cost him far more than the 1149 votes which lost him the election. But there were other causes which contributed to his defeat: the activity of the "Mugwumps," the activity of the Prohibition party, the continual harping on the Mulligan letters,[1] the hostility of Conkling,[2] and a heavy rainstorm on election day, which reduced the Republican vote in the upper parts of New York State.

Cleveland's Path of Thorns. The election of the first Democratic President since the Civil War was regarded by the Republicans as a calamity. They had been telling the country for twenty years that the Democrats were unpatriotic and inefficient, and now they prophesied that Cleveland would bring ruin upon the government, just as the Federalists in 1800 had seen disaster in the election of Thomas Jefferson. Congress would be dominated by "brigadier generals" from the South. The Confederate debt might be honored. Pensions to Union veterans might be stopped. The vast number of offices at the President's disposal would be filled with men hostile to the great industrial machine which the Republicans had been building up for twenty years by the tariff, the banks, the grants of public land to the railroads, and the various favors of Congress and the courts to private corporations.

Cleveland believed that it was time for the animosities of the Civil War to be laid aside; but when he appointed two members of his cabinet from the states of the secession and chose foreign

---

[1] These were a batch of correspondence between Blaine and Warren Fisher of Boston, a promoter of the Little Rock and Fort Smith Railroad. The letters were written while Blaine was Speaker of the House (1869–1875), and they contained the financial transactions between Blaine and Fisher in regard to marketing the bonds of the road. Blaine believed that the letters had been destroyed; but a former clerk of his partner Stanwood, one James Mulligan, had kept them and had produced them in 1876 to help defeat Blaine for the Republican nomination at Cincinnati. Now after eight years, they were resurrected and republished with commentaries and additions, to show that "no honest man could vote for James G. Blaine."

[2] Conkling never forgave Blaine for his attack on the Republican machine in New York (p. 481). When urged to take the stump for Blaine in the campaign of 1884, he replied, "I do not engage in criminal practice." His Utica district in New York, normally a Republican stronghold, went for Cleveland.

ministers and consuls equally from the North and from the South, he was assailed as a sympathizer with the "rebellion." He was sincerely desirous of extending the reform of the civil service; but his party, after having been deprived of patronage for a quarter of a century, was clamorous for offices. He wished to relieve the people of undue taxation, but his efforts for tariff reform were thwarted by the big manufacturing interests. He was confronted, during his whole term, with a Republican Senate which tried to hamper him in his constitutional right of dismissing Federal officers. Although he labored faithfully for economy, reform, and honesty in the government, he found his path beset with thorns.

The Pension Vetoes. Cleveland's chief concern was to limit the expenditures of the government to the objects necessary for the public welfare and to keep taxation down to the point necessary to meet such expenditures. The pensions paid to the veterans of the Civil War had increased from $15,000,000 in 1866 to $56,000,000 in 1885. In the latter year there were nearly 350,000 names on the pension rolls. In so far as these names represented soldiers or sailors actually wounded or disabled in the war, the pensions were, as Cleveland said, "cheerfully approved by the people." He himself signed more pension bills than any of his predecessors. But there was an immense amount of fraud in the system. Pension agents were abroad in the land, seeking fees by persuading ex-soldiers or their survivors to make claims on the government for pension for illness or accidents in no way connected with their military service. One man had broken his leg by falling into a cellar, another had been thrown from a buggy, a third had been killed by a snowslide in Colorado twenty years after the war, a fourth had been shot by a neighbor who was aiming at an owl. Over seven hundred pension bills were passed in Cleveland's administration, and he insisted on giving each of them his personal examination, with the result that he vetoed two hundred and thirty-three of them. He was unmercifully criticized by the Republicans for "weighing the merits of the veterans in an apothecary's scales," and was accused of "insulting" the army when he vetoed a Dependent

Pension Bill which granted a pension of twelve dollars a month to every dependent soldier and sailor who had served three months, regardless of whether he had received any injury or had even participated in a battle. So great was the abuse heaped upon him by certain officers of the Grand Army of the Republic that he canceled his engagement to visit their encampment at St. Louis. Congress upheld his veto, however, and even the rank and file of the veterans at St. Louis approved it by a vote of 318 to 173.[1]

Labor Unrest. The middle years of the decade of the 1880's were vexed by so many conflicts between capital and organized labor that they have been called the period of "the great upheaval." Strikes increased from 485 in 1884 to 645 in 1885 and 1411 in 1886, involving in the latter year nearly ten thousand establishments and a half a million workers. The situation was made worse by the arrival of radical agitators in the flood of immigrants who came to our shores. The social revolutionists and anarchists of Chicago had formed the International Working People's Association in 1883, advocating violence in the class struggle. Their membership was largely recruited from the embittered revolutionaries of continental Europe. Of the eight anarchist newspapers published in the city, only one was printed in the English language. The labor strife culminated in a deed of horror on May 5, 1886. An open-air meeting in Haymarket Square, Chicago, called by the anarchists to protest against the forcible repression of a strike in the McCormick reaper works and to demand an eight-hour day, was ordered by the police to disperse. The reply was the explosion of a dynamite bomb thrown into the midst of the police squad, killing one man instantly and mortally wounding seven others.

[1] Cleveland's unpopularity with the officials of the G. A. R. was increased by his "rebel-flag order" of April 30, 1887, instructing the Adjutant General to return to the Southern states a number of flags which had been captured from the Confederate armies and had been lying for years in the attic of the War Office building at Washington. The storm of protest that arose over this "recognition of the lost cause," and the realization, on further thought, that the disposition of the flags belonged to Congress and not to the President, led Cleveland to revoke the order. More than twenty years later a Republican Congress under Roosevelt voted unanimously to return the flags.

Though no proof could be found as to who threw the bomb, eight anarchist leaders were arrested and tried for murder, and four of them were hanged the next year.[1] These severe labor troubles induced President Cleveland to send a special message to Congress on April 22, 1886, in which he cited the provision of the Constitution authorizing the national government to protect the states "against domestic violence" (Art. IV, Sect. 4), and recommended the creation of a national commission of three members to serve as a tribunal in labor disputes. Congress failed to act on the President's suggestion, but several of the states (Massachusetts, New York, Iowa, Kansas) passed laws in 1886 and 1887 creating boards for the settlement of labor disputes by arbitration.

The Interstate Commerce Act. One of the most serious problems of the time was the control of the railroads. During the five years preceding Cleveland's election the railroad mileage had increased four times as fast as the population, and more than one hundred and thirty thousand miles of track wove a network, with thinning lines west of the Missouri River, which covered every state and territory in the Union. The railroads had done great service in carrying to the rich Western lands thousands on thousands of settlers who had sent back millions on millions of bushels of wheat and corn to the populous seaboard cities and to the countries of Europe. But they had also been guilty of grave offenses, such as influencing legislatures to show them favors in taxation, charging rates to pay dividends on "watered stock," [2] and giving some shippers, such as the Standard Oil (p. 462), better treatment than others. We have seen how the granger laws tried to curb the railroads and why they failed to

---

[1] One of the men under the death sentence committed suicide in his cell. The three others serving a life sentence in jail were pardoned by Governor Altgeld of Illinois in 1893, on the ground that no evidence of their guilt had been produced at the trial.

[2] "Watered stock" means shares of stock issued in excess of the actual value of the property or its probable earnings. It was a common trick of the unscrupulous railroad manipulators in Wall Street, like Vanderbilt, Jay Gould, and Daniel Drew, to bribe or browbeat the legislature into allowing them to issue millions of dollars' worth of new stock, which they sold to the public before it declined to a fraction of its face value.

THE HAYMARKET RIOT AT CHICAGO [1]

[1] From *Harper's Weekly*, May 15, 1886.

do so (p. 469 and note). After the Wabash decision of 1886 it devolved upon Congress to deal with the railroads, if they were to be dealt with at all. Senator S. M. Cullom of Illinois, who for more than a decade had worked for the cause of the farmers as a member of the legislature and as governor of his state, was made the chairman of a Senate committee for the investigation of the interstate railroads in 1885.

The committee traveled through the country, examining railroad officials, shippers, and farmers; and the result of its long labor was the creation of a national Interstate Commerce Commission of five members, appointed by the President, with power to supervise the interstate railroads. The most important of the twenty-four sections of the act were as follows: special rates, rebates, and other favors to powerful shippers were forbidden; rates were to be proportioned to the distances over which the freight was carried, and not to be raised for "short hauls" on which no competition existed; "pooling," or the agreement between the roads to divide the profits of the total traffic among themselves according to a fixed ratio, was made illegal; rates must be open to public inspection, and the roads must produce their schedules, waybills, and ledgers at the request of the Commission. Violators of the law were subject to a fine not exceeding five thousand dollars for each offense. This Interstate Commerce (or Cullom) Act of February, 1887, was the most important piece — and, in fact, the only really important piece — of legislation in Cleveland's first administration.[1]

---

[1] The lack of harmony in Cleveland's Congress prevented the carrying out of any party program, such as tariff reform. But a number of "nonpartisan" bills were passed, most of them orginating in the Republican Senate. For example, the Presidential Succession Act of 1886 provided that in case of the death or disability of both President and Vice-President, the succession should go to the members of the cabinet in order of the creation of their departments, instead of to the President *pro tempore* of the Senate and the Speaker of the House, who might both be of the opposite party to that of the President. An Electoral Count Act of 1887 made a repetition of the crisis of 1877 impossible by providing that if more than one set of electoral returns were sent in, the set which had the seal of the governor of the state should be accepted. The Dawes Act of the same year conferred a homestead and citizenship on the heads of Indian families who renounced their tribal allegiance. In 1886 a victory of Cleveland over the Senate led to the repeal of the last remnants of the Tenure of Office Act of 1867 (p. 434).

It showed the people that the government had at last awakened to its responsibility to recognize the problems of the new industrial age. It created the first of the numerous commissions and boards in the national government which have dealt in the last fifty years with economic questions. It was the first law of Congress, coming exactly a hundred years after the framing of the Constitution, to apply a clause of the Constitution to the regulation of "big business."

Cleveland's Fight for Tariff Reform. What Cleveland wanted above all else was reform in the revenue system, "to relieve the people of unnecessary taxation . . . and prevent the accumulation of a surplus in the Treasury to tempt to extravagant waste." Owing to our flourishing foreign trade and the high protective tariff, the surplus was piling up in the Treasury at the rate of about one hundred million dollars a year. Of course, the money could be spent in various ways (increased appropriation for coast defenses, the navy, pensions, river and harbor improvements, and so forth) or it could be used to reduce the national debt of over a billion dollars. But Cleveland was opposed to spending the people's money for the sake of getting rid of it; and to pay off the debt by repurchasing the national bonds would not only encourage speculation in the bonds but also remove the basis for the national-bank notes (p. 438) which were needed for the expanding business of the country. Therefore the surplus must be reduced not by paying more out of the Treasury but by taking less in. And the tariff was the point of Cleveland's attack, not only because it was by far the largest source of the government's income (there being as yet no income tax) but because it was a government favor to the manufacturing class.

Cleveland began his fight on the tariff in his first message to Congress (1885) and devoted his entire annual message of 1887 to the subject. Against the manufacturers' plea that the high tariff made high wages possible, he contended that it was more to the point that the high tariff made high prices possible. He showed that of the 17,392,099 workers who were engaged in all industries according to the census of 1880, only 2,623,089 were employed in protected industries. The other 85 per cent of the workers were burdened with artificial taxes on almost all the necessities of life without any compensation in the shape of increased wages. It was not until July, 1888, that Cleveland was able to get the Mills Bill through the House, reducing the tariff by 6 or 7 per cent and putting a number of new articles on the free list. But the Republican Senate took no notice of the Mills Bill, and the tariff rates remained unchanged

The Campaign of 1888. The reason why the Senate ignored the Mills Bill is plain. The national nominating conventions had been held while the bill was being debated in the House, and the Republican platform had pronounced squarely for the maintenance of the high protective tariff. The issue would be fought out at the polls and not in Congress. Blaine, who was traveling in Europe, had attacked Cleveland's "free trade" policy in a long cablegram from Paris, and might easily have had the nomination at Chicago. But, being unwilling to undertake the strenuous work of another campaign in his rather poor state of health, he resolutely declined the honor. At his suggestion the convention selected from the dozen "favorite sons" who were seeking the nomination General Benjamin Harrison of Indiana, a United States Senator, an able lawyer, an honored veteran of the Civil War, and a grandson of the old Whig President, William Henry Harrison. Cleveland was renominated by acclamation by the Democratic convention at St. Louis. The campaign was waged almost wholly on the tariff issue and was happily free from the disgusting personal abuse which had marked the contest of 1884. The Republicans concentrated their efforts on the two "doubtful" states of Indiana and New York, both of which had gone for Cleveland in 1884. They carried the former state by a liberal use of campaign funds, and the latter by the opposition of the highly protected manufacturing interests to Cleveland's tariff policy. These two states (the only ones that shifted their vote of four years before) were enough to give the victory to Harrison by an electoral vote of 233 to 168. Cleveland's popular vote, however, exceeded Harrison's by more than 100,000.

GROVER CLEVELAND   BENJAMIN HARRISON

The New Administration. Benjamin Harrison was not a leader of the "magnetic" type, like Clay, Jackson, Blaine, or Roosevelt. His reserved manner, his disapproval of the scramble for political appointments, and his scorn for the arts of cultivating popularity gave him the reputation of being an austere and frigid person. Moreover, he belonged to that type of President who takes the title "Chief Executive" quite literally — that is, who regards it as the duty of the President to "execute," or carry out, the laws which Congress makes, rather than to urge legislation upon Congress. Consequently the figure of Harrison recedes somewhat into the background behind the brilliant and aggressive Blaine, who had recommended him for the nomination and had received in return the first place in the cabinet; and masterful men in Congress, rather than the formal chief in the White House, shaped the policy of the administration.

When Harrison's Congress met in December, 1889, it was the first time in fifteen years that the Republicans had had a clear majority in both houses. This meant that the deadlock in the legislature which had yielded but two laws of first-rate importance in a decade (the Civil Service Act of 1883 and the Interstate Commerce Act of 1887) was broken. The session of

1889–1891 produced a remarkable amount of legislation, thanks largely to the forceful management of the House by its Speaker, Thomas B. Reed of Maine. This big, jovial man, with a drawling voice and a gift for stinging sarcasm, was determined not to let the Democrats obstruct the business of the House. When they refused to answer the roll call in order to prevent the formation of a quorum, he counted them present just the same, even though they took refuge in the corridor, the coatroom, or the barber shop. When they made motions intended to delay business, he ruled them out of order. The Democrats raged and stormed, even rushing up to the Speaker's desk to shake their fists in his face and call him "Czar" and "tyrant"; but he waited smilingly for the hubbub to cease and then went on with the order of the day. The Republican House adopted the Reed rules in February, 1890; and when the Democrats regained control of the House, five years later, they paid "Czar Reed" the compliment of keeping his rules in force.

The Republican Reaction. Although the election of 1888 gave the Republicans only a narrow majority in Congress and actually registered a Cleveland victory in the popular vote, the Republicans proceeded to reverse the entire policy of the Cleveland administration. They were not troubled by the surplus in the Treasury: there were plenty of ways to spend it. They revived the Dependent Pension Bill which Cleveland had vetoed (p. 489), with the result that the applications for pensions rose from 36,000 in 1889 to 363,000 in 1891, and the expenditures for pensions increased during Harrison's administration from $81,000,000 to $135,000,000 annually — a sum greater than the combined cost of the army and navy in any year of peace in the nineteenth century. The new Secretary of the Navy, Benjamin Tracy of New York, pushed the work begun under President Arthur on the construction of our "White Squadron." We had but three steel vessels in commission at the close of Cleveland's administration, and were practically without modern coast defenses. But before the end of Harrison's term nineteen ironclads were put into commission. The first-class battleship *Oregon* was authorized in June, 1890, to be followed by the

Massachusetts, the *Indiana*, and the *Iowa*. Altogether, appropriations for the navy reached $30,000,000 under Harrison, and our country advanced from the twelfth to the fifth place among the naval powers of the world. At the same time large sums were appropriated for coast defenses, lighthouses, harbor improvements, and Federal buildings.

The expenditures of Harrison's first Congress mounted to $1,000,000,000; and when the Democrats cried out against the "billion-dollar Congress," Speaker Reed quietly replied that this was a "billion-dollar country." Indeed, the Eleventh Census (1890), compiled in twenty-five volumes, revealed the astonishing prosperity of the United States at the end of its first century under the Constitution. Our population was 62,500,000, and our national wealth $65,000,000,000. During the decade of the 1880's the products of our mills and factories had increased from $5,300,000,000 to $9,300,000,000, and the number of wage-earners from 2,700,000 to 4,300,000. The most important feature of our industrial growth was the concentration of capital in the hands of fewer and fewer establishments. The number of manufacturing plants was decreasing, but the size and capitalization and output of products in each unit was rapidly increasing.[1] This tended to the monopoly (or control) of industry in the hands of the big-business corporations, or "trusts," as they began to be called.

The Sherman Antitrust Act. The protest against monopoly grew stronger every year. Henry George attacked the monopoly of land in his *Progress and Poverty*, and Henry D. Lloyd's *Story of a Great Monopoly* exposed the methods of the Standard Oil Company. Investigations into the conduct of the oil, sugar, and beef trusts led to a demand for action by Congress to protect business against "unlawful restraint and monopoly." Of

---

[1] For example, the number of leather factories declined 70 per cent in the decade 1880–1890, while the product of leather increased over 500 per cent. There were 1943 plants engaged in the manufacture of agricultural machinery in 1880 and but 910 plants in 1890; yet the capital invested in this industry had more than doubled in the decade. The same story of concentration and consolidation could be told of the textile mills, the sugar refineries, the liquor distilleries, the meat-packing houses, and so forth (compare page 460).

course, the Republican party, which profited most by the contributions of big business to its campaign funds, was not eager to "curb the trusts." Blaine declared that business was a purely private affair with which the government had no right to meddle. It was not until a dozen states had passed laws against monopolies that Congress at last acted on the mild suggestion of President Harrison, in his first annual message, that it might consider "how far the restraint of those combinations of capital called 'trusts' is a matter of federal jurisdiction."

On July 2, 1890, Congress passed the Sherman Antitrust Act, declaring that "every contract, combination . . . or conspiracy in restraint of trade" was illegal, and punishing with a fine of five thousand dollars or a year's imprisonment any violation of the law. But the terms "combination," "conspiracy," "restraint," were all capable of such different interpretations by clever corporation lawyers that the Sherman Law remained a dead letter. Seven of the first eight cases tried under it in the courts resulted in a victory for the corporations. The trusts grew more rapidly than ever. From the Civil War to 1890 there had been organized only 24 large corporations, with a total capital of less than $450,000,000; but in the ten years following the Sherman Act 157 new trusts were formed, with a capitalization of over $3,000,000,000.

The McKinley Tariff. The Sherman Antitrust Act was a concession which the Republicans made to public opinion; but the McKinley Tariff Act, passed the same year, was their chief pride. They had won the election on a platform endorsing high protection, and they proceeded to prove their argument that a protective tariff was a benefit to the businessman, the laborer, and the farmer alike. In April, 1890, William McKinley of Ohio, chairman of the Ways and Means Committee of the House, introduced a bill increasing the duties on practically every article that competed with American production — food, clothing, furniture, carpets, fuel, tools, kitchenware, thread, etc. Articles of necessity which were not produced in our country, such as tea, coffee, spices, and drugs, were admitted free. Sugar was also put on the free list, but a bounty of two cents a pound was to be paid to our producers of raw sugar so that they could compete with the more cheaply raised sugar of Cuba and Hawaii in selling to the refiners. McKinley boasted that his bill was "protective in every paragraph and American in every line and word," but it met opposition not only from the Democrats but even from certain Republican quarters.

Secretary of State Blaine had resumed the policy begun under Garfield of bringing the United States and the countries of Latin America into a closer commercial union (p. 483). We had but 8 per cent of the $600,000,000 foreign trade of these countries, and Blaine was convinced that we could have 80 per cent of that trade if we adopted the policy of "reciprocity," that is, of admitting their products to our country free of duty in exchange for the opening of their markets to our goods. Reciprocity was opposed by the orthodox high protectionists, who feared that it would be an entering wedge for free trade. But Blaine wrote letters to the President and the Senators and even appeared in person before the Finance Committee of the Senate to urge his views. The bill as it stood, he said, would not open the South American markets to a barrel of our pork or a bushel of our wheat; if passed thus, it would protect the party "into speedy retirement." After a long fight Blaine got his reciprocity provision into the bill.

Another check to the bill came from the Western Senators. In November, 1889, the states of North and South Dakota, Montana, and Washington were admitted to the Union, and Wyoming and Idaho were added the next year. These new states were expected to contribute ten Senators and five or six Representatives to the slim Republican majority in Congress and to furnish as many electoral votes for the Republican column in the next Presidential election. But they brought embarrassment as well as strength to the party; for they were mining states, and their new Senators demanded that "something must be done for silver" before they would support the McKinley tariff. We shall note in the next paragraph the concession that was made to them to get their votes. Finally, the Southern Senators were ready to make an alliance with the

Westerners to kill the McKinley bill unless all further attempts of the Republicans to control the elections in the South were abandoned.[1] The bill had passed the House on May 21, 1890, by a strict party vote; but before all these difficulties in the Senate could be smoothed out, the summer had passed. It was not until the first of October, only thirty-five days before the mid-term elections, that the bill was finally signed by President Harrison.

The Sherman Silver-Purchase Act. The most serious threat to the McKinley bill came from the "silverites," who comprised about one seventh of the Senate, although they represented states which had but one fortieth of our population. Since the Bland-Allison Act of 1878 our government had for a dozen years been purchasing silver at the rate of two million dollars a month, and yet the price of the metal had steadily declined, owing to the immense production of the mines. The agitation for the free coinage of silver at the ratio of sixteen to one was kept up continually; and the Senate, in June, 1890, actually passed an amendment to that effect, which was killed in the House only by the heroic efforts of Speaker Reed. Now (July 4, 1890), partly to head off the danger of free silver and partly to get the necessary votes to pass the McKinley bill, the Republicans agreed to purchase four and a half million ounces of silver a month, or more than double the amount of the Bland-Allison Act, and to issue money (the silver certificates) to the full amount of the silver purchased. But even this generous purchase of silver by the government failed to keep up its price, and the Treasury found itself storing an accumulating stock of silver bullion which was constantly declining in value.

---

[1] The Republicans, after capturing the Presidency and both branches of Congress in 1888, made a last attempt to enforce the laws passed in Grant's administration to maintain their party's strength in the South. On July 2, 1890, the House passed a Federal Election Bill, providing that, on the application of five hundred voters in any district, supervisors from Washington should have the right to inspect and verify the votes cast in a Federal election. The South immediately protested that they would allow no interference with the white man's rule; and when the Southern Senators joined the Westerners to block the tariff legislation, the Republicans gave way and dropped the Federal Election bill (August 16). Thus ended the futile attempt of twenty years to enforce a policy which ran counter to the public sentiment of a large section of the country.

The Democratic Landslide of 1890. Whenever a party passes a number of important laws, it makes trouble for itself by inviting criticism at many points from the opposing party. For example, the great number of measures for the regulation of banking, industry, agriculture, and labor put through Congress by President Franklin D. Roosevelt in 1933 furnished the Republicans with ammunition for attacks on his administration all along the line in 1936. It was so with the Republican legislation of 1890. The extravagance of the "billion-dollar Congress," the "tyranny" of "Czar Reed," the pension bills, the appropriations for rivers, harbors, and coast defenses, the silver legislation, all offered "talking points" against the Harrison regime. Most serious of all was the McKinley tariff. During the whole summer while the bill was being debated in the Senate, the Democrats were making dire predictions of the ruin which would overtake the country if the bill passed. Peddlers were even sent into the country districts to sell pots and pans to the housewives at high prices, which they said were necessitated by the new tariff. The women shoppers in the stores, said Reed, "heard the clerks behind the counter explain how this article or that would not be sold hereafter at the former price, because of the McKinley bill; then they went home and told their husbands, and their stories had a tremendous effect at the ballot boxes." The election of November 6 brought one of those complete defeats of the party in power that are known as "landslides." The Democrats returned 235 members to the House, and the Republicans but 88. McKinley himself, after seven consecutive terms, was defeated for re-election. For the remaining two years of Harrison's term nothing in the way of legislation could be accomplished. All interest in those years centered in the foreign policy of Secretary Blaine.

The Bering Sea Controversy. Blaine had inherited from the Cleveland administration a dispute with Great Britain over the seal fisheries in Bering Sea. Our claim was that Bering Sea, which was almost entirely enclosed by Alaska and the Aleutian Islands, was a *mare clausum* (closed sea) appertaining to Alaska and hence under the jurisdiction of the United States, like

THE SAMOAN QUARREL[1]

Chesapeake Bay, for example. The British claimed that Bering Sea was the "high sea," over which our authority extended only to the ordinary three-mile limit from the shore. Attempts to settle the question by an international conference for the protection of the seals, which were being rapidly exterminated by the hunters of British Columbia, failed through the opposition of the Canadian government. Blaine kept up a spirited and insistent correspondence on the subject with the British prime minister, Lord Salisbury, who was equally insistent on not rec-

[1] From a cartoon by J. Keppler in *Puck*, February 6, 1889.

ognizing our right to police Bering Sea or to dictate to Great Britain what were the proper methods of seal-hunting. After three years of argument and protest we agreed on February 29, 1892, to submit the question to arbitration. The tribunal which met at Paris the next year decided against the claims of the United States. Bering Sea was declared to be the high sea, beyond our jurisdiction, and we were assessed $473,000 damages for our seizures of British vessels therein.

Quarrels with Germany, Italy, and Chile. Blaine was intensely interested in extending our influence in the Pacific. In his first occupancy of the State Department (1881) he had intervened to keep England from securing a dominant position in the Hawaiian Islands, which he declared to be "a part of the American system." Now he came into conflict with the German chancellor, Prince Bismarck, who was attempting to establish a German protectorate over the Samoan Islands. In the strife between rival chieftains the German consul raised his flag over Apia, and German sailors trampled the American flag in the streets of the town. British, American, and German warships were assembled in the harbor of Apia, with their decks cleared for the clash which threatened, when a terrific hurricane struck them (March 16, 1889), capsizing or driving on the coral reefs every vessel except the British cruiser *Calliope*, which valiantly fought her way to the open sea. Sobered by this disaster, the powers agreed upon a conference at Berlin, in which Bismarck, after considerable blustering, consented to a joint protectorate of the three powers in the island.[1]

A dispute with Italy arose in the spring of 1891, when eleven Italians were taken by a mob from the city jail in New Orleans and lynched for the murder of the chief of police, who had been active in suppressing the "Mafia," a secret band of Italian desperadoes. The Italian government demanded that the United

[1] The agreement lasted for ten years, of constant bickering, until in 1899 Great Britain withdrew from Samoa in return for concessions in Africa, and the islands were divided between Germany and the United States. We still retain Tutuila, with the harbor of Pago Pago, which was ceded to us as early as 1872. The German share of the islands, on the dissolution of the German colonial empire after the World War, became a mandate of the British dominion of New Zealand.

States authorities punish the lynchers; and when Blaine rather tartly replied that in our system of government the state and not the Federal authorities dealt with criminal cases, diplomatic relations between the two countries were severed. However, President Harrison adopted a conciliatory tone, expressing his regret for the "deplorable incident" at New Orleans and our "respect and friendship for the people of Italy." When it turned out that only three of the murdered men were Italian citizens, King Humbert accepted with thanks the twenty-five thousand dollars voted by Congress for the families of the victims, and diplomatic relations were cordially resumed.

The most serious of our foreign quarrels was with the republic of Chile. In January, 1891, civil war broke out in Chile between President Balmaceda and the Congressional Party. Patrick Egan, our minister to Chile, was a "Blaine Irishman," disliked by the influential English and German residents, who were supporting the Congressionalists against Balmaceda. In his zeal for the defeated Balmaceda, Egan, upheld by Secretary Blaine, drew upon the United States the hostility of the Congressionalists. On October 16, 1891, a number of American sailors on shore leave from the cruiser *Baltimore* were set upon by a mob in the streets of Valparaiso and viciously stoned, clubbed, and stabbed. Two were killed and eighteen severely wounded. When the Chilean government not only refused to heed our demands for an apology but even put the blame for the affray on the Americans, Harrison sent a special message to Congress on January 25, 1892, which was virtually an invitation to declare war on Chile. Our navy yards on both coasts were busy day and night. A squadron of eight cruisers was ready in the Pacific. War and peace hung in the balance. Then the Chilean government yielded to the show of superior force, apologized for the offensive language of their foreign minister toward our President, and paid an indemnity of seventy-five thousand dollars to the families of the killed and wounded sailors.

The Passing of Blaine. Blaine's popularity was enhanced by his vigorous administration of the State Department. While some censured him for his sharp language, the man in the street was

BLAINE AS "BULL IN THE CHINA SHOP"[1]

delighted when he "twisted the British lion's tail," declared that the German chancellor's irritability was no measure of American rights, and warned the Italian minister that the United States would take no advice from a foreign government as to what its duties and responsibilities were. As early as the summer of 1890 Blaine was put forward for the Presidential nomination in 1892, with the prediction that he would carry the country by "a phenomenal majority." He gave no support to the movement himself, declaring emphatically early in 1892 that he was not a candidate. However, three days before the Republican convention at Minneapolis (June 4, 1892) he resigned his cabinet position in a curt note to the President. His motives have never been fully known. Illness, family bereavement, lack of sympathy with his chief, an eleventh-hour desire for the Presidency, have all been advanced as causes of his action. At any rate he let his name go before the convention, in which he received only 182 votes to 535 for Harrison on the first ballot. He retired to his Maine home much broken in health, and died in

[1] From a cartoon by Thomas Nast.

Washington a few weeks before the close of Harrison's administration (January 27, 1893).

Blaine's character is one of the hardest to estimate in all our history. He was brilliant, able, genial, and brave. The American people made an idol of him, but they did not quite trust him. There were too many incidents in his career that called for apologies and explanations. He could be mercilessly clear in his exposure of others, but he never could wholly dispel the fog that hung about his own dealings with the railroads, the Peruvian guano claims, and the political spoilsmen. He missed the highest honor of the Republic, for which he was a prominent contender in five successive Presidential campaigns from 1876 to 1892. On the whole he was the most conspicuous political leader from Abraham Lincoln to Theodore Roosevelt.

TERMS TO BE MASTERED

patronage	free coinage	reciprocity
"Stalwarts"	"Mugwumps"	high seas .
"spoils system"	watered stock	indemnity

FOR SUPPLEMENTARY READING

J. F. RHODES, *History of the United States from Hayes to McKinley*, chaps. i–xvii; H. T. PECK, *Twenty Years of the Republic*, chaps. i–v; H. J. FORD, *The Cleveland Era* (Chronicles of America, Vol. XLIV); ALLAN NEVINS, *Grover Cleveland, A Study in Courage*, chaps. x–xxiv; D. S. MUZZEY, *James G. Blaine, A Political Idol of Other Days*, chaps. vi–xvi; C. R. FISH, *The Civil Service and the Patronage* (Harvard Historical Studies, Vol. IX), pp. 209–245; IDA TARBELL, *The Tariff in Our Times*, chap. viii; H. C. THOMAS, *The Return of the Democratic Party to Power in 1884* (Columbia University Studies, Vol. LXXXIX); ALICE F. TYLER, *The Foreign Policy of James G. Blaine*; LOUIS ADAMIC, *Dynamite, the Story of Class Violence*; H. S. COMMAGER, *Documents of American History*, Vol. II, pp. 97–133; The Pageant of America, Vol. IX, pp. 106–192; HART, *Contemporaries*, Vol. IV, Nos. 160–177; MUZZEY, *Readings*, pp. 494–526.

TOPICS FOR REPORTS

1. **Civil-Service Reform.** THEODORE ROOSEVELT, *American Ideals and Other Essays*, No. VII; JAMES BRYCE, *The American Commonwealth*, Vol. II, chap. lxv; F. M. STEWART, *The National Civil Service Reform League*; W. D. FOULKE, *Fighting the Spoilsmen*; G. W. CURTIS, *Orations and Addresses*, Vol. II, pp. 477 f.; text of act of 1883 in Commager, Vol. II, pp. 111–113.

2. **The Exclusion of Chinese Immigrants.** E. P. OBERHOLTZER, *History of the United States since the Civil War*, Vol. IV, chap. xxviii; E. E. SPARKS, *National Development* (American Nation Series, Vol. XXIII), pp. 229–250; MARY R. COOLIDGE, *Chinese Immigration*; S. P. ORTH, *Our Foreigners* (Chronicles of America, Vol. XXXV), chap. ix; LUCILE EAVES, *California Labor Legislation*, chaps. iii–vi; COMMAGER, Vol. II, pp. 109–111.

3. **For and against a Third Term for Grant.** EDWARD STANWOOD, *History of the Presidency*, Vol. I, chap. xxvi; T. C. SMITH, *The Life and Letters of James Abram Garfield*, Vol. II, pp. 953–984; ADAM BADEAU, *Grant in Peace*, pp. 319 f.; series of articles for and against a third term in the *North American Review*, Vol. CXXX, pp. 116, 197, 224, 370.

4. **"Czar" Reed.** MARY P. FOLLETT, *The Speaker of the House of Representatives*, pp. 179–216; W. A. ROBINSON, *Thomas B. Reed, Parliamentarian*, chaps. ix–xii; H. J. FORD, *The Cleveland Era* (Chronicles of America, Vol. XLIV), pp. 86–107; EVERETT KIMBALL, *The National Government of the United States*, pp. 333–342; D. S. ALEXANDER, *History and Procedure of the House of Representatives*, pp. 155–212; T. B. REED, "Reed's Rules," in *North American Review*, Vol. CLII, pp. 148–156.

QUESTIONS SUGGESTED BY THE CHAPTER

1. Why was the Republican party so strong after the Civil War? **2.** What was James Bryce's opinion of American parties? **3.** Why was Hayes unpopular with the "Stalwarts"? **4.** Why did Hayes veto the silver act of 1878? **5.** What did Hayes do to improve the civil service? **6.** What is meant by the "crime of '73"? **7.** Under what clause of the Constitution does the government regulate the railroads? **8.** Why was Cleveland unpopular with the Grand Army of the Republic? **9.** Why should not the government have used its surplus in the 1880's to pay off the national debt? **10.** Contrast Cleveland's and Harrison's policy of dealing with the surplus in the Treasury. **11.** What were the arguments for the exclusion of the Chinese? **12.** Why did Blaine quarrel with President Arthur? **13.** Why did many Republicans desert Blaine in the election of 1884? **14.** Name three causes which contributed to Blaine's defeat in 1884. **15.** What was the cause of the Haymarket riot? **16.** How do you account for the large amount of legislation in 1890? **17.** Compare the silver acts of 1878 and 1890 in respect to (a) the amount of silver bought and (b) what was done with it. **18.** When was the last attempt made to enforce the Fourteenth and Fifteenth Amendments? **19.** What new states were added to the Union in Harrison's administration? How many are there in the Union now? Are there likely to be any more? **20.** What delayed the passage of the McKinley tariff bill so long? **21.** Name three controversies with foreign nations when Blaine was Secretary of State in the Harrison administration. **22.** Contrast Blaine and Cleveland.

For rise of parties + use of
minority parties see Scholastic
April 15, 40

CHAPTER TWENTY

〖⌒〗

THE RISING OF THE WEST

A Change of Scene. While the politicians at Washington were wrangling over tariff, currency, and trust legislation, and the parties were impressing Mr. Bryce with the idea that they existed mainly for the purpose of getting into office when they were out and staying in when they were in, an important movement was gathering to a head in the South and West. In thousands of country schoolhouses and town halls groups of farmers, labor agitators, free-silverites, men burdened with mortgages on their homes and impoverished by the decline in the prices of their crops, were meeting to denounce the tyranny of the bankers and capitalists of the East and to demand that the government pay some attention to the distress of the most numerous classes of the people, namely the farmers and laborers, on whose toil the prosperity of the country was built. They accused both Republican and Democratic leaders of indifference to their needs, and deserted the ranks of the old parties by the thousands to join new organizations such as the Farmers' Alliance, the Agricultural Wheel, the Corn-growers' Association, and the People's Party, to fight for relief from debt and despair. At first they were ignored by the politicians in the seats of power or scornfully dismissed as "wild-eyed revolutionists," "leather-lunged orators," and "political rain-makers." But as their numbers grew and they began to make their way into the state legislatures and into Congress, fear took the place of ridicule in the minds of the Eastern conservatives, and sectional hostility succeeded indifference and neglect. The government began to realize that it was no tempest in a teapot, caused by a few "wild-eyed revolutionists," but a storm of menacing violence that was rising in the West.

IMMIGRANTS FROM POLAND

The Western Land Boom. To understand that storm we must note the experience through which the agricultural West was passing in the decade of the 1880's. Encouraged by the homestead grants, the opening of new lines of railroads, the flood of immigrants from Europe, and the return of good times after the panic of 1873–1878, a stream of settlers had poured into the states west of the Missouri. The population of Kansas was 364,000 in 1870; by 1890 it had reached 1,427,000. Nebraska grew from 122,000 to 1,508,000; Dakota Territory, from 14,000 to 511,000. "A territory greater than the original area of the United States was peopled in half a dozen years," wrote Senator Peffer of Kansas in the *Forum* of December, 1889. A spirit of unbounded optimism seized upon the settlers. Mr. Bryce, who made a trip to the great wheat lands over the newly completed Northern Pacific Railroad in 1883, wrote: "The confidence of these Westerners is superb. Men seem to live in the future rather than in the present. . . . They see the country not merely as it is but as it will be twenty, fifty or a hundred years hence."

Every little hamlet saw itself becoming a metropolis with paved streets, tall business buildings, a marble-columned opera house, and rows of sumptuous private mansions. Speculation in land ran riot. In Wichita, Kansas, during the summer of 1887 a real-estate boom, like those of Los Angeles and Miami in the 1920's, threw the little town into a fever of excitement. Lots bought for a few hundred dollars sold for as many thousand two months later, and the transactions for the summer totaled over thirty million dollars. The farmer as well as the townsman bought land in June to sell at double the price in August. Then, too, exceptionally abundant rain in the middle 1880's tempted him to extend his acres westward beyond the safe average line of sufficient rainfall; and when Nature restored the balance by a succession of dry years, he was "starved back." Between 1886 and 1890 the corn crop shrank over $70,000,000. The farms in western Kansas and Nebraska were abandoned by the thousands as wagons carrying the disappointed families and their goods streamed eastward to the Missouri River.

The Farmer's Grievances. The causes of the farmer's distress were various. (1) The best homestead lands were so rapidly taken up in the boom years that the census of 1890 made the fateful announcement that the American frontier had ceased to exist. (2) The enormous production of grain, cotton, hogs, and cattle created a surplus for export which had to compete with the falling prices in the world market. (3) The mortgages on farm property rose from $343,000,000 to $586,000,000 in the decade 1880-1890, until they covered 60 per cent of the farms in Kansas, 55 per cent in Nebraska, and 47 per cent in Iowa. And the demand of the bankers for the payment of the interest and renewal charges on these mortgages in dollars that had the value of two bushels of wheat instead of one seemed to the farmer like a deliberate plot to keep him in the mire of debt.

The farmer's grievance against Wall Street was intensified when he learned how rival speculators were wrecking the railroads which should have been used only for the service of the public. The bankers enjoyed a sort of partnership with the government, a partnership which dated from the days of Alex-

ander Hamilton. For example, a group of bankers, by
National Banking Act of 1863, could buy, say, $1,000,000
government bonds, on which they received 6 per cent interest
in gold, or $60,000. Then they could get, from the Treasury,
bank notes up to the value of 90 per cent of the bonds, and lend
these notes (or credit) to business men or farmers, making another $60,000 or more on their original investment of $1,000,000.
The manufacturers were benefited by the protective tariff.
Organized labor was helped by the restriction on the immigration of contract gangs and Chinese coolies. Only the farmer,
once the choice homesteads were taken up, seemed to get no
favors from the government. He was the Cinderella in the
national family.

The Farmer's Demands. Ever since colonial days there had
been a difference in economic interest, and consequently a
political rivalry, between the settlers who remained in the commercial and industrial centers of the Atlantic seaboard and the
pioneers who went westward to begin life anew beyond the
Alleghenies and beyond the Mississippi. It was the latter class
who had cleared the dense forests, braved the Indians, and
developed those traits of courage, self-reliance, inventiveness,
and optimism which were regarded as truly American. "Europe
extends to the Alleghenies; America lies beyond," wrote Ralph
Waldo Emerson. The descendants of these pioneers now asked
for their due share of the prosperity which they had done so
much to create. We have seen how, when the pinch of poverty
came in the 1870's, they fought as farmers for fair rates from
the railroads and elevators and as debtors for a cheaper currency (pp. 466-470). It was not until the distressing conditions
of the later 1880's, however, that their protests became sufficiently widespread and well organized to cause alarm in the old
political parties.

The Farmer and the Laborer. At first the attempt was made
to unite the farmers and the laborers into a strong political
party, on the ground of their common interest in loosening the
hold of the money power on the government. In fact, the label
"Farmer-Labor" has been retained to the present day as a

party of protest. But the industrial wage-
st and the independent farmer of the West
nything in common. The former was inter-
ges, shorter hours of work, and the right of
in with the employer. He lived from hand to
ay envelope, and, having no property in land,
cared little about its price or distribution. The farmer, on the
other hand, was not concerned with wages, since he and his
family did the work, with only occasional hired "hands." His
hours of labor were prescribed for him by Nature and not by a
"boss." He sold not his time but his produce, and therefore
he was interested in rates of transportation. He labored under
a constant burden of mortgage debt, and hence wanted lower
interest charges. In short, the grievances of the farmer and the
laborer, though both were real, were not alike. They combined
no better than oil and water. Some "labor planks" were kept
in the platforms of the agrarian parties, to be sure, such as the
demand for an eight-hour day and the restriction of immigration ;
but more and more the Western malcontents put their emphasis
upon demands for the relief of the farmer and debtor. The newly
founded American Federation of Labor (p. 465) would take no
part in the agrarian movement, because the farmers were not
wage-earners ; and the Farmer-Labor convention at St. Louis
in 1889, which called for the union of "the organized toilers
and the organized tillers," was attended by only three delegates
from the Knights of Labor.

The Populist Party. The convention at St. Louis was but one
of a series of protest meetings which led to the formation of the
Populists, or "People's party." In May, 1891, it held at Cincinnati a convention of over fourteen hundred delegates from
thirty-two states, including Knights of Labor, free-silverites,
Greenbackers, members of the Farmers' Alliance, and enemies
of the banks, the railroads, the trusts, and the tariff.[1] It invited

[1] The conservative papers of the old parties compared the Cincinnati convention
to the Cave of Adullam, mentioned in the first book of Samuel, Chapter XXII,
where "everyone that was in distress and everyone that was in debt and everyone
that was discontented gathered themselves."

all progressives to meet in conference early in 1892 in order to call a national convention of the People's party for the nomination of a Presidential ticket.

The Southern Populists. The farmers and cotton-growers of the South were in sympathy with the Westerners in their fight against the monopoly of the moneylenders and the railroads. Indeed, the Farmers' Alliance and the Agricultural Wheel had originated in the South, where a great change was taking place in the social order. The old leisurely planter class, ruined by the war, lost influence to small farmers and the workers in the new industries, like lumbering, cotton-spinning, and iron-smelting. The wage-earners in the South increased 200 per cent in the decade 1880–1890, and the mills in the Carolinas spun half the cotton raised in those states. Birmingham, Alabama, was fast rising as "the Pittsburgh of the South" in the production of iron and steel. A symbol of the social shift was the victory of the farmers' and laborers' champion, "Pitchfork Ben" Tillman, over the old cavalier planter General Wade Hampton in the election for governor of South Carolina in 1890.

In spite of their agreement with the Populist demands, however, the Southerners were opposed to the formation of a new Populist party. Their first concern was for the preservation of white supremacy, which had been recovered at so great a cost after the Civil War and which was still being threatened by the attempt of some Northerners to enforce the Fourteenth and Fifteenth Amendments.[1] Therefore they worked *within* the Democratic party, trying to get control of its primaries. When the Populists, in spite of their opposition, did put a third party in the field in 1892, Alabama was the only Southern state that

[1] To offset this threat most of the Southern states, beginning with Mississippi in 1890, framed new constitutions to exclude the Negroes from the polls on other grounds than "race, color, or previous condition of servitude." The famous "grandfather clause" of the Louisiana constitution of 1898, for example, after prescribing educational and tax qualifications for voting which shut out practically all the Negroes (reducing their registration from 127,000 in 1896 to 5300 in 1900), restored the ballot to the poor and illiterate whites by exempting from the qualifications any person or the descendant of any person who had had the vote previous to the year 1867. In 1915 the Supreme Court declared the grandfather clause unconstitutional.

gave as much as 30 per cent of its vote to the new ticket. The Southerners were Democrats first and Populists second.

The Omaha Platform. No more dismal picture of the condition of America was ever drawn (at least until the days of the great depression just forty years later) than that presented by the Populists in the platform of their national convention at Omaha, Nebraska, July 4, 1892. They declared:

> We meet in the midst of a nation brought to the very verge of moral, political and material ruin. Corruption dominates the ballot box, the legislature, the Congress, and even touches the ermine of the bench. . . . Business is prostrated; our homes covered with mortgages; labor impoverished; and the land concentrated in the hands of capitalists. . . . The fruits of the toil of millions are boldly stolen to build up colossal fortunes for a few. . . . We have witnessed for more than a quarter of a century the struggles of the two great parties for power and plunder. . . . Neither do they now promise us any substantial reform. . . . They propose to sacrifice our homes, lives and children on the altar of mammon.

After this terrible indictment, the platform formulated the demands of the party: the free coinage of silver at the ratio of sixteen to one; the abolition of the national banks; a graduated income tax; government ownership of railroads, telegraphs, and telephones; the return to the government of unused lands granted to the railroads; restriction of immigration; an eight-hour day for labor; postal savings banks; a revenue tariff; and the election of United States Senators by a popular vote. General James B. Weaver of Iowa, the candidate of the Greenback-Labor party of 1880, was nominated for the Presidency.

The Election of 1892. The Republicans and the Democrats had held their conventions in June, the former renominating Harrison, in spite of the feeble attempt to stampede the convention to Blaine (p. 505), and the latter putting up Cleveland for the third successive time. Cleveland had alienated the machine politicians of the party by his courageous independence, and they tried, under the leadership of Governor David B. Hill of New York, to prevent his nomination; but he was so strong with the rank and file of the party that he won on the first ballot, with 617 votes to 114 for his nearest competitor, Hill. A strike in the Carnegie steel works at Homestead, Pennsylvania, in the summer of 1892, attended with violence and bloodshed, seriously damaged the cause of the Republicans, who were preaching the security and prosperity of labor under the McKinley tariff. The Democrats swept the country in the election of November, retaining their control of the House and winning a majority in the Senate, which they were not to have again until the inauguration of Woodrow Wilson in 1913.

Weaver carried the four states of Colorado, Kansas, Nevada, and Idaho, with 22 electoral votes to 277 for Cleveland and 145 for Harrison. But the Populist showing of a million popular votes was an exaggeration of the party's actual strength: first, because in several Western states the Democrats either had put no ticket in the field or had supported the Populist nominees; secondly, because Colorado, Idaho, and Nevada (the only states in which Weaver had more than 50 per cent of the vote) were carried by the silver interests rather than by the farmers' program. No state of the great industrial area east of the Mississippi and north of the Ohio gave Weaver as much as 5 per cent of its vote. Cleveland would have won the election by a large margin even if all the Weaver states had gone for Harrison. Yet the campaign showed that Populist influence had pervaded the West. The new party elected three United States Senators and eleven members of Congress; and it more than held its own in the mid-term elections of 1894, when the Republicans regained control of the House. In short, the Populists had leavened the Democratic party with radicalism, and in the next Presidential election, as we shall see, they completely captured the party.

The Plight of the Treasury. Grover Cleveland was faced with harassing problems when he was inaugurated for a second time on March 4, 1893. Business was poor. For the first time in fifteen years our exports fell below our imports, leaving a balance of $35,000,000 to be met in gold. Depreciated silver was accumulating in the Treasury vaults at the rate of about $50,000,000 a year (p. 500). Before the passage of the Sherman Silver Purchase Act of 1890 nearly 85 per cent of the customs duties were paid in gold, but by 1893 over 95 per cent of them were paid in silver. In those three years the Treasury lost $132,000,000 in gold, while the silver in its vaults increased by $147,000,000. Furthermore, foreign holders of our bonds, fearing that the radicals might get control of our government and force the payment of the bonds in silver, sent them back to America for gold while yet there was time. Banks and private individuals also hoarded gold, using the cheaper currency of silver certificates or greenbacks to pay their bills and taxes, until gold threatened to disappear from circulation.[1] An act of Congress in 1882 had provided that the Treasury keep on hand a fund of $100,000,000 in gold to "redeem" the greenbacks which might be presented for "specie payment." Now to the $346,000,000 in greenbacks there were being added $50,000,000 a year of silver certificates, for which the Treasury had also to pay gold if it was demanded. Thus in 1893 there was about $500,000,000 of paper money in circulation (increasing at the rate of $50,000,000 a year), all depending on the $100,000,000 gold reserve fund in the Treasury to keep its value on a "parity," or equality, with gold.

The Repeal of the Sherman Silver Act. Though Cleveland was interested mainly in renewing the battle for tariff reform, he regarded it as his first duty to preserve the credit of the government. For neither our businessmen at home nor the banking houses of Europe would have confidence in the United States so long as there was danger that we would not pay our obligations in gold. Therefore Cleveland called Congress to meet in extra session on August 7, 1893, and asked for an immediate repeal of the Sherman Act. He spoke of the distrust which pervaded all business circles and which threatened "to cripple our merchants, stop the wheels of manufacture, bring distress and privation to our farmers and withhold from our working men the wage of labor." The House readily voted for

[1] Sir Thomas Gresham, an official of the mint in the time of Queen Elizabeth, declared that when coins of different value were used for money, the cheaper kind would drive the more valuable one out of circulation. "Gresham's law" meant simply that people always pay in as cheap a medium as possible. If a man has a gold "dollar" worth one hundred cents and a silver "dollar" worth only seventy cents, he will keep the former and pay his bills with the latter.

the repeal, but there was a bitter contest in the Senate. Seven silver states of the West, representing but 2 per cent of the population of the country, sent fourteen of the eighty-eight Senators to Congress. These silver Senators, supported by the Populists and by the Southerners, who joined them in return for their help in defeating the "Force Bill" (p. 500, note 1), fought against the repeal of the Sherman Act until the end of October, when it was finally passed by the close vote of 48 to 37. Three fourths of the Republicans in the House and two thirds in the Senate voted for the repeal.

Tariff Reform is Defeated. Having thus put an end to the purchase of fifty million dollars' worth of depreciated silver a year by the government, Cleveland turned to the tariff. When the regular session of Congress convened in December, 1893, William L. Wilson of West Virginia introduced a bill for the removal of the duties on raw materials (wool, iron ore, coal, copper, sugar) and a considerable reduction in the duties on manufactures (china, glass, silk, cotton and woolen goods). The Wilson bill promptly passed the Democratic House by a vote of 182 to 106, but when it reached the Senate it met the fate of tariff bills generally. The "coal Senators" of West Virginia, the "iron Senators" of Alabama, the "sugar Senators" of Louisiana, the "wool Senators" of Ohio, all fought for the protection of their own interests. Under the lead of Senator Gorman of Maryland the bill was loaded with over six hundred amendments, which restored most of the McKinley rates. President Cleveland was so disgusted with the Wilson-Gorman bill, which he called a piece of "party perfidy and dishonor," that he refused to sign it. Still, because it contained a few reductions (like free wool and lumber) he did not veto it. It became a law (August, 1894) without his signature. Thus ended in defeat Cleveland's long struggle to secure a real reform of the tariff.

The Panic of 1893. An industrial depression in the summer of 1893 brought failures, strikes, and lockouts in its train. More than six hundred banks closed their doors, and the losses of eight thousand business houses that failed between April and October totaled nearly three hundred million dollars. Great railroad companies, such as the Erie and the Philadelphia and Reading, went into the hands of receivers. The worst of the panic was over by autumn; but it took the country many months to recover, and the winter was attended with great suffering. Tramps and vagrants swarmed over the land. An "army" of the unemployed, led by Jacob Coxey of Ohio, marched to Washington to demand that Congress issue five hundred million dollars in paper money, to be spent in furnishing work for the idle in road-building and similar projects. The invasion of Washington by "Coxey's army" ended in a farce. As the men marched across the lawn of the Capitol on May Day morning their leaders were arrested for "walking on the grass"; and the "army" straggled away, to be lost in the city crowd.

The Pullman Strike. There was nothing farcical, however, in the conflict between capital and labor which broke out in Chicago, that same month of May, when the workers in the Pullman Palace Car Company shops struck on account of a reduction in wages. About four thousand of the Pullman employees belonged to the American Railway Union, founded in 1893 under the presidency of Eugene V. Debs. The union, after a vain attempt to get Mr. Pullman to arbitrate, ordered its men not to "handle" Pullman cars. By July only six of the twenty-three railroads entering Chicago were operating freely. United States mail trains carrying Pullman cars were not allowed to move. President Cleveland sent troops to Chicago, and the Federal court issued an injunction[1] forbidding the strikers to interfere with the United States mails. The injunction was received with hoots and jeers. Debs had appealed to the strikers to refrain from violence; but they could not be restrained, especially as their ranks were swelled by thousands of vagrants and loafers who had been attracted to Chicago by the Columbian Exposi-

[1] An injunction is an order issued by a court, without a regular trial, forbidding some act which in the court's opinion would cause more harm than a regular trial could cure. Disobedience to an injunction is a kind of "contempt of court," which means, except where a special law to the contrary has been made, that the judge can punish it without a jury trial and without hearing witnesses according to the regular rules for witnesses. Since 1914 a law has required trial by jury for violations of certain classes of injunctions of Federal courts.

tion of the previous summer. Trains were ditched, freight cars destroyed, buildings looted and burned. At some points the Federal troops opened fire on the mob in order to protect their own lives. Debs and his chief associates were arrested for contempt of court in not obeying the injunction. The strike was broken by the drastic action of the government; but it left ugly consequences. The President was severely taken to task by Governor Altgeld of Illinois for sending Federal troops to quell the disorder when the state militia were fully able to handle the situation. The imprisonment of Debs by a court order, without jury trial or conviction, was denounced as "tyranny," and even in conservative circles there was criticism of "government by injunction" as a dangerous and unjust procedure.

The Morgan Bond Transaction. The repeal of the Sherman Act had, to be sure, stopped the inflow of depreciated silver into the Treasury but had not replenished the diminishing gold fund. It was like plugging a leak which had been flooding the kitchen floor, and now the floor had to be mopped up. The drain on the Treasury sent the gold reserve down to $70,000,000 before the close of 1893. Twice during the next year Secretary Carlisle sold $50,000,000 of bonds for gold, without helping matters any. In January, 1895, the reserve was down to what Cleveland called the "frightfully low" figure of $41,000,000. The explanation of this loss of gold is simple. As soon as the subscribers to the bonds had paid their gold into the Treasury, they drew it out again by presenting greenbacks or silver certificates to be exchanged for gold. To stop this "endless chain" of put in and take out, which left the government with no more gold but only with the interest debt on the millions of bonds that it had issued, Cleveland decided that he must find gold somewhere which would stay in the Treasury. Early in 1895 he summoned J. P. Morgan to the White House and made a "deal" with him, by which Morgan and his European associates agreed to furnish $62,000,000 in gold in return for 4 per cent government bonds. Morgan made a profit of over $4,000,000 on the sale of the bonds, and the cry went up from the Populists that Cleveland had entered into an unholy alliance with the bankers of New York and London. But if Morgan drove a hard bargain with the government, he at least supplied the needed gold for the Treasury when the public would not; and Cleveland always defended his transaction with Morgan as a proper move to save the country's credit. The next year, after the defeat of the free-silverites under William J. Bryan, confidence was restored and the gold came out of hiding. Before we describe the great battle between silver and gold, the West and the East, the plow-holder and the bondholder, however, we must notice two events in our foreign relations in Cleveland's second term.

The Hawaiian Revolution. The Hawaiian Islands, in the mid-Pacific, had for many decades been an object of special interest to the United States. American missionaries, merchants, and planters had been establishing families and fortunes in the islands ever since the days of Andrew Jackson. As early as 1854 there had been talk of annexing the islands to the United States. In January, 1893, a revolution occurred in Hawaii. The new queen, Liliuokalani, was deposed for attempting to overthrow the constitution, and a provisional government was set up with the help of marines landed from the American cruiser *Boston* in the harbor of Honolulu. The islands were declared a "protectorate" of the United States, and our flag was raised over the government building. A few days later a treaty of annexation was sent by President Harrison to the Senate for ratification (February 15, 1893); but before the Senate acted, Cleveland succeeded Harrison in the White House. Cleveland sent a special commissioner to Hawaii, whose report convinced him that our minister Stevens had acted illegally in encouraging the revolution. He withdrew the treaty from the Senate, ordered our flag to be lowered from the state building, and was ready to restore the queen to her throne on condition that she should pardon the revolutionists. When she replied that she would cut off their heads, Cleveland dropped the matter. The provisional government maintained itself without difficulty until the Republican administration which followed Cleveland annexed the Hawaiian Islands to the United States in July, 1898. Two years later Congress made them an organized territory and conferred American citizenship on their white inhabitants.

The Venezuela Boundary Dispute. If Cleveland was abused by a certain type of patriot for "hauling down the American flag" in Hawaii, he was criticized by a milder type for the belligerent vigor with which he defended the Monroe Doctrine against Great Britain's claim to some twenty-three thousand square miles of rich mineral country in South America. The land lay within territory which had been disputed for many years between British Guiana and the republic of Venezuela. Relying on the guarantee of the Monroe Doctrine to protect the Latin-American countries against encroachments by European powers, Venezuela begged the United States to defend her boundary line. Our State Department again and again asked Great Britain to arbitrate the matter, but was met with refusal. In February, 1895, Congress passed a joint resolution urging arbitration; and when Secretary of State Olney sent a sharp dispatch to London on July 20, declaring that the United States was "practically sovereign on this continent," and that we should "resent and resist any sequestration of Venezuelan soil by Great Britain," Lord Salisbury again replied in polite terms that the Monroe Doctrine was no part of international law and that the boundary dispute was none of our business. But the American people believed that the maintenance of the Monroe Doctrine *was* their business. In December, 1895, Cleveland sent a message to Congress recommending that we take the decision of the boundary line between British Guiana and Venezuela into our own hands, "fully alive to the responsibility incurred and keenly realizing all the consequences that may follow" — in other words, even at the risk of war with England. Congress adopted the President's advice by a unanimous vote, and appropriated one hundred thousand dollars for the expenses of a boundary commission. This action caused a wave of protest against war with their American kindred to sweep over Great Britain. A petition signed by three hundred and fifty members of Parliament was sent to Washington praying that the Christmas season might not be desecrated by preparations for war between the two great English-speaking peoples and asking that all disputes between them be settled by arbitration. Lord Salisbury gave way and even consented courteously to furnish the American commission with such papers as it needed. In January, 1897, Great Britain agreed to submit her entire claim to arbitration; and in October, 1899, the tribunal sitting at Paris determined (favorably, on the whole, to Great Britain's claim) the boundary line which had been in dispute for more than half a century.

Democratic Dissensions. The only thoroughly popular act of President Cleveland in his second administration was pushing the electric button which opened the Columbian Exposition, or World's Fair, at Chicago, on May Day, 1893. He had offended the industrialists of the East by his attack on the protective tariff, and the Populists of the West by his insistence on maintaining a gold basis for our currency. He had alienated organized labor by his forcible repression of the Pullman strike, and capital blamed him (as it always does the administration in power) for the panic which broke upon the country a month after his inauguration. The Republican victory in the mid-term elections of 1894 was attributed to his splitting his party on the issues of tariff, currency, and labor, and the radical Democrats accused him of being "a tool of Wall Street." Two decisions of the Supreme Court in the spring of 1895 added to the radical discontent. The Wilson-Gorman tariff (p. 517) had provided for a tax of 2 per cent on incomes above four thousand dollars, in order to make up for an anticipated loss of fifty million dollars in customs duties. The blanks for the income tax were all ready for distribution when the Supreme Court decided by a vote of five to four that such a tax, being a direct tax, could not be levied except in proportion to the population (Constitution, Art. I, Sect. 2, par. 3). A week later the Court, by a unanimous decision, upheld the injunction under which Debs had been imprisoned at the time of the Pullman strike (p. 518). For these decisions the Court was criticized by the radicals as the "rich man's ally," and the demand was made that it be deprived of the power to declare laws of Congress unconstitutional, or even that it be abolished altogether.

William J. Bryan. Among the Democratic Congressmen who lost their seats in the landslide of 1894 was a young lawyer from Lincoln, Nebraska, of remarkable oratorical powers, who was characterized by Cleveland as "a Populist pure and simple, without the remotest notion of the principles of Democracy." Bryan believed that the root of all the economic evils of the country was the dictatorship of Wall Street, which had control of the gold supply and insisted that gold should be the only standard of value. He devoted his energies to a crusade for the free coinage of silver, and went up and down the states of the West preaching his doctrine with unflagging zeal. He brushed aside the arguments of the trained economists. Their poisoned arrows of ridicule and abuse never penetrated his armor of righteous conviction. He was Martin Luther and William Lloyd Garrison rolled into one. His demand was that the government should buy any amount of silver that should be brought to the mint and make it legal currency at the rate of sixteen ounces of silver to one of gold. As sixteen ounces of silver were worth only about $11 in 1896, while an ounce of gold was worth $20.67, the free-silverites were asking that our government should sanction "dollars" that were worth only a little more than 50 cents. When it was pointed out that our government would lose its credit in the eyes of the world if it used a debased currency like Mexico or Turkey, they replied that the United States was rich and powerful enough to use whatever metal it pleased, without regard to what England, France, or Germany did. Moreover, they said, the supply of gold was not sufficient for the business of the country, and what there was of it was hoarded by the bankers to increase its value in terms of the farmers' products and the laborers' wages. The relief of the "common man," the masses, was more important than our reputation in the eyes of the foreign bankers.

Hanna and McKinley. At the same time there came into prominence a man who was the very opposite of Bryan in every respect. Marcus A. Hanna was a wealthy business man of Cleveland, Ohio. He believed that the welfare of the country depended on a close alliance between the government and "big

WILLIAM McKINLEY WILLIAM J. BRYAN

business." The prosperity of the farmer and the laborer was assured only by the prosperity of the capitalist. He favored a high protective tariff and a gold currency. Hanna was not ambitious for political honors himself, but gave his time and money generously to the advancement of Ohio statesmen who were in sympathy with his ideas. After backing John Sherman for the Presidential nomination in three conventions, he turned to William McKinley, to whom he became personally attached with a devotion which grew stronger until McKinley's death. When McKinley lost his seat in Congress in the landslide of 1890 (p. 501), it was largely through Hanna's efforts that he was elected governor of Ohio ; and a few years later he owed to the same friend his rescue from financial ruin. In 1894 Hanna gave up his large business interests to devote himself entirely to "grooming" McKinley for the Republican nomination two years later. Several months before the Convention met at St. Louis, June 16, 1896, he had enough delegates pledged to McKinley to secure his nomination on the first ballot, by a vote of 661 to 84 for his nearest competitor, ex-Speaker Thomas B. Reed, of Maine.

The "Cross of Gold." Bryan had been as diligent in recommending a platform for the Democrats as Hanna had been in grooming a candidate for the Republicans. In March, 1895, just as he was leaving Congress, he had secured the signatures of thirty-one members from the West and South to a manifesto inviting the radical Democrats, the Populists, the silverites, and the laborers to unite and seize control of the party, to "make it an instrument in the accomplishment of needed reform." The Democratic convention met at Chicago on July 7, 1896. It elected a free-silverite as chairman and adopted a platform endorsing the free coinage of silver at the ratio of sixteen to one. When conservatives like Governor Russell of Massachusetts and Senator Vilas of Wisconsin attempted to speak, they were shouted down by a howling mob. A motion commending the "honesty and courage" of President Cleveland, who had been the leader of the party for a dozen years, was rejected by a vote of 357 to 564. Richard P. ("Silver Dick") Bland of Missouri, who had been regarded as the champion of free silver for more than a score of years, led on the first ballots, but he was speedily overtaken by Bryan, who had come to the convention with the confidence that he would be the nominee. Bryan's nomination on the fifth ballot was due to a speech which he had rehearsed many times during his missionary work in the cause of free silver, and which he delivered with intense fervor before a hot and tired convention. "We are fighting," he cried, "in the defense of our homes, our families, our posterity. . . . We have petitioned, and our petitions have been scorned. We have entreated, and our entreaties have been disregarded. We have begged, and they have mocked when our calamity came. We beg no longer, we entreat no more, we petition no more. We defy them! Having behind us the producing masses of this nation and the world . . . we will answer their demand for a gold standard by saying to them: 'You shall not press down upon the brow of labor this crown of thorns! You shall not crucify mankind upon a cross of gold!'" The applause which had interrupted the orator at every sentence burst into a frenzy before the echo of the last defiant challenge had died. The man of the hour had been found, the "savior of democracy," "the new Lincoln." Bryan's nomination followed immediately amid scenes of the wildest enthusiasm.

A Complicated Situation. Neither of the great parties accepted unanimously the nominee of its convention. The silver Republican delegates, led by Senator Teller of Colorado (who had been present at the birth of the party), seceded from the St. Louis convention. They did not put a separate ticket into the field, but drifted generally into the Bryan ranks. The gold Democrats, however, nominated a ticket which had the support of President Cleveland and all his cabinet members but one, but which polled only 135,000 votes on election day. The Populist and National Silverite parties nominated Bryan. McKinley's position was rather embarrassing. He had voted for the Bland-Allison and Sherman Silver bills, and many utterances of his in favor of "bimetallism" [1] could be quoted. The delegates from Wyoming, in fact, had come to the convention instructed to vote for "McKinley and free silver." But Hanna managed the situation cleverly, holding back the insertion of the "gold plank" in the platform until the nomination of his candidate was assured. McKinley wished to have the campaign conducted on the tariff issue. "In thirty days you will hear nothing of free silver," he remarked to Judge Day, who visited him shortly after the nomination. "In thirty days you will hear of nothing else," replied the judge; and he was right.

The Campaign of 1896. At first the Republicans treated Bryan's candidacy with contempt. They had a campaign fund of several million dollars, collected by Hanna from the bankers, merchants, and manufacturers. With this they could hire hundreds of good speakers and send out millions of tracts, pam-

---

[1] This was the term used for the employment of both gold and silver as legal currency. The Republicans were willing to accept bimetallism if the leading European countries, like France and England, would do so. That is, they favored "international bimetallism." Senator E. O. Wolcott of Colorado, a silver Republican, went to Paris and London to try to persuade those governments to agree to bimetallism in return for tariff favors from the United States. But his efforts were fruitless. Several international conferences on the subject were held between 1878 and 1893, but none of the European countries that had the gold standard would abandon it.

phlets, speeches, and posters printed in a dozen languages. McKinley himself remained quietly at his home in Canton, Ohio, receiving delegations of visitors on his "front porch," while Bryan traveled eighteen thousand miles up and down the country in his railroad car (most inappropriately named the "Idler"), making over six hundred speeches. It was estimated that he spoke to five million people, probably the greatest number that ever listened to a single human voice before the invention of the radio. As the campaign progressed and Bryan's eloquence won thousands to the cause of free silver, the Republicans realized that they had a hard battle. They changed their tune from contempt and ridicule to abuse, denouncing Bryan as an anarchist, a blasphemer, and a lunatic who was encouraging "the uprising of disorder in all its forms against the institutions of the American Republic." Wage-earners in many of the Eastern factories were paid off on the Saturday before election with the notice that they would not be needed further if Bryan was elected. The exceptionally heavy vote of nearly fourteen million in November showed the effect of the "campaign of education" which had been waged, and the result of the voting revealed the sectional character of the struggle. McKinley carried the populous industrial states of the Northeast, together with the border states of Kentucky, West Virginia, Maryland, and Delaware, and five states west of the Mississippi — twenty-three in all, with an electoral vote of 271. Bryan's 176 votes came from the "solid South" and the eight mining states of the West, plus South Dakota, Kansas, Nebraska, and Missouri — twenty-two in all.

The Significance of the Election. The election of 1896 was the most important one in the thirty years of our history since the Civil War. In the first place, it demonstrated the firmness of the Union. Though the Populists used violent language, and some scareheads talked about the "secession" of the West, there was no thought in the minds of Bryan and his followers of an appeal to arms. Tillman of South Carolina was hissed down in the Chicago Convention when he hinted that the farmers of the West might adopt the course of the slaveholders of the South

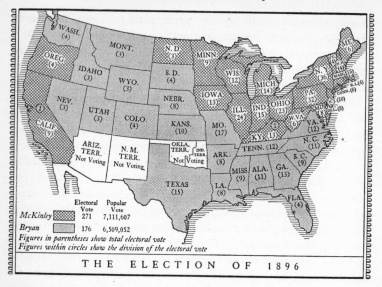

THE ELECTION OF 1896

	Electoral Vote	Popular Vote
McKinley	271	7,111,607
Bryan	176	6,509,052

Figures in parentheses show total electoral vote
Figures within circles show the division of the electoral vote

in 1860. Again, the election of 1896 marked the end (at least for a generation) of the effort made ever since the close of the Civil War to commit the government to the support of an inflated currency for the relief of the debtor class. But most important of all, the election marked the victory of the party of "big business," which was destined to control all the branches of the government for a period of a dozen years. Mark Hanna's triumph meant that the great trusts were to be the "power behind the throne." Many thousands of Americans were doubtless ready in 1896 to support a platform which advocated a sane control of the monopolies of coal, oil, and lumber lands and a reform of the tariff which unduly taxed the poor man's food and clothing. Many wished to see the railroads and express companies regulated in the interests of the public, and our legislatures and courts freed from the pressure of highly paid lobbies. But neither of the great parties offered such a platform in 1896. The Republicans were guided by men whose god was Mammon and who resented the interference of the government in business. The Democrats, deserting the sound reform principles of Grover

Cleveland, were led by the glittering oratory of the free-silver champion to commit their party to a doctrine that was intensely sectional and economically mischievous. The majority of the voters were convinced that the choice of McKinley was the safer course.

Summary. In this unit we have studied the development of our country in the three decades following the Civil War. This period is sometimes called "the emergence of modern America," because it deals with the building of the great industrial and agricultural empire which is the pride of America today. After the chapter on the restoration of the Southern states to the Union and their escape from the reconstruction policy forced upon them by the victorious North, we studied the rapid growth of our banking, manufacturing, mining, and farming industries. Then we traced the political history of the country from Hayes to Harrison, noting the futile strife of the parties and the clashes between organized labor and capital. Finally we followed the rise of the Populist movement in the South and West, which culminated in the great battle between the sections and resulted in the triumph of the business interests in the election of 1896.

TERMS TO BE MASTERED

national-bank notes	injunction	bimetallism
Populists	gold reserve	Omaha platform
"grandfather clause"	income tax	silver certificate

FOR SUPPLEMENTARY READING

J. D. HICKS, *The Populist Revolt*; J. F. RHODES, *History of the United States from Hayes to McKinley*, chaps. xviii–xx; H. A. SANFORD, *The Story of Agriculture in the United States*, chaps. xiii, xxi, xxiii, xxiv; H. T. PECK, *Twenty Years of the Republic*, chaps. vii–xi; ALLAN NEVINS, *Grover Cleveland, A Study in Courage*, chaps. xxvii–xxxvii; F. E. HAYNES, *Third-Party Movements in the United States*, chaps. x–xviii; D. R. DEWEY, *National Problems* (American Nation Series, Vol. XXIV), chaps. xvi–xx; F. W. TAUSSIG, *The Silver Situation in the United States* (American Economic Association Publications, Vol. VIII, pp. 1–18); W. J. ASHLEY, *The Railroad Strike of 1894*; IDA M. TARBELL, *The Tariff in Our Times*, chap. ix; S. J. BUCK, *The Agrarian Crusade* (Chronicles of America, Vol. XLV), chaps. vii–x; F. L. McVEY, *The Populist Movement* (American Economic Association Studies, Vol. I, No. 3); MARK SULLIVAN, *Our Times*, Vol. I, pp. 137–182; *America*, Vol. X, pp. 28–97; HART, *Contemporaries*, Vol. IV, Nos. 170, 171, 178, 179; MUZZEY, *Readings*, pp. 526–545.

Topics for Reports

1. The Farmer's Burden. J. D. Hicks, *The Populist Revolt*, chap. iii; Carl Becker, *Kansas* (Turner Essays), pp. 85–111; A. M. Simons, *The American Farmer*, pp. 12–60; F. J. Turner, "The Problem of the West," in *Atlantic Monthly*, Vol. LXXVII, pp. 289 f; J. P. Dunn, " The Mortgage Evil," in *Political Science Quarterly*, Vol. V, pp. 65 f.; C. W. Davis, "Why the Farmer Is Not Prosperous," in *Forum*, Vol. IX, pp. 231 f.

2. The Pullman Strike. Grover Cleveland, *Presidential Problems*, pp. 79–117; Allan Nevins, *Grover Cleveland*, chap. xxxiii; The Pageant of America, Vol. V, p. 300; John Mitchell, *Organized Labor*, pp. 324–336; H. T. Peck, *Twenty Years of the Republic*, pp. 375–388; F. J. Stimson, "The Modern Use of Injunctions," in *Political Science Quarterly*, Vol. X, pp. 189–202; Muzzey, *Readings*, pp. 526–532.

3. The Venezuela Boundary Dispute. Grover Cleveland, *Presidential Problems*, pp. 173–281; A. D. White, *Autobiography*, Vol. II, pp. 117–126; J. H. Latané, *Diplomatic Relations of the United States and Spanish America*, chap. vi; James Bryce, "British Feeling in the Venezuela Question," in *North American Review*, Vol. CLXII, pp. 145–153.

Questions Suggested by the Chapter

1. How was the Western land boom encouraged in the 1870's and 1880's? **2.** Why were the farmers hostile to the bankers? **3.** Explain why the farmer and the labor elements did not fuse easily. **4.** Why did the Southern farmers oppose the formation of a new party? **5.** Why does the Treasury keep a gold reserve? **6.** How have the Southern states evaded the Fifteenth Amendment? **7.** How can Congress levy an income tax now, considering the fact that the Supreme Court declared it unconstitutional in 1895? **8.** How many different kinds of paper money can you find in circulation? **9.** Why were the Republicans embarrassed on the money question in 1896? **10.** Do you think that Cleveland was justified in seeking help from Morgan in 1895? **11.** How had Cleveland offended labor? the Eastern manufacturers? the Populists? **12.** Do you think that the Monroe Doctrine justified our interfering in the dispute between Venezuela and Great Britain? Give your reasons for or against.

Books Worth Reading on Unit Five

Thomas Dixon, *The Leopard's Spots*; T. N. Page, *Red Rock*; P. L. Ford, *The Honorable Peter Stirling*; Ellen Glasgow, *The Deliverance* and *The Voice of the People*; A. W. Tourgee, *A Fool's Errand*; G. W. Cable, *John March, Southerner*; Hamlin Garland, *A Son of the Middle Border*; O. E. Rölvaag, *Giants in the Earth*; W. A. White, *A Certain Rich Man*; Frank Norris, *The Octopus* and *The Pit*; Owen Wister, *The Virginian*; M. Wilson, *The Able McLaughlins*; George F. Milton, *The Age of Hate*; J. T. Flynn, *God's Gold*; Paxton Hibben, *The Peerless Leader*; Thomas Beer, *The Mauve Decade* and *Hanna*.

★ ★

Read together in class

How our Country Acquired Distant Possessions and Put Democratic Government to the Test

On February 8, 1935, a convention of two hundred distinguished men at Manila, in the far-distant Philippine Islands off the southeastern coast of China, completed a constitution for the new Republic of the Philippines, to be started on its independent course ten years hence. The convention met by authority of an act of the American Congress passed in the spring of 1934. In the southern Pacific Ocean the people of the American portion of Samoa (p. 503) are now petitioning Washington to be taken from under the command of a naval officer and to be given a representative government of their own. The island of Puerto Rico in the Greater Antilles, which fringe the Caribbean Sea, is asking to be admitted as the forty-ninth state of the American Union. In August, 1935, our State Department announced its intention of terminating our treaty right to intervene in the cities of Panama and Colón in the Republic of Panama, just as, the year before, we had renounced our right to intervene in the island of Cuba to preserve order. These recent events in regions of the world separated from us and from each other generally by thousands of miles remind us that the sovereignty and flag of the United States have been carried into distant parts of the world. What were the motives that led to this expansion of America beyond the limits of our own continental domain? How have we dealt with the distant possessions which came under our flag? What effects has our venture on what President McKinley called the "new and untried paths" of *empire had upon the interpretation of our constitution and our inherited ideal of "government by the consent of the governed"? What bearing did the opening of new markets in our colonies and dependencies for the growing surplus of our manufactured goods have upon the increasing power of the moneyed classes in our government? What encouragement to military and naval power was furnished by the planting of our flag on the islands of the Pacific and the Caribbean? How was the rule of millions of distant alien peoples by force (which is the essence of "imperialism") to be reconciled with the self-rule of the people (which is the principle of democracy)? These were the questions which chiefly occupied the attention of the American people from the opening of the Spanish-American War in 1898 to the outbreak of the World War sixteen years later. They will be the subject of our study in the present unit.*

CHAPTER TWENTY-ONE

DOMINION OVER PALM AND PINE

Cuba. As they were driving back from the Capitol to the White House after the inauguration on March 4, 1897, Cleveland remarked to McKinley : "I am deeply sorry, Mr. President, to pass on to you a war with Spain. It will come within two years. Nothing can stop it." The war came in a little more than a year. The cause of the trouble was the island of Cuba, the "pearl of the Antilles," which had been the proud possession of the crown of Spain since its discovery by Columbus four hundred years before. The oppressive rule of the Spanish officials in Cuba bred a smoldering discontent, which broke out from time to time in insurrection. The one which started in 1895 was devastating. Bands of insurgents roamed the country, destroying the plantations; and the cruel governor-general, "butcher" Weyler, herded the old men, the women, and the children into prison camps, where they died like flies of starvation and disease.

The island of Cuba was at our door. More than fifty million dollars of American capital was invested in the railroads, mines, and sugar and tobacco plantations there, and our trade with the island had grown to nearly one hundred million dollars. Many Cubans had been naturalized in the United States, and Cuban refugees organized *juntas* (clubs) in New York and other American cities which furnished money, arms, and munitions to aid in throwing off the yoke of Spain. The platforms of both our great parties in 1896 condemned the Spanish misrule in Cuba, and both houses of Congress passed resolutions in favor of Cuban independence. Cleveland, in his final message to Congress in December, 1896, devoted six pages to the Cuban situation, declaring that there might be "a limit to our patient waiting for Spain to end the contest," and that if the useless sacrifice of life and property went on much longer our recognition of Spanish sovereignty in the island would be "superseded by a higher obligation" (namely, that of pacifying the island ourselves). McKinley strove to persuade the Spanish ministry to grant Cuba some degree of self-government, but was met only by the rebuke that the United States should mind its own business and stop giving aid and comfort to rebels.

War with Spain. In February, 1898, two incidents occurred which roused the hostility of the United States to Spain to a point where further diplomatic negotiations proved vain. On the ninth of that month W. R. Hearst's *New York American* published a letter which had been stolen from the Havana post office. The letter was written by Señor Dupuy de Lome, the Spanish minister at Washington, to a friend in Cuba. It denounced the American government and characterized President McKinley as "a cheap politician who truckled to the masses." Six days later (February 15) the battleship *Maine*, on a friendly visit in the harbor of Havana, was sunk by a terrific explosion, carrying to the bottom two officers and two hundred and fifty-eight seamen. The government at Madrid immediately accepted the resignation of Dupuy de Lome and expressed its sorrow over the "accident" to the *Maine*. But the American public, roused to fury by the "yellow press," was convinced that the battleship had been blown up by the Spaniards. There was a clamor for vengeance. Men, women, and children wore buttons inscribed with the motto "Remember the Maine!" The desks of the Congressmen at Washington were "piled high," as one of them wrote, with letters and petitions demanding war with Spain.

On March 8 Congress unanimously voted the President fifty million dollars as "an emergency fund for national defense." Neither McKinley nor the Spanish court wanted war. In Easter week (early April) the queen regent, yielding to the entreaties of the Pope, made all the concessions she could to the Cubans without endangering the throne of her young son Alfonso XIII. She decreed a cessation of hostilities and offered to consider some degree of liberty for the Cubans. At this point President

THE ISLAND OF CUBA

McKinley failed to back up his good intentions with courageous action. He had already prepared a message to Congress saying that he had "exhausted every effort to relieve the intolerable condition" in Cuba and inviting Congress to take such action as it saw best. Instead of tearing up this message (which meant sure war) and writing a new one when word of the queen mother's concessions came, he simply added a short paragraph dismissing the concessions as unimportant and sent the original message to the belligerent Congress (April 11). Eight days later Congress, by a vote of 324 to 19 in the House and 67 to 21 in the Senate, passed resolutions recognizing the independence of Cuba, demanding the immediate withdrawal of Spain from the island, and authorizing the President to employ the military and naval forces of the United States in carrying out the resolution. At the same time Congress adopted the Teller Resolution,

DEWEY ON THE FLAGSHIP *MANILA*

to the effect that the United States had no intention of annexing Cuba, but would "leave the government and control of the island to its own people" when the Spaniards had been expelled. Of course, it is possible that further negotiations on the basis of the queen mother's concessions of Holy Week might not have prevented eventual war; but at any rate they should have been made the occasion for renewed and redoubled efforts for peace on the part of the administration at Washington.

Dewey's Victory at Manila. Our navy, thanks largely to the energy of the Assistant Secretary Theodore Roosevelt, was in the pink of condition. The Asiatic fleet of seven vessels, under the command of Commodore George Dewey, was at the British

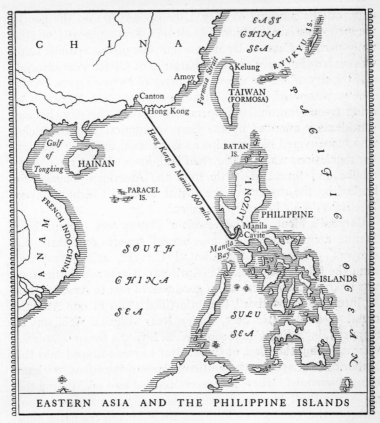

EASTERN ASIA AND THE PHILIPPINE ISLANDS

port of Hong Kong, on the Chinese coast, when the war broke out. As a belligerent Dewey could not remain in a neutral port unless he "interned" his fleet, or put it into the hands of the authorities there. Therefore he had either to sail seven thousand miles for home or to seek the enemy. On April 25 he received a cable from the Navy Department ordering him to proceed at once to the Philippine Islands to commence operations against the Spanish fleet there; and a few hours later his drab-painted warships were steaming southeast across the China Sea toward the ancient Spanish colony of the Philippines, six hundred and twenty-eight miles distant. Entering Manila Bay early on the morning of May 1, he opened fire on the poorly manned vessels of Admiral Montojo's fleet anchored off the navy yard at Cavite. By noon every one of the Spanish ships was sunk or in flames, the land batteries of Cavite were silenced, and the city of Manila was at the mercy of Dewey's guns. While Dewey was waiting for the transports from San Francisco to bring troops for the land operations against the city, he was considerably annoyed by the German admiral Von Diedrichs, who maneuvered his warships as he pleased, ignoring the harbor regulations which Dewey had laid down. But after a sharp rebuke and threat of battle from the American commodore, backed by the support of the British admiral Chichester, Von Diedrichs decided to obey the rules.[1]

Cervera's Fleet. As the vessels of Dewey were approaching Manila a Spanish fleet of four armed cruisers and three destroyers, commanded by Admiral Cervera, sailed westward from the Cape Verde Islands (April 29). Cervera's destination was unknown, and there was a good deal of fear in America that he intended to bombard the unfortified cities of our Atlantic coast. Our Atlantic fleet, under Rear Admiral William T. Sampson, including Commodore W. S. Schley's flying squadron, was patrolling the coast of Cuba. But Cervera slipped into the harbor of Santiago, on the southern shore of the island, without being discovered. There Sampson "bottled him up" during the entire month of June by drawing a blockading squadron — consisting of the cruisers *New York* and *Brooklyn* and the battleships *Massachusetts, Texas, Iowa, Indiana,* and *Oregon* [2] — around the mouth of the harbor in a semicircle.

---

[1] Great Britain was the only important European power that sympathized with the United States in the Spanish war. This was partly due to the popularity of John Hay, our ambassador at London, and partly to the fact that England was without European friends in the late 1890's. She was at odds with Germany over naval rivalry and the Kaiser's encouragement of the Boers in South Africa; with France over conflicting claims in the Sudan; and with Russia over the threatened advance of the Czar's power southward to Persia, Afghanistan, and India. The German government was suspected of having sent a strong fleet to Manila Bay in order to seize the Philippines when the Spanish empire should have gone to pieces.

[2] The *Oregon* had just completed a marvelous voyage of fourteen thousand miles from Bremerton (in the state of Washington) around Cape Horn to Florida.

Our Army in Cuba. Meanwhile about sixteen thousand troops had been sent from the American camps in Florida to invade Cuba. Major General W. R. Shafter was in command. The most picturesque division of this army was the first volunteer cavalry regiment, popularly known as the "Rough Riders," made up of Western cowboys, ranchmen, Indians, and hunters, with a sprinkling of Harvard and Yale graduates. Colonel Leonard Wood commanded the "Rough Riders," and Theodore Roosevelt resigned his post as Assistant Secretary of the Navy to become their Lieutenant Colonel. The American troops stormed the fortified hills of El Caney and San Juan, above Santiago, but then found themselves in a dangerous situation. Disease had attacked the men unused to the tropical climate and had taken a far greater toll than the rifles of the enemy. The reinforcements which would be necessary to drive the Spaniards from Santiago would be weeks in reaching the island. The army's food supply was so bad that a number of the volunteer officers joined in a round robin of protest to Washington and asked to have the sick men sent home to Montauk Point on Long Island. Indeed, General Shafter, himself sick with fever and gout in his camp several miles from the city, was inclined to withdraw the army from the heights which it had so laboriously gained and from which it might be driven by a well-directed fire from Cervera's fleet in the harbor below.

The Destruction of the Spanish Fleet. But fortune smiled on the American cause. On Sunday morning, July 3, the Spanish ships steamed out of the harbor and started to run westward along the southern shore of Cuba. Admiral Sampson was absent at the moment, with his flagship the *New York*, conferring with General Shafter on the critical situation of the American army. Commodore Schley, on the *Brooklyn*, was left as ranking officer. Following the orders left by Sampson, the American ships closed in on the Spaniards in a wild chase along the coast, pouring a deadly fire into them all the while. The Spaniards replied, as at Manila, with a rapid but ineffectual discharge. One by one the Spanish cruisers, disabled or in flames, turned and headed for the breakers, until the last of them, the *Cristóbal Colón*, bearing the proud name of the man who four centuries earlier had discovered for Spain the Western world whose last remnants were now slipping from her grasp, was driven on the beach by the relentless fire of the *Brooklyn* and the *Oregon*, forty-five miles west of the harbor of Santiago. Only one man was killed and one seriously wounded on the American fleet, while ten thousand dollars repaired all the damage done by the Spanish guns. But the enemy's fleet was completely destroyed, over five hundred men killed, wounded, or drowned, and seventeen hundred taken prisoners. The Spanish loss would have been far larger had not the American sailors rescued hundreds, including the brave Admiral Cervera himself, from the burning decks and the wreck-strewn waters — a courtesy which brought a warm letter of gratitude from the Spanish admiral to Admiral Sampson. A few days later the Spanish general surrendered the city of Santiago, now at the mercy of Sampson's guns, and turned over his entire army as prisoners of war to General Shafter.

The Capture of Manila. The total loss of two fleets and an army brought Spain to sue for terms of peace, through the French minister at Washington, Jules Cambon. The preliminaries were signed at Washington and hostilities were suspended on August 12. The news stopped General Miles's advance against the Spanish forces in Puerto Rico, and the governor immediately surrendered the island to the American general. But before the news of the armistice reached the distant Philippines an event of great importance had occurred there. An American army, which had been sent out to the islands to support Dewey, entered the city of Manila on August 13 and raised the American flag over the governor's palace.

Peace with Spain. The preliminaries of peace, signed at Washington, had provided that Spain should immediately relinquish all claims to Cuba and should cede Puerto Rico and an island in the Ladrones group in the Pacific (Guam) to the United States, and that we should hold the city, bay, and harbor of Manila "pending the conclusion of a treaty of peace which should determine the control, disposition, and government of the Philippines." The American commissioners appointed by

THE WRECK OF THE SPANISH SHIP *REINA MERCEDES*,
OFF MORRO CASTLE

the President to conclude the final treaty of peace met the Spanish negotiators at Paris late in September, but it was more than two months before they could persuade them to accept the terms demanded by the United States. The delay came over the Philippines. Since the war had been undertaken by the Americans for the liberation of Cuba and since the city of Manila had not been taken until *after* the peace preliminaries had been signed and hostilities suspended, the Spanish commissioners claimed that the Philippines should remain in their possession and that the American "occupation" of the islands should cease forthwith.

In his first instructions to our delegates, President McKinley, through his new Secretary of State, John Hay, had been inclined to ask only for the cession of the island of Luzon and for equal commercial rights with Spain in the other islands of the Philippine archipelago. But various considerations led him gradually to change his mind and demand the cession of the whole of the Philippines to the United States.[1] The Spanish

[1] These considerations were (1) fear that if we left the Philippines in Spain's possession they would be oppressed like Cuba, (2) fear that if we left them to

commissioners made a stubborn resistance; but when we threw into the scales an offer of twenty million dollars, they agreed to the "sale" of the islands to the United States.

The Philippine Insurrection. Meanwhile an ugly situation was developing in the Philippines. The Filipinos had been in revolt against Spain at the same time as the Cubans, and in 1897 Spain had bought off the leaders of the revolt, including an able young man named Emilio Aguinaldo, with a promise of one million dollars. Aguinaldo had retired to Singapore. While at Hong Kong, Dewey made an agreement to convey Aguinaldo back to the Philippines on an American ship and furnished his insurgents with arms. Filipino troops entered the city of Manila with the American army on August 13; but they were not allowed to take part in the occupation of the city, and the next month were ordered to withdraw. Aguinaldo now claimed that Dewey had promised to turn over the Philippines to him when the power of Spain should have been crushed. He organized a Filipino republic, had himself proclaimed dictator, and prepared to maintain his position by force of arms. For several months Aguinaldo's troops hung about the outskirts of Manila, nursing their sullen wrath against the Americans. Then, on February 4, 1899, just two days before our Senate ratified the peace treaty with Spain, the first battle occurred. The superior quality and training of the American army made victory in the open field very easy; but when the Filipinos took to a guerrilla warfare among their native swamps and jungles the wearying task of subjugating them dragged on for more than two years, while atrocious methods of torture were employed by both sides. Even the capture of Aguinaldo himself in his mountain retreat by a party of American scouts disguised as insurgents (February, 1901), and Aguinaldo's proclamation two months later acknowl-

themselves they would become a prey to anarchy, (3) the pressure of the commercial interests eager to open new markets for our surplus products, (4) the desire of the "imperialists" like Lodge and Roosevelt to share in the spheres of interest which the Western powers were rapidly establishing in the Far East, and (5) McKinley's own growing conviction, fortified, as he declared, by God's answer to his anxious prayers, that it was our duty to take the Filipinos under our beneficent rule, "to educate and uplift and civilize and Christianize them."

edging American sovereignty in the islands, did not end the insurrection. It was not until April, 1902, that the last rebel surrendered and the Philippines were officially declared "pacified." Aguinaldo himself became completely reconciled to American rule in the Philippines, leaving to other leaders, like Quezón and Roxas, the task of agitating for Philippine independence.

The Anti-Imperialists. When the Senate, by a bare two-thirds majority, ratified the treaty with Spain early in 1899, the United States was fairly launched upon a "new and untried" course. We had annexed the Hawaiian Islands in the mid-Pacific, and "picked up" the smaller islands of Guam, Wake, and Baker. We had undertaken the responsibility of providing an orderly government for Cuba. We had acquired nearly a million subjects of Spanish and Negro blood in Puerto Rico. We had become the masters and protectors of eight million people in the Philippines, ranging from the cultured Tagalogs of Manila to the naked Negrito dwarfs, the savage head-hunting Igorrotes, and the brutal Moros of the Sulu peninsula. Many prominent Americans of the intellectual class — college presidents, clergymen, lawyers, and statesmen — protested against this departure from our traditional ideals of democracy. A flood of pamphlets appeared condemning our faithlessness to the doctrine of the Declaration of Independence. William Vaughn Moody's bitter ode of glory "To a Soldier Fallen in the Philippines" charged his country to

Let him never dream that his bullet's scream went wide of its island mark,
Home to the heart of his sinning land, where she stumbled and sinned in
the dark.

Thomas B. Reed retired from the Speakership in disgust, referring to the treaty as "buying ten million Malays at two dollars a head."

From the very earliest days the United States had pursued a policy of steady expansion. But that expansion had been westward into the virgin lands which beckoned to the pioneer. Louisiana and Oregon, Texas and California, were acquired as frontier regions to be filled with American settlers and to round out the domain of the United States. But the new possessions were already inhabited by millions of alien and distant people, differing from us in language, race, and customs. They had been brought into subjection and were held in obedience by the army and navy of the United States. This, said the opponents of annexation, was nothing less than "imperialism," the system by which Rome dominated the ancient world. Against the "jingoes" [1] who were boastful of the spread of the American flag and marines to any part of the world, against the great industrialists and bankers who wanted new markets for the disposal of surplus goods and the investment of surplus funds, against even the moralists like McKinley, who argued that it was our duty to "take up the white man's burden" and do our part in civilizing the "backward" people of the earth, the anti-imperialists insisted that all our institutions were designed for the free citizens of a republic and not for the rulers of an empire.

The Election of 1900. The anti-imperialists, however, fought a losing battle. The opportunity was given to the American people in the election of 1900 to pronounce on the issue, and their verdict was heavily in favor of the administration. McKinley was renominated at Philadelphia in June by a unanimous shout. Theodore Roosevelt, who had been elected governor of New York in the autumn of 1898 as a reward for his service in the Spanish war, was nominated for the Vice-Presidency, in spite of his vigorous protest against being "shelved" in that inconspicuous office. Once nominated, however, he threw himself into the campaign with vigor, declaring to the Republican manager, Mark Hanna, that he felt "as strong as a bull moose," and traveling up and down the country denouncing as weaklings and "mollycoddles" those who would haul down our flag or "scuttle" out of the Philippines. The Democrats met at Kansas City on July 4 and unanimously nominated William J. Bryan, who had been defeated on the free-silver issue four years be-

[1] The word is taken from a popular song of the London music halls in 1878:

We don't want to fight, yet by jingo, if we do
We've got the ships, we've got the men, and got the money too.

fore. Although Bryan was strong enough to get a free-silver plank inserted into the platform, the campaign was waged not on that dead issue[1] but on the opposition to imperialism. A huge American flag hung from the rafters of the convention hall, bordered with the motto "The flag of a Republic forever, of an Empire never." Placards and banners were displayed with the inscriptions "Lincoln abolished slavery; McKinley restored it" (referring to the fact that slavery existed in the southern islands of the Philippines) and "The war for the liberation of Cuba ended with the enslavement of the Philippines."

Anti-imperialistic leagues were formed all over the country, and distinguished opponents of our Philippine policy (Charles Francis Adams, Senator George F. Hoar, Carl Schurz, Moorfield Storey, Professors William James, William G. Sumner, and Felix Adler) pointed out the political and moral evils of the attempt to govern alien peoples against their will. Point was given to their arguments by the Philippine insurrection (p. 542), which was at its height during the summer of 1900. The Republicans indignantly denied that they were imperialists. We were the liberators, not the oppressors, of the Filipinos. "The Republican party," said McKinley in his speech of acceptance, "broke the shackles of four million slaves and made them free, and to the party of Lincoln has come another supreme opportunity, which it has bravely met in the liberation of ten millions of the human family from the yoke of imperialism." The country endorsed the doctrine of our "manifest destiny" in the election of November. McKinley's vote fell off in New England, where the anti-imperialists were strongest, but he carried most of the West, including Bryan's own state of Nebraska, and his popular plurality reached 860,000. For better or worse, we had entered into the race for colonial supremacy and world trade. We had voted down the counsel of men who urged us to maintain the letter and the spirit of the Constitution. We were no longer confronted by the choice as to whether we should play a great part in the events of the world or not. The only ques-

[1] The Republican Congress had already (March 14, 1890) passed an act making gold the sole standard of currency.

tion was, in the words of Theodore Roosevelt, "whether we should play that part well or ill."

The Reorganization of Cuba. The administration had already begun to grapple with the practical task of devising governments for the former Spanish islands. We had pledged ourselves by the Teller Resolution (p. 536) to turn the government of Cuba over to the natives after order was restored; and to the amazement of Europe we kept our promise. Under the military governorship of General Leonard Wood (1899–1902) the ravages of the revolution were repaired. Towns and cities were restored to industry, an educational system was started, and under honest administration the finances of the island were set in order. Through the brilliant work of Major Walter Reed of Virginia, an army surgeon, the mosquito which carried the germs of yellow fever was discovered, and the disease which had made Havana a pesthole was stamped out. In the summer of 1900 General Wood ordered an election for the choice of delegates to a convention to frame a constitution for the Cuban Republic. While the convention was in session Secretary of War Root sent instructions to Wood that certain provisions must appear in the constitution, as a recognition of the special interests and responsibilities of the United States in the island. The most important of these provisions were (1) that Cuba should make no treaties with foreign powers impairing its independence, nor permit any foreign power to acquire Cuban territory; (2) that it should not contract any debts whose interest could not be met out of the current revenues; (3) that it should allow the United States to intervene whenever necessary to preserve the independence or the stability of the government; (4) that the government of Cuba should sell or lease to the United States land for coaling and naval stations.

The convention, not relishing the idea of American intervention in Cuba, drew up a constitution patterned on that of the United States but with no mention of the provisions prescribed by Secretary Root. Whereupon Senator O. H. Platt of Connecticut embodied these provisions in an amendment to the army appropriation bill, and the Cuban convention, in spite of a protest sent to Washington, was obliged to add the Platt Amendment to its constitution. After the Cubans had held their election, General Wood handed over the government (with a surplus of seven hundred thousand dollars in the treasury) to the newly inaugurated president, Tomás Palma, and the American troops were withdrawn from the island.[1]

Puerto Rico. The island of Puerto Rico, fourth in size of the West Indies, with a population of 935,000 (589,000 whites), came willingly under the rule of the United States. But it was impossible to give statehood or even a territorial status to a people containing but 17 per cent of literates, alien in blood and speech and without any experience in self-government. By the Foraker Act of April, 1900, Puerto Rico was organized as a sort of compromise between a colony and a territory. A governor and a council of eleven (including five Puerto Ricans) were appointed by the President, and a legislature of thirty-five members was elected by the natives. The Spanish courts were entirely swept away and replaced by a judiciary system like that of the United States. The island was put under the protection of our laws, and works of sanitation, education, roadbuilding, and agricultural development were undertaken. Owing partly to the loss of her free trade with Spain and Cuba and partly to a terrible hurricane in August, 1899, which destroyed most of her coffee bushes, the island was in such serious economic distress that President McKinley, high protectionist as he was, advised Congress in his message of December that it was "our plain duty to abolish all customs tariffs between the United States and Porto Rico, and give her products [sugar, coffee, tobacco, fruits] free access to our markets." The most

[1] From time to time the United States found it necessary to intervene in Cuba under the Platt Amendment. When a revolution broke out there in 1906, on the re-election of President Palma, we administered the government for three years, until General Gómez was peacefully chosen president under new election laws. Again in 1912 and 1917 we were obliged to land marines on the island to prevent civil war; and in the spring of 1921 the Liberals appealed to President Harding to send American troops to supervise the elections. But although the Platt Amendment was ratified in a "permanent" treaty with Cuba in May, 1903, we have refrained from applying it in late years; and in 1934 we formally renounced our right to intervene in the political affairs of the island.

that Congress would do, however, was to grant the island a reduction of 85 per cent of the high duties levied under the Dingley tariff of 1897. But in the midsummer of 1901 we gave the island free trade. In 1917 President Wilson signed a bill giving Puerto Rico full territorial status. Her inhabitants were made citizens of the United States, and the appointive council of eleven was replaced by a Senate elected by the people of the island. Lately they have been asking to be admitted as a state of the Union.

The Philippines. It is in the Philippines that the real test of our colonial administration has been made. Nearly eight million people, inhabiting a group of islands seven thousand miles from our nearest shores, had been turned over to American rule without their consent. An armed rebellion against our authority was on foot in the islands, which was eventually to cost our government a thousand lives and $135,000,000. In the absence of any legislation by Congress, President McKinley, as commander in chief of our army and navy, exercised full power over the Philippines. This power he delegated in 1900 to a commission of five members, headed by Judge William H. Taft of Ohio, who were instructed by Secretary Root "to make rules and orders, having the effect of law, for the raising of revenue by taxes, customs duties, and imposts; the appropriation and expenditure of the public funds of the Islands; the establishment of an educational system; the establishment of an efficient civil service; the organization of courts; the establishment or organization of municipal and departmental governments, and all other matters of a civil nature for which the military governor is now competent to provide." A year later Congress adopted the Spooner Amendment, which vested in the President as absolute power over the Philippines as ever a Roman proconsul had over a distant province of the Empire. The President now appointed Taft as civil governor of the Islands and made each of the four associate commissioners the head of an executive department.

In July, 1902, Congress passed the Philippine Act, providing for the faint beginnings of self-government. A census of the

THE RESIDENCE OF A WELL-TO-DO PHILIPPINE FAMILY

Islands was to be taken as soon as the commission should inform the President that the insurrection was at an end; and two years after the census was completed the commission should hold elections in the Christian provinces for a Philippine assembly, which should be added to the commission as a lower house of the legislature. The suffrage was given to all males of twenty-three years of age or over who had held municipal office or possessed property or paid taxes of a certain amount or could read, speak, or write the English or Spanish language. In 1907 the elections were held, resulting in the choice of an assembly of eighty-one members, about three fourths of whom were Nationalists, or advocates of Philippine independence. Ex-governor Taft (now Secretary of War in place of Root), who had won great popularity in the Philippines by his conciliatory and progressive administration, went out to Manila in person to open the first session of the new assembly in October. Congress had already (1902) made a tariff concession to the Philippines by letting the exports from the islands enter the ports of the United States at a reduction of 25 per cent from the Dingley rates.

The Colonies and the Constitution. The practical work of pacification, political organization, and social improvement had thus gone on under the authority of the President and Congress. But the important question of the constitutional relations of these new possessions to the United States could be decided only by the Supreme Court. If Puerto Rico and the Philippines had become parts of the United States when our flag was raised over them, did their inhabitants thereby come under the protection and privileges of the Constitution of the United States? Or, as it was popularly phrased, did the Constitution follow the flag? If so, it was clear that the Filipinos and Puerto Ricans had the rights enumerated in the first ten amendments to the Constitution (the Bill of Rights). Before the court spoke on this question, both the President and Congress had proceeded upon the assumption that the Constitution does not "follow the flag."

The Insular Cases. It was a difficult question, therefore, that the Supreme Court faced when the so-called "insular cases," testing the right of the United States to collect duties on goods from Puerto Rico and the Philippines, came up before it in the spring term of 1901. If it decided that the Constitution applied in all its vigor to the inhabitants of the islands, it would make them forthwith citizens of the United States — a preposterous idea. If, on the other hand, it excluded the Constitution entirely from the new possessions, it would sanction a doctrine abhorrent to most of the American people: namely, that there was some authority above and beyond the Constitution, which could rule alien people under our flag. Faced by this dilemma, the court, by a vote of five to four, decided that the islands were "not a part of the United States within the revenue clauses of the Constitution," and hence Congress might levy duties on their products. In other words, the Constitution itself contained some parts which were not of the same binding quality as other parts. No doubt, the court realized that the

President and Congress had already determined the policy which was acceptable to the business interests of the country, and it had been endorsed by the people in the election of 1900. As Mr. Dooley humorously put it, whether or not the Constitution followed the flag, the Supreme Court followed the election returns.

The Hague Conference. The acquisition of distant colonies was by no means the only sign of the increasing prestige of the United States in world affairs during the McKinley administration. Since our virtual separation from the Old World, after the second war with England in 1812–1815, we had from time to time been engaged in controversies with foreign powers over such questions as the Monroe Doctrine or our boundaries or fishing rights; but with the turn of the century we became a "world power" in earnest. This was due to no deliberate planning or intention. A spirited foreign policy was probably the last thing in the mind of McKinley or Hanna when the Republicans came into power in 1897. They expected to run a "business administration" devoted to the furtherance of American prosperity. But, as it turned out, exactly two thirds of the pages of McKinley's annual messages to Congress were concerned with the problems arising out of our relations to foreign powers and our new dependencies in the Pacific and the Caribbean.

In the spring of 1899 the Czar of Russia invited the powers to a conference at the Hague, in Holland, to discuss measures for relieving the European nations of the burden put upon them by the maintenance of huge armies and fleets. A generation earlier we should have politely declined the Czar's invitation to participate in the conference, on the ground that we were not "burdened" with armaments and that the wars of Europe were no concern of ours. But now President McKinley accepted the invitation heartily and sent a strong delegation to the Hague. The conference adopted a number of rules for the mitigation of the cruelties of war on land and sea; but its most important work was the outcome of the labors of the American delegation, who won over the German emperor to the idea of a court of arbitration, before which the nations could present their disputes

THE CARNEGIE PEACE PALACE AT THE HAGUE

for a peaceful settlement. The United States was the first of the great nations to submit a case to the Hague Court (1902), and within five years after the establishment of the tribunal the European nations had made thirty-three treaties providing for the voluntary submission to arbitration of all disputes which did not affect "the vital interests, the independence or the honor of the two contracting parties."[1]

The "Open Door" in China. Six weeks after the Hague Conference adjourned, the United States scored another diplomatic victory. After its decisive defeat by Japan in the war of 1894–1895, the huge Chinese Empire lay "like a stranded whale" at the mercy of the great powers, who proceeded to cut up its territory into "spheres of influence." Germany, France, Russia, and England forced the Chinese government to grant them "leases" of vast regions, in which they seized the valuable rail-

[1] The student will recall the earlier contribution of the United States to the peaceful settlement of disputes by arbitration in the Geneva tribunal of 1872 (p. 444). It had been a policy recommended by us since the days of Washington.

road and mining rights and even extinguished China's political sovereignty. Our conquest of the Philippines, just at the moment that this dismemberment of China was threatened, had brought us close to the Asiatic coast, and the prospect of new markets in the Far East made us eager to preserve equal opportunities for trade in China. Besides, we were friendly to China and had a genuine desire to see her fairly treated. Therefore our able Secretary of State, John Hay, dispatched an identical note to the powers, asking them not to interfere with the rights of any of the twenty-two ports in China, nor to disturb the regular collection of the Chinese duties, nor to close their "spheres of influence" against other nations by increased railroad rates or harbor dues. As none of the powers wished to appear more grasping than the rest, each answered accepting the terms of Hay's note, provided the others would. Whereupon Hay notified each of the powers that all of them had accepted his proposal, and the "open door" in China was assured.

The Boxer Rebellion. However, the exploitation of China by the Europeans had roused the wrath of the natives. A patriotic society called the "Righteous Fists of Harmony" (abbreviated to "Boxers") quickly spread over the northern provinces of China, carrying murder and pillage in its train. The Boxers, secretly supported by the Dowager Empress, were determined to drive the "foreign devils" out of China. When crops failed in the drought of 1899, they stirred the ignorant and superstitious masses to murder the Christians, who had "irritated heaven" so that no rain would fall. Peking was surrounded by a fanatical army of Boxers and cut off from communication with the outside world. The German minister, Baron von Ketteler, was murdered in the street while on his way from his legation to the Foreign Office to lodge a protest. Whereupon the entire diplomatic corps, with their families and many native Christians, — in all about four hundred persons, — took refuge in the enclosure of the British legation, which they fortified by trenches and barricades against the horde of Boxers, who rained a continual fire upon them.

Sixty-five of the besieged party were killed and one hundred and thirty-five wounded before a relief army composed of American, British, French, German, Russian, and Japanese troops fought its way up from the coast and captured the city of Peking. The imperial court fled, and the city was brutally plundered by the European troops. The powers would have taken vengeance by overthrowing the government of China and dividing her territory among themselves; but Secretary Hay again intervened, insisting that the integrity of China be preserved and that the government be obliged only to punish the ringleaders of the rebellion and pay a money indemnity for the destruction of lives and property. The sum was fixed at $334,000,000, of which the United States asked but $24,000,000; and when it was found that less than half this sum would pay for the damages to our citizens and the cost of our part in the relief expedition, Congress remitted the balance. The Chinese government, "profoundly impressed with the justice and great friendliness of the United States," used the money to send hundreds of its young men to be educated in American colleges and universities.

Big Business Triumphant. While our country was thus entering on the "new and untried paths" of empire at the turn of the century, it was enjoying a period of remarkable prosperity at home. The causes of discontent which had led to the bitter battle between the East and the West were largely removed. Gold was discovered in 1897 on the Klondike River and at Cape Nome in Alaska; and within five years one hundred million dollars of the precious metal was mined. The consequent fall in the value of gold enabled the farmers to sell their corn and wheat at higher prices. They began to paint their barns, pay off their mortgages, and put money in the bank. Our exports of manufactured goods increased from 17.8 per cent of the total exports in 1890 to 32 per cent in 1900. In 1897 the Republican Congress passed the Dingley tariff, restoring the high rates of the McKinley Act of 1890 (p. 498), and for a dozen years of almost uninterrupted prosperity the Dingley tariff remained unchanged. According to the Commercial Year Book, 157 new trusts were organized in the last few years of the nineteenth century, with a capitalization of $3,150,000,000, or more

THE KLONDIKE GOLD RUSH, 1897

than the total capitalization of all the industries established in the preceding thirty years. There was no disposition on the part of President McKinley to interfere with what John Hay called "the insolent prosperity" of the United States. He agreed with Mark Hanna that the success of big business was the best index of the country's welfare. He instituted no suits against the trusts under the Sherman Antitrust Act (p. 498). He made no recommendations to Congress for the regulation of the railroads.

The United States Steel Trust. The foremost example of the business consolidations which were taking place in the railroad, meat-packing, coal, leather, lumber, sugar, and other industries was the United States Steel Corporation, which was launched by J. P. Morgan and Company in 1901. Eleven companies, including Andrew Carnegie's great plants, were merged to form this gigantic trust, which was capitalized at the amazing figure of $1,404,000,000. It owned not only the mills for the production of steel but the mines which furnished the iron ore, the lake steamers which brought the ore from the mines, and the railroads which carried it to the mills. The trust was started at a time when capital was abundant, and its stock was eagerly purchased by the public. It was no accident that our interest in new colonies across the sea coincided with the development of big business. So long as we had remained an agricultural people chiefly, our surplus crops had gone to feed the old manufacturing countries of Europe. But the rapid growth of the industrial system in America brought a change. Our own people could not now absorb the goods turned out of our mills and factories by large-scale standardized production. We also needed supplies of raw material which we could not raise at home, such as rubber, silk, dyewoods, coffee, and drugs. The tropical countries could furnish us with these materials, while their millions of "backward" people could be educated to take our cotton and woolen goods, our shoes and hats, our sewing machines and harvesters. Whether or not the Constitution followed our flag into the new possessions, it was certain that the business promoter did.

The Assassination of McKinley. Fortune seemed to smile on the President as he took the oath of office for his second term on March 4, 1901. The country had endorsed his administration by a generous vote of confidence. At the end of April he left Washington with members of his cabinet and several invited guests for a grand tour of the country to the Pacific coast, and was received at every stopping place with demonstrations of the people's affection. On September 5 he attended the Pan-American Exposition at Buffalo, New York, and in a noble speech outlined the policy of friendly co-operation, or reciprocity, in trade with the nations of the world. "We must not," he said, "repose in the fancied security that we can forever sell everything and buy little or nothing. . . . The period of exclusion is past. The expansion of our trade and commerce is the pressing problem. Commercial wars are unprofitable. A policy of good will and friendly trade relations will prevent reprisals. Reciprocity treaties are in harmony with the spirit of the times; measures of retaliation are not. . . . Let us ever remember that our interest is in concord, not conflict, and that our real eminence rests on the victories of peace and not those of war." It was his last public utterance. The next day, as he was holding a reception in the Temple of Music, he was shot by a young Polish anarchist named Czolgosz, whose brain had been inflamed by reading the tirades of the "yellow press" against "Czar McKinley." After a week of patient suffering the President died — the third victim of an assassin's bullet since the Civil War. The tribute paid to him by President Benjamin Ide Wheeler of the University of California, in conferring on him the degree of Doctor of Laws in the spring of 1901, is engraved upon the McKinley Memorial at Canton, Ohio: "A statesman singularly gifted to unite the discordant forces of government and mold the diverse purposes of men toward progressive and salutary action."

Terms to be Mastered

imperialism	guerrilla war	"the open door"
"yellow press"	civil government	sphere of influence
internment of ships	insular cases	merger

FOR SUPPLEMENTARY READING

J. F. RHODES, *The McKinley and Roosevelt Administrations*, chaps. ii–vii; J. H. LATANÉ, *America as a World Power* (American Nation Series, Vol. XXV), chaps. i–x; WALTER MILLIS, *The Martial Spirit*; GEORGE DEWEY, *Autobiography*, chaps. xiii–xviii; THEODORE ROOSEVELT, *The Rough Riders*; C. R. FISH, *The Path of Empire* (Chronicles of America, Vol. XLVI), chaps. v, vii–xvi; *The Pageant of America*, Vol. IX, pp. 193–214; W. F. WILLOUGHBY, *Territories and Dependencies of the United States*; H. HAGEDORN, *Leonard Wood, a Biography*, Vol. I, chaps. vii–xvii, Vol. II, chaps. i–iii; F. W. ATKINSON, *The Philippine Islands*; P. H. CLEMENTS, *The Boxer Rebellion*; H. S. COMMAGER, *Documents of American History*, Vol. II, pp. 181–198; HART, *Contemporaries*, Vol. IV, Nos. 180–194; MUZZEY, *Readings*, pp. 546–555.

TOPICS FOR REPORTS

1. **The Anti-imperialists.** M. A. DE W. HOWE, *Portrait of an Independent, Moorfield Storey*, pp. 191–230; MOORFIELD STOREY, "What shall we Do with our Dependencies?" in *Harvard Law Review*, Vols. XI, XII; W. A. ROBINSON, *Thomas B. Reed, Parliamentarian*, chap. xvii; G. F. HOAR, *No Power to Conquer Foreign Nations* and *Autobiography of Seventy Years*, Vol. II, pp. 304–320; EDWARD ATKINSON, *The Cost of War and Warfare from 1899 to 1902*; HART, *Contemporaries*, Vol. IV, Nos. 186, 190, 191.

2. **American Rule in the Philippines.** F. W. ATKINSON, *The Philippine Islands*, pp. 337–372; H. P. WILLIS, *Our Philippine Problem*; H. HAGEDORN, *Leonard Wood, A Biography*, Vol. II, chaps. i–iii, xviii, xix; J. H. LATANÉ, *America as a World Power*, pp. 153–174; M. M. KALAW, *The Case of the Filipinos*, chaps. iv, vi, and Appendix G; J. S. REYES, *The Legislative History of America's Economic Policy toward the Philippines* (Columbia University Studies, Vol. CVI, No. 2).

3. **The United States Steel Corporation.** B. J. HENDRICK, *The Age of Big Business* (Chronicles of America, Vol. XXXIX), pp. 58–85; CARL HOVEY, *The Life Story of J. P. Morgan*, pp. 194–223; IDA TARBELL, *The Life of Elbert Gary*; B. J. HENDRICK, *The Life of Andrew Carnegie*, Vol. II, chaps. i–v.

QUESTIONS SUGGESTED BY THE CHAPTER

1. Why is President McKinley held responsible by some for the Spanish-American War? **2.** Why was the war started in the Philippine Islands? **3.** Why did Great Britain sympathize with the United States in the War? **4.** What motives influenced McKinley to take the Philippines? **5.** How did the case differ from that of Puerto Rico? **6.** To what extent have we "liberated" the Filipinos? **7.** Explain the phrase "Does the Constitution follow the flag?" **8.** How did we show ourselves friendly to China in 1899? **9.** What connection is there between imperialism and big business? **10.** How did the discovery of gold in the Klondike affect the farmer? **11.** Distinguish between Thomas C. Platt and the author of the Platt Amendment. **12.** How did our expansion after 1898 differ from that of the nineteenth century? **13.** What did the Supreme Court decide as to the extension of the Constitution to the Philippines? **14.** What happened in the Philippines in 1935?

CHAPTER TWENTY-TWO

THE ROOSEVELT ERA

Theodore Roosevelt. The death of McKinley brought into the Presidency a man who was to fill the stage of our political life in the first decade of the twentieth century and to become in his time probably the best-known man of the world. Roosevelt was born in New York on October 27, 1858, of Dutch stock.[1]

Graduating from Harvard in the class of 1880, he spent two years on a ranch in North Dakota strengthening his rather frail constitution. After serving in the New York legislature, on the national Civil Service Commission, and as president of the police board of New York City, he was made Assistant Secretary of the Navy in 1897 by President McKinley. How he resigned this position to enter the Spanish War and was elected governor of New York (1898) and Vice-President (1900) we have already mentioned. Unquenchable energy was the master trait of Roosevelt's character. The range of his interests, activities, and curiosities was enormous. His published works on history, politics, ethics, travel, and sport fill thirty volumes. It is estimated that he wrote one hundred and fifty thousand letters, which, distributed over the forty years from his majority to his death, would make an average of more than ten a day. Though born to comparative wealth, he was a man of the most democratic and genial nature. Cowboys, ambassadors, labor leaders, Senators, clergymen, and prize fighters were likely to meet one another in the reception room of the White House or to sit down at his table together. He loved power, and he wielded it with a sublime confidence that his policies

---

[1] The Dutch *oo* is pronounced like a single long *o*, as in "note." Therefore the surname of Theodore Roosevelt and of his distant cousin Franklin D. is pronounced "rō′zĕ vĕlt" — not "rōō′zĕ vĕlt."

were right in themselves and that they would prove of the utmost benefit to the American people.

His Conception of the Presidency. The "elder statesmen" of the Republican party and the bankers of Wall Street were not enthusiastic over Roosevelt's accession to the Presidency. In spite of the fact that he announced his intention of carrying out the policy of his predecessor and that he invited the members of McKinley's cabinet to retain their portfolios, the seasoned politicians, with Mark Hanna at their head, were apprehensive lest this "young man" of forty-two, with his self-assurance and his record of independence of the bosses, might disturb the well-oiled machinery of the business man's government as it had been stabilized under the "safe" administration of McKinley. They and the country were soon to learn that Roosevelt regarded the Presidency as the directing force in the government. As the "first officer" of the land and the representative of the whole American people, he believed that it was his duty and privilege to tell Congress what it should do. He did not search the Constitution for a specific grant of authority to act in any matter that appealed to him as necessary for the public welfare. "I caused to be done," he wrote in his autobiography, "many things not previously done by the President and the heads of the executive departments. I did not usurp power, but I did greatly broaden the use of the executive power. In other words, I acted for the common well-being of all our people, whenever and in whatever manner was necessary, unless prevented by direct constitutional or legislative prohibition." He liked to compare himself in this respect to Andrew Jackson and Abraham Lincoln.

The Northern Securities Case. Roosevelt was not opposed to big business as such. He realized that concentration in industry was inevitable, and he had too much energy and initiative himself to condemn the great captains of industry who had thrown the railroads across the country and raised America to the first rank among the industrial nations of the world. But he believed that the great corporations, especially those that practically monopolized the necessities of life, such as coal, oil,

THEODORE ROOSEVELT

beef, and sugar, should be "supervised and within reasonable limits controlled." They should conduct their business honestly and in strict conformity with the law. In his first message to Congress he began with a discussion of the trusts, declaring that the corporations engaged in interstate commerce should submit to a full and free investigation of their business practices. The country was not left long to speculate on whether this paragraph of the message was more than idle words.

A few weeks later the financial world was startled by the announcement in the newspapers that the President had instructed his Attorney-General, Philander C. Knox, to bring suit against the Northern Securities Company for violation of the Sherman Antitrust Law. This company represented a combination of two great railroads of the West — the Northern Pacific, controlled by J. P. Morgan, and the Great Northern, built by James J. Hill. The roads were parallel, running from the upper Mississippi Valley through the new states of the Northwest to the Pacific. Hill had come as a penniless lad in 1856 from a little Canadian village to the town of St. Paul in Minnesota, and had made a large fortune in mining, shipping, and railroads.

His Great Northern was a magnificent property, honestly built and managed. It had prospered even in the panic of 1893, when nearly two hundred roads, with a capitalization of two and a half billion dollars, went into the hands of receivers.

The object of Hill's combination with Morgan in 1901 was not to monopolize the traffic of the Northwest but to protect the "securities" (the stocks and bonds) of the two railroads from the raids of speculators in Wall Street. The "northern securities" were then taken off the stock market and exchanged for shares in a holding company with that name, incorporated in New Jersey. But the people of the Northwest complained that the merger of the two lines, by stifling competition, would put them at the mercy of whatever freight or passenger rates the Morgan-Hill combination might see fit to charge. Roosevelt asked his Attorney-General Knox for an opinion on the combination, and, on receiving the answer that it was a violation of the Sherman Act, he ordered the Northern Securities Company to be dissolved. Suit was brought in the circuit court of St. Paul, which rendered a decision in 1903 against the company. The next year the Supreme Court, by a vote of five to four, upheld the decision and ordered the company to restore to their original holders the stocks and bonds of the merged lines.

Roosevelt the " Trust-buster." The prosecution of the Northern Securities Company marked a new policy at Washington. For more than ten years the Sherman Act had stood on the statute books, but the government had not pushed a single case under it to victory against the great corporations. A member of the Supreme Court had called it a "dead letter." But now there was great anxiety among the big-business interests as to where the President might strike next. Mr. Morgan had hurried to Washington on the news of the prosecution of the Northern Securities Company to see if the matter could not be "fixed up" between his lawyers and the government, without a lawsuit. Failing in this, he had asked the President whether he intended to attack his other interests, such as the Steel Corporation. "He seemed to regard me as a rival operator," said Roosevelt. Morgan had to get such comfort as he could from

TRUST CARTOON[1]

the assurance that no business, whether big or small, had anything to fear so long as it conformed to the provisions of the law. A series of acts followed in 1903 for the better definition and enforcement of the Sherman Act. Suits dealing with the trusts were given precedence on the court calendar. A new Department of Commerce and Labor was added to the cabinet. An act was passed punishing the receiver as well as the giver of railroad rebates. Suit was brought by the government against the beef trust. These activities confirmed the fears of the standpat conservatives that Roosevelt would be a disturbing figure in the White House. But for every enemy that these acts made for the President in Wall Street or in the business lobbies at Washington, they made him a score of friends among the people at large. His declaration that the government must be "the senior partner in every business" was hailed as the warning that no private business interests would be allowed to flout the law. He was represented as carrying a "big stick" and was christened the "trust-buster."

[1] After a cartoon by F. B. Opper in the *New York American*, January 10, 1910.

The Anthracite-Coal Strike. In the autumn of 1902 Roosevelt demonstrated his readiness to act for the "public welfare" even where he had no law to fall back on, as in the case of the trust prosecutions. In May nearly one hundred and fifty thousand anthracite-coal miners in Pennsylvania had gone on a strike after John Mitchell, the president of the United Mine Workers, had tried in vain to get the mine-operators to listen to the grievances of the workers or to submit their complaints to arbitration. The grievances of the miners were real. They were obliged to produce over three thousand pounds of coal to a "ton," to "top" the cars nine inches above the edge, to buy blasting powder from the company at more than twice its cost, and at some of the collieries to accept their wages in certificates which were good only for the purchase of supplies (at a high price) from the company's stores. As the strike continued through the summer, in spite of the operators' assurance that it would be broken in a few days or weeks, the situation became threatening for the public. Anthracite was the fuel almost exclusively used for heating homes in the days before the oil-burners. When the price of coal rose from five dollars to twenty-five or thirty dollars a ton for those who were fortunate enough to get any, Roosevelt decided to act to avert the suffering which a coal famine would bring in the approaching winter.

On October 3 he summoned Mr. Mitchell and the mine-operators to the White House to a conference. "I appeal to your patriotism," he said, "to the spirit that sinks personal considerations and makes individual sacrifices for the common good." He asked that the work at the mines be resumed at once, pending an investigation and arbitration of the dispute. Mr. Mitchell at once sprang to his feet and accepted the proposition. But the operators flatly refused. They said they had nothing to arbitrate, and, with some insolence, they called upon the President to suppress the strike by force and prosecute the miners for violating the Sherman Law. Then Roosevelt took the matter into his own hands. He selected a commission to investigate the conditions in the anthracite fields and made plans to send General Schofield to Pennsylvania with a force of

United States troops to direct the resumption of work in the mines under government authority. At the same time he sent Secretary Root to New York to talk to Mr. Morgan, on whose financial backing the operators depended. Just what Root said to Morgan on their all-day conference on the latter's yacht *Corsair* in the Hudson is not recorded; but he returned to Washington with the signed promise of the operators to submit the dispute to arbitration.

Work was resumed in the mines on October 23. The strike had lasted one hundred and sixty-three days and cost close to a hundred million dollars in the loss of freight and wages. After several months the arbitration commission made its report, granting the miners a 10 per cent increase in wages, recognizing the union, and providing for a board of conciliation composed of men representing the operators, the union, and the public to settle future disputes. Under this plan peace reigned in the anthracite mining industry until after the World War.

Roosevelt's Imperialism. Although the President did not please the "elder statesmen" of the party in his determination to bring the big-business corporations to heel in obedience to the law, and, as he wrote Governor Taft in the Philippines, was "having a regular stand-up fight with Hanna and Aldrich in the Senate" to get them to accept any trust regulation, he was nevertheless in full sympathy with the most ardent of the imperialists. He not only accepted but welcomed every opportunity to assert and to uphold by force, if necessary, the prestige of the United States in any part of the world. He defended the conduct of our officers in the Philippines when they were charged with cruel treatment of the native soldiers. He spoke of Cuba as "a part of our international political system." When several of the European powers started to bombard the ports of Venezuela in 1902, to force that republic to pay its debts to them, he warned Germany (whom he mistakenly supposed to be the ringleader) that he would send Admiral Dewey with an American fleet to prevent any violation of the Monroe Doctrine, and forced the powers to submit their claims to the Hague tribunal.

CARTOON — THE MONROE DOCTRINE[1]

He exchanged letters with Senator Lodge of Massachusetts discussing the prospects of the penetration of our trade into Korea and China. When Russia and Japan were engaged in war in 1904, he notified France and Germany that if they came to the aid of the Russians he would "promptly side with Japan and proceed to whatever length was necessary on her behalf." England was an ally of Japan's, and this extraordinary threat of Roosevelt's meant practically a triple alliance between England, Japan, and the United States against Russia, France, and Germany. Indeed, the next year he sent to Japan an envoy who negotiated a secret agreement by which we recognized Japan's rule in Korea in return for her pledge to respect our sovereignty in the Philippines. And when both Russia and Japan were exhausted by the war, he brought the envoys of the two countries together at Portsmouth, New Hampshire (August, 1905), to arrange the terms of peace.

Our Interest in an Isthmian Canal. It was in the acquisition of the Panama Canal, however, that Roosevelt showed his most

[1] After a cartoon in *New York Herald*, December 16, 1902.

audacious exhibition of imperialism, and won both hearty praise and bitter denunciation from his fellow countrymen according as they viewed the ethics of the transaction. For many years the desirability of a canal across the Isthmus of Panama had been realized by our government. A French company headed by Ferdinand de Lesseps, who had built the Suez Canal, secured from Colombia in 1878 the right to dig a canal across the Isthmus, but abandoned the work ten years later after the scandalous mismanagement of its finances had brought it to bankruptcy. For a decade thereafter the French machinery rusted at Panama while the United States was absorbed in the Populist revolt and the battle over free silver. The Spanish war, however, revived our interest in the canal. The fourteen-thousand-mile voyage of the *Oregon* (p. 538, note 2) revealed the danger of the isolation of our Atlantic and Pacific coasts in time of war; and the acquisition of islands in the distant Pacific made necessary a short cut from our Eastern ports to Hawaii and the Philippines, that would save the long voyage around Cape Horn. In March, 1899, a month after the ratification of the treaty with Spain, Congress created a commission, with an appropriation of one million dollars, to investigate the relative merits of the Panama and Nicaragua routes for a canal.

The Negotiations for the Canal. The first step necessary to secure a canal under American control was the abrogation of the Clayton-Bulwer Treaty of 1850 with Great Britain, by which that power and the United States had agreed to a joint guarantee of any canal built across the Isthmus. England, as we have seen (p. 538, note 1), was very friendly to the United States at the turn of the century, and she agreed, in the Hay-Pauncefote Treaty of November, 1901, to give up her rights under the Clayton-Bulwer Treaty and allow the United States to build the canal and have "the exclusive management and policing of it." The next step necessary was to buy out the rights of the French Panama Company, if we intended to use the Panama route. At first the company charged the exorbitant price of $109,000,000 for its rights and property, which our commissioners thought worth only $40,000,000. The high French de-

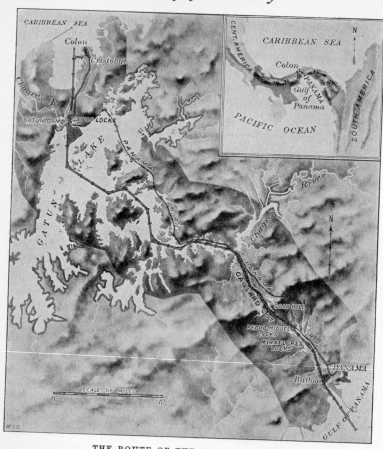

THE ROUTE OF THE PANAMA CANAL

mand seemed to make the cost of a canal through Panama prohibitive, and the House had already voted by a majority of 308 to 2 to use the Nicaraguan route when the French company suddenly agreed to our figure of $40,000,000. Then Congress reconsidered the matter and, in June, 1902, voted in favor of the Panama route if the President could secure the concession from Colombia (of which Panama was a province) "within a reasonable time."

There remained, then, only the negotiations with Colombia, which nobody thought would be difficult. Secretary Hay concluded with the Colombian representative at Washington a treaty by which we agreed to pay Colombia $10,000,000 in gold and an annual subsidy of $250,000, beginning nine years after the ratification of the treaty, for the perpetual lease of a strip of land six miles wide across the Isthmus. To the surprise and disgust of President Roosevelt, the Colombian senate, which was under the control of a corrupt usurper, rejected the treaty. It demanded that Colombia should receive $10,000,000 of the $40,000,000 which we were to pay to the French company and $5,000,000 more from the United States, making, in all, $25,000,000. Roosevelt refused to add a dollar to our generous offer, and the Colombian senate adjourned without budging from its position. It looked as if the President would not be able to get Colombia's consent to the Panama route "within a reasonable time," or, indeed, within any time at all.

The Panama Revolution. Panama was as eager as the United States to have the canal built; and when our offer was rejected by Colombia, revolutionists in Panama began to plot the revolt of that province from Colombia. Philippe Bunau-Varilla, the chief engineer of the old French Panama Company (which was also eager to get its $40,000,000), sailed for America to set the revolution on foot. A certain Dr. Guerrero came from Panama to Washington to try to get aid from our government in launching the revolution. He failed in this; but in New York he met Bunau-Varilla, who assured him that the United States would support Panama. On the evening of November 3, 1903, an uprising took place in the city of Panama. The Colombian authorities were seized and imprisoned. Some four hundred Colombian troops had already been landed at Colón, on the Atlantic side of the Isthmus. But our gunboat *Nashville* was also at Colón, with orders from Washington to prevent the Colombian troops from crossing the Isthmus to put down the revolution. They re-embarked two days later and returned to Cartagena, on the Colombian coast.

The next day our government recognized the independence

of Panama. Bunau-Varilla came to Washington as the first minister of the new republic. On November 18 he concluded with our Secretary of State the Hay-Bunau-Varilla Treaty, which was a duplicate of the previously proposed treaty with Colombia except that we acquired a ten-mile strip of land from Panama and secured the right to intervene at any time in the cities of Panama and Colón to preserve order. In 1936 a new treaty was negotiated which contained a clause surrendering this right.

Were we Responsible for the Revolution? Roosevelt's critics have accused him of "fomenting" the revolution in Panama and have called it "an ineffaceable blot of dishonor" on his administration. But to the end of his life he was emphatic in his denial of the charge. In a special message to Congress on January 4, 1904, recounting the whole affair in great detail, he said, "No one connected with this government had any part in preparing, inciting or encouraging the late revolution of the Isthmus of Panama"; and in this he was supported by the leading men in his cabinet, Elihu Root and John Hay. It is true that he sent warships to the Isthmus, and that their presence there prevented the Colombian troops from quelling the revolution. But Roosevelt defended this action on the ground of a treaty which we had made with Colombia (then New Granada) in 1846, by which we had the right to intervene in Panama to prevent disorders that might interfere with free transit across the Isthmus. The commander of the *Nashville* was obeying the letter of this treaty when he refused to let the Colombian troops cross the Isthmus to begin a civil war. But the crucial point was whether that treaty gave us the right to prevent Colombia herself from putting down a revolt in her own province. On former occasions we had intervened in Panama at the request of Colombia in order to *preserve* her authority there, whereas in 1903 we intervened to prevent her from trying to *restore* her authority. Our action, therefore, in spite of Roosevelt's denial, was virtually an alliance with the insurgents of Panama; and this was Colombia's grievance.

Far from apologizing for his action, Roosevelt boasted of it. "I took the Canal Zone," he said in an address at Berkeley,

California, in March, 1911, "and let Congress debate." And in his autobiography he wrote, "In actual fact the canal would not have been built at all save for the action which I took." When a Democratic administration came into power after the canal was dug, Secretary of State Bryan negotiated a treaty (April 7, 1914) with Colombia, providing for the payment of twenty-five million dollars to that republic and expressing "sincere regret that anything should have occurred to mar the cordial friendship" between the two nations. Roosevelt denounced the treaty as "a crime against the United States and an attack on its honor." But in April, 1921, after Roosevelt had passed away, the treaty, with the expression of "sincere regret" left out, was ratified by a Republican Senate, and our payments of the indemnity to Colombia began.

The Election of 1904. Four former Vice-Presidents (Tyler, Fillmore, Johnson, and Arthur) had succeeded to the Presidency on the death of their chiefs; but none had been able to get the nomination of his party for the ensuing term. There was a movement, favored by Wall Street and some of the big-business interests, to replace Roosevelt in 1904. They wanted Mark Hanna, who would not worry them with any trust prosecutions or talk about the "senior partnership" of the government in business. Hanna seemed at least so far willing as to oppose a resolution of the Ohio state convention of 1903 endorsing Roosevelt for nomination the next year. But Hanna died in February, 1904, and Roosevelt was nominated by acclamation at the Republican convention at Chicago in June. The Democrats turned from Bryan, twice defeated, to a conservative, Judge Alton B. Parker of New York, who made it clear by a telegram to St. Louis that he was in favor of the gold standard. His views were accepted by the convention, in spite of a protest by Bryan.

Judge Parker proved a man of straw against President Roosevelt, who was at the height of his popularity. In the election in November the Republicans carried the entire North and West with 336 electoral votes, leaving Parker with only 140 votes from the "solid South." Roosevelt won even Missouri, which had not voted for a Republican President since 1868. Parker's popular vote of a little over 5,000,000 (to Roosevelt's 7,624,000) fell more than a million behind Bryan's in 1900, showing that the radical Democrats either stayed away from the polls or voted for the Socialist candidate Debs, whose vote rose from 95,000 in 1900 to 403,000 in 1904. Immediately after the election Roosevelt published a statement acknowledging the great honor the American people had done him and declaring that, since the more than three years which he had already spent in the White House were virtually a first term, he would "under no circumstances be a candidate for or accept another nomination."

Increased Control over the Railroads. After being elected "President in his own right," Roosevelt continued his policy of law enforcement at home and intervention abroad with redoubled energy. In a speech at Philadelphia in January, 1905, he said:

We do not intend that the republic shall ever fail, as those republics of ancient times failed in which there came to be a government by classes, which resulted either in the poor plundering the rich or in the rich exploiting and in some form or other enslaving the poor. For either event means the destruction of free institutions and of individual liberty.

About the same time he wrote to Senator Lodge, "I get very much puzzled at times on questions of finance and the tariff, but when it comes to such a perfectly simple matter as keeping order, then you strike my long suit." It was clear at the outset of the new term that he would have trouble with the men who believed that reform had gone far enough already and that it was time to give the business world a "rest." Therefore, when he proposed in his message of December, 1904, that the Interstate Commerce Act (p. 400) be strengthened, there was instant opposition.

The leader of the Senate at that time, Nelson W. Aldrich, disapproved any further "meddling" of the Interstate Commerce Commission with the railroads; and even warm friends of the President, like Lodge and Knox, were unwilling to give the commission the power to fix railroad rates. It was not till

June 29, 1906, after a sixteen months' struggle with the Senate, that Roosevelt got the Hepburn Bill enacted into law. It increased the membership of the Interstate Commerce Commission from five to seven and extended its authority over express companies, sleeping-car companies, oil pipe lines, bridges, ferries, and terminals. It forbade rebates and free passes. It required advance notice of any change in schedule rates and provided that the books of the railroad companies should be open to inspection by the commission. Most important of all, it gave the commission the power to reduce an unreasonable rate, on the complaint of a shipper, until the court should pronounce on its fairness. The Hepburn Act, in short, made the Interstate Commerce Commission an effective body for the first time in its history of nineteen years.

The "Muckrakers." The same month that saw the passage of the Hepburn Act was marked by social legislation which showed the interest of the administration in public health and morals. Partly as a protest against the blunted ethics of an age of "insolent prosperity," and partly as a result of Roosevelt's constant plea for equal justice and the "square deal," a company of writers in the early years of the twentieth century turned their talents to what Professor Paxson calls a "literature of exposure." A number of new, low-priced magazines (*McClure's, Munsey's,* the *Cosmopolitan,* the *American, Collier's*) ran exciting stories of the lawlessness of the beef barons and the lumber kings. Lincoln Steffens's *The Shame of the Cities* laid bare the corrupt government of the great metropolitan centers like New York, Philadelphia, Chicago, St. Louis, and San Francisco. Thomas W. Lawson's *Frenzied Finance,* Frank Norris's *The Octopus,* and Winston Churchill's *Coniston* revealed the iniquities of the stock market, the wheat pit, and the railroads. A novel of Upton Sinclair's called *The Jungle* showed the revolting conditions that prevailed in the Chicago stockyards, and led to the passage, on Roosevelt's recommendation, of a Meat Inspection Act giving Federal officials the authority to see that all meat shipped in interstate commerce came from healthy animals and was packed under sanitary conditions.

A Pure Food and Drugs Act followed, forbidding the manufacture and sale of adulterated or poisonous foods, drugs, and liquors, and requiring on the containers of patent medicines a label showing what the contents actually were. A third piece of social legislation was the Employers' Liability Act, making corporations engaged in interstate commerce responsible for injuries received by their employees. Roosevelt deemed these measures for safeguarding health as important as the antitrust legislation. "The public welfare," he said, "outweighs the right to private gain, and no man may poison the public for private profit."

Roosevelt's Attitude toward the Corporations. When a temporary halt in prosperity came in the summer of 1907, and the prices of gilt-edged securities dropped sharply on Wall Street, Roosevelt was blamed for the panic by the capitalistic newspapers. They called him "Theodore the Meddler," and attributed the bank failures and business distress to his "hostility" to the railroads and the large corporations. Many even of his supporters urged him to "go slowly" for a time. But the President refused to "deviate a hand's breadth" from his course. The panic, he insisted, was caused not by the government's enforcement of the law but by the corporations' violation of it. "I do not for a moment believe," he wrote to the Attorney-General, "that our acts have brought on the business distress . . . but if it were true that to cut out the rottenness from the body politic meant a momentary shock to an unhealthy seeming prosperity, I should not for a moment hesitate to put the knife to the cancer." During his administration he brought twenty-five indictments against the trusts, as against five in the administrations of Harrison, Cleveland, and McKinley, and he constantly urged that the Sherman Antitrust Law should be made more definite and drastic.

On account of his interest in social reform he was accused by the conservatives of being a socialist. But he had really no sympathy with the socialist doctrine of the public ownership of the means of production and distribution, though he did advocate taxes on incomes and inheritances, and wrote to Jacob

Riis that he wished wealth might be diffused in such a manner as should "measurably avoid the extremes of swollen fortunes and grinding poverty." He had "no respect or admiration" for the typical millionaire "to whom money is the be-all and end-all of existence," and he declared that he had never found pleasure or profit in the companionship of such men. Still, he believed in the individual initiative and management of business so long as it obeyed the law. The proper way to deal with big-business corporations was not to destroy them nor to absorb them into the State, but to supervise and regulate them by strict governmental authority. He was not a socialist, but a socially-minded individualist.

Our Interest in the Caribbean Region. While the President was engaged in domestic reforms he was also incessantly busy in world affairs. We have already seen how he brought about peace between Russia and Japan in 1905 (p. 566). France and Germany were on the point of coming to blows over the control of the North African state of Morocco when he persuaded them to agree to a conference at Algeciras, Spain, in the spring of 1906, at which the two delegates from the United States took the leading part in securing a peaceful settlement of the dispute — a part which was not known to the public until Roosevelt's long secret letter of April 28, 1906, to Whitelaw Reid in London was published in 1921. In the Latin-American republics Roosevelt, resuming the work begun by Blaine twenty years before (p. 483), started that penetration of American influence which has resulted in binding a dozen of them to the United States with more or less intimate ties. His action in Venezuela and Panama we have described (pp. 565–571). With the construction of the Panama Canal [1] we naturally became interested in the stability of the governments of the countries in its neighbor-

---

[1] The "dirt began to fly" at Panama in May, 1904; and in August, 1914, the canal was opened to traffic. It was built not by private contractors but by government employees under the sole direction of Colonel George W. Goethals, a West Point engineer. Dr. William C. Gorgas, who had eliminated yellow fever from Havana, was made chief sanitary officer, and in a few years he had banished fever and malaria from the Canal Zone, making the Isthmus almost as healthy a region as any part of the United States.

hood and began the process of converting the Caribbean Sea into an American lake.

The island republic of Santo Domingo had become bankrupt through successive revolutions. Its revenues were less than one third of the interest on its debt of thirty-two million dollars, and its European creditors threatened to collect by force unless the United States would guarantee the honest and efficient management of the finances of the republic. Roosevelt announced in his message of December, 1904, to Congress that in case of "chronic wrongdoing or impotence" on the part of a Latin-American state we were bound by the Monroe Doctrine to intervene, "however reluctantly," and to "exercise an international police power." With the consent of the president of Santo Domingo, he negotiated a treaty making the United States the receiver for the bankrupt republic and appointed an official to collect the revenues. The Senate refused to ratify the treaty; but Roosevelt went on with the policy under an "executive agreement" until the Senate gave way in 1907. Under our management of her finances the solvency of Santo Domingo was restored and her creditors were satisfied. Heretofore we had only forbidden Europe to interfere with the governments of the republics of the New World; now we stepped in ourselves. This exercise of the "police power" to prevent disturbances in Latin America is called "the Roosevelt corollary of the Monroe Doctrine."

In the same year that the Senate ratified the Santo Domingo treaty, Roosevelt and President Diaz of Mexico co-operated in establishing the Central American Court of Justice, to which the five republics between Mexico and the Isthmus of Panama agreed to submit all their disputes with one another. In 1908 a further step toward the security of the Caribbean countries was taken in the creation of a Central American International Bureau to further the interests of education, trade, agriculture, and industry.

A Controversy with Japan. Serious trouble with Japan was threatened in 1906 when the board of education of San Francisco ordered Japanese, Chinese, and Korean children to attend separate schools provided for them. Up to the close of the nineteenth century not more than twenty-five thousand Japanese immigrants had come to our Pacific shores; but the crowded condition of the islands of Japan and the economic distress caused by the war with Russia sent the immigration up to seventy-five thousand by 1906. The Japanese government protested against the San Francisco order as a violation of the treaty rights of 1894, which gave Japanese residents here the status of citizens of "the most favored nation." Certain newspapers of California and Japan whipped up the quarrel by mutual insults and appeals to race prejudice. Roosevelt summoned the mayor of San Francisco and several of the anti-Japanese leaders to Washington and warned them that they must leave the settlement of an international question in the hands of the Federal government, at the same time assuring them that he would at once "take action that would meet the needs of California." The result was the "Gentlemen's Agreement" of 1907, by which Japanese children under sixteen years of age were admitted to the regular public schools and the Japanese government agreed to prohibit the immigration of Japanese laborers to this country. Again in 1909 Roosevelt had to intervene with a threat of Federal action to prevent the California legislature from passing bills to exclude the Japanese from holding land. But it was only a truce. Four years later the legislature at Sacramento passed the act, directed especially against the Japanese, forbidding aliens to hold land in the state.

Our Fleet Sent Round the World. It was perhaps chiefly to impress Japan with the naval strength of the United States that Roosevelt decided to send a fleet of battleships around the world. Many people protested against leaving our own shores unprotected, and some even predicted that Japan would attack our Pacific coast as soon as the fleet had put to sea. But the President, as commander in chief of the navy, had a right to send the vessels where he pleased. He had money enough, he said, to send them as far as San Francisco, and they would remain there if Congress refused to appropriate the funds for the rest of the voyage. The fleet of twenty-eight battleships left Hampton Roads, Virginia, on December 16, 1907, and circled the world by way of the Strait of Magellan, San Francisco, Hawaii, Australia, the Philippines, China, Japan, the Suez Canal, and the Mediterranean. At every port of call the men and officers were received with enthusiasm, and nowhere with greater cordiality than at Yokohama and Tokyo. When they returned to Hampton Roads on February 22, 1909, without the slightest accident in their long voyage, President Roosevelt was there to greet them. "You have touched the coast of every country," he said; "you have shown yourselves the best of all possible ambassadors and heralds of peace. Wherever you have landed you have borne yourselves so as to make us at home feel proud of being your countrymen." Whether or not it was a contribution to world peace, the voyage of the battleships was a striking illustration of Roosevelt's reiterated doctrine that a show of force was the best guarantee of peace, and a spectacular climax to a spectacular administration.

Conservation. We have left to the last the mention of Roosevelt's greatest service to the nation. "When the historian of the future shall speak of Theodore Roosevelt," wrote Senator La Follette at the close of the administration, "he is likely to say that he did many notable things . . . but that his greatest work was inspiring and actually beginning a world movement for staying territorial waste and saving for the human race the things on which alone a peaceful, progressive, and happy life can be founded." In his first message to Congress (1901) Roosevelt spoke of the conservation of our natural resources in forests, minerals, and water power as "the most vital internal question of the United States." Our government had lavishly given away its unoccupied lands in the days when they were supposed to be inexhaustible, and our people had wasted the natural resources of the country by careless mining of the coal, reckless cutting of the forests, neglecting to fertilize the fields, letting the oil flow from the wells to film the surface of the rivers, and lighting the natural gas as it burst from the ground. It was evident that a campaign of education in the responsibility of the present generation for the welfare, and even for the existence, of future generations was necessary. It was evident, too, that this campaign would have to be waged against the opposition of those "pioneer pillagers" who had fastened their grip on the land, lumber, coal deposits, water sites, phosphate beds, ores, and oil fields, and who wished to remain undisturbed in the monopoly of these resources. To cite but a single item: whereas at the close of the Civil War three fourths of the standing timber in the country was owned by the government, forty years later four fifths of it was in private hands. President Roosevelt took up the work of the conservation of our natural resources in a program of four points: (1) the enlargement and protection of the national forests, (2) irrigation projects for the reclamation of arid lands, (3) the improvement of our internal waterways, and (4) the enlistment of all the states in the Union in co-operation with the national government in furthering the work.

The Forests and Mineral Lands. In 1891 Congress had rather casually passed what Professor Beard has called "one of the most noteworthy measures ever passed in the history of the nation": it had given the President power, at his discretion, to withdraw from sale and set apart as forest reservations in any state or territory "public lands wholly or in part covered with timber." Cleveland had shown his interest in the matter by setting aside the San Joaquin forest of 25,000,000 acres, in California, as a national domain; but the total area of forest lands reserved by Roosevelt's three predecessors was less than 50,000,000 acres. His addition of more than 140,000,000 acres brought the number of national forests up to one hundred and forty-nine, and the total acreage to nearly 200,000,000 — an area equal to that of Great Britain and France combined. He also withdrew from sale millions of acres of public land containing mineral wealth in the form of coal, oil, and phosphates. In 1905 he had the forests transferred from the Public Land Office to the care of a special forest service under the direction of his most valuable supporter in the conservation policy, Gifford Pinchot. Scientific reforestation and fire prevention were seriously taken in hand. Timber began to be cut in a man-

THE ROOSEVELT DAM

ner to preserve and perpetuate the forests instead of wasting them. Had our government adopted this wise policy a generation earlier, it would have been able in Roosevelt's day to draw from its sale of timber and water power, its leases of coal and oil lands, a revenue which would have gone far toward meeting the expenses of the national treasury.

Irrigation Projects. An act of 1894 had allowed states in the arid regions of the country to take over large tracts of public land for improvement by irrigation. But since these were the poorer states, the ones which could least afford the capital for the construction of dams, reservoirs, and canals, the work lagged. Then Roosevelt stepped in with government aid. In June, 1902, he secured the passage of the Reclamation Act, which devoted the proceeds of the sales of public lands in sixteen states and territories of the West (the so-called "cowboy states") to a special irrigation fund. The irrigated lands were to be sold to settlers at moderate prices on a ten-year installment plan, the proceeds going constantly to renew the fund. Under the

Ewing Galloway

IRRIGATED LAND

operation of this act large tracts of land, formerly worth only a cent or two an acre for cattle grazing, became worth hundreds of dollars an acre for agriculture. Fruits came to the Eastern markets from Arizona farms which a few years before had been sandy wastes covered with patches of scrubby grass or sagebrush. The acreage of irrigated lands was less than 1,000,000 in 1880; forty years later it had increased to over 20,000,000. From the small beginnings in 1902 the irrigation projects have grown to immense proportions, combining with the work of irrigation the harnessing of rivers and the construction of reservoirs for the production of electric power. As a monument to the man who started these projects stands the great Roosevelt Dam (1911), two hundred and eighty feet high, on the Salt River in Arizona, which makes a storage reservoir with a capacity of fifty-six billion gallons, covering an area of twenty-seven square miles. Canals from the reservoir irrigate over 700,000 acres for the production of alfalfa, sugar beets, and semi-tropical fruits. This was the forerunner of the huge works that are today under construction by the Federal government on the Tennessee, Colorado, and Columbia rivers.

The Conference of the Governors. Another feature of the conservation policy was the improvement of transportation over the 26,500 miles of navigable rivers in the United States. The rapid growth of the railroads had reduced the importance of the rivers as commerce-carriers and condemned to decay most of the 4500 miles of canals. In 1907 Roosevelt appointed an Internal Waterways Commission, with a view to making the rivers and canals a great arterial system, as they are, for example, in Germany and France. He himself was the guest of the commission on a trip down the Mississippi that autumn, and shortly afterward he called together the governors of the states and territories to discuss the subject of conservation. The meeting took place in the East Room of the White House in May, 1908. The governors of thirty-four states and five territories, the members of the Supreme Court and the cabinet, Congressmen, delegates from sixty-eight national societies interested in conservation, and a number of special guests were present. The conference lasted three days and resulted in the appointment of a National Conservation Committee, with Gifford Pinchot at its head, and forty state conservation commissions appointed by the governors. Congress hampered the work of the national committee by refusing to appropriate money for its expenses, but Roosevelt persuaded the staffs of various government departments to volunteer their services. His conduct won popular approval, and the Supreme Court upheld the constitutionality of his program in every case that came before it.

The Second Hague Conference. In 1904 Roosevelt had proposed a second peace conference at the Hague; but the Russo-Japanese War caused the postponement of the meeting till 1907, when it was called by the Czar. Delegates from forty-four nations met on June 15 in the magnificent Peace Palace built by Andrew Carnegie. The conference adopted the "Drago Doctrine" (proposed by the Argentine foreign minister Luis Drago), namely, that nations should not use force to collect their debts "unless the debtor nation refused to accept arbitration." Resolutions were also adopted for the better protection of the rights of neutrals in time of war. The American delegation tried to secure the limitation of naval armaments and the creation of a permanent court of international justice to supplement the arbitration court established by the First Hague Conference (p. 551). Neither of these suggestions found favor in 1907. But after the World War they were both at least partially realized: the former in the Washington Conference of 1921-1922, which limited the tonnage of battleships, and the second in the World Court established by the League of Nations in 1921. For his efforts in behalf of international peace Roosevelt was awarded the Nobel peace prize of forty thousand dollars.[1] He kept the medal and diploma, but turned the money over to a trust foundation for the promotion of industrial peace in this country. It was finally distributed among various charitable and relief agencies when the United States entered the World War in 1917.

The Election of 1908. In spite of his insistence that he would not be a candidate for a third term, Roosevelt had hard work to prevent the Republican convention at Chicago in June, 1908, from forcing the nomination upon him. He would have liked to see Elihu Root, whom he considered the ablest statesman in the country, nominated; but Root was too closely connected with big-business corporations to make a good candidate, however good a President he would have made. After some consideration of Governor Charles E. Hughes of New York, Roosevelt decided to back his Secretary of War, William H. Taft, for the nomination. " I think that of all men in the country," he wrote to Dr. Lyman Abbott, "Taft is the best fitted . . . to carry on the work upon which we have entered during the past six years." Roosevelt's recommendation was equivalent to a nomination. Taft was chosen on the first ballot, with 702 votes to 68 for his nearest competitor, Senator P. C. Knox of Pennsylvania. The Democrats, meeting at Denver, Colorado, nominated Bryan by as imposing a majority, denouncing the Republicans as the party of privileged monopolies. Since the Democratic plat-

[1] The prize was provided by the will of the Swedish scientist Alfred Nobel, who had made an enormous fortune in the invention of explosives!

form contained a plank condemning government by injunction (p. 518), which had recently been applied in two cases of severe labor disputes, Samuel Gompers, departing from the custom of the American Federation of Labor not to mix in politics, came out openly for Bryan and pledged the labor vote of 2,000,000 to his support — a pledge which he was unable to redeem. The Socialists nominated Debs for the third time, and the waning Populists, the Prohibitionists, and the Socialist Labor party put tickets into the field.

Taft won by a popular majority of 1,270,000 and an electoral vote of 321 to 169 for Bryan. But it was more a victory for Roosevelt's candidate than for the Republican party. Democratic governors were chosen in several states which gave Taft substantial majorities. In New York, Taft won by 202,600 votes, but the Republican governor Hughes was re-elected by a plurality of less than 70,000. The meaning of this was clear. The people of the country still repudiated Bryan, but in their state elections they were registering protests against the political bosses of the party which had been in power for a dozen years. They showed greater independence in voting in 1908 than they ever had shown before. It was a portent of unrest which was realized by few of the conservative leaders — least of all, perhaps, by the gifted and genial gentleman who was forced by a raging snowstorm to take his oath of office and deliver his inaugural address in the shelter of the Senate chamber on March 4, 1909.

Ex-President Roosevelt. As soon as his successor was installed in office, Colonel Roosevelt, now a private citizen for the first time in twenty years, sailed for a long hunting trip in East Africa. One reason for his going was to avoid any appearance of wishing to control the Taft administration. He wrote to his friend George O. Trevelyan in England, three days after the election: "Taft is a strong, forceful, efficient man, absolutely upright, disinterested and fearless. In leaving, I have the profound satisfaction of knowing that he will do all in his power to further every one of the great causes for which I have fought." When Roosevelt "emerged from the jungle" in the spring of 1910, he at once became the center of observation of the whole

Western world. His progress from Egypt through Italy, Austria, Germany, France, Holland, and England was a continuous ovation, such as no American save General Grant had received before. He delivered addresses at the University of Cairo, the Sorbonne, the University of Berlin, and Oxford University. He represented the United States at the funeral of King Edward VII in London. When he landed at New York on June 18, 1910, he was welcomed by a huge and enthusiastic crowd at the Battery. In reply to the mayor's greeting he said: "I am glad to be back among the people I love. I am ready and eager to do my part, so far as I am able, in helping solve problems which must be solved if we of this, the greatest democratic republic on which the sun has ever shone, are to see its destinies rise to the high level of our hopes and its opportunities."

TERMS TO BE MASTERED

executive power	gold standard	employers' liability
Northern Securities Company	rate-fixing	conservation
arbitration commission	social legislation	"Gentlemen's Agreement"
"literature of exposure"	Nobel prize	Roosevelt corollary

FOR SUPPLEMENTARY READING

J. F. RHODES, *The McKinley and Roosevelt Administrations*, chaps. vii–xvii; J. B. BISHOP, *Theodore Roosevelt and His Times*, Vol. I, chaps. xiv–xxvii, Vol. II, chaps. i–ix; H. F. PRINGLE, *Theodore Roosevelt, a Biography*, pp. 514–527; MARK SULLIVAN, *Our Times*, Vol. II, pp. 236–253; H. HOWLAND, *Theodore Roosevelt and His Time* (Chronicles of America, Vol. XLVII), chaps. vi–ix; H. H. KOHLSAAT, *From McKinley to Harding*, chaps. xvii–xxxvi; H. C. HILL, *Roosevelt and the Caribbean*; The Pageant of America, Vol. IX, pp. 215–244 (illustrations); JOHN MOODY, *The Masters of Capital* (Chronicles of America, Vol. XLI), chaps. ii, iv, vii; W. F. JOHNSON, *Four Centuries of the Panama Canal*, chaps. viii–xviii; H. U. FAULKNER, *The Quest for Social Justice* (A History of American Life, Vol. XI), chaps. i–iv; *America*, Vol. X, pp. 215–278; THEODORE ROOSEVELT, *Autobiography*, chap. xi; JOHN MITCHELL, *Organized Labor*, chaps. xvii, xviii; GIFFORD PINCHOT, *The Fight for Conservation*; H. S. COMMAGER, *Documents of American History*, Vol. II, pp. 198–233; MUZZEY, *Readings*, pp. 556–576.

TOPICS FOR REPORTS

1. **The Northern Securities Case.** B. H. MEYER, "History of the Northern Securities Case" (University of Wisconsin Bulletins, Vol. I, pp. 215–330); GEORGE KENNAN, *Life of E. H. Harriman*, Vol. I, pp. 387–404; J. G. PYLE, *Life of James*

J. Hill, Vol. II, pp. 112–187; E. A. PRATT, *American Railroads*, pp. 223–234; J. W. GARNER, "The Northern Securities Case" (American Academy of Political and Social Science, Proceedings, Vol. XXIV, pp. 125–147).

2. **The Coal Strike of 1902.** JOHN MITCHELL, *Organized Labor*, pp. 355–396; J. B. BISHOP, *Theodore Roosevelt and his Times*, Vol. I, pp. 196–220; E. D. DUR-RAND, "The Coal Strike and its Settlement," in *Political Science Quarterly*, Vol. II, pp. 385–415; THEODORE ROOSEVELT, *Autobiography*, pp. 504–518; MARK SUL-LIVAN, *Our Times*, Vol. II, pp. 420–446; H. F. PRINGLE, *Theodore Roosevelt, a Biography*, pp. 264–278.

3. **Were we Unjust to Colombia?** H. C. HILL, *Roosevelt and the Caribbean*, chap. iii; J. B. BISHOP, *Theodore Roosevelt and his Times*, Vol. I, chaps. xxiv, xxv; THEODORE ROOSEVELT, "The Panama Blackmail Treaty," in *Metropolitan Maga-zine*, Vol. XLI, pp. 8 f.; J. F. RHODES, *The McKinley and Roosevelt Adminis-trations*, pp. 261–278; L. T. CHAMBERLAIN, "A Chapter of National Dishonor," in *North American Review*, Vol. CXCV, pp. 145–174; W. R. THAYER, "John Hay and the Panama Republic," in *Harper's Magazine*, Vol. CXXXI, pp. 167–175.

4. **Roosevelt's Conservation Policy.** F. A. OGG, *National Progress* (American Nation Series, Vol. XXVII), pp. 96–130; C. A. and W. BEARD, *The American Leviathan*, chap. xvii; S. E. WHITE, "The Fight for the Forests," in *American Magazine*, Vol. XLV, pp. 252 f.; THEODORE ROOSEVELT, *Autobiography*, chap. xi; G. W. JAMES, *Reclaiming the Arid West*; F. H. NEWELL, *Irrigation in the United States*; C. R. VAN HISE, *The Conservation of Natural Resources in the United States*.

QUESTIONS SUGGESTED BY THE CHAPTER

1. Trace Roosevelt's political career before 1900. **2.** Why were the "elder statesmen" of the Republican party suspicious of him? **3.** Why did the public sympathize largely with the miners in the strike of 1902? **4.** Why did Morgan and Hill form the Northern Securities merger? **5.** How did Roosevelt bring the coal strike of 1902 to an end? **6.** What clause in the Constitution gives Congress power to regulate the railroads? **7.** Why was interest in an Isthmian canal stim-ulated at the close of the nineteenth century? **8.** Why was Roosevelt called a Socialist by some critics? **9.** How did he differ from the Socialists? **10.** Who were the "muckrakers"? **11.** Where and by whom was the Panama revolution planned? **12.** Do you think our government "fomented" the revolution? **13.** How did Roosevelt justify sending warships to Panama in 1903? **14.** When and how was our controversy with Colombia settled? **15.** Why did we have diplomatic negotiations with England over the building of an Isthmian canal? with France? with Colombia? **16.** Did the Democrats make a mistake in nominating Parker in 1904? **17.** Why was Roosevelt called "Theodore the Meddler" in 1907? **18.** Why is the conservation of our forests important? **19.** Why did our river transportation decline in the second half of the nineteenth century? **20.** What objects did Roosevelt have in sending the fleet around the world? **21.** Why was there opposition to his plan? **22.** What was the "Gentlemen's Agreement" of 1907? **23.** Compare the Japanese immigration of the early twentieth century with the Chinese immigration of a generation before. **24.** What did Roosevelt do to merit the Nobel prize?

CHAPTER TWENTY-THREE

THE PROGRESSIVE MOVEMENT

Political and Social Ferment. The country to which Roosevelt returned in the summer of 1910 was in the midst of a political and social agitation such as it had not known since the uprising of the Populists in the 1890's. "In no period after the Civil War," says Professor Ogg, "was the American system of government more clearly on trial than in the opening decade of the present century." "Shall the people rule? is the overshadowing issue which manifests itself in all the questions now under discussion," said the Democratic platform of 1908. The combination of Populists and Democrats (the "Popocrats") in 1896 had put all their eggs in one basket by making free silver the sole issue of the campaign. Bryan's defeat on that issue, followed by the decisive victories of the Spanish War, the great wave of business prosperity, the interest of the country in the problems arising out of the government of our new possessions, and the heightened prestige of the United States in Europe and the Far East had, for a brief period at the turn of the century, somewhat drowned the voices of the reformers. But their demands for the relief of the farmers' tax burdens, the better reward of labor, the curbing of the trusts and of the business lobbies at Washington, and a greater share of the common people in determining the policies of government continued to be raised, especially in the communities of the West. Men imbued with these ideas were coming into Congress. Governors in several states were elected on reform platforms. No one had done more to encourage this movement than President Roosevelt himself, with his zeal for bringing the corporations into obedience to the law and with his insistence that "government agencies are justified in the way in which they are used for the practical betterment of living and working conditions among the mass of the people."

Popular Rule. "Democracy" means "the rule of the people." In a small community, such as a New England town, all the adult male citizens had the opportunity to participate directly in government by speaking and voting in town meetings. But tens or hundreds of thousands of citizens cannot meet in an assembly to make laws. They elect representatives to do this for them. About sixty-eight hundred men (one in nineteen thousand of our population), sitting at Washington and the various state capitals, frame the country's laws. Legislative bodies had always been regarded as the most democratic part of our government, because, as Andrew Jackson said, they came "fresh from the hands of the people." But now there was a growing feeling that they were not faithful to their trust. In 1907 a series of articles appeared in the *Cosmopolitan*, under the title of "The Treason of the Senate," in which the author undertook to prove that seventy-five of the ninety members of the United States Senate were really representing not the people but the railroads, the meat-packers, the sugar, oil, and steel interests. The Populists, twenty years before, had asked for the passage of certain reforms rather than any change in the machinery of government; but the new Progressives, as soon as they got control in some of the Western states, began to put into operation political devices for making their officials and legislators more responsive to the popular will.

Direct Primaries. It had long been the custom for the Democratic and Republican machines in cut-and-dried party caucuses, attended by a few professional politicians, to "prepare the slate," that is, to select the candidates for office. Thus the voters on election day found themselves confronted with a choice between candidates in whose nomination they had had no part and in whose election they often had little interest. The direct primary gave the people a voice in the *selection* as well as the *election* of their public servants, by substituting for the secret caucus a vote of the regularly enrolled members of the party in making nominations. After a long battle, Governor La Follette of

Wisconsin got the legislature to adopt the direct primary system in 1903, and since that date all but five of the states of the Union have made provision for the nomination of all or part of their candidates for office by a popular vote. The direct-primary idea was extended into national politics in 1910, when Oregon adopted a scheme of "Presidential preferential primaries." The people of the state expressed their choice by ballot for the man they preferred to have nominated for the Presidency, and thus "instructed" their delegates to the national convention whom to vote for. A dozen states had adopted this system by 1912.

The Initiative, Referendum, and Recall. Many states passed measures to give the people a voice in the making of the laws as well as in the choice of their officials. By the "initiative," if a certain proportion (usually 5 to 8 per cent) of the voters sign a petition to have a certain law passed, their proposition must be voted on either by the legislature or by the people directly. By a similar petition, any law passed by the legislature must be submitted to the voters of the state for approval or rejection; thus the "referendum" is a popular exercise of the veto power. Since South Dakota adopted the initiative and referendum in 1898, half the states of the Union have followed its example. Oregon has made the most complete test of the referendum, having submitted three times as many measures to popular vote since its adoption of the device in 1902 as any other state. In 1910 it asked the people to pronounce on thirty-two measures, including such a variety of subjects as woman suffrage, liquor laws, the salmon fisheries, employers' liability, railroad legislation, and tax reform. Another device of popular government is the "recall," by which a certain proportion (seldom less than 25 per cent) of the people may start a movement for the removal of an elected or appointed official. Just as the referendum is a popular veto, so the recall is a popular impeachment. It was first adopted by Los Angeles in 1903, and has been used chiefly in city governments. The most serious objection to the recall has been its application to judges, who, it is felt, should not be controlled by the shifting currents of political opinion. Though included in the constitutions of about a dozen states, the recall has never been used to remove a state judge, and only once (by North Dakota in 1921) invoked for removing a governor or other high official.

The Popular Election of Senators. The momentum of the campaign for direct government carried through a reform in the Federal machinery which had been discussed for nearly a century, namely, the election of United States Senators by a popular vote instead of by the state legislatures (Constitution, Art. I, Sect. 3, par. 1). Without doubt, many Senators, or their big-business backers, used methods far from righteous to influence the members of the legislatures in their votes. It would be impossible, argued the advocates of direct election, for a sugar, a lumber, or an oil Senator to bribe or intimidate the whole electorate of the state, as he might the two or three hundred lawmakers at the state capital. More than once the House of Representatives, by majorities far in excess of the necessary two thirds, passed an amendment for the direct election of Senators. But the Senate refused to comply. Then, beginning with Oregon in 1904, state after state adopted the plan of allowing the voters at the primaries to indicate their choice of a Senatorial candidate and pledging the members of the state legislature to vote for the candidate of the "people's choice." More than enough states to ratify a Federal amendment had thus virtually provided for the popular election of Senators by 1910. The Senate then gave way and passed the amendment that its own members should be elected by a popular vote, as were the members of the House. This seventeenth amendment to the Constitution, being duly ratified by three fourths of the states, went into effect in 1913.

Woman Suffrage. At the same time the movement was under way for doubling the electorate by a constitutional amendment giving women the right to vote. Wyoming had come into the Union in 1890 with woman suffrage, and Colorado (1893), Utah (1896), and Idaho (1896) had adopted the reform. The movement for direct government roused the women to renew the agitation for enfranchisement, which had lagged for a decade. Moreover, the number of women engaged in gainful occupations

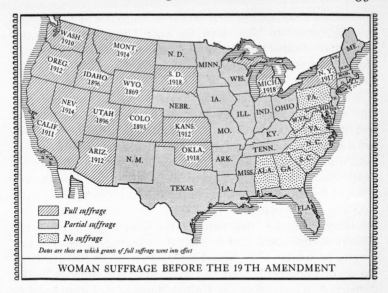

Full suffrage
Partial suffrage
No suffrage

Dates are those on which grants of full suffrage went into effect

WOMAN SUFFRAGE BEFORE THE 19TH AMENDMENT

was growing at a rapid rate, and this new economic status of women gave them an equal interest with men in laws dealing with conditions in factories and mills, hours of labor, sanitation, employers' liability, and the like. Large numbers of women were also employed in various fields of welfare work, such as children's courts and institutions of correction and charity, which were becoming more numerous as the state extended its activities in the regulation of the social and economic conditions of the people. Women had entered the professions as doctors, lawyers, and preachers. By 1910 more than one hundred thousand young women were attending colleges and universities. Tens of thousands were filling positions in the civil service. About one in five of the employees in mills and factories were women. In 1903 a National Trades Union League was formed to contend for equal pay for equal work with men, an eight-hour day, and full equality with men in the rights of citizenship. Women resented being classed with children, idiots, and criminals in the denial of the vote. In mild imitation of their sisters in England, who smashed windows, hacked monuments, horsewhipped ministers, and went on hunger strikes to compel Parliament to give them the vote, the more "militant" suffragists paraded the streets with banners, picketed the White House, and annoyed public men who were opposed to "votes for women."

The final victory for a national woman-suffrage amendment, which had been proposed by Susan B. Anthony as early as 1869, was due to the steady campaign waged in the states. Washington was won in 1910, and in the next two years California, Kansas, Arizona, and Oregon gave the ballot to women. By 1916 a dozen states, which chose about one sixth of the Presidential electors, had adopted woman suffrage, and the politicians realized that the woman vote was a factor to be reckoned with, like the labor vote, the Irish vote, or the farmer vote. The large Eastern states, which had resisted the movement, began to fall in line, beginning with New York in 1917; and in 1919 both houses of Congress passed the Nineteenth Amendment to the Constitution, forbidding the United States or any state to deny the right to vote to any citizen on account of sex. Tennessee ratified the amendment as the thirty-sixth state in 1920, in time to allow the women of the country to take part in the Presidential election of that year. In 1840, even after the democratic reforms of the Jacksonian period, only one fourth of the adult population of the country had the ballot; eighty years later the proportion had risen to four fifths.[1]

[1] The following diagram shows the extension of the suffrage since Washington's day. The shaded portions represent the proportion of the voting population to the total population of twenty-one years of age or over.

SUSAN B. ANTHONY

Municipal Reform. As far back as the 1880's James Bryce called the government of our cities "the one conspicuous failure of American democracy," and twenty years later his severe judgment was echoed and confirmed in Lincoln Steffens's *Shame of the Cities.* The Industrial Revolution was so rapidly converting America into a land of city dwellers that by 1910 more than a third of our population lived in cities of over twenty-five thousand. Immigrants crowded into the slum districts of the great urban centers. The foreign-born formed only 7.5 per cent of the population in the country regions, but in the cities of five hundred thousand or over they comprised 33.6 per cent. They were sometimes naturalized at the rate of one a minute, and tens of thousands of ignorant voters (coming in ever-greater numbers from the poorer countries of southern and eastern Europe) remained in the large cities to become the easy prey of political bosses and a difficult problem for the agencies of Americanization.

It was an accident that started the reform of the machinery of city government. In 1900 the city of Galveston, Texas, was almost destroyed by a tidal wave. Like a bankrupt corporation, it was put in the hands of receivers. Mayor, council, and board of aldermen were removed, and a commission of five able citizens was chosen to manage the city. The experiment proved so successful that other cities took it up. The form adopted by Des Moines, Iowa, in 1908 has been most widely copied. The commissioners (usually five in number) are selected by the whole people of the city, and each one is responsible for an administrative department, such as finance, public health, or public works. No franchise can be granted or contract let without popular approval. The small number of officials to be elected gives the voters a much better chance to become familiar with the merits of the candidates. The commission form of government has been extended to more than four hundred cities. Other cities have adopted a still more concentrated form of government, in which a city manager is hired as an expert, nonpartisan administrator, invited usually from a different part of the country. He has general supervision over the commissioners and is charged with the appointment and dismissal of subordinates, like the manager of a big business concern. The object of these new plans is to take the government of the cities out of the hands of corrupt bosses and rings and put it into the hands of administrative experts.

The Socialists. All these devices for the reform of national, state, and city government were looked on by the Socialists as useless tinkering with a bad political and social system. The only remedy, they said, for the evils of society lay in an entire change in the economic system, in which the wealth of the country should be more justly distributed. "The capitalist class," said the platform of the new Socialist party in 1901, "owns the government, the press, the colleges, and schools." By their control of land, money, credit, and all the tools of production, they had monopolized the country's wealth and reduced the great mass of workers who produced that wealth to mere "wage slaves," without money, land, homes, or tools, living from hand to mouth and constantly on the verge of destitution. There was wealth enough for all under proper methods of production and distribution. The public, and not the small privileged class, should own the land, the railroads, the telegraph and telephone lines, the mills and factories, the banks and power plants. Production of goods should be regulated by the State to fit the needs of the people, instead of being determined by capitalists, whose only thought was the accumulation of profits. The Socialists entered the field of national politics in 1900 with Eugene V. Debs of Indiana as their candidate for the Presidency. He headed the Socialist ticket in four successive campaigns, from 1900 to 1912, his vote increasing from 88,000 to 900,000 in the dozen years. However, the Socialists have never carried a state in a Presidential election or elected a state governor or a United States Senator. They have sent only two members to Congress. The size of their vote is far in excess of their party membership, a good part of it being a "protest vote" against the behavior of the Republicans and the Democrats rather than an endorsement of Socialist doctrines.

The I.W.W. Just as the Socialists condemned the "bourgeois" attempts to remedy economic evils by tinkering with the machinery of government, so the more extreme revolutionists regarded the Socialist program of reform by the peaceful method of the ballot as futile. Neither had they any faith in the efforts of the labor unions of the American Federation to get better wages, shorter hours, and the recognition of collective bargaining with the capitalists. In January, 1905, they organized at Chicago a radical association called the Industrial Workers of the World (the I.W.W.), and declared in their manifesto that "the working class and the employing class have nothing in common" and that a bitter struggle must go on between labor and capital until the workers "take possession of the earth and the machinery of production and abolish the wage system." They advocated (like the old Knights of Labor) "one big union" in place of the conservative federation of unions under Gompers, which, they said, "fostered the idea of a harmony of interests between the employing exploiter and the employed slave." As their name implies, their allegiance was to an international and not to an American program, and their ranks were recruited largely from the unskilled, foreign-born laborers who imported the revolutionary ideas of the European class strife. They approved "direct action," that is, terrorism, mass strikes, sabotage (the crippling of machines), destruction of property, and the incitement of the workers to revolution. The I.W.W. never had a membership of more than a few tens of thousands, and they should not be confused with the Socialist party or the labor unions, which condemn their methods as severely as do the capitalists.

Social Legislation. The object of all the advocates of changes in our government, whether by reform or revolution, was to secure for the people a fuller participation in shaping the laws and especially to gain better conditions for the working classes. During the first dozen years of the new century an immense amount of social legislation was passed. By 1912 three fourths of the states had child-labor laws, forbidding the employment of children under a certain age or in dangerous industries or for an excessive number of hours per day. Workingmen's compensation acts recognized the responsibility of employers for injury to workers due to defective machinery or hazardous jobs. In several states compulsory insurance systems were established, by which employers and workers both contributed to a fund for the relief of the sick or the pensioning of the aged or disabled. The eight-hour day in industry became almost universal. Commissions were appointed in various states to make a careful study of wages and the cost of living, and the first minimum-wage law was passed by the state of Massachusetts in 1912. State after state in the West and South prohibited the manufacture and sale of intoxicating liquors, until by the close of the first decade of the century about two thirds of the area of the United States was "dry." A better distribution of the burdens of government was sought through the recommendation of laws imposing taxes on the profits of corporations, on the inheritance of fortunes, and on incomes above a certain figure.

President Taft. It was a far different country, then, that Mr. Taft was called to govern on March 4, 1909, from the country which Theodore Roosevelt found at the beginning of the century. It was an America awakened and seething with social unrest. "The whole country," wrote Franklin K. Lane to Roosevelt in April, 1910, "is insurgent." The new President was not a reactionary, as many of his critics have called him. Indeed, as compared with Cleveland or McKinley, he seems almost a radical. He approved the major policies of Roosevelt. He added tens of thousands of postal employees to the classified civil-service lists. He brought forty-five indictments against the trusts, as against twenty-five in Roosevelt's administration. He extended the conservation policy by the addition of over a million acres of forest reserves in the Appalachian Mountains and by the reservation of the mineral wealth in coal, oil, asphalt, and phosphates beneath the surface of the public lands entered for sale. Treaties of arbitration and reciprocity were negotiated by his Secretary of State, P. C. Knox. Laws were passed establishing postal savings banks and the parcel post, taxing the profits of corporations, and creating a new Department of Labor in the cabinet. The President himself recommended an amendment to the Constitution providing for an income tax.

Yet, because Taft moved forward slowly when the reformers were calling for rapid action, he seemed to many to be moving backward. He was an administrator of great capacity, a lawyer of great distinction, a man of contagious courtesy, open, sympathetic, buoyant, and conciliatory. By temperament and training he was deliberate and cautious. He walked sedately, whereas Roosevelt had charged ahead with confidence and dash. His mental attitude was that of the judge accustomed to weigh arguments and less disturbed by postponing a decision than by making a wrong or hasty one. He surrounded himself with a cabinet of lawyers well on in years. The schemes of "direct government" that were being pushed by the more radical reformers seemed to him to contain many dangers. Wise legislation, he thought, should be preceded by careful investigation by boards and commissions. The courts, with their slow and dignified examination of the evidence in the case, should take precedence over the legislatures, which might easily be led by eloquent demagogues to adopt measures that pleased the shifting and unstable whims of the people. Roosevelt was a crusader; Taft was a judge. The one was a dynamo, the other a balance wheel.

Taft Disappoints the Tariff Reformers. The administration had come into power pledged to a "substantial downward revision" of the Dingley tariff, which had stood unchanged for a dozen years. The bulletins of the Bureau of Labor showed that the cost of necessary articles of consumption had risen some 40 per cent under its operation, while wages had advanced less than 20 per cent. The high tariff was ensuring enormous profits to the manufacturer, but its benefit to the consumer and laborer was dubious. Taft himself declared in a campaign speech that the time had come for tariff revision. On March 15, 1909, he called Congress in extra session to redeem his pre-election promise. The bill brought in by Chairman Payne, of the Ways and Means Committee of the House, partially redeemed the party pledge by enlarging the free list and cutting the duties on steel, iron, lumber, refined sugar, and chemicals. It passed the House by a party vote of 217 to 161; but when it reached the Senate, under the charge of Nelson W. Aldrich of Rhode Island, the leader of the big-business interests, it underwent 847 alterations, of which more than 600 were increases in rates. A group of progressive Senators worked like Trojans to defeat the bill, but were not able to prevent its passage. President Taft signed the bill in August, 1909.

The Payne-Aldrich Bill was a plain betrayal of the party pledge of "downward revision." The President made no attempt to restrain the high protectionists of the Senate from mutilating the bill; and when he did take a hand in it during the conference stage, it was the tariff reformers that he summoned to the White House to convert, and not Mr. Aldrich. He signed the bill without protest, and the next month, in a speech at Winona, Minnesota, he called it the "best tariff ever passed by the Republican party." The country did not agree with him, however. "Cynical comments were heard on all sides," says Miss Ida Tarbell. The press was filled with scathing editorials on the "hoax" of tariff revision. The administration at once lost the support of all the Progressives.

The Insurgents. When the first regular session of Congress met in December, Taft was eager to press measures for railroad and trust legislation, currency reform, and conservation. But he soon discovered what a determined opposition he had roused in Congress. It was not alone the signing of the Payne-Aldrich Bill that made him trouble. During the summer of 1909 a controversy had arisen between Gifford Pinchot, Chief of the Forest Service, and Richard A. Ballinger, Taft's Secretary of the Interior, over Ballinger's alleged favoritism to the Guggenheims in their claims to valuable mineral lands in Alaska. Taft stood by his secretary; and when Pinchot violated the rules of government etiquette by writing a criticism of his superior to a Senator, Taft dismissed him. Ballinger was exonerated by a Congressional committee of investigation, but the sympathy of the progressives was with Pinchot, who hastened to Egypt to meet Roosevelt and give his former chief his side of the story. Convinced by the Ballinger-Pinchot incident and the Payne-Aldrich Tariff that Taft was a "tool of the interests," thirty Republican members of the House (enough, in combination with the Democrats, to defeat any measures of the administration) signed a pledge to work to "restore the principles of representative government." These "Insurgents" began with a fight to free the House from the control of the "stand-pat" Speaker, Joseph G. Cannon of Illinois. In March, 1910, Representative George W. Norris of Nebraska moved that the Committee on Rules, which the Speaker appointed and of which he was the chairman ex officio, should henceforth be elected by the House and that the Speaker be not a member of it. As the Rules Committee practically controlled the business of the House by determining the order of bills on the calendar, this Norris resolution meant shearing Speaker Cannon of all his power except merely presiding over the debates of the House and recognizing the speakers. Cannon declared the Norris resolution "out of order," but the insurgent Republicans joined with the Democrats to pass it after an all-night's bitter battle. Then Cannon defiantly invited the House to depose him from the Speakership; but a motion to that effect, introduced by a Democratic Congressman, was defeated by a vote of 155 to 192. The insurgents were content to let "Uncle Joe" Cannon remain in office, when shorn of his power.

The "New Nationalism." The cause of the insurgents in Congress and of the Progressives throughout the country was strengthened by the return of Roosevelt in the summer of 1910. He announced his intention of remaining "out of politics," for a time at least, in order to study the situation. But he could no more keep out of politics than a fish can live out of water. He entered into the campaign in New York State as chairman of the Republican convention at Syracuse. In spite of his lavish praise of Taft a year before, he had now become convinced that the President was "a first-class lieutenant, but no leader, with no real conviction or appreciation of the really vital problems before the country." In a famous speech on "The New Nationalism" in the autumn of 1910, Roosevelt put himself squarely on the side of the Progressives, advocating strict regulation of the trusts, publicity of campaign funds, genuine tariff revision, income and inheritance taxes, workmen's compensation laws, the protection of women and children in industry, direct primaries, the initiative and referendum, and the recall of elected officials. "The Constitution does not give the right of suffrage to any corporation," he declared. We must "equalize opportunity, destroy privilege and give the highest value to the individual."

In discussing "the conflict between the men who possess more than they have earned and the men who earn more than they possess," he quoted Lincoln to the effect that "labor is the superior of capital and deserves much higher consideration." We were "face to face with a new conception of the relations of property to human welfare." The present rules of the political and economic game, which allowed the corporations to evade the law by the "vulpine legal cunning" of their counsel, must be changed. Urging the "Square Deal," — in language which anticipated that of his distant cousin, President Franklin D. Roosevelt, more than twenty years later, in launching the "New Deal," — he declared that "the power of the national government extended to the protection of the whole people against the special interests." "I am a Progressive," he wrote a few months later; "I could not be anything else. ... We must work and we must fight for the restoration of popular rule."

The Election of 1910. The revolt against the Taft administration culminated in the mid-term elections of 1910. The President's unpopularity was increasing. The trust prosecutions dragged. An act passed to extend the power of the Interstate Commerce Commission over the railroads, disappointed the reformers by not providing for a valuation of the property of the roads, on which alone the determination of fair freight rates and a proper limitation of their issues of stocks and bonds could be based. In our foreign affairs Secretary of State Knox was pursuing a policy of "dollar diplomacy," that is, of using our diplomatic influence in Latin America, China, and Japan for the advancement only of our commercial and financial interests, at the expense of friendly cultural relations with those countries. The Democrats won an overwhelming victory at the polls, getting control of the House for the first time in sixteen years, and greatly reducing the Republican majority in the Senate. As there were about a dozen Republican insurgents in the Senate, this meant that the administration was left without support in either branch of Congress. Democratic governors replaced Republicans in eight states. The election marked a sharp division between the two halves of the Taft administration. In 1909 and 1910 he had the opportunity to put himself at the head of the progressive forces; but he disapproved what he called their "dangerous changes in the form of our government," and sided with the conservatives. When he signed and defended the Payne-Aldrich Tariff, he was represented in cartoons as putting the "big stick" in the corner and approaching the Senator from Rhode Island with the humble petition "Please, Mr. Aldrich!"

The Progressives Organize. The insurgent Republicans did not delay long after the disastrous defeat of 1910 to organize for the reform and capture of the party. In January, 1911, they met at the house of Senator La Follette in Washington and formed the National Republican Progressive League. They adopted La Follette's Declaration of Principles to the effect that "popular government in America" had been "thwarted by the special interests," and agreed on a program including direct primaries, direct election of United States Senators, the initiative, referendum and recall, and strict laws for the punishment of corruption and bribery in elections. A few weeks later they held another meeting and decided to support a Progressive candidate for the Presidential campaign of 1912. "There is but one man," said Senator Cummins, "who should be considered, and that man is Senator La Follette." A Progressive conference of about three hundred delegates at Chicago in the autumn of 1911 approved the program of the League and endorsed La Follette as "the logical candidate for the Presidency of the United States." The Progressives disclaimed any intention of seceding from the Republican party; their object was to capture the party for progressive ideas, as the Populists had captured the Democratic party for free silver in 1896 (p. 525), and not to disrupt it. But disruption was inevitable in both cases. The Republican Progressives had already repudiated President Taft (as the "Popocrats" did President Cleveland in 1896) and condemned the party machine to which they declared he was slavishly bound.

Canadian Reciprocity. President Taft only made more trouble for himself during the months that the Progressives were organizing. In January, 1911, he negotiated a reciprocity agreement with Canada, by which many of the food products of our northern neighbor were to be admitted to the United States free of duty, while the rates on our manufactures imported by the Canadians were to be lowered. In order to get this pet scheme of his through, he called together the hostile Congress (which would not meet ordinarily until December) in extra session on April 4. The Western farmers, however, among whom the insurgents had their chief support, opposed the free admission of Canadian grain, vegetables, eggs, butter, and cattle;

while the high protectionists of the East resisted reciprocity in any form as a dangerous breach in the protective walls. Taft got his measure through Congress, with the help of Democratic votes, only to have it killed by the Canadian government, which saw in it an attempt to bring Canada too closely under the political and economic influence of the United States.[1] Besides opposing the President on his reciprocity program, the insurgents took advantage of the extra session to join with the Democrats in a series of attacks on the Payne-Aldrich tariff. Bills were passed lowering the rates on woolens, cottons, chemicals, and iron, and removing those on agricultural implements, wire fencing, and cotton bagging, essential to the farmers. Taft vetoed all these "pop-gun bills," as hasty and unscientific measures.

Roosevelt and La Follette. It was not the President, however, who was causing the chief worry to the Progressives, but the popular Colonel. Since his return from Europe, Roosevelt had approved the Progressive measures in his speeches, but had neither joined the League nor given any support to the movement for La Follette as President. Was it because he was unwilling to split the Republican party or because he had no intention of playing second fiddle to the Wisconsin Senator? His devoted followers in the League, like the Pinchot brothers and ex-Secretary of the Interior James R. Garfield, wanted him to come out as a candidate for the nomination in 1912, but he would say neither Yes nor No to their urging. In a curiously contradictory letter to William B. Howland, he said that Taft could be beaten by "a strong candidate," but that La Follette had no strength east of the Mississippi. "I am not a candidate," he continued, "and I never will be a candidate. But I have to tell the La Follette men and the Taft men that, while I do not

[1] This apprehension in Canada was reinforced by unwise remarks of some people of high position in the United States. "Champ" Clark, the new Speaker of the House, favored reciprocity because he "hoped to see the day when the American flag would float over every square foot of the British North American possessions clear to the north pole"; and President Taft, in a letter to Roosevelt in January, 1911, spoke of reciprocity as "procuring a current of business between the two countries that would make Canada only an adjunct of the United States."

wish the nomination, yet I do not think it would be right or proper for me to say that under no circumstances would I accept it if it came." His attitude exasperated La Follette, who complained with considerable logic that he could not see why Roosevelt kept talking about not being a candidate unless he really meant to be one. He bitterly accused Roosevelt of having approved the Payne-Aldrich Act and of balancing every rebuke to the trusts with a rebuke to the labor unions. As for him, he preferred Taft's honest conservatism to Roosevelt's "rhetorical radicalism" and "mock heroics."

The long period of suspense came to an end early in 1912. On February 10, Roosevelt received a letter (said to have been composed in the office of the *Outlook*, on whose staff the Colonel was serving as contributing editor), signed by the Progressive governors of seven states, urging him to sink his personal objections for the sake of "the happiness and prosperity of the country," and to accept the nomination "as a plain patriotic duty." A few days later Taft made a speech before the Republican Club of New York in which he attacked the Progressives as "emotionalists" and "neurotics," who would "hurry us into a condition which would find no parallel except in the French Revolution or in that babbling anarchy that once characterized the South American republics." This was too much for Roosevelt. On February 24 he replied to the governors, "I will accept the nomination for the Presidency if it is tendered to me." His "hat was in the ring."

The "Theft" of the Roosevelt Delegates. President Taft had little hope of being re-elected. When he was introduced as "our next President" at a meeting in the West in 1911, he replied that the chairman was "a better Republican than prophet." A dozen of the states had already adopted the system of instructing their delegates to the national convention to vote for the candidate of the people's choice. More than a third of the delegates to the Republican convention at Chicago in June, 1912, were from these states; and of the 382 thus chosen, 278 were instructed for Roosevelt, 68 for Taft, and 36 for La Follette. So far, then, as the people had a chance to express their wish,

Roosevelt was the candidate they desired. But the machinery of the convention was in the hands of the administration leaders, and they were determined not to let the Progressives capture the party as the Populists had captured the Democratic party in 1896. The seating of delegates was in the control of the national committee, which had been elected four years before. This committee assigned 238 of the contested seats to Taft delegates, and only 19 to the Roosevelt claimants. As a result, the regular Republicans were able to elect their candidate for chairman, Elihu Root, by the narrow margin of 558 votes to 502 for the Progressive Governor McGovern of Wisconsin; but when Root advanced to the platform to make his "keynote speech," he was greeted with cries of "Thief!" by the Roosevelt men. The latter then either left the convention hall or refused to vote, and Taft was nominated on the first ballot with 561 votes to 107 for Roosevelt and 41 for La Follette. Had only 22 of the contesting Roosevelt delegates been seated, Taft would have failed to get the nomination.[1]

The Republican Split. Roosevelt had hastened to Chicago from his home at Oyster Bay, Long Island, to protect his interests. But as he was not a delegate to the convention and had no privilege on the floor, he could not prevent the "steam roller" of the administration from flattening out opposition, as it had done four years before when his own hand was on the throttle. On the evening of Taft's nomination the Roosevelt followers gathered in Orchestra Hall and passed resolutions condemning the "fraud" of the convention and inviting Roosevelt to lead a third party. The Colonel entered the hall amid a storm of applause. In a brief but stirring speech he advised the delegates to go back to their homes to sound the sentiment of the people, and to reassemble later in the summer in a con-

[1] Senator Borah of Idaho, a member of the national committee, who attended all its sessions, believed that 52 delegates were "stolen" from Roosevelt. A. W. Dunn, the dean of the Washington newspaper correspondents, who also sat in the committee room for eight days, "watching the wheels go round," estimated that 51 Roosevelt men were deprived of seats in the convention to which they were entitled. Even La Follette conceded that "some justification could be found" for counting 49 of the contested seats for Roosevelt.

vention to nominate a Progressive candidate on a Progressive platform, who would appeal to every section of our country and "to Republicans and Democrats alike in the name of our common American citizenship." "If you wish me to make the fight," he said, "I will make it, even if only one state should support me. I am in this fight for certain principles. The first and most important of these goes back to Sinai and is embodied in the commandment, 'Thou shalt not steal.' Thou shalt not steal a nomination . . . thou shalt not steal from the people the birthright of the people to rule themselves. . . . We stand at Armageddon and we battle for the Lord."

The Bull-Moose Convention. On August 5, 1912, in response to the Progressive committee representing forty states, some two thousand delegates assembled at Chicago to launch the new party. The meeting was "more like a religious revival than a political convention." It was permeated with a spirit of crusading zeal. "The Battle Hymn of the Republic" and "Onward Christian Soldiers" were sung over and over again. Miss Jane Addams of the Hull-House settlement led the women delegates and made one of the keynote speeches. When Roosevelt entered the hall, he was received with a burst of singing and cheering which lasted for nearly an hour. He was nominated for the Presidency by acclamation, with Governor Hiram Johnson of California for his running mate; and the convention adjourned after singing "Praise God from whom all blessings flow." The party platform declared that "the first task of the statesmanship of the day" was to destroy the "invisible government" of special privilege. It advocated all the political and social reforms that have been described in the early paragraphs of this chapter. It adopted the Bull Moose [1] as its emblem, and entered with zeal upon its campaign to make a clean sweep of the old abuses and "build a new and nobler commonwealth." Thus the Progressive Republicans, failing to introduce the leaven of reform into the party, had repudiated the administration. The insurgents had become seceders. For a third time since the Civil War the nomination of a Republican

[1] For the origin of the Bull Moose symbol see page 544.

candidate unacceptable to the reform element of the party had provoked a revolt. In 1872 the Liberal Republicans had tried to defeat Grant with Horace Greeley and the aid of the Democrats. In 1884 the Mugwumps had deserted Blaine to vote for Cleveland. In 1912 the Progressives were to trust to the popularity of their candidate to defeat Taft.

The Opportunity of the Democrats. Three days after the Republican convention at Chicago had adjourned in schism and torrid heat, the Democrats met in joy and more torrid heat at Baltimore (June 25, 1912). Their hopes were high; for it was evident as soon as the split occurred among the Republicans that the Democrats had only to nominate a candidate who would satisfy the progressive element in their own party in order to win the election, whether Roosevelt ran on an independent ticket or not. For if he did, he would draw his votes chiefly from the Republicans who were dissatisfied with the Taft administration; and if he did not, many of those dissatisfied Republicans would vote for a reform Democrat, as the Mugwumps had voted for Cleveland in 1884. There were many aspirants for the nomination, but the results of the primaries narrowed the serious contestants to four: Governor Judson Harmon of Ohio, Governor Woodrow Wilson of New Jersey, Representative Oscar Underwood of Alabama, and the Speaker of the House, J. Beauchamp ("Champ") Clark of Missouri. Harmon, however, was handicapped by the fact that he was reckoned as a conservative at a time when a "progressive" nomination was imperative; and Underwood was further handicapped by coming from a state of the lower South.

It was evident from the beginning that the fight was between Clark and Wilson, each of whom had more votes on the first ballot than all the other candidates combined. The most notable feature of the convention was the influence exercised by Bryan. Though not a candidate for the nomination himself, he dictated the platform and controlled the proceedings at Baltimore as thoroughly as he had done at Denver four years before. He censored the delegates, even proposing to exclude certain representatives of the big-business interests from the floor. He carried by a

WOODROW WILSON AND WILLIAM H. TAFT

large majority a resolution that the convention should nominate no candidate identified with "the privilege-hunting and favor-seeking class." And when the opportune moment came, he swung the delegates from the man who had led on every ballot, and whose nomination was virtually conceded by his nearest rival, to the man of his own choice.

The Nomination of Woodrow Wilson. Champ Clark had defeated Wilson in the primary elections by more than 200,000 votes. He led Wilson by a large margin ($440\frac{1}{2}$ to 324) when the balloting began at Baltimore; and when the New York delegation, led by Charles F. Murphy, the boss of Tammany Hall, transferred its votes from Harmon to Clark on the tenth ballot, the latter had a majority of the delegates, though not the two-thirds vote necessary to nominate in a Democratic convention. At this point Governor Wilson conceded the nomination of his rival and prepared a telegram of congratulations to him. But at this point also Mr. Bryan stepped in. Though the Nebraska delegation was pledged by the primaries to support Clark, and had done so till now, Bryan swung it over to Wilson, declaring that no candidate who received the vote of Tammany Hall should receive the vote of Nebraska. Other states fell in behind Nebraska; and Wilson crept up on Clark until on the twenty-eighth ballot he passed him and on the forty-sixth received 990 votes, far more than the two thirds necessary for the nomination.

In only one other Democratic convention in our history has a candidate (Van Buren, in 1844) won a majority of the votes without eventually getting the nomination. Clark, like Roosevelt, could claim that he was the popular choice of his party as expressed in the primaries, but, unlike Roosevelt, he did not bolt the party. The day following his defeat he gave a statement to the press, thanking his friends for their support and declaring, "I lost the nomination solely through the vile and malicious slanders of Colonel William J. Bryan of Nebraska." Governor Thomas R. Marshall of Indiana was nominated for the Vice-Presidency. The platform branded the Payne-Aldrich Tariff as a robbery of the people, and the trusts as "indefensible and intolerable private monopolies." It endorsed the progressive measures of direct government, farm credits, the creation of a Department of Labor in the cabinet, a single Presidential term, and a recognition of the independence of the Philippines as soon as a stable government should be established in the Islands.

The Campaign of 1912. A deplorable feature of the campaign was the exchange of bitter personal vituperation between the erstwhile bosom friends Taft and Roosevelt. The latter accused the President not only of having failed to redeem his pledge to carry out the progressive policies of the Roosevelt administration but of having broken his promise to retain certain members of that administration in his cabinet and of having "stolen" the nomination at Chicago. Taft indignantly denied the accusations and countered with the charges of "hysteria" and "dangerous emotional radicalism" against his former chief. Wilson conducted a dignified campaign, criticizing both Roosevelt and Taft for supporting a tariff which encouraged the trusts and for associating with men who had no faith in the people to work out their own salvation. "They are willing to act *for* the people," he said, "but not *through* the people"; to allow the middle class to have some share in prosperity, but not to originate it; to let prosperity trickle down on the people in thin streams, but not to well up from their own generous energies. He

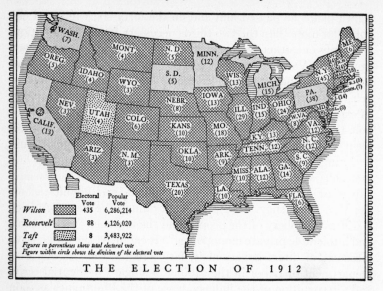

Electoral Popular
Vote Vote
Wilson 435 6,286,214
Roosevelt 88 4,126,020
Taft 8 3,483,922
Figures in parentheses show total electoral vote
Figure within circle shows the division of the electoral vote

THE ELECTION OF 1912

preached the doctrine of free competition. There would be no salvation of the country until the evil partnership between the government and the trusts was dissolved. He believed in the common man, in individual enterprise, and in states' rights. These and other tenets of Jeffersonian democracy are to be found in the little volume of principles, entitled *The New Freedom*, which contains the gist of his campaign speeches.

In the election, Wilson carried forty of the forty-eight states, receiving the unprecedented total of 435 votes in the Electoral College. Roosevelt carried Pennsylvania, Michigan, Minnesota, South Dakota, Washington, and California, with 88 votes. Taft won only Vermont and Utah, with 4 votes each. However, Wilson's popular vote of 6,286,214, as against 4,126,020 for Roosevelt and 3,483,922 for Taft, was but 42 per cent of the total, and outside the old slaveholding South he did not have a majority of the popular vote in a single state of the Union, except Arizona. The Socialists, with Debs as their candidate for the fourth time, polled nearly 900,000 votes — their high-water mark. The outstanding feature of the election was the

Roosevelt vote. That a man without the support of either of the great party machines, heading a third party hastily formed and with some disaffection in its own ranks (for La Follette gave Roosevelt no support), should have polled over 30 per cent of the popular vote, or four times as large a vote as any independent party had received since the Civil War, was no small triumph. With the Presidency the Democrats won also both branches of Congress. Only once before (1893–1895) since the election of James Buchanan, in 1856, had they controlled both the executive and the legislative department of the government. They also elected governors in twenty-one of the thirty-five states in which governors were chosen in 1912. It was a Democratic year.

Taft retired from the Presidency with cheerful resignation. He had not really wanted the office very much. His ambition was for a seat on the Supreme Court, an honor which, to his great credit, he had twice declined in the Roosevelt administration, from a sense of duty to his work in the Philippines. He had his reward in 1921, when President Harding appointed him Chief Justice of the Supreme Court, — a position which he held until his death, in 1930. He is the only man in our history who has held the two most distinguished offices in our government.

TERMS TO BE MASTERED

direct government	suffragists	dollar diplomacy
"Popocrats"	city manager	"steam roller"
sabotage	insurgents	"the New Freedom"

FOR SUPPLEMENTARY READING

F. A. MAGRUDER, *American Government*, chaps. xxiv, xxvi; EVERETT KIMBALL, *State and Municipal Government in the United States*, chaps. iv, vi, xxiii–xxv; S. P. ORTH, *The Boss and the Machine* (Chronicles of America, Vol. XLIII), chaps. ix, x; WOODROW WILSON, *The New Freedom*; E. P. OBERHOLTZER, *The Referendum, Initiative, and Recall in America*; W. E. DODD, *Woodrow Wilson and his Work*, chaps. i–v; H. U. FAULKNER, *The Quest for Social Justice* (A History of American Life, Vol. XI), chaps. ii, iii, v; MARK SULLIVAN, *Our Times*, Vol. IV, chaps. xiv, xvi–xxi; C. G. BOWERS, *Beveridge and the Progressive Era*, pp. 333–383, 416–454; *The Pageant of America*, Vol. IX, pp. 205–214; R. S. BAKER, *Woodrow Wilson, Life and Letters*, Vol. III, chaps. v–vii; HART, *Contemporaries*, Vol. V, Nos. 94–98, 119, 120.

Topics for Report

1. **Oregon's Experiments in Direct Government.** A. H. Eaton, *The Oregon System*; J. D. Barnett, *Operation of the Initiative, Referendum, and Recall in Oregon*; B. J. Hendrick, "The Initiative in Oregon," in *McClure's Magazine*, Vol. XXXVIII, pp. 235 f., 435 f., 505 f.; Jonathan Bourne, Jr., "The Recall in Oregon," in *The Outlook*, Vol. XCVI, pp. 329 f.; G. H. Haynes, "The People's Rule in Oregon," in *Political Science Quarterly*, Vol. XXVI, pp. 32–62.

2. **How Women Got the Vote.** A. M. Schlesinger, *New Viewpoints in American History*, pp. 137–158; S. B. Anthony and I. H. Harper, *History of the Movement for Woman Suffrage*, Vol. IV; W. H. Allen, *Woman's Part in Government*; K. Porter, *History of Suffrage in the United States*, pp. 135–145, 228–254; R. C. Dorr, *What Eight Million Women Want*; P. W. Slosson, *The Great Crusade and After* (A History of American Life, Vol. X, chap. v); E. A. Hecker, *The Significance of the Woman Suffrage Movement* (American Academy of Political and Social Science, Annals, May, 1910).

3. **Immigration Problems.** S. P. Orth, *Our Foreigners* (Chronicles of America, Vol. XXXV); F. J. Warne, *The Tide of Immigration*, chaps. xxi–xxiv; A. M. Schlesinger, *New Viewpoints in American History*, pp. 13–21; H. P. Fairchild, *Immigration*, chaps. ii–iv; E. A. Ross, *The Old World in the New*; K. Berkovici, *On New Shores*; R. L. Garis, *Immigration Restriction*, chap. iv.

4. **How Wilson was Nominated at Baltimore.** R. S. Baker, *Woodrow Wilson, Life and Letters*, Vol. III, pp. 332–363; W. G. McAdoo, *Crowded Years*, pp. 137–159; W. F. McCombs, *Making Woodrow Wilson President*; Champ Clark, *My Quarter Century of American Politics*, Vol. II, pp. 392–443; J. P. Tumulty, *Woodrow Wilson as I Know him*, pp. 105–126; E. H. Abbott, "The Game at Baltimore," in *The Outlook*, Vol. CI, pp. 522–527.

Questions Suggested by the Chapter

1. Why did Populism decline after 1896? **2.** How had Theodore Roosevelt encouraged the movement for popular government? **3.** What forms of control over legislatures were advocated by the Progressives? **4.** What are the objections to the recall of judges? **5.** Why did the women want the vote? **6.** Compare the methods of the English and the American suffragists. **7.** Could women vote before the passage of the Nineteenth Amendment? Explain your answer. **8.** What were the advantages of the commission form of city government? **9.** How widely has the city-manager type of municipal government been used? **10.** How did the I. W. W. differ from the Socialists? **11.** Give some recent examples of social legislation. **12.** Why has labor been hostile to the courts? **13.** By what acts did Taft lose the support of the Progressives? **14.** Describe the Progressive revolution in the House in 1910. **15.** Why didn't Roosevelt join the Progressives in 1910? **16.** Why did Canada reject the reciprocity treaty of 1911? **17.** Do you think Taft was fairly nominated in 1912? **18.** Do you think Roosevelt was justified in splitting the Republican party in 1912? **19.** Why were the Progressives called the Bull Moose party? **20.** Why did Roosevelt and Champ Clark both claim to be the "people's choice" for the nomination of their respective parties in 1912?

CHAPTER TWENTY-FOUR

WOODROW WILSON AND THE "NEW FREEDOM"

The New President. Woodrow Wilson dominated the second decade of the twentieth century as Theodore Roosevelt had dominated the first. He was born at Staunton, Virginia, December 28, 1856, of Scotch-Irish stock, with Presbyterian ministers among his ancestors on both sides. He graduated from Princeton in 1879, the year before Roosevelt graduated from Harvard. But while Roosevelt plunged into practical politics, Wilson, after a half-hearted attempt to practice law, decided to remain in the shades of academic life. He studied history and political science at Johns Hopkins, taught at Bryn Mawr, Wesleyan, and Princeton, and wrote books on the government of the United States and European countries. After two years as professor at Princeton he was elected president of the university, and entered upon a determined campaign to raise the standard of scholarship and make the institution more democratic. He was in constant conflict with certain of the trustees, professors, and alumni over his educational policies, until he was virtually forced to resign in 1910.

Meantime Colonel George Harvey, editor of *Harper's Weekly* and the *North American Review*, an anti-Bryan Democrat, who was "tired of having to vote the Republican ticket," had begun to boom Wilson for the Presidency. As a steppingstone to that high office, Harvey and other friends of Wilson secured for him the nomination for the governorship of New Jersey in 1910, just as he was ready to retire from Princeton. The leaders of the Democratic machine in the state were willing to accept him for the votes that his rare eloquence would win, "trusting," as Professor Dodd says, "to his mere academic character and political inexperience to make him either too timid or too conservative for the real work of reform." They were right about his vote-getting capacity, for he was elected by a majority of 49,000 in a state which had given Taft a majority of 82,000 two years before. But they were sadly mistaken about his character. He immediately entered upon a program of reform in the face of bitter opposition from the Democratic bosses, who thought that the "professor" would be an easy tool in their hands. He put through legislation for direct primaries, employers' liability, the strict regulation of public utilities, election reforms, and the elimination of corrupt practices, earning the reputation of being the most independent and progressive governor in the Eastern states. A tour of the Western states in the autumn of 1911 enabled him to present his progressive views to a wide audience in the finished and convincing oratory of which he was a supreme master. When the campaign of 1912 opened, he was a figure of national importance.

His Political Philosophy. In his classroom lectures, his magazine articles, and his books (*Congressional Government, The State*, and *The History of the American People*) Wilson had matured his views on political theory and practice. He had as positive ideas as a Jackson or a Roosevelt on the dignity and responsibility of the Presidential office. "The Presidency," he said in an address at Staunton in December, 1912, "is an office in which a man must put on all his war-paint." He must be the "big chief," directing and controlling legislation by his constant pressure upon Congress, but directing it always in the interest of the people at large. There were three possible kinds of government, he thought: the "invisible" government of the bosses, for the sake of the special interests; the "mass meeting" government of populace, subject to the influence of demagogues; and the "responsible" government by a leader who was given ample power, but held to strict accountability in the use of his power, by a free and enlightened citizenry. The people should select good leaders and "back them to the limit."

Though a Jeffersonian in his faith in "the average intelligence of the American people," Wilson could not, in the highly indus-

trialized America of the twentieth century, follow Jefferson's
doctrine of the noninterference of the government with business
(*laissez faire*). As if with prophetic vision of that tremendous
extension of the authority of the Federal government into every
sphere of business which we have witnessed under the "New
Deal," he wrote in 1912, "We are just upon the threshold of a
time when the systematic life of this country will be sustained
or at least supplemented at every point by governmental activity." "We have great tasks before us," he continued, "and
we must enter upon them as befits men charged with the responsibility of shaping a new era." In his inaugural address of
March 4, 1913, to a huge throng gathered before the east front
of the Capitol at Washington, he spoke of the abundant forces,
material and moral, in American life; of the evil that had crept
in with the good; of the inexcusable waste amid unparalleled
riches. We must return to the standards which we had "so
proudly set up in 1776," and which we had "always carried in
our hearts." Then having squared our public life with our traditions of freedom and opportunity for all, we should be in a
position to make our influence felt among the nations of the
world, not by the fear of our battleships, but by the powerful
plea of a good example. In conclusion, he abjured the spirit of
narrow partisanship: "This is not a day of triumph; it is a day
of dedication. Here muster not the forces of party but the forces
of humanity. . . . I summon all honest men, all patriotic men,
all forward-looking men to my side. God helping me, I will not
fail them if they will but counsel and sustain me."

Difficulties Confronting the President. In spite of his
courageous words, President Wilson knew that he was facing
a very difficult task. He was now the leader of the American
people; yet three fifths of the votes had been cast at the polls
for other candidates (see page 610). He was the head of the
Democratic party; yet the Democrats had given him fewer
votes in victory than they had given three times to Bryan in
defeat.[1] He had little sympathy with Bryan's views, and in a

---

[1] Bryan's popular vote in 1896, 1900, and 1908 was 6,509,052, 6,358,737, and
6,407,982 respectively. Wilson's popular vote in 1912 was 6,286,214.

letter of 1907 had expressed the hope that some way might be found to "knock Bryan into a cocked hat"; yet he had now to reckon with the large element of Bryan's followers in the party. As an "academic" person, with little active experience in politics, he was looked on with rather scornful misgivings by the seasoned political war horses in Congress. As the first President of Southern birth since Andrew Johnson, he was disliked by Northerners who resented his warm defense of the South in fighting its "war for independence"; and though the complexion of the administration was decidedly Southern, — five of the members of the cabinet and the chairmen of the most important committees in both houses of Congress being of Southern birth, — it by no means meant that the Southern leaders would approve his policies. They had voted for him as a Democrat, not as a Progressive. They represented a conservative section of the country, which had little sympathy with such innovations as direct government and woman suffrage, or such social legislation as child labor and employers' liability laws.

But if the President had handicaps to contend with, he had also certain advantages to offset them. His very absence from the turmoil of the political arena had spared him the enmities and jealousies of political rivals. He was not identified with any unpopular measures or political defeats. He had a thorough knowledge of the machinery of our government. He was strong-willed, eager, optimistic, and capable of making up his mind with precision and finality and of keeping his counsels almost to the point of secretiveness. Finally, he had a party majority in both houses of Congress, including a number of new men, who would not be so jealous of executive control as those who had served many years in Congress.

The Cabinet. Wilson's cabinet selections did not serve to increase confidence in him. He was practically obliged to offer the Secretaryship of State to the man who had made his nomination possible, albeit Mr. Bryan had no conspicuous gift for diplomacy. As a matter of fact, he was never allowed to do more than hold the ends of the reins, while President Wilson did the driving. The Treasury post was given to William G. McAdoo, who in 1903 had moved from Tennessee to New York and had been engaged in many business enterprises, the chief of which was the building of the "tubes" connecting New York and New Jersey under the Hudson River. Lindley M. Garrison, a New Jersey lawyer, was made Secretary of War, and the Navy department was given to Josephus Daniels, editor of the Raleigh *News and Observer*, who had been most influential in securing the North Carolina delegation. Colonel Edward M. House of Texas, a most intimate though recent friend of Wilson, might have had any cabinet position he pleased, but he preferred to remain out of office as a private counselor to the President. However, he recommended his fellow Texan Albert S. Burleson for the position of Postmaster-General. It was noticeable that during his entire Presidency of eight years Wilson made no appointment of a cabinet member from New England or from the important states of the Old Northwest.[1]

The Program. Instead of making his inaugural address the usual general oration on the prosperity, peace, and prestige of the United States, Wilson took the people into his confidence by announcing the specific reforms that he intended to accomplish, in order to restore the ideals which we had "so proudly set up in 1776," and to release the "generous energies" of the American people. The chief evils to be remedied were three:

1. A tariff which cuts us off from our proper part in the commerce of the world, violates the just principles of taxation, and makes the government a facile instrument in the hands of private interests.

2. A banking system based on the necessity of the Government to sell its bonds fifty years ago, and perfectly adapted to concentrating cash and restricting credits.

3. An industrial system which . . . holds capital in leading strings, restricts the liberties and limits the opportunities of labor, and exploits, without renewing, the natural resources of the country.

On this triple wall of privilege the President forthwith began his attack.

[1] The other members of the original cabinet were Franklin K. Lane of California (Interior), J. C. McReynolds of Tennessee (Attorney-General), D. F. Houston of Missouri (Agriculture), W. C. Redfield of New York (Commerce), and W. B. Wilson of Pennsylvania (Labor).

The Reform of the Tariff. Wilson called the new Congress together in extra session on April 7, 1913. Instead of sending a message from the White House (as all the Presidents since Washington and John Adams had done), to be read in a droning voice by the clerk, while the members of Congress snoozed or conversed, Wilson went in person to the Capitol and delivered a brief and forceful address to an attentive audience. Believing in tackling one thing at a time, he spoke only of the reform of the tariff. "We must abolish everything that bears even the semblance of privilege or any kind of artificial advantage," he said, and make our producers "better workers and mechanics than any in the world" by constantly sharpening their wits in competition with those of foreign producers. It was not "free trade" that he advocated but free opportunity for American business. Our Treasury would continue to depend for its income largely upon duties laid on imports, but those duties must be for the sake of revenue and not for the enrichment of great industries which no longer had need of "protection."

The Democrats had had control of the House since 1911, and a new tariff bill was ready to be introduced by Oscar W. Underwood of Alabama, the chairman of the Committee on Ways and Means. As it passed the House in May by a vote of 281 to 139, it contained 958 reductions, chiefly on articles of necessity like food and clothing, while the rates on luxuries, such as gems, furs, silks, perfumes, wines, and automobiles, were generally increased. There were about 300 articles on the free list, and the average rate of the Payne-Aldrich duties (p. 598) was lowered from 41 to 29 per cent. When the Senate threatened to repeat its tactics of 1894 and 1909 and "amend" the bill into a highly protective measure,[1] Wilson came out with a public rebuke of the "insidious lobby" at work in Washington. It was due to his insistence on an honest revision of the tariff that the Senate, after four months of wrangling, passed the bill with little change by a vote of 44 to 37. The Underwood-Simmons Bill was the

[1] F. M. Simmons of North Carolina, who had succeeded Aldrich as chairman of the Finance Committee of the Senate, was no supporter of Wilson's progressive program. He had voted for the Payne-Aldrich Tariff.

first piece of genuine tariff reform since the Civil War. On signing it (October 3) Wilson congratulated the American people that the fight for free business "which had lasted a long generation through had at last been won handsomely and completely."

An Income Tax is Levied. To make up for the anticipated loss of revenue from tariff duties, an income tax (made constitutional by the adoption of the Sixteenth Amendment in February, 1913) was levied. Net incomes above $3000 for a single person and $4000 for a married couple were subject to a tax of 1 per cent up to $20,000, 2 per cent from $20,000 to $50,000, and so on up to 6 per cent on incomes above $500,000. Complete free trade with the Philippines was established, and our merchant marine was encouraged by a 5 per cent reduction of the duties on merchandise imported in American ships. How the tariff of 1913 would have affected business and prices in America under normal conditions it is impossible to say. To meet the huge expenses of our preparation for and participation in the World War, which broke out the year after the Underwood-Simmons Bill was passed, the income, corporation, and excess-profits taxes were so greatly increased that the tariff sank into comparative insignificance. It furnishes less than 10 per cent of the national revenue today.

The Banking and Currency Problem. We now approach an important subject which is very difficult for persons not experts in finance to understand, but which we must try to explain as simply as possible. The money of our country, except for the relatively small amount of coins (gold, silver, nickel, and copper) in circulation, consisted of four different kinds of paper "notes" or "bills." There were (1) gold certificates, or "yellowbacks," of large denominations, based on the gold bullion in the Treasury; (2) the United States notes, or "greenbacks," to the amount of $346,000,000, issued during the Civil War (p. 438); (3) the silver certificates, based on the silver purchased by the government under the acts of 1878 and 1890; and (4) the notes issued by the national banks on the basis of government bonds (p. 438). All these kinds of currency together did not furnish enough money and credit to conduct the rapidly expanding business of the country. It was like trying to sail an ocean steamer in a shallow river. Moreover, none of these types of currency were "elastic," that is, capable of increasing to meet the expansion of business; for (1) only relatively small amounts of gold were being brought to the Treasury, (2) the "greenbacks" had been fixed at their present amount at the time of the "resumption of specie payments" (p. 439), (3) the government had ceased to purchase silver, except for the coinage of "change" (p. 516), and (4) the national-bank notes were decreasing just at the time when the business activity of the country was increasing.[1]

This scarcity of credit enabled the big bankers to establish a kind of "money trust." Men wishing to start a business enterprise had to come to them "hat in hand" to get the necessary capital. Furthermore, the thousands of banks and trust companies of the country were not connected by any system of common responsibility, so that if there was a "run" on a bank (that is, a demand of a large number of depositors for their money at the same time), the bank's reserves might be exhausted and failure result.

The Federal Reserve Act. For a score of years before Wilson came into office, statesmen and financiers had been working on plans for a more adequate currency and a more centralized banking system. In 1912 a bill for the establishment of a central national bank, like that of Hamilton's day, was introduced into the Republican Senate. But the Democrats opposed this "Aldrich plan," and when they came into power, a year later, their chairman of the Banking and Currency Committee in the House, Carter Glass of Virginia, brought forward a bill on which he had been working for a year. President Wilson, Secretaries Bryan and McAdoo, Senator Owen of Oklahoma (the chairman

---

[1] This was partly because the government bonds on which the notes of the national banks were based began to fall due and be paid off in the 1880's, and partly because the higher price of the bonds, as the credit of the government rose, offset the profit which the bankers could make by lending notes based upon them. Thus, when business was booming, the price of bonds high, and the rate of interest low was just the time that the bankers were least inclined to add notes to the currency.

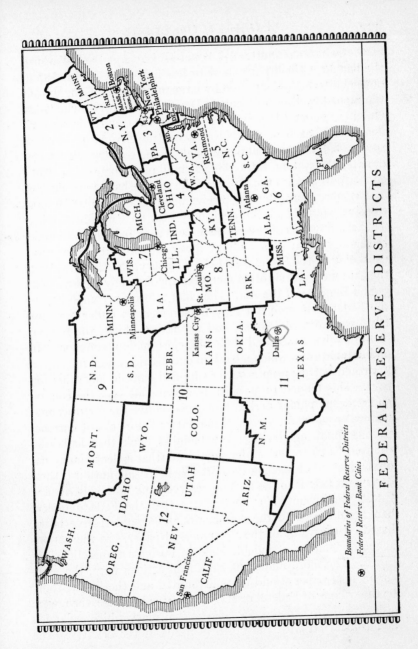

FEDERAL RESERVE DISTRICTS

Boundaries of Federal Reserve Districts
Federal Reserve Bank Cities

of the Senate committee), Colonel House, and Paul Warburg, the banker, all had parts more or less important in the shaping of the bill, which was passed by large majorities in Congress and was signed by the President on December 23, 1913. The Glass-Owen (or Federal Reserve) Act divided the country into twelve districts, in each of which was a central city with a Federal reserve bank. Every national bank in the country was obliged to enter the system, subscribing a small percentage of its capital and surplus to form the capital of the reserve bank in its district. The reserve banks did not receive deposits from or make loans to private individuals but dealt only with the "member banks." The whole system of reserve banks and their branches was under the management of a Federal Reserve Board at Washington, consisting of the Secretary of the Treasury, the Comptroller of the Currency, and six other members appointed by the President.

The Benefits of the Act. The chief reforms accomplished by the Federal Reserve Act may be summed up under the three R's: reservoir, rediscount, and regulation. First, the reserves of the twelve banks and their branches made a common pool, or reservoir, from which a bank in one district whose funds were low could borrow from a better-supplied bank in any other district. This tended to stabilize the banks all over the country and prevent panics and failures. Secondly, the "rediscount" feature provided for a more abundant and more elastic currency by the following device. Any member bank that had "discounted" a customer's promissory note (that is, lent him money on it), instead of keeping the note idle in its safe until it became due might take it to the Federal reserve bank in the district and get it "rediscounted." That means that the Federal reserve bank could issue to the member bank Federal reserve notes, based on the value of the "commercial paper," as the various acknowledgments of indebtedness in business transactions are called. The more numerous such transactions were, the more commercial paper would be rediscounted and the larger would be the volume of Federal reserve notes issued. These, then, were a new kind of currency, an "elastic" currency which expanded and contracted with the business needs of the country. The third benefit of the Federal Reserve System was its influence in preventing industrial and financial panics by regulating the discount rate. If, for example, the Federal Reserve Board charged 6 per cent instead of 4 for rediscounting commercial paper, it would discourage the member banks from accumulating too much of that paper, or, in other words, of making loans too recklessly in a period of overspeculation. Similarly, by reducing the discount rate from 4 per cent to 2, the Board would stimulate loans for the recovery of business in a period of depression.

In 1936 the Federal reserve notes constituted three fifths of the total amount of money in circulation in the United States. Their volume was over $3,000,000,000, as against $882,786,000 of national-bank notes. Of course, a sound currency and banking system cannot *alone* insure a people's prosperity. Many other factors, such as the condition of its agriculture and industry, its foreign trade, its moral disposition, enter into the situation. But during the score or more years of its operation the Federal Reserve System has proved its worth as a steadying influence on the business of the country.

The Trust Problem. After keeping Congress in continuous session for two hundred and sixty days (April 7–December 23, 1913), President Wilson gave the members a Christmas vacation of less than a month, while he himself went down to Pass Christian, Mississippi, for a still shorter rest. On January 20, 1914, he called them together again, to tackle the third of the major evils mentioned in his inaugural address, namely, the trusts. This problem Wilson considered the most important of all. "You cannot solve the tariff and currency," he had said in an address at Lincoln, Nebraska, in October, 1912, "under the domination which is proposed by one branch of the Republican party [Taft] and tolerated by the other [Roosevelt]." It was also the most difficult problem; for while the Constitution gives Congress the clear power to determine the tariff and regulate the currency, it contains no mention of corporations, capital, labor, factories, profits, business methods, competition, and the like. Clever lawyers, citing the fifth and fourteenth amendments to the Constitution, which guarantee that no person should be deprived of "life, liberty or *property* without due process of law," contended that, as a corporation was a "person" in the eyes of the law, neither Congress nor a state legislature could deprive it of its property by excessive taxation or the regulation of wages or prices. We have seen how seldom the government won cases in the courts under the Sherman Antitrust Act of 1890 (p. 498).

In his address of January 20 Wilson appealed to Congress for "a common effort to square business methods with public opinion" and proposed a five-point program: (1) the creation of a Federal Trade Commission to regulate all forms of big business except interstate commerce and banking, which were already provided for by the Interstate Commerce Commission and the Federal Reserve Board; (2) the prohibition of interlocking directorates in corporations with a capital and surplus in excess of one million dollars; (3) a better definition of the Sherman Antitrust Law; (4) the elimination of unfair practices in business competition; and (5) the regulation of the issue of railroad securities.

The Federal Trade Commission. The Federal Trade Commission was established by an act of September 26, 1914. It consisted of five men, appointed by the President to serve seven years and to have the power of investigating the big business corporations. Although the commission could demand reports from the corporations and even publish such information about their business methods as it believed the public should know; although it could order them to refrain from illegal practices and, in case of disobedience, could apply to a Federal court to discipline them — nevertheless the purpose of the commission was rather to help business to obey the law than to punish it for disobeying. It was to be, as Wilson said, "a clearing house for facts, by which both the public mind and the managers of great business undertakings should be guided." The commission furnished a body of experts who, by warning and advice, could prevent the well-intentioned corporations, or the "good trusts," from making mistakes which might bring them into the courts to fight against government prosecutions. On the whole, the

Federal Trade Commission was favorably received by the business interests of the country.

The Clayton Act. The next month a long and complicated act, — or, rather, a series of acts, — in twenty-six sections, received the name of Henry D. Clayton of Alabama, the chairman of the Judiciary Committee of the House. It was designed "to supplement existing laws against unlawful restraints and monopolies." It defined and forbade a number of illegal practices in business, such as cutting prices to "freeze out" a competitor or bribing a rival company's employees. It prohibited the absorption of the stock of one company by another to the extent of creating a monopoly. It forbade anyone to serve as a director in two or more banks whose capital and surplus equaled five million dollars or in two or more corporations with capital, surplus, and profits aggregating one million dollars. Finally, it contained provisions very favorable to organized labor and the farmer. Section 6 declared that "the labor of human beings is not a commodity or article of commerce," and exempted "labor, agricultural, or horticultural organizations instituted for the purpose of mutual help and not conducted for profit" from prosecution under the antitrust laws. Section 20 stated that a peaceable strike or boycott is not to be held a violation of the law, and forbade courts to grant an injunction against labor in any dispute "concerning the terms or conditions of employment, unless necessary to prevent irreparable injury to property."

An Extraordinary Congress. The second session of the Sixty-third Congress adjourned on October 24, 1914, after two hundred and eighty-five days of continuous work. Altogether, President Wilson had kept the lawmakers at Washington for seventeen of the eighteen months since April, 1913, and their debates in the period fill eighteen thousand pages of the *Congressional Record*. The three major reforms which we have just studied claimed most of the attention of Congress, but there were other measures of importance. Labor profited not only by the sections of the Clayton Act which we have just cited but also by the Newlands Act, which set up a board of mediation to persuade the parties in labor disputes to resort to arbitration. In the first three years of its existence the board averted strikes on forty-two Eastern railroads and adjusted over sixty labor controversies. A Seamen's Bill greatly improved the condition of the sailors in our merchant marine in respect to quarters, food, and wages. The Smith-Lever Act made an appropriation of five hundred thousand dollars a year, to be divided equally among the states in aid of the "land grant" colleges, which had been established in 1862 for the promotion of education in agriculture and the mechanical arts. Congress also provided a civil government for the Panama Canal Zone, and repealed an act of 1912 which violated the Hay-Pauncefote Treaty of 1901 (p. 567) by exempting American vessels in the coastwise trade from paying tolls for passage through the canal. Measures were introduced to aid the farmers by the construction of better roads, the establishment of farm-loan banks, and the extension of rural credits.

In August, 1914, the President wrote to Representative Underwood, "The American people have been served by this Congress as they have never been served before"; and ex-President Eliot of Harvard, reviewing the first year and a half of the administration in an article in *Harper's Weekly*, agreed with this judgment. At the same time, the very volume and variety of legislation aroused opposition, which, combined with criticism of Wilson's foreign policy (especially in regard to Mexico), led to a large gain for the Republicans in the mid-term election of November, 1914. The Democratic majority was reduced from 147 to 29 in the House, and the Republicans regained control of several of the state governments. This was due partly to the fact that many of the Progressives of 1912 were returning to the Republican ranks, the vote for Progressive candidates in 1914 being only 1,800,000 as against 4,126,000 cast for Roosevelt in 1912.

Diplomatic Problems. While he was holding Congress to its long task of reform legislation, the President had a number of difficulties to settle with foreign countries. In April, 1913, the Japanese ambassador, Baron Chinda, protested against the proposed law of the California legislature to exclude aliens from holding land in the state (p. 577). Wilson tried to get California to modify the law, and even sent Secretary Bryan to Sacramento to remonstrate with the legislature. But the law was passed, and signed by Governor Johnson. Japan continued to protest; and the ill feeling, fanned by the jingo press of Tokyo and San Francisco, might have broken out in hostilities had not the advent of the World War checked Japanese immigration and turned the attention of the Mikado's people to schemes of expansion in China. There was considerable tension with Great Britain over the Panama tolls question, which Wilson told Congress threatened to tie his hands in dealing with "other matters of greater delicacy and nearer consequence,"[1] when the Senate gave way and voted for the repeal of the exemption of American coastwise vessels.

During the summer of 1913 Secretary Bryan negotiated treaties with more than thirty nations, pledging them to submit disputes to the investigation of an international commission, in case diplomacy failed, and to refrain from hostilities for a year until the report of the commission should be received. But these "cooling off" treaties were ignored when the World War broke out. A beginning of the restoration of cordial relations with Colombia was made, as we have seen (p. 571), by the negotiation of a treaty in 1914. The most persistent and serious of all the diplomatic problems that Wilson had to handle in the first two years of his administration was caused, however, by the disorders in Mexico.

The Mexican Revolution. In 1910 the aged president-dictator of Mexico, Porfirio Diaz, who had ruled the country with a rod of iron for over thirty years, was driven from power by a revolution of liberals headed by Francisco Madero. But Madero proved too weak to control the revolutionary spirit

[1] Just what these "other matters" were Wilson never explained. It may be that he was referring to the situation in Mexico, in which he needed England's support, or that he was thinking of the visit which Colonel House was shortly to make to England, France, and Germany for the sake of helping these nations to reach some kind of understanding that would avert a European war. We could not in good conscience advise them to deal justly with one another if we ourselves refused to obey the terms of the Hay-Pauncefote Treaty.

which he had aroused, and Mexico was torn by a war of rival factions, each trying to get control of the capital and the treasury. In February, 1913, a cruel and ignorant general with Indian blood in his veins, Victoriano Huerta, proclaimed himself president. Madero was arrested and, while being conducted to jail, was murdered in the street, probably by Huerta's orders. President Taft had forbidden the shipment of arms and ammunition to any of the factions and had strengthened the guard on our Mexican border, in order to keep the disorder confined to the other side of the Rio Grande.

A few days after Madero's murder, Wilson assumed office. Huerta had managed to hold his own against several other revolutionists, and claimed that four fifths of the provinces of Mexico acknowledged his rule. Over a score of foreign governments recognized him as *de facto* president of Mexico. Our ambassador at Mexico City, Henry Lane Wilson, urged President Wilson to do the same, declaring that not to recognize Huerta meant "chaos" in Mexico. Encouraged by Diaz's policy of granting "concessions" to foreign capitalists, Americans had invested about a billion dollars in Mexican mines, railroads, plantations, and oil fields. It was the protection of this capital that appealed to those Americans who favored the recognition of the Huerta regime.

"Watchful Waiting." But President Wilson had decided ideas on our obligations to the Latin-American countries under the Monroe Doctrine. In his first statement on foreign policy, just a week after he took office, he said:

It shall be one of the chief objects of this administration to cultivate the friendship and deserve the confidence of our sister republics of Central and South America. . . . Coöperation is possible only when supported at every turn by the orderly processes of just government, based upon law, not upon arbitrary or irregular force. . . . We can have no sympathy with those who seek to seize the power of government to advance their own political interest or ambition.

Formerly we had not refused to recognize revolutionary governments, but now Wilson declared that he would not "extend the hand of welcome to anyone who obtains power in a sister republic by treachery and violence." Ambassador Wilson resigned, and the President sent a special messenger to Mexico to make the following demands on Huerta: (1) the immediate cessation of hostilities; (2) a general amnesty; (3) a new election in which Huerta must not be a candidate; and (4) the promise of all the factions to abide by the result of the election. When Huerta indignantly refused these terms, Wilson let him alone, trusting to the steady pressure of the disfavor of the United States to embarrass him with the countries of Europe and South America. "We shall not be obliged," he said in his message of December, 1913, to Congress, "to alter our policy of watchful waiting, and when the end comes we shall hope to see order restored in distressed Mexico by the concert and energy of such of her leaders as prefer the liberation of their people to their own ambitions."

Veracruz. Shortly after this announcement, however, Wilson abandoned his policy of noninterference in Mexico. In February, 1914, he allowed arms to be sent to Huerta's chief rival, Carranza, and early in April a serious incident followed. A boatload of American marines from the gunboat *Dolphin* of Admiral Mayo's fleet landed at Tampico to purchase a supply of gasoline. They were promptly seized by Huerta's commander in Tampico and marched off to jail amid the hoots and jeers of the crowd. Admiral Mayo demanded the immediate release of the marines, an apology from Huerta, and a salute to the American flag. Huerta released the men and apologized for his commander's act, but refused to salute the flag. He maintained that we could not with consistency ask him to fire a salute to our flag when we refused to recognize him as the president of Mexico. Wilson backed up Admiral Mayo and, on April 20, asked Congress for the permission to use armed force "to obtain from General Huerta the fullest recognition of the rights and dignity of the United States." He did not wait for the consent of Congress, because he received a wireless message from Admiral Mayo, soon after midnight on the twenty-first, stating that a German steamer laden with arms and munitions for Huerta was expected to dock at Veracruz in a few hours. After consulting

SOLDIERS ARRIVING AT VERACRUZ, 1914

with Secretaries Daniels and Bryan over the telephone, he sent to Mayo the reply "Take Veracruz at once." A detachment of American marines was landed in the morning, while the battleships *Utah* and *Florida* shelled the customhouse and the arsenal. Eighteen of the marines and about sixty Mexicans were killed before the Americans got control of the city.

This was certainly very different from "watchful waiting"! Most of the European nations believed that it was the prelude of a march of an American army upon Mexico City, like the landing of General Scott at Veracruz sixty-seven years before (p. 331). To avert war between Mexico and the United States, the greater republics of South America now offered their mediation. Delegates from Argentina, Brazil, and Chile (the "ABC powers") met representatives from Mexico and the United States at Niagara Falls, Canada, and prevailed upon Huerta to leave Mexico (July 15). Then Carranza entered Mexico City in triumph, and in November Wilson withdrew our troops from Veracruz. It looked for the moment as if our diplomacy, supplemented by the incident at Veracruz, had brought order out of the Mexican "chaos" predicted by Ambassador Wilson. But the end was not yet. We shall see in a later chapter how for more than a decade after Huerta's departure for Europe our relations with Mexico continued to vex three American Presidents.

An Interrupted Program. That same month of August, 1914, in which Carranza's entry into Mexico City seemed to President Wilson to mark the dawn of a "new freedom" for the nation south of the Rio Grande, two events occurred that interrupted or seriously modified his crusade for the "New Freedom" at home. The first of these events was the sudden outbreak of the World War in Europe. Wilson had come into the Presidency with the conviction that there had never been a more favorable time for the pursuit of the reforms on which his heart was set. In a speech of October, 1913, he waxed eloquent over the approaching millennium :

It seems to me that this is a day of infinite hope . . . for I am fain to believe that, in spite of all the things we would wish to correct, the nineteenth century, that now lies behind us, has brought us a long stage toward the time when, slowly ascending the tedious climb which leads to the final uplands, we shall get our ultimate view of the duties of mankind.

Five weeks later, in his first annual message to Congress, he spoke of the "many happy manifestations . . . of a growing cordiality and sense of community among nations, foreshadowing an age of settled peace and good will." The terrible havoc that burst on the world but a few months after these optimistic words he no more expected than he expected the end of the world. His mind was filled with plans for the social and cultural improvement of his fellow countrymen, once the necessary political and economic reforms were accomplished. He wrote to the poet Percy MacKaye of his hopes for the creation of a National Institute of Arts and Letters, the founding of a national university, and the cultivation of the drama, pageantry, and colorful folkways. The European war overtook him, said one of his biographers, somewhat as "the flood may have interrupted Mrs. Noah in the midst of her spring house-cleaning." From the time the last session of the Sixty-third Congress assembled, in December, 1914, until the return of peace, all other business had to yield the floor to the problems of our abstention from, preparation for, or participation in the great struggle beyond the sea. Woodrow Wilson is known to the "man in the street" only as a war President.

"Yankee Imperialism" in the Caribbean. The second event of August, 1914, that had consequences for the New Freedom was the opening of the Panama Canal. In January, Colonel George W. Goethals, the chief engineer, had been appointed the first governor of the Canal Zone. Percy MacKaye wrote the ode in honor of his inauguration :

> A man went down to Panama
> Where many a man had died,
> To slit the sliding mountains
> And lift the eternal tide.
> A man stood up in Panama,
> And the mountains stood aside.

On August 3 the steamer *Ancon* went through the locks with her decks crowded with officials and guests of the American and Panama governments. At first sight there would seem to be little connection between this event and the New Freedom. Wilson believed in the freedom of the people of every country to work out their own destiny without interference from their stronger neighbors. He was opposed to the "dollar diplomacy" of the Taft administration, and at the very beginning of his term he had refused to give the government's approval to the participation of American bankers in a large six-power loan to China because it involved the control of the Chinese customs duties for the guarantee of the interest on the loan. He had declared that the United States would never seek another square foot of territory through annexation or conquest.

Yet, if our interest in preserving order in the Caribbean region for the protection of the Canal did not result in the actual annexation of territory there, it did lead to our constant interference with the politics and finances of the Central American and island republics. Under Wilson, as under Roosevelt and Taft, the penetration of American control in Santo Domingo,

THE PANAMA CANAL TODAY

Haiti, Nicaragua, Honduras, and the countries of the Spanish Main went on steadily and, for the most part, quietly. No change of policy in the direction of a newer "freedom" for these regions marked the replacement of the "dollar diplomat" Knox by the "anti-imperialist" Bryan in the State Department. As one critic put it, "Yankee imperialism grew steadily by homeopathic doses cleverly administered" while the attention of the people of the United States was absorbed in the World War and the problems of the peace.

American Dictation in Haiti. We have not the space to describe all the instances of American intervention and dictation in the Caribbean countries, which took the forms of landing marines, controlling elections, establishing American police forces, collecting the customs duties, censoring the press, selecting officials, and even forcing the countries to take American loans. The case of Haiti may serve as an example. On June 14, 1914, France and Germany were on the point of intervening in the island to collect their debts when we demanded a financial protectorate over Haiti, such as Roosevelt had established over Santo Domingo in 1905 (p. 576). On the refusal of the Haitian government, American marines landed, marched to the National Bank, and seized the five hundred thousand dollars of public gold deposited there. A few months later Admiral Caperton arrived at Haiti with orders from Washington which read:

The United States expects to be intrusted with the practical control of the customs and such control over the financial affairs of Haiti as the United States may deem necessary for efficient administration. . . . It has no designs upon the political and territorial integrity of Haiti.

Nevertheless, we forced the republic to elect a president of our own choice, who had agreed in advance to accept a constitution drafted in Washington and any treaty that the United States might see fit to present to him. When the Haitian assembly protested against the constitution, which gave the Americans extraordinary privileges in the island, it was dissolved, and the people of Haiti were forced to accept the constitution by a popular vote. A revolt against the constitution was promptly quelled by the American marines. It was not till the New York *Nation* published a series of articles in the autumn of 1920 on the American occupation of Santo Domingo and Haiti that the general public knew much of what had been going on in the island for a period of five years.

The "Colossus of the North." Intervention of this sort in Haiti and other countries in the Caribbean region has been justified by our government as necessary to prevent revolution and chaos which might invite European powers to gain a foothold there. For nearly a century the Monroe Doctrine had stood as a general warning to Europe to leave the republics of the New World alone; but the building of the Panama Canal gave special point to the warning, and furnished the chief excuse for our not leaving those republics alone ourselves. American bankers supported the policy of intervention because it both gave them the opportunity of placing loans in the Caribbean countries at high rates of interest and assured them of our govern-

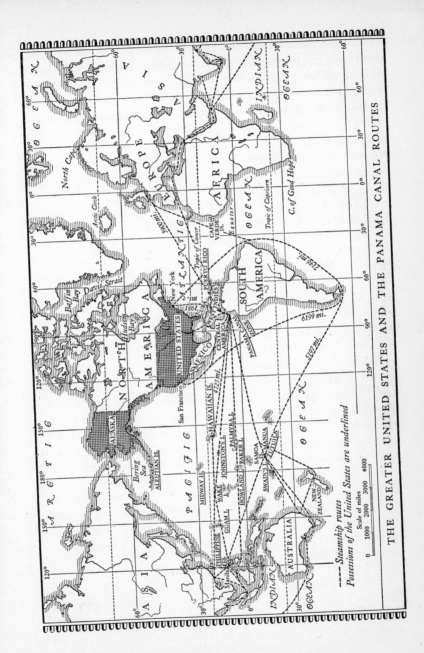

THE GREATER UNITED STATES AND THE PANAMA CANAL ROUTES

--- Steamship routes
Possessions of the United States are underlined

Scale of miles
0   1000   2000   3000   4000

ment's aid in safeguarding the principal and interest of the loans. No doubt, American intervention and control has often brought material benefit to the Caribbean republics. Money that was wasted on recurrent revolutions has been available for works of sanitation, road-building, industrial and agricultural improvements, hospitals, and schools. More stable political conditions have attracted American and foreign capital to develop rich resources of sugar, fruit, rubber, coffee, petroleum, hard woods, and asphalt.

Yet the interference of the "Colossus of the North," as the United States is called, with the politics and finances of the Caribbean countries has aroused a jealous fear in Latin America lest we intend, under the cover of the Monroe Doctrine, to extend our rule over the whole region between the Rio Grande and the South American mainland. Every intervention of the United States to influence elections, dictate candidates, enforce conventions, and suppress uprisings has lent weight to the arguments of those Latin-American politicians and publicists who are determined to see nothing but a cynical policy of aggression in our behavior. "The famous Monroe Doctrine," writes a noted Argentine author, "which appeared for a century to be our guarantee of political independence against European conquest, has revealed itself gradually as a right of the North Americans to intervene in our affairs . . . so that the phrase 'America for the Americans' means now nothing more than America — our Latin America — for the North Americans. . . . The danger of the United States comes from her superiority. She is to be feared because she is great, rich and strenuous." Our government has been sincerely anxious to allay such fears. In an address at Philadelphia in celebration of the centennial of the Monroe Doctrine (November, 1923) Secretary of State Hughes said:

By promoting stability [in Latin America] we do not threaten independence, but seek to conserve it. We are not aiming at control, but endeavoring to establish self-control. We are seeking to establish a *pax Americana* [American peace], maintained not by arms, but by mutual respect and good will.

That we in the United States believe such oft-repeated sentiments is of comparatively little importance. The important
thing is to convince the people of Latin-America of the sincerity
of these professions. A better knowledge of the history of the
Latin-American countries, a more sympathetic understanding
of the character of their people, and a deeper appreciation
of their culture on our part will contribute to that "friendly
co-operation and mutual good will" which has been the text
of so many sermons of our State Department.

Summary. In this unit we have seen first how a war with
Spain, begun for the liberation of Cuba, resulted in the acquisition of colonies or dependencies in the tropical regions of the
Caribbean Sea and the Pacific. We have studied the problems
which the government of such regions under our Constitution
raised. We have seen how the prestige and power of our country abroad was furthered by the "imperialism" of Theodore
Roosevelt, at the same time that he was awakening a spirit of
reform at home by his crusade for social justice. This movement
gathered to a head in the rise of the Progressives, who advocated
a number of changes in our political machinery, to bring the
government under a more direct control of the people. We have
seen how Roosevelt himself led the new Progressive party in the
campaign of 1912 and, by taking millions of votes from the
conservative Republican candidate Taft, assured the victory
of the Democrats under Woodrow Wilson. Finally, we have
studied the great reform measures of Wilson, who was also a
"progressive," in the remarkable sessions of the Sixty-third
Congress (1913–1914), and have seen how his crusade for the
New Freedom (except in the countries of the Caribbean) was
interrupted by the outbreak of the World War. To that great
cataclysm and its profound effects upon America we must now
turn our attention.

TERMS TO BE MASTERED

invisible government	elastic currency	"watchful waiting"
laissez faire	member banks	arms embargo
income tax	rediscount	"Yankee imperialism"

For Supplementary Reading

W. O. Woods, *The Story of Uncle Sam's Money*; H. P. Willis, *The Federal Reserve*, chaps. ii, iii, vi, viii, xii; H. R. Mussey, "The New Freedom in Commerce," in *Political Science Quarterly*, Vol. XXIX, pp. 600–625; W. H. Stevens, "Unfair Competition," in *Political Science Quarterly*, Vol. XXIX, pp. 383–406; W. E. Dodd, *Woodrow Wilson and his Work*, chaps. v, vi; F. A. Ogg, *National Progress* (American Nation Series, Vol. XXVII), chaps. xii–xvi; R. S. Baker, *Woodrow Wilson, Life and Letters*, Vol. IV; W. H. S. Stevens, "The Clayton Act," in *American Economic Review*, Vol. V, pp. 38–54; C. L. Jones, *The Caribbean Interests of the United States*, chaps. ii, vii–x; W. M. Shuster, "The Mexican Menace," in *Century Magazine*, Vol. LXV, pp. 593–602; Edith C. O'Shaughnessy, *A Diplomat's Wife in Mexico*; J. F. Rippy, *The United States and Mexico*, chaps. xx, xxi; The Pageant of America, Vol. IX, pp. 268–292 (illustrations); H. S. Commager, *Documents of American History*, Vol. II, pp. 262–275; Hart, *Contemporaries*, Vol. V, chaps. xv, xvi, xxi.

Topics for Reports

1. **The New Banking System.** E. E. Agger, "The Federal Reserve System," in *Political Science Quarterly*, Vol. XXIX, pp. 265–281; H. P. Willis, "The New Banking System," in *Political Science Quarterly*, Vol. XXX, pp. 591–617; P. M. Warburg, *The Federal Reserve System*, Vol. I, chap. i; D. S. Muzzey, *The United States of America*, Vol. II, pp. 546–555; Charles Seymour (ed.), *The Intimate Papers of Colonel House*, Vol. I, pp. 158–175; W. G. McAdoo, *Crowded Years*, pp. 219–259.

2. **American Marines in Haiti.** G. H. Stuart, *Latin America and the United States*, pp. 219–238; Stephen Bonsal, *The American Mediterranean*, pp. 47–138; W. A. McCorkle, *The Monroe Doctrine and its Application to Haiti* (American Academy of Political and Social Science, Annals, Vol. LIV, pp. 28–56); C. L. Jones, *Caribbean Interests of the United States*, pp. 125–157; New York *Nation*, Vol. CXI, pp. 35, 254, 308, 366, 493.

3. **Pershing's Pursuit of Villa.** George McAdam, "Pershing's Story of the Villa Chase," in *New York Times*, November 13, 1921; G. Mason, "Invasion or Intervention," in *World's Work*, Vol. XXXII, pp. 40–62; F. A. Ogg, *National Progress*, pp. 295–304; *The Literary Digest*, Vol. LII, pp. 801–804 (with map); George Marvin, "The First Line of Defense in Mexico," in *World's Work*, Vol. XXXII, pp. 416–424.

4. **The Building of the Panama Canal.** J. B. and F. Bishop, *Goethals, Genius of the Panama Canal*, chap. xi; Mark Sullivan, *Our Times*, Vol. I, pp. 457–473; J. B. Bishop, *The Panama Gateway*, pp. 175–197, 222–248; M. D. Gorgas and B. J. Hendrick, *William Crawford Gorgas*, chaps. v–vii; H. J. Haskin, *The Panama Canal*, chaps. ix–xi; W. F. Johnson, *Four Centuries of the Panama Canal*, chaps. ix–xxi.

QUESTIONS SUGGESTED BY THE CHAPTER

1. What did Wilson emphasize in his first inaugural address? **2.** What difficulties confronted Wilson at the outset of his administration? **3.** What three major evils did Wilson seek to remedy? **4.** Compare Wilson's objections to a protective tariff with Cleveland's. **5.** Why is the tariff of 1913 called the first genuine tariff reform since the Civil War? **6.** Why did Wilson call the currency system an "outgrown" one? **7.** What kinds of paper money are in circulation today? **8.** Show how the Federal Reserve Act made the currency more "elastic." **9.** What part of Wilson's trust program failed of enactment? **10.** What was the Federal Trade Commission created for? **11.** What practices in business did the Clayton Act make illegal? **12.** How did the Clayton Act favor labor? **13.** How do you account for the Democratic losses in the campaign of 1914? **14.** Do you think our vessels should pay tolls in passing through the Panama Canal? **15.** Why did not Wilson recognize Huerta as president of Mexico? **16.** Why are we more interested now in the Caribbean region than we were in the nineteenth century? **17.** Why did Wilson depart from his policy of "watchful waiting" in Mexico in 1914? **18.** What are the A B C powers? **19.** Compare the Monroe Doctrine with the doctrine of Pan-Americanism. **20.** Why have the Latin-American countries grown more jealous of the intervention of the United States? **21.** How did we coerce the republic of Haiti? **22.** On an outline map, shade the possessions and the protectorates of the United States in the Caribbean region. **23.** What quarrel did we have with Japan in 1913?

BOOKS WORTH READING ON UNIT SIX

JOSEPH HERGESHEIMER, *Bright Shawl*; WINSTON CHURCHILL, *Mr. Crewe's Career*; FRANK NORRIS, *The Octopus* and *The Pit*; H. HAGEDORN, *The Rough Riders*; ELBERT HUBBARD, *A Message to Garcia*; F. P. DUNNE, *Mr. Dooley in Peace and War*; SINCLAIR LEWIS, *Main Street* and *Babbitt*; JANE ADDAMS, *Twenty Years at Hull-House*; JOHN CHAMBERLAIN, *Farewell to Reform*; C. C. REGIER, *The Era of the Muckrakers*; UPTON SINCLAIR, *The Jungle*; JACOB RIIS, *How the Other Half Lives*; GERTRUDE ATHERTON, *Senator North*; KONRAD BERKOVICI, *Around the World in New York*; ZONA GALE, *Miss Lulu Bett*; MEREDITH NICHOLSON, *The Valley of Decision*; J. K. WINKLER, *Morgan the Magnificent* and *John D., A Portrait in Oils.*

How our Country was Transformed by the World War

"*I have seen two Americas*," said *James Bryce, when he came to Washington as British ambassador in 1913: "the America before and the America since the Spanish War." But the changes in the life of the people of the United States which followed that brief and decisive conflict were slight as compared with the revolution in industry and agriculture, in the activities of the government at home and its concerns abroad, in the outlook, temper, manners, and morals of the mass of our countrymen, which was brought about by the World War. In this unit we shall study first the efforts made by President Wilson to keep the United States out of the conflict. We shall see why those efforts failed and how, finally drawn into the war, we contributed to the victory of the Allies, both by the participation of American troops on the battle front and by the enormous amounts of money, food, and military supplies that we furnished to the foes of Germany. We shall see how the whole resources of the country were put at the disposal of President Wilson, giving him and his agents a control over manufactures, crops, transportation, exports, wages, prices, the press, and even the styles of clothing and articles of diet permitted to the people, such as no man in our history had ever exercised before. Following Wilson to Paris at the close of the war, we shall see how he worked for the kind of peace treaty which he hoped would make future wars on a large scale impossible, through the Covenant of the League of Nations, which he succeeded in getting adopted as the first article of the Treaty of Versailles. Finally, we shall return with him to America and describe his losing fight with the Senate to get the treaty ratified. His administration ended in disappointment, disorder, and defeat, which formed a striking contrast to the optimism and success with which it had begun. Stricken down with paralysis in the midst of his fight for the treaty, he lingered on, a broken and pathetic figure, until his death early in 1924.*

CHAPTER TWENTY-FIVE

THE STRUGGLE FOR NEUTRALITY

The Tension in Europe. In the early years of the twentieth century Europe was an armed camp. In spite of the attempts of the Hague peace conferences of 1899 and 1907 to lighten the burden of military armaments; in spite of the multiplication of international organizations for scientific, educational, and economic co-operation; in spite of the growth of peace societies; in spite of the many books that were being written condemning war not only as a relic of barbarism but as a stupid and wasteful way of settling disputes between nations — the preparation for war (always called preparation for *defense*) went on apace. The nations all clung to the delusion, as they still do, that to be armed to the teeth is the surest way of preserving peace. The German Kaiser, for example, who walked in "shining armor" and rattled the sword in the scabbard, posed as an "apostle of peace" and was even presented with a medal by the American Peace Society on the twenty-fifth anniversary of his accession to the throne (1913).

Two great groups of European nations faced each other in 1914, in jealous rivalry for territory, trade routes, colonies, new sources of raw materials, and new markets for their manufactured products. France and Russia had made an alliance in 1894, and ten years later the traditional enemies England and France had arrived at a friendly understanding, the *Entente Cordiale*. All three countries were hostile to Germany: France because, with lingering memories of her humiliation in the Franco-Prussian War of 1870, she saw the German Kaiser perfecting a war machine which should be irresistible whenever he chose to set it in motion; England because the German naval officers were drinking toasts to *der Tag* (the day) when

643

their new fleet should wrest the command of the seas from Great Britain; and Russia because her designs on the Balkan states and Constantinople were threatened by the German "thrust to the East," an ambitious plan to establish Teutonic influence over a wide swath of territory from "Berlin to Baghdad." Facing the "Triple Entente" of England, France, and Russia was the "Triple Alliance" of Germany, Austria, and Italy, formed in 1883, from which, however, Italy had become almost detached on account of her rivalry with Austria. Germany looked upon the Entente as a plot to surround her with an "iron ring" of hostile powers and thwart her ambition for colonial expansion and "a place in the sun." Indeed, Colonel House, who was on a mission to Europe in the summer of 1914, in the interest of preserving peace, wrote to President Wilson on May 29, "Whenever England consents, France and Russia will close in on Germany and Austria."

The Outbreak of the World War. It was an event in the Balkans (the "tinderbox of Europe") which started the conflagration. On June 28, 1914, Francis Ferdinand, the heir to the Austrian throne, was assassinated with his wife while driving through the streets of Sarajevo, in the Austrian province of Bosnia. Holding the Serbian revolutionary societies responsible for the murders, the Austrian government (backed by Germany) declared war on Serbia and marched upon her capital (July 28). Russia then mobilized her army to protect her fellow Slavs in the Balkans and check the Teuton "thrust to the East," whereupon Germany declared war on Russia (August 1). This was bound to involve Russia's ally France, against whom Germany declared war two days later. And when the mighty German military machine was launched across the neutral soil of Belgium, in order to strike a fatal blow at Paris before the Russian army could get into action, Great Britain came to the assistance of France (August 4). In vain had the foreign ministers of the great capitals of Europe labored during the last week of July to avert the catastrophe of a general war. In vain had they pleaded for time for the submission of the Austro-Serbian case to the Hague Tribunal or to the arbitration of

FRANZ FERDINAND AND HIS WIFE AT SARAJEVO

Great Britain, France, Germany, and Italy. The precarious structure of peace, built on the old doctrine of the "balance of power," fell like a house of cards. Bulgaria and Turkey joined the Central Powers; Japan and Italy came to the side of the Allies. Eventually, of all Europe only the Scandinavian countries, Holland, Spain, and Switzerland remained neutral.

Wilson's Proclamation of Neutrality. The United States, of course, had no part in the European rivalries, fears, and hatreds that had precipitated the war. We cared little whether Slav or Teuton controlled the Balkan Peninsula. Probably not one in ten thousand of our citizens could locate Bosnia or Baghdad on the map. Three thousand miles of "cooling ocean" lay between us and inflamed Europe. Moreover, our land was the hospitable refuge of immigrants from all the belligerent countries. Nearly 9,000,000 of our population were either of German birth or of German parentage. Russians, Italians, Poles, Hungarians, and Irishmen worked side by side in our mines, mills, and factories. The very year of 1914 was the peak year of immigration, bringing 1,200,000 foreigners to our shores.

Following the custom since the days of Washington, President Wilson issued on August 4 a proclamation of neutrality, which he supplemented two weeks later with an appeal to the American people to be "neutral in fact as well as in name" and to curb any thought or action that might be "construed as a preference of one party to the struggle above another." America, he said, must be calm and cool, completely detached from the struggle, "neither sitting in judgment on others nor disturbed in her own counsels," keeping herself ready, when the time should come, to lend her help in the re-establishment of peace. Theodore Roosevelt, agreeing with Wilson in nothing else, agreed in this. Writing in the *Outlook* (September 23) he rejoiced that we were not involved in the "bitter and vindictive hatreds" of Europe, expressed indifference over the invasion of Belgium, and advised against our "taking sides one way or the other" — statements which caused him no little embarrassment soon afterwards, when he himself took the side of the Allies with characteristic zeal.

American Rights Threatened. Before the war had continued many weeks, however, it became evident that we could not view it like disinterested spectators sitting at a play. The German drive on Paris, delayed by the valiant resistance of the little Belgian army, was checked at the river Marne, only forty miles from the capital, on September 6, and thereafter the French and German armies faced each other for many months in the long line of trenches, with little active fighting. The British navy got control of the seas by the destruction of Admiral von Spee's fleet off the Falkland Islands in December, and attempted to force Germany into surrender by shutting off her importations of munitions and food. The Germans replied by sending out their submarines to torpedo the British war and merchant vessels. As the war took millions of men from the fields and factories of Europe, the demand of the belligerent countries for American food, clothing, metals, and war supplies of every sort increased enormously. We became again, as in the Napoleonic Wars, the great neutral commerce-carrier of the world; and again, as in the Napoleonic Wars, the infringement of our rights upon the high seas finally brought us into the struggle.

Our Controversy with England. During the first six months of the war our grievances were against Great Britain. Determined to starve Germany into submission, the British government altered or interpreted the rules of war to suit its own convenience, to the great injury of neutral commerce. In the first place, British Orders in Council kept adding to the list of "contraband" (or goods which might be seized on their way to the enemy) until it covered over forty articles, including rubber, cotton, wool, leather, copper, chemicals, wheat, and a score or more of other commodities which had formerly been free from seizure. An American merchant could not ship a cargo to Europe and be sure that it would not be declared contraband before it reached the other side of the ocean. Secondly, the British ignored the rule of blockade, which required that vessels be actually stationed near the ports of the enemy country to intercept the contraband goods. On account of the danger from the submarines, British warships stopped neutral merchant vessels on the high seas and, instead of searching them there for contraband, took them into a British port. Thirdly, the British seized vessels bound for neutral countries, such as Holland, Norway, Sweden, or Denmark, on the ground that the cargoes were actually going to Germany.[1]

Lively protests against this "indefensible and intolerable conduct" were sent to London by Secretaries Bryan and Lansing; but our ambassador to England, Walter H. Page, was so thoroughly convinced that the victory of the Allies was necessary to preserve Europe and the world from the domination of Prussian militarism that he refused to press the protests upon Sir Edward Grey, the British foreign minister. The offenses of Great Britain against our neutral rights might have led to

[1] No doubt England was justified in this suspicion. Our exports to Sweden, for example, grew from $337,000 to $2,558,000 in the first year of the war, and those to Denmark from $558,000 to $7,100,000. Of course the Danes did not eat thirteen times as much food or wear thirteen times as much clothing in 1915 as they did in 1914. The goods sent to Scandinavia or Holland could be easily transported by boat or rail to Germany. England could also point to the example of the United States in the Civil War, when Union vessels seized cargoes, bound for Cuba or Nassau, which were really destined to find their way through the blockade to the Confederate ports.

serious consequences had not Germany replied to the British attempts to starve her people by adopting a policy which threatened American lives.

The Submarine Peril. It was a rule of international law that if a warship seized or destroyed a merchant vessel, it had to place the passengers and crew in a position of safety. The Germans, with their surface fleet either sunk or bottled up behind the Kiel Canal, relied upon submarines to destroy the British sea power. But the submarine could not obey the rules of international law. Being a frail craft, it could be sunk by a single gunshot. Nor did it have room on board to care for the passengers and crew of a vessel attacked. It had to strike swiftly and secretly by launching its deadly torpedo. It was called "the stiletto of the seas."

On February 4, 1915, the Germans issued a proclamation declaring the waters around the British Isles a war zone, in which their submarines would operate freely, and warned neutral vessels against the danger of entering this zone. They denied any intention of destroying the lives of neutrals, but maintained that so long as we tolerated the illegal acts of Great Britain we ought not to complain of their using the only means they had of combating them. They professed to be willing to modify the submarine decree if we would compel Great Britain to observe the rules of blockade and capture. It was unfair, they said, to hold one nation to obedience to international law and let another nation flout it at will. But President Wilson would not "bargain" on the subject. In a note of February 10 he protested to the German government against marking off any part of the high seas as a war zone and warned it that if American ships were destroyed or American lives lost by the submarine's disregard of the rules of visit and search, such an act would be viewed by us as an "indefensible violation of neutral rights," for which we should "hold the Imperial German Government to a strict accountability."

The *Lusitania*. Unless Americans abandoned their right to sail on British ships, it was inevitable that sooner or later they would be the victims of a submarine attack. Three or four

THE *LUSITANIA*

Americans had already been numbered among such victims when a brutal deed was committed which shocked the whole civilized world. In the early afternoon of May 7, 1915, the magnificent Cunard liner *Lusitania*, nearing the end of her eastern voyage from New York, was torpedoed ten miles off the southern coast of Ireland, and sank in twenty minutes, carrying to their death 1198 men, women, and children, of whom 124 were Americans. Many in our country were for an immediate declaration of war against Germany. Colonel House, who was in London at the time, wrote to Wilson two days after the catastrophe: "America has come to the parting of the ways. . . . We can no longer remain neutral spectators."

But the President was determined to remain neutral. The country was unprepared for war and disunited in opinion. In the West the feeling was strong that our citizens should keep out of harm's way by refraining from traveling on ships that were liable to be torpedoed. Many even wished the President to forbid such travel by proclamation. Therefore, instead of calling Congress in extra session and sending in a war message, President Wilson chose to deal with the crisis by diplomacy. On

> ## NOTICE!
>
> TRAVELLERS intending to embark on the Atlantic voyage are reminded that a state of war exists between Germany and her allies and Great Britain and her allies; that the zone of war includes the waters adjacent to the British Isles; that, in accordance with formal notice given by the Imperial German Government, vessels flying the flag of Great Britain, or of any of her allies, are liable to destruction in those waters and that travellers sailing in the war zone on ships of Great Britain or her allies do so at their own risk.
>
> **IMPERIAL GERMAN EMBASSY**
> **Washington, D. C., April 22, 1915**

May 13 he sent a note expressing his confidence that the German government would disavow the sinking of the *Lusitania*, and declaring that our government would not "omit any word or act necessary to its sacred duty" of protecting the rights of its citizens. Germany expressed regret that American lives had been lost, but refused to be held responsible therefor. The *Lusitania*, they claimed, was a ship of war of the British navy because she was carried on the reserve list. They also maintained that she had guns mounted on her decks (which was not true) and that she was carrying a large stock of ammunition in her hold (which was true). Finally, the German embassy at Washington had warned American citizens, on the very day the *Lusitania* sailed, not to travel on ships liable to be torpedoed in the war zone.[1] By disregarding this warning and entrusting themselves to the

[1] On April 22 the German government had ordered Ambassador von Bernstorff at Washington to publish this general warning, but he had delayed to do so. There was no deliberate intention to single out the *Lusitania* for destruction. The German submarine commander, Lieutenant Schwieger, discovered her by accident as he was on his way home to his base at Wilhelmshaven to replenish his fuel, and torpedoed her in obedience to the general orders applying to the war zone. As to the "warning" which appeared among the shipping news in the papers of May 1, it was both too late to influence American passengers who were sailing on the *Lusitania* that day and a breach of diplomatic courtesy as well. "A foreign minister is here," says John Bassett Moore, our greatest authority on international law, "to correspond with the Secretary of State.... He has no authority to communicate his sentiments to the people by publication, and any attempt to do so is contempt of this government."

care of the captain of a British liner, the Americans had "invited their own destruction." The interchange of notes over the sinking of the *Lusitania* continued during the summer, but the German government never disavowed the act.

German and Austrian Plots. Because the Allies were able to get war supplies from America while the Central Powers were not, the latter complained that we were not really neutral. They therefore asked us to put an embargo on the exportation of war materials so as not to aid either side. We refused, however, to interfere with the purchase of arms and munitions in this country by the Allies, pointing out that belligerents always had the right to purchase war supplies in neutral countries, and that to suspend this right because one of the belligerents (Germany) was unable to use it would be an unfair act against the other belligerent. Failing to get our government to stop the shipment of supplies of war material to the Allies, the Central Powers sought to stop it themselves. Their emissaries placed bombs on board munition ships, blew up bridges, and fomented strikes in munitions plants. A letter from Dr. Constantin Dumba, the Austrian ambassador at Washington, to his chief in Vienna, recommending a plan to "disorganize and hold up for months, if not entirely prevent, the manufacture of munitions in Bethlehem and the Middle West," was intercepted in September, 1915, and its publication led to the demand for Dumba's recall. A few weeks later our State Department asked for the withdrawal of the military and naval attachés of the German embassy, Captain von Papen and Captain Boy-Ed, on account of their "improper activities." Ambassador von Bernstorff maintained steadily that he and his subordinates had no part in such activities; but the seizure of a portfolio of papers left by accident in a Ninth Avenue elevated car in New York by Dr. Albert, the financial adviser of the German embassy, told a different story. Among the papers were found letters and memoranda, over the signatures of Von Papen and Bernstorff, encouraging plans for "fomenting internal discord among the American people to the advantage of the German Empire." The British and French were also active in propaganda work in America; but as they were in much better favor here than the Germans and had no difficulty in getting war supplies, they used their propaganda for describing German "atrocities" and fortifying the American conviction that the Allies were fighting solely for the preservation of liberty and democracy.

The Two Currents. The President's counsel of neutrality "in thought as well as in act" went unheeded. The sympathizers with each of the belligerent groups in Europe grew more and more ardent and vocal week by week. Since the beginning of the war, advocates of military preparedness had been active. In December, 1914, a National Security League was formed to rouse the people to the need for more adequate national defense. The next summer an officers' training camp was established at Plattsburg, New York, largely through the efforts of General Leonard Wood. A National Defense Society, founded in August, 1915, condemned the administration for its "supineness," and four months later the American Rights Committee urged the immediate entrance of the United States into the war.

At the same time the pacifists were organizing the League to Limit Armaments (1914), the American Union against Militarism (1915), and the Woman's Peace party (1915), with Jane Addams as its leader. Bryan, who resigned from the State Department in June, 1915, rather than sign the second *Lusitania* note, threw all his influence against preparedness, declaring that in case of necessity we could "raise a million men between sunrise and sunset." Henry Ford chartered the steamer *Oscar II* in December, 1915, and sent a peace delegation to Europe to get the soldiers "out of the trenches by Christmas."

President Wilson refused to be swept along by these currents. He undoubtedly sympathized with the Allies, but at the same time he had misgivings about the purity of their cause. He wanted to keep America out of the war, but he was not willing to sacrifice American rights. He had advised against preparedness in his message of December, 1914, but the events of the next twelve months brought a gradual change of mind. In January, 1916, he began a tour of the Middle West, recommending military preparation "as effective and prompt as possible, without losing a day." He realized, as he declared in several of his speeches on this trip, that he might not be able much longer both to "defend the country's honor" and to keep it out of war.

Military Preparedness. From March to December, 1915, Congress was not in session, and the President was left free to handle the war problems by diplomacy alone. But when the houses met he was confronted by more than five hundred Representatives and Senators all of whom had their opinions of what should be done and their eye to the effect of their actions on the votes of their constituents. The respective chairmen of the committees on military affairs in the House and the Senate were at odds over the kind of army that should be raised. Senator Chamberlain favored a greatly enlarged "national," or regular, army, and Representative Hay advocated the use of the militia, which was raised and officered by the states. Secretary of War Garrison supported the Chamberlain plan; and when President Wilson refused to accept it (without committing himself to the Hay plan either), Garrison resigned and was soon afterward replaced by the efficient mayor of Cleveland, Ohio, Newton D. Baker. During the spring months of 1916 Congress wrangled over the army bill, each party trying to make capital for the approaching Presidential campaign.

The National Defense Act which resulted (June 3) authorized the increase of the regular army until it should reach a strength of 223,000 men in five years, the "Federalization" of the national guard (or militia) of 425,000, the establishment of civilian training camps and of military training schools in the colleges, and the construction of a $20,000,000 plant for the production of nitrates and other materials for munitions. Since a strong navy has always been a cherished American policy, it was easy to get Congress to adopt Secretary Daniels's $600,000,000 program in August, authorizing the building of ten dreadnoughts, six battle cruisers, and one hundred and forty minor vessels, over a period of three years. Our neutrality had passed through the stages of calm aloofness from the European struggle, of protest against the violation of our commerce, of remonstrance over the destruction of American lives, to a fourth stage in which we began to prepare to defend by force the rights for which we could not secure respect by argument.

Economic Preparedness. Besides the military and naval bills, Congress passed, during the session of 1916, a number of measures designed to make industry, agriculture, shipping, and railroad transportation more efficient in case war should come. A Council of National Defense was created, consisting of six cabinet members assisted by seven expert advisers, including Daniel Willard, president of the Baltimore and Ohio Railroad, Samuel Gompers, president of the American Federation of Labor, and Julius Rosenwald, head of the Sears Roebuck Company. A Rural Credits Act of July 17 established twelve Federal Farm Loan Banks, on the pattern of the Federal Reserve Banks (p. 620), authorized to lend the farmers money on long-term mortgages at not over 6 per cent. This government relief to the farmers, who were burdened with a mortgage indebtedness of over $3,500,000,000, on which they were often obliged to pay 10 per cent interest to the private bankers, was of the utmost importance in mobilizing our basic industry in the event of war. A third subject to which Congress turned its attention was the improvement of our merchant marine, which had steadily declined since the Civil War until in 1914 less than 10 per cent of our foreign trade was carried in ships under the American flag. At the end of August, 1916, a Ship Purchase Act was passed, creating a United States Shipping Board of five members, with power to build, purchase, or lease vessels "suitable for use as naval auxiliaries," and to operate them for a period of five years after the termination of the war.

Finally, on September 8, Congress, under pressure from the President, passed the famous Adamson Act. The freight trainmen were demanding an increase of wages in the form of their actual ten hours' pay for eight hours of work, with an hour and a half's extra pay for every hour of work beyond eight. They were backed by the other railroad brotherhoods and the American Federation of Labor. When their demands were refused by the railroad officials, they declared a nation-wide strike, to begin on Labor Day, September 4. Such a strike, by stopping the shipment of food and munitions to the Allies, might well have meant the winning of the war by Germany. President Wilson went before Congress on August 29 to urge a law granting the trainmen's demands in order to avert the strike. On September 1 the act was passed by the House (239 to 56), while a delegation of the brotherhoods sat in the gallery to enjoy their triumph. It was the first time that organized labor had compelled the government to do its will, and the opponents of the President condemned his "cowardly surrender to the brotherhoods" as a "bid for the two million votes of organized labor" in the approaching Presidential election. The Adamson Act also provided that the President might take over the railroads and operate them in case he should deem it necessary for military purposes. The railroads contested the constitutionality of the Adamson Act, but it was upheld by a five-to-four decision of the Supreme Court in March, 1917.

The Campaign of 1916. While Congress was busy with these measures of preparedness, the Presidential campaign was being waged. The Democrats, in spite of the declaration of their platform of 1912 against a second term, had no idea of replacing Wilson, who was nominated by acclamation at St. Louis. The problem before the Republicans was to select a candidate who would win the Progressives back to the fold. The Progressive convention met at Chicago on the same day (June 7) as the Republican convention, with the hope that the Republicans would nominate Roosevelt. But they had not yet wholly forgiven the Colonel for leading the revolt which had made possible the election of Wilson in 1912. The man on whom they finally united was Charles Evans Hughes, ex-Governor of New York and, since 1910, an associate justice of the United States Supreme Court. The Progressives nominated Roosevelt, who to their sorrowful disgust declined the nomination and came out in support of Hughes. The paramount issue, he said, was to defeat the "weak" and "vacillating" Wilson.

The campaign was fought on the issue of the defense of American rights both in the European war and in Mexico.

Wilson's position was strengthened by two victories which he had won earlier in the year. In February, 1916, Senator Gore of Oklahoma and Representative McLemore of Texas had introduced resolutions into Congress forbidding American citizens to sail on armed belligerent merchant ships which were liable to be sunk by German submarines. But President Wilson held firmly to the position he had taken in the *Lusitania* notes. "Once accept a single abandonment of our rights," he wrote to Senator Stone, chairman of the Committee on Foreign Relations, "and many other humiliations will follow." He demanded an immediate vote on the resolutions, in order that the country might know who stood by the administration. Congress backed him up by laying the resolutions on the table (that is, setting them aside) by the decisive votes of 276 to 142 in the House and 68 to 14 in the Senate. The next month, when the Germans sank the French passenger steamer *Sussex* without warning in the English Channel, causing the death of two Americans, Wilson sent an ultimatum to Germany that we would sever diplomatic relations with her unless she should "now immediately declare and effect an abandonment of the present methods of submarine warfare against passenger and freight-carrying vessels." The ultimatum brought from the German government the promise that merchant ships would not be sunk "without warning and without saving human lives." It was this "*Sussex* pledge" that led the chairman of the Democratic convention at St. Louis to boast that President Wilson, "without firing a single gun or shedding a drop of blood," had "wrung from the most militant spirit that ever brooded over a battlefield a recognition of American rights and a concession to American demands." "He kept us out of war" was the Democratic slogan.

A temporary cessation of submarine activity in the summer of 1916, although due to the internal situation in Germany, gave strength to the Democratic claim that the President had forced the Kaiser to mend his ways. Wilson did not take the stump but remained at his summer cottage, "Shadow Lawn," at Long Branch, New Jersey, addressing weekly delegations of pilgrims in the defense of the policies of his administration. Hughes toured the country, denouncing the administration for its bungling diplomacy, its Mexican policy, and its lack of appreciation of the danger of the European situation. He reiterated the statement, "I stand for the firm and unflinching maintenance of all the rights of American citizens on land and sea." But when asked just what he would do if elected, — whether he would compel England to recognize our rights or go to war with Germany, — he was silent. Wilson too stood for "the firm and unflinching maintenance of our rights."

The Re-election of Wilson. The election proved to be the closest in our history since the Hayes-Tilden campaign of 1876 (p. 447). Before midnight of election day it was known that Hughes had carried the populous Eastern states, together with Indiana, Illinois, Michigan, and Wisconsin. At half past nine the President telephoned to his private secretary at Asbury Park: "Well, Tumulty, it looks as if we have been badly licked. . . . I have no regrets. We have tried to do our duty." Telegrams of congratulation poured in upon Hughes that evening, and he went to bed confident of his election. The *New York Times*, a strong Wilson paper, announced in its early edition the next morning the "sweeping victory" of Hughes. But as the day advanced and the returns from the remoter districts of the West came in, Wilson's prospects grew brighter. One after another, states that had been assigned to Hughes were transferred to the Wilson column. By Thursday night it was certain that Wilson had carried California by a slim margin, and therewith the election. Hughes won every state east of the Mississippi and north of Mason and Dixon's line, except New Hampshire and Ohio. His defeat was due to his failure to win the Progressive vote of the West, and especially of California. He lost the 13 electoral votes of the latter state, which would have given him a majority of three in the Electoral College, by a piece of stupidity on the part of his campaign managers.[1]

[1] Governor Hiram Johnson, the former Progressive candidate for Vice-President on the "Bull Moose" ticket of 1912, was running for United States Senator in California, where the Progressive sentiment was very strong. Hughes visited California on his campaign tour and was even in the same hotel with Johnson at

The electoral vote was 277 for Wilson to 254 for Hughes, and the popular vote 9,128,837 to 8,536,380. The Republicans chose governors in a number of states which appeared in the Wilson column, reduced the Democratic majority from 16 to 12 in the Senate, and wiped it out completely in the House (to which each party elected 214 members). Except for Mr. Wilson himself, it was very much like a Republican victory. But the Presidential vote was, after all, the important element in the crisis. It was a vote of confidence in the President. If the country was indeed approaching the brink of war, as an increasing number of our people believed, it was a decision, in the homely phrase of Abraham Lincoln, not to "swap horses while crossing the stream."

Wilson's Efforts for Peace. Meantime, for all the preparedness measures and the excitement of the political campaign, Wilson was endeavoring to bring the influence of America to bear upon ending the strife in Europe. He was from the beginning not so much interested in the progress of the war as in the prospects for peace. In a speech before the League to Enforce Peace at Washington, on May 27, 1916, he said:

With the causes and the objects of the war we are not concerned. The obscure fountains from which its stupendous flood has burst forth we are not interested to search for or explore. . . . The longer the war lasts, the more deeply do we become concerned that it should be brought to an end and the world permitted to resume its normal life and course again.

When Ambassador Page returned from London on a visit in August and tried to impress on the President the sinister purpose of the German militarists and the desperate plight of the Allies, he found him "utterly cold, utterly unresponsive, interested only in ending the war."

In February, 1916, the President had sent Colonel House to England to confer with Sir Edward Grey on the possibility of getting the Central Powers and the Allies to discuss terms. He

Long Beach; but the shortsighted, standpat Republicans of the state did not allow him even to meet Johnson, who was giving him support for President. The result was that Johnson was elected to the Senate by a majority of 300,000, and Hughes lost the state by 3773 votes out of a total of over 900,000 cast.

even expressed his willingness to go to Europe and sit at the conference himself as mediator, and held out hopes to the Allies that the United States would "probably" enter the war on their side if Germany refused to confer. But it was rather France and England that were cold to the proposition. They had made a number of secret treaties for the division of the spoils of war and did not wish to reveal them or revise them. They argued that if they won the war, as they expected to do, they could impose harsh terms on Germany more easily without the interference of the "idealistic" American President, and that if their case grew desperate the German submarine campaign would probably bring the United States into the war anyway. In other words, while they paid a price for the aid of Italy and Rumania in the promise of additions of territory, they expected to (and did) get the help of the United States for nothing.

Taking his re-election as an endorsement of his efforts for peace, Wilson again attempted to mediate. On December 18 he sent a note to all the belligerent powers, asking that they "state their views as to the terms on which the war might be concluded . . . in order that we may learn how near the haven of peace may be, for which all mankind longs with an intense and increasing longing." In his note the President wrote, "The objects which the statesmen of the belligerents on both sides have in mind in this war are virtually the same, as stated in general terms to their own people and to the world." This was a perfectly true statement, but it was interpreted by the Allies as Wilson's *own* opinion that their cause was no better than the Germans'. A note from Belgium protested against "the President's assumption that the statesmen of the two opposing camps were pursuing the same objects of war," and, according to Ambassador Page, King George broke down and wept. The replies to the President's note were not encouraging. The Germans expressed their willingness to attend a conference at some neutral place, but would not state in advance "their views as to the terms on which the war might be concluded." The Allies replied that they had already stated their objects clearly enough.

Wilson Defines a Peace Acceptable to America. On January 22, 1917, President Wilson addressed the Senate in a remarkable speech, stating the conditions on which America would "give its formal and solemn adherence to a league of peace." The present war must first be ended, he said, but it must be ended by terms that would create a peace worth guaranteeing and preserving, a "peace representing security by the organized major force of mankind." "First of all," he said, "it must be a *peace without victory*." This startling statement, so offensive to both the Allies and the Central Powers, he begged to be allowed to explain:

Victory would mean a peace forced upon the loser, a victor's terms imposed upon the vanquished. It would be accepted in humiliation under duress, at an intolerable sacrifice, and would leave a sting, a resentment, a bitter memory upon which terms of peace would rest not permanently, but only as upon quicksand. Only a peace between equals can last.

Prophetic words, whose truth was to be sadly demonstrated in the years that followed the war! But they were received at the time with scorn by both sides. What were the nations fighting for if not for "victory" and the chance to impose "the victor's terms"! The Germans replied that they would soon dictate the terms of peace — in Paris. The editor of the *London Daily Mail* sneered at Wilson's warning as "an abstract pontifical statement of a future international morality." The rest of the President's speech, advocating the limitation of armaments, the freedom of the seas, government by the consent of the governed, and the security of small and weak nations, was lost in the single phrase "peace without victory." But Wilson clung to his idealism. "These are American principles," he concluded. "We can stand for no others. They are also the principles of foward-looking men and women everywhere. . . . They are the principles of mankind, and must prevail."

The Break with Germany. Two opposite policies were struggling for control in Germany in 1916. The diplomats, headed by the chancellor, Von Bethmann-Hollweg, and by Von Bernstorff in America, were for keeping the United States out of the war by all possible sacrifices. It was they who had counseled the moderation of the submarine warfare and had secured for us the *Sussex* pledge (p. 656). The militarists, on the other hand, urged the ruthless prosecution of the war, regardless of the effect on the United States. They despised our "contemptible little army" as less to be feared than Rumania's — even if it could be landed in Europe. The militarists got control in the autumn of 1916. A fleet of larger and wider-cruising submarines was built, which was to bring Great Britain to her knees. "Give us only two months of this warfare," said Zimmermann of the Foreign Office to our Ambassador Gerard, "and we shall end the war."

On January 31, 1917, the German government issued a proclamation enlarging the war zone and removing all former restrictions on submarine warfare. It offered to let the United States send one passenger ship a week to the English coast through a narrow lane of safety, the ship to be plainly marked with large stripes of red and white on hull and funnels and to carry a red-and-white checkered flag at each masthead. In vain did Von Bernstorff plead against this order, informing the chancellor of his promising negotiations with Colonel House and the President for bringing England to consent to a "peace of equals." The reply came back from Berlin: "Far-reaching military preparations have already been made which cannot be undone, and the U-boats have already sailed with new instructions." There was nothing left for the ambassador to do but to hand to Secretary Lansing the fateful notice of the renewal of the submarine warfare, which he knew meant the end of his mission in Washington and of the neutrality of the United States. The *Sussex* pledge had been broken, and President Wilson had "no alternative consistent with the dignity and honor of the United States" but to sever relations with the German Empire. On February 3, 1917, he announced this decision to a joint session of Congress, attended by the members of the Supreme Court, the diplomatic corps, and a throng of invited guests who crowded the galleries. "We do not desire any conflict with the German government," he said; "we are the sincere friends of the German people, and earnestly desire to remain

THE GERMAN SUBMARINE ZONE OF JANUARY 31, 1917

at peace with the government which speaks for them. We shall not believe that they are hostile to us until we are obliged to believe it." On the same day Von Bernstorff received his passports.[1]

"Armed Neutrality." The rupture of diplomatic relations with Germany led to redoubled efforts on the part of the pacifists to prevent "the overt act" that would lead to war. Bryan, addressing a large peace meeting at Madison Square Garden, New York, declared that it would be a "crime" for us to go to war with "a nation that wishes us no harm." Let the people demand that no declaration of war be made without submitting the question to a popular referendum. "Wire immediately to

[1] Colonel House wrote to Von Bernstorff on his departure from Washington: "It is too sad to see that your government should have declared the unrestricted U-boat war at a moment when we were so near to peace."

the President, your senator, your congressman," he said; "a few cents now may save many dollars in taxes, and possibly a son." The general approval of the President's action, however, was hearty and instantaneous. The Senate supported him with only five dissenting votes. Great industrial plants signified their readiness to put their men and machinery at his service. The American Federation of Labor agreed to waive the law prescribing an eight-hour day for workers in the government employ.

Meanwhile, in February, the German U-boats had sunk two hundred ships, with a tonnage of 456,000. To send American vessels to sea unarmed, to meet such risk as these figures showed, would have been folly. Wilson therefore asked Congress, on February 26, for the power to arm American merchant ships. While the bill granting this power and appropriating one hundred thousand dollars for its enforcement was pending in the House, the news leaked out of a plan of Zimmermann's to attract Mexico to the German side, in case the United States entered the war, by offering to restore to her the "lost provinces" of Texas and New Mexico. The revelation of the Zimmermann plot swept away the opposition to the Armed Ship Bill in the House, which passed it on March 1 by a vote of 403 to 13. But in the Senate it encountered the stubborn resistance of a dozen men, headed by La Follette, who, taking advantage of the rule of unlimited debate, prevented its passage before the expiration of Congress on March 4. President Wilson bitterly reproached this "little group of willful men, representing no opinion but their own," who had "rendered the great government of the United States helpless and contemptible." Relying on the advice of Attorney-General Gregory and Secretary of State Lansing, he took upon himself the responsibility of arming our merchant vessels. The American liner *St. Louis* soon afterward left New York with guns fore and aft, and safely traversed the submarine zone.

Wilson stood "firm in armed neutrality," as he said in his second inaugural address of March 4, 1917. But within a fortnight two events occurred which brought us closer to the verge

NEUTRALITY CARTOON[1]

of war. On March 15 a revolution in Russia overthrew the absolute government and drove Czar Nicholas from his throne. The prospect of our joining the Allies then was made infinitely more inviting by the thought that we should not be pledged "to fight side by side with the autocratic and intolerable government of the Romanoffs." On the day after the Czar's overthrow, German submarines sank three American vessels, one of them with the loss of American lives. The "overt act" had come. Our neutrality was at an end.

The Declaration of War with Germany. The growing seriousness of the situation had determined the President to call the Sixty-fifth Congress in extra session on April 16. But the events which we have just mentioned led him to advance the date by two weeks. On the evening of April 2, 1917, President Wilson, escorted by a troop of cavalry, drove through the rain to the Capitol and, in the most momentous words ever uttered within its walls, addressed the eager, cheering, flag-waving throng that packed the floor and galleries of the House.

[1] After a cartoon by J. T. McCutcheon in the *Chicago Tribune*.

PRESIDENT WILSON READING THE WAR MESSAGE

With a profound sense of the solemn and even tragical character of the step I am taking, and of the grave responsibility which it involves, but in unhesitating obedience to what I deem my constitutional duty, I advise that the Congress declare the recent course of the Imperial German Government to be in fact nothing less than war against the government and people of the United States; that it formally accept the status of belligerency which has been thrust upon it; and that it take immediate steps not only to put the country in a more thorough state of defense, but also to exert all its power and employ all its resources to bring the government of the German Empire to terms and end the war.

He reviewed the long course of outrages that had served to convince us that the Prussian autocracy was not and never could be our friend. He protested that we had no quarrel with the German people. He insisted that our motive should be "not revenge or the victorious assertion of the physical might of the nation, but only the vindication of human rights," and that our ultimate aim should be "a steadfast concert of peace, maintained by a partnership of democratic nations."

The world must be made safe for democracy. We have no selfish ends to serve. We desire no conquest, no dominion. We seek no indemnities for ourselves, no material compensation for the sacrifices we shall freely make. We are but one of the champions of the rights of all mankind. We shall be satisfied when those rights have been made as secure as the faith and the freedom of nations can make them.

It is a distressing and oppressive duty, gentlemen of the Congress, [he concluded] which I have performed in thus addressing you. There are, it may be, many months of fiery trial and sacrifice ahead of us. It is a fearful thing to lead this great and peaceful people into war, into the most terrible and disastrous of all wars, civilization itself seeming to be in the balance. But the right is more precious than peace, and we shall fight for the things which we have always carried nearest our hearts — for democracy, for the right of those who submit to authority to have a voice in their own government, for the rights and liberties of small nations, for a universal dominion of right by such a concert of free peoples as shall bring peace and safety to all nations and make the world itself at last free. To such a task we can dedicate our lives and our fortunes, everything that we are and everything that we have, with the pride of those who know that the day has come when America is privileged to spend her blood and her might for the principles that gave her birth and happiness and the peace which she has treasured. God helping her, she can do no other.

That same evening resolutions were introduced into both houses of Congress declaring that the United States accepted the war which had been thrust upon her by the German government. On April 4, after a heated debate in which the war was described by the pacifists as "useless" and "senseless," a product of Wall Street for the protection of our loans to the Allies, and a pledge of vassalage to Great Britain, the Senate passed the resolution by a vote of 82 to 6 — Stone, Lane, and Vardaman (Democrats), and La Follette, Gronna, and Norris (Republicans). The debate in the House lasted through the following day and night. Shortly after 3 A.M. on the morning of the sixth, the resolution was passed by a vote of 373 to 50. President Wilson signed the resolution the same day. It was Good Friday. For the first time in over a century the United States was at war with a first-class foreign power.[1]

[1] We broke off diplomatic relations with Austria-Hungary on April 8, but we did not go to war with her until the following December. With the other allies of Germany (Turkey and Bulgaria) we did not go to war at all, nor did we even break off relations with Bulgaria.

TERMS TO BE MASTERED

Triple Entente
Triple Alliance
mobilization

"place in the sun"
contraband
peace without victory

balance of power
armed neutrality
"overt act"

FOR SUPPLEMENTARY READING

CHARLES SEYMOUR, *Woodrow Wilson and the World War* (Chronicles of America, Vol. XLVIII), chaps. ii–v; J. B. MCMASTER, *The United States in the World War*, Vol. I, chaps. i–xiii; B. J. HENDRICK, *Life and Letters of Walter H. Page*, Vol. I, chaps. xii, xiii, Vol. II, chaps. xiv–xx; F. A. OGG, *National Progress* (American Nation Series, Vol. XXXVII), chaps. xii–xxi; WALTER MILLIS, *Road to War*; W. E. DODD, *Woodrow Wilson and his Work*, chaps. vi–ix; R. S. BAKER, *Woodrow Wilson, Life and Letters*, Vol. IV, chap. ix, Vol. V; J. W. GERARD, *My Four Years in Germany*; J. VON BERNSTEIN, *My Three Years in America*; C. J. H. HAYES, *A Brief History of the Great War*, chaps. i, x–xv; The Pageant of America, Vol. IX, pp. 293–310; Viscount Grey of Falloden, *Twenty-five Years, 1892–1916*, Vol. II, chaps. xxi–xxiv; *America*, Vol. XI, pp. 250–254, 261–268, 300–305; Vol. XII, pp. 23–66, 78–83, 117–183; H. S. COMMAGER, *Documents of American History*, Vol. II, pp. 282–312; HART, *Contemporaries*, Vol. V, Nos. 167, 173, 184–186.

TOPICS FOR REPORTS

1. **The Adamson Act.** E. J. CLAPP, "The Adamson Act," in *Yale Review*, Vol. VI, pp. 258–275; T. R. POWELL, "The Supreme Court and the Adamson Law," in *University of Pennsylvania Law Review*, Vol. LXV, pp. 3–27; F. A. OGG, *National Progress*, pp. 353–363; E. G. ROBBINS, "The Trainsman's Eight-Hour Day," in *Political Science Quarterly*, Vol. XXXI, pp. 541–557; *The Review of Reviews*, Vol. LIV, pp. 389–393.

2. **Measures of National Defense.** J. B. MCMASTER, *The United States in the World War*, Vol. I, pp. 230–254; H. HAGEDORN, *Leonard Wood, A Biography*, Vol. II, chaps. vii–x; THEODORE ROOSEVELT, *The Foes of Our Own Household*; FREDERICK PALMER and NEWTON D. BAKER, *America at War*, Vol. I, chaps. ii–vii; E. E. ROBINSON and V. J. WEST, *The Foreign Policy of Woodrow Wilson*, Part III, Nos. 43, 44, 46, 50, 51; J. S. BASSETT, *Our War with Germany*, pp. 71–70, 114–130; E. H. CROWDER, *The Spirit of Selective Service*.

3. **The True Story of the *Lusitania*.** C. E. LAURIAT, JR., *The Lusitania's Last Voyage*; T. A. BAILEY, "The Sinking of the Lusitania," in *American Historical Review*, Vol. XLI, pp. 54–73; G. S. VIERECK, *Spreading Germs of Hate*, pp. 59 f.; WALTER MILLIS, *Road to War*, chap. v; *America*, Vol. XI, pp. 261–265; O. G. VILLARD, "The True Story of the Lusitania," in the *American Mercury*, Vol. XXXV, pp. 41–51.

4. **Wilson's Peace Efforts of 1916.** CHARLES SEYMOUR (ed.), *The Intimate Papers of Colonel House*, Vol. II, chaps. iv–vii, ix, xii–xv; VISCOUNT GREY OF FALLODEN, *Twenty-five Years, 1892–1916*, Vol. II, chap. xxiii; B. J. HENDRICK, *Life and Letters of Walter H. Page*, Vol. II, pp. 148–213; WALTER MILLIS, *Road to War*, chaps. vii, viii; *America*, Vol. XI, pp. 300–305.

Questions Suggested by the Chapter

1. Why was Germany an object of suspicion in 1914 to France? to Great Britain? to Russia? 2. Why did Germany support Austria in the coercion of Serbia? 3. What reasons did President Wilson urge for our neutrality? 4. In what ways did Great Britain interfere with American commerce? 5. Contrast the attitude of Ambassador Page and Secretary Bryan toward the war. 6. How did Germany justify the use of the submarine? 7. How did Germany justify the sinking of the *Lusitania*? 8. Contrast the methods of propaganda of the Allies and Germany in this country. 9. What were the provisions of the National Defense Act of 1916? 10. Specify four stages of our neutrality. 11. Why did Wilson urge Congress to pass the Adamson Act? 12. Show the resemblance between Great Britain's treatment of our commercial rights in 1812 and in 1914. 13. Name two events which strengthened Wilson's chances of re-election in 1916. 14. Compare Hughes's loss of California in 1916 with Blaine's loss of New York in 1884. 15. Why were the Allies cold to Wilson's efforts for peace in 1916? 16. Why did we break off relations with Germany in February, 1917? 17. What was the Zimmermann "plot"? 18. What reasons did Wilson give for asking Congress to declare war on Germany? 19. Compare the vote on the declaration of war with that on the eve of the War of 1812 and the Spanish-American War. 20. With what other country besides Germany did we go to war? 21. Do you think Wilson was right in making a distinction between the German government and the German people? Explain your answer. 22. What did Wilson mean by "peace without victory"? 23. How did the Allies interpret the phrase?

CHAPTER TWENTY-SIX

OUR PART IN THE FIGHTING

America's War Aims. If our object in entering the war was to avenge the slaughter of American citizens by the submarines, there was more cause for our going to war when the *Lusitania* was sunk than there was two years later. If it was to "make the world safe for democracy," there was as much need of intervention when Belgium was crushed under the invader's iron heel in 1914. The purposes and methods of the German government had not changed since the days when President Wilson had relied on polite notes to persuade it to observe the rules of humane warfare — if such a thing exists. It was Wilson himself who had changed, under the steady pressure of public opinion. Once we were actually in the war, he dropped the language of pacifism and advocated the total destruction of the German military power. There was no more talk of being "too proud to fight" or of "peace without victory"; now it was to be "force, force, to the uttermost." He was still most concerned at heart with the kind of peace that should emerge from the war, but the immediate task was to bring the war to an end as quickly as possible. To that task we must devote all our resources in man power, materials, and money. It is an error to speak, as so many persons do, of "our Allies" in the war. We were associated with *the* Allies in the fight against the Central Powers; but we made no alliance with any European power ourselves, no treaty of any kind binding us to the continuation of the war or to the division of spoils at its end. We really had our own war with Germany (and Austria), begun and ended at different times from that of the Allies, and fought with a different object in view when once the military power of Germany should be crushed.

669

How Europe Regarded our Entrance into the War. The German high command viewed our declaration of war with indifference. In their eyes we were already furnishing all the help we could to the Allies by our shipments of munitions and supplies. The Germans believed that Wilson was brandishing a "wooden sword." Even if the Americans should raise an army of a million, the war would be over before the army could be trained; for it was to be only a matter of a few months at most before the new submarine warfare would force England to sue for peace. The Allies, on the other hand, welcomed the entrance of the United States into the war with great rejoicing. They were hard pressed and war-weary. Though the situation on the western front had not changed much since the armies had settled down in the trenches after the battle of the Marne (September 6, 1914), German arms had won decisive victories in the east, driving back the Russians and crushing the Rumanians. Their agents were busy in Russia trying to detach that great country from its alliance with France and England, thereby freeing hundreds of thousands of German troops for use on the western front.

Confronted with these dangers, the Allies hailed us as saviors. President Wilson's war message was translated into French and posted in the public places of Paris. The Italian parliament called it a "hymn of humanity." The American flag bedecked the streets of London, Paris, and Rome. It was raised with the Union Jack over the Houses of Parliament on "America Day" (April 20), when the king and queen joined the great assembly in St. Paul's Cathedral to give thanks for our aid. Commissions were immediately sent to the United States by Great Britain and France (followed by the Belgians, Russians, Italians, Rumanians, and Japanese) to bring the grateful greetings of their countries and to advise us how best we might meet their needs. The English mission was headed by the Honorable Arthur J. Balfour, who was invited to address the houses of Congress. The French sent over as spokesman the eloquent René Viviani, the minister of justice, who was accompanied by Marshal ("Papa") Joffre, the hero of the Marne.

U. S. BATTLESHIP *NEW YORK*

American Naval Co-operation. Our navy was mobilized on the day that war was declared, and eighty-seven ships of the German merchant marine in our ports were taken over by our government. Even before the actual declaration of war, Rear Admiral W. S. Sims, president of the Naval War College at Newport, had been sent to England, at the urgent request of Ambassador Page, to consult with the British admiralty on the part we might play in the blockade of Germany. On May 4 a small fleet of destroyers arrived at Queenstown, and in another month our battleships followed. American vessels laid down 55,000 mines, constituting four fifths of the great barrage of the North Sea from the Orkney Islands to the coast of Norway. Furthermore, to help repair the frightful ravages of the submarines, which had sunk between 3,500,000 and 4,000,000 tons of Allied and neutral ships from January to July, 1917, our

Emergency Fleet Corporation, organized under the United States Shipping Board (p. 654), undertook the construction of 10,000,000 tons of merchant marine to carry food, locomotives, cars, trucks, munitions, and troops to the Allies. By the end of the war our service fleet had grown to more than 2000 ships, which had carried to French ports alone 7,500,000 tons of cargo, of which only 1.6 per cent was lost in transit. The cost of our navy and auxiliary-service ships during the two years 1917 and 1918 was $3,833,000,000, a sum equal to the total cost of the United States navy from the second administration of Washington to the World War.

American Troops in France. It was not the intention of the administration to send any American soldiers to Europe before the spring of 1918. Our regular army of only a little over two hundred thousand men would hardly have been a drop in the bucket if added to the millions of European troops on the western front; and our officers were needed at home to train the host of recruits who must be called to the colors. We intended meantime to make our contribution to the Allied cause by furnishing the "sinews of war" in the shape of generous credits for the purchase of supplies of all sorts. But on the plea of Viviani and Joffre, backed by Balfour, that the presence of even a few thousand men in the uniform of the United States would do more than anything else to make America's participation in the war seem like a reality to the armies which had borne the incessant burden for thirty-three months, the President decided to send a small American Expeditionary Force (the "A.E.F.") to France at once. As commander he selected Major General John J. Pershing, a West Point graduate who had a splendid record of service in Cuba, the Philippines, and Mexico.

General Pershing and his staff landed in England on June 8. After five days of lavish entertainment, including a reception by the king at Buckingham Palace, they crossed over to Paris, which, like London, was decked with the Stars and Stripes. A dramatic incident of Pershing's arrival in Paris was his visit to the grave of Lafayette, on which he placed a wreath of flowers. The debt of gratitude we owed to France for her aid

GENERAL PERSHING AT THE GRAVE OF LAFAYETTE

in the American Revolution was about to be paid. Toward the end of June fifteen thousand of our regular troops arrived at Brest, and on the Fourth of July a battalion of these troops paraded through the streets of Paris amid the cheers of the throng. A few weeks later General Pershing established his headquarters at Chaumont, one hundred and forty miles southeast of Paris, where his soldiers were to be trained in trench warfare before taking their place in the "quiet sector" of the front between Verdun and Belfort (see map, p. 674).

Raising an Army. On April 5, while the House was still debating the war resolution, Secretary of War Baker had submitted to Congress the draft of an army bill prepared by the general staff. It called for the immediate completion of the full strength of the regular army (293,000) and the national guard (425,000) by voluntary enlistments, and for the conscription of a new national army of 500,000 to 1,000,000 soldiers by a "selective draft" apportioned among the states according to population. In spite of objections in Congress to the drafting of men for war, the President and the War Department were convinced that it was the fairest way to recruit the new national army. It would bring home to all the young manhood of the nation that the war was a common undertaking in which they must be ready to take their part; and the "selective" feature provided ample means of exempting men who were needed as the sole support of dependents or as indispensable workers in industries necessary for the prosecution of the war.

The Selective Service Act (passed on May 28 by almost unanimous vote in both houses of Congress) increased the pay of the private soldier from fifteen dollars to thirty dollars a month, allowed the President to enlist a volunteer infantry force if he so wished,[1] and required all male citizens between the ages of twenty-one and thirty-one to register for military service, just as they registered at the polls for voting. On registration day (June 5) 9,586,508 young men were enrolled in the 4557 registration districts of the country. Six weeks later numbers were drawn by lot in Washington, each number drawn calling into the service the man with the corresponding registration number in his district. When all the numbers had been drawn, it was found that 1,374,000 men had been drafted. They were required to report to their district boards at once for physical examination and to claim exemption from service for any of the reasons provided in the law. About 687,000 of the drafted men were retained for the service. They were distributed during the summer and autumn among sixteen camps in various parts of

[1] This feature of the act was prompted by Theodore Roosevelt's call at the White House with an offer to raise a volunteer division for immediate service in France. The Colonel claimed that three hundred thousand men were ready to enlist under his command, and asked to have several of the best officers of the regular army associated with him. Many people in America and Europe believed that his presence on the field of battle would be a great encouragement to the Allies. But President Wilson, while paying tribute to Roosevelt's "vigor and enthusiasm," declined the offer. To accept it, he said, "would seriously interfere with the prompt creation and early use of an effective army, and would contribute virtually nothing to the effective strength of the armies now engaged against Germany.... The business in hand is undramatic [a dig at Roosevelt!], practical, and of scientific definiteness and precision.... The first troops sent to France will be taken from the present forces of the regular army and will be under the command of trained soldiers only [another dig!]."

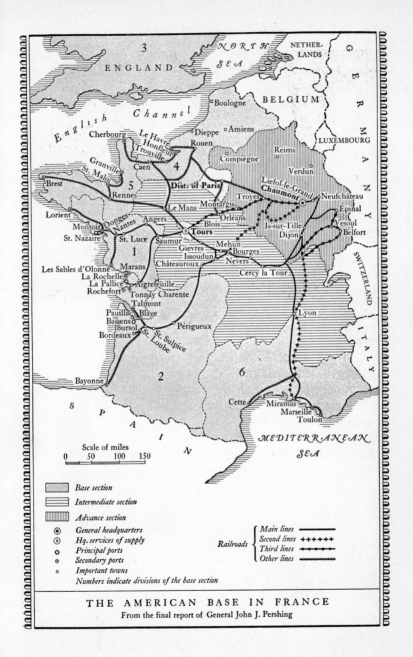

THE AMERICAN BASE IN FRANCE

From the final report of General John J. Pershing

SECRETARY BAKER DRAWING THE FIRST NUMBER IN THE SECOND
MILITARY DRAFT, JUNE 24, 1918

the country, while the national guard (militia) called into the
Federal service were sent to sixteen other camps. These thirty-
two training camps, with their hospitals, shops, lighting and
heating plants, water supply, sewage systems, and amusement
halls, were built in a few months' time at a cost of two hundred
million dollars. On the eve of the departure of the first con-
tingent of the national army for their camps, President Wilson
sent them the following message :

> The eyes of the world will be upon you, because you are in some special
> sense the soldiers of freedom. Let it be your pride, therefore, to show all
> men everywhere not only what good soldiers you are, but also what good
> men you are, keeping yourselves fit and straight in everything and pure
> and clean through and through. . . . My affectionate confidence goes with
> you in every battle and every test.

Raising a Revenue. Nobody had any definite idea of what
the war would cost us, but it was evident that, with the huge
expenses for our army, navy, and air forces, together with the
assistance in money and materials to the Allies, it would

run into unprecedented figures. When Professor Seligman, of Columbia University, suggested that the cost of the first year might be ten billion dollars, his estimate was "greeted with a smile of incredulity."

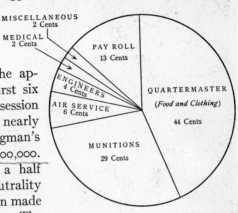

MISCELLANEOUS
2 Cents

MEDICAL
2 Cents

PAY ROLL
13 Cents

ENGINEERS
4 Cents

AIR SERVICE
6 Cents

QUARTERMASTER
(*Food and Clothing*)
44 Cents

MUNITIONS
29 Cents

HOW THE AMERICAN DOLLAR WAS SPENT IN THE WAR

As a matter of fact, the appropriations for the first six months of the extra session of Congress reached nearly double Professor Seligman's estimate, or $18,897,000,000. During the two and a half years of American neutrality great fortunes had been made here out of war profits. The balance of our exports over our imports had risen from $470,600,000 in 1914 to $3,630,690,000 in 1917. Nearly four times as many men reported incomes above a million dollars in 1917 as in 1914. The radicals in Congress were in favor of "conscripting the wealth" as well as the men of the country. Senator Johnson of California proposed a tax of 80 per cent on war profits, which he estimated would bring into the Treasury between three and four billion dollars.

A revenue bill designed to produce $1,800,000,000 in taxes was introduced into the House on May 9, 1917. It provided for an increased income tax, excess-profits taxes ranging from 20 to 60 per cent, and a variety of taxes on amusements, luxuries, transportation, and business transactions. But these taxes were trivial as compared with the revenue bill of the autumn of 1918. That bill called for over $6,000,000,000, the largest sum ever levied by a government on its people at one time. The normal rate on incomes above $4000 was raised to 12 per cent, with graded surtaxes reaching 65 per cent on incomes above $1,000,000. Corporations paid $12\frac{1}{2}$ per cent on net incomes, in addition to the taxes on excess and war profits. Altogether, the

THE SECRETARY OF THE TREASURY, WILLIAM G. McADOO

government raised $11,280,000,000 by taxation from April, 1917, to October, 1919. Such a figure is almost beyond the reach of the mind. We cannot think in terms of billions. But we can gain some idea of their meaning when we reduce them to familiar terms. The cost of the war in those two and a half years was over $35,000,000 a day, or $25,278 a minute!

The Liberty Loans. Rich as our country was, it was clear that the whole staggering cost of the war could not be paid by the taxation of its current wealth. The larger part of it (two thirds, according to the plan of the government) would have to be financed by the issue of government bonds. Before our entrance into the World War very few American citizens had bought government bonds. If they had money to invest, they found much more attractive rates of interest in the stocks and bonds of the railroads, the steel companies, the public utilities (gas, water, telephone, electric light), and various other corporations. It was part of the administration's purpose, however, to enlist the capital as well as the man power of the whole country in support of this "democratic" war. Hence Secretary of the Treasury McAdoo, instead of selling the government bonds in large amounts to the bankers, as had been the usual custom, offered them to the general public. An issue of $2,000,000,000, bearing 3½ per cent interest, was authorized by Congress in April, 1917, as the First Liberty Loan. It was opened to popular subscription in amounts as low as $50 ("baby bonds"). Posters on billboards, placards in store windows, appeals in papers and magazines, special features in theaters and movie houses, urged every American citizen to "buy a bond." Artists furnished cartoons, and clever writers provided slogans like "Buy bonds or wear them!" When the loan was closed, it was found that subscriptions totaling $3,035,000,000 had been made by over four million persons. Three other Liberty Loans followed, at intervals of about six months; and each one, like the first, was heavily oversubscribed. In addition to paying taxes of $11,280,000,000 and subscribing double that amount to Liberty Bonds, the American people contributed as a free-will offering $4,000,000,000 to various organizations for the physical and moral welfare of the soldiers, such as the Red Cross, the Salvation Army, the Knights of Columbus, the Jewish Welfare Board, the Young Men's Christian Association, and the War Camp Community Service.

Number of Loan [1]	Date	Amount Asked	Rate	Amount Subscribed	Number of Subscribers
First	May, 1917	$2,000,000,000	3½	$3,035,000,000	4,000,000
Second	Oct., 1917	3,000,000,000	4	4,617,000,000	9,400,000
Third	April, 1918	3,000,000,000	4¼	4,176,000,000	18,300,000
Fourth	Oct., 1918	6,000,000,000	4¼	6,988,000,000	21,000,000

The Allies' Call. In the autumn of 1917 and the spring of 1918 events occurred in Europe which called for the immediate

[1] A fifth great popular loan, the Victory Loan "to finish the job," was announced by the Treasury in April, 1919. It called for $4,500,000,000 at 4¾ per cent interest, and was taken by 15,000,000 subscribers. Like the four Liberty Loans, it was heavily oversubscribed.

help of the American soldiers on the battle front. In October, 1917, the Italians suffered a terrible defeat at Caporetto by the Austro-German army, being driven back from the Alps to the neighborhood of Venice. Ten divisions of French and British troops were diverted from the western front to save Italy from the possible fate of Serbia and Rumania. Then, in November, the Bolshevists got control of the Russian revolution and proceeded to detach their country from the Allies. The Communist dictators, Lenin and Trotsky, entered into negotiations with the Germans at Brest-Litovsk, with the result that Russia withdrew from the war and half a million German troops were freed for service in France. Here, with a considerable superiority over the Allies, they began a great series of "drives" in March, 1918, to pierce the British and French lines and reach the Channel ports and Paris. The Germans failed to reach their objectives, but they conquered three thousand square miles of territory and took one hundred and fifty thousand prisoners before they were stopped at Château-Thierry, on the Marne, only forty-two miles from the outskirts of Paris. In the midst of this great German offensive the prime ministers of Great Britain, France, and Italy, in conference at Versailles, June 2, sent the following message to President Wilson :

General Foch has presented to us a statement of the utmost gravity, which points out that the numerical superiority of the enemy in France, where one hundred and sixty-two Allied divisions oppose two hundred German divisions, is very heavy, and that, as there is no possibility of the British and French increasing the number of their divisions, there is great danger of the war being lost, unless the numerical inferiority of the Allies can be remedied as rapidly as possible by the advent of American troops. . . . He places the total American forces required for this at no less than a hundred divisions and urges continuous fresh American levies, which, in his opinion, should be not less than three hundred thousand a month.

America's Response. There were only about three hundred and fifty thousand American soldiers in France when the German drives began. General Pershing had put them all at the disposal of General Ferdinand Foch, who had been made generalissimo of the Allied armies on March 26, declaring that "the

AMERICAN OPERATIONS IN FRANCE

American people would hold it an honor for our troops were they engaged in the present battle." The honor was granted. Early in April our First Division, under General Robert Bullard, left its "quiet sector" near Toul for the scene of conflict, and on May 28 American soldiers stormed and captured the high fortified position of Cantigny — our first military contribution to the victory of the Allies. At the same time American troops of the Second and Third Division joined the French north of the Marne to help stop the German drive on Paris. Though some of these troops had been in France less than two months and had had no training in the front lines, they acquitted themselves nobly, driving the enemy from strongly fortified positions at Belleau Wood, Bouresches, and Vaux, and capturing fourteen hundred prisoners. For the brilliant conduct of the fourth brigade of marines, led by General J. G. Harbord, the French army orders of June 30 changed the name of Belleau Wood to "the Wood of the Marine Brigade."

Now, in response to the cry of distress from Versailles, our War Department made plans to place three million troops in France by the spring of 1919, in addition to furnishing a continuous supply of food, clothing, rolling stock, motor trucks, mechanics, and engineers over "the longest line of communication in the history of warfare."[1] At the end of June, 1918, there were 722,000 American soldiers in France : at the end of October they had increased to 1,843,000. Nearly half of them were transported across the Atlantic in American-built ships. Only a few hundred were lost at sea, the most serious disaster being the torpedoing of the Cunarder *Tuscania* off the coast of Ireland. All but one hundred and seventy-five of the two thousand soldiers, engineers, and aviators on board were rescued by the *Tuscania's* convoy. This was the answer to the German threat that the submarines would prevent an American army from ever reaching the shores of France. Their own great liner *Vaterland*, seized at the port of New York and converted into the troopship *Leviathan*, ferried almost one hundred thousand American soldiers across the sea to help break the Hindenburg line.

The Saint-Mihiel Salient. By mid-July the German drive of four months had been checked at all points, and General Foch began a counterdrive of another four months, which was to end in the surrender of the German armies, the abdication of the Kaiser and the crown prince, and the establishment of a republic in Germany. In these closing months of the war the American troops played a major part. When the German drive began in March, they were holding but twelve miles of the western front

[1] Early in 1918 General Pershing established a " Service of Supply" for facilitating the distribution of the enormous amount of material sent to France. The headquarters of the " S. O. S." were at Tours, which was connected by American-built railroads and telegraph lines with the ports of debarkation on the French coast of the Bay of Biscay. From Tours radiated the lines of communication with the troops at the front. All along these lines cantonments, training schools, and recreation huts were built. Seventy American storage depots dotted the map of France, one of them near Tours covering six square miles and housing in its three hundred buildings one hundred million dollars' worth of supplies (map, p. 675).

in "quiet sectors"; but by October their line had been extended to one hundred and one miles, or nearly a quarter of the entire front from Switzerland to the North Sea. In none of the Allied defensive engagements from March to June had as many as thirty thousand American troops been engaged; but in the final offensive of September–October more than a million took part, earning from General Foch the laconic praise "The American soldiers are superb."

The two chief exploits of our army were in the Saint-Mihiel salient and the Meuse-Argonne forest. Since September, 1914, the Germans had held a triangle of high ground two hundred miles in area, jutting into the French lines southeast of Verdun. The position was of great importance, since it served to protect the fortifications of Metz and the rich Briey coal fields. Early in September, 1918, General Pershing, with his forces increased to over a million men, got the consent of General Foch to undertake the wiping out of the Saint-Mihiel salient. Four divisions of French troops were included in Pershing's command, ready to assault the apex of the salient as the American troops pinched the flanks. In addition, about 2000 French and British guns, 273 tanks, and 192 airplanes were put at Pershing's disposal. In the three days' fighting (September 12–15) the Americans swept through wire entanglements and over fortified ridges, clearing the entire salient, and capturing 16,000 prisoners, 443 guns, and a vast quantity of military stores left by the Germans in their hasty retreat.

The Battle of the Argonne. A few days after Generals Pershing and Pétain had entered the town of Saint-Mihiel together, amid the cheers of the inhabitants, began the battle of the Meuse-Argonne, a titanic struggle of more than six weeks, in which 1,200,000 American troops were engaged. The object of the attack was the city of Sedan, through which ran the great four-track railway paralleling the German front, the artery of the enemy's supplies from Belgium, Luxemburg, and Lorraine. The scene of the struggle was the Argonne forest, twenty-five miles deep, a mass of barbed-wire entanglements, pathless wastes pitted with shell craters, and dense undergrowth hiding the ravines and ridges which sheltered nests of machine guns. The French officers had declared the forest impenetrable. Yet our army never faltered. After a fortnight of incessant fighting they had cleared the Germans out of the Argonne (October 4), and at the end of another month of steady hammering against some of the best of the Kaiser's troops they reached the banks of the Meuse at a point opposite Sedan. The American losses had been heavy (117,000 dead or wounded); but we had driven the enemy back 30 miles and broken his whole line of defense from Metz to Sedan, liberating 150 towns and villages, and capturing 26,000 prisoners and nearly 4000 cannon and machine guns. Four days after the "Rainbow Division" had reached the banks of the Meuse (November 7), the Germans signed the armistice, and the war was over.[1]

The "Fourteen Points." Early in January, 1918, the British prime minister, Lloyd George, addressed Parliament and President Wilson addressed Congress, announcing the terms which would be acceptable as a basis for peace. The statements were made in response to the publication by the Russian Bolshevists of the secret treaties revealing the imperialistic designs of the Allies, and to the suggestions from various sources that the Austrian and German people were anxious for peace if only they could be assured that the Allies were not determined on their political and economic destruction. President Wilson's address of January 8 proposed fourteen points as the "only possible program for world peace." The first five points dealt with general reforms in international relations: "open covenants, openly arrived at," the removal of economic barriers, the freedom of the seas, the reduction of armaments to the lowest point consistent with national security, and the adjustment of colonial

---

[1] Some idea of the magnitude of the engagements at Saint-Mihiel and Argonne can be formed by comparing them with two battles fought in our Civil War. General Pershing commanded five and one-half times as many troops at Saint-Mihiel as General Meade did at the battle of Gettysburg. The Meuse-Argonne battle lasted six times as long as the battle of the Wilderness, and twelve times as many American troops were engaged in it as General Grant had in the Wilderness campaign. The weight of ammunition fired in the Meuse-Argonne drive exceeded that fired by the Union armies during the whole Civil War.

claims with due regard to the interests of the populations concerned. Points six to thirteen contained special territorial and political recommendations concerning Russia, Belgium, Alsace-Lorraine, Italy, the Balkan states, the Turkish Empire, and Poland. The last point, the most important in the eyes of President Wilson, read, "A general association of nations must be formed, under specific covenants, for the purpose of affording mutual guarantees of political independence and territorial integrity to great and small states alike." As to Germany, the President said:

We have no jealousy of Germany's greatness. We grudge her no achievement or distinction of learning or of pacific enterprise such as have made her record very bright and very enviable. We do not wish to injure her or block in any way her legitimate influence or power. . . . We only wish her to accept a place of equality among the people of the world — the new world in which we live — instead of a place of mastery.

In his Metropolitan Opera House speech in New York, on the launching of the Fourth Liberty Loan (September 27), President Wilson repeated these assurances, but insisted that America was determined to fight the war to a finish against the "military masters of Germany." Again he emphasized his fourteenth point, declaring that an association of the nations must be a part, "and in a sense the most important part," of the treaty of peace.

Germany's Desperate Condition. In February, 1918, the German militarists greeted Wilson's "Fourteen Points" with scorn. They were preparing the great drive which was to win the war. The terms of peace would be announced not from London or Washington but from Berlin. "Forward with God!" was the Kaiser's cry. But the events of the summer and autumn brought other counsel. The submarine campaign was failing. More ships were being launched than were destroyed. Hundreds of thousands of fresh troops were coming from America every month. The Hindenburg line was receding week by week, although the German generals in their reports to headquarters tried to cover up the plain fact of retreat by such phrases as "rectifying the front" or "shortening lines." The Kaiser still spoke of his "invincible, heaven-favored armies," and in a speech at the great Krupp gun factory, on September 12, claimed a sure victory for his "death-defying navy and mighty generals." But the mighty generals knew better. A month earlier his general in chief, Ludendorff, had told him that the game was up. The only German soldiers going "forward" were the long files of stolid prisoners marching to the rear of the Allied armies to the good-natured chaffing of the "Yanks," who hailed them as they passed with "You're on your way to Paris now" or "Kaiser Bill will miss you."

The eastern allies of Germany were deserting her cause, like rats leaving a sinking vessel. Turkey had dropped out. On September 20 (the day the Meuse-Argonne drive started) Bulgaria signed an armistice with the French general Franchet d'Esperey, and crowds gathered before the Bulgarian embassy in Berlin shouting "Down with the Kaiser!" Six days later the Austrians asked for terms of peace. For four years Germany had waged an almost superhuman fight against heavy odds; but she had now come to the end of her rope. Her people were starving from the blockade and were being goaded to revolution both by the peace propaganda of the Russian Bolshevists and by the tons of leaflets, dropped from the Allies' airplanes, telling them that they were being deceived by their military leaders. The Kaiser now abandoned the Junkers and spoke of his desire that "the people should co-operate more effectively than heretofore in deciding the fate of the Fatherland." He advocated a democratic reform of the Prussian constitution, and called to the chancellorship Prince Maximilian of Baden, a liberal and an avowed champion of peace. It was to Wilson that the German government turned in its distress, knowing that America had no imperialistic ambitions to gratify, no European territory or colonies to demand, no ancient grudges or enmities to satisfy.

The Armistice. On October 4, when the American troops were nearing Sedan, Chancellor Max approached Wilson through the Swiss minister at Washington, asking him to invite all the belligerent states to agree to "the immediate conclusion of an armistice on land and sea." "The German government," said the chancellor, "accepts the program set forth by the President of the United States in his message to Congress of January 8 [the Fourteen Points] and in his later pronouncements, especially his speech of September 27, as a basis for the peace negotiations." President Wilson neither refused nor complied with the request immediately. Before he could act as a peace broker he wanted to be sure that the chancellor was speaking not for the "military masters and monarchical autocrats" of Germany but for the people. The chancellor assured him that the proposed reforms in the German government were "in complete accord with the wishes of a people free from arbitrary and irresponsible influences"; and the chancellor's word seemed to be confirmed when, toward the end of October, Ludendorff resigned his command and the Reichstag subjected the military power to the civil authority. When Wilson was at last satisfied of the good faith of the new German government, he submitted the correspondence to the Allied governments, with the suggestion that, if they were disposed to effect peace on the terms indicated, they should authorize their military representatives to conclude the armistice.

The terms were drawn up by the Supreme War Council of the Allies, and on November 7 were presented by Marshal Foch to German envoys who were conducted, blindfolded, within the Allied lines. When the German credentials had been verified, Marshal Foch, without ceremony, read the terms of the armistice. They called for the immediate withdrawal of all German troops from the soil of France, Belgium, Alsace-Lorraine, and Luxemburg. German armies were also to be withdrawn from all German territory west of the Rhine, and a strip ten kilometers (about six miles) wide on the east bank of the river, extending from Switzerland to Holland, was to be a neutral zone. Allied and American troops were to occupy the three great Rhenish cities of Cologne, Coblenz, and Mainz. Furthermore, the Germans were to surrender all their submarines, fifty destroyers, and twenty-four battleships and cruisers; and to hand over vast stores of cannon, machine guns, airplanes, locomotives, freight cars, and motor trucks. They were to remove all their troops from Austria-Hungary, Turkey, Russia, and Rumania, and to renounce the treaties of Brest-Litovsk and Bucharest which they had forced, respectively, upon the latter two countries. They were to repatriate all prisoners taken, to make reparation for the damage done by their invading armies, and to pay all the expenses of the Allied and American armies of occupation. The time accorded the German delegates for signing the armistice was seventy-two hours.

The terms were severe, and a protest against signing came from the Kaiser's headquarters at Spa. But Germany's hour of extremity had come. She was not able to resume the war. The terms must be accepted. The revolution which stalks in the wake of fallen autocracies was threatening the country. The red flag was flying in half of the cities of Germany. There was mutiny in the fleet at Kiel. The Kaiser and the crown prince signed letters of abdication on November 9, and the next day fled across the border to Holland for safety. The frightful sacrifices of the German people for the sake of the Hohenzollern autocracy were at an end.

The End of the War. A few hours before the expiration of the time limit set, the German delegates signed the armistice, and at 11 A.M. on November 11, 1918, the last gun was fired on the front. Compared with the sacrifice of millions of men who had borne the brunt of the fighting for four years, the losses of the Americans in the last months of the war were slight. Less than fifty thousand of our soldiers were killed in battle, somewhat over fifty thousand died of disease at home and abroad, and of the two hundred and forty thousand wounded nearly five sixths were restored to duty again. A Man-Power Act of August 31, 1918, had called for the registration, for military service, of all American men between the ages of eighteen and forty-five; and under this act thirteen million were registered on September 12. But as the armistice was concluded less than a month afterward, not 1 per cent of these newly registered men were called into the service. Less than one in twenty-five of our male population participated in actual warfare, as compared with one in six of the French.

	In Dollars	Men Killed in Battle
Germany	39,000,000,000	1,600,000
British Empire	38,000,000,000	900,000
France	26,000,000,000	1,385,000
United States	22,000,000,000	49,000
Austria	21,000,000,000	800,000
Russia	18,000,000,000	1,700,000
Italy	13,000,000,000	462,000

COMPARATIVE COST OF THE WAR TO SEVEN CHIEF BELLIGERENTS

Throughout the world the cessation of the four years of carnage was hailed with wild demonstrations of joy — in Berlin and Vienna, as well as in London, Paris, and New York. Shortly after noon of armistice day President Wilson drove to the Capitol through Pennsylvania Avenue, which was lined with cheering crowds, to announce to a joint session of Congress the terms of the armistice and "the attainment of the object upon which all free men had set their hearts."

It is not possible now [he truly said] to assess the consequences of this great consummation. We know only that this tragical war, whose consuming flames swept from one nation to another until all the world was on fire, is at an end; and that it was the privilege of our own people to enter it at its most critical juncture, in such fashion and such force to contribute in a way in which we are all deeply proud to the great result.

On the same day he issued the following proclamation to the American people:

My Fellow Countrymen: The armistice was signed this morning. Everything for which America fought has been accomplished. It will now be our fortunate duty to assist by example, by sober friendly counsel, and by material aid in the establishment of just democracy throughout the world.

Terms to be Mastered

the A. E. F.	conscription of wealth	the "Fourteen Points"
"quiet sector"	"baby bonds"	armistice
selective draft	service of supply	Bolshevists

For Supplementary Reading

J. J. Pershing, "Final Report to the Secretary of War," in *New York Times Current History of the War*, Vol. XI, pp. 50–68, 338–350; L. P. Ayres, *The War with Germany, A Statistical Summary*; Charles Seymour, *Woodrow Wilson and the World War* (Chronicles of America, Vol. XLVIII), chaps. vi–xiv; T. G. Frothingham, *American Reinforcement in the World War*; S. Thomas, *The History of the A.E.F.*; Frederick Palmer, *Newton D. Baker, America at War*, Vol. II, and *Our Greatest Battle*; W. S. Sims and B. J. Hendrick, *The Victory at Sea*; P. W. Slosson, *The Great Crusade and After* (A History of American Life, Vol. XII), chaps. i, ii; The Pageant of America, Vol. VII, pp. 208–351 (illustrations); J. J. Pershing, *My Experiences in the World War*; America, Vol. XII, pp. 35–183; Arthur Bullard, *Mobilizing America*; Hart, *Contemporaries*, Vol. V, Nos. 167, 173, 184–186.

Topics for Reports

1. **Mobilizing the Nation.** J. B. McMaster, *The United States in the World War*, Vol. II, pp. 32–84; E. W. Young, *The Wilson Administration and the Great War*, pp. 28–106; Frederick Palmer, *Newton D. Baker, America at War*, Vol. I, chaps. ix–xviii; The Pageant of America, Vol. VII, pp. 238–267; J. S. Bassett, *Our War with Germany*, chap. vii.

2. **Saint-Mihiel and the Argonne.** Frederick Palmer, *Our Greatest Battle*; R. S. Tompkins, *The Story of the Rainbow Division*, pp. 120–144; J. B. McMaster, *The United States in the World War*, Vol. II, pp. 116–140; The Pageant of America, Vol. VII, pp. 327–351; *New York Times Current History of the War*, Vol. IX, pp. 43–53 (Pershing's Report).

3. **The United States Shipping Board.** E. N. Hurley, *The New Merchant Marine*; E. E. Day, "The American Merchant Fleet; a War Achievement, a Peace Problem," in *Quarterly Journal of Economics*, Vol. XXXIX, pp. 567–606; Clark, Hamilton, and Moulton, *Readings in the Economics of War*, pp. 368–379; A. Hurd, "The World's Shipping: the Balance of Power," in *Fortnightly Review*, Vol. CXIV, pp. 584–597; H. B. Drury, "The Labor Policy of the Shipping Board," in *Journal of Political Economy*, Vol. XXIX, pp. 1–28.

4. **The American Front in France.** J. B. McMaster, *The United States in the World War*, Vol. II, chap. iii; *America*, Vol. XII, pp. 54–60, 81–83, 90–157; J. S. Bassett, *Our War with Germany*, chaps. x–xii; Shipley Thomas, *The History of the A.E.F.*; De Chambrun and De Marenches, *The American Army in the European Conflict*, pp. 277–306; Charles Seymour, *Woodrow Wilson and the World War*, chap. viii.

Questions Suggested by the Chapter

1. Explain how we were an "associated" and not an "allied" power in the war. 2. What change of policy did Wilson show after we had entered the war? 3. Why did Germany make light of our entrance into the war? 4. How did the Allies greet our entrance? 5. What contribution did our navy make to winning the war?

6. What made Wilson decide to send soldiers to France in the summer of 1917? **7.** How was our new national army raised? **8.** Why did not Wilson accept Roosevelt's offer to raise volunteers for the war? **9.** How much money did the government raise during the war by taxes? by bonds? **10.** What new method of selling its bonds did the government adopt? **11.** Why were American troops so sorely needed in France in the summer of 1918? **12.** How do you account for the fact that so few ships carrying American troops were torpedoed? **13.** What were the two chief engagements of American troops in the war? **14.** When, where, and why did Wilson announce his Fourteen Points? **15.** What was Wilson's fourteenth point? **16.** Have any of the first five points been realized? **17.** Why did the Kaiser change his policy at the end of September, 1918? **18.** Why did he apply to Wilson rather than to France or England for an armistice? **19.** What were the terms of the armistice? **20.** Explain the difference between an armistice and a treaty of peace. **21.** How did our losses in the war compare with those of the European powers? **22.** How did Wilson show his "idealism" in his announcement of the armistice?

CHAPTER TWENTY–SEVEN

THE INFLUENCE OF THE WAR ON
AMERICAN LIFE

The People and the Government. No other event in our history ever wrought such sweeping changes in the conduct of business, the position of labor, the condition of the farmer, the burden of the taxpayer, and the whole mental and moral outlook of the American people as the World War. It may be that we are now, twenty years later, experiencing a similar revolution in the upheaval of the "New Deal," but many of the measures of the New Deal can be traced back to the effects of the war. First of all, the World War brought the government very close to the people and made them "government-minded." Our traditions had been those of private initiative and management in business, of making and spending our money as we pleased, of full liberty in the expression of opinion. Before income taxes were levied, very few Americans except the importers of dutiable goods had ever paid a dollar into the national treasury. Only one man in a hundred of military age had worn the uniform of the United States army. Probably not one person in a thousand had ever seen a United States government bond. But the war changed all this. Over twenty million persons, or one in five of our population, subscribed to the Fourth Liberty Loan. At the close of the war there were nearly four million men in uniform. Seven million people were paying a billion dollars of income taxes into the Treasury. The government at Washington, acting through scores of boards, commissions, and committees, was controlling the entire production and distribution of the important industries of the country, dictating to the people what they should eat and wear, rationing their sugar and fuel, and limiting their railroad travel and their Sunday automobile rides. Men gave up high-salaried positions and went to Washington to work for a dollar a year, to aid the President in the exercise of the powers conferred upon him by Congress. The government went into the banking, the railroad, the shipping, the insurance, and the employment-agency business. It conscripted labor like soldiers. It determined the price the manufacturer should be paid for his steel and the farmer for his wheat. Never had a nation of such self-dependent individualists been put under a regime of such rigid paternalism.

America's Resources. All this control was exercised with the sole aim of helping the Allies win the war. The part which our soldiers played in the closing months of the war was, as we have seen, magnificent. But, after all, the 1,200,000 American troops in the great battle of the Meuse-Argonne were only about 15 per cent of the total fighting force on the western front. It was upon America's almost inexhaustible resources in the factories, mills, mines, forests, and fields that the Allies depended for their chief aid. Clemenceau spoke of the men who directed these resources toward the winning of the war as "the organizers of the industrial victory." Without our metals, timber, coal, food, textiles, locomotives, and trucks the fighting arm of the Allies would have been paralyzed. It is true that there were only a few American-made airplanes and guns at the front when the war ended; but had it not been for the millions of tons of steel, the copper and the chemicals, the spruce and the cotton, shipped from America to supply the factories and foundries of England and France, the necessary guns, airplanes, and shells could not have been manufactured. All this we furnished in addition to supplying our own rapidly growing army with an enormous amount of material, over a line of three to four thousand miles.[1] To fill these demands a full inventory of America's resources had to be made. Her production had to be "speeded up" and her

[1] For example, the army purchased twice as many blankets in 1918 as the total number manufactured in the country in 1914. In the first fourteen months of the war it requisitioned 30,700,000 pairs of shoes, 26,500,000 flannel shirts, and 13,900,000 woolen coats. The cost of the clothing for the army was over a billion dollars, or an average of $500 for each soldier. In the operations of Pershing's army at Saint-Mihiel 5000 telephones and 50,000 miles of field wire were used.

transportation system by rail and ship to be handled so as to make the maximum contribution to the armies at the front.

Extraordinary Powers Conferred on the President. Though our President, as commander in chief of the army and navy, has enormous military power, the framers of the Constitution certainly never intended to give him the authority to control the political and economic life of the country. They were so wary of the creation of a "dictator" that they hemmed in the power of the President in civil affairs by a number of "checks and balances." But Congress, in the emergency of the war, conferred "dictatorial" powers on President Wilson, just as twenty years later it conferred such powers on President Franklin D. Roosevelt in the emergency of the great depression, which was "as serious as a war." The Democratic caucus of the House voted to set aside all bills except those which were recommended from the White House. Representative A. P. Gardner of Massachusetts, a stanch Republican, declared, "Whatever the President says he needs, that I shall vote to give him." Congress had already, in the National Defense Act of 1916 (p. 653), authorized Wilson to appoint a board on the "mobilization of the industries necessary for military preparedness," and out of this had come the Council of National Defense, with its seven civilian advisers on raw materials, finished products, munitions, transportation, labor, engineering, and medicine. With our entrance into the war, measure after measure was passed by Congress increasing the President's power, until the climax was reached in the Overman Act of May 20, 1918, which made him a virtual dictator for the rest of the war. He was authorized to create any new organs of administration that he saw fit, to change the old ones regardless of existing laws, and to redistribute their personnel, functions, and funds according to his judgment.

The Espionage Act. It would be impossible to describe all these measures in detail, but we may select three laws of the extra session of April–October, 1917, as examples. The Espionage Act, of June 15, gave the President the authority to control the exports of commodities necessary for the Allies and conferred upon him certain powers of censorship. Direct trade with Germany had been prevented from the beginning of the war by the British blockade; but the Central Powers had still been able, as we have seen (p. 647, note), to draw large supplies from neutral countries. The Exports Board under the Espionage Act was therefore given the right to regulate trade with neutrals. For example, in the midsummer of 1917 one could see several Dutch ships, loaded with grain, lying for weeks in the Hudson River because they were unable to get clearance papers allowing them to sail until they gave assurance that their cargoes were not eventually destined for Germany.

The act also imposed severe penalties upon persons disclosing any information concerning places connected with the national defense, "enemy aliens" (that is, Germans or Austrians not naturalized in the United States) being forbidden to go up in airplanes or balloons, to come within a hundred yards of wharves or piers, or to be found in waters within three miles of the shore. It was made a penal offense to advocate resistance to the laws of the United States, to refuse to do military duty, or to obstruct the draft. Provision was made for the "conscientious objectors." Drafted men who could prove that they belonged to "any well-organized religious sect whose creed or principles forbade its members to participate in war in any form" were allowed to enter the various types of noncombatant service, such as the Medical Corps and the construction and repair departments. All but about five hundred conscientious objectors who were drafted accepted one or another of these assignments. Altogether some fifteen hundred to two thousand offenders against the Espionage Act were sent to prison, among them Eugene V. Debs, who ran for President for the fifth time on the Socialist ticket [1] in 1920 while still serving his sentence in the Atlanta jail for encouraging resistance to the draft.

---

[1] The Socialist party was split by the war. On July 1, 1917, by a referendum vote of 21,639 to 2752, it condemned our entrance into the war as "a conspiracy of capitalism." Thereupon several prominent American Socialists, including John Spargo, William E. Walling, J. G. Phelps Stokes, Upton Sinclair, and Allan Benson (the Presidential candidate of the party in 1916), withdrew from the party, declaring that it had been "scuttled by German nationalist jingoes and anarchistic impossibilities."

The Lever Act. The most imperative need of the Allies was food. Just after we entered the war President Wilson made an appeal to the American people to "turn in hosts to the farm" and "help solve the problem of feeding the nations." In May, 1917, he appointed Herbert C. Hoover [1] as voluntary food-controller, to "mobilize the forces of the country in saving food and eliminating waste." The saving of an ounce of sugar a day by every person in the United States would mean over a million tons at the end of the year. A pound of wheat a week saved meant 150,000,000 bushels in twelve months. The grain harvests of the Allied countries would fall 500,000,000 bushels below their normal yield. We must send over at least 225,000,000 bushels to ward off starvation. The Lever Act, of August 10, 1917, gave the President authority to "requisition foods, feeds, fuel, and other supplies necessary to the support of the army or any other public use connected with the common defense." He could fix prices, regulate distribution, buy, store, and sell fuel, grain, and vegetables, and require producers to sell to the government through the agencies which he might designate. He was given a monopoly of the purchase of wheat through a Federal Food Administration Grain Corporation, which fixed the price at $2.26 a bushel; and the use of grain for the manufacture of distilled liquors was forbidden during the period of the war.

The President appointed Mr. Hoover as Food Administrator and President H. A. Garfield of Williams College as Fuel Administrator under the Lever Act. State and local food and fuel administrators were chosen. The country was asked to observe "wheatless, meatless, and heatless days." The sugar bowls were removed from the tables of hotels and restaurants. Housewives and bakers were pledged to make "victory bread" from corn, rice, or barley flour instead of wheat. Front lawns were turned into vegetable gardens. Society ladies took lessons in canning and preserving. The Department of Agriculture sent

[1] Hoover was a California mining engineer who since 1914 had directed the Commission for the Relief of Belgium, which kept millions of the civilian population of Belgium and the invaded districts of northern France from starvation.

UNLOADING SHIPS IN FRANCE

out millions of leaflets instructing the people how to make their contribution to the winning of the war in the homely matters of kitchen, pantry, and garden. The value of our food products sent to the Allies in the year 1918 was over two billion dollars. Dr. Garfield used heroic methods during the terribly severe winter of 1917–1918. When two hundred and fifty ships loaded with cargoes for the Allies were lying at their docks in January, 1918, because their coal bunkers were empty, he ordered all the manufacturing plants east of the Mississippi that were not engaged in the production of goods essential to the war to shut down for a period of five days and for ten successive Mondays thereafter. There were angry protests from the manufacturers against this governmental "tyranny," but President Wilson upheld his Fuel Administrator's order.

The Trading-with-the-Enemy Act. The third major grant of dictatorial power to the President by Congress was the Trading-with-the-Enemy Act, of October 6, 1917. It prohibited dealing with persons residing in countries or doing business in countries at war with the United States. It authorized the President to put an embargo on imports (as the Espionage Act had on exports) and to establish a censorship on communication by mail, cable, or wireless with foreign countries. It provided for the creation of a custodianship of alien property in the United States. Every citizen of an enemy country (Germany) or its ally doing business in the United States was obliged to take out a Federal license, and every newspaper here printed in a foreign language was obliged to furnish the Postmaster-General with English translations of any matter that it published concerning the war. The Alien Property Custodian collected enemy property in this country to the amount of some seven hundred million dollars. For this property he acted as a trustee, depositing in the Treasury, to be invested in United States bonds, such moneys or securities as he took over. Business properties might be transferred, in the discretion of the custodian, to be operated by American citizens. The eventual disposition of the property was to be determined by Congress. This drastic measure was resented by German firms doing business in the United States, not only because it confiscated their property (much of which they never got back) but also because it revealed many of their patented and protected secret methods of manufacture. For example, many chemical processes, such as the manufacture of dyestuffs, were appropriated by the Americans from German models.

The Railroads. In the first months of the war the railroads had formed a voluntary association to promote efficiency in transportation. But they proved unequal, in the face of the rising costs of labor and materials, to furnish the equipment and the service necessary for the war needs of the country. Therefore, on December 26, 1917, President Wilson, acting under the authority of the Adamson Act (p. 654), took over the railroads of the country, which represented an investment of seventeen and a half billion dollars and employed nearly two million men. On January 4, 1918, the President addressed a joint session of Congress on the policy of the government management of the roads, pointing out the need for unified control and promising the owners that their interests would be "as scrupulously looked after as they could be under a private board of directors." The Railroad Bill, signed on March 21, provided that the roads should be restored to their owners not later than twenty-one months after the close of the war; that they should be paid a yearly rental, by the government, based on their average net income for the three years preceding June 30, 1917; and that freight and passenger rates might be fixed by the President, subject to the approval of the Interstate Commerce Commission.

Secretary McAdoo was made Director-General of the railroads, which were operated as a single system. Competition was abolished, terminals and rolling stock were pooled, hundreds of passenger trains were cut out of the schedules, and the public was asked to abstain from all but the most necessary travel. A week after the Director-General assumed his duties, he met the representatives of the railroad brotherhoods and promised labor "a square deal." "Every railroad employee," he said, "is now in effect a government employee, and as much in duty bound to give his best service to his country as if he wore the uniform of the United States army and occupied the trenches at the front." On May 20 he authorized 182 roads to spend $938,000,000 for repairs and equipment during the coming year, and on the twenty-sixth he granted the employees a wage increase of $300,000,000, raising freight and passenger rates to meet the expense. Congress voted a revolving fund of $500,000,000 for loans to the roads. The large express companies were also merged into a single concern (the American Railway Express), and the telegraph and telephone lines passed under the control of the Postmaster-General. The management of the railroads cost the government several hundred millions of dollars, but the deficit was reckoned as one of the necessary expenses of the war.

The Farmers and the War. If the slogan "Food will win the war!" was true, it was evident that every encouragement must be given to the American farmer to produce the maximum of wheat, corn, hogs, and cattle. We have already seen how the government, in its measures of preparedness many months before we entered the war, came to his financial relief by the enactment of the Rural Credits Act and the establishment of the Federal Farm Loan Banks (p. 654). During the war the unprecedented demand for food for our soldiers and for the armies and the civilian population of the Allies sent agricultural prices skyrocketing. The average prices received by the producers of the following commodities, according to a report of the Department of Agriculture a few years after the war, were as follows:

YEAR	WHEAT (Per Bushel)	CORN (Per Bushel)	APPLES (Per Bushel)	COTTON (Per Pound)	BUTTER (Per Pound)	HOGS (Per Hundred-weight)
1913	0.779	0.753	0.81	0.133	0.275	7.68
1918	2.00	1.59	1.335	0.318	0.473	17.50
1920	2.143	1.213	1.328	0.255	0.541	13.98
1922	0.904	0.616	1.096	0.20	0.362	8.23
1923	0.932	0.857	1.00	0.272	0.414	7.81

Encouraged by such prices, the farmers began to pay off their mortgages, to paint their barns, and to buy expensive farm machinery. Though the price of land rose too, $2.26 wheat enabled them to extend their acreage until, as in the prosperous days of the early 1880's, they were cultivating land that would not have paid them under ordinary conditions. We shall see in a later chapter how, when the demand and the prices for their products declined sharply after the war was over, they were plunged into a distress from which the agricultural program of the New Deal tried to rescue them.

Labor and the War. Because of the enormous demands on the industries of the country, labor assumed an importance and received a consideration during the war which it had never had before. Men were taken away from the mills and factories by the hundreds of thousands to fill the ranks of the army. Immigration, which had been above one million in 1914, sank to a little over one hundred thousand in 1918. Women filled the gap to some extent, taking up the men's work in the factories and fields; but still the shortage of labor led to serious difficulties in industry. Wages were raised to unheard-of levels by the bidding of the government and of private firms against each other for workers. Carpenters, plumbers, steel workers, and machinists were paid twelve dollars or fourteen dollars a day, and the increased buying power of the laboring class often led to the extravagant purchase of silk shirts and fur coats. To prevent the wasteful "turnover" in labor, the government went into the employment-agency business and allocated practically all the skilled labor of the country to its most useful work.

From the first, labor supported the war wholeheartedly. "This is labor's war," said Samuel Gompers, who was a member of the advisory board of the Council of National Defense. Under his leadership the unions of the American Federation of Labor agreed not to engage in strikes during the war. Early in April, 1918, a National War Labor Board was created to act as a court of arbitration in labor disputes. Some fifteen hundred cases were submitted to the War Labor Board, and in the few instances in which labor refused to accept the decisions the President used the pressure of public opinion to compel the men to return to their work or, in extreme cases, took over the plant. At the same time a War Labor Policies Board was set up, to investigate the conditions of labor employed in the various departments of the government and to determine fair standards of production, distribution, and wages.

The War Finance Corporation. Capital as well as labor was taken under the protection and the regulation of the government during the war. By an act of April 5, 1918, a War Finance Corporation was organized for the purpose of "conserving capital and directing investments." It was given a fund of five hundred million dollars and authorized to lend through the Federal reserve banks to industries important for the winning of the war. The Capital Issues Committee of the Federal Reserve Board scrutinized the loans carefully. In the first three months of its operation it passed on applications for nearly five hundred million dollars from various industries, on the principle of whether it was "compatible with the national interest that their securities be offered for sale." It was something new in our history for the government to presume to determine what industries were or were not "compatible with the national interest." At the same time that the government's favor was extended to approved industries, its hand of restraint was laid upon them. The War Labor Board, in its decisions, not only held labor to its promise not to strike but also forbade capital to discharge laborers for their activities in the unions.

The War Industries Board. The central directing agency of America's economic life in the war was the great War Industries Board, which was created by the National Council of Defense (p. 654) in the summer of 1917. Its object was to bring under government supervision and control all the manufacturing industries of the country. Bernard M. Baruch, a financier of intense and quiet energy, who had made a large fortune in Wall Street, was invited by President Wilson to become chairman of the board. "Barney Baruch," said the chairman of a Congressional investigating committee later, "had more power during the war than any other man in the world." By the President's letter he was authorized to act "as the general eye of all the supply departments in the field of industry." The task was immense. Agents of the Allies during the years 1914–1917 had been bidding wildly in this country for supplies of all sorts, sending our exports up from $1,500,000,000 to approximately $4,500,000,000. They were spending $500,000 a day here.

As soon as we entered the war, our own military and naval departments joined in the competition. The War Department issued sixty thousand orders for supplies in the first three months. To bring order out of this chaos of conflicting bidding and "rush orders," to stimulate production of the essential industries and curtail the production of the unessential ones, to determine the "priority" of deliveries, to keep prices fair, to supervise the Allies' purchases, to allocate shipping — these were a few of the duties of the War Industries Board. "Should locomotives go to Pershing to help him get ammunition to the front, or should they go to Chile to haul nitrates, without which there would be no ammunition? Should steel go to destroyers whose mission was to sink the submarines, or to merchant ships, which the submarines had thinned to the point of breaking down the food supplies of the Allies? Should nitrates go to munitions, without which the guns were useless, or to fertilizers, without which the artillerymen would be foodless? Should cranes go to the American wharves for loading ships for France, or to French wharves for unloading the same ships?" About the War Industries Board gathered thirty-five committees on materials ranging from "alcohol" to "zinc." Twenty-one regional advisers, from Boston to San Francisco, co-operated with the central board. More than seven hundred businessmen and technical experts came to Washington to serve on the various divisions of the board, many of them leaving positions with large salaries to work for the government at a dollar a year. In some instances great manufacturers handed to Mr. Baruch or his agents contracts with the price of the materials left blank for the government to fill in.

The Co-operation of the People. The success of such government agencies as the War Industries Board, the Food and Fuel Administration, and the War Labor Board depended, of course, on the voluntary co-operation of the American people; for we sought to establish no regime of military coercion. Our soldiers were employed in fighting the enemy, not in cowing their fellow countrymen into submission to the government's orders. It was a dictatorship of consent that President Wilson wielded, — the consent of the great manufacturers to allow the government to control their supplies of raw materials and the production and distribution of their products; the consent of the people at large to have their bill of fare regulated, their heating and lighting rationed, their amusements and travel curtailed, in the emergency of the war.

Heretofore business and patriotism had occupied separate compartments in the American mind. Now they were fused. Great steel and copper producers made contracts with the government at prices 50 per cent lower than those prevailing in the inflated market. The industries which were not essential to the war, such as the manufacture of pleasure automobiles, assented to the reduction of their profitable output to one half or one quarter of its prewar amount. The plea "Will you take this material or let the boys in France have it?" seldom failed to bring the generous response. If here and there a manufacturer stood out for his "rights," asserting that he had coal and raw material in plenty and would use them as he pleased in his business, the hint that the Fuel Administration might find it necessary to commandeer his coal, or that the Railroad Administration would find it impossible to spare the cars to transport his products, brought him quickly to his senses. If the workers in a munitions factory insisted on their "right" to strike, in spite of the agreement to submit labor controversies to arbitration during the war, an order from the President to take over the factory and "conscript" the workers was sufficient to restore normal conditions. If individuals indulged their selfish desires in food, clothing, amusements, or social display against the conservation agencies in Washington, they were quickly made to feel the rebuke of popular disapproval.

Mobilizing Public Opinion. We have seen how the government recruited an army of millions of men, raised billions of money by taxes and loans to support it, and brought all the material resources of the country — food, railroads, shipping, manufactures, labor, capital — under its control. In addition to this military, financial, and industrial mobilization, the government also undertook to mobilize the public opinion of the country. From the beginning of the war the propagandists of both sides had been busy trying to win the sympathy of the rich and powerful neutral nation across the Atlantic. British and French publicists had deluged our country with appeals to accept the Allies' interpretation of the great struggle, namely, that the German militarists, thirsting for world domination, had deliberately prepared and launched an unprovoked attack on the democratic, peace-loving nations of the Entente; that they had committed unspeakable atrocities on sea and land; and that if they should win the victory it would mean an end to the liberty of mankind, including even the United States.

The German propaganda, conducted at first by Dr. Bernard Dernburg, a former colonial secretary of the empire, was less effective for several reasons: (1) the British and French controlled the cables and censored or doctored the news of the situation in Europe as they pleased (so that, for example, we heard nothing of the Russian atrocities in East Prussia, but much of German atrocities in Belgium); (2) the failure of the Germans to get the United States to put an embargo on munitions led them to supplement argument with deeds of lawlessness which alienated such sympathy as they had here in the early months of the war; and (3) the sinking of the *Lusitania*, with the loss of over a hundred American lives, destroyed the credit of Germany in the eyes of everyone except those who believed that she could do no wrong. The calm, judicious President Eliot of Harvard, on hearing of the outrage, said, "We shall all now heartily wish the success of the Allied cause."

On our entrance into the war on the side of the Allies our government quite naturally supported and reinforced the Allied doctrine of the origin and the purpose of the war. President Wilson immediately appointed a Committee on Public Information, with the journalist George Creel at its head, to "sell the war to America." Beginning May 10, 1917, a daily *Official Bulletin* was published by Mr. Creel, containing the war news which the administration wished to have disseminated. Professors in American universities, popular magazine writers, newspaper correspondents, and patriotic penmen generally were enlisted by Creel to set the Allied case before the people in articles, books, and pamphlets (such as the "Red, White and Blue" series).

Opposition to the War. So long as the United States remained neutral, any citizen had, of course, the right to oppose our entrance into the war. But after the declaration of April 6, 1917, any attempt to obstruct the government in the prosecution of the war was equivalent to giving aid and comfort to the enemy, and as such was regarded as treason to the United States. If we may take the overwhelming vote of Congress in favor of the war resolution as an index of the sentiment of the people of the country, the pacifists were in the decided minority. At any rate, as over against the millions of people who worked with greater or less zeal to make the war a success, there were probably only a few hundreds or thousands at most who worked actively to make it a failure. Of course, no resolution of Congress or executive order or even persecution could alter the honest conviction of the "conscientious objectors," but the government made provision for them to enter some branch of the noncombatant service. The comparatively small disloyal group was made up of extreme partisans or paid agents of Germany and Austria in this country and of certain radical elements among the labor agitators who condemned the war as a crime of the capitalist class against the workers.

The Sedition Act. To guard against danger from the treasonably inclined and the enemy aliens here, Congress had passed the Espionage Act (p. 694) in the summer of 1917. The next spring, at the President's request, Congress supplemented this with a Sedition Act which equaled in severity the famous Sedition Act against which Jefferson and Madison had protested in 1798 (p. 205). It imposed penalties on any persons who "used abusive language about the government or institutions of the country," and empowered the Postmaster-General to refuse the delivery of mail to anyone who, in his opinion, was using the postal service in violation of the act. In spite of the fact that the Sedition Act itself violated the constitutional guarantee of free speech (which the President had declared only a little earlier to be the inalienable privilege of the American people), and that a majority of the Republicans in the Senate voted against it, the influence of the administration was strong enough to put it through Congress without delay. And it was far more harshly enforced than its prototype of 1798. "Individual critics of the war and the Wilson program," says Professor Beard, "were rounded up by the government, often without warrants of arrest, hustled to jail, held incommunicado without bail, tried in courts where the atmosphere was heavily charged with passion, lectured by irate judges, and sent to prison for long terms — in one case an adolescent girl for twenty years."

The Censorship of the Press. A strict censorship of the press was advocated by the President, and a clause to that effect was put into the Espionage Act; but the House rejected the clause by a vote of 144 to 184. Freedom of the press was guaranteed by the Constitution. Henry Watterson, the veteran Democratic editor of the Louisville *Courier-Journal*, wrote: "That the war involves autocracy, I understand well enough; but in the field, not in the White House. ... I reject, loathe, and spit upon the plea that because of the war the press should abdicate its duty to the people." The Postmaster-General had been authorized by the Espionage Act to exclude from the mails any seditious or treasonable publications, and now, in spite of the rejection of the censorship clause by Congress, he proceeded to suppress a number of newspapers. Most of the criticism for which these papers were silenced was anything but "seditious" in character. It protested against the "denatured news from the government news-factories" and had for its object, as Theodore Roosevelt said, "to tell the truth and speed up the war." "The real purpose of the propaganda in which Creel is the most active figure," wrote the Philadelphia *North American*, which as an anti-administration but prowar paper felt the heavy hand of the censor, "is to overlay the facts of history with studied inventions. ... For Washington authority behind it causes it to find reflection in the press of the Allied countries, which pay glowing tribute to President Wilson for having overcome the reluctance and stimulated the patriotism of his fellow countrymen, so that at last they have been aroused to defend themselves and civilization."

The Activities of the Department of Justice. The enforcement of the Espionage and Sedition Acts by the Department of Justice was unnecessarily harsh, to say the least. Alleged seditious meetings were broken up and the headquarters of suspected organizations raided, generally without proper warrants. Furniture was destroyed, papers were seized, and often the members of the organization who happened to be in the rooms were seized and marched off to jail without any formal complaint being lodged against them. Even "innocent bystanders" were sometimes beaten by the police. One of the worst features of this campaign of suspicion was the encouragement it gave to busybodies to spy upon their neighbors. The Department of Justice is said to have enlisted two hundred thousand private citizens in this work of voluntary information and denunciation. Huge card catalogues were compiled of the names of citizens whom their spying neighbors suspected of not agreeing with the policies of the administration, which was equivalent in their eyes to being "pacifists," "pro-Germans," and "traitors." Our country had a bad case of the "jitters," which was probably caused less by the actual fear of the Kaiser's conquest of America than by the behavior of the Russian Bolshevists, who had ousted the moderate government of Kerensky, in November, 1917, and set up the "dictatorship of the proletariat" under Lenin and Trotsky — a communist regime which confiscated private property, exiled the capitalists of the old order, and put to death the Czar and his family, the members of the nobility, and the "counterrevolutionists" and conservatives generally. The "Reds," or the sympathizers with the communistic revolution in Russia, though they were few in this country, were magnified by the fearful into a great host who were plotting to overthrow our government; and the attitude of suspicion which had originally been roused against the German spies and emissaries in America was easily transferred to the "tools of Moscow."

Mistaken Zeal. It is not easy to determine the limit to which the government of a liberty-loving people in a republic should go in repressing freedom of speech and writing in a great national emergency. Obviously it will depend upon the degree of danger apprehended; and on that point there will always be a wide difference of opinion. As we look back from the postwar days it is not difficult to see that the government was overzealous in repression and persecution. The great mass of our people were loyal to the cause for which we were fighting, and even to most of the policies of the Wilson administration. Though the majority of the Socialists condemned the war (p. 695, note), there was no organized attempt of the party to hinder its prosecution. Labor was solidly behind the President. "Traitors" were as rare as white crows. "When all the immense inquisitorial activities [of the Department of Justice] were sifted down to the bottom," says Beard again, "... not a single first-class German spy or revolutionary workingman was caught and convicted of an overt act designed to give direct aid or comfort to the enemy." It would have been enough for the government to punish actual unlawful acts or deeds of violence, letting opposition to the war or the government in speech or writing play itself out. That there were some Americans who put loyalty to the idea of peace above loyalty to their country, some even who worked for the defeat of the cause for which their country was fighting, was true. But they were after all comparatively few; and the most effective answer to them was not an overzealous campaign of suspicion and persecution, which invariably tends to confound the innocent with the guilty, but the spectacle of the millions of Americans who rallied to the support of the government's war policies and the call to the colors.

Terms to be Mastered

paternalism	"victory bread"	priorities
emergency powers	alien property	industrial mobilization
enemy aliens	revolving fund	*Official Bulletin*
noncombatant service	labor turnover	"Reds"

For Supplementary Reading

G. B. Clarkson, *Industrial America in the World War*; Samuel Gompers, *American Labor and the War*; Isaac Lippincott, *The Economic Development of the United States*, Part V; C. R. Van Hise, *Conservation and Regulation in the United States during the World War*; E. L. Bogart, *War Costs and their Financing*; D. R. Dewey, *The Financial History of the United States*, chap. xxii; W. F. Willoughby, *Government Organization in War Time and After*; George Creel, *How we Advertised America*; Norman Thomas, *The Conscientious Objector in America*; Zechariah Chafee, Jr., *Freedom of Speech*; *America*, Vol. XII, pp. 78–80, 158–183; H. S. Commager, *Documents of American History*, Vol. II, pp. 312, 317–325; Charles Seymour, *Woodrow Wilson and the World War*, chap. vii; E. R. A. Seligman, *Essays on Taxation*, pp. 717–782.

Topics for Reports

1. **The War Industries Board.** G. B. Clarkson, *Industrial America in the World War*, chaps. i–v (organization), chap. ix (controlling prices), chap. xv (labor), chap. xviii (steel), chap. xxvii (textiles), chap. xxix (transportation), chap. xxxi (summary).

2. **War Propaganda.** H. D. Lasswell, *Propaganda Technique in the World War*; A. Ponsonby, *Falsehood in War Time*; G. S. Viereck, *Spreading Germs of Hate*; Walter Millis, *Road to War*, pp. 201–217; J. B. McMaster, *The United States in the World War*, Vol. I, pp. 23–44; J. S. Bassett, *Our War with Germany*, pp. 30–39; Hart, *Contemporaries*, Vol. V, Nos. 167, 173.

3. **Labor and the War.** Samuel Gompers, *Seventy Years of Life and Labor*; L. L. Lorwin, *The American Federation of Labor*, chaps. vi, vii; Mary Beard, *A Short History of the American Labor Movement*, chap. xii; "Our Industrial Victory," in *National Geographic Magazine*, Vol. XXXIV, pp. 212–229; Alexander Bing, *War-Time Strikes and their Adjustment*; Ordway Teal, "The American Labor Situation in War-Time," in *Century Magazine*, Vol. XCV, pp. 354–359; Ida C. Clark, *American Women and the World War*.

4. **Censorship during the War.** W. A. Dunning, "Disloyalty in Two Wars," in *American Historical Review*, Vol. XXIV, pp. 625–630; G. R. Brown, "The Lynching of Public Opinion," in *North American Review*, Vol. CCIII, pp. 795–802; Glenn Frank, "Is Free Speech Dangerous?" in *Century Magazine*, Vol. C, pp. 355–360; Peyton C. March, *The Nation at War*, pp. 119–130; R. E. Annin, *Woodrow Wilson, A Character Study*, pp. 277–291; C. M. Case, *Non-Violent Coercion*; Norman Thomas, *The Conscientious Objector in America*.

Questions Suggested by the Chapter

1. What measures of the war tended to make the people "government-minded?" **2.** Who were the "dollar-a-year men"? **3.** What were the chief raw materials that America furnished to the Allies? **4.** What was the Council of National Defense? **5.** What was the attitude of the great majority of the Socialist party toward the war? **6.** Why was Eugene V. Debs sent to jail? **7.** What powers were given to President Wilson in the Lever Act? **8.** What were the war services of Mr. Hoover? of Mr. Gompers? **9.** Why was the government's operation of the railroads expensive? **10.** Do you think that the government had more or less reason to exercise censorship in the World War than in the Civil War? Explain your answer. **11.** What heroic measures did the Fuel Administrator take to conserve coal? **12.** What benefit did our industries receive from the taking over of alien property? **13.** On what terms did the government take over the railroads? **14.** What did the government do for the railroads? **15.** How do you account for the rise in American prices during the war? **16.** What was the effect of the war on women in industry? **17.** What is meant by Wilson's "dictatorship of consent"? **18.** In what way did the war interfere with the daily life of the noncombatant citizen? **19.** Why was the Allies' propaganda more effective than that of the Germans? **20.** On what was the opposition to the Sedition Act based? **21.** Why was Bernard M. Baruch called "the most powerful man in the nation" in 1918? **22.** What do you think of the conduct of the Department of Justice during the war?

CHAPTER TWENTY-EIGHT

OUR PART IN THE PEACE

The President Goes to Paris. A week after the armistice was signed President Wilson made the official announcement of his intention "to sail for France immediately after the opening of the regular session of Congress, for the purpose of taking part in the discussion and settlement of the main features of the treaty of peace. It is not likely that it will be possible for him to remain throughout the sessions . . . but his presence is necessary at the outset in order to obviate the manifest disadvantage of discussion by cable in determining the greater outlines of the final treaty." At the conclusion of his speech at the opening of Congress on December 2, 1918, he said:

I realize the great inconvenience that will attend my leaving the country, particularly at this time, but the conclusion that it was my paramount duty to go has been forced upon me. The peace settlements which are now to be agreed upon are of transcendent importance both to us and to the rest of the world, and I know of no business or interest which should take precedence of them. . . . I shall be in close touch with you and with affairs on this side of the water, and you will know all that I do. I shall make my absence as brief as possible, and shall hope to return with the happy assurance that it has been possible to translate into action the great ideals for which America has striven.

The President sailed from New York on December 4, on the *George Washington*, accompanied by Mrs. Wilson and a large number of expert advisers on history and geography, to add to the staff that had been working for some months in Paris under the direction of Colonel House. He landed at Brest, on the French coast (December 13), and spent the next few weeks in a triumphal progress through France, Great Britain, and Italy, in which he was received with the highest honors by the heads of the states and hailed by the people as "the savior of Europe."

Why the President Went. It was an unprecedented thing for a President to go abroad during his term of office, and Wilson was severely criticized for doing so. Not only was he needed at home, said the critics, to deal with the important questions that faced our country in getting back to a peace basis, but by absenting himself he practically abdicated his office; for the Constitution reads (Art. II, Sect. 1, par. 6), "In case of the removal of the President from office or of his death, resignation, or inability to discharge the powers and duties of the said office, the same shall devolve on the Vice President." Obviously, they said, Mr. Wilson could not discharge the powers and duties of the President of the United States if he were thousands of miles away in Paris.

But these arguments had no more weight with Wilson than did the meaner suggestions that he was intoxicated with power and was going to Europe to receive the adulation of the governments and people abroad. He went because he believed that he could serve America (and the whole world) best by going. The victory in war would have been won in vain unless it were followed by the right kind of peace. And the "most essential part" of the treaty of peace was the establishment of a League of Nations which would make future wars impossible. On this Wilson's heart was set. The punishment of Germany, indemnities, acquisition of territory and colonies, and all the "spoils of war" for which he knew the Allies were thirsting would only be the breeders of more war. The whole weight of the influence of the United States must be thrown into the scales to secure a just and lasting "peace of equals," as the whole weight of its power and resources had been thrown into the scales to secure the victory in war. Nobody but the President himself, the symbol of America in the eyes of Europe, could wield this influence. No Senator or Representative or member of the executive or judicial branches of our government would be on a par with the prime ministers of the Allied governments at the peace table. Therefore, although Wilson appointed four peace commissioners to serve with himself (Secretary of State Lansing, General Tasker H. Bliss, Colonel House, and a Republican,

Henry M. White, a former ambassador to London and Paris), according to Secretary Lansing's account they had but a minor part in formulating the terms of the treaty. President Wilson could trust no one, not even Colonel House, who had made the first draft of the League of Nations covenant, to represent him at Paris while he himself stayed at home. He was virtually the sole American peace commissioner.

American Prestige in Europe. When the war came to an end, the United States occupied a position of eminence in the eyes of Europe and the world such as no other nation of modern times has enjoyed. The Central Powers had appealed to us to intercede with their other enemies to bring about the cessation of hostilities, and trusted most to us for mercy in the terms of peace. The Allies had drawn upon our wealth for loans totaling ten billion dollars, and agreed with Marshal Joffre's testimony that "it was the weight of America thrown into the balance at the critical moment that turned the scales and won the victory." The smaller and weaker nations of the world looked to us for the championship of their rights in the great settlement following the war. Our prestige was due both to material and to moral causes. To the countries of the Old World, exhausted in money and man power, America was a fresh and vigorous nation come to their relief. When the order came to stop firing on the western front, we were only just beginning to get into our war stride. We were planning to have an army of five million in France by 1920. In the month of the armistice we constructed one hundred and seventy-one vessels, with a tonnage of 357,668. We were manufacturing more machine guns and rifles than Great Britain and France combined, and were planning to send ten thousand airplanes a month to France after January, 1919. Though our debt had increased nearly twentyfold, it was still only about 10 per cent of our national wealth, whereas the war debt of Great Britain and France stood at 40, of Germany at 50, and of Italy at over 60 per cent of the national wealth.

Great areas of Europe had been temporarily lost to needed cultivation through the ravages of bombs and shells. Towns and villages had been wiped out by the thousands, and their starving inhabitants thrown on the mercy of charity. The ten million slain in battle far outnumbered all the hosts ever marshaled by an Alexander the Great or a Napoleon Bonaparte. But the United States had not seen the march of an invading army or the menace of starvation or, looming through the clouds of bankruptcy and famine, the specter of revolution and anarchy. Above all, we came to the peace table as the one powerful nation with wholly unselfish aims, — with no desire for territory, no boundaries to adjust, no colonies to claim, no reparations to demand. We did not have to live as a neighbor to a conquered foe whose vengeance we feared, nor to calculate the effect of the creation of new, independent states out of the fragments of the dismembered empires. Remote and secure, we could regard the peace conference rather as the opportunity for formulating the principles on which the nations should base their future policies than for wrangling over the terms on which they should settle their present difficulties. This favored position of the United States must be taken into account when criticism is made of the "selfish" and "vindictive" temper of the Allies.

President Wilson's "Mandate." Nevertheless, for all the prestige of his country and his own personal renown in Europe, President Wilson was in an embarrassing position at Paris. Two weeks before the mid-term Congressional elections of November, 1918, he had issued an appeal to the country to vote for none but Democrats, though a few months earlier he had said, "Politics is adjourned ; the elections will go to those who deserve them." He now declared that the Republicans had hampered him in the prosecution of the war and that the election of a Republican majority to Congress would be interpreted in Europe as a repudiation of his leadership. "I am your servant," he added, however, "and I will accept your judgment without cavil." In view of the fact that the Republicans had cast a larger percentage (72) of votes in the House than had the Democrats (67) for the war measures between April, 1917, and May, 1918, the President's charge that they had obstructed his policies was hotly resented by them. "A more ungracious, more unjust, more mendacious accusation was never made by the most reckless stump orator," said Will H. Hays, the chairman of the Republican National Committee. Ex-Presidents Roosevelt and Taft (now reconciled) signed a joint protest against the President's insinuation that the Republicans, who "were good enough to pay taxes for the war and give their lives for the country," were not good enough to share in the government.

The result of Wilson's partisan appeal was the return of a Republican majority to both houses of the Sixty-sixth Congress. Such a defeat of the administration in the countries of western Europe would have meant the replacement of the actual ministry by the leaders of the opposition. But in our system the head of the government serves through his term of four years whether his party wins or loses in the mid-term elections. The British prime minister, Lloyd George, went to the peace conference supported by a large majority in Parliament in the "khaki election," waged on the platform of hanging the Kaiser and making Germany pay the whole cost of the war. The French chambers backed by a vote of more than three to one Clemenceau's announced program of ending the German menace forever. But Wilson sailed for France a month after the American people had elected a majority of the "opposition" party to both House and Senate. "The President goes abroad," said the *New York Tribune*, "a rebuked and discredited leader in his own nation." In spite of his party's defeat, President Wilson proceeded as though he had received as complete an endorsement of his program by the people as had Lloyd George.

At the first full session of the conference, on January 25, 1918, he made the following amazing statement of the mission of the American delegation :

If we return to the United States without having made every effort in our power to realize this program [the League of Nations], we should return to meet the merited scorn of our fellow citizens. . . . They expect their leaders to speak, their representatives to be their servants. We have no choice but to obey their mandate. But it is with the greatest enthusiasm and pleasure that we accept that mandate. . . . We would not dare abate a single item of the program which constitutes our instructions.

Nothing could have been more misleading to the European statesmen than these words. President Wilson had no "mandate," no "instructions" of any sort from the American people. His only mandate was his own strong conviction that he was doing the best thing for the American people, and the only instructions that the peace commissioners received were those which he gave them.[1] It may be that the majority of the President's "fellow citizens," whose "merited scorn" he was anxious not to incur by returning to America without the League of Nations, were in sympathy with his program. But we have no means of knowing whether they were or not. They have never directly voted on that issue.

The Peace Conference. Seats were provided for seventy delegates from twenty-eight nations at the great horseshoe table in the hall of the foreign-ministry building at Paris, for the opening of the peace conference on January 18, 1919. Nearly all the seats were filled when President Wilson rose, after a brief address of welcome by President Poincaré of France, to nominate Clemenceau as president of the conference. No representatives from the defeated powers were invited to attend. It was not, therefore, to be a "peace of equals," for which Wilson had contended just a year before in his speech to the Senate (p. 660), but "a victor's terms imposed upon the vanquished."

The direction of affairs, the appointment of the fifty-eight special committees, the hearings of the claims that the delegates of the various countries had to present, were all taken in hand, in spite of the protests of some of the delegates of the smaller nations, by a Supreme Council of ten, consisting of President Wilson and Colonel House for the United States and the prime ministers and foreign ministers of Great Britain, France, Italy, and Japan. But after more than two months had

---

[1] In a speech at Pueblo, Colorado, on September 25, 1919, President Wilson repeated his assertion about the mandate, and gave the following definition of it: "I had gone over there [to France] with, so to say, explicit instructions. Don't you remember that we [!] laid down fourteen points which should contain the principles of a settlement? They were not my points [!]. In every one of them I was trying to read the thoughts of the people of the United States."

passed without much progress toward a settlement of the confusing claims and counterclaims, the council was narrowed down to four men — President Wilson, Lloyd George, Clemenceau, and Orlando. The "Big Four" held one hundred and forty-five meetings between March 24 and May 7, during which "the whole treaty was put into shape; territorial, financial, economic, and colonial clauses alike." No stenographic reports of their meetings were kept. The press was furnished only with such brief communications as they chose to make public. Delegates to the conference and expert advisers were summoned for hearings or advice at the will of the "Big Four." As Wilson spoke no foreign language, the discussions were conducted in English; and as Orlando spoke no English, the major work of the council was done by Wilson, Lloyd George, and Clemenceau. "Open covenants openly arrived at" was the first of Wilson's Fourteen Points on which the treaty was supposed to be based. But three men in secret session took practically the whole responsibility for preparing the most fateful treaty in the history of the world.

The League of Nations. President Wilson had come to Paris with the chief purpose of writing into the peace treaty the covenant of a League of Nations, which should guarantee the future peace of the world. In accepting the honorary doctor's degree conferred upon him by the Sorbonne, on his arrival in Paris, he had made the League his topic, declaring it to be the "mandate of mankind" to the delegates, and warning them a month in advance of their meeting that unless they heeded that mandate they would make themselves "the most conspicuous and deserved failures in the history of the world." A few delegates — Lord Robert Cecil of England, General Jan Smuts of South Africa, and Léon Bourgeois of France, for example — were enthusiastic advocates of the League; but most of them regarded it with indifference, being intent on the punishment of Germany and on reaping the gains which their nations had been promised in the secret treaties made during the war. It would be well enough to consider the League *after* the main business of settling the account against Germany was over.

Lloyd George   Orlando   Clemenceau   Wilson

THE BIG FOUR

But Wilson was determined that the League should come first. If postponed, he knew that it would be abandoned. His influence was strong enough [1] to secure the appointment by the Supreme Council of a commission of ten members (January 25, 1919) to draft the covenant of the League, which was to be "an integral part of the general treaty of peace, open to every civilized nation which could be relied upon to promote its objects."

[1] Wilson had to make concessions, however, to get the League. For example, Clemenceau had no trust in a League of Nations for the protection of France against the vengeance of a recovered Germany. He would accept it only if it were supplemented by a "tripartite treaty" between Great Britain, the United States, and France, by which the two former powers agreed to come to the aid of France in case she should be attacked by her former foe. Though such a treaty ran counter to Wilson's emphatic declaration that there should be no "special alliances" within the League, he signed it and promised to submit it to the Senate at the same time with the peace treaty. But he withheld it for several days, and it was never acted upon by the Senate.

The Covenant was based on a number of drafts, reports, and suggestions contributed by President Wilson, Colonel House, General Smuts, Lord Cecil, and others. It consisted in its final form of twenty-six articles, the most important of which concerned the reduction of armaments, guaranties of security for all the member nations, the arbitration of disputes, and "sanctions" (punishment) to be imposed on nations which should go to war in defiance of the Covenant. The machinery of the League was to be in the hands of two bodies: an Assembly consisting of delegates from all the member states, and a small executive Council of nine members (later enlarged to sixteen), of whom five were to be always representatives of the United States, Great Britain, France, Italy, and Japan. Article X, which Wilson declared to be the "heart of the Covenant," read:

> The members of the League undertake to respect and preserve as against external aggression the territorial integrity and existing political independence of all the members of the League. In case of any such aggression, or in case of any threat or danger of such aggression, the Council shall advise upon the means by which this obligation shall be fulfilled.

The President Defies Opposition. Wilson read the completed Covenant of the League to a full session of the conference on February 14, 1919, and immediately afterward sailed for home to sign the bills passed during his absence by the Sixty-fifth Congress, which would expire on the fourth of March. He had cabled the request that Congress should refrain from making the Covenant a subject of debate until he had had the opportunity of discussing it with the members of the Senate and House Committees on Foreign Affairs, whom, at Colonel House's suggestion, he had invited to dine with him at the White House on February 26. But the President's request had not been heeded. As soon as the Covenant was published, certain Senators had begun an attack on it. They felt aggrieved that Wilson had neither appointed a single one of them to the peace commission nor let them know anything of what was going on in Paris. Landing at Boston on February 24, he met their attacks with his first note of defiance, foreshadowing his purpose of appealing to the American people rather than to Congress for support: "The people are in the saddle," he said, "and they are going to see to it that, if the present governments do not do their will, some other government shall."

Nor did the dinner at the White House two days later help matters any. He told the members of the committees that the League endangered no American interests, that fourteen nations had already signified their approval of it, and that our failure to ratify it would cause "deep sorrow" throughout the world. But he made no converts. Just before Congress came to an end, thirty-seven Republican Senators (four more than enough to defeat the treaty in the next Congress) signed a round robin declaring that they would not vote for ratification if the treaty contained the Covenant of the League of Nations.

On March 4 the President again left Washington to return to the conference at Paris. That same night he appeared on the platform of the Metropolitan Opera House in New York, where he repeated his defiance of the Republican Senators. One of the first things he would tell the conference, he said, was that "an overwhelming majority of the American people" favored the League. The men who criticized it had "never felt the great pulse of the heart of the world"; they had no appreciation of the temper of those "splendid boys in khaki" who had gone across the sea to win liberty for mankind. No peace would be "vital" without the League, and he had no intention of bringing back a "cadaver" (corpse) with him. "When the treaty comes back," he insisted, "gentlemen on this side will find the Covenant not only in it, but so many threads of the treaty tied to the Covenant that you cannot dissect it from the treaty without destroying the whole vital structure." The next morning the President sailed again on the *George Washington* for France.

The Treaty Completed. The President was as good as his word. When he got back to Paris he found that some members of the conference had grown indifferent to the League during his month's absence, and were willing to postpone it until after the conclusion of the peace. But he rallied the wavering members to his support and secured the adoption of the Covenant as the first article of the treaty on April 28. The treaty, as completed and presented to the German envoys for their signature at the Trianon palace at Versailles on May 7, was a document consisting of eighty thousand words, which imposed the most severe terms upon the vanquished nation. Germany was obliged to surrender all her colonies, to restore Alsace-Lorraine to France, and to cede other portions of her empire to Poland, Denmark, and Belgium. She was reduced to military impotence, with an army fixed at a maximum of one hundred thousand men. Her warships, submarines, and docks were surrendered. Her fortifications in large areas were destroyed. Her bill of damages was fixed at two hundred billion gold marks, to be paid in "gold, goods, ships, or other specific forms of payment within two years." Finally, she was made to confess her sole responsibility for the war.

The German statesmen declared that the acceptance of this "murderous volume" was impossible. President Ebert, of the new German republic, said that history had "no precedent for such a determination to annihilate a vanquished nation." The noted professor Hans Delbrück thought that, rather than agree to the terms, Germany would open her gates to Bolshevism. But protests were of no avail. The Germans were not allowed to enter into any discussion with the Allies on the terms: they might have only two weeks in which to present in writing, in English and in French, any "such practical suggestions as the German plenipotentiaries had to submit." In the end the German assembly ordered its envoys to sign the treaty, "yielding to superior force, and without renouncing our view of the unheard-of injustice of the peace conditions." The ceremony was performed on June 28 (the fifth anniversary of the assassination at Sarajevo, which had started the war) in the great Hall of Mirrors in the palace of Versailles, where, forty-eight years before, the Hohenzollern king of Prussia, William the Great, had been proclaimed the first emperor of the proud Germany which now lay crushed at the feet of her former victim.

Criticism of the League. The name "Woodrow Wilson" stood first among the signatures to the Treaty of Versailles. There were some things in the treaty that Wilson did not like, such as the occupation of the Chinese province of Shantung by Japan; but he had to make concessions to the demands of the Allies in order to get their support for his League, and he believed that the League would remedy the injustices in due time.

The Sixty-fifth Congress had expired on March 4, without passing the appropriation bills for the army and navy, the civil service, the District of Columbia, and other regular expenses of the government. These bills had been held up by a Republican filibuster in the Senate for the purpose of forcing President Wilson immediately to call in extra session the new Republican Congress elected in November, 1918. But the President refused to be deterred from returning to Paris to finish the work of the treaty. "A group of men in the Senate," he said, "have deliberately chosen to embarrass the administration of the government. . . . It is plainly my present duty to attend the peace conference at Paris." However, the appropriation bills had to be passed before the expiration of the fiscal year, on June 30; and on May 8 (the day after the completed treaty was presented to the Germans) Wilson sent the cable summoning Congress in extra session.

Wilson sailed for home himself the day after the treaty was signed, and on July 10 sent it to the Senate for ratification. He had again asked the Senate not to discuss the treaty before he brought it back from Paris; but they had paid no attention to his request. For more than a month the articles of the treaty, especially the first article, or the Covenant of the League of Nations, had been hotly debated in Congress.[1] The chief point of attack on the Covenant was Article X, which seemed to pledge the United States to send its soldiers to Europe, Asia, or Africa to defend the "territorial integrity" or the "political inde-

[1] It had been impossible to keep the treaty secret until it should be submitted to the Senate. The Germans had published it as soon as it was signed, and several copies of it had found their way to the United States. Senator Borah even had it incorporated into the *Congressional Record* of June 9, a month before the President submitted it to the Senate.

pendence" of any member state of the League, at the bidding of a council of nine men at Geneva, eight of whom were foreigners. What, then, would become of the constitutional right of Congress "to declare war"? Other parts of the Covenant, like Articles XI and XVI, seemed to force our country to join in applying punishment, military or economic, to any state of the League which should resort to war in defiance of its pledges, and to bind us to submit to the arbitration of a foreign tribunal questions affecting our national defense, the tariff, immigration, and other "domestic" problems. Again, there was complaint that the President had "subordinated" the United States to Great Britain by allowing her five self-governing colonies (Canada, Newfoundland, South Africa, Australia, and New Zealand) to have separate votes in the Assembly of the League, thus giving her six votes to our one. No doubt there was much exaggeration of these dangers of the League, due to political opposition to President Wilson.[1] Still, there was enough truth in them to persuade millions of Americans that by joining the League we should be abandoning the advice of Washington and Jefferson to steer clear of "entangling" political alliances.

Wilson Defends the League. During the two months that the treaty was in the Senate Committee on Foreign Relations, the President labored to convince its opponents that their objections were trivial and their fears unfounded. On August 19 he invited the members of the committee to lunch at the White House, and in a three-hour conference heard their arguments and endeavored to answer them. Nothing could happen in the League Council without our consent, he said, because the vote there had to be unanimous, and a representative of the United States was to have a permanent seat on the Council. He would naturally vote according to his instructions from home, so that Congress would still preserve its constitutional right of declaring

[1] For example, Senator Sherman of Illinois indulged in the following burst of oratory on March 3: "The League will embargo our commerce, close our exchanges, destroy our credits, leave our merchantmen rotting at the piers, shut the Isthmian Canal, order Congress to declare war, levy taxes, appropriate money, raise and support armies and navies, and dispatch our men to any quarter of the globe to fight and die, because an alien Executive Council has willed it."

war. We should be pledged under the Covenant to do nothing that we should not wish to do anyway, as a great peace-loving and justice-loving nation. Our domestic interests were sufficiently safeguarded by the amendments which had been added to the Covenant before its final adoption. The Monroe Doctrine was explicitly recognized in Article XXI. Our right to withdraw from the League was guaranteed. Our obligations would be "moral" rather than "legal." The President saw no objection to the Senate's accompanying its ratification of the treaty with "interpretations of the sense in which the United States accepts the engagements," provided such interpretations were not made a part of the ratifying act itself. But the text of the Covenant must stand without further amendments, especially Article X, which was "the heart of the League." He patiently met the cross-questioning of Senators Brandegee, Knox, Johnson, Lodge (the chairman of the committee), and others; but the opponents of the Covenant left the conference unconverted.

Wilson Appeals to the Country. Convinced by the conference of August 19 that he could not get the Republican support in the Senate necessary for the ratification of the treaty, the President started on a tour of the country (September 3) to explain the Covenant of the League to the people directly. If popular pressure could not be brought to bear on the Senate to secure a favorable vote, at least public sentiment might be roused to turn out the Republican majority at the elections of the ensuing year. The President spoke to large and enthusiastic audiences all the way out to the Pacific coast, but the "irreconcilable" Senators Borah, Johnson, and McCormick, who followed on his trail to denounce the League, spoke to equally large and enthusiastic audiences. Certainly, before his tour came to its sad end, President Wilson must have realized that his confident assertion that "an overwhelming majority of the American people were in favor of the League" could not be proved.

The President had suffered a severe attack of influenza at Paris, and was still under the care of his physician, who advised him strongly not to undertake the speaking tour. But Wilson would not be deterred. He showed signs of exhaustion as he turned homeward from California, and as he was approaching Wichita, Kansas, on September 25, he was stricken down with paralysis. He was hurried back to Washington, where for several days he lay in a critical condition. The metropolitan papers of October 4 announced that his death was probably a matter of but a few hours. He recovered, however, sufficiently to see some callers and to attend to a few matters of business, and he lived for nearly four and a half years, till February 3, 1924. But his physical power as well as his political power was at an end.

The Treaty Rejected. There were 49 Republicans and 47 Democrats in the Senate. They were divided into four groups on the question of ratification, which required a two-thirds vote (64). The first group consisted of about 25 Democrats, with one Republican, McCumber of North Dakota, who favored accepting the Covenant without any change whatever, as President Wilson wished. The rest of the Democrats and a few Republicans would ratify it with mild reservations. Most of the Republicans, led by Chairman Lodge, stood out for decided amendments to the Covenant, protecting the authority of Congress and the sovereignty of the United States, and would ratify the treaty only on condition that the other powers accepted these amendments. Finally, there was a group of about a dozen "irreconcilables," all but three of them Republicans, led by Borah, Johnson, La Follette, and Brandegee, who were opposed to our entering a League of Nations on any terms whatever. The sympathy of many prominent citizens in private life, such as ex-President Taft, Elihu Root, Mr. Hughes, and Mr. Hoover,[1] was with the advocates of mild reservations or amendments.

On September 10, exactly a week after the President had

---

[1] The most prominent citizen in private life, Theodore Roosevelt, had died on January 6, 1919, twelve days before the opening meeting of the peace conference. He probably would have been as heartily opposed as his bosom friend Lodge to the "Wilsonian" League, though he had, like Lodge, earlier commended the idea of such an association. In a speech at Oslo (Christiania), Norway, on his return from the jungle, in 1910, he had said, "The ruler or statesman who should bring about a League of Peace would earn a place in history for all time and his title to the gratitude of mankind."

started on his tour, the treaty was reported out of the committee by Chairman Lodge, with a number of reservations and amendments, to be debated for two months in the Senate. The chief points in the Lodge resolution were: (1) that the United States should be held under no obligation to fulfill Article X or to take any part in punishing an offending member of the League without the express authority of Congress; (2) that the United States should be the sole judge of whether we fulfilled our obligations to the League and of whether or not we should submit any question to its arbitration; and (3) that the treaty should not be binding upon us until at least three of the four principal powers associated with us in the war (England, France, Italy, and Japan) had accepted our conditions of ratification. President Wilson, however, insisted that the treaty be ratified without amendments or reservations. If changes were needed in the Covenant as time advanced, they could be made by the League itself in the machinery provided for its amendment in Article XXVI. The President wrote to his spokesman in the Senate, Gilbert Hitchcock of Nebraska, urging the Democrats all to vote against the proposed changes. "I trust that all true friends of the treaty will refuse to support the Lodge resolution," he said; "it does not provide for the ratification, but rather for the nullification of the treaty."

On the same day (November 19) the vote was taken on the treaty with the Lodge amendments. All but 5 of the 47 Democrats obeyed the President's request and voted No, together with the 13 "irreconcilables," making a negative vote of 55, against 39 in the affirmative. Immediately after the decisive defeat of the amended treaty, Senator Underwood of Alabama proposed the ratification of the treaty without change, as Wilson wished. On this resolution practically all the Republicans (46) voted No, and they were joined by 7 Democrats, thus defeating the resolution by the equally decisive vote of 38 to 53. The Republicans would not allow the treaty to be ratified without changes, and the Democrats would not allow it to be ratified with changes. Unable to break the deadlock, the six months' extra session of Congress adjourned.

A Final Attempt at Ratification. The President made no reference to the treaty or the League in the message which he sent from his sickroom on the opening of the regular session of Congress a fortnight later. But an official notice was issued from the White House a few days afterwards to the effect that he considered his responsibility in the matter at an end: "He has no compromises or concessions of any kind to make, but intends ... that the Republican leaders of the Senate shall continue to bear the undivided responsibility for the fate of the treaty and the present condition of the world in consequence of that fate." He sent a letter to be read at the Jackson Day banquet at Washington, January 8, 1920, in which he said:

Personally I do not accept the action of the Senate as the decision of the nation.... We cannot rewrite the treaty.... If there is any doubt as to what the people of the country think on this vital matter, the clear and only way out is to submit it at the next election to the voters of the nation, to give the election the form of a great and solemn referendum as to the part the United States is to play in completing the settlement of the war.

But many Democrats both in the Senate and out disagreed with the President. It is the constitutional duty of the Senate, and not of the people, to pass upon treaties. Accordingly, the majority of the Democratic Senators were in favor of making another attempt in the spring of 1920 to secure ratification by a compromise set of resolutions which should be acceptable to both sides. Republican and Democratic Senators in conference worked out a plan, and again the treaty came up for a vote, on March 19, 1920. This time, though half the Democrats rejected the President's advice and voted for the treaty with mild reservations, giving the treaty a majority of 57 to 39, it still fell 7 votes short of the necessary two thirds, 15 "irreconcilables" joining with 24 Democrats to vote No. The treaty was then returned to the President with the formal announcement that the Senate had been unable to obtain the constitutional majority for ratification. Shortly after, Congress passed the Knox resolution, declaring that the war with Germany was at an end; but the President vetoed it as "an ineffaceable stain on the gallantry and honor of the United States" (May 27,

1920). The House failed to pass the resolution over the veto, and we remained technically at war with Germany until July 2, 1921, after the advent of the Republican President Harding.

The Establishment of the League. Meanwhile the ratification of the Treaty of Versailles by the German assembly and by the principal Allied nations, and its formal proclamation at Versailles, had automatically brought into existence the League of Nations. The first meeting of the Council was held at Paris, on January 16, 1920, on the call of President Wilson, as provided in the terms of the Covenant. Of the thirty-two nations named in the Annex of the Covenant as eligible to the League, the only important one to remain outside was the United States. A permanent secretariat of about a hundred persons was organized, the budget was established, the National Hotel on the shore of the Lake of Geneva was purchased for the permanent headquarters, and a vast number of projects were started for the recovery of Europe from the war, through the co-operation of men of international good will. By October 1, 1920, the League had thirty-four members, and thirteen more states had applied for admission. The first meeting of the Assembly at Geneva, comprising the representatives of forty-one nations, was opened on November 15, 1920 — just thirteen days after the "great and solemn referendum" at the polls had seemed to confirm America's determination to have no part or parcel in it.

A Momentous Decision. The refusal of the Senate of the United States to ratify the Treaty of Versailles, and the consequent failure of her representatives to take the seats provided for them in the Council and Assembly of the League of Nations, was one of the most momentous decisions ever made by our country. To one part of our population the decision seemed (and still seems) like a deplorable anticlimax. We had been gloriously present in the conflict of war, but in the hour of victory we remained in our tent. We had gone forth to "make the world safe for democracy," but now we doubted that our own democracy could be safe in close association with the other nations of the world. To another part of our population our behavior seemed in keeping with American traditions since the days of Washington, Jefferson, and Monroe. We had only asked for proper guaranties that the authority of Congress should not be overridden by the decisions of an international body (the Council) in which our representative would have only a single vote. The champions of the President saw in the action of the Republican Senators only a political plot to discredit him and the Democratic party, under the excuse of preserving American rights. The advocates of the Lodge resolutions, on the other hand, accused the President of an obstinate determination to browbeat the Senate into accepting his own version of the Covenant, without "the dotting of an *i* or the crossing of a *t*."

Although the motives of many of the Republican Senators in opposing the Covenant as it stood may have been narrowly partisan, the fact remains that President Wilson, who yielded so much at Paris to get his Covenant adopted, would yield nothing at home to get it ratified. He preferred to have the treaty rejected rather than to accept the reservations which a majority of the Senate approved. For this he is commended by some and blamed by others. But both his supporters and his opponents must acknowledge that the choice was his. On the final test the Republicans voted 34 to 15 in favor of ratification on terms which they believed would be acceptable to the nations associated with us in the war. It was the 24 Democrats who, in obedience to the President's advice, still voted against the treaty with reservations, and so prevented it from receiving the two-thirds vote necessary for ratification.

Thus ended a chapter of unusual glory and inspiration in our history. The generous enthusiasm, the unselfish devotion and co-operation, of 1917 and 1918 gave place to a reaction of political rivalry and economic strife in 1919. It seemed as if the idealism of the nations had been exhausted by the efforts of the war. "The vision for which we fought" was clouded by the emergence of selfish material aims, and the prophecies of a new and better world remained unfulfilled. In the Old World wars did not cease with the conclusion of the Treaty of Versailles. Armies and navies were not reduced. Imperial ambitions were not quenched in the blood bath of Europe's agony. And in our own land the path immediately before our feet was to lie through the valley of humiliation and the slough of despond — through a welter of industrial chaos, social ferment, class struggle, bitter propaganda, commercial profiteering, and reckless business plunging. It was the aftermath of war.

Summary. This unit has dealt with the tremendous five-year period of 1914–1919, which saw the world plunged into the madness of the most terrible of wars in its history. The United States tried hard to keep out of the struggle, which at first seemed so remote from us in its causes and objects as well as in its location across the sea. But little by little the war encroached upon American rights and honor, first by interference with our commerce and then by the destruction of American lives by the submarines. We passed, in the two and a half years from August, 1914, to April, 1917, through five stages of neutrality: impartial detachment, protests to Great Britain against illegal interference with our shipping, remonstrances with Germany over the death of our citizens on torpedoed merchant vessels, military preparedness to defend the rights which we were unable to secure by diplomacy, and finally the severance of diplomatic relations with the German Empire, which was the certain prelude to war. By throwing its immense resources in money, materials, and man power into the scales at a critical moment for the Allies, the United States tipped the balance in favor of victory against the Central Powers. At the same time, in order to utilize all these resources with maximum efficiency for winning the war, President Wilson was given dictatorial powers by Congress over practically all the activities of American life — manufacturing, agriculture, transportation, labor, the press, and even the freedom of individuals in their habits of travel, amusements, dress, and diet. Our country was transformed suddenly from the scene of thousands of independent competing businesses into one great workshop under government direction. America's co-operation in the war meant much more to President Wilson than winning the victory on the field of battle. He must also win a victory in the settlement that followed the war —

the victory of a just and lasting peace, guaranteed by the common consent of the nations to abide by the terms of a written pledge, or "covenant," for the prevention of future wars. For this purpose he went in person to the peace conference at Paris, where he succeeded in getting the Covenant of the League of Nations adopted as the first article of the Treaty of Versailles. But his victory at Paris was turned into defeat at home, where a combination of Senatorial partisanship and Presidential determination led to the rejection of the treaty and the League. The war was over; but its effect upon the government and people of the United States cannot even yet be wholly estimated. We turn now to the study of America during the decade following the war.

TERMS TO BE MASTERED

peace of equals
mandate
the "Big Four"

covenant
sanctions
filibuster

irreconcilables
reservations
censorship of the press

FOR SUPPLEMENTARY READING

F. A. MAGRUDER, *National Government and International Relations*, Appendix (for text of Covenant of the League); CHARLES SEYMOUR, *Woodrow Wilson and the World War* (Chronicles of America, Vol. XLVIII), chaps. ix–xiv; F. L. ALLEN, *Only Yesterday*, chap. ii; E. M. HOUSE and C. SEYMOUR (ed.), *What Really Happened at Paris*; The League of Nations, "What it Means and Why it Must Be," in *National Geographic Magazine*, Vol. XXXV, pp. 43–66; B. M. BARUCH, *The Making of the Reparation and Economic Sections of the Treaty*; CHARLES SEYMOUR, *The Intimate Papers of Colonel House*, Vol. IV, chaps. vii–xiii; D. F. FLEMING, *The United States and the League of Nations*; A. TARDIEU, *The Truth about the Treaty*; R. S. BAKER, *Woodrow Wilson and the World Settlement*; E. W. YOUNG, *The Wilson Administration and the Great War*, chaps. xiv–xvi; The Pageant of America, Vol. IX, pp. 314–321; *America*, Vol. XII, pp. 200–226; FREDERICK PALMER, *Bliss, Peacemaker*, chaps. xxxi–xxxvi; ROBERT LANSING, *The Peace Negotiations, a Personal Narrative*.

TOPICS FOR REPORTS

1. **Wilson's Associates on the Peace Commission.** CHARLES SEYMOUR, *The Intimate Papers of Colonel House*, Vol. IV, pp. 201–249; ALLAN NEVINS, *Henry White, Thirty Years of American Diplomacy*, chaps. xx–xxiii; FREDERICK PALMER, *Bliss, Peacemaker*, pp. 353–403; ROBERT LANSING, *The Peace Negotiations, a Personal Narrative*, chaps. i, ii, xiv, xvi, xvii.

2. **The French Demand for Security against Germany.** F. S. NITTI, *The Wreck of Europe*, pp. 114f.; H. W. STEED, *Through Thirty Years*, Vol. II, pp. 309–317; C. T. THOMPSON, *The Peace Conference Day by Day*, pp. 282f.; A. TARDIEU, *The Truth about the Treaty*, pp. 202f.; HOUSE and SEYMOUR (ed.), *What Really Happened at Paris*, pp. 464f.

3. **Wilson's Conference with the Senate Committee on Foreign Relations.** H. C. LODGE, *The Senate and the League of Nations*, Appendix, pp. 297–379 (a stenographic report).

4. **The Senate and the League.** J. C. MALIN, *The United States after the World War*, chaps. ii–iv; R. S. BAKER, *Woodrow Wilson and the World Settlement*, Vol. I, pp. 314–339; D. F. FLEMING, *The United States and the League of Nations*, chaps. ix–xvi; S. P. DUGGAN (ed.), *The League of Nations*, pp. 273–303; W. E. DODD, *Woodrow Wilson and his Work*, pp. 354–400; ORDWAY TEAL, *The People's Part in Peace*, pp. 7–26; J. B. McMASTER, *The United States in the World War*, Vol. II, pp. 378–451 and Appendix E.

QUESTIONS SUGGESTED BY THE CHAPTER

1. Why did President Wilson go to Paris? 2. Had a President ever been out of our country before? If so, when? 3. To what was America's prestige due at the close of the war? 4. How did Wilson offend the Senate? 5. How did he offend the Republicans? 6. What did Wilson mean by speaking of his "mandate" from the American people? 7. Compare Wilson's political position with that of Lloyd George at the time the peace conference met. 8. What concession to France did Wilson make in order to get the League established? 9. What did Article X provide? 10. Why did Germany call the Treaty of Versailles "a murderous volume"? 11. How did the Republican Senators notify Wilson early in 1919 of their intention to defeat the treaty? 12. How did the treaty interfere with the independence of the United States, according to its critics? 13. What did Wilson hope to accomplish by his speaking tour of September, 1919? 14. What were the Lodge reservations to the treaty? 15. How did Wilson receive the defeat of the treaty in November, 1919? 16. How did the vote of March, 1920, differ from that of the previous November? 17. What was the Knox resolution? 18. Do you think that Wilson was right in refusing to accept reservations to the treaty? 19. When and where was the League of Nations organized? 20. What were the main objections of the Senate to the Covenant of the League? 21. What attempt did Wilson make to win the consent of the Senate to the treaty? 22. Do you think war would be less likely if it could be declared only by a popular vote? Give reasons for your answer.

BOOKS WORTH READING ON UNIT SEVEN

H. G. WELLS, *Mr. Britling Sees it Through*; E. M. REMARQUE, *All Quiet on the Western Front*; WILLA CATHER, *One of Ours*; W. B. CLARK, *When the U-Boats Came to America*; L. J. THOMAS, *Count Luckner, the Sea Devil*; R. D. PAINE, *The Corsair of the War Zone*; A. G. EMPEY, *Over the Top*; R. NICHOLS and M. BROWNE, *Wings over Europe*; L. STALLINGS, *The First World War* (photographs); V. B. IBÁÑEZ, *The Four Horsemen of the Apocalypse*; SIR PHILIP GIBBS, *Now it Can be Told*; R. RAEMAEKERS, *America in the War* (cartoons).

How our Country Sought to Return to "Normalcy"

The war was like a great storm at sea. "Our ship of state" was driven far off the course which it had followed for a century, past the familiar headlands and beacons of the Constitution: the limitation of executive power, the noninterference of the government with private initiative and competition in business, the guarantees of freedom of speech and of the press. When the storm had subsided, the task was to right the ship to an even keel and get her back on the course. This task Warren G. Harding, the genial Republican President who succeeded Wilson in the White House in the spring of 1921, called the "return to normalcy," that is, to the "normal" or usual American attitude toward foreign entanglements, the conduct of government, methods of business, and individual freedom. But it was impossible for the United States to ignore the tremendous changes which the war had wrought in our financial, political, industrial, and social life. The Allies owed us billions of dollars, represented by Liberty Bonds, on which the interest had to be paid by taxes levied upon the American people. Millions of American soldiers were returning to civil life to find jobs. Millions more of immigrants from the impoverished countries of Europe were preparing to come to our shores, to add to the confusion which a bitter struggle between labor and capital was already making in our industrial life. Certain groups in our country wanted to see the government retain or even increase the control over private business which it had established during the war. Others demanded that the government relax or even abolish that control. How could these conflicting claims and demands be adjusted? We shall see in this unit how, after two years of confusion and turmoil, our country entered upon a period of what it believed to be an enduring prosperity. Poverty was to be abolished. There was to be a "chicken in every pot," and "two cars in every garage." We shall also see on what false and flimsy bases this seeming prosperity was built, and how, when it was put to the test by the touch of sober reality, it collapsed like a house of cards.

CHAPTER TWENTY-NINE

THE AFTERMATH OF THE WAR

The Reaction. The character of a nation, like that of an individual, is the result of years of development. It cannot be suddenly and wholly changed by any single event, however important. The new experience is grafted onto the old life, as a new branch is grafted onto a tree. The quality of the fruit is different, but the nature of the fruit is not changed from apples to pears or peaches. So the sudden revolution which the war brought in the political, business, and social habits of the American people was bound to be followed by a reaction. The armistice released the Republicans from the support they had given Wilson in the war, and political opposition to the administration began to flare up, as we have seen in the Senate's rejection of the treaty. Business was eager to get back to its old competitive basis. Labor was determined to maintain its high wages, and capital its unwonted profits. The extraordinary powers conferred on the President by the war legislation must return to the people's representatives in Congress, and the executive boards and commissions must cease to control production, transportation, prices, wages, food, fuel, and the general habits and occupations of the people.

Many seemed to think that the domestic problems raised by the return to a condition of peace would be easily solved. President Wilson himself expressed this opinion in his address to Congress just before his departure for Paris, in December, 1918:

Our people do not wait to be coaxed or led. They know their own business, and are quick and resourceful at any readjustment. . . . From no quarter have I seen any general scheme of "reconstruction" emerge which I thought it likely we could force our spirited businessmen and self-reliant laborers to accept with due pliancy and obediency.

This optimistic statement may have been partly the President's excuse for leaving the country just when the problems of "re-construction" were bound to arise; but it was also in keeping with his life-long conviction as a Jeffersonian Democrat that the government should interfere as little as possible with in-dividual freedom — at least in time of peace. Others, however, realized that the readjustment would be neither quick nor easy. When, for example, the Secretary of Commerce attempted to carry on the work of the War Industries Board (p. 702) through a voluntary co-operation of the industries of the country with the government, he met with such antagonism from the business interests that he gave up the plan in a few weeks. Indeed, it was only because we were still technically at war with Germany for nearly two years after the armistice that our government could invoke the war legislation, such as the Lever Act (p. 696), to exercise some control over business.

Military Demobilization. The return to civil life of the 3,634,000 men in the army proceeded rapidly. Nearly half the young men in American training camps were discharged within five months after the signing of the armistice. More than two thirds of our soldiers in France were back at home before the peace treaty was signed in June, 1919. After January, 1920, the only part of Pershing's forces remaining in Europe was the little American army of occupation of the Rhine region at Co-blenz. Major General Pershing, returning early in September, 1919, had been enthusiastically received by the people and Congress and raised to the rank of a full general.

Our government had been generous to the American soldier. His pay of $30 a month was nearly three times that of the Brit-ish soldier and more than ten times that of the French soldier. Of this $30 the government allotted $15 to the soldier's wife and added sums ranging from $15 to $30 a month, according to the size of his family. If a man was totally disabled, he might re-ceive as much (after December, 1919) as $100 a month from the Treasury. The government also allowed every enlisted man to take out an insurance policy up to $10,000 at a low premium rate, to run for five years after the war was over. These policies, issued to four and a half million men, totaled more than $37,000,000,000, an amount larger than that of the policies of all the private American life-insurance companies combined. The average allowance of the government to the dependents of soldiers killed was $360 a year, as compared with $202 in England, $50 in France, and $11 in Italy. For those who found difficulty in getting work the government employment agency tried to supply jobs, placing nearly five hundred thousand men from December, 1918, to September, 1919. A Federal Board for Vocational Training, established to educate disabled service men for such occupations as they were capable of filling, was less successful. However, the figures of the Veterans' Bureau show that up to February 1, 1922, the government had spent nearly $2,500,000,000 for the disabled and was then paying $1,000,000 a day to the ex-service men or their dependents. All these forms of aid and compensation were designed to take the place of the pension system, which had led to such abuses and frauds after the Civil War.

The American Legion. On November 11, 1919, the first anniversary of the signing of the armistice, the ex-service men organized the American Legion at a convention at Minneapolis. Membership in the Legion was open to privates and officers on equal terms. Its general purpose, like that of the G. A. R. formed by the veterans of the Civil War, was to maintain the spirit of patriotism which had inspired so many of the men to offer their lives for their country, and to exert the power of their united efforts for legislation favorable to their interests. As stated in its declaration, its objects were "to uphold and defend the Constitution of the United States, to maintain law and order, to foster 100 per cent Americanism, and to preserve the memories and incidents of the Great War." In 1920 it formulated plans of asking subsidies from Congress in the shape of effectual vocational training for the disabled veterans, lands for those who wanted farms, aid for house-building, and a cash bonus. On May 29, by the decisive vote of 289 to 92, the House passed a bill providing for a cash bonus to the ex-service men; but a vote in the Senate was not reached in the session. We shall note later the persistent and finally successful efforts of the ex-service men to get a cash bonus.

Economic Demobilization. While the soldiers were coming home the government was relinquishing many of the extraordinary powers which it had assumed during the war. At the end of 1918 the War Industries Board was disbanded, and the dollar-a-year men began to shut their government desks and go back to their private offices. Shortly afterward the President's orders terminated the government control over food and fuel. In May, 1919, the cables (which the Postmaster-General had taken over just after the armistice) were returned to their owners, and in August the telephone and telegraph lines. On December 24 President Wilson announced that the railroads would be returned to private management on the first of the following March. The War Labor Board had already ceased to exist.

When the war ended there were government contracts outstanding for billions of dollars' worth of supplies of all kinds: munitions, ships, buildings, trucks, airplanes, etc. Where work had not yet begun on these contracts, they were canceled; in the other cases they were adjusted by a Board of War Claims, with a total estimated saving of some $7,000,000,000 to the government. There were also vast supplies of clothing, food, and equipment of various sorts in the storehouses of the Service of Supply (p. 682, note) in France and in the camps in America. A Liquidation Commission of March 2, 1919, negotiated an agreement with the French government by which the latter was to pay the United States $400,000,000 for all the permanent structures, such as buildings, roads, bridges, and railways, built in France by American capital. The supplies accumulated abroad, valued at $1,700,000,000, were sold at about fifty cents on the dollar. Partly to stem the rising tide of prices that followed the war, our government sold to the people at home, without profit, a great variety of commodities such as shoes, blankets, clothing, underwear, canned food, kitchen utensils, and plumbers' fixtures, left over in the training camps.

The Shipping Problem. Of course the government's losses on these sales were large, being estimated at $80,000,000 on the

UNITED STATES SHIPS LAID UP IN NEW JERSEY AFTER THE WAR

camps and cantonments alone. But by far the greatest loss was on ships. When we entered the war, at the height of the submarine ravages, the cry from the Allies was "Ships will win the war!" The Emergency Fleet Corporation of the United States Shipping Board then began an enormous program of construction of iron, wooden, and concrete vessels. When the armistice was signed there were 381,000 workers in American shipyards, as against 44,000 at the beginning of the war; and the Shipping Board controlled a fleet of 1196 vessels, with a gross tonnage of 6,500,000. But this was scarcely more than a third of the tonnage planned for. By 1920 our merchant marine had increased 600 per cent over the figures of 1914, and the total government appropriations for the Emergency Fleet Corporation up to the end of 1920 reached the huge sum of $3,225,000,000.

With our foreign trade hard hit by the distress of the European nations at the close of the war, the United States found itself with millions of tons of shipping that it could not profitably use or dispose of. The Merchant Marine (Jones) Act, of June 5, 1920, directed the Shipping Board to sell the government vessels "as soon as practicable." But in spite of easy terms of payment and the creation of a government fund of $25,000,000 for loans to private owners for the establishment of new routes of trade, buyers could not be found. Not only were there already far too many ships for the amount of trade, but the La Follette Seaman's Act of 1915 prescribed conditions of food and wages for American sailors which made it impossible for us to compete with foreign shipping. England could operate her merchant fleet 25 per cent cheaper, Sweden from 30 to 40 per cent cheaper, and Japan from 40 to 50 per cent cheaper than could the United States. So the Merchant Marine Act remained practically a dead letter, and such of the ships as were not operated (at a steady loss) by the government were laid up to rust or rot at Hog Island in the Delaware or in Haverstraw Bay in the Hudson. In 1922 George D. Perry, a San Francisco merchant, bought two hundred and twenty-six of them for $750,000. They had cost the government an average of $700,000 apiece. And in August, 1926, the government accepted Henry Ford's bid of about $800 apiece for two hundred iron vessels as "junk." Such was one item of the expense of a war which cost the American people $1,000,000 an hour from April, 1917, to April, 1919, — a sum equal to the total expenses of the government since George Washington's administration and sufficient to have continued the American Revolution, at its rate of expenditure, for a thousand years!

Profiteering. Neither our "spirited businessmen" nor our "self-reliant laborers" showed any disposition to give up the gains that they had won during the war. Profiteering, which Senator Kapper of Kansas denounced as "open, scandalous, and shameful," invaded every branch of industry. Manufacturers and dealers who had been content with profits of 10 to 20 per cent before the war now wanted to make 50 or 100 per cent. A report of the Federal Trade Commission in August, 1919, revealed sickening instances of the gouging and cheating of the people by the profiteers. There was plenty of food and clothing in the country; but tens of millions of eggs, millions of pounds of butter, and great quantities of meat and vegetables were hoarded by dealers and packers, to be sold at exorbitant prices. Every rise in prices was accompanied by a demand for increased wages, and every rise in wages was made the excuse for an increase of prices. The consuming public, caught in this "vicious circle," saw the purchasing price of its dollar decline from 100 cents in 1914 to 76.2 cents in 1917 and 48 cents in 1920. Clothing cost almost three times as much, food twice as much, rent half again as much in 1920 as in 1914. In August, 1919, President Wilson declared in a special message to Congress that the excessive prices were "the result of improper practices on the part of the manufacturers and the dealers," and recommended the extension of the Lever Act so as "to insure competitive selling and to prevent unconscionable profits." But Congress, no longer looking to the President for guidance, ignored his advice. About a thousand actions brought by the Department of Justice against alleged profiteering resulted in only one hundred and eighty convictions and the assessment of $275,000 in fines. Senator Lenroot of Wisconsin complained that the Attorney-General "was setting a few mousetraps around the country when he ought to be setting beartraps."

Industrial Turmoil. The generous truce between capital and labor came to an abrupt end as soon as the emergency need for co-operation in winning the war had passed. A perfect epidemic of strikes broke out in 1919, involving four million workers and costing two billion dollars of loss in sales and wages. Dock men, ship hands, firemen, garment workers, textile workers, carpenters, miners, telegraph operators, steel workers, expressmen, railroad men, policemen, actors, waiters, bakers, and barbers followed one another out of their jobs. The statistics of the Department of Labor for the single week of September 11–18, 1919, showed one hundred and fifty-one strikes under way and fifty-three threatened. One of the worst features of the situation was the large number of "outlaw" strikes (that is, strikes not authorized by the unions), conducted by radical agitators imbued with the Bolshevist theory of turning the capitalists out and putting the industries in the hands of the workers.

President Wilson tried in vain to quiet the strife. Just before starting on his western tour in behalf of the League of Nations he invited representatives of capital, labor, and the general public to meet in a conference at Washington, to "consult together on the vital questions concerning our industrial life." Wilson himself was too ill to greet the fifty-odd delegates to the conference, which the chairman, Secretary of the Interior Franklin K. Lane, hailed as "the most important extra-legal body that has been called in this country, certainly in our own time." He declared that it was "bound to be a success." But his prophecy was false. Instead of trying to find a common basis of agreement, the representatives of capital and labor fell to quarreling about the justice of the great steel strike which had broken out two weeks before the conference met. Mr. Gompers demanded "the right of wage-earners to organize without discrimination and to bargain collectively . . . with employers in respect to wages, hours of labor and conditions of employment." The employers insisted that they would deal only with their own workers in the separate shops. Whereupon Gompers and the labor group withdrew from the conference, declaring that "further attempts to reach an agreement would be futile."

After the failure of the industrial conference the American Federation of Labor and the railroad brotherhoods called a labor conference "to define the general policies to be adopted by labor in seeking to promote its interests." The conference repudiated Bolshevism and the I.W.W. (p. 595) as "destructive to American ideals," reiterated the principles of voluntary arbitration and collective bargaining, and recommended that the government retain control of the railroads for at least two years "in order that a thorough test may be made of government operation under normal conditions." The "reconciliation" of capital and labor seemed to be as impossible as "squaring the circle."

The Great Steel Strike. The rock on which the President's industrial conference split was a nation-wide strike of the steel workers, involving about 370,000 men. It arose out of the attempt to unionize the laborers in the steel industry, the most important industry of the country which still insisted on dealing with its workers individually. Judge E. H. Gary, of the United States Steel Corporation, acting for the manufacturers generally, refused even to hold an interview with the representatives of the unions in the industry. He explained his position in a statement of September 17: "We do not combat labor unions as such, but we do not negotiate with labor unions, because it would indicate the closing of our shops to nonunion labor, and large numbers of our workmen are not members of the unions and do not care to be."

The Interchurch Report of 1920 on the steel strike justified the demands of the workers for the abolition of the seven-day week and the twenty-four-hour shift, and spoke of the "intolerable and brutal conditions under which the men are compelled to work." Nevertheless, the strike was a failure from the start and was called off before the end of the year. The main reason for this was the attempt of its chief promoter, William Z. Foster, to introduce the very kind of "un-American" agitation that was condemned by the labor unions in their conference at Washington. Such sympathy as there was for the condition of the workers was largely offset by the tactics of the agitators. "Behind this strike," said an investigating committee of the Senate, "is massed a considerable element of I.W.W.'s, anarchists and revolutionists, and the Russian soviets; some radicals are attempting to use the strike to elevate themselves to power within the ranks of organized labor." The committee recommended a law of Congress to provide for "the effective education and Americanization of illiterate foreigners" and to "compel aliens to become naturalized within five years or be deported."

The Government and the Coal Strike. The most serious of the many strikes of 1919 was inaugurated on November 1, when, in spite of Wilson's plea for the maintenance of a full supply of fuel for the world's needs, 435,000 in the bituminous coal fields laid down their tools to enforce their demands for a

60 per cent increase in wages and the guaranty of a minimum of thirty hours of work a week. The workers had made an agreement with the mine-owners which was to last "until the close of the war." They now claimed that the war was over and the agreement at an end. The owners, however, refused to listen to any revision of the agreement unless they were allowed to advance the price of coal 20 per cent, which would have added $150,000,000 to the people's coal bill. The President issued a statement condemning the strike "under present conditions" as "not only unjustifiable, but unlawful."

As we were still technically at war with Germany, the Lever Act of 1917, which made it a penal offense "to conspire or take action leading to the interference with the production of coal," was still in force. Under its authority President Wilson revived the fuel administration and again called Dr. Garfield to Washington. Troops were ordered to West Virginia, Wyoming, Utah, and New Mexico. Attorney-General Palmer secured an injunction from a Federal judge in Indianapolis ordering the officials of the United Mine Workers to terminate the strike within three days. The protest of the labor officials against this injunction was bitter. John L. Lewis, the president of the United Mine Workers, called it "the most sweeping abrogation of the rights of citizens, guarded under the Constitution and defended by statutory law, that has ever been issued by any Federal court." Nevertheless, the officials decided, after a seventeen-hour session at Indianapolis, to call off the strike. "We will comply with the mandate of the court," said Mr. Lewis. "We do it under protest. We are Americans. We cannot fight the government. That is all." The men were slow in returning to work, however, and the cold days of December came on with only about 40 per cent of the normal production of coal. Meanwhile Dr. Garfield and Secretary of Labor Wilson were quarreling between themselves and with both the mine-owners and the workers over a proper scale of wages. It was not until March, 1920, that a settlement was made on the basis of a 27 per cent increase. The strike had cost $125,000,000, of which nearly half was in loss of wages.

The Boston Police Strike. Another strike, local in situation but sinister in character, added to the social chaos of the autumn of 1919. On September 9, Police Commissioner Curtis of Boston suspended nineteen policemen for breaking the orders of the department in organizing a union affiliated with the A.F. of L. Thereupon 90 per cent of the police force of 1544 men went on a strike. For two or three days a reign of terror threatened the city. The criminal element emerged boldly. Rioting, holdups, and looting of stores followed. Guards were rushed to the city from the navy yard at Charlestown, and Harvard students volunteered for the preservation of order. At the request of the mayor of Boston, Governor Calvin Coolidge mobilized five thousand of the state militia; but not, said his critics, until after the police commissioner and the mayor had the situation well in hand. At any rate, Coolidge backed the commissioner in his refusal to reinstate the striking policemen, and replied to Gompers's telegram asking that leniency be shown them: "There is no right to strike against the public safety by anybody, anywhere, any time." President Wilson wrote to Governor Coolidge, commending him for this ringing declaration, and the quiet, modest chief magistrate of the Bay State, whose name had scarcely been known outside its borders, suddenly found himself a figure of national importance. He was reelected by an enormous majority by the people of Massachusetts in the autumn of 1919; and the next summer, at the Republican national convention at Chicago, he was nominated for the Vice-Presidency on the first ballot, with 674 votes to 146 for his nearest competitor.

The Railroad Situation. The government operation of the railroads during the war had been very costly. The deficit amounted to over $200,000,000 in 1918, and a further deficit of $192,000,000 was accumulated in the first four months of 1919. Thirty per cent of the railroad stock was paying no dividends. Obviously, the government could not simply hand the roads back to their owners in this condition and still keep its promise to return them in as good condition as they were in before it took them over. But there was a wide diversity of opinion as to the terms on which the railroads were to be restored to their owners. The Director-General wanted the government to continue its management of the lines for five years longer, to ease the transition from the war to a peace economy. The owners wanted to have the roads returned immediately, but with some backing still by the government in the shape of a Federal Transportation Board, which could recommend fair rates, prohibit strikes and lockouts, and compel the settlement of labor disputes by arbitration. The stockholders wanted the government to guarantee a 6 per cent return on their investments, while any profit of the roads above that figure should be equally divided between the owners, the employees, and a fund for improvements. The workers, through Glenn E. Plumb, the counsel for the railroad brotherhoods, proposed a scheme of public ownership. The government should buy the roads and operate them through a national corporation composed one third of railroad employees, one third of officials, and one third of members appointed by the President. The employees should receive half of any profits above 5 per cent; but if there was a deficit, it should be made up by public taxation. Labor disputes were to be settled by an arbitration board of five employees and five officials.

The Plumb Plan was endorsed by the A. F. of L., and received a good deal of support as being in line with President Wilson's suggestion of a "genuine democratization of industry, based on the full recognition of the right of those who work in whatever rank to participate in some organic way in every decision which directly affects their welfare." Its opponents, however, regarded it as dangerously like the Russian soviet plan of the control of industry by the workers. Bills introduced by J. J. Esch of Wisconsin in the House and Albert Cummins of Iowa in the Senate, in November and December, 1919, were so far apart that it seemed hardly possible that a compromise could be reached before the date of March 1, 1920, set by the President for the return of the railroads.

The Railroad Transportation Act. By dint of nine weeks of hard labor the conflicting views were reconciled in the Esch-

Cummins Railroad Transportation Act, which was signed by the President on February 28, 1920. Its main provisions were as follows: (1) the enlargement of the powers of the Interstate Commerce Commission (increased to eleven members) to fix rates to yield a return of 6 per cent for two years on the estimated value of the roads, and to supervise their issues of stocks and bonds; (2) the creation of a Railway Labor Board of nine members appointed by the President (three from the owners, three from the workers, and three from the public) to settle labor disputes; (3) the appropriation of two hundred million dollars to help the roads to get back to their prewar status, and of three hundred million dollars, as a revolving fund out of which loans to the roads might be made; (4) the prohibition of any increase in rates or decrease in wages before September 1, 1920; (5) the provision that no man should serve on the board of directors of more than one road after December 31, 1921. The act was never acceptable to labor. The railroad brotherhoods asked President Wilson to veto it, and in June, 1920, the convention of the American Federation of Labor at Montreal voted 19,058 to 8348 in favor of the government ownership of the roads. A decision of the Railway Labor Board in July, granting a wage increase of 20 per cent, was denounced by Gompers as "grossly inadequate." Nor was the board able to prevent a strike of three hundred thousand railway shopmen in the summer of 1922, which was attended with violence in the shape of attacks on "scab" workmen and attempts to wreck trains and bridges.

The Eighteenth Amendment. The prohibition of the manufacture and sale of intoxicating liquor was a subject which had enlisted the interest of reformers, especially among the women and church members, ever since the middle of the nineteenth century. The state of Maine had a "dry" law as early as 1851. In 1872 a Prohibitionist party entered the field with a Presidential candidate, and in 1883 Miss Frances Willard was the moving spirit in founding the Women's Christian Temperance Union. Twelve years later the powerful Anti-Saloon League was formed at Westerville, Ohio, with the purpose of carrying on a nation-wide political and moral crusade against the liquor traffic. The league had the support not only of those who deplored the suffering and poverty caused by strong drink but also of many industrial leaders who realized the loss of efficiency and the danger in the operation of the delicate and speedy machinery of modern production which resulted from befuddled or drunken workers.

By the end of 1917 half the states of the country, representing all sections from New England to the Pacific coast, had passed prohibition laws; and in December of that year both houses of Congress, by more than two-to-one majorities, adopted a resolution for a prohibition amendment to the constitution of the United States. Still, it is a question whether the ratification of such an amendment by the necessary thirty-six states could have been secured without the pressure of the war. It was the need for conserving the grain, cereals, and fruit of the country for food that prompted the clauses of the Lever Act of 1917 and the Food Stimulation Act of 1918 forbidding the use of these products for distilled beverages during the period of the war. On January 16, 1919, the thirty-sixth state ratified the Eighteenth Amendment, which was to go into effect one year later. It prohibited "the manufacture, sale, or transportation of intoxicating liquors within, the importation thereof into, or the exportation thereof from the United States and all territory subject to the jurisdiction thereof for beverage purposes." It left to Congress the definition of the word "intoxicating," and the Volstead Act of October, 1919 (passed over President Wilson's veto), declared that $1\frac{1}{2}$ per cent of alcohol made a beverage intoxicating.

Objections were at once raised to the amendment on several counts: it was a violation of personal freedom; it was not referred for ratification to the *people* in those states where the referendum prevailed;[1] it outraged the principle of states' rights; and, as a law dealing with the habits of citizens and

[1] Only 6780 persons out of the 105,000,000 citizens of the country voted directly on the Eighteenth Amendment in Congress and the state legislatures. But the votes of these representatives of the people were so overwhelmingly in favor of the amendment that its advocates claimed that it was truly representative of the

not with the framework of government, it had no proper place in the permanent constitution of the United States. The Supreme Court, however, in decisions of June, 1920, unanimously upheld the constitutionality of both the amendment and the Volstead Act.

During the thirteen years in which it was in force (for it was repealed by the Twenty-first Amendment in 1933) the Eighteenth Amendment was the subject of constant argument in the press, on the platform, and at the dinner table. Its opponents maintained that it was a complete failure, in spite of the expensive attempts to enforce it. They pointed to the bootleggers and rumrunners who were amassing fortunes by violating the amendment and imperiling the health of the citizens by the poisonous liquor which they sold at exorbitant prices. Worst of all, it was encouraging widespread contempt for law by the defiant and unpunished violation of its provisions. The supporters of the amendment, on the other hand, pointed to statistics to show the decrease in the amount of liquor consumed (from 22.69 gallons per capita in 1914 to 3.01 gallons in 1920) and in the number of arrests for drunkenness; increase in the length of life as reported by the life-insurance companies; empty jails and workhouses; reduced police forces; and swelling savings-bank accounts. But each side was only the more convinced of its own position by the arguments of its opponents, which it called false in logic and unfounded in fact. The upshot of the matter was to prove the difficulty, if not the impossibility, of enforcing a law which large numbers of the people regarded as unwise and unjust.

The "Reds" in America. It would have been a difficult enough task to restore the industrial and political balance of the country after the war even if all our citizens had been inspired with the spirit of patriotic co-operation. But instead of dying out with the return of peace, suspicion, intolerance, and persecution con-

---

will of the people at large. For example, 85 per cent of the Senate and 78 per cent of the House voted for the amendment. The adverse vote in 34 state senates and 21 assemblies was less than 10 per cent, and in South Dakota, Kansas, Idaho, Washington, Wyoming, and Utah there was not a dissenting vote in either house.

tinued to bring confusion into the social order. In most of Europe east of the Rhine, revolution followed on the heels of the war. The Russian Bolshevists aimed at nothing less than the conquest of the world by communism. They had allies in this country in the extreme "left wing" Socialists and the I. W. W., who endorsed the Moscow program for the destruction of capitalism and the appropriation of wealth by the working class. Their radical agitators sought to get control of the labor unions and turn them from the peaceful methods of arbitration or orderly strikes to revolutionary violence. The Bolshevist government of Lenin and Trotsky sent an official agent named Martens to this country. Neither Martens nor the government which sent him was recognized by our State Department; yet he opened offices in New York and engaged in an active campaign of propaganda. Radical associations were formed in many of our cities, bearing the strange name of the "All-Russia Soviet of America."

In February, 1919, an attempt was made at Seattle, Washington, to paralyze the whole industrial life of the city by a general strike which grew out of the grievances of the workers in the shipyards. During the summer a number of outrages were committed. A bomb exploded on the doorstep of the home of Attorney-General Palmer in Washington, wrecking the façade of the building but injuring no one besides the man who threw it. Bombs destined for other officials were discovered in the mails. On the anniversary of the signing of the armistice (November 11) a parade of the American Legion was fired upon at Centralia, Washington, and four men were killed. The I. W. W. were held responsible for most of the acts of violence. Twenty-seven members of the organization tried before a judge in Kansas City were sentenced to terms of imprisonment varying from three to nine years and to fines ranging from three thousand dollars to ten thousand dollars. President Wilson, in his message of December, 1919, spoke of these "evidences of world-wide unrest" which were manifesting themselves in America, and warned us to stop the "spread of this contagious thing before it saps the very vitality of the nation." "With the free expression of opinion and with the advocacy of orderly political change, however fundamental," he continued, "there must be no interference; but toward passion and malevolence tending to incite crime and revolution . . . there should be no leniency. . . . The instrument of all reforms in America is the straight road of justice. . . . Let those beware who would take a shorter road of disorder and revolution."

The "Soviet Ark." The government was preparing, meanwhile, to send the "Reds" on a long road. Early in November, 1919, by orders of the Secretary of Labor, over two hundred and fifty radical agitators were arrested in a dozen cities, and on December 21 the transport *Buford*, dubbed "the Soviet Ark," sailed from New York, carrying two hundred and forty-nine aliens who were "a menace to law and order here" to Soviet Russia. The Department of Justice declared that there were ten times that number of "Reds" in the country who deserved deportation. Ellis Island was crowded with them. About eight hundred were confined in Federal prisons.

The treatment of the radicals by the Departments of Labor and Justice roused a lively discussion in the country. Some believed that the government was too lenient. The American Legion, in its second annual convention in 1920, demanded the dismissal of the Assistant Secretary of Labor, Louis F. Post, because he opposed the policy of deportation; and Representative Johnson of Washington declared that the mere fact of membership in the I. W. W. or the Communist party was ground enough for sending a person out of the country. " Deprive these organizations of their aliens," he cried, "and they will either become American or fade away. The United States is not going to be run by aliens who do not vote." On the other hand, the Attorney-General was attacked as a panic-stricken reactionary who was doing more harm to our free institutions by his "illegal arrests" and "shocking raids" than all the "Reds" in the country put together. Liberals denounced the repression of free speech and assembly, guaranteed in the Constitution. Several prominent attorneys signed a manifesto on May 27, 1920, reading: "American institutions have not been protected by the

Attorney-General's suppressions. On the contrary, those institutions have been seriously undermined and revolutionary unrest vastly intensified." Some even accused Attorney-General Palmer of deliberately fomenting radical agitation in order that he might pose as the defender of an endangered American patriotism and so prepare the way for his nomination for the Presidency in the coming Democratic convention.

The Lusk Laws. Perhaps the most conspicuous example of the determination to enforce patriotism by law was furnished by the activities of the Lusk Committee of the New York legislature. On April 24, 1920, this committee, headed by Senator Lusk, filed a report of over forty-two hundred pages in four volumes on *Revolutionary Radicalism, its History, Purpose and Tactics.* It condemned in one sweeping charge all pacifists, internationalists, socialists, anarchists, and communists as "seeking to undermine and destroy not only the government under which we live, but also the very structure of American society." The committee secured the passage of bills requiring all persons or societies conducting any "school, institute, class or course of instruction in any subject" to procure a license from the Regents of the University of the State of New York; and denied a license to any teacher who had "advocated, either by word of mouth or in writing, a form of government other than the government of the United States or of this state." These bills for the suppression of the freedom of teaching were vetoed by Governor Alfred E. Smith, but were revived under his Republican successor, Governor Nathan Miller, who signed them.

Furthermore, on the recommendation of the Lusk Committee, the New York legislature, by a vote of 140 to 6, refused seats to five members of the Socialist party regularly elected on the party ticket in 1920, on the ground that a Socialist could not be a loyal citizen of the United States. Governor Smith, ex-Governor Hughes, and Theodore Roosevelt (the son of the ex-President, serving his first term in the legislature) were among the thousands of prominent persons who protested against this injustice, born of the fear and intolerance nurtured by the war.

Said Mr. Hughes, who could by no means be suspected of radical or "anarchistic" tendencies:

This is not, in my judgment, American government. I count it a most serious mistake to proceed not against individuals charged with the violation of the law, but against masses of our citizens combined for political action (the Socialist party), by denying them the only resource of peaceful government, that is, action through duly elected representatives in legislative bodies.

He doubted whether, in the light of such repressive measures, our system of government could survive another great war.

The Breakup of the Wilson Administration. It was in the midst of such political, industrial, and social confusion that the administration of the stricken President went to pieces. No one seemed to know who was directing the policy of the executive department. There were rumors that Private Secretary Tumulty and Mrs. Wilson were "running the government." Congress, Republican in both branches, ceased to look to the White House for guidance or advice. The cabinet disintegrated. Six of the members resigned between December, 1918, and February, 1920. The only original cabinet appointees who retained their posts to the end of the administration were Postmaster-General Burleson, Secretary of the Navy Daniels, and Secretary of Labor Wilson, the first two of whom were far from popular with the country at large. Even Colonel House, who had been the President's most faithful adviser and intimate friend, received no response to his letters addressed to the White House after his return from Europe in the autumn of 1919.

The Political Situation in 1920. Such was the distracted state of the country when the national conventions met in the early summer of 1920 to choose candidates to compete for the power which had already passed out of the hands of President Wilson. Of the two strong men who had filled the stage so completely in the first and second decades of the century, one was in his grave and the other was a hopeless paralytic. Theodore Roosevelt had made his peace with the Republican party and was already being talked of as the inevitable nominee when death overtook him in his sleep, before dawn on January 6, 1919. The two men who could claim to take his place in the Republican convention which met at Chicago on June 8, 1920, were General Leonard Wood of New York, his old favorite in the army, and Senator Hiram Johnson of California, his running mate in the campaign of 1912. The men of the Hanna tradition, who wanted a candidate favorable to big business, inclined toward the wealthy, efficient Governor of Illinois, Frank B. Lowden.

A group of liberals, including a large element among the women voters, thought Wood too military, Johnson too radical, and Lowden too conservative. They started a boom for Herbert Hoover, whose management of the Belgian relief and the American food administration during the war had stamped him as an able executive without political partisanship. But his support of the League of Nations and his service under Wilson ruined his chances with the Senatorial group, who, as it proved, controlled the convention. A month before the convention met they had already selected one of their number to be brought forward in case of a deadlock, namely, Warren G. Harding of Ohio, a signer of the round robin of March 3, 1919 (p. 721), and a Lodge follower on the League of Nations.

General Wood led on the first ballot, with 287½ votes to 211½ for Lowden, 133½ for Johnson, and 65½ for Harding. Thirteen other candidates had less than 100 votes apiece. When, the vote having remained essentially unchanged for nine ballots, Senator Borah announced that the Liberals would bolt the party if either Wood or Lowden were nominated, Senators Lodge (the chairman of the convention), Smoot, Watson, Wadsworth, and others held a meeting at the Hotel Blackstone on the night of June 11 and sent out the word that Harding was to be the man. He was nominated the next day with 692 votes, and Governor Calvin Coolidge of Massachusetts was named for the Vice-Presidency on the first ballot.

The Democrats, meeting at San Francisco on June 28, were in a quandary. President Wilson refused to indicate any choice, either of his son-in-law McAdoo or of his cabinet minister Palmer, both aspirants for the nomination. He only begged the convention to nominate a man who supported the League of

EUGENE DEBS   NORMAN THOMAS

Nations. Bryan, once the "peerless leader," had apparently lost interest in politics and transferred his extraordinary influence from the fight for free silver and the destruction of the trusts to a crusade against rum and evolution. He was out of sympathy with Wilson for entering the war, for vetoing the Volstead Act, and for his refusal to compromise with the Senate, thereby "preventing the ratification of the treaty of Versailles" and "assuming the responsibility for the nation's failure to enter the League of Nations." On the forty-fourth ballot the deadlock between McAdoo and Palmer was broken by the nomination of Governor James M. Cox of Ohio, with Franklin D. Roosevelt, the Assistant Secretary of the Navy, as running mate.

The Socialists for the fifth time nominated Eugene V. Debs, who was behind the bars of the Federal prison in Atlanta for violation of the Espionage Act, and in their platform challenged "the whole rotten capitalistic society." A Farmer-Labor party appeared, demanding the public ownership of mines, railways, and public utilities, our immediate withdrawal from the Philippines and the West Indies, the recognition of the Irish republic and the Russian soviet government, the repeal of all wartime legislation against sedition, the payment of a soldiers' bonus, and old-age pensions. The prohibitionists tried to induce Bryan to accept a unanimous nomination, but after his refusal they turned to A. S. Watkins of Ohio.[1]

The Campaign of 1920. Neither Harding nor Cox could be called a figure of national importance or a popular party leader. The campaign was waged on the issue of endorsing the whole Wilson administration, which the Republican platform characterized as "unconstitutional and dictatorial . . . founded upon no principle and directed by no definite conception of our nation's rights and obligations . . . with the result that, after a period of unexampled sacrifice, our motives are suspected, our moral influence is impaired, and our government stands discredited and friendless among the nations of the world." In reply to this the Democrats pointed with pride to the record of the administration, which, they said, had "fought the cleanest war ever fought in the history of civilization" and, against low and unworthy political opposition, had "striven to redeem the word that America had given to the world." Their platform advocated "prompt ratification of the Treaty of Versailles, without reservations which would imperil its essential integrity."

Governor Cox visited President Wilson and received his blessing. He tried to make the League of Nations the sole issue of the campaign. But however important that question was in the eyes of the more thoughtful of our citizens, it was obscured for millions of voters by questions which seemed to touch them more nearly. High rents and prices, empty coal bins, arrogant plumbers and plasterers, dissatisfied "doughboys," insolent bootleggers, bolshevist bombs, Lusk laws, government injunctions, were all dancing before the people's eyes in a confused medley. The times were out of joint. We had done our part, and more than our part, in the war. It was time now to set our own house in order. The Republicans promised to "allay

[1] A peculiar feature of the campaign was the selection of the Republican, Democratic, and Prohibition candidates for President, besides the Vice-Presidential candidates of the Farmer-Labor party (Hayes) and the single-taxers (Barnum), from the state of Ohio. Only twice before had the candidates of the two major parties come from the same state: Lincoln and Douglas from Illinois in 1860, and Roosevelt and Parker from New York in 1904.

unrest, suspicion, and strife in the country" and to secure the "co-operation and unity of all its citizens."

Holding the administration responsible, as they have always done, for the misfortunes arising from varied and complex social conditions, the people went to the polls in November and condemned Wilson's leadership by a majority of 7,000,000. Harding carried every state of the North and the West, all the border states except Kentucky, and even invaded the old states of the secessionist South by capturing Tennessee. "It was not a landslide," said Tumulty, "it was an earthquake." The electoral vote was 404 for Harding to 127 for Cox. The Republicans won the House by the largest majority ever recorded in our history (309 to 132) and secured a margin of 22 votes in the Senate (59 to 37). Vice-President-elect Coolidge hailed the victory as "the end of a period which has substituted words for things, and the beginning of a period of real patriotism and national honor." But President Wilson declared that the people had disgraced themselves in the eyes of the world by repudiating a "fruitful leadership for a barren independence." "They will have to learn now by bitter experience just what they have lost. . . . We had a chance to gain the leadership of the world. We have lost it, and soon we shall be witnessing the tragedy of it all."

Terms to be Mastered

economic reconstruction	outlaw strike	the "Soviet Ark"
cash bonus	closed shop —	Anti-Saloon League
profiteering —	Plumb Plan	collective bargaining —

For Supplementary Reading

Walter Weyl, *The End of the War*; E. L. Bogart, *War Costs and their Financing*, chaps. iii–x, xiv; J. M. Beck, *The Passing of the New Freedom*; M. Olds, *The High Cost of Strikes*; W. B. Donham, *Business Adrift*; A. M. Simons, *The Vision for which we Fought*; J. T. Adams, *Our Business Civilization*, chaps. v, vi; C. Merz, *The Dry Decade*, chaps. i–iii; Peter Odegard, *Pressure Politics: the Story of the Anti-Saloon League*; P. W. Slosson, *The Great Crusade and After* (A History of American Life, Vol. XII), pp. 72–92, 105–129; F. L. Allen, *Only Yesterday*, chaps. i–v; P. F. Brissenden, *The History of the I.W.W.*; Will Irwin, *How Red is America?* H. S. Commager, *Documents of American History*, Vol. II, pp. 334–337, 345–347.

Topics for Reports

1. The Steel Strike of 1919–1920. Interchurch World Movement, *Report on the Steel Strike of 1919*; W. Z. Foster, *The Great Steel Strike*; Edward Berman, *Labor Disputes and the President of the United States*, pp. 166–177; S. A. Shaw, "Closed Towns," in *The Survey*, Vol. XLIII, pp. 58–64; M. M. Vorse, *Men and Steel*; "The Truth about the Steel Strike," in the *New Republic*, Vol. XXIII, pp. 266–268.

2. The Railroad Problem. F. H. Dixon, "The Interstate Commerce Act as Amended," in *Quarterly Journal of Economics*, Vol. XXI, pp. 22–49; E. R. Johnson and T. W. Van Metre, *Principles of Railroad Transportation*, pp. 564–577; W. J. Cunningham, *American Railroads: Government Control and Reconstruction*, chaps. i–xiii; E. W. Young, *The Wilson Administration and the Great War*, pp. 83–106.

3. Why Prohibition Failed. Martha B. Bruère, *Does Prohibition Work?* chaps. i, x, xiii, xvi–xix; Charles Merz, *The Dry Decade*, chaps. vi, vii, ix; Peter Odegard, *Pressure Politics: the Story of the Anti-Saloon League*; J. T. Greenan, *Readings in American Citizenship*, chap. xviii ("The Long Dry Spell"); F. L. Allen, *Only Yesterday*, chap. x.

4. The Soldiers' Bonus. Talcott Powell, *Tattered Banners*, pp. 170–248; E. Streeter, "The Battle of the Bonus," in *The Outlook*, Vol. CXXXVI, pp. 276–279; H. MacNider, "A Bonus for ex-Soldiers," in *New York Times Current History*, Vol. XVI, pp. 545–550; J. R. Quinn, "Defending the Soldier," in *The Forum*, Vol. LXXI, pp. 354–357; E. W. Young, *The Wilson Administration and the Great War*, pp. 420–428.

Questions Suggested by the Chapter

1. What was Wilson's idea of the relation of business to the government after the war? **2.** What measures did the government take for the benefit of the soldiers during the war? **3.** Compare these measures with the pension system of the Civil War. **4.** What were the objects of the American Legion? **5.** What did the government do with the supplies of food and clothing which it had on its hands at the close of the war? **6.** Why could the government not operate its merchant marine profitably? **7.** What did it do with the ships? **8.** What kept the prices of food and clothing too high after the war? **9.** What caused the failure of the President's industrial conference in 1919? **10.** What was the attitude of the A. F. of L. toward Bolshevism? **11.** What caused the steel strike of 1919? **12.** How did the government end the coal strike of 1919? **13.** How did Calvin Coolidge spring into national fame? **14.** What was the Plumb Plan? **15.** On what terms did the government restore the railroads to their owners? **16.** Why were the railroad brotherhoods dissatisfied with the Transportation Act of 1920? **17.** Show how the war hastened national prohibition. **18.** What was the Volstead Act? **19.** Why did the Eighteenth Amendment arouse so much opposition? **20.** Why was it repealed in 1933? **21.** How did Wilson distinguish between reform and revolution in his message of December, 1919? **22.** For what was the Department of Justice criticized by the liberals? **23.** Why was the exclusion of the Socialist members from the New York legislature "un-American"?

CHAPTER THIRTY

THE "PROGRAM OF NORMALCY"

The Republican Reaction. "Normalcy" was the new word which President-elect Harding coined in his campaign speeches to designate what he believed to be the regular, long-established, desirable, and "normal" attitude of the United States toward government and business at home and our relations to countries abroad. We had, according to him and his supporters, been pursuing an "abnormal" policy under the Wilson administration. Not only had the government, in the stress of the war, departed from its proper sphere in marshaling the whole industry of the country under its control, but it had also pursued a will-o'-the-wisp in attempting to convert the cynical nations of Europe to the ideals of democracy. Our business was at home. Just before his nomination Senator Harding had announced his political creed in a speech before the Ohio Society of New York: "Stabilize America first, prosper America first, think of America first, exalt America first!" And in his inaugural address he said: "We seek no part in directing the destinies of the Old World. . . . We asked the sons of this republic to defend our national rights, not to purge the Old World of the accumulated ills of rivalry and greed." He had no sympathy with the Wilsonian plea that our refusal to enter the League of Nations would "break the heart of humanity."

The reaction which gave the Republicans an unbroken lease of a dozen years of power after the war was based first of all on the desire to forget the war. It was evident enough before the Senate finally rejected the Treaty of Versailles that the world had not been made "safe for democracy." Revolutions and civil wars were raging over half of Europe. Dictators were rising to power on the ruins of royal thrones. Persecution of racial and religious minorities was sowing hatred and strife. Millions of our citizens who had supported the great crusade for democracy, "the war to end war," now began to question whether the game had been worth the candle. The American Revolution had secured our independence as a nation; the Civil War had rid the land of the curse of slavery; but what had this remote war, "with whose causes and objects we had nothing to do," brought us except a huge debt, oppressive taxes, high cost of living, industrial confusion, social unrest, and even the jealous ingratitude of the nations whom we had aided with billions of money and millions of soldiers! It was time, said these disillusioned Americans, to be done with such knight-errantry. Senator Harding summed up what he believed should be the creed of "forward-looking Americans," in contrast to President Wilson's, in a speech at Boston in the spring of 1920: "America's present need is not heroics but healing; not nostrums but normalcy; not revolution but restoration; not surgery but serenity." His triumphant election in November foreshadowed a return to the "good old days" of McKinley and Hanna, when the big-business interests of the country were unhampered by government interference, labor was kept in its place, and prosperity was measured by the abundance of crumbs which dropped from the rich men's tables.

The New Administration. President Harding was a man of superb figure and physique. He looked "every inch a king." To a Washingtonian dignity in appearance he added a most un-Washingtonian genialty of manner, a hail-fellow-well-met companionship of the "good mixer" among "the boys" with whom he enjoyed a Saturday night's game of poker. He was the proprietor of a newspaper in the small town of Marion, Ohio, and a true "son of the middle border." "We are just plain folks," said Mrs. Harding. Main Street moved into the White House. But behind the façade of his handsome face, his genial manners, and his winning voice President Harding had but meager qualifications for the responsibilities of the high office to which he had been elected. Both mentally and morally he failed to measure up to high standards. He was no student of the history or science of government, and consequently he lacked the knowledge and convictions necessary to make him a real leader among the men whom he gathered about him. Moreover, his pliant good nature and his attachment to personal friends like the crooked politicians of the "Ohio gang" and plunderers of the public wealth brought discredit upon his administration and bitter sorrow (perhaps even death) to himself.

The start of the new administration was promising. If many thoughtful citizens were disturbed over the elevation of the Ohio "small-town man" to the Presidency, they were reassured by his appointment of one of the wisest and ablest Republicans in the country, the present Chief Justice Charles Evans Hughes, to the first place in the cabinet, and of Herbert Hoover as Secretary of Commerce. Andrew W. Mellon, a millionaire banker of Pittsburgh, Pennsylvania, was given the Treasury portfolio, and proved, in spite of no previous experience in public office, to be an extremely able secretary, holding the office for a longer period (from 1921 to 1932) than any other Secretary of the Treasury in our history except Albert Gallatin (1801–1814). Senator Albert B. Fall of New Mexico, Harding's desk mate in the Senate, was appointed Secretary of the Interior. Though revelations of Fall's dishonesty came out after he had left the cabinet in 1923, his appointment in 1921 was so acceptable that it was ratified with great applause in the Senate on inauguration day, without even the customary reference of his name to the committee. The other cabinet members were also confirmed unanimously on the same day.[1]

---

[1] They were John W. Weeks of Massachusetts (War), Edwin C. Denby of Michigan (Navy), Will H. Hays of Indiana (Postmaster-General), Henry C. Wallace of Iowa, the father of the later secretary Henry A. Wallace (Agriculture), James J. Davis of Pennsylvania (Labor), and Harry M. Daugherty of Ohio (Attorney-General). The latter's name was the only one to arouse unfavorable criticism at the time. Daugherty belonged to the "Ohio gang" of politicians. He had "groomed" Harding for the Presidency and managed his campaign. Though he himself urged the name of the present Supreme Court Justice George Sutherland of Utah for the Attorney-Generalship, he yielded to Harding's insistence that he should join the cabinet — a step which he called, in his later book on *The Inside Story of the Harding Tragedy*, "the tragic blunder of my life." Vice-President Coolidge was invited to attend the cabinet meetings.

The Harding Program. In spite of his desire to co-operate with Congress and of his large majorities in both houses, President Harding found the road back to "normalcy" a long and difficult one. He called Congress in extra session in April, 1921, to begin the work of financial reconstruction. In his message he recommended the creation of a national budget bureau to sift the demands of the various departments for appropriations and reduce them to a single system, to be presented by the President to Congress. The enactment of an emergency tariff law, the readjustment of the war taxes, economy and retrenchment in government expenditures, generous treatment of disabled soldiers, and aid to the farmers were stressed.

As to foreign affairs, the President repeated the sentiments of his inaugural address : we craved the friendship of the world and harbored no hates ; we were ready to "associate ourselves" with the nations of the world "for counsel and conference, for the suggestion of plans of mediation, conciliation and arbitration, but every commitment had to be made in the exercise of our national sovereignty." This sounded something like a willingness to work with the League of Nations. But it was only an empty formula, to placate prominent Republicans who favored international co-operation and who had even signed a declaration during the campaign that the election of Harding offered the best chance of getting us into the League. It was a sadly mistaken prophecy. The Harding administration "threw the League into the wastebasket." For many months after the inauguration our State Department refused even to acknowledge the receipt of communications from Geneva.

The Knox resolution for the declaration of peace with Germany, which President Wilson had indignantly vetoed a year before (p. 728), was immediately introduced into the Senate and passed. It was signed by President Harding on July 2, 1921 ; and after diplomatic relations with Germany were resumed Alanson B. Houghton of New York was appointed ambassador to Berlin. Peace was also concluded with Austria and Hungary. But the policy of the Wilson administration in regard to Russia was maintained. Litvinov's overtures to Secretary Hughes for the recognition of the Bolshevist government and the resumption of trade relations with Russia were rebuffed. It was not until November, 1933, that a new Democratic administration recognized the Russian government.[1]

The Fordney-McCumber Tariff. It was not to be expected that the Republicans would let the Democratic tariff of 1913 stand. Every change of party rule since the Civil War had been followed immediately by an attempt to lower or raise the tariff. There was an additional reason after the World War for the restoration of protective duties. During the war many new industries had developed in the United States, — in dyestuffs, glass, chemicals, and drugs for example, — and the great increase of agricultural products in Canada threatened our Western farmers with serious competition. For their protection an emergency tariff was passed in May, 1921, raising the duties on wheat, corn, meat, and wool; and this was followed in the regular session by the Fordney-McCumber tariff of 1922, which more than restored the high rates of the Payne-Aldrich tariff of 1909 (p. 598). A unique feature of the new bill was the "flexible clause," which gave the President power to raise or lower the rates by 50 per cent whenever he found, upon investigation by the Tariff Commission, that they did not fairly equalize the difference between the costs of production here and in the competing foreign countries. By that clause Congress partially delegated to the President its own constitutional right to raise a revenue (lay taxes).

The Democrats denounced the bill as a "monstrosity" which would add $4,000,000,000 to the cost of living at a time when retail prices were 60 per cent higher than they had been in 1914, and which would discourage foreign trade at a time when the large debts owed to us by the European nations would have to be paid chiefly in goods. The revival of high protection was also

[1] The recognition was accorded on the distinct promise of the Russian negotiator, Litvinov, that there should be no attempt to spread communist propaganda in America. In the summer of 1935, however, our Secretary of State, Mr. Hull, had to protest rather sharply to Russia for encouraging, or at least permitting, the Third International, the communist organization at Moscow, to extend its missionary activities to this country.

condemned by the Democrats as a hindrance to the restoration of good feeling between the nations through economic co-operation, one of the first of President Wilson's Fourteen Points being the "removal of economic barriers." The high tariff did invite other countries to increase their selfish nationalism by erecting tariff walls against us and one another; but the predictions of the dire effects of the Fordney-McCumber tariff upon our prosperity turned out to be wrong. Prices actually declined and foreign trade increased during the years following the passage of the bill, while the Treasury receipts grew from $356,000,000 in 1922 to nearly $600,000,000 in 1928. It was argued by the opponents of the bill, however, that an increase of some $200,000,000 in customs revenues in a total budget of $3,500,000,000 by no means made up for the mistake of refusing to take the lead in persuading the nations to lower their tariff barriers for the sake of the encouragement of international trade.

Tax Revision. A subject on which there was a wide difference of opinion in Congress and among the people at large was the readjustment of the tax schedules after the war. Four fifths of the taxes during the war had been laid on the capital and the enormous earnings of big business. People of small incomes in America were subject to very much lower taxes than people of the same class in the European countries. For example, the highest rate levied on incomes of married people with incomes of not more than $4000 was 6 per cent in America, while an Englishman with an income above $800 paid a tax of $22\frac{1}{2}$ per cent. In 1920 more than 90 per cent of the income-tax payers in this country (with net incomes between $1000 and $5000) paid only 15.4 per cent of the total tax. On the other hand, the surtaxes on incomes over $1,000,000 reached as high as 65 per cent.

As business recovered from the slump of 1920-1921 the high taxes began to bring surpluses of hundreds of millions of dollars into the Treasury. The question was, Where should the taxes be reduced? The agricultural sections of the country, which had suffered most from the decline of prices after the war, wanted the more fortunate industrial interests to continue to pay heavily. There was a "bloc" (or group) of members from the agricultural states in Congress who backed this "soak the rich" program. They fought for maintaining surtax rates as high as 50 per cent. Secretary Mellon, however, favored the reduction of the tax on large incomes to a maximum of 25 per cent. He argued that the very high tax on these incomes was causing men of large wealth to put their money into the tax-exempt bonds of states and cities, rather than into the expansion of industry; and he cited the fact that the receipts of the Treasury from surtaxes on incomes above $300,000 had declined on this account from $248,000,000 in 1919 to $85,000,000 in 1921. The only way, he said, to induce capital to go into productive ventures was to lower the surtaxes sharply. Another evil effect of the placing of so much money in tax-exempt bonds was to encourage states and cities to increase their bonded debts to dangerously high figures and to spend money lavishly for roads, public buildings, palatial schoolhouses, courthouses, and the like. The state and municipal debts were growing at an alarming rate, while the national debt was being reduced. The contest between those who insisted that the big incomes should pay the bulk of the taxes and those who wanted capital relieved from the burden so that it would be encouraged to go into industry continued through Harding's brief administration (1921–1923).

The tax bill which resulted from the long months of discussion and which was signed by President Coolidge on June 2, 1924, was a compromise. It reduced the normal income-tax rates to 2 per cent on the first $4000, 4 per cent on the next $4000, and 6 per cent on more than $8000; but it left surtaxes running as high as 40 per cent. Growing prosperity in the few years immediately following led to further reductions in both normal and surtax rates. The important thing for the student to note is not the exact proportion of the taxes which the rich and the poor were asked to pay, but the fact that the war brought a great change in the *kind* of taxes on which the government depended chiefly for its income. The Republicans could not, if they wished, go back to the days of Hanna and McKinley, when the indirect taxes from imports and excises (levied on liquor, tobacco, playing cards, perfumery, etc.) furnished enough money to run the government. These taxes the consumer paid, without realizing it, in the prices of the goods he bought. But now (since the Sixteenth Amendment, of 1913) the government required him to pay a part of his income *directly* into the Treasury. He knew that he was being taxed; and, since no one likes to pay taxes, the rich, the middle class, and the poor were each interested in legislation which would put the chief burden on "the other fellow."

The Soldiers' Bonus. The question of tax reduction was complicated by the demands of the ex-service men for a cash bonus. We have seen (p. 739) that the government hoped, by its system of allotments and insurance for the soldiers of the World War, to avoid a repetition of the pension abuses which had followed the Civil War. Generous provision was made for the disabled, but the men who returned to civil life uninjured received nothing but the $60 bonus paid them on discharge. They compared their war pay of $30 a month (from which $15 was deducted for the wife at home and another $6.60 for premium on the insurance policy of $10,000) with the $150 or $200 a month which their neighbors had been earning meantime in a factory or shipyard. Uncle Sam was rich. He could afford to make up some of this difference to the boys who had been ready to risk their lives on the battlefields of France.

In March, 1922, the House for a second time (see page 739) passed a cash bonus bill, amid cheers from the crowded galleries where a delegation of ex-service men was massed. This time the Senate concurred by a vote of 47 to 22. President Harding had already expressed his disapproval of the bill, which it was estimated would cost the government nearly $3,000,000,000. In a letter to Chairman Fordney he said, "Any compensation legislation enacted at this time ought to carry with it the provision for raising the needed revenue." He reminded Congress that the Treasury had $6,000,000,000 of obligations to meet in the next sixteen months. On September 19 he vetoed the bonus bill, declaring that the soldiers themselves, while serving in the war, did not expect a bonus. The House immediately passed the bill over the veto (258 to 54), but the Senate failed of the necessary two-thirds majority to override the President's veto by a margin of four votes (44 to 28).

Undeterred by this second failure, advocates of the bonus continued their pressure upon Congress by a powerful lobby. In the spring of 1924, they got an "adjusted compensation" bill through both houses of Congress. The bill provided not for the direct payment of cash to the veterans but for the issuance to them of "certificates," or paid-up insurance policies, falling due in twenty years. The amount payable then to the soldier was based on an allowance of $1.25 a day if he had served abroad during the war and $1.00 a day if he had served at home. The maximum amount that a soldier could receive in 1945 under this arrangement was $1590. Nearly 3,500,000 ex-service men were entitled to receive these certificates, and their total claims on the government amounted to nearly $3,500,000,000. The men might borrow on them (as on a life-insurance policy) up to 22½ per cent of their face value, a figure later raised to 50 per cent. By the year 1931 the government loans to veterans on their certificates had reached $330,000,000. President Coolidge vetoed the "adjusted compensation" bill on May 15, 1924, but four days later it was passed by large majorities in both houses over his veto. This was not the end of the bonus question, however. Dissatisfied with the prospect of waiting until 1945 for the payment of their certificates, the veterans began to press, when hard times came in the early 1930's, for the immediate conversion of them into cash by the government. We shall see in a later chapter what forms this pressure took.

The European War Debts. Besides the tariff, tax revision, and the bonus, a fourth financial problem of the administration was the question of whether and how the Allied nations should pay their debts to the United States, which on September 30, 1922, amounted to over $9,000,000,000. More than 90 per cent of this was owed by Great Britain ($4,136,000,000), France ($2,293,000,000), and Italy ($1,648,000,000). Various reasons were advanced by people in America as well as in the Allied countries why we should wipe these debts off the books. First, it was argued that, as we had delayed entering the war until it was nearly over, we should consider this money contribution as a fair offset to the suffering and loss of life which the Allies had endured in the "common cause." In the second place, we had made many times $9,000,000,000 out of the war during the two and a half years of our neutrality. Thirdly, the good will of Great Britain and the other debtor countries in future trade relations was worth more to us than the money they owed us. And, finally, since they could repay the huge sums only by the shipment of goods to our country, how could we demand payment and at the same time protect our home industries by high tariffs? Our government, however, took (and has since maintained) the ground that the war debts should not be canceled. They were represented by Liberty Bonds sold to our people, the interest on which had to be raised from our people by taxation. At the same time, our government has always been willing to consult the "capacity to pay" of the debtor nations and to make the terms of payment as easy for them as possible.

Early in 1922 President Harding appointed a committee to negotiate with our debtors, and, the following January, Great Britain agreed to pay in installments spread over a period of sixty-two years, with interest at an average of 3.3 per cent. The arrangement with France was much more liberal, cutting the principal of the debt down about 50 per cent and the interest rate to 1.6 per cent. With Italy the settlement was still more generous, canceling over 70 per cent of the debt and charging an interest of .04 per cent only on the balance. By 1927 we had made contracts with sixteen debtor nations to pay us eventually about $11,500,000,000. At first most of them paid their semiannual installments in June and December; but one by one they began to default on these payments, until Finland remained the only country to pay. Although the agreements have not been canceled and our government still holds officially that the debts should be paid, the question has become practically dead. We have no way to *force* the governments of the European countries to pay except to try to collect the money at the point of the bayonet; and that, of course, we should not dream of doing. Neither we nor our debtors any longer reckon payments on the war debts as items of the budget. The billions that we lent to the Allies have, in fact, become a contribution of the United States toward the winning of the war.

Labor Troubles. There was no such violent and widespread epidemic of strikes in Harding's term as had marked the year 1919, when 2665 labor conflicts had involved over 4,000,000 workers. Yet there were serious troubles in the mining and transportation industries. An attempt to unionize all the labor in the West Virginia coal fields in the spring of 1921 led to such scenes of rioting that Governor Morgan was obliged to declare martial law in Mingo County and President Harding sent Federal troops to restore order in the region. The next April 600,000 miners went out on strike, bringing operations to a standstill in 6000 of the 7800 bituminous and anthracite mines of the country, and causing a daily loss of 1,500,000 tons of coal. There was considerable violence, notably at Herrin, Illinois, where a battle between the strikers and the strikebreakers resulted in the death of nineteen miners.

In 1919 President Wilson had broken the coal strike by invoking the wartime Lever Act (p. 696); but now that peace with Germany had been concluded, there was nothing left for President Harding to rely upon but the powers of persuasion. He called the mine-owners in conference at Washington and urged them to make a settlement. "I cannot permit you to depart," he said, "without reminding you that coal is a national necessity. . . . The freedom of action on the part of the workers and the employers does not measure in importance with the public welfare and national security." On the day after the conference he sent telegrams to the governors of twenty-eight coal-producing states, offering them Federal protection should they find it necessary to take over and operate the mines. The persistent pressure of public opinion brought the strike to an end after four months, and Congress, on the President's request, established a National Coal Commission, to study the situation fully and to recommend measures for securing a steady supply of coal at a fair price to the consumers and for averting further strikes in the industry. President John Lewis of the United Mine Workers asserted before the Coal Commission, in May, 1923, that the only way to do away with repeated coal strikes was to unionize the industry completely.

In the midst of the coal strike three hundred thousand railroad shopmen, dissatisfied with the rulings of the Railway Labor Board under the Esch-Cummins Act (p. 749), laid down their tools. They were supported by the railroad brotherhoods and the American Federation of Labor. The strike was even more serious than the coal strike, because the personal safety of the traveling public depended on keeping the locomotives and cars in proper repair in the railroad shops. Attorney-General Daugherty took the ground that the strike was the work of communist agitators who took their instructions direct from Russia. He declared that if the "Red Borers" were allowed to get control of the railroads, "from that hour our time-tables and freight rates would be made out in Moscow, and the first step would be taken in a revolution to overthrow our government and substitute a Soviet regime." Whether he really believed that such a danger threatened, or was merely using the "Red menace" to divert the growing criticism of his management of the Department of Justice, is uncertain. At any rate, he induced President Harding to go before Congress with a special message, on August 18, denouncing the strike:

We must assert the doctrine that in the Republic the first obligation and the first allegiance of every citizen, high and low, is to his government. . . . We have a state of lawlessness shocking to every conception of American ideals. . . . Deserted continental trains in the desert regions of the Southwest have revealed a cruelty and contempt for law on the part of railroad employees, who have conspired to paralyze transportation. And lawlessness and violence in a hundred places have revealed the failure of the striking unions to hold their forces to law obedience. . . . I am resolved to use all the power of the government to maintain transportation and sustain the right of men to work. . . . There are existing laws by which to settle the prevailing disputes. There are statutes forbidding conspiracy to hinder interstate commerce. There are laws to assure the highest possible safety in railway service. It is my purpose to invoke these laws, civil and criminal, against all offenders alike.

Two weeks later the Attorney-General went in person to Chicago and secured from a Federal judge an injunction forbidding the strikers to picket shops, to hinder the inspection or repair of locomotives or cars, to obstruct the movement of trains, to trespass on the premises of the railroads where repair work was going on, to intimidate any of the employees of the roads, or even to communicate by telegraph or telephone to encourage to strike. This "most sweeping injunction ever issued in the history of labor disputes in America" was assailed by labor as a violation of constitutional rights and an attempt to reduce the workers to a "condition of slavery." The strikers had committed no crime, said Mr. Gompers, in "quitting work when conditions became intolerable." But the courts upheld the injunction, as in the case of the Pullman strike of 1894. The shopmen's strike was quelled by this drastic action of the government. According to figures made public early in 1924 by the Department of Justice, it had caused nineteen deaths by violence, wrought the destruction of millions of dollars' worth of railroad property, reduced the income of the roads by 20 per cent in 1923, and cost the government nearly two million dollars for special deputies sworn in by the Attorney-General to preserve order.

The Immigration Laws. Because America has made it her boast to be a land of refuge for the oppressed and of opportunity for the seekers of new fortunes, our doors have until quite recently stood wide open to the immigrants from the Old World. In 1914 the high-water mark was reached, with a total of 1,218,480 immigrants, of whom more than 800,000 came from Italy, Russia, and Austria-Hungary, and 260,000 were illiterates of fourteen years of age or over. During the war the numbers of immigrants fell off; but when the war was over, there was danger that we might be flooded by refugees from the distressed countries of Europe. "The world is preparing to move to America," wrote the Commissioner of Immigration. The war had also revealed some alarming facts in regard to our foreign population. Many immigrants were neglecting to become naturalized American citizens, retaining their real allegiance to the lands from which they had come. Radical labor agitators were suspected of "taking their orders from Moscow." Over one thousand newspapers in the United States were printed in foreign languages, and over 10 per cent of the people here could not speak English. American labor leaders were disturbed over the influx of hordes of foreigners who were accustomed to work for low wages, and patriotic citizens generally were alarmed at the numbers of newcomers who had no knowledge of American institutions or ideals. If we were not to become what Theodore Roosevelt called "an international boarding-house," some step must be taken to limit the unrestricted immigration of the prewar days.

The method adopted was the quota system. On May 19, 1921, President Harding signed the Emergency Quota Act, which limited the number of immigrants that any country could send to the United States in any given year to 3 per cent of its people who were here according to the census of 1910. But this law was unsatisfactory, because a large number of immigrants from the eastern and southern countries of Europe had come here before 1910 and hence had large quotas (Russia, 34,284; Poland, 25,827; Italy, 42,057). To turn the balance more in favor of the northern countries, such as the British Isles, Germany, Norway, and Sweden, which had sent us so many welcome immigrants in the nineteenth century, a new law was passed in 1924, fixing the quota at 2 per cent of the number of the nationals of each country in the United States according to the census of 1890. The new law cut down the Russian quota to 2248, the Italian to 3845, and the Polish to 5982, while it permitted 63,574 to come from the British Isles, 51,227 from Germany, and 9561 from Sweden. The new law also provided that after July 1, 1927, only 150,000 immigrants should be admitted annually, divided among the several countries in proportion to the numbers of their nationals here according to the census of 1920.

Because the act of 1924 forbade the entrance into our country of all aliens who were ineligible to citizenship, it drew from the Japanese ambassador at Washington a respectful but forceful protest to our State Department. Japanese exclusion, said the ambassador, was not only a violation of the "Gentlemen's Agreement" of 1907 (p. 577) but also an affront to his nation from which "grave consequences" might arise. Though the Japanese quota under the new act would have been but 142 immigrants a year, and President Coolidge asked that the exclusion clause be taken out of the act, Congress refused to change the law. The net result of the immigration laws was to put a stop to the steady flow of aliens to our shores. The foreign-born population of 13,225,000 in 1920 increased only 0.6 per cent in the next decade. "The doors of the United States as the historic haven of the oppressed in all lands were now closed."

The Washington Conference. The principal event in the Harding administration was the Washington conference for the limitation of naval armaments and for the insurance of better relations in the area of the Pacific. Although many months had passed since the signing of the armistice, the burden of military and naval expenditures had not been lightened. There were more men under arms in Europe than there had been in 1914, and our own naval program called for the construction of over 800,000 tons of warships to bring us to an equality with Great Britain. As the nation with the largest naval construction program in the world, we had the opportunity of showing our sincerity in the cause of peace by starting the movement for the reduction of naval armaments.

On May 15, 1921, Senator Borah proposed an amendment to the huge naval appropriation bill of $494,000,000, authorizing the President to invite Great Britain and Japan, our chief naval competitors,[1] to a conference in Washington to discuss the possibility of ending the mad competition. The amendment

[1] The relative position of the three chief naval powers in 1921 was as follows:

	TONNAGE COMPLETED	TONNAGE PROJECTED	TOTAL
Great Britain . . .	1,588,442	76,890	1,665,332
United States . . .	779,173	842,109	1,621,282
Japan	340,596	328,460	669,056

passed without a dissenting vote, and the President sent invitations in August not only to Great Britain and Japan, but also to France and Italy as important naval powers, and to China, Holland, Belgium, and Portugal as nations with large interests in the Far East. Delegates from eight European and Asiatic powers therefore met at Washington for the opening of the conference on November 12, 1921. After a graceful speech of welcome by President Harding, Secretary Hughes, the chairman, came straight to the point with the proposal of "a practical program which shall at once be put into execution." He suggested a "naval holiday" for at least ten years, during which no new battleships should be built, and proposed "scrapping" a number of capital ships (that is, warships of over 10,000 tons or carrying guns of over eight inches bore) either already built or in process of construction. The United States was ready to scrap 30 ships totaling 845,700 tons. Great Britain was asked to scrap 19 ships of 583,375 tons, and Japan 17 ships of 448,928 tons, a total reduction of about 2,000,000 tons in the world's navies. Hughes proposed a naval ratio of 5 : 5 : 3 for the United States, Great Britain, and Japan in capital ships, and France and Italy agreed to an allotment a little more than half that of Japan (175,000 tons to 313,000). Great Britain wanted to have the submarine abolished entirely as "an inhuman agent of warfare," but France held out for the nonlimitation of submarines and cruisers. Secretary Hughes's attempt to include the discussion of land armaments was also vetoed by Premier Briand of France, who made an impassioned plea for the necessity of a strong army to defend his country against a populous and vindictive Germany. So the naval disarmament was limited to large battleships. The United States gave up the building program of 1916, which would have made us by 1924 the strongest naval power in the world, and Great Britain abandoned her long-established policy of maintaining a navy equal to the combined strength of her two strongest possible rivals.

The Treaties. Besides the five-power treaty for the limitation of capital warships, the conference framed a number of other treaties. It prohibited the use of the submarine as a commerce-destroyer, condemned poison gas in warfare, provided for Japan's return of the province of Shantung to China, guaranteed the integrity of China and the continuance of the open-door policy, regulated the Chinese customs duties, and allotted the use of the cables in the Pacific. A four-power treaty between the United States, Great Britain, France, and Japan bound the signers to respect one another's possessions in the Pacific and to submit to a joint conference any dispute arising out of these possessions. It was the nearest thing to an "alliance" with foreign powers that we had entered into since the French alliance of 1778. On the adjournment of the conference President Harding submitted the sheaf of treaties to the Senate, asking for a speedy ratification to prove that our professed desire for world peace was not "a hollow mockery." The treaties were all ratified within a few weeks, the only one that caused any opposition in the Senate being the four-power pact of the Pacific.

The Washington Conference has been severely criticized, and even called futile, because it failed to stop competition in submarines, cruisers, destroyers, aircraft, and land armaments. Critics pointed out that we spent 174 per cent more on our navy in the year following the conference than we had in 1914, and declared that we had made real sacrifices by scrapping uncompleted modern battleships whereas Great Britain had scrapped only old ones. We were left, they said, with a navy actually inferior to that of Japan, and it would cost us $800,000,000 to build up to Great Britain's strength. But in spite of all that it failed to accomplish, the Washington Conference was a step forward in international co-operation and good will. Especially were the treaties for "the pacification of the Pacific" a notable contribution to world peace.

Wickedness in High Places. President Harding sincerely wished (in his better moments) to be a good executive. He was impressed by the responsibilities of his high office and declared that he meant to surround himself with "the best minds" of the party — men like Hughes, Hoover, Root, and Taft. But, unfortunately, he had been surrounded with men of an entirely different type in his career as an Ohio politician. He was not able to associate mentally or morally with the best minds, because his own mind and character were on a lower level. He had been put into the Presidency not because he was a leader but because the Senatorial clique and the self-seeking politicians who had secured his nomination believed that he would be easy to manage — as he was. The result of the elevation to the highest position in the land of a man without statesmanship or strong moral fiber, but with a good-natured and dogged devotion to his old political pals, was a tragedy both for him personally and for the nation. It opened the way for advancement to high places of crooks and grafters. Rascality always exists; but in no other administration in our history (with the possible exception of President Grant's) has our government been so disgraced by rascals as it was during the two short years of Harding's term.

An ex-Congressman and ex-service man, Colonel Thomas W. Miller, was given the post of Alien Property Custodian and proceeded to accept graft for supporting false claims to the property of the American Metal Company, for which he was later sentenced to eighteen months' imprisonment. Colonel Charles R. Forbes, a member of the executive committee of the American Legion in the state of Washington, was entrusted with the administration of the Veterans' Bureau, from which he stole several hundred thousand dollars' worth of supplies before he was discovered and sent to Leavenworth jail. "Jess" Smith, a notorious member of the "Ohio gang," came to Washington, where he acted as collector and distributor of the graft taken from violators of the prohibition law. He committed suicide in the apartment which he shared with the Attorney-General when he suspected that his game was up, as did Forbes's chief counsel, Cramer. Attorney-General Daugherty himself was threatened with impeachment, and was brought to trial on suspicion of sharing with Jess Smith and with his brother Mal S. Daugherty in the graft; but the indictment was dismissed after the jury had twice failed to come to a verdict. President Coolidge then demanded his resignation.

The Oil Leases. The most sensational of all the scandals of the administration — one which did not come out until after

Harding's death — was the attempted theft of the nation's oil reserves. Oil had come to play the chief role in our natural resources, and a group of wealthy oil magnates, such as Jake Hamon, national Republican committeeman from Oklahoma, Harry F. Sinclair of New York, and Edward L. Doheny of Los Angeles, had exercised an influence in the Republican convention of 1920 which rivaled that of the Senatorial clique. Oil was a prime necessity of our government. The oil-burning ships of the navy used 137,500 barrels in 1911 and 6,934,500 barrels in 1919. In 1912 the government had set aside, for the navy, oil reserve No. 1 at Elk Hills, California; and in 1915 reserve No. 3 at Teapot Dome, Wyoming. They were under the charge of the Secretary of the Navy. When wells drilled in the neighborhood threatened to draw the oil off from these reserves, the government, instead of taking out its own oil and storing it in tanks for the use of the navy, decided to lease the lands to private operators who should contract to build tanks and supply the navy with fuel oil.

Since the leasing of public lands was a customary duty of the Department of the Interior rather than of the Navy Department, Secretary Fall, with the consent of Secretary Denby of the Navy, secured an executive order from the President transferring the business of leasing the reserves from Denby's department to his own. Fall then proceeded secretly and without asking for competitive bids to lease the Teapot Dome reserve to Sinclair, who had made a very large contribution to the Republican campaign fund, and the Elk Hills reserve to his intimate friend Edward L. Doheny. Doheny is said to have remarked that he expected to make one hundred million dollars out of the lease. At the same time Secretary Fall's private fortunes, which had been in a bad way, began to show marvelous improvement. He paid up his back taxes, restocked his ranch at Three Rivers, New Mexico, and acquired additional land. On March 4, 1923, he resigned from the cabinet. In spite of the tricky measures adopted by the group of oil barons to keep secret their plundering of the national navy reserves, suspicion was aroused in the summer of 1923, culminating in the appointment of a Senate committee in October, under Thomas J. Walsh of Montana, to investigate the leases. From the 3586 pages of testimony taken by the committee a sordid story emerged. Fall had accepted a "loan" of one hundred thousand dollars from Doheny, without interest or security. Sinclair, Doheny, and their associates had organized a bogus company with a Canadian name to cover up their theft and had attempted to distribute hush money in the shape of bonds to various influential members of the Republican party, somewhat as the Crédit Mobilier had done in the Grant Administration (p. 446). Sinclair and Doheny were brought to trial in a District of Columbia court for "conspiracy to defraud the government," but escaped conviction through clever lawyers (1926). The next year the oil leases were canceled by the Supreme Court of the United States, which used the words "fraud," "conspiracy," and "corruption" in its decision. Two of the "conspirators" fled to Europe to escape testifying. Fall was finally convicted of accepting a bribe from Doheny, and in July, 1931, was sent to serve a year's sentence in the Federal jail at Santa Fe, New Mexico.

The Death of President Harding. On June 30, 1923, the President and Mrs. Harding, with a party of sixty-five, started for a tour across the country and a visit to Alaska. The President was far from well when he left Washington, his splendid physique having been undermined by two years of desperate labor to fulfill duties for which he knew he was not fitted. But more serious than his physical health was his mental state. Though the scandals of the administration had not yet come to light, he was aware of the suspicions that hovered over the men to whom he had so unwisely given his confidence. Again and again he asked Secretary Hoover and others of his companions on the trip what a man should do who had been betrayed by his friends. He dreaded the revelations which he knew were waiting on his return to Washington. On the boat back from Alaska he was taken ill with what seemed to be ptomaine poisoning. When he reached San Francisco his condition became worse, though it was not considered dangerous. The country was therefore shocked when the news came that he had died suddenly in the early evening of August 2 while his wife was reading a story to him in his room at the Palace Hotel. Throngs stood with bared heads at the railroad stations as the funeral train crossed the country. The President of the United States had passed away, and the voices of criticism were drowned in the genuine manifestations of sorrow at the moment. Eulogies were pronounced on the dead President, and a project was started of erecting a marble memorial tomb at Marion.

The history of the Harding Memorial is perhaps the best index to the judgment which the American people came to hold of the man as the years passed. The beautiful monument was completed not long after his death. But year after year went by before a President of the United States could bring himself to go to Marion to dedicate the memorial, and when at last President Hoover did so on June 16, 1931, it was to speak not of a great leader or benefactor of his country but of a "man whose soul was seared by a great disillusionment," and whose trust had been betrayed by men who had been "proved in the courts of the land" to be the betrayers also of their country. The Harding administration marked what William Allen White has called "the zero hour of our courage and faith."

TERMS TO BE MASTERED

"normalcy"	surtaxes	"naval holiday"
the "Ohio gang"	"adjusted compensation"	the Four-Power Pact
budget bureau	capacity to pay	oil reserves
"flexible clause"	immigration quota	capital ships

FOR SUPPLEMENTARY READING

W. A. WHITE, *Masks in a Pageant*, pp. 389–434; H. M. DAUGHERTY and THOMAS DIXON, *The Inside Story of the Harding Tragedy*; C. W. THOMPSON, *Presidents I've Known*, chap. xxv; F. L. ALLEN, *Only Yesterday*, chap. vi; R. L. BUELL, *The Washington Conference*; W. MCDOUGALL, *Is America Safe for Democracy?*; H. E. BARNES, *World Politics in Modern Civilization*, pp. 555–574; The Pageant of America, Vol. XV, pp. 339–341, 343–347; *America*, Vol. XII, pp. 237–245; R. L. GARIS, *Immigration Restriction*, chaps. vi, vii; GINO SPERANZA, "The Immigration Peril," in the *World's Work*, Vol. XLVII, pp. 57 f., 147 f., 256 f., 399 f., 479 f.; E. A. ROSS, *The Old World in the New*, pp. 95–119; MARK SULLIVAN, *Our Times*, Vol. VI, chaps. i–xii; H. S. COMMAGER, *Documents of American History*, Vol. II, pp. 352, 361–365, 371–374.

Topics for Reports

1. Should we Cancel the War Debts? C. A. Beard, "A Bankruptcy Fire Sale," in the *American Mercury*, July, 1927; F. W. Peabody, *A Square Deal to our War Partners*; Charles Merz, "The War-Debt Tangle Approaches a Climax," in *New York Times*, Sunday, January 24, 1932; R. L. Buell, "Our Stake Abroad," in *New York Times*, Sunday, February 7, 1932; A. E. Smith, "War Debts," in the *New Outlook*, Vol. CLXI, pp. 9 f.; W. Lippmann and W. O. Scroggs, *The United States in World Affairs*, 1931, pp. 132–183.

2. The Washington Conference on Naval Limitation. Charles Seymour, "The Washington Conference," Encyclopædia Britannica, Vol. XXXII, Twelfth Edition; A. H. Abbott, "The League's Disarmament Activities and the Washington Conference," in *Political Science Quarterly*, Vol. XXVIII, pp. 1–24; H. C. Bywater, "The Limitation of Naval Armaments," in the *Atlantic Monthly*, Vol. CXXIX, pp. 259–269; H. G. Wells, *Washington and the Riddle of Peace*; A. Bullard, *The ABC's of Disarmament and the Pacific Problems*.

3. The Restriction of Immigration. James Bryce, *The American Commonwealth*, Vol. II, pp. 469–490; P. F. Hall, *Immigration*, pp. 309–323; John P. Gavit, *Americans by Choice*; R. Mayo-Smith, *Emigration and Immigration*, pp. 266–302; Adams and Sumner, *Labor Problems*, pp. 80–111; "Our Foreign-Born Citizens," in *National Geographic Magazine*, Vol. XXXI, pp. 95–130; A. H. Eaton, *Immigrant Gifts to American Life*.

4. Teapot Dome. M. E. Werner, *Privileged Characters*, chap. ii; Mark Sullivan, *Our Times*, Vol. VI, pp. 272–349; F. L. Allen, *Only Yesterday*, chap. vi; John Ise, *The United States Oil Policy*; M. E. Ravage, *Teapot Dome*; H. S. Commager, *Documents*, Vol. II, p. 371.

Questions Suggested by the Chapter

1. Who were the most distinguished members of Harding's cabinet? **2.** What was Harding's attitude toward the League of Nations? **3.** What was the object of the emergency tariff of 1921? **4.** When did the United States recognize Russia? **5.** What effect did our high protective tariff have upon our foreign trade? **6.** How did our income taxes compare with those of England after the war? **7.** What were Secretary Mellon's arguments for reducing the high surtaxes? **8.** Why did Harding veto the bonus bill of 1922? **9.** What substitute for a cash bonus was passed over Coolidge's veto in 1924? **10.** What arguments were advanced in favor of canceling the war debts? **11.** What European country continued to pay the interest on its war debt to the United States? **12.** Why was it easier for Wilson to stop the coal strike of 1919 than for Harding to stop that of 1922? **13.** Why did our government restrict immigration after the war? **14.** What types of warships did the Washington Conference not limit? **15.** What provisions did the conference make concerning the Pacific? **16.** Why was the conference criticized as "futile"? **17.** What was there "fraudulent" about Secretary Fall's leases of the oil reserves? **18.** Why was Fall sent to jail? **19.** To what traits in Harding's character do you attribute his failure? **20.** For what was Charles R. Forbes sent to jail?

CHAPTER THIRTY-ONE

(💲)

WORSHIPING THE GOLDEN CALF

Calvin Coolidge, Conservative. Very early in the morning of August 3, 1923, the news of President Harding's death came to the Coolidge farmhouse in the sleepy little village of Plymouth Notch, Vermont, where the Vice-President was spending his summer vacation. The family was roused from bed and came down to the parlor, where, by the light of the kerosene lamp, John Coolidge, justice of the peace, administered the oath of office of President of the United States to his son. There have been striking transitions in the White House, like that from the cold, austere, and studious John Quincy Adams to the dictatorial frontiersman Andrew Jackson or from the wise and patient Lincoln to the obstinate, egotistical Johnson; but none more remarkable than the replacement of Harding by Calvin Coolidge. Instead of the handsome, genial, expansive "good mixer," surrounded by boon companions and baffled by the problems of statesmanship which exceeded his powers of understanding and his strength of character, we had a plain, silent, well-educated President, a Puritan Yankee, who placed responsibility and thrift at the top of the list of virtues and was as honest as the granite of his Vermont hills. After graduating from Amherst College in 1895, Coolidge made his home in Northampton, Massachusetts, studying law in the old-fashioned way in the office of a successful firm and gradually entering politics. For a score of years from 1899 on, he advanced steadily through elective offices (city councilman, city solicitor, member of the legislature at Boston, mayor of Northampton, state senator, lieutenant governor) until in 1918 he became governor of the commonwealth. We have seen how his rather belated summons of the state militia in the Boston police strike of 1919

WARREN G. HARDING   CALVIN COOLIDGE

(p. 747) brought him national recognition and the nomination in 1920, on the Republican ticket, for the Vice-Presidency.

Coolidge had never been in Washington before he went to preside over the Senate the next spring. Indeed, he had scarcely been beyond the borders of Massachusetts, and "home" for him and his charming, vivacious wife and his two sons John and Calvin, Jr., was still the half of the double house in Northampton which he rented for twenty-seven dollars a month. For all his personal parsimony, however, Coolidge was "a little brother of the rich." He believed in the Hamiltonian doctrine of close and cordial relations between the government and the moneyed powers. He shared neither Roosevelt's zeal to bring the great trust magnates to the heel of the law nor Wilson's ideal of the new freedom for the little man in industry. "The business of America is business," he said in an address of December, 1923; and by "business" he meant big business. He sought no indictments of the trusts, and his appointments to important boards like the Tariff Commission and the Federal Trade Commission contained no names of reformers or disturbers of the methods of business approved by Republican leaders from

Hanna to Mellon. In short, the new President was a conservative, quietly resisting the "socialistic" tendencies of groups in Congress such as the "farm bloc" or the "soak the rich" advocates, and rejoicing in the renewed prosperity of the middle 1920's, which brought large surpluses into the Treasury and a consequent steady reduction of the public debt and taxes.

The Coolidge Policies. In his first address to Congress,[1] on December 6, 1923, President Coolidge set forth at considerable length the policies from which he did not depart during the five and a half years of his administration. As to foreign affairs, we had "definitely refused to adopt and ratify the League of Nations" and had no intention of reopening the question, although we might join the World Court of International Justice under proper guaranties for the interests of the United States. Our government offered no objections to carrying on trade with Russia, but we could not recognize the Soviet regime. The debts owed us by the Allies were not to be canceled. Our country had no desire to be "an oppressive creditor," but "would maintain the principle that financial obligations between nations are also moral obligations which international faith and honor require should be discharged." Our main problems, however, were domestic ones. For seven years the people had borne a tremendous burden of national and local taxation without complaint. This burden must now be lightened by the stimulus of business and the reduction of government expenses. The protective tariff (of 1922) was bringing the country "an abounding prosperity," and, except for the occasional adjustment of rates allowed to the President by the "flexible clause" (p. 765), the tariff should not be changed — as, indeed, it was not during the Coolidge administration. The government must take adequate care of the veterans of the war, through hospital relief and compensation for the disabled, support for their dependents, and vocational training for the unemployed. "But," added the President, "I do not favor the granting of a bonus."

[1] President Coolidge followed Wilson and Harding in appearing before Congress in person to deliver this first annual message, but after that he went back to the old custom of sending his messages to be read by the clerk.

The great plant which the government had developed at Muscle Shoals, on the Tennessee River, for the production of water power and nitrates should be sold to private operators, subject to the right of the government to retake it in time of war. Immigration should continue to be restricted, in order that America "be kept American." The debt-burdened farmers must find relief not by looking to the government to fix their prices or buy their products but by "simple and direct methods put into operation by the farmer himself," such as better planning of crops and co-operative marketing. Loans should be available to them, however (through the Federal Farm Banks), as "a temporary and emergency expedient." Other paragraphs on the railroads, shipping, the enforcement of prohibition, the civil service, the army and navy,[1] the Department of Justice, education and welfare, reclamation, and highways completed the long message. It was no clarion call to a "new freedom" or a "new deal," but rather a counsel to hold fast to the old virtues of honor, courage, and "work done squarely and unwasted days," which had made our country what it was.

Social Demoralization. In sharp contrast to the President's counsel and example, however, were many signs of a low tone of public and private morals. The decade of the 1920's was one upon which, in spite of its material prosperity, the American people must look back with a sense of shame. Probably it was a reaction from the tense idealism of the war that was chiefly responsible for the moral let-down. Young people, feeling that their elders had made a terrible mess of the world, began to question the entire moral and religious bases of a society which they saw permeated with suspicion, hypocrisy, and greed. A flood of books appeared glorifying rebellion against the accepted

[1] The problem of furthering world peace while increasing national armaments (a problem as difficult as squaring the circle) was never better illustrated than in the President's short paragraph on the army and navy:

The army is the guarantee of the security of our citizens at home; the navy is the guarantee of the security of our citizens abroad. Both of these services should be strengthened rather than weakened. Additional planes are needed for the army, and additional submarines for the navy. . . . We want no more competitive armaments. We want no more war. But we want no weakness that invites imposition. A people who neglect their national defense are putting in jeopardy their national honor.

ideas of sexual conduct, exalting cynicism and pessimism, and "debunking" (or showing up the weaker sides of) the men whom generations of young Americans had been taught to revere as heroes.

The enormous gains to be made out of the violation of the prohibition law produced a class of desperate criminals who did not stop at murder to protect their ill-gotten millions; and the high-powered automobile, from which a shower of machine-gun bullets was sprayed upon a victim, allowed the murderers to make their "get away" all too easily. Chicago, under the terrorism of the infamous Al Capone, was the outstanding center of crime, but the other great cities were not far behind in their record of lawlessness. The rate of homicides in the United States was more than fifteen times that in England, and the rates of insurance against burglary and robbery (which cost the American people about $300,000,000 a year) were higher than those of any other country in the world. In the ten years between 1914 and 1924 the premiums paid in burglary insurance in the United States rose from $1,377,000 to $26,513,000. Nor did the law begin to cope with the "crime wave." According to an estimate of the New York Crime Commission in 1925, more than four out of five of the indictments for major crimes failed to bring any punishment. One newspaper cynically remarked that the felon's chances of escape were about ninety-seven in a hundred. Sensational murder trials were treated by the country like Roman holidays, while respectable journalists, authors, and even clergymen reaped golden profits from reporting the scandalous details to an eager public. The Ku Klux Klan of the post-Civil-War days was revived and quickly enrolled a membership of several millions whose mission was the persecution of Negroes, Jews, and Roman Catholics. At the height of its power in the middle 1920's the Klan controlled the politics of half a dozen states of the Union. It is not a pleasant thing to contemplate such facts, but without noticing them one cannot understand the plight to which our country was brought at the close of the decade by the worship of the false gods of greed, intolerance, and contempt for law.

The Election of 1924. The Presidential year opened with the country all astir over the investigation of the oil scandals of the Harding administration. Because Coolidge had sat with the Harding cabinet, the Democrats attempted to discredit him; but the people at large believed him (as they did Hughes and Hoover) when he denied any knowledge of the things that had gone on in the departments of Denby, Daugherty, and Fall. He was nominated on the first ballot at Cleveland, by 1065 votes to 34 for Senator La Follette of Wisconsin and 10 for Senator Johnson of California. After Governor Lowden of Illinois had declined, General Charles G. Dawes, Director of the Budget, was named for Vice-President. The Democrats met at Madison Square Garden, New York, on June 24. For five days the delegates wrangled in the sweltering heat over whether the platform should advocate our entrance into the League of Nations (defeated by a vote of 353 to 742) or denounce the Ku Klux Klan (defeated by 541 to 546). Though there were a dozen candidates for the nomination, the contest was narrowed down to ex-Secretary William G. McAdoo of California, the champion of the "drys" and the rural sections of the South and West, and Governor Alfred E. Smith of New York, a "wet" and a Roman Catholic, who was supported by the delegates from the industrial regions of the East, with its large cities and teeming foreign population. After the deadlock had continued for 102 ballots, the wearied convention turned to John W. Davis of West Virginia, an able conservative lawyer, who had served as ambassador to London in the later years of the Wilson Administration. Governor Charles W. Bryan of Nebraska, brother of the "Peerless Leader," was named for Vice-President, to satisfy the more radical elements of the party.

On the adjournment of the Republican convention, Senator La Follette of Wisconsin repudiated Coolidge, who, he said, "had literally turned his back on the farmer," and organized an Independent-Progressive party, which was launched at Cleveland on July 4, with La Follette and Senator Burton K. Wheeler (Democrat) of Montana as the candidates. The Socialist party, which had cast nearly a million votes for Debs in

ROBERT M. LA FOLLETTE   SAMUEL GOMPERS

1920, endorsed the La Follette ticket, as did the Farmer-Labor party and the American Federation of Labor. La Follette stood for the abolition of private monopoly, the government ownership of the railroads, the popular election of Federal judges, the prohibition of injunctions, generous measures of relief for the farmers, a child-labor amendment to the Constitution, the outlawry of war, an amendment giving Congress the power to override a decision of the Supreme Court which should declare a law unconstitutional, and various measures of "direct government" (initiative, referendum, recall) advocated since the close of the nineteenth century.

La Follette's candidacy caused great anxiety in the ranks of the two major parties. It was predicted that he would carry enough states of the West to prevent a majority in the Electoral College and thus throw the election into the House of Representatives. But election day confirmed the usual fate of third parties. Though La Follette rolled up a popular vote of 4,667,312 (half a million larger than Roosevelt's "Bull Moose" vote in 1912), he carried only his own state of Wisconsin, with 13 electoral votes. Coolidge swept the country, with a popular plurality of 7,000,000, and with 382 electoral votes to 136 for Davis, who carried only Oklahoma and the states of the former Southern Confederacy. The Republicans won a majority of 60 in the House and 15 in the Senate. A novel feature of the election was the choice of 123 women for seats in state legislatures, and the election of two women governors, Mrs. Miriam A. Ferguson of Texas and Mrs. Nellie T. Ross of Wyoming.

The President and Congress. President Coolidge met determined resistance in Congress both in his domestic and in his foreign policies. Those members who had joined the La Follette revolt were punished by being deprived of their positions on influential committees, and they retaliated by antagonizing the administration. The Senate refused to ratify a number of Presidential appointments, including even a cabinet member; and in both houses the administration's plans for tax revision, prohibition enforcement, the funding of the European debts, railroad consolidation, the naval program, and intervention in Latin America encountered bitter hostility. The mid-term elections of 1926 saw the Republican majority wiped out in the Senate and reduced from 60 to 36 in the House.

However, in spite of such rebuffs as the passage of the bonus bill over his veto (p. 769), the rejection of his recommendation to lease Muscle Shoals to private corporations, the refusal of the Senate to heed his advice to join the World Court, the passage of bills for farm relief which he twice vetoed effectively, President Coolidge went calmly on his way, neither scolding Congress, like Cleveland, nor driving it, like Wilson, nor appealing constantly to the people for justification, like Theodore Roosevelt. And he retained the confidence of the people of the country, partly because of their respect for his integrity and diligence, and perhaps even more because they were inclined to attribute to him the mounting prosperity which the country enjoyed during his administration. President Coolidge had the rare good fortune to be carried along on a wave of business recovery and unprecedented material comfort. The Federal taxes were constantly reduced (from forty-five dollars per capita in 1921 to thirty-six dollars in 1928)[1]; but in spite of the cuts in income taxes, surpluses appeared on the Treasury books at the close of every fiscal year. The national debt, which at the close of the World War had stood at about $26,000,000,000, was reduced by June 30, 1928, to $17,500,000,000.

The Farmer's Burden. Not all the industries of the country shared in the prosperity of the Coolidge administration. It was a "spotty" prosperity. That is, there were spots, such as the textile, leather, and soft-coal industries, where conditions failed to improve. The darkest spot on the sun of prosperity, however, was the distress of agriculture. The farmers had been growing poorer while the rest of the country was growing richer. In the five-year period from 1922 to 1927 it was estimated that more than one million people had left the farms for the cities and that the value of farm property had declined from $79,000,000,000 to $59,000,000,000. The net income of the farmer was rated at less than $800 a year as against $1300 for the schoolteacher, $1650 for the government employee, and $1675 for the preacher — all poorly paid positions. The farmers, who constituted a quarter of the working population of the country and on whose labor the general prosperity of the country depended, received less than 10 per cent of the national income.

There were a number of causes for the farmer's distress. (1) During the war the demand for American food and the high prices paid for it tempted the farmer to plant lands which it would not pay to cultivate in ordinary times and to buy (often on credit) expensive farm machinery. When the war was over and millions of men returned to the farms in Europe, the American farmer could not sell all his surplus abroad, and what he did sell had to be at the price in the "world market," which was determined by the competition of agricultural countries such as Russia, the Argentine, and Canada. The Canadian wheat

---

[1] It is true that at the same time the state and local taxes were rising ominously, from twenty-eight dollars per capita in 1921 to fifty dollars in 1928. This was due partly to extravagance in the construction of roads and public buildings and partly to the encouragement of the issue of tax-exempt state and city bonds.

output, for example, increased nearly tenfold in the decade after the war. The result was a rapid decrease (deflation) in the price of farm products. Between 1919 and 1927 these prices fell nearly 40 per cent. (2) At the same time the prices which the farmer had to pay for his necessities (tools, fences, clothing, machinery, paint, etc.) rose about 30 per cent. The spread between his income and his expenses thus widened year by year. (3) Furthermore, his burden of debt was increased by constantly mounting local taxes and interest charges on his mortgages. The taxes on farm property, taking 100 as the index figure for 1914, were 130 in 1919 when the farmer was prosperous, and 258 in 1927 when he was in the Slough of Despond. His mortgage indebtedness grew in the same years from $1,762,000,000 to over $4,000,000,000. (4) Finally, the great advance in "technology" (the improvement of machines such as drillers, huskers, reapers, combines, and tractors) had made it possible with far fewer workers to produce enormous quantities of food and so add to the surpluses which were already smothering the farmer. When we read that the number of gasoline tractors replacing horses and mules on the farms rose from eighty thousand in 1919 to over eight hundred thousand ten years later, we can realize the effect on the farmer's market for hay and oats.

The McNary-Haugen Bills. As in the Granger movement after the Civil War and the Populist revolt in the 1890's, the farmers now turned to the government for relief. The manufacturer was favored by a high tariff for the protection of his prices and profits. The unionized laborer saw the threat to his wage standards removed by the national laws restricting immigration. Why should the farmer continue to be the Cinderella in the family of American industry? The "farm bloc" in Congress and their supporters in the agricultural organizations of the country, such as the National Grange and the Fruit Growers' Association, began a campaign for government aid as soon as President Harding's first Congress assembled in 1921, and kept it up during the whole decade. Under Harding they got some little relief in the bills prohibiting certain kinds of speculation in grain, protecting dairymen against the competition of impure milk in interstate trade, and making easier terms for borrowing from the Federal Farm Loan Banks. But it was not the chance to borrow more money that the farmers wanted. They had already borrowed far too much and could not hope to "borrow their way out of debt." The government took the ground of willingness to help the farmers to help themselves, by encouraging and helping them to finance co-operative efforts for the better marketing of their crops; but the farmers asked for more direct government aid.

Their demands were presented to Congress in several McNary-Haugen bills, so named from Senator McNary of Oregon and Representative Haugen of Iowa, chairman of the agricultural committees in the Senate and the House respectively. The bills were too complicated to explain here in detail, but the gist of them was that the government should take the surpluses off the hands of the farmer so that he could sell his produce at home at a price protected by the tariff (which was forty-two cents a bushel on wheat, for example). The loss which the government incurred through "dumping," or selling the surpluses abroad at the world price, could then be made up by an assessment on the farmers, called the "equalization fee."[1] Another form of relief suggested in the bills was the so-called "debenture plan," by which the national treasury was to give the farmer a share in the benefits of the protective tariff.[2] The first McNary-

---

[1] The working of the equalization fee can be shown by the following illustration. Suppose the wheat crop of the country to be 800,000,000 bushels, of which only 600,000,000 bushels could be used at home. Suppose also the price of wheat in the world market to be $1 a bushel. The farmers would then have a wheat crop worth $800,000,000. But with a tariff of 42 cents a bushel to protect him from the competition of wheat imported, say, from Canada, the farmer could get $1.42 a bushel for his wheat (or $1,136,000,000 for the crop) *if he sold it all in the United States*. The plan was therefore for the government to buy the 200,000,000 surplus bushels at the protected price of $1.42 and sell them abroad at the world price of $1 a bushel. The government's loss on this transaction would be $84,000,000. But this could be made up by assessing a fee of about 10 cents a bushel on the farmers, leaving the net price which they received for their crop still some 30 cents a bushel higher than the world price.

[2] The debenture plan proposed not that the government buy the surpluses but that it give the farmer a bounty on the produce which he sold abroad at the world prices. This bounty was to take the form of debentures, or certificates of in-

Haugen Bill was introduced into the House early in 1924, but was defeated by the decisive vote of 153 to 223. A second attempt to pass the bill in May–June, 1926, resulted in another defeat, but by narrower margins. The "farm bloc" still persisted, and in February, 1927, both branches of Congress passed the bill.

The Coolidge Vetoes. President Coolidge vetoed the bill in a long message in which he maintained that the bill gave special favors to producers of a few commodities, such as wheat, corn, cotton, rice, hogs, and tobacco; that it delegated to the proposed Farm Board the powers of taxation, which belonged to Congress alone; that it would stimulate further overproduction of the favored commodities; and that it would create a large number of Federal agents "intruding into the affairs of the American farmers and offering infinite opportunities to fraud and incapacity." He accompanied the veto with an opinion from the Attorney-General to the effect that the bill was unconstitutional. The President expressed his sympathy with the farmers, who, he said, had "not been receiving their fair share of the national income since the war." But, he continued, "to saddle agriculture with unjust and unworkable schemes of government control is to invite disaster worse than any that has yet befallen our farmers." Any sound and workable proposal to help the farmer, he declared, would have "the earnest support of the government." Congress failed to pass the bill over the veto. Again, in April–May, 1928, both the Senate (53 to 23) and the House (204 to 121) passed the McNary-Haugen Bill, with the equalization fee. And again the President successfully vetoed it, using the same arguments that he had urged a year before. These vetoes aroused a great deal of resentment in the

debtedness, issued by the Treasury. For example, for each bushel of wheat exported the farmer was to receive a bounty equal to one half the tariff duty (that is, twenty-one cents). These debentures would be honored by the government for the payment of customs duties on imports. They would be equivalent to money, then, and the farmers could sell them to importing merchants. Therefore, while the government would not be out of pocket by the equalization-fee plan, it would be a loser by the debenture plan. For it would be accepting as part of the payment of customs duties the certificates (debentures) which it had given gratis to the exporting farmers.

West and led to prophecies that the great agricultural states of the Mississippi Valley and the Northwest would refuse to support in the next nominating convention of the Republican party any candidate but "a friend of the farmer," like ex-Governor Lowden of Illinois or Senator George Norris of Nebraska.

Railroads and Shipping. Besides the questions of veterans' bonus, revenue adjustment, and agricultural relief, a number of other problems left by the war clamored in vain for solution in the Coolidge administration. The railroads saw their profits cut into deeply by the competition of unregulated and virtually untaxed motorbus and truck service, but Congress and the railroad executives failed to unite on a plan for the grouping of the stronger roads into a unified system. The Railway Labor Board set up by the Transportation Act of 1920 (p. 748) provoked so much criticism that it was abandoned in favor of a Mediation Board for the voluntary arbitration of labor disputes.

The Shipping Board continued its efforts to get its vessels transferred to private ownership. The Jones-White Merchant Marine Act of 1928 went far beyond its predecessor of 1920 (p. 742) in its offers of loans to private companies and its generous subsidies for carrying ocean mail. It authorized the sale of government-owned vessels at bargain prices. For example, in 1929 the P. W. Chapman Company of New York bought the five finest ships of the United States Line (the *Leviathan, George Washington, America, Republic,* and *President Harding*), together with five ships of the American Merchant Line, for a little over sixteen million dollars. At the close of the decade 75 per cent of the merchant vessels of over one thousand tons flying the American flag were owned by private corporations.

The "Blotting Paper" Industries. To describe the progress of industry and invention during the 1920's would require a volume in itself. Certain industries, such as the automobile, the radio, and the motion-picture industry, grew so rapidly that they absorbed millions of workers and thus got the name of "blotting paper" industries. For example, the automobile industry, which was not important enough even to find mention in the census of 1910, increased the output of cars from seven million in 1919 to twenty-four million ten years later. It now is our leading industry, with billions of dollars invested and an annual production of about five million cars. The first broadcasting radio station (KDKA) was opened at Pittsburgh in November, 1920, to carry the news of the Harding-Cox election. Two months later Herbert Hoover's voice was heard in the first public radio address, pleading for funds for the relief work in Europe; and within three years short-wave transmission was carrying music and messages across the seas. An interesting indication of the shift of interest from the passions of the war to the new wonders of invention is cited by Frederick L. Allen in his fascinating book *Only Yesterday*. While the *Reader's Guide to Periodical Literature* for 1919–1921 contained two columns of titles on "Radicals" and but one fourth of a column on "Radio," in 1922–1924 the titles on "Radio" filled nineteen columns and those on "Radicals" but half a column. Some ten million radio receiving sets (more than those of all the rest of the world put together) were in use in the United States in 1928, and a Federal Radio Commission established by Congress (1927) had the task of assigning wave lengths to widely competing broadcasting stations. The motion-picture industry antedated the war, but it was not till the postwar decade that it blossomed out, with speech and music added to the films, to become by 1926 the fourth-largest industry of the country, attracting to its twenty-five thousand theaters an attendance estimated at one hundred million a week. Great feature pictures cost often as much as a million dollars to produce, and Hollywood, California, the center of the industry, drew beauty and talent from all parts of the world.

The Conquest of the Air. The greatest triumph of invention, however, has been the conquest of the air, both for the instantaneous communication of sound and even of photographs by radio, and as a path of travel for dirigibles and airplanes. Though the first successful flight in a heavier-than-air machine was made by Wilbur and Orville Wright at Kittyhawk, North Carolina, in December, 1903, little progress in aviation was made until the World War. At the close of hostilities we had

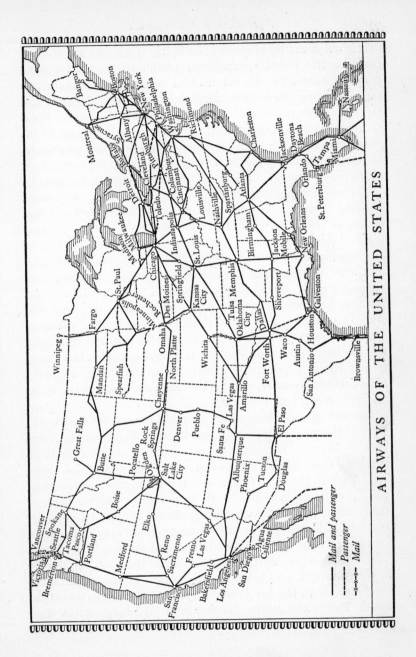

AIRWAYS OF THE UNITED STATES

Mail and passenger
Passenger
Mail

over eight hundred planes at the battle front and twenty-four plants in this country, capable of producing twenty thousand planes a year. The air service had become a permanent and expanding branch of our national defense in both the army and the navy. Air routes for carrying mail, merchandise, and passengers developed rapidly in the postwar decade, though in the passenger service we lagged far behind Europe, where practically all the important cities were connected by a network of air routes over which passenger planes flew on regular schedules.

The whole world was thrilled on the 21st of May, 1927, when a young American air-mail pilot named Charles A. Lindbergh landed at the flying field of Le Bourget, Paris, after a nonstop flight of thirty-three hours from New York. In spite of the gifts and trophies showered upon him and the attempts to "lionize" him after the sensational methods of the day, Lindbergh remained a quiet, modest citizen, devoted to his profession and refusing to capitalize his popularity by going on the vaudeville stage or endorsing a brand of cigarettes. His sterling character was a wholesome influence, especially on the young people, in an age too much given to cynicism, jazz, and mawkish interest in murder trials. Unfortunately, his feat was imitated by a number of less skillful aviators, who took off for a flight across the ocean and were never heard of again.

Another splendid hero of the air was Commander Richard E. Byrd of the navy, who, with Floyd Bennett, flew over the North Pole on May 19, 1926, and the next year (a month after Lindbergh's "Lone Eagle" flight) flew with three companions from New York to the coast of France. Byrd's greatest achievement was his exploration of the South Polar region. With a party of thirty men, provided with four airplanes, a hundred dogs, ice tractors, radio equipment, and motion-picture apparatus, at an expense of over eight hundred thousand dollars, Byrd established his base at "Little America," near the Ross Ice Barrier of the Antarctic, on Christmas Day, 1928. Flying twelve thousand feet above the Liv Glacier, Byrd and his pilot crossed the South Pole; and before his return to Washington (as Rear Admiral) in March, 1930, he had made invaluable studies of the geography and climate of the great Antarctic Continent. In the autumn of 1933 Admiral Byrd started from Boston on a second South Polar expedition of two years. From this he brought back more valuable information, and he was rewarded with more medals and decorations. His plans are now (1936) shaping for a third expedition, and Little America bids fair to become as familiar to the people of great America as Alaska or Puerto Rico.

The World Court. Every one of our Presidents from Wilson to Franklin D. Roosevelt has favored our adherence to the Permanent Court of International Justice, established by the League of Nations at the Hague, Holland, in 1920. The American lawyer Elihu Root was the chief framer of the statute of the court, and an American member (first John Bassett Moore, then Charles E. Hughes, then Frank B. Kellogg) has sat on the court ever since it was opened. But because the court was created by the League of Nations and could be called on for "advisory opinions" on disputes between members of the League, many in the United States were fearful that we might be drawn into the political controversies of Europe if we joined the court.

The Senate finally consented by a vote of 76 to 17 (January 27, 1926) to accept membership in the court, subject to certain reservations, the most important of which were that we should have the right to withdraw at will, that the statute (constitution) of the court should not be amended without our consent, and that no request for an advisory opinion "touching any dispute or question in which the United States has or claims an interest" should be entertained by the court without our consent. In the assembly convened at Geneva on September 1, 1926, the fifty-four member nations of the court accepted all the reservations except the last. But President Coolidge stood by the Senate in its refusal to modify the reservation, and no further steps were taken during his term toward joining the court. Late in 1928 the venerable Elihu Root went to Geneva and aided in a revision of the statute of the court which met the approval of our State Department, and our acting minister to Switzerland was authorized to sign a treaty for our joining (December 9, 1929).

President Hoover submitted the treaty to the Senate, but it was not until May 12, 1932, that the Foreign Relations Committee, by a vote of 11 to 9, reported the treaty out. A tremendous campaign of opposition was waged, headed by Senators Borah and Johnson and the influential Catholic priest Father Coughlin of Detroit. Telegrams by the tens of thousands were sent to the Senators, begging them to keep us out of the "trap" of European politics. When the vote was taken on January 29, 1935, it failed of the necessary two thirds by seven votes (52 to 36). Although friends of the court insist that we shall eventually join, its opponents are equally certain that the Senate vote laid the matter to rest forever.

The Briand-Kellogg Peace Pact. The principal event of the Coolidge administration in the field of foreign policy was the signing at Paris, on August 27, 1928, by the representatives of fifteen powers, of a pact for the "outlawry of war." The parties to the pact solemnly agreed to "renounce war as an instrument of national policy in their relations with one another" and to seek the solution of all disputes or conflicts, "of whatever nature," by pacific means. The pact originated in a proposition of M. Aristide Briand, the French foreign minister, that France and the United States should make such a treaty; but our Secretary of State, Mr. Kellogg, extended the invitation, in April, 1928, to Great Britain, Italy, Germany, and Japan. Eventually, more than sixty nations, representing practically the whole civilized world, joined in signing the pact. But since no penalities were provided against nations that resorted to force, and war for self-defense was still regarded as legitimate, the Briand-Kellogg Pact seemed rather like a pious wish than a real preventive of war. Each nation, it was agreed, "is free at all times and regardless of the treaty provisions to defend itself, and is the sole judge of what constitutes the right of self-defense and the necessity and extent of the same." As every modern war is a war of self-defense in the eyes of the nation that starts it, the critics of the pact declare that it is a worthless piece of paper. It did not prevent Japan from resorting to force to seize Manchuria in 1931 or Italy from invading Ethopia in the autumn of

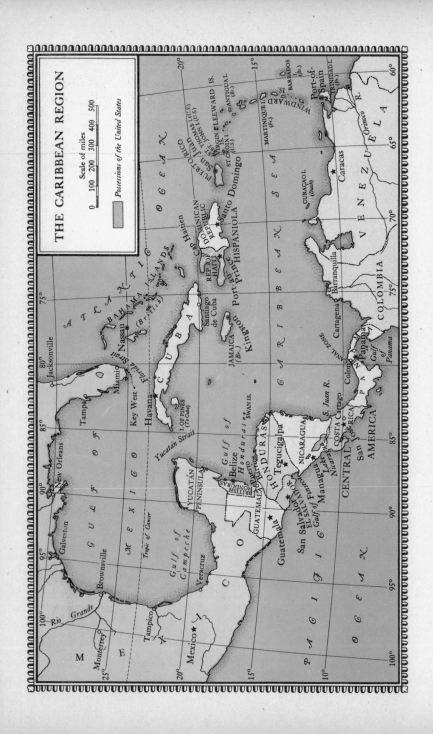

THE CARIBBEAN REGION

Scale of miles
0   100 200 300 400 500

▭ Possessions of the United States

1935. However, the very fact that the nations have put themselves on record against "war as an instrument of national policy" counts for something in the long struggle for peace and good will on earth.

President Coolidge worked hard in 1927 to get the representatives of the naval powers at Geneva to agree to a treaty with the United States limiting the construction of submarines, cruisers, and destroyers (not covered by the Washington Conference of 1921). But when the powers turned a cold shoulder to his proposal, he committed himself squarely to the cause of naval preparedness. A program for the construction of fifteen new cruisers and an airplane-carrier, estimated to cost $274,000,000, passed Congress by a five-to-one vote; and in February, 1929, Coolidge signed the bill, with the provision that five new cruisers should be begun in each of the years 1930, 1931, and 1932. The cruiser bill was signed just three weeks after the Senate had ratified the Briand-Kellogg Peace Pact with only a single dissenting vote — that of Senator Blaine of Wisconsin.

Mexico and Nicaragua. Relations with Latin America during the Coolidge administration showed a strange mixture of "dollar diplomacy" and a sincere desire to play the part of the "good neighbor." Our brokers and bankers, taking advantage of the abundant capital seeking investment, sold hundreds of millions of dollars' worth of Peruvian, Chilean, and Brazilian bonds (bearing attractive rates of interest) to the American people. Our investments in Latin-American securities increased from $114,000,000 in 1923 to $359,000,000 in 1927. Many of these "securities" were anything but secure, as their purchasers later learned to their sorrow. The anxiety to safeguard our "stake," or investments, in Latin America by the promotion of our trade and our financial influence there is evident in all our political and diplomatic relations with the republics to the south.

Mexico and Nicaragua furnish interesting examples. There was constant friction with Mexico over Article XXVII of the constitution of 1917, which threatened American property in mines and oil fields by declaring that "only Mexicans by birth or naturalization" had the right to acquire land or obtain concessions in the republic, and that all concessions granted under the Diaz regime (1876–1910) were subject to revision. President Coolidge recognized the Mexican government in 1924, on the assurance that American interests would be protected; but when, two years later, the Mexican Congress passed laws for the enforcement of Article XXVII, the conflict broke out again. Secretary Kellogg (who had succeeded Hughes in the State Department in March, 1925) greatly offended President Calles by accusing Mexico of "being on trial before the world" as a violator of international law, and President Coolidge refused to arbitrate the dispute, declaring that Mexico's action was a clear case of "confiscating property legally owned by American citizens." In the spring of 1927 President Coolidge made the best appointment of his administration by sending his old Amherst classmate Dwight W. Morrow, a partner in the Morgan firm, as ambassador to Mexico. Mr. Morrow's tact and sympathy completely won the confidence of the Mexican government and people, and the renewed friendship was strengthened when Colonel Charles A. Lindbergh, after a nonstop flight of twenty-two hundred miles from Washington, landed at Mexico City (December 14, 1927) as an "American ambassador of good will."

The administration was severely criticized for dispatching some five thousand American marines to Nicaragua to put down a revolt against the party there which was supposed to be friendly to our commercial and financial interests. More than seventy Americans were killed or wounded in the guerrilla warfare against the rebel leader Sandino. Petitions came from the American Federation of Labor, peace societies, and committees of clergymen, educators, and publicists denouncing our enforcement of "dollar diplomacy" by arms. Senator Wheeler declared in a speech at Cleveland (February 11, 1928) that war was "being waged in Nicaragua by Calvin Coolidge privately in defiance of the Constitution," and that Nicaragua had been "reduced from a sovereign state to a protectorate of Wall Street." When Sandino had been finally overcome, both sides agreed to abide by a fair election held under the supervision of an American brigadier general and a large force of American inspectors and guardsmen. It was not until January 2, 1933, that our armed forces, which had been in Nicaragua almost continuously for twenty years, were finally withdrawn.

The Sixth Pan-American Congress. While American marines were hunting out the nests of the Sandino rebels in Nicaragua, the sixth of the series of Pan-American congresses, which had been inaugurated by Secretary Blaine in 1889, met at Havana, Cuba (on January 16, 1928). About one hundred and fifty delegates from twenty Latin-American countries attended the six weeks' session, adopting a mass of resolutions on international law, trade, aviation, immigration, and education. President Coolidge went to Havana to open the congress with a message of good will to our sister republics. Ex-Secretary Hughes, the chairman, with great skill kept the congress clear of political controversies. "We have no policy of aggression," he assured the congress. "Nothing could be happier for the United States than that all the countries in the region of the Caribbean should be strong and self-sufficient ... settling their problems with peace at home and the fulfillment of their obligations abroad." One of the resolutions provided for the negotiation of arbitration treaties between the Latin-American states in a supplementary Pan-American conference to meet at Washington the following December. The treaties which emerged from this conference in January, 1929, were called by Secretary of State Kellogg "the most advanced ever adopted by the nations of the world."

The Campaign of 1928. On the completion of his fourth year of office (August 2, 1927), President Coolidge handed to the newspapermen at his camp at Rapid City, South Dakota, the brief statement "I do not choose to run for President in 1928." Four months later he told the National Republican Committee that he really meant what he said and that they should "select a candidate from among the numbers of distinguished men available," expressing no choice himself for his successor. Mr. Hughes, probably the next most influential man in the Republican party, also announced that he would not be a candidate. The leaders then turned to Herbert Hoover, the efficient Secretary of Commerce since 1921, who was nominated at Kansas City (June 12) on the first ballot, with 837 votes out of a total of 1088. Senator Charles E. Curtis of Kansas was named for Vice-President. The Democrats, meeting two weeks later at Houston, Texas, nominated Governor Alfred E. Smith of New York on the first ballot (849½ votes out of 1100), with Senator Joseph T. Robinson of Arkansas as running mate. Both platforms pledged their parties to the enforcement of prohibition and the relief of the farmers, although the Republican convention rejected the principle of the McNary-Haugen bills. The Socialist convention at New York (April 13) had put up Norman Thomas on a platform advocating the government ownership of natural resources and public utilities, old-age pensions, unemployment and accident insurance, the cancellation of the war debts, Philippine independence, the entrance of the United States into the League of Nations, and the recognition of Soviet Russia.

Mr. Hoover made only half a dozen speeches, and in these he dwelt on the general prosperity under Republican rule and promised its continuance; while Governor Smith toured the West and South, discussing in his homely, forcible language spiced with humor the questions of farm relief, the tariff, the power trusts, and prohibition. The governor had need of all the help that his colorful personality could furnish, for he was severely handicapped in the rural sections of the country because he was a member of Tammany Hall, an avowed "wet," and a member of the Roman Catholic Church. The combination was too much for him. Hoover carried forty of the forty-eight states on election day, November 6, including four states of the "solid South" (Virginia, North Carolina, Florida, and Texas) which had never before appeared in the Republican column. Besides six states of the old Confederacy, Smith won only Massachusetts and Rhode Island; but his popular vote of 15,000,000 to 21,400,000 for Hoover showed that he was a stronger candidate than either Cox in 1920 or Davis in 1924. Thomas, whose able campaign speeches deserved better attention than they received in the exciting battle between the two major parties, polled

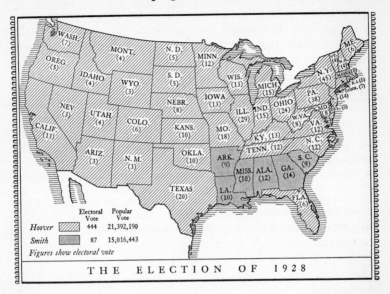

	Electoral Vote	Popular Vote
Hoover	444	21,392,190
Smith	87	15,016,443
Figures show electoral vote		

THE ELECTION OF 1928

only 267,835 votes. Soon after the election Hoover sailed on the battleship *Maryland* for a visit to the Central and South American republics, his object being, as he said at a state banquet in Peru, "to better prepare himself for the task of reënforcing the peace and friendship" between North America and Latin America. The President-elect's tour, covering ten of the Latin-American countries, was a recognition of the importance of firsthand acquaintance with a region in which our investments had grown from less than one and a half billion dollars in 1913 to over five billion dollars in 1928, and with which our trade had passed the one-billion-dollar mark.

On the Top of the Wave. It was in the midst of a cold, drizzling rain that President Hoover delivered his inaugural address of March 4, 1929, from the east portico of the Capitol, to be carried by radio to every corner of the land. Except for an earnest warning against the menace of a widespread disregard for law, the President's remarks were pervaded with optimism. We had "reached a higher degree of comfort and security than ever existed before in the history of the world." We had taken "a practical part in supporting all useful international under-takings" and were ready to contribute all we could to the advance of the cause of peace. He hoped that we would enter the World Court. At home our task was, through the spirit of co-operation and without "undue government restraints," "to establish more firmly the stability and security of business and thereby remove poverty still further from our borders." He closed with a jubilant outburst of faith:

Ours is a land rich in resources, stimulating in its glorious beauty, filled with millions of happy homes, blessed with comfort and opportunity. In no nation are the institutions of progress more advanced. In no nation are the fruits of accomplishment more secure. In no nation is the Government more worthy of respect. No country is more loved by its people. I have an abiding faith in their capacity, integrity, and high purpose. I have no fears for the future of our country. It is bright with hope.

TERMS TO BE MASTERED

"debunking"	deflation	debenture
Ku Klux Klan	"farm bloc"	Little America
"spotty" prosperity	"equalization fee"	Briand-Kellogg Pact

FOR SUPPLEMENTARY READING

J. M. MALIN, *The United States after the War*, chaps. xxix, xxx, xxxiii, xxxiv; ARTHUR KAPPER, *The Agricultural Bloc*; W. A. WHITE, *Masks in a Pageant*, chaps. xlii, xliii; F. L. ALLEN, *Only Yesterday*, chaps. vii–ix, and *The Lords of Creation*, chaps. viii, ix; J. I. ARNOLD, *Problems of American Life*, chaps. xxxi, xxxii; CHARLES MERZ, *The Great American Bandwagon*, chap. vi; R. C. ENGBERG, *Industrial Prosperity and the Farmer*, chaps. i–iv; PETER ODEGARD, *The American Public Mind*, chap. vii; MARK SULLIVAN, *Our Times*, Vol. VI, chaps. xiii–xv; H. F. PRINGLE, *Alfred E. Smith, A Critical Study*, pp. 291–391; ALFRED E. SMITH, *Up to Now*, pp. 384–418; C. W. THOMPSON, *Presidents I've Known*, chaps. xxvi–xxviii; W. A. WHITE, *Calvin Coolidge*; J. T. SHOTWELL, *War as an Instrument of National Policy*; *America*, Vol. XII, pp. 246–262; H. S. COMMAGER, *Documents of American History*, Vol. II, pp. 374–377, 388–396, 401; R. V. PEEL and T. C. DONNELLY, *The 1928 Campaign*.

TOPICS FOR REPORTS

1. **The McNary-Haugen Bills.** G. N. PEEK, "The McNary-Haugen Plan for Relief," in *New York Times Current History Magazine*, November, 1928; E. R. A. SELIGMAN, *The Economics of Farm Relief*; W. M. JARDINE, "The Farmer's Place under the Sun," in the *Century Magazine*, Vol. CXII, pp. 543–550; J. D.

BLACK, "The McNary-Haugen Movement," in the *American Economic Review,* Vol. XVIII, pp. 405 f.

2. **The World Court.** *Statute and Rules of the Court,* Publications of the Permanent Court of International Justice (World Peace Foundation, 40 Mt. Vernon Street, Boston, Massachusetts), Series D, No. 1; M. O. HUDSON, *The Work of the Permanent Court of International Justice during Four Years* (World Peace Foundation Pamphlets, Vol. IX, No. 2); *The United States and the Permanent Court of International Justice* (International Conciliation Pamphlets, No. 186).

3. **The Conquest of the Air.** The Pageant of America, Vol. IV, pp. 331–347; *National Geographic Magazine:* Vol. XLVI, pp. 93–122, "Man's Amazing Progress in Conquering the Air"; Vol. LII, pp. 347–368, "Our Transatlantic Flight," by Richard Byrd; Vol. LVII, pp. 653–688, "The First Airship Flight around the World"; C. A. LINDBERGH, *We*; G. H. WILKINS, *Flying the Arctic*; W. POST and H. GATTY, *Around the World in Eight Days.*

4. **Strained Relations with Mexico.** J. F. RIPPY, *The United States and Mexico,* chaps. xxii, xxiii; J. R. CLARK, "The Oil Settlement with Mexico," in *Foreign Affairs,* Vol. VI, July, 1928; C. W. HACKETT, *The Mexican Revolution and the United States*; E. TURLINGTON, *Mexico and her Foreign Creditors*; FRANK TANNENBAUM, *The Mexican Agrarian Revolution*; HAROLD NICHOLSON, *Dwight Whitney Morrow.*

QUESTIONS SUGGESTED BY THE CHAPTER

1. Contrast the characters of Harding and Coolidge. **2.** How many Vice-Presidents have succeeded to the Presidency on the death of the President? **3.** How did Coolidge show his conservatism? **4.** Why was the farmer less able than the industrial worker to recover from the postwar deflation? **5.** Compare our intervention in Nicaragua under Coolidge with that in Santo Domingo under Theodore Roosevelt. **6.** What was the "Root formula"? **7.** How did Coolidge wish to dispose of the government plant at Muscle Shoals? **8.** What new party appeared in the election of 1924? What success did it have? **9.** To what extent was our national debt reduced in the Coolidge administration? **10.** On what questions did Coolidge meet with opposition in Congress? **11.** What favors had the government shown to the manufacturer and the laborer to the neglect of the farmer? **12.** What was the object of the McNary-Haugen bills? **13.** What reasons did Coolidge give for his vetoes of the bills? **14.** What inducements to purchase its ships did the government offer to private concerns? **15.** What was the first national event to be broadcast on the radio? **16.** What were the exploits of Lindbergh? of Richard Byrd? **17.** What services did Elihu Root perform for the World Court? **18.** Contrast the votes of the Senate in 1926 and in 1935 on joining the World Court. **19.** Give two instances of the violation of the Briand-Kellogg Pact by foreign nations. **20.** What were the causes of friction between the United States and Mexico in the Coolidge administration? **21.** When and where was the sixth Pan-American Congress held? **22.** What special handicaps did Alfred E. Smith have in the campaign of 1828? **23.** What states of the "solid South" voted for Hoover in 1928? **24.** What was the tone of Hoover's inaugural address?

CHAPTER THIRTY-TWO

THE ECLIPSE OF PROSPERITY

No More Poverty. Never had the nation been more content with its present or more confident of its future than it was in the spring of 1929. Trade was booming, industry was flourishing, wages were high, corporations were paying fat dividends, and the Federal taxes, in spite of lowered rates, were still bringing surpluses into the Treasury. If there were some spots which the tide of prosperity had not yet reached, they would soon feel its irresistible rise. If a million or two men had been thrown out of employment by the introduction of labor-saving machines, the increased demand for the products of those machines would quickly provide jobs to absorb the unemployed. If a few voices were raised here and there warning against the mania for stock speculation which had seized the people, they were powerless to prevent rich and poor alike from staking their savings and their borrowings on the gamble in the stock market, where shares were rising day by day to fantastic heights. The loans made by the banks to brokers, to carry their customers' speculative (or "margin") accounts, had risen within a few years from $2,800,000,000 to $3,500,000,000, and were to pass the $6,000,000,000 mark before the end of the summer of 1929. Everybody saw the pot of gold at the end of the rainbow. "We in America," said Mr. Hoover in his acceptance speech at Palo Alto, on August 11, 1928, "are nearer to the final triumph over poverty than ever before in the history of any land. We have not reached the goal, but, given the chance to go forward with the policies of the last eight years, we shall soon, with the help of God, be in sight of the day when poverty will be banished from this nation." No warnings of conservative financiers or clear-eyed students of social conditions that we were living in a fools' paradise of easy wealth for all could stem the tide of confidence that flowed from the White House and the Treasury, from Wall Street and Main Street. Poverty was now to be conquered, as smallpox and yellow fever had been conquered.

The New Administration. The man whom the American people had so decisively elected to lead the way to permanent prosperity was a fitting symbol of their hopes and dreams. Herbert Hoover, born on a small farm in Iowa in 1874 and orphaned at the age of ten, had made his way through Stanford University and gradually amassed a large fortune as a mining engineer in Australia, China, South Africa, Russia, Nicaragua, and California. On the outbreak of the World War he had turned his back on private gain and devoted his organizing talents to the unselfish task of feeding ten million destitute inhabitants of Belgium and northeastern France. When we entered the war he came home to accept from President Wilson the post of Food Administrator. During his seven and a half years as Secretary of Commerce in the Harding and Coolidge administrations, he raised that department to a major branch of the government, introducing economy and efficiency into methods of production, enlarging our foreign trade, and increasing the bureaus of the department to include patents, mines, and radio. He reveled in blueprints, graphs, and statistics.

We had had generals, lawyers, and politicians in the Presidential chair, but Mr. Hoover was to be our first business executive, fitly corresponding to the age in which, in the words of Stuart Chase, "the business man had become the dictator of our destinies and the final authority on the conduct of American society." Secretary Mellon (called "the greatest Secretary of the Treasury since Alexander Hamilton") remained at the head of the Treasury until February, 1932, when he was appointed ambassador to Great Britain. Secretary of Labor James J. Davis also held over from the Coolidge cabinet until he resigned in 1930 to run for the Senate. The other members of the cabinet were new appointees.[1] But none of them were selected from

[1] Colonel Henry L. Stimson of New York was recalled from the governorship of the Philippines to become Secretary of State. James W. Good of Iowa (suc-

those states of the "solid South" which had broken their Democratic tradition by voting for Hoover.

The Federal Farm Board. The darkest spot on the "bright hopes" of our country was the plight of the farmer. Both parties had promised him relief in the campaign of 1928; and on April 15, 1929, President Hoover called the Seventy-first Congress in extra session to redeem this pledge and also to make such "limited revision" of the tariff as a few depressed industries like textiles demanded. After the House had twice defeated the attempt of the Senate to include the debenture plan (p. 793, n. 2), an Agricultural Marketing Bill was passed by large majorities and was signed by the President on June 15. It created a Federal Farm Board of nine members, including the Secretary of Agriculture, and provided for a fund of $500,000,000 from which loans, at not over 4 per cent interest, should be made to co-operative associations of farmers to help them market their grain, cotton, livestock, dairy products, and fruits to better advantage. It aimed to encourage the scientific management of farming on a large scale, akin to the organization of manufacturing industries.

For a few months it seemed to promise success. Loans amounting to $165,000,000 were made to 132 co-operatives. But when farm prices continued to sag, borrowing only added to the farmers' burdens. Though the Agricultural Marketing Act did not authorize the government to buy and sell farm products, the board actually did purchase from the farmers over 300,000,000 bushels of wheat and 1,300,000 bales of cotton in the vain attempt to hold up the prices of those commodities. But by the close of 1931 wheat had sunk from $1 to 61 cents a bushel, and cotton from 16 to 6 cents a pound; and the government's loss on the purchase of these two articles was $185,000,000. It was

ceeded on his death in December, 1929, by Patrick J. Hurley of Oklahoma) was made Secretary of War. The Attorney-General was William D. Mitchell of Minnesota; the Postmaster-General, Walter F. Brown of Ohio; the Secretary of the Navy, Charles Francis Adams, great-grandson of John Quincy Adams, of Massachusetts; the Secretary of the Interior, Ray Lyman Wilbur, president of Leland Stanford University, California; the Secretary of Agriculture, Arthur M. Hyde of Missouri; the Secretary of Commerce, Robert P. Lamont of Illinois.

evident that the agricultural problem was no nearer solution in 1932 than it had been in 1922, and that a solution, if there was one, was possible only by reaching some agreement with the other agricultural countries. As the farmer's distress was largely due to world-wide conditions brought on by the war, it could be remedied — so it was believed by many of our best economists — only by international agricultural planning. It was difficult, however, after the war to get international agreement on any subject (agriculture, arms reduction, tariffs, or money), since each nation seemed doubly determined to look out for its own interests only. We are therefore still attempting to solve the farmer's problem by an adjustment between agricultural production and prices in the United States.

The Hawley-Smoot Tariff. The dominance of the industrial interests of the country over the agricultural was illustrated by the new tariff bill. Instead of the "limited revision" recommended by President Hoover and the party platform, an increase of duties on more than one thousand articles, raising the rates far above those of the Fordney-McCumber Act of 1922, appeared in the bill submitted by Chairman W. C. Hawley (Oregon) of the Ways and Means Committee and passed by the House on May 28, 1929, by a vote of 267 to 147. The "farm bloc" and their sympathizers in the Senate (Borah, Norris, La Follette, Blaine, Frazier, Nye) fought hard to protect the farmer by the insertion of the debenture plan into the bill. The importers, the bankers who had lent large sums abroad, and the merchants who were interested in stimulating our foreign trade were opposed to higher duties. But the high-protectionist manufacturers, with their powerful lobbies, were in the saddle. Joseph Grundy, president of the Pennsylvania Manufacturers' Association, confessed that he was spending two thousand dollars a month to boost the tariff rates. More than a year passed, during which the "Grundy tariff" was assailed from all parts of the country, before the bill got through the Senate, in May, 1930. On the thirtieth of that month a petition signed by more than a thousand economists begged Hoover to veto the bill; but when it passed in final form, by

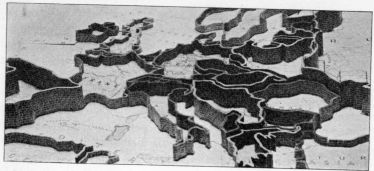

PROTECTIVE TARIFF WALLS IN EUROPE   © Barratts

votes of 44 to 42 in the Senate and 222 to 153 in the House, the President put his signature to it.

The evil effects of surrounding the country with a Chinese wall of high protection were soon evident. Before the close of 1931 about twenty-five foreign countries had raised their own tariff walls against American goods, by way of reprisal. Our debtors in Europe, whose only means of payment was the shipping of merchandise to us, found their goods shut out by our tariff barrier. In the seventeen months preceding the signing of the Hawley-Smoot tariff our exports had been $6,829,000,000 and our imports $5,766,000,000; in the next seventeen months these figures dropped to $4,000,000,000 and $3,262,000,000 respectively. Surpluses of both manufactured and agricultural products accumulated in our country, which the people, owing to hard times and the growing number of the unemployed, were unable to purchase. We were threatened with being suffocated in our own plenty: millions of surplus bushels of wheat, and millions of men hungry; millions of extra pairs of shoes, and men going barefoot; billions of idle dollars lying in the banks, and industry paralyzed. There were, to be sure, other reasons than the high tariff for this distressing condition. For example, widespread poverty in Europe, revolutions in Latin America, riots and civil war in India and China, all contributed to cut down our foreign markets. Still, the mistaken idea that we could forever sell to nations without buying from them in return was a hindrance rather than a help to the recovery of world trade.

The Wickersham Commission. It was no misgiving about the continuance of economic prosperity that disturbed President Hoover when he entered the White House, but rather the widespread disregard and violation of the law, made evident by the operations of bootleggers, highjackers, and racketeers and the failure of the courts to convict and punish criminals. Worst of all, great masses of our people, fed on the glorification of crime in the tabloid press, had a sneaking admiration for the man who "got away with it." On April 22, 1929, the President told the Associated Press meeting in New York that this was "the dominant national problem." A month later he appointed a Commission on Law Observance and Enforcement, of eleven distinguished citizens, including ex-Attorney-General George W. Wickersham (chairman), ex-Secretary of War Newton D. Baker, and Dean Roscoe Pound of the Harvard Law School. Meeting the commission at the White House, May 28, he told them that "no nation can long survive the failure of its citizens to respect and obey the laws which they themselves make."

After eighteen months the commission submitted the first installment of its report (January 19, 1931), concerning the subject in which public opinion was most interested, namely, the enforcement of the prohibition law. Ten of the eleven members signed the body of the report, which opposed the repeal of the Eighteenth Amendment or the modification of the Volstead Act. Yet in the *individual* opinions appended to the report only four members were in favor of continuing the law as it stood, while five recommended modifications and two favored the outright repeal of the amendment. This inconsistency led to the description of the report by one paper as "the most astonishing document ever submitted to our government by a responsible committee," and to its reception by the people with more amusement than respect. The commission subsequently made reports on a dozen other subjects, such as the causes of crime, the machinery of the criminal courts, the deportation of aliens, and police methods. They contained much valuable information, but, as the chairman of the commission sadly confessed in May, 1932, they "received little or no attention, due to the overwhelming public interest in the two reports that concerned prohibition."

The Stock-Market Crash. The Wickersham Commission had hardly begun its work when an event occurred which shook the country from one end to the other. For the first few months of the Hoover administration the prosperity of the years 1924–1929 seemed undiminished. Many believed that poverty would be abolished. The prices of stocks soared to fantastic heights in the "Hoover bull market," and the public rushed to buy securities which they could sell in a few days at large profits. The fever of speculation spread to all classes, from bankers and business magnates to clerks, chauffeurs, and cooks. Professional men, schoolteachers, and shopkeepers staked their savings of years on the chance of doubling them in Radio common, United States Steel, or Anaconda Copper. People sold their Liberty Bonds and mortgaged their homes to get money to entrust to their brokers. Billions of dollars were drawn from the banks into Wall Street.

Warnings of the shaky foundations of this Tower of Babel went unheeded until it came crashing down. On October 29, 1929, the market broke, and the wild rush to buy stocks gave way in a moment to a still wilder rush to sell them before they should go lower. Prime securities, such as General Electric and American Telephone and Telegraph, tumbled as if they had been bogus issues of the Bullfrog Gold Mine. Over 16,400,000 shares of stock were thrown on the market for what they would bring on that fateful October 29. Fortunes were wiped out, and scores of impoverished victims committed suicide. In spite of reiterated assurances from President Hoover, Secretary Mellon, and others in high places that the market crash was only a temporary panic, that business conditions were "fundamentally sound," that the crisis would be over in a few weeks, that a great revival of prosperity was "just around the corner," that the panic was only "psychological," and that nobody should lose confidence and "sell America short," it became evident as the months passed without relief that we had entered into the worst slough of depression in our entire history. Foreign trade fell from $9,600,000,000 in 1929 to $4,500,000,000 in 1931. Factories shut down by the hundreds, the army of the unemployed grew rapidly, the bread lines lengthened, mortgages were foreclosed, banks failed, dividends were passed, and the prices of wheat, cotton, oil, copper, silver, and other commodities kept on sinking, as the buying power of the people was paralyzed.

Efforts for Relief. It was a hard discipline for a people nourished on the myth of never-ending prosperity to face such distress as we had in our pride imagined afflicted only the old war-torn countries of the world. The government, while attempting to restore confidence to the people by its optimistic predictions of recovery, began to take steps to relieve the economic distress. In November, 1929, President Hoover summoned a group of businessmen to the White House and asked them not to interrupt their programs for expansion or to reduce wages. In December, 1930, he submitted to Congress a vast program for road construction, public buildings, flood relief, and airways development, and signed twenty-two bills appropriating over three hundred million dollars for emergency construction, loans by the Farm Board, and drought relief.[1] Finally, on January 22, 1932, he signed the bill creating a two-billion-dollar Reconstruction Finance Corporation, empowered to extend loans to banks, railroads, building and loan associations, insurance companies, and agricultural associations. The management of the corporation was vested in a board of seven directors under the chairmanship of General Charles G. Dawes, who had just resigned the post of ambassador to London. Democrats and Republicans alike joined in passing the bill in a nonpartisan spirit of devotion to help "start the country forward all along the line." To these projects of public relief were added a number of "plans" (suggested by professional men and businessmen, such as President Butler of Columbia,

---

[1] Nature conspired with man to make the situation worse. In the midsummer of 1930 a terrific heat wave and drought ruined the crops and destroyed most of the livestock on half a million farms in eighteen states, from Virginia to Oklahoma.

Professor Charles A. Beard, Gerard Swope, and Owen D. Young) advocating reforms in the organization and management of industry to make it serve social welfare rather than private profit.

The Impoverished Treasury. It would have been fairly easy for the national treasury to provide the relief needed if it had continued to enjoy the abundant revenues and fat surpluses of the Coolidge administration. But the depression, which had stopped the wheels of industry, had also dried up the sources of income. Federal taxes were supplying only 50 per cent of the government's expenses at the close of the year 1931, and the Treasury was faced with a deficit of over $2,000,000,000 for the coming year. Appropriations for the army and navy, the veterans' service, and the interest on the public debt were absorbing every dollar of the national income. Yet, as revenue declined, the demands on the Treasury increased. For example, in February, 1931, both houses of Congress overrode by huge majorities President Hoover's veto of the bill extending cash loans to the veterans up to 50 per cent of their insurance certificates (p. 769), at an estimated cost of a billion dollars. Agitation continued for the full cash payment of the certificates (two billion dollars), though the convention of the American Legion at Detroit in September rejected this demand by a vote of 902 to 507. Even the $238,000,000 which we should have collected from our foreign debtors was lost to the Treasury when President Hoover, in order to prevent Germany from a total financial collapse, proposed on June 20, 1931, a "moratorium" (postponement) for one year of "all payments on intergovernmental debts . . . both principal and interest."

The mid-term elections, coming in the midst of the depression, naturally turned against the administration. The Seventy-second Congress, which met in December, 1931, showed the Democrats in control of the House (219 to 214) for the first time since Woodrow Wilson's day, and the Senate almost exactly balanced. Political rivalry then complicated the situation. Though the Democrats professed themselves ready to co-operate in measures of relief, President Hoover charged that they were working to make his administration a failure in order that they might oust the Republicans from power in 1932. The leaders of both parties agreed that new taxes must be levied if the deficits were to be wiped out and the budget balanced. But they wrangled over the question whether the taxes should "soak the rich" or be distributed more generally among the consumers. The tax bill which finally emerged, in April, 1932, was declared by Secretary of the Treasury Ogden Mills "inadequate to check the growing deficit," which, in fact, mounted in the first four months (July–October) of the fiscal year 1932 by almost seven hundred million dollars.

The London Naval Treaty. When the Briand-Kellogg Pact was signed in 1928 (p. 800), the folly of the mad competition in naval construction became apparent. Early in October, 1929, the British prime minister, J. Ramsay MacDonald, came to America and conferred quietly with Secretary Stimson and President Hoover at the latter's fishing camp on the Rapidan River, in Virginia. Declaring that war between England and the United States was "unthinkable," they agreed to start negotiations for further naval limitations. Invitations were sent by the British government to the five naval powers of the Washington Conference of 1921 to meet in London in January, 1930.

The conference produced a treaty, signed by the United States, Great Britain, and Japan (France and Italy refusing to agree to the terms), which established a "parity," or equality, between the United States and Great Britain in all types of warships and continued the "naval holiday" in battleship-building to 1936. Our Senate ratified the treaty by a vote of 58 to 9. Nevertheless, the treaty was far from satisfactory, because (1) it left out the two naval powers France and Italy, (2) it allowed the signatory nations to build up their fleets if France or Italy threatened their security (the "escalator clause"), and (3) it still made it possible for us to build more than one million tons of war vessels, costing a billion dollars, before reaching the treaty limits. Still there was hope that neither the United States nor Great Britain would actually build up to the treaty strength. "We look forward," said Secretary Stimson at the close of the parleys, "to periodically recurring conferences, confident that we shall obtain ever increasing security with ever decreasing armaments." The agitation of the "big-navy men" on both sides of the water for building up to the full treaty limits has continued unabated.

The Campaign of 1932. The Republican national convention met at Chicago on June 14, 1932, and renominated Hoover and Curtis on the first ballot. The platform stood pat on the merits of the Hoover administration, warned against the danger to business if the Democrats should come into power, and rejected the pleas of President Butler and Senator Bingham of Connecticut for a plank favoring the repeal of the prohibition amendment. The Democrats met on June 27 in the same Coliseum building that the Republicans had vacated a few days before. Governor Franklin D. Roosevelt of New York, who had been Assistant Secretary of the Navy under Wilson and the Vice-Presidential candidate with J. M. Cox in 1920, was the leading candidate. He was opposed by ex-Governor Smith and Tammany Hall in his own state, while John N. Garner of Texas, the Speaker of the House, and five other "favorite sons" from various states were put in nomination. On the first ballot Roosevelt was more than 100 votes short of the necessary two thirds (700); but on the fourth Garner released his 90 delegates, and McAdoo of California, who had been supporting Garner, threw the delegation of that state to Roosevelt, who was nominated with 945 out of the 1154 votes of the convention. Garner was named for Vice-President. Roosevelt immediately flew from Albany to Chicago to deliver his speech of acceptance to the assembled delegates.

There was little doubt of the outcome of the campaign. Suffering under the severest depression in our history, with more than ten million men out of employment, with business prostrate, mortgages on homes and farms being foreclosed, the savings of millions of people wiped out by bank failures and stock losses, and taxes taking one dollar out of every three of the national income, the voters of the country were easily per-

THE BONUS ARMY AT THE CAPITOL

suaded that the Republican administration was responsible for all their ills. In the midsummer a "Bonus Expeditionary Force" of more than ten thousand veterans marched on Washington, like "Coxey's army" of forty years before (p. 518), and encamped on the banks of the Potomac and the grounds of the Capitol, determined to remain until Congress voted them the full cash payment of their certificates. They were not dislodged until the government moved upon them with tear gas and army tanks. A thousand farmers in Iowa picketed the roads to prevent by violence their products' reaching the cities at prices which did not pay them for raising the grain and livestock. And many a sheriff who attempted to auction off a farmer's property for nonpayment of interest or taxes found an ominous group of neighbors gathered around the front porch with shotguns to forbid the sale. The country was in a dangerous revolutionary temper.

Roosevelt and Hoover. Governor Roosevelt toured the country from coast to coast, attacking the administration for encouraging the reckless speculation which had brought on the panic and for its failure to find a remedy. He was eloquent, persuasive, and smilingly confident. He promised a "new deal" and a rapid recovery of prosperity for business and agriculture under a Democratic administration. He spoke to an electorate ready for a change of leaders. Prominent Republicans, like President Butler in the East and Senator Borah in the West, were not uttering a word in support of Hoover; others, like Senators Johnson of California and Norris of Nebraska, were declaring openly for Roosevelt. Late in September, Calvin Coolidge called for a "fighting campaign," and President Hoover made a strenuous effort to stem the tide that was running against him stronger every week. Four times he left his pressing duties at Washington to visit the cities of the West, addressing large audiences in carefully prepared speeches, defending his administration for saving the people from what might have been a much worse calamity, attributing the real causes of the depression to world causes which we could not control, predicting dire consequences if the Republicans were turned out, and denouncing the Democratic Congress for its refusal to co-operate with him in measures for economic recovery. But his speeches were rather heavy and complaining, whereas Roosevelt inspired confidence by his friendly personal appeal to his audiences.

Roosevelt's Election. The verdict at the polls on November 8 was an overwhelming victory for Governor Roosevelt. He carried every state in the union but six (Maine, Vermont, New Hampshire, Connecticut, Delaware, and Pennsylvania), with 472 electoral votes to Hoover's 59. His popular majority of 6,000,000 was equal to that of Hoover four years before. The Socialist candidate, Norman Thomas, fell behind Debs's vote of 920,000 in 1920, while the half-dozen other candidates (Communist, Labor, Prohibition, etc.) divided only about 300,000 votes among them. The Democrats won a majority of 191 in the House and 22 in the Senate. The four months' interval between the election and the inauguration of the new President was a period of "dead center." Hoover graciously invited the President-elect to come to Washington to confer with him on the question of a readjustment of the war debts, and Roosevelt accepted the invitation with equal courtesy. They failed, however, to agree.[1]

The final session of the Seventy-second Congress (December, 1932, to March, 1933) proved to be the last for the "lame ducks,"

---

[1] The most important foreign question of the closing months of Hoover's administration was the attitude of our European debtors toward the payment of their installments. Premier Laval of France had visited Washington in October, 1931, and from his conversations with President Hoover had evidently carried back to Paris the idea that if the European creditors of Germany would not demand reparation payments from her, we would not call upon them for the payment of their installments to us. When, therefore, Germany's creditors reduced her reparations from several billions to $714,000,000, at Lausanne, July 9, 1932, they made no provision in their budgets for paying us their December installments. We denied any pledge to relieve them of their payments. After a lively exchange of notes between Washington and the debtor capitals, Great Britain paid the $95,500,000 due in December, and Italy, Finland, Latvia, Lithuania, and Czechoslovakia paid about $3,000,000. But France "deferred" her payment of $19,000,000, and Poland, Belgium, Hungary, and Estonia also failed to pay. President Hoover wished to re-establish the debt commission of 1922, but Roosevelt opposed it. Finland is the only debtor country that has continued to pay its (small) installments.

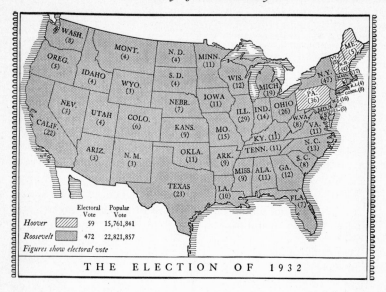

	Electoral Vote	Popular Vote
Hoover	59	15,761,841
Roosevelt	472	22,821,857

Figures show electoral vote

THE ELECTION OF 1932

that is, those members of the House and Senate who had been defeated for re-election in November. For in January, 1933, the Twentieth Amendment to the Constitution was ratified, which provided that henceforth the Congress elected in November should begin its sessions on the third of the following January, and the President should be inaugurated on the twentieth of January. Hence the President's term of office now expires on January 20 instead of March 4. The "lame duck" Congress also passed a Twenty-first Amendment to the Constitution, repealing the Eighteenth Amendment. Special conventions met in the states during the summer and autumn, and with two exceptions (North and South Carolina) ratified the amendment by large majorities. It went into effect on December 5, 1933, when the thirty-sixth state (Utah) ratified. The experiment of prohibition, which had been tried with such varying fortunes for a dozen years, was at an end. The President-elect hoped that the short session of Congress would enact legislation for the relief of the farmers and the balancing of the budget, so that he should not have to call an extra session on his inauguration in March,

1933. But when that date arrived, the country was already facing a crisis which made immediate action necessary.

Summary. In this unit we have studied the fortunes of our country during the fourteen years following the end of the World War. Those fortunes touched extremes of heights and depths that had never been reached in our history before. The immediate result of the war was a period of two or three years of such political, economic, and social confusion as usually follow a great war. Intense idealism gave place to disillusionment as "the vision for which we had fought," the reign of democracy in a warless world, was clouded over by the return of the old rivalries of selfishness, greed, and hate between the nations. President Wilson's administration went out under a cloud of disappointment for him and his followers, who had hoped that the United States would join the League of Nations and take the lead in the crusade for international peace. His Republican successors were more interested in rescuing our own country from the evils which the war had brought : depression in business and agriculture when the high war prices slumped ; strikes and labor wars in industry ; the menace of the "Reds" and "Bolshevists," who were accused of aiming to overthrow our government ; and the spread of various forms of intolerance, persecution, and crime. Both our public morality (as revealed in the scandals of the Harding administration) and our private morality (as shown by the thirst for novels, news, and plays dealing with highly spiced adventures) reached a low point in the early years of the 1920's. A better morale emerged with improving economic conditions under the honest, patient, and prudent Calvin Coolidge. A wave of prosperity in the middle and later years of the decade seemed to be bearing the country to the desired shore of comfort and security for all its people. A boundless optimism replaced the pessimism of a few years before. That the foundations of our prosperity were somewhat shaky nobody cared to be told. Yet it was true that our large foreign trade was possible only because we ourselves lent the people of Europe and Latin America billions of dollars with which to pay for the commodities they bought from us ; that the advance of "tech-

HERBERT C. HOOVER AND FRANKLIN D. ROOSEVELT

nology" (improved machinery) was making possible the production of far more goods by fewer workers, thereby throwing out of employment increasing numbers of men and reducing the power of the masses to buy the goods produced; that the manufacturing interests, supported by a high tariff, were judging the total condition of the country by their own prosperity, while the farmers were sinking deeper and deeper into the slough of debt; and that the prices of stocks in the mad orgy of speculation bore no fair relation to the real value of the properties represented. When the crash came, in the autumn of 1929, the country woke from its dream of the conquest of poverty to the stern reality. It was President Hoover's hard lot to struggle for three fourths of his term with the deepening depression which five years of folly had brought. He struggled manfully and conscientiously; but his efforts to restore prosperity by bolstering up the very system of big business, banking, and finance which was largely held responsible for the depression were without avail. And his lack of political tact and adaptability prevented his winning the confidence of Congress and the people. He was soundly defeated for re-election in November, 1932; and when he left the White House, four months later, the country was at the lowest depths of faithlessness to its past, discouragement with its present, and apprehension for its future.

TERMS TO BE MASTERED

brokers' loans	moratorium	"lame ducks"
farmers' co-operatives	"escalator clause"	"Grundy tariff"
mortgage foreclosure	bull market	balanced budget

FOR SUPPLEMENTARY READING

EDWIN EMERSON, *Hoover and his Times*; WILL IRWIN, *Herbert Hoover, A Reminiscent Biography*, chaps. xxv, xxvi; C. A. BEARD and G. H. E. SMITH, *The Future Comes*; P. H. DOUGLAS and A. DIRECTOR, *The Problem of Unemployment*; STUART CHASE, *The Economy of Abundance* and *Men and Machines*; J. A. HOBSON, *Poverty in Plenty*; GEORGE SOULE, *The Coming American Revolution*, pp. 153–203; GILBERT SELDES, *The Years of the Locust*; BRANDER MATTHEWS, *The Tocsin of Revolt*; F. L. ALLEN, *Only Yesterday*, chaps. xii–xiv, and *The Lords of Creation*, chaps. x–xiv; Anonymous, *Washington Merry-Go-Round*; F. MORLEY (ed.), *Aspects of the Depression*, pp. 120–146, 166–196, 270–278, 287–297.

TOPICS FOR REPORTS

1. **Why the Depression Came.** GEORGE SOULE, *The Coming American Revolution*, pp. 75–149; M. L. ERNST, *America's Primer*, pp. 75–127; J. T. ADAMS, *Our Business Civilization*, chaps. i, ii; STUART CHASE, *The Nemesis of American Business*, chaps. i, iv, ix; W. Z. RIPLEY, *Main Street and Wall Street*, chaps. x, xi.

2. **Our Protest against Japan's Seizure of Manchuria.** QUINCY WRIGHT, "The Manchurian Crisis," in *American Political Science Review*, Vol. XXVI, pp. 45–76; A. L. LOWELL, "Manchuria, The League and the United States," in *Foreign Affairs*, Vol. X, pp. 351–368; TYLER DENNETT, "America's Far-Eastern Diplomacy," in *New York Times Current History Magazine*, Vol. XXXVII, pp. 15 f.; C. P. HOWLAND, "Washington's Stand on the Far-East Crisis," in *Asia*, Vol. XXXII, pp. 230–236; SHERWOOD EDDY, *The World's Danger Zone*.

3. **The Radio.** W. KAEMPFFERT, *A Popular History of American Invention*, Vol. I, pp. 351–378; F. L. DARROW, *Masters of Science and Invention*, chap. xxvi; C. A. and W. BEARD, *The American Leviathan*, pp. 437–446; H. L. JOME, *The Economics of the Radio Industry*; H. P. DAVIS, *The History of Broadcasting in the United States* (Harvard School of Business Administration, 1928); *Radio Markets of the World* (Department of Commerce, Trade Information, *Bulletin No. 600*).

Questions Suggested by the Chapter

1. What does buying stock "on margin" mean? **2.** What new type of President did Hoover represent in the White House? **3.** How did the Federal Farm Board attempt to aid the farmer? **4.** What made the farmer's products decline in price in spite of the government's attempt to keep the price up? **5.** What effect did the tariff of 1930 have on our foreign trade? **6.** Why was there distress in the country in the midst of abundant production? **7.** What is meant by "home market"? **8.** What did Hoover consider the "dominant national question" at the beginning of his administration? **9.** Why was the Wickersham report on prohibition received with ridicule? **10.** How did the Hoover administration treat the stock-market crash of 1929? **11.** What was the purpose of the Reconstruction Finance Corporation? **12.** Why did the surplus change to a deficit in the national treasury in 1931? **13.** What effect did the mid-term elections of 1930 have on the administration? **14.** Show how the London naval conference of 1930 encouraged rather than limited naval construction. **15.** To what do you attribute Roosevelt's overwhelming victory in 1932? **16.** What signs of violence were manifested by the farmers in 1932? **17.** What prominent Republicans supported Roosevelt? **18.** Why did our debtor nations think themselves absolved from their obligations to pay us after the Lausanne agreement? **19.** What was the Twentieth Amendment? **20.** When and how did the experiment of national prohibition come to an end? **21.** What gave a false impression of the prosperity of our foreign trade in the 1920's? **22.** To what did President Hoover attribute the depression? What measures did he take to meet it?

Books Worth Reading on Unit Eight

J. W. Krutch, *The Modern Temper*; Van Wyck Brooks, *America's Coming of Age*; G. E. Sokolsky, *The Tinder Box of Asia*; Calvin Coolidge, *Autobiography*; N. M. Butler, *Is America Worth Saving?*; A. Blumenthal, *Small-Town Stuff*; George Santayana, *The Last Puritan*; W. C. Redfield, *Dependent America*; Frank H. Simonds, *Can America Stay at Home?*; M. Nicholson, *The Valley of Democracy*; N. Hapgood and H. Moskowitz, *Up from the City Streets: Alfred E. Smith*; Glenn Frank, *Thunder and Dawn*, and *America's Hour of Decision*; Abraham Epstein, *Insecurity, A Challenge to America*; A. H. Quinn, *The Soul of America*.

This book comes from the press at a critical moment in American history. Our country is in the midst of the most radical experiment that it has ever tried. It is nothing less than the attempt of the government at Washington to control the whole industrial and agricultural life of the nation, with the purpose of bringing about a more equal distribution of the national income, better prices for the farmer, and higher wages for the laborer. It puts the enormous credit of the national government behind a number of agencies for the relief of unemployment, better housing, the safety of bank deposits, and the security of the disabled, the poor, and the aged. Never before has the central government undertaken the responsibility for the social and economic welfare of the whole nation. In doing so now, the Roosevelt administration runs counter to many private business interests which have been built up with more regard to profits for the producers than to the welfare of the consuming public. It also makes new laws for which it is difficult to find authority granted to Congress by the Constitution of the United States. Finally, it is increasing the national debt by leaps and bounds. On all these counts the administration is being attacked as dictatorial, wildly experimental, and recklessly wasteful by its Republican (and even by some prominent Democratic) critics; and is as ardently defended by its supporters as promising a more abundant life for the mass of our people. The Presidential campaign of 1936 approaches. It will be fought with a bitterness probably unequaled since the days of the Civil War. The battle is already

on. The great and absorbing question is, Will the American people at the polls endorse the New Deal and return President Roosevelt to the White House, or will they turn the present administration out and put an end to the great experiment in social reconstruction which has been tried at Washington for the past three years?

CHAPTER THIRTY-THREE

THE "NEW DEAL"

The New Administration. President Roosevelt was sworn into office by Chief Justice Hughes shortly after noon on March 4, 1933. In his brief inaugural address he condemned the evil practices in industry and finance which had brought us to distress in the midst of plenty, and, in words of confidence recalling Woodrow Wilson's inaugural of twenty years before, asked the people to join him in a "national consecration" to the work of restoring prosperity through united and unselfish effort. "This great nation," he said "will endure as it has endured, will revive and prosper. . . . We face the arduous days that lie before us in the warm courage of national unity. . . . We aim at the assurance of a rounded and permanent national life. We do not distrust the future of essential democracy." He called for faith and courage in the people: the only thing we had to fear was fear itself. In his campaign of the previous summer he had specified the chief evils in our economic system. The farmers, who with their families comprised nearly half our population, were receiving but 7 per cent of the national income, and the prices of their products must be increased to the average prewar figures if the basic industry of the country was to be kept from going on the rocks. More of the profits from business must go to the workers to enable them to consume the goods which were being turned out in such abundance, rather than having the lion's share return to the capitalists to be reinvested in still more plants to produce a still greater surplus of unconsumed goods. And the riot of unrestrained competition, which led to cutthroat prices and sweatshop wages, must give way to a planned and controlled industrial system which should guarantee a decent living wage, shorter hours, and the consequent extension of employment.

Many believed that prominent Democrats, like Newton D. Baker, Owen D. Young, or Alfred E. Smith (who had made his peace with Roosevelt and supported him — albeit half-heartedly — in the campaign), would be invited into the cabinet; but the list, which was immediately confirmed by the Senate, included none of them. Cordell Hull of Tennessee, an old-fashioned Democrat, devoted to tariff reform, was made Secretary of State. The Treasury portfolio was given to William B. Woodin of Pennsylvania, a former Republican and an intimate friend of the President. Failing health compelled Woodin to resign in December, 1933, and his place was taken by Henry Morgenthau, Jr., who had been governor of the Farm Credit Administration since its establishment in May. The other members of the cabinet who were most conspicuous on account of the particular interests of their departments in the measures of the New Deal were Harold L. Ickes of Illinois (a Progressive in 1912 and a Republican in 1916), Secretary of the Interior; Henry A. Wallace of Iowa (son of Harding's Henry C. Wallace), Secretary of Agriculture; and Miss Frances Perkins of New York (the first woman to hold a cabinet seat), Secretary of Labor.[1]

Meeting the Banking Crisis. It must be borne in mind that the President had two tasks to perform, which sometimes clashed with each other. His platform and his campaign speeches pledged him to "national planning" for a better balance between production and distribution of wealth, for the recovery of agriculture, and for economy in government expenses to balance the budget. At the same time, there were pressing needs to be met immediately if he was to make good his assurance that "nobody was going to be allowed to starve." How could the large expenditures necessary to care for the

---

[1] The remaining cabinet members were Governor George H. Dern of Utah (War), Senator Claude A. Swanson of Virginia (Navy), Homer S. Cummings of Connecticut (Attorney-General), Daniel C. Roper of Washington, D.C. (Commerce), and James A. Farley of New York, Chairman of the Democratic National Committee (Postmaster-General). Thus three of the cabinet members were from the President's own state. Mr. Roper, the former Commissioner of Internal Revenue, was the only member who had ever held an executive office in the national government.

thirteen million unemployed and to rescue the farmers from the bog of debt be reconciled with economy? And just how much of the "emergency" relief measures were intended to be a part of the "planning" for a new and juster economic order? It is on these questions that the chief battle between the supporters and the opponents of the New Deal has been waged.

The immediate crisis facing President Roosevelt was the plight of the banks. Even during the prosperous years of the 1920's the poverty of the rural sections of the country had caused the failure of more than five thousand of the smaller and weaker banks. But when the depression sent down the values of the real estate and the business assets on which the loans of the banks were based, and fear of even worse times drove people by the thousands to draw out their deposits to hoard, the banks went down like card houses. In 1930, banks to the number of 1345 closed their doors; in 1931 the figure rose to 2298; in 1932 it was 1456. In the eight days preceding Roosevelt's inauguration over one and a half billion dollars was drawn out of the banks still open. Not even the strong, rich banks of New York could stand the strain. On inauguration day Governor Lehman of New York closed all the banks of the state, and within a few hours his action was followed by all the rest of the states of the Union.

After a White House conference between the President, the Secretary of the Treasury, the Attorney-General, and Professor Raymond Moley (at that time the President's most intimate adviser), lasting well through the night of March 5, President Roosevelt issued an order that all the banks of the country, including the Federal reserve banks, were to remain closed for four days. At the same time he summoned Congress to meet in extra session on March 9. That very afternoon the House, without a roll call, and the Senate, with only seven dissenting votes, passed the Emergency Banking Bill, which approved the President's action and gave the Secretary of the Treasury the power to investigate the condition of all the banks and to permit them to reopen for business at his discretion. The examination of the banks showed four fifths of them to be in a much better condition than the panicky public had imagined.

They were reopened rapidly, confidence was restored, and deposits began to flow in again. By midsummer 14,000 of the 18,500 banks of the country, holding 94 per cent of the deposits, were doing business; but the big banks were ordered to cease the stock-market operations which they had been carrying on through their so-called "affiliates."

The Gold Standard Abandoned. Ever since the passage of the Gold Standard Act in March, 1900, the government had been ready to exchange for gold all the currency of the country. But now President Roosevelt, by a series of orders, began to "manage" the currency. On April 5 the hoarding of gold was forbidden. People were ordered to deliver all their gold to the Federal reserve banks, and the banks were not allowed to pay out gold to their depositors. On April 20 the export of gold was forbidden, except by license from the Secretary of the Treasury. And on June 6, by resolution of Congress, all public and private obligations, even those which specified payment in gold in the contract, were declared to be payable "dollar for dollar in any coin or currency which at the time of payment is legal tender for public and private debts." Congress also gave the President power to reduce the gold content of the dollar by as much as 50 per cent, and on January 31, 1934, he issued a proclamation fixing the gold value of the dollar at 59.06 cents. The main object of this "devaluation" of the dollar was to raise the prices of goods, though it was also expected to help our export trade by enabling foreign countries to pay for our commodities in a cheaper currency. The holders of the bonds of the government and of private corporations denounced the "bad faith" of the administration in making the bonds payable in dollars worth only 59.06 cents in gold. Cases were carried to the Supreme Court, and the decision of that final tribunal was eagerly awaited. When it came, on February 18, 1935, it upheld the government by a vote of five to four.[1] Thus the abandon-

---

[1] Chief Justice Hughes joined the so-called "liberal" members of the Court (Brandeis, Stone, Roberts, and Cardozo) in supporting the administration; while Justices McReynolds, Van Devanter, Sutherland, and Butler held to the sanctity of gold payments. The court further made it impossible for claimants to sue in the Court of Claims for the recovery of the gold value of their bonds.

ment of the gold standard was approved, by the narrowest margin, by the highest court in the land.

The Budget. In his election campaign Roosevelt had scored the extravagance of the Republicans and promised to cut down expenditures by 25 per cent. A beginning was made in the Economy Act of March 20, 1933, which gave the President power to readjust the pension and benefit payments to veterans of the Spanish-American and the World War, and to reduce the salaries of government officials by 15 per cent. Savings of some seven hundred and fifty million dollars a year were expected from these measures, and another two hundred million dollars or so was to be saved by cutting out a number of "unnecessary" boards and bureaus in the government. Since these savings were not enough to balance the budget, new taxes were imposed — on gasoline, beer, excess profits, and dividends from corporations.

But the Economy Act, which was hailed with enthusiasm by the country, failed to produce the results anticipated. The veterans and the officeholders resented the reductions. They were strong enough to get Congress to pass over the President's veto, in March, 1934, the Independent Offices Bill, putting back most of the veterans on the benefit list and restoring the salaries of the government employees. President Roosevelt divided the budget into an "ordinary" and an "extraordinary" part, the former comprising the regular expenses of the government, and the latter the emergency expenses. There was to be, for the present at least, no attempt to balance the extraordinary budget. Bonds were issued by the billions for the projects of relief and recovery under the New Deal. The public debt would be increased, of course, but it was argued that it was well worth adding ten billion dollars to the debt if thereby the recovery of business would add two or three times that sum to the national income. England, with less than half our population and wealth, had a debt of over thirty billion dollars, and her credit was not impaired. We need not feel uneasy, then, if our debt rose to something over twenty-seven billion dollars in 1935. The government could borrow all the money it wanted at less than 3 per cent. The opponents of the mounting debt, however, urged that whether it was called an "ordinary" or an "extraordinary" one made little difference. It threatened, if it went on at the present rate, to undermine the credit of the government, and it would have to be paid in the end by increased taxation.

The Agricultural Adjustment Act. The extra session of Congress sat from March 9 to June 16, 1933. In those hundred days or so it passed such an amazing number of bills that a diligent person could hardly find time to read them, to say nothing of digesting them. The two principal measures were those for the relief of agriculture and for the recovery of industry. Both of them were marked by the enormous control of the government in these fields. On May 12 the Agricultural Adjustment Act was signed by the President. It was a very long and complicated measure, but the gist of it can be explained briefly. Its professed object was to raise the prices of agricultural products to the level which they had enjoyed in the five-year period before the war (1909–1914). Since the chief cause of depressed prices was the great surplus of agricultural products which could not find a market, the act aimed at reducing the surplus by limiting the production of a number of articles, such as wheat, corn, cotton, hogs, tobacco, and milk. For example, the wheat-growers were asked to take several million acres out of cultivation, and the cotton-growers to "plow under" about 30 per cent of their ripening crop, or the equivalent of four million bales of cotton. About six million little pigs were slaughtered, to prevent their growing up into five-hundred-pound porkers. For thus reducing their output the farmers were to receive cash bonuses from the Treasury. The money for these payments was to come from a "processing tax," levied upon the industries which converted the raw agricultural products into salable goods, — for instance, the milling of the wheat into flour or the making of the cotton into cloth or the curing and packing of the pork. Of course, the tax would be "passed along" to the consumer of the finished articles in the higher prices that he would have to pay for them (for example, for a loaf of bread, a cotton shirt, or a Virginia ham). In other words, the processing tax would act for the

PLO____ 'G COTTON UNDER

benefit of farmers somewhat as the tariff did for the benefit of the manufacturers. Indeed, it was called "the farmer's tariff."[1]

A huge organization called the Agricultural Adjustment Administration (the AAA) was set up to carry out the act. Up to the summer of 1935 it had paid to the wheat, cotton, corn, and tobacco farmers nearly six hundred million dollars in government checks and had collected over five hundred million dollars in processing taxes. The farmer's buying power was certainly increased; but critics of the act declared that it was a mistake to seek prosperity by destroying crops. Other parts of the act of May 12, 1933, provided for the extension of easier credit to the farmer and for Federal aid to keep him from losing his farm and home through the foreclosure of his mortgage. Since there

[1] The student will note the difference between this farm program and the McNary-Haugen bills, which also aimed at giving the farmer a share in the benefits of the protective tariff. While those bills asked the help of the government in *disposing* of the surpluses of farm products, the present act sought to *prevent* such surpluses from accumulating. It tackled the difficulty at its source.

was a large group in Congress which believed that an inflation (increase) of the currency was the only way to restore prosperity, it was necessary, in order to get the agricultural bill through, to adopt the amendment of Senator Thomas of Colorado, giving the government the authority to issue three billion dollars of paper money and to reduce the gold content of the dollar by 50 per cent. We have seen how Roosevelt did the latter. He did not, however, inflate the currency by issuing paper money. He frankly declared that the agricultural act was a venture on a "new and untried path," and told Congress that if the act "failed to produce the hoped-for results," he would be the first to acknowledge it and advise Congress further. On January 6, 1936, however, the Supreme Court put an end to this experiment in agricultural relief by declaring the AAA unconstitutional, by a vote of six to three.

The NRA. The industrial workers were in as serious a situation as the farmers when Roosevelt came into power. About thirteen million men, whose families made up fully a quarter of our population, were out of work. How to get business started so as to reabsorb this army of the unemployed was the problem which the government tackled in the National Industrial Recovery Act of June 16, 1933. The objects of the act were to encourage co-operation and planning in industry, to maintain fair wages, to eliminate child labor and to multiply jobs by spreading out the work among more men, to strengthen the labor unions, and to get rid of unfair methods of competition. The government did not take over the industries, to run them itself, as the Socialists and Communists advocated, but assumed a direct control over them. Representatives of the various industries were invited to Washington in the summer of 1933, to work out with the National Recovery Administrator, General Hugh S. Johnson, a series of "codes" of fair dealing, covering wages, hours of labor, and methods of business. Those industries which refused the invitation might be put under a "blanket code" issued by the President. Those which violated the terms of the codes (the "chiselers") might have the Blue Eagle, which was the approving symbol of the NRA, taken away from them.

Beginning with cotton, nearly four hundred codes were drawn up before the end of Roosevelt's first year, and the energetic General Johnson declared that 90 per cent of the industries of the country were supporting the NRA. Under section 7, *a*, of the act, labor was given the right to bargain with employers through representatives "of their own choosing," nor could the employer discharge a workman for refusing to join the "company union" (controlled by the employers) or for joining the American Federation of Labor or any other labor organization. It was an experiment in business and labor co-operation under the strong hand of the government. Some resented it as "coerced," or forced, co-operation, and a few powerful manufacturers, such as Henry Ford, declared their intention to ignore the NRA. But most of them came to heel under the pressure of public opinion and the threats of General Johnson to "crack down" upon the chiselers. Objection was made to the NRA not only on the score that the government was exceeding its powers under the Constitution in this wholesale regulation of business but also that the codes bore unfairly on the small business man, who did not have the capital necessary to pay the higher wages or to hire more workers, or the credit necessary to borrow from the banks.

Emergency Relief. It was not enough, however, to pass laws for the recovery of agriculture and business. An immediate crisis faced the country in the millions of men without employment or hope of employment. Private charity and local relief were insufficient to take care of the destitute. President Roosevelt had declared that no American must be allowed to starve. So the strong credit of the national government must be put behind the relief efforts. An Unemployment Relief Act of March, 1933, gave the President authority to employ men in work on the improvement and conservation of the natural resources of the country. Under this law a Civilian Conservation Corps (the CCC) was organized, which enrolled about three hundred thousand idle young men in camps situated in all parts of the country, to engage in outdoor work, at thirty dollars a month, on useful projects such as planting trees, constructing trails and fire-prevention lanes in the national parks and forests, and eradicating insect pests and plant diseases. A Federal Emergency Relief Act of May 12 appropriated five hundred million dollars for direct aid to the victims of unemployment. Half the sum was to supplement the relief funds of the states which could still afford contributions; but as the state funds failed, the burden on the national treasury grew heavier and heavier.

By the end of June, Harry L. Hopkins, the head of the Federal Emergency Relief Administration (the FERA), had assigned over fifty million dollars to forty-five states, and in addition the government, through the Federal Surplus Relief Corporation, had purchased large quantities of pork, flour, butter, beans, wheat, and corn to distribute to the hungry. The object of the administration was to transfer the unemployed from the emergency relief of a "dole," or pure charity, to some sort of work in which they could preserve their self-respect. To this end huge projects of Public Works and Civil Works (the PWA and CWA) were started on highways, sanitation, parks and playgrounds, waterways, public buildings, landscaping, etc., including both manual and clerical work. Over a million men were taken off the relief rolls and put to work on these projects by the end of January, 1934. The next month an additional appropriation of nearly a billion dollars was made for continuing the work, and at the close of the year still another $525,000,000. Altogether the government had authorized between two and a half and three billions to be spent for this emergency program; but even that huge sum sank into insignificance when the new Congress of 1935 passed the administration's bill for $4,880,000,000 for public works.

Long-Term Planning. In addition to measures for emergency relief and for the recovery of agriculture and business, there were a number of national projects for the improvement of large areas of the country and for what the President called the future "security of the men, women, and children of the nation." The sum of twenty-five million dollars was allotted by the NRA for the building of "subsistence homesteads." In congested regions such as the West Virginia coal fields, where the workers were living in squalid shanties, neat little houses with small plots of land for gardening were provided at a very small cost, to be paid over a period of twenty-five years. It was hoped that in this way many little model communities would grow up in the neighborhood of the cities, and that, with the aid of the Emergency Housing Corporation, the slums which have so long been a disgrace to our cities would gradually be wiped out.

A few days before the adjournment of Congress (August, 1935), the President signed the Social Security Bill, which the New York *Sun* called "the most important legislation of the Roosevelt Administration." "Today a hope of many years' standing is in large part fulfilled," said the President in signing the bill; "we have tried to frame a law which will give some measure of protection to the average citizen and his family against the loss of a job and against poverty-ridden old age." Federal aid, matching state aid up to fifteen dollars a month, will be paid to needy persons over sixty-five years of age. Federal funds will also be available to help those who are unable to work, such as the sick, the crippled, or the blind. A system of nation-wide unemployment insurance financed by a tax of 1 per cent in 1936 and 3 per cent after 1938 on the pay rolls of the employers, together with a system of old-age insurance financed by a tax on both the employers and the workers (3 per cent after 1949), will bring a new sense of security to millions of Americans who have been living in the shadow of fear for the future of themselves and their children.

Still another instance of long-term planning for the betterment of the people is the work which the government is doing to develop large areas of the country through its water projects: the Grand Coulee and Bonneville power plants on the Columbia River, the great Boulder Dam on the Colorado, and especially the grand project of improvement of the valley of the Tennessee. It was on May 18, 1933, that the act was passed creating the Tennessee Valley Authority, a board of three men headed by President A. E. Morgan of Antioch College. The purpose of the act was "to improve the navigability and to provide for the flood control of the Tennessee River; to provide for the reforestation and proper use of the marginal land in the Tennessee Valley; to provide for the agricultural and industrial development of the said Valley; to provide for the national defense by the creation of a corporation for the operation of the Government properties at and near Muscle Shoals in the state of Alabama." The TVA might manufacture fertilizers and other compounds of nitrogen. It might generate and sell electric power, over its own transmission lines or leased lines, to states, cities, corporations, or even individuals.[1] In time of war its resources might be wholly taken over by the government. Its work of reclamation, farm and forest reconstruction, and furnishing of electrical power at much cheapened rates was expected to benefit half a dozen or more states in the valley of the Tennessee and its tributaries.

Opposition to the New Deal. As business conditions slowly improved and the unemployed began to find jobs (though many of them at "made" work in which their wages from the public funds scarcely differed from a "dole"), it was natural that opposition to the government's extensive program should develop. Some declared that the emergency was now over and that business could stand on its own feet. Some argued that the President had gone too fast and far in his innovations. Some thought that he had yielded too much to the advice of the theorists of his "brain trust"[2] in his farm program, his devaluation of the dollar, his restrictions on the freedom of industry, and his recom-

[1] The Supreme Court, in a decision of February 17, 1936, upheld by a vote of 8 to 1 the right of the government to sell power through the TVA.

[2] "The brain trust" was the nickname given by Mr. Kieran of the *New York Times* to a group of men, mostly college professors, whom Governor Roosevelt had consulted freely during his campaign and after his election. Professors Raymond Moley, Rexford Tugwell, and A. A. Berle of Columbia were prominent members of the "brain trust" at first. It was never a constant group. Some of the men, like Professor O. M. Sprague of Harvard, broke with the President when their advice was not taken. Professor Moley was Assistant Secretary of State for a while, but retired to edit the magazine *Today* when his ideas clashed with those of Secretary Hull. Professor Tugwell is still (1936) Undersecretary of Agriculture. The chief complaint against these men was that they were amateur politicians, foisting their half-baked theories upon the country, while some of their bitter enemies foolishly charged them with plotting to overthrow our republican form of government and set up a communist regime.

BOULDER DAM

mendations for the expenditure of mounting billions of dollars for public works and emergency relief.

Moreover, 1934 was the year of the mid-term Congressional elections, and the Republicans, who had generally supported the emergency legislation of the spring of 1933, were now bent on the recovery of their former party strength in Congress. The leading Republican paper, the *New York Herald-Tribune*, declared in April, 1934, that the administration's policies had been "a succession of unrelated and hastily devised remedies," and that it had "produced an economic chaos with no end in sight." Nevertheless, President Roosevelt was still "going strong" at the midway mark of his administration. He had taken the people into his confidence by several radio addresses, explaining in friendly, simple, and cheerful "talks" the aims which he had in view. He had published a book in April, 1934, entitled *On Our Way*, in which he reviewed the measures of the year past. In the elections of November 6 he was overwhelmingly endorsed at the polls. The Democrats secured 322 of the 425 seats in the House and 69 of the 96 Senators for the Seventy-fourth Congress, which, according to the Twentieth Amendment, was to meet on January 3, 1935.

The new year brought signs of returning prosperity. Retail sales were increasing; savings-bank deposits, for the first time in three years, were on the upward trend; farm prices were higher; the output of automobiles reached a peak figure. Of course, the criticisms of the New Deal increased as the election year of 1936 approached. They came from radicals, such as Dr. Townsend of California, Father Coughlin of Detroit, and Senator Huey Long of Louisiana (assassinated in the state capitol on September 8, 1935), with their schemes for redividing the nation's wealth, and from the Republicans, who were eager to return to power. The latter dwelt on President Roosevelt's failure to redeem the campaign promises of a balanced budget, declared that the huge extraordinary appropriations (some eight billion dollars by 1935) were piling up an intolerable burden of debt for future generations to meet, criticized much of the relief program as coddling the lazy and weakening the moral fiber of the nation, deplored the invasion of the citizen's liberty by increasing government control, and charged the President and Congress with reckless disregard for the limitations set upon their power by the Constitution.

The Supreme Court and the New Deal. Meanwhile the opponents of the Roosevelt policies sought to bring various parts of the New Deal to the Federal courts, to test their constitutionality. The first case (though a minor one) to reach the Supreme Court, in January, 1935, was a setback for the administration. The judges, by a vote of 8 to 1,[1] decided that section 9, *c*, of the NIRA, giving the President the right to prohibit the interstate transportation of "hot oil" (or oil produced in excess of the state's quota) was unconstitutional. A month later, however, the Court, as we have noted (p. 832), upheld by a 5-to-4 decision

---

[1] The dissenter was Justice Benjamin Cardozo of New York, who had been appointed by President Hoover early in 1932 to succeed Justice Oliver Wendell Holmes, on the latter's retirement at the age of ninety-one. Justice Holmes, honored through the world for his legal learning and his humane interpretation of the law, died at his home in Washington on March 6, 1935. He was the son of the New England physician-poet.

GRIEF [1]

the cancellation of the "gold clause" in the bonds of the government and of private corporations. The most sensational decision came on May 27, 1935, when the Court, in the Schechter case, declared the NIRA unconstitutional, without a dissenting voice. The case itself was of small importance, involving the violation of the live-poultry code by a firm of dealers in Brooklyn, New York; but the decision was momentous. It declared that Congress had no right to fix wages and hours in intrastate business and that no economic emergency justified the invasion of the rights of the states by the Federal power. Thus the seven hundred and fifty codes of the NRA were outlawed by the highest court of the land, and the Blue Eagle was shorn of his beak and talons.

We have already noted how the Court, in its decisions of Jan-

[1] From a cartoon by Elderman in the *Washington Post*.

uary and February, 1936, annulled the AAA and upheld the TVA (pp. 836, 840, note 1). Whether further decisions will uphold or condemn other measures of the New Deal remains to be seen. It is possible that if the Court continues to nullify the New Deal, the President and Congress will seek a constitutional amendment giving them power to apply national remedies to nation-wide economic crises. For, as the President said in his comment on the Schechter decision, "we are no longer in the horse-and-buggy age."

Foreign Relations. President Roosevelt was so absorbed in the problems of relief and recovery at home that he paid comparatively little attention to foreign affairs. The questions of the Allies' debts to us, of international plans for disarmament, of international trade, or the tariff were not pushed. The President spoke in his inaugural address of our wishing to play the part of a "good neighbor" to the other nations, which might be interpreted as a neighbor who stays at home and minds his own business. When the disarmament conference of 1932 at Geneva petered out, we took no steps to revive it. We sent a delegation, headed by Secretary of State Hull, to the London Economic Conference of the summer of 1933; but Roosevelt's refusal to allow our delegates to join with those of the gold-bloc countries in devising an international standard of currency practically broke up the conference. Our one positive stroke of diplomacy was the recognition of the Soviet Republic of Russia in November, 1933. As for Latin America, we refrained from forcible intervention in a revolution which overthrew President Machado of Cuba in the summer of 1933, and gave up in 1935 the Platt Amendment, which had been the legal basis for our intervention in the island on five previous occasions. In November, 1933, we participated in the seventh Pan-American Conference, at Montevideo, Uruguay, with Secretary Hull again leading our delegation. The representatives of twenty-one republics of the New World made some progress in "neighborliness" in the matter of the exchange of goods and ideas; but their major task of ending the persistent war between Bolivia and Paraguay over the Gran Chaco region was left to 1935.

When we have brought our domestic problems nearer solution, — in a better adjustment between agriculture and industry, in diffusing buying power more widely through the nation, and in reviving a sense of security and confidence among our own people, — we may turn with renewed interest to our duties and privileges as a member of the community of nations.

"A Backward Glance o'er Traveled Roads." In these pages we have traced the development of the American people from a few scattered settlements on the Atlantic shore in the seventeenth century to a great continental nation of over twenty-five million, with colonial possessions in the Caribbean and the far Pacific. We have seen how in the colonial days the enterprising descendants of these settlers, increased by new emigrants from the British Isles and the continent of Europe, pushed westward to the barriers of the Appalachians and beyond, successfully disputing with the French the Ohio "gateway to the West" and subduing the Indians and the forest in their progress down the "Western waters" into the rich lands between the Alleghenies and the Mississippi.

We have seen how the independent spirit of our forefathers chafed under the political control of a government three thousand miles distant, and resented that government's regulation of their commerce and industry in the interests of a world-wide empire, until they finally renounced their allegiance to the British crown and, after a revolutionary struggle of seven years, won the recognition of their freedom and their independent status among the nations of the world. We have seen how leaders like Washington, Madison, Morris, Wilson, Jay, and Hamilton grappled with the difficult task of overcoming mutual jealousies among the economic interests and the social classes of the new states, to persuade them to accept the constitution of a real union, strong enough to ensure the preservation of order, the protection of property, and the vindication of the honor of the United States in the eyes of such European nations as were still disposed to regard us as a people "in a position of colonial dependence and fear."

We have seen how, by purchase, conquest, and treaty, vast new regions were acquired beyond the Mississippi and beyond the Rockies for the constantly westward-moving explorers, missionaries, fur traders, mining prospectors, ranchers, and farmers, until by the middle of the nineteenth century the imperial domain of the United States reached unbroken from the Atlantic to the Pacific, and from the Canadian border to the Gulf of Mexico.

We have seen how the conflicting economic interests of the commercial East, the planter South, and the new pioneer West led to impassioned debates in Congress over the tariff, public lands, internal improvements, and banking, culminating in the great issue of slavery, which led eventually to the secession of the South and to four years of civil war for the preservation of the Union and the liberation of the slaves.

We have seen how after the Civil War the attention of the government was more and more absorbed by economic problems arising out of the exploitation of the unbounded natural resources of the country : the concentration of capital in "big business," the demands of organized labor, the complaints of the associated farmers, the criticism of the arbitrary conduct of the railroads, the crusade for cheap currency.

We have seen how, at the turn of the century, the United States entered upon the "new and untried path" of empire, with its complex problems of the government of distant peoples, alien in race, language, ideals, and customs.

We have seen how our country was drawn into the greatest war of history, sending its soldiers for the first time to fight on the battlefields of Europe and seeing its President sail to spend months in conference with the statesmen of the Old World at Paris, writing the terms of a European peace. We have seen how our country refused to adhere to the League of Nations or the World Court, for fear that its independence might be impaired by entanglements in the political, economic, diplomatic, and military quarrels of Europe.

We have seen how the Wilsonian program of international idealism was superseded under his Republican successors Harding, Coolidge, and Hoover by a strong devotion to the idea of "national interests." And, finally, we have seen how, after a period of unexampled prosperity based on the unsound foundations of speculation, our country was plunged into the abyss of depression from which the bold experiments of the New Deal attempted to rescue it.

The Strength of America. Every one of these stages of development has brought new responsibilities to the government and people of the United States, and every one has aroused in timid minds the fear lest cherished ideals and institutions might be sacrificed. Just as one hundred and sixty years ago there were many who predicted that the colonies were rushing headlong into anarchy and ruin by repudiating their allegiance to "the best and kindest of kings," so today there are many who contend that we should lose our priceless independence by joining the League of Nations. There have been few sessions of Congress in which anxious orators have not predicted that the passage of this or that measure would mean the "downfall of the Republic." And still the Republic endures. Its industrial and financial strength is the wonder of the world. With only 5.8 per cent of the world's area and 6.3 per cent of its population, the United States has 73 per cent of the world's automobiles (one for every five inhabitants of the country), 32 per cent of the telegraph lines and 60 per cent of the telephone lines, 32 per cent of the harnessed water power, and 33 per cent of the railway mileage. We produce 48.8 per cent of the world's cotton, 59.9 per cent of its petroleum and 27.5 per cent of its steel, 24.4 per cent of its zinc and 26.3 per cent of its copper, 32 per cent of its coal and 26.9 per cent of its iron. Every region of our country, from the coastal lowlands of the Atlantic and the Gulf through the central plains to the towering ridges of the Rockies and beyond to the fertile valley of the Pacific states, produces its mounting surplus of food, raw materials, and manufactured goods, to be distributed from one end of the land to the other by the most effective transportation system through the greatest area of free trade in the world. Eight hundred thousand retail stores serve the ultimate consumers. With a friendly people of ten million on the north, of like race, language, and political ideals with ourselves;

with neighbors on the south too weak and disturbed in their internal politics to be a menace to our safety, even if they wished; with the broad oceans east and west separating us from the coast of Europe and Asia, — we have no such problems of national defense as confront the crowded, jealous nations of the Old World. For more than a century the four-thousand-mile border between the United States and Canada has not seen a fortress or a garrison.

"The Foes of our Own Household." This rich and powerful republic has no fear of foes from without. But there are dangers that threaten within. We have been a wasteful people in the midst of our abundance, consuming the resources which we should be conserving for a future generation. It is estimated that the reckless plundering of our mines, oil fields, and forests entails an annual waste of 750,000,000 tons of coal, 1,000,000,000 barrels of oil, 600,000,000,000 cubic feet of natural gas, and 5,000,000,000 feet of lumber. Strikes and lockouts, preventable illness and accidents, the maladjustment of labor supply to labor demand, have resulted, even in normal times, in the unemployment of about 15 per cent of the man power of the nation, and fully another 15 per cent of the workers have been engaged in the manufacture of useless luxuries to flatter our vanity, or positively harmful "goods." More than three million people a year are made sick by food adulterations; another million are drug addicts; and no one knows how numerous are the dupes of the patent medicines, cure-alls, and beautifiers which have made us the victims of "the gaudiest collection of quacks in the world's history." Our preoccupation with material success has threatened to blind us to the value of the patient, honest cultivation of mind and character. The conquest of the forces of nature has far outrun the organization of intelligence. If we have the enviable record of leading the world in economic prosperity, we have also the unenviable record of leading the world in recklessness, instability, and crime. Every year our losses by preventable fires exceed the cost of the Panama Canal. Fatal accidents claim one victim every five minutes. The number of suicides mounts steadily. The losses paid by burglary-insurance companies have increased 600 per cent in the last decade. The number of divorces granted in the United States was 56,000 in 1900 and 160,000 in 1932 — or one divorce for every 6.2 marriages in the latter year, a ratio one and a half times as high as that of France and Japan, and more than fifteen times as high as that of England. Murders and homicides are more numerous here than in any other country of the world.

American Ideals. These are appalling facts. They are sicknesses in the body of the nation and, like illness in the human body, they must be realized to be remedied. If our Republic ever fails to fulfill the high hopes of the men who founded it and who sustained it in the days of weakness and trial, the fault will be with a generation that has lost the inspiration of their ideals. We shall continue to go through the forms of democratic government in vain if we lose the sense of responsibility, individual and collective, which is the cement which prevents freedom from crumbling into license. The fathers set up an ideal of liberty within the wholesome restraint of law. They conceived of a republic in which the opportunity to make the most of one's talent and industry should be open to all, irrespective of birth, creed, or condition. They forbade Congress to prohibit the free exercise of religion or to abridge freedom of speech or of the press. They declared that no person should be deprived of the rights of life, liberty, and property without due process of law. They expressly reserved to the people of the states the exercise of powers not specifically delegated to the central government, never meaning to interfere with local self-government or personal freedom. These are the principles of American democracy, and they must be respected if America is to continue to be a land of liberty.

Passing the Torch. Paraphrasing the words of Abraham Lincoln, the teacher of American history today says to the boys and girls in the classrooms of our broad land, "In your hands, my young fellow students and citizens, lies the future of our country." If the coming generation is more faithful to the ideals of economy, industry, and honesty, of order, freedom, and disinterested service, than the present generation has been, then we shall be going forward toward the fulfillment of the destinies of the Republic. If the coming generation is even a little less faithful to these ideals, then we shall be headed down the road to degeneracy, defeat, decay. Could there be a more inspiring call than the stake of America's very life and honor for the youth of our schools to pledge themselves to study her past history with diligence in order that they may judge her present policies with understanding and meet her future problems with courage? A feature of the ancient Greek games was the relay race in which the runner at the end of his lap handed on the lighted torch to his successor. It is a parable of all education and a symbol of ever-renewing life. The torch of our history was kindled at the sacred altar of liberty. Let it be your pledge and mine to bear it

> High like a beacon,
> Till our strong years be sped
> And sinews weaken;
> Till others in our stead
> Take from our loosening hand
> The torch full-streaming which we pass at Death's command.

Terms to be Mastered

planned economy	extraordinary budget	emergency relief
managed currency	processing tax	subsistence homesteads
devaluation of the dollar	industrial codes	unemployment insurance

Books on the New Deal

1. Favorable. F. D. Roosevelt, *Looking Forward* and *On our Way*; H. A. Wallace, *America must Choose* and *New Frontiers*; H. L. Ickes, *Back to Work*; Donald Richberg, *The Rainbow*; E. K. Lindley, *The Roosevelt Revolution, the First Phase.*

2. Neutral. Schuyler Wallace, *The New Deal in Action*; L. M. Hacker, *A Short History of the New Deal*; C. A. Beard and G. E. H. Smith, *The Future Comes*; Sir Arthur Steele-Maitland, *The New America*; B. Faÿ, *Roosevelt and his America.*

3. Hostile. Ralph Robey, *Roosevelt versus Recovery*; B. Stolberg and W. J. Vinton, *The Economic Consequences of the New Deal*; William MacDonald, *The Menace of Recovery*; David Lawrence, *Beyond the New Deal*; Herbert Hoover, *The Challenge to Liberty*; J. P. Warburg, *It's Up to Us.*

QUESTIONS SUGGESTED BY THE CHAPTER

1. Compare Roosevelt's inaugural address of 1933 with Wilson's inaugural address of 1913. **2.** Why did so many American banks fail? **3.** What did Roosevelt do to meet the bank crisis? **4.** What measures in regard to gold did the government take in Roosevelt's first year? **5.** What steps toward economy in government were taken in the early days of the administration? **6.** Why was not the budget balanced? **7.** How did the administration defend the increase in the public debt? **8.** What was the object of the AAA? **9.** Compare the AAA and the McNary-Haugen bills in regard to the method of relief proposed for the farmers. **10.** What was the fate of the AAA? **11.** What did the Thomas Amendment provide? **12.** Name three aims of the NIRA. **13.** What was the Blue Eagle? **14.** How did the NIRA seek to benefit labor? **15.** What did the government do for the relief of unemployment? **16.** For what purpose was the TVA established? **17.** Why was it opposed by the owners of power corporations? **18.** What did the Social Security Act of 1935 provide? **19.** What signs of returning prosperity were there in 1935? **20.** What was the decision of the Supreme Court in the Schechter case? **21.** What did Roosevelt mean by the doctrine of "the good neighbor"? **22.** State the main issue in the Presidential campaign of 1936.

TOPICAL ANALYSIS

★

APPENDIXES

I. *Declaration of Independence*[1]

IN CONGRESS, JULY 4, 1776

A DECLARATION BY THE REPRESENTATIVES OF THE UNITED STATES OF AMERICA, IN CONGRESS ASSEMBLED

WHEN, in the course of human events, it becomes necessary for one people to dissolve the political bands which have connected them with another, and to assume, among the powers of the earth, the separate and equal station to which the laws of nature and of nature's God entitle them, a decent respect to the opinions of mankind requires that they should declare the causes which impel them to the separation.

We hold these truths to be self-evident: — That all men are created equal; that they are endowed by their Creator with certain unalienable rights; that among these are life, liberty, and the pursuit of happiness. That, to secure these rights, governments are instituted among men, deriving their just powers from the consent of the governed; that, whenever any form of government becomes destructive of these ends, it is the right of the people to alter or to abolish it, and to institute a new government, laying its foundation on such principles, and organizing its powers in such form, as to them shall seem most likely to effect their safety and happiness. Prudence, indeed, will dictate, that governments long established should not be changed for light and transient causes; and accordingly all experience hath shown that mankind are more disposed to suffer while evils are sufferable, than to right themselves by abolishing the forms to which they are accustomed. But when a long train of abuses and usurpations, pursuing invariably the same object, evinces a design to reduce them under absolute despotism, it is their right, it is their duty, to throw off such government, and to provide new guards for their future security. Such has been the patient sufferance of these colonies; and such is now the necessity which constrains them to alter their former systems of government. The history of the present King of Great Britain is

[1] The original copy of the Declaration of Independence is kept in the Library of Congress in Washington. The Declaration was adopted July 4, 1776, and was signed by the members representing the thirteen states August 2, 1776. John Hancock, whose name appears first among the signers, was president of the Congress.

i

a history of repeated injuries and usurpations, all having in direct object the establishment of an absolute tyranny over these states. To prove this, let facts be submitted to a candid world.

He has refused his assent to laws the most wholesome and necessary for the public good.

He has forbidden his governors to pass laws of immediate and pressing importance, unless suspended in their operation till his assent should be obtained; and when so suspended, he has utterly neglected to attend to them.

He has refused to pass other laws for the accommodation of large districts of people, unless those people would relinquish the right of representation in the legislature — a right inestimable to them, and formidable to tyrants only.

He has called together legislative bodies at places unusual, uncomfortable, and distant from the depository of their public records, for the sole purpose of fatiguing them into compliance with his measure.

He has dissolved representative houses repeatedly, for opposing, with manly firmness, his invasions on the rights of the people.

He has refused, for a long time after such dissolutions, to cause others to be elected, whereby the legislative powers, incapable of annihilation, have returned to the people at large for their exercise; the State remaining, in the mean time, exposed to all the dangers of invasions from without, and convulsions within.

He has endeavored to prevent the population of these States; for that purpose obstructing the laws for the naturalization of foreigners; refusing to pass others to encourage their migration hither, and raising the conditions of new appropriations of lands.

He has obstructed the administration of justice, by refusing his assent to laws for establishing judiciary powers.

He has made judges dependent on his will alone for the tenure of their offices, and the amount and payment of their salaries.

He has erected a multitude of new offices, and sent hither swarms of officers to harass our people and eat out their substance.

He has kept among us in times of peace, standing armies, without the consent of our legislatures.

He has affected to render the military independent of, and superior to, the civil power.

He has combined with others to subject us to a jurisdiction foreign to our constitutions, and unacknowledged by our laws; giving his assent to their acts of pretended legislation:

For quartering large bodies of armed troops among us;

For protecting them, by a mock trial, from punishment for any murders which they should commit on the inhabitants of these States;

For cutting off our trade with all parts of the world;

For imposing taxes on us without our consent;

For depriving us, in many cases, of the benefits of trial by jury;

For transporting us beyond seas, to be tried for pretended offences;

For abolishing the free system of English laws in a neighboring province, establishing therein an arbitrary government, and enlarging its boundaries, so as to render it at once an example and fit instrument for introducing the same absolute rule into these colonies;

For taking away our charters, abolishing our most valuable laws, and altering, fundamentally, the forms of our governments;

For suspending our own legislatures, and declaring themselves invested with power to legislate for us in all cases whatsoever.

He has abdicated government here, by declaring us out of his protection, and waging war against us.

He has plundered our seas, ravaged our coasts, burned our towns, and destroyed the lives of our people.

He is at this time transporting large armies of foreign mercenaries to complete the works of death, desolation and tyranny, already begun with circumstances of cruelty and perfidy scarcely paralleled in the most barbarous ages, and totally unworthy the head of a civilized nation.

He has constrained our fellow-citizens, taken captive on the high seas, to bear arms against their country, to become the executioners of their friends and brethren, or to fall themselves by their hands.

He has excited domestic insurrection among us, and has endeavored to bring on the inhabitants of our frontiers the merciless Indian savages, whose known rule of warfare is an undistinguished destruction of all ages, sexes, and conditions.

In every stage of these oppressions we have petitioned for redress in the most humble terms; our repeated petitions have been answered only by repeated injury. A prince whose character is thus marked by every act which may define a tyrant, is unfit to be the ruler of a free people.

Nor have we been wanting in our attentions to our British brethren. We have warned them, from time to time, of attempts by their legislature to extend an unwarrantable jurisdiction over us. We have reminded them of the circumstances of our emigration and settlement here. We have appealed to their native justice and magnanimity; and we have conjured them, by the ties of our common kindred, to disavow these usurpations, which would inevitably interrupt our connections and correspondence. They, too, have been deaf to the voice of justice and consanguinity. We must, therefore, acquiesce in the necessity which denounces our separation, and hold them, as we hold the rest of mankind, enemies in war, in peace friends.

We, therefore, the Representatives of the United States of America, in General Congress assembled, appealing to the Supreme Judge of the world for the rectitude of our intentions, do, in the name and by the authority of the good people of these colonies, solemnly publish and declare, That these united Colonies are, and of right ought to be, free and independent states; that they are absolved from all allegiance to the British crown, and that all political connection between them and the state of Great Britain is, and ought to be, totally dissolved; and that, as free and independent states, they have full power to levy war, conclude peace, contract alliances, establish commerce, and do all other acts and things which independent states may of right do. And, for the support of this declaration, with a firm reliance on the protection of Divine Providence, we mutually pledge to each other our lives, our fortunes, and our sacred honor.

The foregoing Declaration was, by order of Congress, engrossed, and signed by the following members:

JOHN HANCOCK

NEW HAMPSHIRE
JOSIAH BARTLETT
WILLIAM WHIPPLE
MATTHEW THORNTON

MASSACHUSETTS BAY
SAMUEL ADAMS
JOHN ADAMS
ROBERT TREAT PAINE
ELBRIDGE GERRY

RHODE ISLAND
STEPHEN HOPKINS
WILLIAM ELLERY

CONNECTICUT
ROGER SHERMAN
SAMUEL HUNTINGTON
WILLIAM WILLIAMS
OLIVER WOLCOTT

NEW YORK
WILLIAM FLOYD
PHILIP LIVINGSTON
FRANCIS LEWIS
LEWIS MORRIS

NEW JERSEY
RICHARD STOCKTON
JOHN WITHERSPOON
FRANCIS HOPKINSON
JOHN HART
ABRAHAM CLARK

PENNSYLVANIA
ROBERT MORRIS
BENJAMIN RUSH
BENJAMIN FRANKLIN
JOHN MORTON
GEORGE CLYMER
JAMES SMITH
GEORGE TAYLOR
JAMES WILSON
GEORGE ROSS

DELAWARE
CÆSAR RODNEY
GEORGE READ
THOMAS M'KEAN

MARYLAND
SAMUEL CHASE
WILLIAM PACA
THOMAS STONE

CHARLES CARROLL, of Carrollton

VIRGINIA
GEORGE WYTHE
RICHARD HENRY LEE
THOMAS JEFFERSON
BENJAMIN HARRISON
THOMAS NELSON, JR.
FRANCIS LIGHTFOOT LEE
CARTER BRAXTON

NORTH CAROLINA
WILLIAM HOOPER
JOSEPH HEWES
JOHN PENN

SOUTH CAROLINA
EDWARD RUTLEDGE
THOMAS HEYWARD, JR.
THOMAS LYNCH, JR.
ARTHUR MIDDLETON

GEORGIA
BUTTON GWINNETT
LYMAN HALL
GEORGE WALTON

Resolved, That copies of the Declaration be sent to the several assemblies, conventions, and committees, or councils of safety, and to the several commanding officers of the continental troops; that it be proclaimed in each of the United States, at the head of the army.

★

II. *Constitution of the United States*

PREAMBLE

WE, the people of the United States, in order to form a more perfect union, establish justice, insure domestic tranquillity, provide for the common defense, promote the general welfare, and secure the blessings of liberty to ourselves and our posterity, do ordain and establish this CONSTITUTION for the United States of America.

ARTICLE I. LEGISLATIVE DEPARTMENT

SECTION 1. CONGRESS

All legislative powers herein granted shall be vested in a Congress of the United States, which shall consist of a Senate and House of Representatives.[1]

SECTION 2. HOUSE OF REPRESENTATIVES

Election of Members. The House of Representatives shall be composed of members chosen every second year by the people of the several States, and the electors in each State shall have the qualifications requisite for electors of the most numerous branch of the State Legislature.

Qualifications. No person shall be a representative who shall not have attained to the age of twenty-five years, and been seven years a citizen of the United States, and who shall not, when elected, be an inhabitant of that State in which he shall be chosen.

Apportionment. Representatives and direct taxes shall be apportioned among the several States which may be included within this Union, according to their respective numbers,[2] which shall be determined by adding to the whole number of free persons, including those bound to service for a term of years, and excluding Indians not taxed, three-fifths of all other persons.[3] The actual

---

[1] The term of each Congress is two years. Under the twentieth amendment to the Constitution, ratified in 1933, Congress assembles at noon of the third day of January of each year.

[2] The apportionment under the census of 1910 is one representative for every 212,407 persons.

[3] The word "persons" refers to slaves. The word "slave" nowhere appears in the Constitution. This paragraph has been amended (Amendments XIII and XIV) and is no longer in force.

enumeration shall be made within three years after the first meeting of the Congress of the United States, and within every subsequent term of ten years, in such manner as they shall by law direct. The number of representatives shall not exceed one for every thirty thousand, but each State shall have at least one representative : and until such enumeration shall be made, the State of New Hampshire shall be entitled to choose three ; Massachusetts, eight ; Rhode Island and Providence Plantations, one ; Connecticut, five ; New York, six ; New Jersey, four ; Pennsylvania, eight ; Delaware, one ; Maryland, six ; Virginia, ten ; North Carolina, five ; South Carolina, five ; and Georgia, three.

Vacancies. When vacancies happen in the representation from any State, the executive authority [1] thereof shall issue writs of election to fill such vacancies.

Officers. Impeachment. The House of Representatives shall choose their Speaker [2] and other officers ; and shall have the sole power of impeachment.

SECTION 3. SENATE

Number of Senators : Election. The Senate of the United States shall be composed of two senators from each State, chosen by the Legislature thereof, for six years ; and each senator shall have one vote. [Repealed in 1913 by Amendment XVII.]

Classification. Immediately after they shall be assembled in consequence of the first election, they shall be divided as equally as may be into three classes. The seats of the senators of the first class shall be vacated at the expiration of the second year ; of the second class, at the expiration of the fourth year ; of the third class, at the expiration of the sixth year, so that one-third may be chosen every second year ; and if vacancies happen by resignation, or otherwise, during the recess of the Legislature of any State, the executive [1] thereof may make temporary appointments until the next meeting of the Legislature, which shall then fill such vacancies. [Modified by Amendment XVII.]

Qualifications. No person shall be a senator who shall not have attained to the age of thirty years, and been nine years a citizen of the United States, and who shall not, when elected, be an inhabitant of that State for which he shall be chosen.

President of Senate. The Vice-President of the United States shall be president of the Senate, but shall have no vote, unless they be equally divided.

Officers. The Senate shall choose their other officers, and also a president *pro tempore*, in the absence of the Vice-President, or when he shall exercise the office of President of the United States.

Trials of Impeachment. The Senate shall have the sole power to try all impeachments : When sitting for that purpose, they shall be on oath or affirmation.

[1] Governor.

[2] The Speaker, who presides, is one of the representatives ; the other officers — clerk, sergeant-at-arms, postmaster, chaplain, doorkeeper, etc. — are not.

When the President of the United States is tried, the Chief-Justice shall preside: and no person shall be convicted without the concurrence of two-thirds of the members present.

Judgment in Case of Conviction. Judgment in cases of impeachment shall not extend further than to removal from office, and disqualification to hold and enjoy any office of honor, trust, or profit under the United States; but the party convicted shall nevertheless be liable and subject to indictment, trial, judgment, and punishment, according to law.

SECTION 4. BOTH HOUSES

Manner of electing Members. The times, places, and manner of holding elections for senators and representatives shall be prescribed in each State by the Legislature thereof; but the Congress may at any time, by law, make or alter such regulations, except as to the places of choosing senators.[1]

Meetings of Congress. The Congress shall assemble at least once in every year, and such meeting shall be on the first Monday in December, unless they shall by law appoint a different day.

SECTION 5. THE HOUSES SEPARATELY

Organization. Each house shall be the judge of the elections, returns, and qualifications of its own members, and a majority of each shall constitute a quorum to do business; but a smaller number may adjourn from day to day, and may be authorized to compel the attendance of absent members, in such manner, and under such penalties, as each house may provide.

Rules. Each house may determine the rules of its proceedings, punish its members for disorderly behavior, and, with the concurrence of two-thirds, expel a member.

Journal. Each house shall keep a journal of its proceedings, and from time to time publish the same, excepting such parts as may in their judgment require secrecy, and the yeas and nays of the members of either house on any question shall, at the desire of one-fifth of those present, be entered on the journal.

Adjournment. Neither house, during the session of Congress, shall, without the consent of the other, adjourn for more than three days, nor to any other place than that in which the two houses shall be sitting.

SECTION 6. PRIVILEGES AND DISABILITIES OF MEMBERS

Pay and Privileges of Members. The senators and representatives shall receive a compensation for their services, to be ascertained by law, and paid out of the treasury of the United States. They shall in all cases, except treason, felony, and breach of the peace, be privileged from arrest during their

[1] This is to prevent Congress from fixing the places of meeting of the state legislatures.

attendance at the session of their respective houses, and in going to and returning from the same; and for any speech or debate in either house, they shall not be questioned in any other place.

Prohibitions on Members. No senator or representative shall, during the time for which he was elected, be appointed to any civil office under the authority of the United States, which shall have been created, or the emoluments whereof shall have been increased, during such time; and no person holding any office under the United States shall be a member of either house during his continuance in office.

Section 7. Method of passing Laws

Revenue Bills. All bills for raising revenue shall originate in the House of Representatives; but the Senate may propose or concur with amendments as on other bills.

How Bills become Laws. Every bill which shall have passed the House of Representatives and the Senate shall, before it become a law, be presented to the President of the United States; if he approve, he shall sign it, but if not, he shall return it, with his objections, to that house in which it shall have originated, who shall enter the objections at large on their journal, and proceed to reconsider it. If after such reconsideration, two-thirds of that house shall agree to pass the bill, it shall be sent, together with the objections, to the other house, by which it shall likewise be reconsidered, and if approved by two-thirds of that house, it shall become a law. But in all such cases the votes of both houses shall be determined by yeas and nays, and the names of the persons voting for and against the bill shall be entered on the journal of each house respectively. If any bill shall not be returned by the President within ten days (Sundays excepted) after it shall have been presented to him, the same shall be a law, in like manner as if he had signed it, unless the Congress by their adjournment prevent its return, in which case it shall not be a law.

Resolutions, etc. Every order, resolution, or vote to which the concurrence of the Senate and House of Representatives may be necessary (except on a question of adjournment) shall be presented to the President of the United States; and before the same shall take effect, shall be approved by him, or being disapproved by him, shall be repassed by two-thirds of the Senate and House of Representatives, according to the rules and limitations prescribed in the case of a bill.

Section 8. Powers granted to Congress

Powers of Congress. The Congress shall have power:

To lay and collect taxes, duties, imposts, and excises, to pay the debts and provide for the common defense and general welfare of the United States; but all duties, imposts, and excises shall be uniform throughout the United States;

To borrow money on the credit of the United States;

To regulate commerce with foreign nations, and among the several States, and with the Indian tribes;

To establish a uniform rule of naturalization, and uniform laws on the subject of bankruptcies throughout the United States;

To coin money, regulate the value thereof, and of foreign coin, and fix the standard of weights and measures;

To provide for the punishment of counterfeiting the securities and current coin of the United States;

To establish post-offices and post-roads;

To promote the progress of science and useful arts, by securing, for limited times, to authors and inventors the exclusive right to their respective writings and discoveries;

To constitute tribunals inferior to the Supreme Court;

To define and punish piracies and felonies committed on the high seas, and offenses against the law of nations;

To declare war, grant letters of marque and reprisal,[1] and make rules concerning captures on land and water;

To raise and support armies, but no appropriation of money to that use shall be for a longer term than two years;

To provide and maintain a navy;

To make rules for the government and regulation of the land and naval forces;

To provide for calling forth the militia to execute the laws of the Union, suppress insurrections and repel invasions;

To provide for organizing, arming, and disciplining the militia, and for governing such part of them as may be employed in the service of the United States, reserving to the States respectively the appointment of the officers, and the authority of training the militia according to the discipline prescribed by Congress;

To exercise exclusive legislation in all cases whatsoever over such district (not exceeding ten miles square) as may, by cession of particular States, and the acceptance of Congress, become the seat of the government of the United States,[2] and to exercise like authority over all places purchased by the consent of the Legislature of the State in which the same shall be, for the erection of forts, magazines, arsenals, dockyards, and other needful buildings; — And

Implied Powers. To make all laws which shall be necessary and proper for carrying into execution the foregoing powers, and all other powers vested by this Constitution in the government of the United States, or in any department or officer thereof.[3]

[1] Letters granted by the government to private citizens in time of war, authorizing them, under certain conditions, to capture the ships of the enemy.

[2] The District of Columbia.

[3] This is the famous elastic clause of the Constitution.

SECTION 9. POWERS FORBIDDEN TO THE UNITED STATES

Absolute Prohibitions on Congress. The migration or importation of such persons as any of the States now existing shall think proper to admit, shall not be prohibited by the Congress prior to the year one thousand eight hundred and eight, but a tax or duty may be imposed on such importation, not exceeding ten dollars for each person.[1]

The privilege of the writ of habeas corpus [2] shall not be suspended, unless when in cases of rebellion or invasion the public safety may require it.

No bill of attainder [3] or ex-post-facto law [4] shall be passed.

No capitation or other direct tax shall be laid, unless in proportion to the census or enumeration hereinbefore directed to be taken. [Extended by Amendment XVI.]

No tax or duty shall be laid on articles exported from any State.

No preference shall be given by any regulation of commerce or revenue to the ports of one State over those of another; nor shall vessels bound to, or from, one State, be obliged to enter, clear, or pay duties in another.

No money shall be drawn from the treasury but in consequence of appropriations made by law; and a regular statement and account of the receipts and expenditures of all public money shall be published from time to time.

No title of nobility shall be granted by the United States: And no person holding any office of profit or trust under them, shall, without the consent of the Congress, accept of any present, emolument, office, or title, of any kind whatever, from any king, prince, or foreign state.

SECTION 10. POWERS FORBIDDEN TO THE STATES

Absolute Prohibitions on the States. No State shall enter into any treaty, alliance, or confederation; grant letters of marque and reprisal; coin money; emit bills of credit; make anything but gold and silver coin a tender in payment of debts; pass any bill of attainder, ex-post-facto law, or law impairing the obligation of contracts, or grant any title of nobility.

Conditional Prohibitions on the States. No State shall, without the consent of the Congress, lay any imposts or duties on imports or exports, except what may be absolutely necessary for executing its inspection laws; and the net produce of all duties and imposts, laid by any State on imports or exports,

---

[1] This refers to the foreign slave trade. "Persons" means "slaves." In 1808 Congress prohibited the importation of slaves. This clause is, of course, no longer in force.

[2] An official document requiring an accused person who is in prison awaiting trial to be brought into court to inquire whether he may be legally held.

[3] A special legislative act by which a person may be condemned to death or to outlawry or banishment without the opportunity of defending himself which he would have in a court of law.

[4] A law relating to the punishment of acts committed before the law was passed.

shall be for the use of the treasury of the United States; and all such laws shall be subject to the revision and control of the Congress.

No State shall, without the consent of Congress, lay any duty of tonnage, keep troops, or ships-of-war, in time of peace, enter into any agreement or compact with another State, or with a foreign power, or engage in war, unless actually invaded, or in such imminent danger as will not admit of delay.

ARTICLE II. EXECUTIVE DEPARTMENT

Section 1. President and Vice-President

Term. The executive power shall be vested in a President of the United States of America. He shall hold his office during the term of four years, and, together with the Vice-President, chosen for the same term, be elected, as follows:

Electors. Each State shall appoint, in such manner as the Legislature thereof may direct, a number of electors, equal to the whole number of senators and representatives to which the State may be entitled in the Congress: but no senator or representative, or person holding an office of trust or profit under the United States, shall be appointed an elector.

Proceedings of Electors and of Congress. [1 The electors shall meet in their respective States, and vote by ballot for two persons, of whom one at least shall not be an inhabitant of the same State with themselves. And they shall make a list of all the persons voted for, and of the number of votes for each; which list they shall sign and certify and transmit sealed to the seat of the government of the United States, directed to the president of the Senate. The president of the Senate shall, in the presence of the Senate and House of Representatives, open all the certificates, and the votes shall then be counted. The person having the greatest number of votes shall be the President, if such number be a majority of the whole number of electors appointed; and if there be more than one who have such majority, and have an equal number of votes, then the House of Representatives shall immediately choose by ballot one of them for President; and if no person have a majority, then from the five highest on the list the said house shall, in like manner, choose the President. But in choosing the President, the votes shall be taken by States, the representation from each State having one vote; a quorum for this purpose shall consist of a member or members from two-thirds of the States, and a majority of all the States shall be necessary to a choice. In every case, after the choice of the President, the person having the greatest number of votes of the electors shall be the Vice-President. But if there should remain two or more who have equal votes, the Senate shall choose from them by ballot the Vice-President.]

1 This paragraph in brackets has been superseded by the Twelfth Amendment.

Time of choosing Electors. The Congress may determine the time of choosing the electors, and the day on which they shall give their votes; which day shall be the same throughout the United States.[1]

Qualifications of President. No person except a natural born citizen, or a citizen of the United States at the time of the adoption of this Constitution, shall be eligible to the office of President; neither shall any person be eligible to that office who shall not have attained to the age of thirty-five years, and been fourteen years resident within the United States.

Vacancy. In case of the removal of the President from office, or of his death, resignation, or inability to discharge the powers and duties of the said office, the same shall devolve on the Vice-President, and the Congress may by law provide for the case of removal, death, resignation, or inability, both of the President and Vice-President, declaring what officer shall then act as President; and such officer shall act accordingly until the disability be removed, or a President shall be elected.[2]

Salary. The President shall, at stated times, receive for his services a compensation which shall neither be increased nor diminished during the period for which he shall have been elected, and he shall not receive within that period any other emolument from the United States, or any of them.

Oath. Before he enter on the execution of his office, he shall take the following oath or affirmation: — " I do solemnly swear (or affirm) that I will faithfully execute the office of President of the United States, and will, to the best of my ability, preserve, protect, and defend the Constitution of the United States."

SECTION 2. POWERS OF THE PRESIDENT

Military Powers; Reprieves and Pardons. The President shall be commander-in-chief of the army and navy of the United States, and of the militia of the several States, when called into the actual service of the United States; he may require the opinion, in writing, of the principal officer in each of the executive departments, upon any subject relating to the duties of their respective offices; and he shall have power to grant reprieves and pardons for offenses against the United States, except in cases of impeachment.

Treaties; Appointments. He shall have power, by and with the advice and consent of the Senate, to make treaties, provided two-thirds of the senators present concur; and he shall nominate, and by and with the advice and consent of the Senate shall appoint ambassadors, other public ministers and consuls, judges of the Supreme Court, and all other officers of the United

---

[1] The electors are chosen on the Tuesday next after the first Monday in November, preceding the expiration of a presidential term. They vote (by Act of Congress of February 3, 1887) on the second Monday in January for President and Vice-President. The votes are counted, and declared in Congress on the second Wednesday of the following February.

[2] This has now been provided for by the Presidential Succession Act of 1886.

States, whose appointments are not herein otherwise provided for, and which shall be established by law: but the Congress may by law vest the appointment of such inferior officers, as they think proper, in the President alone, in the courts of law, or in the heads of departments.

Filling of Vacancies. The President shall have power to fill up all vacancies that may happen during the recess of the Senate, by granting commissions which shall expire at the end of their next session.

SECTION 3. DUTIES OF THE PRESIDENT

Message; Convening of Congress. He shall from time to time give to the Congress information [1] of the state of the Union, and recommend to their consideration such measures as he shall judge necessary and expedient; he may, on extraordinary occasions, convene both houses, or either of them, and in case of disagreement between them with respect to the time of adjournment, he may adjourn them to such time as he shall think proper; he shall receive ambassadors and other public ministers; he shall take care that the laws be faithfully executed, and shall commission all the officers of the United States.

SECTION 4. IMPEACHMENT

Removal of Officers. The President, Vice-President, and all civil officers of the United States, shall be removed from office on impeachment for, and conviction of, treason, bribery, or other high crimes and misdemeanors.

ARTICLE III. JUDICIAL DEPARTMENT

SECTION 1. UNITED STATES COURTS

Courts established; Judges. The judicial power of the United States shall be vested in one Supreme Court, and in such inferior courts as the Congress may from time to time ordain and establish. The judges, both of the Supreme and inferior courts, shall hold their offices during good behavior, and shall, at stated times, receive for their services a compensation which shall not be diminished during their continuance in office.

SECTION 2. JURISDICTION OF UNITED STATES COURTS

Federal Courts in General. The judicial power shall extend to all cases, in law and equity, arising under this Constitution, the laws of the United States, and treaties made, or which shall be made, under their authority; — to all cases

---

[1] The president gives this information through a message to Congress at the opening of each session. Washington and John Adams read their messages in person to Congress. Jefferson, however, sent a written message to Congress. This method was followed until President Wilson returned to the earlier custom.

affecting ambassadors, other public ministers, and consuls; — to all cases of admiralty and maritime jurisdiction; — to controversies to which the United States shall be a party; — to controversies between two or more States; — between a State and citizens of another State; [1] — between citizens of different States; — between citizens of the same State claiming lands under grants of different States, and between a State, or the citizens thereof, and foreign states, citizens or subjects.

Supreme Court. In all cases affecting ambassadors, other public ministers and consuls, and those in which a State shall be party, the Supreme Court shall have original jurisdiction. In all other cases before mentioned, the Supreme Court shall have appellate jurisdiction, both as to law and fact, with such exceptions and under such regulations as the Congress shall make.

Trials. The trial of all crimes, except in cases of impeachment, shall be by jury; and such trial shall be held in the State where the said crimes shall have been committed; but when not committed within any State, the trial shall be at such place or places as the Congress may by law have directed.

SECTION 3. TREASON

Treason defined. Treason against the United States shall consist only in levying war against them, or in adhering to their enemies, giving them aid and comfort.

No person shall be convicted of treason unless on the testimony of two witnesses to the same overt act, or on confession in open court.

Punishment. The Congress shall have power to declare the punishment of treason, but no attainder of treason shall work corruption of blood, or forfeiture, except during the life of the person attainted.

ARTICLE IV. RELATIONS OF THE STATES TO EACH OTHER

SECTION 1. OFFICIAL ACTS

Full faith and credit shall be given in each State to the public acts, records, and judicial proceedings of every other State. And the Congress may by general laws, prescribe the manner in which such acts, records, and proceedings shall be proved, and the effect thereof.

SECTION 2. PRIVILEGES OF CITIZENS

The citizens of each State shall be entitled to all privileges and immunities of citizens in the several States.

Fugitives from Justice. A person charged in any State with treason, felony, or other crime, who shall flee from justice, and be found in another State,

[1] This has been modified by the Eleventh Amendment.

shall, on demand of the executive authority of the State from which he fled, be delivered up, to be removed to the State having jurisdiction of the crime.

Fugitive Slaves. No person[1] held to service or labor in one State, under the laws thereof, escaping into another, shall, in consequence of any law or regulation therein, be discharged from such service or labor, but shall be delivered up on claim of the party to whom such service or labor may be due.

Section 3. New States and Territories

Admission of States. New States may be admitted by the Congress into this Union; but no new State shall be formed or erected within the jurisdiction of any other State; nor any State be formed by the junction of two or more States, or parts of States, without the consent of the Legislatures of the States concerned as well as of the Congress.

Territory and Property of United States. The Congress shall have power to dispose of and make all needful rules and regulations respecting the territory or other property belonging to the United States; and nothing in this Constitution shall be so construed as to prejudice any claims of the United States, or of any particular State.

Section 4. Protection of the States

The United States shall guarantee to every State in this Union a republican form of government, and shall protect each of them against invasion, and on application of the Legislature, or of the Executive (when the Legislature cannot be convened) against domestic violence.

ARTICLE V. AMENDMENTS

How proposed; how ratified. The Congress, whenever two-thirds of both houses shall deem it necessary, shall propose amendments to this Constitution, or, on the application of the Legislatures of two-thirds of the several States, shall call a convention for proposing amendments, which, in either case, shall be valid to all intents and purposes, as part of this Constitution, when ratified by the Legislatures of three-fourths of the several States, or by conventions in three-fourths thereof, as the one or the other mode of ratification may be proposed by the Congress; provided that no amendment which

---

[1] "Person" here includes slave. This was the basis of the Fugitive Slave Laws of 1793 and 1850. It is now superseded by the Thirteenth Amendment, by which slavery is prohibited.

may be made prior to the year one thousand eight hundred and eight shall in any manner affect the first and fourth clauses in the ninth section of the first article; and that no State, without its consent, shall be deprived of its equal suffrage in the Senate.

ARTICLE VI. GENERAL PROVISIONS

Public Debt. All debts contracted, and engagements entered into, before the adoption of this Constitution, shall be as valid against the United States under this Constitution, as under the Confederation.

Supremacy of Constitution. This Constitution, and the laws of the United States which shall be made in pursuance thereof; and all treaties made, or which shall be made, under the authority of the United States, shall be the supreme law of the land; and the judges in every State shall be bound thereby, anything in the Constitution or laws of any State to the contrary notwithstanding.

Official Oath; Religious Test. The senators and representatives before mentioned, and the members of the several State Legislatures, and all executive and judicial officers, both of the United States and of the several States, shall be bound by oath or affirmation to support this Constitution; but no religious test shall ever be required as a qualification to any office or public trust under the United States.

ARTICLE VII. RATIFICATION OF THE CONSTITUTION

Ratification. The ratification of the Conventions of nine States shall be sufficient for the establishment of this Constitution between the States so ratifying the same.

Done in convention, by the unanimous consent of the States present, the seventeenth day of September, in the year of our Lord one thousand seven hundred and eighty-seven, and of the independence of the United States of America the twelfth.

In witness whereof, we have hereunto subscribed our names.[1]

> GEORGE WASHINGTON,
> *President, and Deputy from Virginia.*

---

[1] There were sixty-five delegates chosen to the convention: ten did not attend; sixteen declined or failed to sign; thirty-nine signed. Rhode Island sent no delegates.

NEW HAMPSHIRE	PENNSYLVANIA	VIRGINIA

NEW HAMPSHIRE

JOHN LANGDON
NICHOLAS GILMAN

MASSACHUSETTS

NATHANIEL GORHAM
RUFUS KING

CONNECTICUT

WILLIAM SAMUEL JOHNSON
ROGER SHERMAN

NEW YORK

ALEXANDER HAMILTON

NEW JERSEY

WILLIAM LIVINGSTON
DAVID BREARLEY
WILLIAM PATERSON
JONATHAN DAYTON

PENNSYLVANIA

BENJAMIN FRANKLIN
THOMAS MIFFLIN
ROBERT MORRIS
GEORGE CLYMER
THOMAS FITZSIMONS
JARED INGERSOLL
JAMES WILSON
GOUVERNEUR MORRIS

DELAWARE

GEORGE READ
GUNNING BEDFORD, JR.
JOHN DICKINSON
RICHARD BASSETT
JACOB BROOM

MARYLAND

JAMES M'HENRY
DANIEL OF ST. THOMAS
JENIFER
DANIEL CARROLL

VIRGINIA

JOHN BLAIR
JAMES MADISON, JR.

NORTH CAROLINA

WILLIAM BLOUNT
RICHARD DOBBS SPAIGHT
HUGH WILLIAMSON

SOUTH CAROLINA

JOHN RUTLEDGE
CHARLES C. PINCKNEY
CHARLES PINCKNEY
PIERCE BUTLER

GEORGIA

WILLIAM FEW
ABRAHAM BALDWIN

Attest : WILLIAM JACKSON, *Secretary*

AMENDMENTS

Religion, Speech, Press, Assembly, Petition. ARTICLE I.[1] Congress shall make no law respecting an establishment of religion, or prohibiting the free exercise thereof ; or abridging the freedom of speech, or of the press; or the right of the people peaceably to assemble, and to petition the government for redress of grievances.

Militia. ARTICLE II. A well-regulated militia being necessary to the security of a free State the right of the people to keep and bear arms shall not be infringed.

Soldiers. ARTICLE III. No soldier shall, in time of peace, be quartered in any house, without the consent of the owner; nor in time of war but in a manner to be prescribed by law.

Unreasonable Searches. ARTICLE IV. The right of the people to be secure in their persons, houses, papers, and effects, against unreasonable searches and seizures, shall not be violated, and no warrants shall issue, but upon

---

[1] These amendments were proposed by Congress and ratified by the legislatures of the several states, pursuant to the fifth article of the Constitution. The first ten were offered in 1789 and adopted before the close of 1791. They were for the most part the work of Madison. They are frequently called the Bill of Rights, as their purpose is to guard more efficiently the rights of the people and of the states.

probable cause, supported by oath or affirmation, and particularly describing the place to be searched, and the persons or things to be seized.

Criminal Prosecutions. ARTICLE V. No person shall be held to answer for a capital, or otherwise infamous crime, unless on a presentment or indictment of a grand jury, except in cases arising in the land or naval forces, or in the militia, when in actual service in time of war and public danger; nor shall any person be subject for the same offense to be twice put in jeopardy of life or limb; nor shall be compelled in any criminal case to be a witness against himself, nor to be deprived of life, liberty, or property, without due process of law; nor shall private property be taken for public use, without just compensation.

ARTICLE VI. In all criminal prosecutions, the accused shall enjoy the right to a speedy and public trial, by an impartial jury of the State and district wherein the crime shall have been committed, which district shall have been previously ascertained by law, and to be informed of the nature and cause of the accusation; to be confronted with the witnesses against him; to have compulsory process for obtaining witnesses in his favor, and to have the assistance of counsel for his defense.

Suits at Common Law. ARTICLE VII. In suits at common law, where the value in controversy shall exceed twenty dollars, the right of trial by jury shall be preserved, and no fact tried by a jury shall be otherwise reëxamined in any court of the United States than according to the rules of common law.

Bail, Punishments. ARTICLE VIII. Excessive bail shall not be required, nor excessive fines imposed, nor cruel and unusual punishments inflicted.

Reserved Rights and Powers. ARTICLE IX. The enumeration in the Constitution of certain rights shall not be construed to deny or disparage others retained by the people.

ARTICLE X. The powers not delegated to the United States by the Constitution, nor prohibited by it to the States, are reserved to the States respectively, or to the people.

Suits against States. ARTICLE XI.[1] The judicial power of the United States shall not be construed to extend to any suit in law or equity, commenced or prosecuted against any of the United States by citizens of another State, or by citizens or subjects of any foreign state.

Method of electing President and Vice-President. ARTICLE XII.[2] The electors shall meet in their respective States, and vote by ballot for President and Vice-President, one of whom, at least, shall not be an inhabitant of the same State with themselves; they shall name in their ballots the person voted for as President, and in distinct ballots the person voted for as Vice-President; and they shall make distinct lists of all persons voted for as President, and of all persons voted for as Vice-President, and of the number of votes for each, which list they shall sign and certify, and transmit sealed to the seat of the government of the United States, directed to the president of the Senate; —

---

[1] Proposed in 1794; adopted in 1798.   [2] Adopted in 1804.

the president of the Senate shall, in the presence of the Senate and House of Representatives, open all the certificates, and the votes shall then be counted; — the person having the greatest number of votes for President, shall be the President, if such number be a majority of the whole number of electors appointed; and if no person have such majority, then from the persons having the highest numbers not exceeding three on the list of those voted for as President, the House of Representatives shall choose immediately, by ballot, the President. But in choosing the President, the votes shall be taken by States, the representation from each State having one vote; a quorum for this purpose shall consist of a member or members from two-thirds of the States, and a majority of all the States shall be necessary to a choice. And if the House of Representatives shall not choose a President whenever the right of choice shall devolve upon them, before the fourth day of March next following, then the Vice-President shall act as President, as in the case of the death or other constitutional disability of the President. The person having the greatest number of votes as Vice-President, shall be the Vice-President, if such number be a majority of the whole number of electors appointed; and if no person have a majority, then from the two highest numbers on the list, the Senate shall choose the Vice-President; a quorum for the purpose shall consist of two-thirds of the whole number of senators, and a majority of the whole number shall be necessary to a choice. But no person constitutionally ineligible to the office of President shall be eligible to that of Vice-President of the United States.

Slavery abolished. ARTICLE XIII.[1] *Section 1.* Neither slavery nor involuntary servitude, except as a punishment for crime, whereof the party shall have been duly convicted, shall exist within the United States, or any place subject to their jurisdiction.

Section 2. Congress shall have power to enforce this article by appropriate legislation.

Negroes made Citizens. ARTICLE XIV.[2] *Section 1.* All persons born or naturalized in the United States, and subject to the jurisdiction thereof, are citizens of the United States and of the State wherein they reside. No State shall make or enforce any law which shall abridge the privileges or immunities of citizens of the United States; nor shall any State deprive any person of life, liberty, or property, without due process of law, nor deny to any person within its jurisdiction the equal protection of the laws.

Section 2. Representatives shall be apportioned among the several States according to their respective numbers, counting the whole number of persons in each State, excluding Indians not taxed. But when the right to vote at any election for the choice of electors for President and Vice-President of the United States, representatives in Congress, the executive or judicial officers of a State, or the members of the Legislature thereof, is denied to any of the male inhabitants of such State, being twenty-one years of age, and citizens of

1 Adopted in 1865.　　2 Adopted in 1868.

the United States, or in any way abridged, except for participation in rebellion or other crime, the basis of representation therein shall be reduced in the proportion which the number of such male citizens shall bear to the whole number of male citizens twenty-one years of age in such State.

Section 3. No person shall be a senator or representative in Congress, or elector of President or Vice-President, or hold any office, civil or military, under the United States, or under any State, who having previously taken an oath as a member of Congress, or as an officer of the United States, or as a member of any State Legislature, or as an executive or judicial officer of any State, to support the Constitution of the United States, shall have engaged in insurrection or rebellion against the same, or given aid or comfort to the enemies thereof. But Congress may, by a vote of two-thirds of each house, remove such disability.

Section 4. The validity of the public debt of the United States, authorized by law, including debts incurred for payment of pensions and bounties for services in suppressing insurrection or rebellion, shall not be questioned. But neither the United States nor any State shall assume or pay any debt or obligation incurred in aid of insurrection or rebellion against the United States, or any claim for the loss or emancipation of any slave; but all such debts, obligations, and claims shall be held illegal and void.

Section 5. The Congress shall have power to enforce, by appropriate legislation, the provisions of this article.

Negroes made Voters. ARTICLE XV.[1] *Section 1.* The rights of citizens of the United States to vote shall not be denied or abridged by the United States, or by any State, on account of race, color, or previous condition of servitude.

Section 2. The Congress shall have power to enforce this article by appropriate legislation.

Income Tax. ARTICLE XVI.[2] The Congress shall have power to lay and collect taxes on incomes from whatever source derived, without apportionment among the several States, and without regard to any census or enumeration.

ARTICLE XVII.[2] The Senate of the United States shall be composed of two Senators from each State, elected by the people thereof for six years; and each Senator shall have one vote. The electors in each State shall have the qualifications requisite for electors of the most numerous branch of the State Legislatures.

Direct Election of Senators. When vacancies happen in the representation of any State in the Senate, the executive authority of such State shall issue writs of election to fill such vacancies: Provided, that the Legislature of any State may empower the Executive thereof to make temporary appointments until the people fill the vacancies by election as the Legislature may direct.

This amendment shall not be so construed as to affect the election or term of any Senator chosen before it becomes valid as part of the Constitution.

[1] Adopted in 1870.   [2] Ratified in 1913.

National Prohibition. ARTICLE XVIII.[1] *Section 1.* After one year from the ratification of this article the manufacture, sale, or transportation of intoxicating liquors within, the importation thereof into, or the exportation thereof from the United States and all territory subject to the jurisdiction thereof for beverage purposes is hereby prohibited.

Section 2. The Congress and the several States shall have concurrent power to enforce this article by appropriate legislation.

Section 3. This article shall be inoperative unless it shall have been ratified as an amendment to the Constitution by the Legislatures of the several States, as provided in the Constitution, within seven years from the date of the submission hereof to the States by the Congress.

Woman Suffrage. ARTICLE XIX.[2] *Section 1.* The right of citizens of the United States to vote shall not be denied or abridged by the United States or by any State on account of sex.

Section 2. Congress shall have power to enforce this article by appropriate legislation.

"Lame Duck" Amendment. ARTICLE XX.[3] *Section 1.* The terms of the President and Vice-President shall end at noon on the twentieth day of January, and the terms of senators and representatives at noon on the third day of January, of the years in which such terms would have ended if this article had not been ratified; and the terms of their successors shall then begin.

Section 2. The Congress shall assemble at least once in every year, and such meeting shall begin at noon on the third day of January, unless they shall by law appoint a different day.

Section 3. If, at the time fixed for the beginning of the term of the President, the President-elect shall have died, the Vice-President-elect shall become President. If a President shall not have been chosen before the time fixed for the beginning of his term, or if the President-elect shall have failed to qualify, then the Vice-President-elect shall act as President until a President shall have qualified; and the Congress may by law provide for the case wherein neither a President-elect nor a Vice-President-elect shall have qualified, declaring who shall then act as President, or the manner in which one who is to act shall be selected, and such person shall act accordingly until a President or Vice-President shall have qualified.

Section 4. The Congress may by law provide for the case of the death of any of the persons from whom the House of Representatives may choose a President whenever the right of choice shall have devolved upon them, and for the case of the death of any of the persons from whom the Senate may choose a Vice-President whenever the right of choice shall have devolved upon them.

Section 5. Sections 1 and 2 shall take effect upon the fifteenth day of October following the ratification of this article.

Section 6. This article shall be inoperative unless it shall have been ratified as an amendment to the Constitution by the Legislatures of three-fourths of the several States within seven years from the date of its submission.

---

[1] Ratified in 1919. In force in 1920.   [2] Ratified in 1920.   [3] Ratified in 1933.

The Repeal of Prohibition. ARTICLE XXI.[1] *Section 1.* The eighteenth amendment to the Constitution of the United States is hereby repealed. '

Section 2. The transportation or importation into any State, Territory, or possession of the United States for delivery or use therein of intoxicating liquors, in violation of the laws thereof, is hereby prohibited.

Section 3. This article shall be inoperative unless it shall have been ratified as an amendment to the Constitution by conventions in the several States, as provided in the Constitution, within seven years from the date of the submission hereof to the States by the Congress.

[1] Ratified in 1933.

★   •

III. *The States, Territories, and Dependencies of the United States*

No.	STATE	DATE OF ADMISSION	POPULATION (CENSUS OF 1930)	*	AREA IN SQUARE MILES	CAPITAL
1	Delaware		238,380	1	2,370	Dover
2	Pennsylvania		9,631,350	34	45,126	Harrisburg
3	New Jersey		4,041,334	14	8,224	Trenton
4	Georgia		2,908,506	10	59,265	Atlanta
5	Connecticut	Original States	1,606,903	6	4,965	Hartford
6	Massachusetts		4,249,614	15	8,266	Boston
7	Maryland		1,631,526	6	12,327	Annapolis
8	South Carolina		1,738,765	6	30,989	Columbia
9	New Hampshire		465,293	2	9,341	Concord
10	Virginia		2,421,851	9	42,627	Richmond
11	New York		12,588,066	45	49,204	Albany
12	North Carolina		3,170,276	11	52,426	Raleigh
13	Rhode Island		687,497	2	1,248	Providence
14	Vermont	1791	359,611	1	9,564	Montpelier
15	Kentucky	1792	2,614,589	9	40,598	Frankfort
16	Tennessee	1796	2,616,556	9	42,022	Nashville
17	Ohio	1803	6,646,697	24	41,040	Columbus
18	Louisiana	1812	2,101,593	8	48,506	Baton Rouge
19	Indiana	1816	3,238,503	12	36,354	Indianapolis
20	Mississippi	1817	2,009,821	7	46,865	Jackson
21	Illinois	1818	7,630,654	27	56,665	Springfield
22	Alabama	1819	2,646,248	9	51,998	Montgomery
23	Maine	1820	797,423	3	33,040	Augusta
24	Missouri	1821	3,629,367	13	69,420	Jefferson City
25	Arkansas	1836	1,854,482	7	53,335	Little Rock
26	Michigan	1837	4,842,325	17	57,980	Lansing
27	Florida	1845	1,468,211	5	58,666	Tallahassee
28	Texas	1845	5,824,715	21	265,896	Austin
29	Iowa	1846	2,470,939	9	56,147	Des Moines
30	Wisconsin	1848	2,939,006	10	56,066	Madison
31	California	1850	5,677,251	20	158,297	Sacramento
32	Minnesota	1858	2,563,953	9	84,682	St. Paul
33	Oregon	1859	953,786	3	96,699	Salem
34	Kansas	1861	1,880,999	7	82,158	Topeka
35	West Virginia	1863	1,729,205	6	24,170	Charleston
36	Nevada	1864	91,058	1	110,690	Carson City

*Number of Representatives in the House by the 1930 apportionment.

No.	STATE	DATE OF ADMISSION	POPULATION (CENSUS OF 1930)	*	AREA IN SQUARE MILES	CAPITAL
37	Nebraska	1867	1,377,963	5	77,520	Lincoln
38	Colorado	1876	1,035,791	4	103,948	Denver
39	North Dakota	1889	680,845	2	70,837	Bismarck
40	South Dakota	1889	692,849	2	77,615	Pierre
41	Montana	1889	537,606	2	146,997	Helena
42	Washington	1889	1,563,396	6	69,127	Olympia
43	Idaho	1890	445,032	2	83,888	Boise
44	Wyoming	1890	225,565	1	97,914	Cheyenne
45	Utah	1896	507,847	2	84,990	Salt Lake City
46	Oklahoma	1907	2,396,040	9	70,057	Oklahoma City
47	New Mexico	1912	423,317	1	122,634	Santa Fe
48	Arizona	1912	435,573	1	113,956	Phoenix
	Totals		122,775,046	435	3,026,789	

TERRITORIES AND DEPENDENCIES	DATE OF ANNEXATION	AREA IN SQUARE MILES	POPULATION
Alaska	1867	586,400	59,278
District of Columbia	1790	70	486,869
Hawaii	1898	6,407	368,336
Philippines	1899	114,400	c. 13,000,000
Puerto Rico	1899	3,435	1,543,913
Guam	1899	206	18,509
American Samoa	1900	76	10,055
Panama Canal Zone	1904	549	39,467
Virgin Islands	1917	133	22,012

*Number of Representatives in the House by the 1930 apportionment.

IV. Presidents of the United States

No.	NAME	STATE	BORN	DIED	TERM OF OFFICE	PARTY
1	George Washington	Virginia	1732	1799	1789–1797	Federalist
2	John Adams	Massachusetts	1735	1826	1797–1801	Republican
3	Thomas Jefferson	Virginia	1743	1826	1801–1809	Republican
4	James Madison	Virginia	1751	1836	1809–1817	Republican
5	James Monroe	Virginia	1758	1831	1817–1825	Republican
6	John Quincy Adams	Massachusetts	1767	1848	1825–1829	Republican
7	Andrew Jackson	Tennessee	1767	1845	1829–1837	Democratic
8	Martin Van Buren	New York	1782	1862	1837–1841	Democratic
9	William H. Harrison	Ohio	1773	1841	March, 1841	Whig
10	John Tyler	Virginia	1790	1862	1841–1845	Whig
11	James K. Polk	Tennessee	1795	1849	1845–1849	Democratic
12	Zachary Taylor	Louisiana	1784	1850	1849–1850	Whig
13	Millard Fillmore	New York	1800	1874	1850–1853	Whig
14	Franklin Pierce	New Hampshire	1804	1869	1853–1857	Democratic
15	James Buchanan	Pennsylvania	1791	1868	1857–1861	Democratic
16	Abraham Lincoln	Illinois	1809	1865	1861–1865	Republican
17	Andrew Johnson	Tennessee	1808	1875	1865–1869	Republican
18	Ulysses S. Grant	Illinois	1822	1885	1869–1877	Republican
19	Rutherford B. Hayes	Ohio	1822	1893	1877–1881	Republican
20	James A. Garfield	Ohio	1831	1881	March–Sept., 1881	Republican
21	Chester A. Arthur	New York	1830	1886	1881–1885	Republican

No.	Name	State	Born	Died	Term of Office	Party
22	Grover Cleveland	New York	1837	1908	1885–1889	Democratic
23	Benjamin Harrison	Indiana	1833	1900	1889–1893	Republican
24	Grover Cleveland	New York	1837	1908	1893–1897	Democratic
25	William McKinley	Ohio	1843	1901	1897–1901	Republican
26	Theodore Roosevelt	New York	1858	1919	1901–1909	Republican
27	William H. Taft	Ohio	1857	1930	1909–1913	Republican
28	Woodrow Wilson	New Jersey	1856	1924	1913–1921	Democratic
29	Warren G. Harding	Ohio	1865	1923	1921–1923	Republican
30	Calvin Coolidge	Massachusetts	1872	1933	1923–1929	Republican
31	Herbert C. Hoover	California	1874		1929–1933	Republican
32	Franklin D. Roosevelt	New York	1882		1933–	Democratic

★

V. *Chief Justices of the United States Supreme Court and Present Members of the Court (1936)*

CHIEF JUSTICES

No.	Name	State	Term of Office
1	John Jay	New York	1789–1795
2	John Rutledge	South Carolina	1795
3	Oliver Ellsworth	Connecticut	1796–1800
4	John Marshall	Virginia	1801–1835
5	Roger B. Taney	Maryland	1835–1864
6	Salmon P. Chase	Ohio	1864–1873
7	Morrison R. Waite	Ohio	1874–1888
8	Melville W. Fuller	Illinois	1888–1910
9	Edward D. White	Louisiana	1910–1921
10	William H. Taft	Connecticut	1921–1930
11	Charles E. Hughes	New York	1930–

PRESENT MEMBERS OF THE SUPREME COURT

Name	State	Appointed by	Date
Chief Justice Charles E. Hughes	New York	Hoover	1930
Justice Willis Van Devanter	Wyoming	Taft	1910
Justice James C. McReynolds	Tennessee	Wilson	1914
Justice Louis D. Brandeis	Massachusetts	Wilson	1916
Justice George Sutherland	Utah	Harding	1922
Justice Pierce Butler	Minnesota	Harding	1922
Justice Harlan F. Stone	New York	Coolidge	1925
Justice Owen J. Roberts	Pennsylvania	Hoover	1930
Justice Benjamin Cardozo	New York	Hoover	1932

INDEX

(For references to Topical Analysis, see pages 853–854)